UNEMPLOYMENT

UNEMPLOYMENT

A PROBLEM OF INDUSTRY

(1909 AND 1930)

BY

W. H. BEVERIDGE

NEW EDITION

AMS PRESS
NEW YORK

Reprinted from the edition of 1930, New York
First AMS EDITION published 1969
Manufactured in the United States of America

Library of Congress Catalogue Card Number: 79-95398

AMS PRESS, INC.
NEW YORK, N. Y. 10003

TO

MY FATHER AND MY MOTHER

—AND TO THEIR MEMORY—

THIS BOOK IS DEDICATED

WITH THE HOPE THAT, IN A DIFFERENT FIELD

OF STUDY FROM THEIRS, IT MAY YET

APPEAR TOUCHED BY SOMETHING

OF THEIR OWN SPIRIT.

PREFACE TO EDITION OF 1930.

THE substance of Part I of this volume was given in lectures delivered in the University of Oxford during Michaelmas Term, 1908. The substance of Part II was given in lectures delivered in the University of Chicago during December, 1929. Some explanation of the appearance as a single work of studies so widely separated in time may seem to be required.

For ten years after the issue of the first edition of this book, in the spring of 1909, my official position in the British Civil Service precluded free public comment by myself on unemployment and policies for dealing with it. The book was reprinted—altogether four times—without change, beyond correction of errors and addition in Appendices of such public documents as the Labour Exchanges Act of 1909, Part II of the National Insurance Act of 1911 dealing with unemployment insurance, and the regulations made under these Acts.

On leaving the Civil Service in the autumn of 1919, one of my first acts was to get a volume of the current edition—already long out of print—dissected and mounted on sheets for additions and corrections; my aim then was to make a new edition revised and up to date throughout. The dissected volume remained in a cupboard untouched from December, 1919, till the summer of 1928; though the official barrier to my writing had gone, administrative occupations in the School of Economics and the University of London proved almost as absorbing as the Civil Service had done before. I had, however, at one time during this period, when a break in these occupations seemed likely, secured the services of Mr. L. C. Robbins (now Professor of Economics in the University of London) to work over the book and the new material available since 1909. He very soon reported to me his conclusion that nothing was to be gained, commensurate with the labour involved, in bringing what had been written in 1908 verbally and formally up to date—changing tenses, replacing older by newer figures in support of the same argument, continuing figures, such as those dealing with Distress Committees in Chapter VIII beyond the point at which they ceased to be significant. He advised—and convinced me—that I should reprint the original book without change, but with later figures available for those who wished them in a Supplement, and with a second part dealing with new developments both of the problem and of policies since 1909. This accordingly is the form taken by the edition of 1930. Part I stands as it was written in 1909, subject to a few corrections of bad style or grammar and of errors of fact and figure.

I hope that the book may still be read as one, and in that hope have kept Part II as short and as relevant to Part I as possible. I have attempted, not to write a comprehensive treatise on unemployment and all that is known of it in 1930, but to show how a theory of unemployment deduced from facts known in 1909, has stood the test of experience, and what has happened to policies based on that theory. This is my excuse for neglecting, as I should not otherwise have had any excuse for neglecting, the international aspects of the problem and the light to be thrown on it by comparisons from other countries. Nor can I pretend to have studied all that has been written of recent years, even about unemployment in this country. I have left out the bibliography which appeared in earlier editions; its place has been amply filled by other students. I have left out all but one of the original Appendices.

Part I of course is dated throughout and contains much that is now out of date, such as the discussion of the sources of information in Chapter III or of the causes of cyclical fluctuation in Chapter IV. Though, however, the sources of information in Chapter III are now, for Britain, superseded by statistics obtained in the working of Labour Exchanges and unemployment insurance, some of the arguments in that chapter may still have relevance for other countries which have to rely on less perfect sources. Though, again, the Distress Committees described in Chapter VIII have vanished, their experience has a permanent application to the policy of relief work.

I have done my best to save readers of Part I from being misled into out-of-date inferences on points of detail, by giving in the Statistical Supplement not simply all the figures up to date, but comments on all the conclusions in that part on which revision or caution seems called for by later experience or criticism. The main arguments of Part I are still, so far as I can judge of them, valid, though I do not claim that it is easy for me to judge them impartially. The most substantial theoretic criticism of which I know was made to me in conversation eight or nine years ago by Professor Verrijn Stuart, who urged that in any new edition I should pay attention to the relation between wages and unemployment; readers of Chapter XVI will see how right Professor Stuart was. In correction of what is said in Chapter XI, it has now to be said that, for unemployment to be always in process of disappearing, it is not sufficient that the demand for labour should be single and the supply of labour perfectly fluid; the price of labour must also be agreed on, at a point within the productivity of the marginal labourer. In correction of what is said in Chapter IX, it has now to be said that the problem of curing unemployment to-day *is* to some extent a problem of securing a general balance between the growth of the demand for labour and the growth of the supply; as soon as wages cease to be plastic the balance is no longer secured automatically by economic forces.

Fuller recognition of the part that can in practice be played by wages in determining the scale of unemployment is the main new feature of Part II. With this goes appreciation of the changed aspect of the population problem, best illustrated by reading successively Chapter I and Chapter XVII. Another point noted in Chapter XVI is one of emphasis alone; changes of industrial structure, long recognised as potential causes, for almost the first time assume importance as actual causes of unemployment in the aftermath of war.

Part II is largely concerned with discussion of activities and policies in which for a time I had some share. As a guide to my personal equation, I should record that, having entered the Board of Trade on a temporary basis in July, 1908, I became Director of Labour Exchanges in July, 1909. In that capacity I was concerned both in devising under Sir Hubert Llewellyn Smith, then Permanent Secretary to the Board of Trade, the unemployment insurance scheme of 1911, and in administering, with the co-operation of Mr. C. F. Rey as General Manager, the joint service of Labour Exchanges and unemployment insurance. From the spring of 1915 onwards I was largely absorbed in the work of the Ministry of Munitions, but retained my position in the Board of Trade, and was concerned in the partial extension of unemployment insurance in 1916. In the autumn of that year I was put in charge, as Assistant-Secretary, of the newly constituted Employment Department of the Board of Trade, combining exchanges, insurance, trade boards, food prices, and one or two other items. At the beginning of 1917, however, all these matters, except the embryo control of food prices, went to the newly established Ministry of Labour; I remained nominally attached to the Board of Trade, but practically absorbed in the Ministry of Food till I left the Civil Service in September, 1919. I was thus without administrative responsibility for any dealing with unemployment after the end of 1916. I served, however, as Chairman of the Civil War Workers Sub-Committee, under the Ministry of Reconstruction, which recommended generalisation of unemployment insurance in February, 1918, and as member of a Departmental Committee appointed by the Minister of Labour to frame a scheme for this purpose in 1919. I was a witness before the Committee of Enquiry into Labour Exchanges in 1920. This is my last practical association of any kind with the problem of unemployment or the means of dealing with it.

Part II has been written largely in hours and circumstances in which the writing of books should not after the age of thirty be attempted, in scraps of time filched from administration and punctured by interviews, after endless afternoons of committees, at sea and when on the sick list for other reasons, in railway trains, and in bed. This preface, but for necessary reference to later events, such as the Sidney Ball Lecture, would have been dated from "The Wolverine (Eastbound and Snowbound)— December 18, 1929." In the last stage of all, three weeks of

abnormal temperature and the subsequent convalescence, acting
as a restraint on administration, made it possible for the text of
the final chapters to reach the printer a month earlier than would
otherwise have been the case.   Part I had much the same experience of birth-times and birth-places, but the parent's age was
different and his practical activities centred round the subject of
his writing.   No one (I hope) can be more conscious than myself
of the looseness of joints and roughness of skin, that a work
born as Part II has been must show.   But since Part I is still
in demand, Part II cannot be allowed to block the way for ever.

Such as it is, Part II could never have appeared without help
of all kinds which twenty years ago would not have been at my
service.   First and foremost here I must thank my statistical
assistant, Miss F. J. Nicholas, who has untiringly collected information and compiled and re-compiled tables, cheerfully hunted at
my request unimportant references and screaming red herrings,
checked nearly every figure, and (I hope) caught and killed every
misprint.

My indebtedness to Mr. L. C. Robbins, when he was my
research assistant, for suggesting the form of this new edition, has
already been acknowledged; in that capacity he did much of the
work also of bringing up to date the figures in the Statistical
Supplement.   In other and later capacities he has been yet more
helpful.   Part II of this volume forms a thesis submitted by myself as an internal student of the University of London, registered
at the School of Economics under statute 113 of the old constitution, for the degree of Doctor of Science in Economics; this was
the only way open to me of becoming in 1930 a full member of
the University of which I had been Vice-Chancellor from 1926 to
1928.   Professor Robbins has been the official supervisor of my
studies and one of the examiners to whom my thesis has been
referred.   While it would be both premature and improper to
thank him for his services as examiner, I may thank him, as my
supervisor and colleague, for invaluable criticisms and suggestions
on nearly every chapter.

The Index, made originally by Mr. A. Andrews-Uthwatt, has
been extended by Miss Elspeth Mair.

I have to thank the Barnett Trustees for allowing me, without derogation of their copyright, to incorporate in Chapters XIV and XVIII most of the Sidney Ball lecture on "The Past and Present of Unemployment Insurance" delivered by me on 7th February, 1930. The last chapter is printed as an article in the current number of the *Political Quarterly*. Parts of other chapters have appeared at various dates, as articles in the *Economic Journal* and *Economica*, and I acknowledge the courtesy accorded me of using them freely.

W. H. B.

94 Campden Hill Road,
July, 1930.

PREFACE TO FIRST EDITION.

THIS volume contains a course of lectures delivered in Oxford, during Michaelmas term of the year now ending, for the Delegates of the Common University Fund. Its object is to combine a record of the principal facts of unemployment with a continuous argument as to the causes of unemployment. It includes a good deal of matter from published sources to which in the lectures I merely gave references, and appendices, the most important of which deal with "Public Labour Exchanges in Germany"[1] (reprinted from the *Economic Journal* for March, 1908) and "Methods of Seeking Employment in Great Britain".

I am only too conscious that the treatment given in the following pages to one of the most perplexing and urgent of industrial problems is in many points defective; that, not once but many times, I have been compelled to leave the record of facts or their analysis incomplete, to give probabilities in place of searching for certainties, to turn back unsatisfied from whole fields of inquiry as fascinating as they are important. Among these last is to be mentioned particularly the problem of the underlying causes of cyclical fluctuation in trade and employment. In so far as the main obstacle to further inquiry into these causes has, in my case, been immersion in actual dealing with distress as member of the Central (Unemployed) Body for London during the past three years, I can only hope that the following discussion may prove to have gained on the side of practical experience something to set against what it has lost on the side of theory. After all, whatever may be the underlying causes of cyclical fluctuation, the fact of cyclical fluctuation has to be reckoned with by governments and individuals for many years to come. No analysis of its causes can hope within the range of practical politics, if indeed ever, to dispense with the need for providing against its results.

[1] Omitted in the new edition.

Another point of incompleteness is involved in the publication of these lectures now rather than six months or a year hence. The trade of the country appears to be passing through a depression more severe, or at least more general, than any that has occurred within recent times.   It is possible, therefore, though, I think, not probable, that the experience of Distress Committees during the present winter may be such as to modify considerably some of the conclusions based upon their working in the past. In any case, however, the modification will be one of emphasis rather than of substance.   The present winter's experience may bring to light more distress that can truly be called exceptional. It cannot diminish the seriousness of the distress that is chronic. I would gladly have delayed publication in order to test, by the experience of a fresh and in some ways abnormal winter, the conclusions already drawn.   Since circumstances make this delay impossible I can only hope that here, too, loss may be counterbalanced by gain and the present volume have additional value as contributing to discussion at a critical moment.

The final chapters serve to define what needs to be done rather than to set out in section and subsection the way of doing it.   They must be judged as a statement of remedial policy, not as a compendium of practical reforms.   The guiding principle of this policy is the reduction of the question of unemployment to a question of wages.   Along that line alone but along that line certainly will the problem of distress through unemployment at last be solved.   It is not in any substantial sense insoluble.   The main part of it lies within ascertainable limits.   It represents, not an immeasurable and irredeemable failure of the existing social system, but incompleteness of organisation at certain points. There is, indeed, something almost fantastic in supposing that a nation capable of raising the edifice of British industry must be forever baffled by the business problem of organising and maintaining adequately the reserve forces of labour.

The question is simply that of determining that the problem shall be solved.   Upon that and that alone depends the practicability of all the essential reforms—of the voluntary or compulsory organisation of the labour market, and of the voluntary or compulsory averaging of earnings.   " Practicability " is never anything but a relative term—dependent upon the urgency with which an object is desired and upon the inconveniences which men are prepared to undergo in its pursuit. It is practicable for most people to run a mile to save a life. It is not practicable for any one to run a mile unless he is prepared to get warm. So it is not practicable for a nation to get a mastery of unemployment without being prepared to submit to some change of industrial methods and customs. The problem of unemployment—this is a point that cannot be too strongly emphasised—is insoluble by any mere expenditure of public money. It represents not a want to be satisfied but a disease to be eradicated. It needs not money so much as thought and organisation. It needs above all to be taken seriously. A problem of industrial organisation is not taken seriously so long as it is left to the Poor Law or to "Distress" Committees, so long as it is forgotten with every temporary improvement of trade, so long as it is made a peg on which to hang all other projects of social or political change.

I have to thank many friends for help in the publication of these lectures—more particularly my aunt Mrs. North, who collected and prepared the material for many of the statistical tables ; Mr. A. Andrewes-Uthwatt, who read a large part of the proofs and compiled the index ; and Mr. J. S. Nicholson, who is mainly responsible for the bibliography and also gave invaluable aid at the last moment in completing statistics and verifying references.

I have to thank also the Editors of the *Albany Review*, the *Contemporary Review* and the *Economic Journal* for placing at my disposal again matter which had already appeared in those periodicals.

W. H. BEVERIDGE.

December, 1908.

CONTENTS.

PART I. (1909).

CHAPTER I.

CHAPTER II.

CHAPTER III.

CONTENTS

CHAPTER VIII.

CHAPTER IX.

LIST OF TABLES.*

* Bracketed figures give references to continuations in the Statistical Supplement of Tables in Part I.

xxvi   LIST OF TABLES

LIST OF CHARTS.

CHAPTER I.

THE PROBLEM AND ITS LIMITS.

Growth of sense of public responsibility in regard to unemployment. Growth of accurate knowledge; general theory of causes now possible. Inquiry must be (a) economic, (b) as to unemployment rather than as to the unemployed. The problem that of the adjustment of supply of and demand for labour.
The forces making for adjustment. Supply influenced by demand; demand ultimately governed by supply. The demand for the products of labour unlimited. This demand, however, is not for the products of labour alone but for those of labour in combination with land and capital. Relations of labour and land. No shortage of latter. No pressure of population on the means of subsistence to-day. Relations of labour and capital. No general displacement of men by machines. The reward to labour rising not falling. The negative conclusion reached: Unemployment does not represent general failure of adjustment between growth of supply of labour and growth of demand. The positive conclusion reached: Unemployment does represent specific imperfections of adjustment. Changes of industrial structure. Fluctuations of industrial activity. The glutting of the labour market. Outline of subsequent discussion.
The positive conclusion more certain and more important than the negative conclusion. A rising demand for labour no cure for unemployment.

THE problem of unemployment lies, in a very special sense, at the root of most other social problems. Society is built up on labour; it lays upon its members responsibilities which in the vast majority of cases can be met only from the reward of labour; it imprisons for beggary and brands for pauperism; its ideal unit is the household of man, wife and children maintained by the earnings of the first alone. The household should have at all times sufficient room and air according to its size—but how, if the income is too irregular always to pay the rent? The children, till they themselves can work, should be supported by the parents —but how, unless the father has employment? The wife, so long at least as she is bearing and bringing up children, should have no other task—but how, if the husband's earnings fail and she has to go out to work? Everywhere the same difficulty recurs. Reasonable security of employment for the bread-winner is the basis of all private duties and all sound social action.

At one time this reasonable security was assumed as axiomatic. The great majority of people were people who had obtained employment. The great majority argued from their own cases that any man who really wanted employment could always obtain it. Only now and again came exceptional circumstances —a war in America, a famine in India, a bank failure in Glasgow —to be met by emergency measures of relief. Not one in a thousand of those who lived by this cheerful belief could have given reasons for his optimism. Now that this optimism is shaken, as it certainly is, there is danger that it may give place to a pessimism as unreasoning and as harmful.

The circular issued by Mr. Chamberlain as President of the Local Government Board in 1886 laid upon local authorities the moral obligation of endeavouring to provide work in times of exceptional distress. This circular was repeated by Sir Henry Fowler in the succeeding depression of 1892 and onwards. In 1904 under the Presidency of Mr. Walter Long semi-official machinery was established for the better administration of special relief funds. In 1905 the Unemployed Workmen Act reversed the principles of 1834 and enshrined in the statute book the policy of relieving the unemployed without the disqualifications of the Poor Law. The Act itself was so drafted as to prevent any direct application of public moneys for relief; the cost of providing work had in the first year to be met entirely from voluntary subscriptions. In the following year and since then this distinction has been disregarded; unemployment has been relieved without the pauper stigma, though at the public cost. In the spring of the present year[1] a Bill to acknowledge the right of every man to have work provided for him by public authority was introduced in the House of Commons and received on its second reading the support of 116 members. The Government of the day, while opposing that Bill, pledged itself to introduce practical alternatives of its own in the near future.

There has been thus a steady, if gradual, growth of the sense of public responsibility for the case of the unemployed. If this sense of responsibility is to issue in further action, it is before all things necessary that that case should be fully understood. In a matter of the first importance there is room for mistakes of the first importance. A community may treat its criminals or its lunatics unwisely without more than local inconvenience; it will touch in any case but an insignificant percentage of its members. It cannot treat the question of employment unwisely without the risk of grave harm in every quarter; its policy there is a policy affecting the great majority of citizens. Fortunately, with the growth of a sense of public responsibility in regard to this problem, there has been a growth of knowledge and understanding. The administration of the Unemployed Workmen Act in

[1] 1908.

particular has afforded a mass of new experience and of discussion. If much, with regard to unemployment, remains obscure, yet much has been done to lighten the past obscurity; many crude ideas are in process of dispersal; it is even possible to suggest the outlines of a general theory of causes and principles for treatment. This is the attempt which will be made in the following pages. The manner of that attempt is governed by two general considerations. First, the inquiry must be essentially an economic one. The evil to be analysed is, in technical language, that of maladjustment between the supply of and the demand for labour. Second, the inquiry must be one as to unemployment rather than as to the unemployed.

The inquiry must be essentially an economic one. The object in view is not the framing of palliatives for present distress, but the discovery of causes and the suggestion, if possible, of preventive measures and final remedies. With this in view the problem must be approached, not from the standpoint of the Poor Law or of charitable administration, but from that of industry. The first question must be, not what is to be done with the unemployed individual, but why he is thus unemployed. His involuntary idleness indicates excess of the supply of labour over the demand for labour. To what extent, under what circumstances, and in what forms is such an excess observable in the industry of to-day? To what economic and social causes may it be attributed? How is the action of the social and economic causes complicated by the influence of personal character? How, if at all, can they be rendered harmless or eliminated? How far, if at all, can this be done without risk of graver harm in other directions?

The inquiry must be one into unemployment rather than into the unemployed. It will appear at once, indeed it is manifest from the start, that any one unemployed individual may represent, and commonly does represent, the concurrence of many different forces, some industrial, some personal. A riverside labourer in Wapping during February, 1908, might be suffering at one and the same time from chronic irregularity of employment, from seasonal depression of his trade, from exceptional or cyclical depression of trade generally, from the permanent shifting of work lower down the river, and from his own deficiencies of character or education. His distress could not be attributed to any one of these factors alone. Classification of men according to the causes of their unemployment is, strictly speaking, an impossibility. The only possible course is to classify the causes or types of unemployment themselves.

1 *

The problem of unemployment is the problem of the adjustment of the supply of labour and the demand for labour. The supply of labour in a country is, in the widest sense, the supply of population. It is at any moment, apart from the possibilities of emigration and immigration, a fairly fixed quantity. Moreover, it is fixed for each moment, not by anything then happening, but by the habits and actions of millions of disconnected households a generation back. The demand for labour, on the other hand, is an aggregate of thousands or tens of thousands of separate demands in the present. It fluctuates with the fortunes and the calculations of the host of rival employers.

Discrepancy between two things so distinct in immediate origin is obviously possible. The problem has merely to be stated in order to shatter the simple faith that at all times any man who really wants work can obtain it. There is nothing in the existing industrial order to secure this miraculously perfect adjustment. The question is rather as to what there is to secure any sort of adjustment at all, and to keep the demand for labour even within measurable distance of the supply. When only one type of labour is in question, there are obvious possibilities of adjustment. Men will tend to leave or to avoid entering an employment that they know to be overcrowded ; they will transfer their services to one in which the demand appears to exceed the supply. In regard to labour as a whole, there is not this possibility. Is there then anything to prevent the supply of labour as a whole from growing to be permanently and largely in excess of the demand, or the demand for labour as a whole from falling off so as to be permanently and largely deficient for the supply? Is it not possible that one or other of these things has happened or is happening in the United Kingdom to-day? If so, there can be little need of elaborate inquiry into the minor causes of unemployment, and there can be no hope of a remedy except in the rapid expansion of industry or in the restriction of the population.

At the threshold, therefore, of the present inquiry lies the general question as to the relations of population and industry. Until the bearings of that are known discussion of particular types of unemployment is useless. Consideration of it involves a brief examination of general social conditions and tendencies to-day.

There are, no doubt, economic forces which tend in the long run to adjust supply and demand in regard to labour as in regard to all other commodities. The supply of labour, even in the most general sense—that of population—is influenced by the state of the demand. People are not born in a country out of

all proportion to the possibilities of living there. The sudden growth of the population at the end of the eighteenth century did not take place till the industrial revolution had made room for it. This adjustment of supply of population to demand, however, is only of the most general character. Much more important is the ultimate dependence of the demand upon the supply. Insufficiency in the supply of labour will tend to cause a rise in its price, and this rise will either check production itself or will stimulate the invention and use of methods of production in which less labour is required. In either case there will be forces at work to reduce the demand for labour and so bring it into accord with the supply. If, on the other hand, the supply of labour is excessive, its price will tend to fall. Its employment will thereby be encouraged; there will be less pressure to try labour-saving machines and processes. The demand will tend to grow up to the supply. This argument, it will be seen, applies not only to the quantity of the demand for labour but to its quality, not only to the demand as a whole but also to its distribution between different trades.

This process of adjustment, moreover, is not and cannot be checked in the long run by deficiency in the demand for the products of labour. The total demand for these products must be regarded as infinite or at least as capable of indefinite expansion. It is impossible to imagine a state of affairs in which every need for material good things was satisfied and labour idle because nothing remained to be done. Least of all could such a description apply to a society in which men were seeking employment; the very fact of their seeking employment would show that some of their demands for commodities were unsatisfied. Over-production of any one particular good thing is possible and not uncommon. Over-production of all the good things of life is, strictly speaking, an impossibility. The satisfaction of one need is followed by the immediate growth of another; the standard of comfort can and does rise indefinitely.

These general economic arguments have their place in the present discussion. They do not, however, carry the matter very far. They leave the field clear for two distinct objections. First, the forces which make for equilibrium in the labour market, though ultimately they cannot be limited through deficient demand for commodities, may yet be limited in other ways. Second, these forces make only for ultimate equilibrium; they get to work very slowly and never complete their work.

The first objection starts from the fact that the demand for commodities is a demand, not for labour as such, but for the joint

products of labour, land and capital in combination. The demand for commodities may be unlimited. The demand for any one of the three factors in production can only expand within limits set by the available amounts of the other two. Each factor is useless unless it is combined in appropriate proportions with the others. Any part of it which cannot be so combined is necessarily in excess and unemployed. The two possibilities have therefore to be considered—of too many men in a country for the available land, and of too many men for the available capital.

It is clearly possible, theoretically, for there to be more men in a country than can find living room there. To the English economists of a past generation this appeared to be a practical and urgent danger in the country that they knew. The supply of labour, *i.e.*, the population, was seen constantly increasing. The supply of land appeared stationary. The ever-increasing pressure of the population on the means of subsistence seemed to follow as an inevitable disaster. To-day economists view the matter very differently.[1] The fear of over-population is dispelled, or at least postponed to a remote future.

On the one hand, there is clearly no insufficiency of land in the United Kingdom to-day. There is land enough and to spare. The greater part of the United Kingdom, instead of being over-populated, is being depopulated by the drift to the towns. The growing nation avails itself of a constantly diminishing proportion of its total territories.

On the other hand, all the statistical tests which might be expected to reveal pressure of population upon the means of subsistence, if such pressure existed, point to the conclusion that there is no such pressure. What in essence would over-population —an increase not of some particular type of people, but of people generally above the capacity of a country—mean in that country? How would it show itself? It would mean, in the language of the economists, that the law of diminishing returns had come to apply to labour generally; that each fresh unit of labour in the country, though perhaps adding to the total product, added less than the one before; that each new-comer could find living and working room only at the cost of diminishing the average living and working room for those already there. It would show itself most decisively by a falling standard of life and diminished productivity of the nation in proportion to its size. Nothing of the sort is witnessed in the United Kingdom to-day. On the contrary, as the population increases so do the wealth and the productivity per head of the population. The estimates of Sir Robert Giffen

---

[1] *Cp.* Marshall, *Principles of Economics,* vol. i., book iv., ch. xiii.

and others are familiar. In 1867 the national income was put at
£814,000,000 for a population of 30,000,000, or at just over £27
per head. In 1901 it is put at £1,700,000,000 for a population
of 42,000,000, or at just over £40 per head. The standard of
income measured in money has risen nearly 50 per cent. The
actual standard of life has risen yet more rapidly; the fall of
prices makes every pound of greater value than before. As to
the total consumption of commodities, no figures are available.
Practically all the figures that can be given show an increase
per head, e.g., those for wheat, tea, sugar, tobacco, and rice.
In regard to production, the same thing holds. There are no
records covering industry as a whole; wherever, for particular
industries, there are records, they show a rising level of productivity per head of population. The following table deals with the
coal, iron, cotton, wool and shipbuilding industries during the
past fifty years.

TABLE I.—PRINCIPAL INDUSTRIES IN UNITED KINGDOM, 1855-1907.

	Coal: Production per head. Tons.	Pig Iron: Production per 100. Tons.	Raw Cotton: Consumption per head. lbs.	Raw Wool: Consumption per head. lbs.	Shipbuilding: Tonnage per 1,000.
1855-1864	2·62	13·5	28·1	—	9·72[1]
1865-1874	3·59	18·0	33·5	10·40	13·52
1875-1884	4·21	21·0	38·6	10·25	15·99
1885-1894	4·62	20·0	40·6	11·85	16·68
1895-1904	5·22	21·5	40·1	12·35	20·36
1905	5·46	22·2	42·8	10·90	24·27
1906	5·74	23·2	43·6	11·80	26·47
1907	6·07	22·9	44·7	13·46	23·52

The table shows clearly that the general tendency in all these
principal manufactures is upward; that for every man in the
country—employed or unemployed—more is being produced in
them now than ten or twenty or fifty years ago.

Any idea of over-population, in the sense in which it was
feared by the economists of eighty years or a hundred years ago,
may be dismissed as for the present unfounded. All the conditions have been changed with the growth of foreign trade and the
indefinite extension of the area from which food and raw material
can be drawn. The land of the United Kingdom is clearly
capable under these modern conditions of holding all and far
more than all the people now there. It remains, therefore, to
consider the other possibility—insufficiency of capital to co-operate
with labour in production.

[1] 1858-64.

Those who believe in this possibility would presumably put the case as follows: Land, capital and labour are always the three requisites of production, but they are not always combined in the same proportions. Certain general changes of proportion are, indeed, manifestly taking place, and one of them has been noticed already. The change from agriculture to manufacturing implies a decrease in the amount of land required in this country for any given volume of production. Land, therefore, in this country tends to go out of employment. Its actual volume is declining relatively to the volumes both of capital and labour (since it remains stationary while they increase), but the part that it is required to play is declining still more. A little land—enough for a factory—goes so much further in production now than formerly—as part of a farm—that land as a whole is becoming a drug on the market. May not the same thing be happening to labour? Is not labour too being required to play a constantly decreasing part in production, so that though production is increasing faster than population, population yet increases faster than the opportunities for employment. One man with a machine may produce more than two men without machines. Increased wealth and productivity per head do not necessarily mean increased opportunities for employment. They may simply be a testimony to the success of the dominant partner—capital— in economising labour and so rendering large parts of the population superfluous.

This is a very common criticism of the existing industrial order. It places the root cause of unemployment in the supersession of men by machines. There is no need to discuss whether it is tenable in theory. It is sufficient to say that it will not stand examination in the light of the facts of to-day. It is, as has been noticed, perfectly consistent with the fact of increasing wealth and heightened productivity per head of the population. It is not consistent with the equally certain fact of a rising reward to labour. If, by the progress of industrial invention, labour generally, not labour in particular forms, were being rendered superfluous and a drug on the market, then its price should be falling. In fact its price is rising, and rising while that of most other things falls or rises at least less rapidly. The following table compares the course of wages and prices during the past thirty years.

TABLE II.—RATES OF MONEY WAGES AND PRICES, 1878-1907.

(BOARD OF TRADE INDEX NUMBERS, 1900 = 100.) R.

Mean of ten years.	Wages.						Prices (wholesale).
	Building.	Coal-Mining.	Engineering.	Textile.	Agriculture.	Mean of five groups.	
	1	2	3	4	5	6	7
1878-1887	85·45	63·66	89·32	91·54	91·42	84·28	119·5
1888-1897	89·65	76·54	93·56	95·15	92·96	89·57	98·3
1898-1907	99·80	87·14	100·30	101·10	100·85	97·83	97·8

The first five columns in the table, dealing with wages in the principal industries and agriculture, show in every case a considerable movement upward. The sixth column gives the mean of all five groups; this has risen from 84·28 to 97·83, or 16 per cent. between 1878-87 and 1898-1907. The last column shows the strikingly different change that has taken place in regard to the prices of ordinary commodities.

It is not easy to get a comparable indication for the position of land in the market. Yet the following figures, compiled from the Returns of Inland Revenue, show clearly the change that has taken place :—

ANNUAL VALUES OF LAND ASSESSED TO INCOME TAX
UNDER SCHEDULE A.

(1900 = 100.)

Mean of—
1878-1887 . . . 126·6
1888-1897 . . . 108·4
1898-1906 . . . 99·7

Land, rapidly losing its importance as a factor in production, has tended to go out of employment. The inevitable symptom of this has been a decline of price. Labour, on the other hand, so far from becoming a drug on the market, stands almost alone in maintaining and increasing its price. The figures here given do not, indeed, fully indicate the change that has taken place. Two considerations make the true increase in the reward of labour greater than appears from the statement of money wages alone.

In the first place, there has been a decrease in the cost of living. This is indicated, though not accurately represented, by the fall of wholesale prices. Official estimates put the decrease in cost of living at 17 per cent. as between the five years from

1878 to 1882 and those from 1898 to 1902.[1] This has meant, of course, a corresponding rise in the value of every pound earned.

Allowing for this change of values, Mr. Bowley gives the following striking estimate for the course of average real wages during the seventy years up to 1900.[2]

AVERAGE REAL WAGES AS PERCENTAGES OF THE LEVEL OF 1900.

Years	circa	1830	1840	1850	1860	1870	1875	1880	1885	1890	1895	1900
Real wages .		45	50	50	55	60	70	70	72	84	93	100

It will be seen that in the last ten years of the table the progress has been greater than in any equal period before except 1885 to 1895.

In the second place, there has been a transference of labour from the lower paid to the more highly paid occupations. The industrial groups which show the relatively largest rises of money wages, *e.g.*, building and coal-mining, are also those which show as between 1881 and 1901 the largest increases in the numbers employed. According to a calculation made by Mr. Bowley the rise of wages in the principal industries between 1881 and 1901 may be put at 16 per cent.; the actual volume of wages paid in these industries—taking account of the greater growth of the best paid ones—has increased by 29 per cent., or nearly twice as much.[3]

The criticism may, indeed, be made that the table given deals only with the rates of wages, not with actual or average earnings. Might not the rate of wages rise while continuity of employment diminished? Might not one section of the supply of labour by collective action or otherwise force up its own price while another and growing section found it impossible to obtain employment at any price? Once again it is unnecessary to discuss theoretical possibilities. The suggestion here made can be ruled out practically by reference to actual conditions. First, the rise of wage rates is not confined to skilled and organised trades. It extends to occupations such as agriculture, where there is no collective action on the part of the wage-earners at all, as well as to many sections of unskilled and semi-skilled workpeople among whom collective action is very slight. Second, there is no evidence of increasing unemployment. The weight of evidence is all the other way. The experience of exceptional distress in 1904 and in 1908 may be paralleled in all essential particulars by the events of 1893-4, 1886, 1878-9, 1867 and earlier periods, when the population was half or two-thirds of what it is at present. Then as now there were emergency relief funds. There was pauperism greater than at present. There was an unem-

---

[1] *British and Foreign Trade.* Second Series of Charts and Memoranda, pp. 31-3.
[2] *National Progress in Wealth and Trade*, p. 33.   [3] *Ibid.*

ployed percentage in the trade unions; the record of 10·7 per cent. for the year 1879 has never since been approached. It is all but impossible to suppose that, while labour generally was becoming a drug on the market, all the sections of labour as to which statistics are obtainable should be increasing their remuneration. It is quite impossible to find any evidence of that piling up of superfluous and wholly unemployed labour outside the magic ring of these fortunate workers which would be the necessary accompaniment of such a process.

The foregoing discussion has necessarily been somewhat summary. Yet it should be sufficient to establish the main negative conclusion—that unemployment cannot be attributed to any general want of adjustment between the growth of the supply of labour and the growth of the demand. If labour generally had become or were becoming a drug on the market, the return to labour would be diminishing. In fact the return is increasing, whether labour be regarded separately or in its combination with land and capital. The popular conception is of industry as rigidly limited—a sphere of cast iron in which men struggle for living room; in which the greater the room taken by any one man the less must there be for others; in which the greater the number of men the worse must be the case of all. The true conception is of a sphere made of elastic material, capable of expansion and being in fact continually forced to expand by the struggling of those within. Each individual appears to be, and no doubt, to some extent is, pressing upon the room of his neighbours; the whole mass presses outwards upon the limits within which it is for the moment confined; the result of a particularly violent struggle of one man for the room of others may be to enlarge appreciably the room for all. This expansion of industry cannot readily be made visible, and is nowhere recorded in direct and comprehensive figures. It is and must always remain something of a mystery. It does not take place evenly. It is perhaps not a thing to be counted on for ever. The sphere may at last lose its elasticity and cease to respond further to the increasing pressure from within. That, if it ever happens, *will* mean over-population, a diminishing return to labour, a falling standard of life, and, unless the growth of numbers be arrested, a gradual but certain return to barbarism for all or the immense majority of the people. For the present it is sufficient to say that that time has not come; it is not within sight; it can barely be imagined. For the present the sphere of industry in the United Kingdom retains its elasticity. It expands, not indeed steadily, but still sufficiently for the people. It absorbs the generations as they come. It yields each fresh man on the whole more living and working room than fell to the lot of those before.

Yet with all this comes the perpetual cry of some who find no living and working room at all. While the number of those who can and do obtain employment rises endlessly, the number of the unemployed never falls to zero. Many who recognise the indisputable facts of the expansion of industry and the rising standard of life, are apt to deny directly or implicitly the existence of an unemployed problem at all. If there are not too many workmen in the country, every man who really wants work must be able to obtain it. If any men fail to find room while all round them fresh room is opening out, they must be men either unfit or unwilling to do so. They must be "unemployable"—the incompetent, the lazy, the sick and infirm. Those who argue thus, however, have to ignore facts at least as indisputable as those which testify to the growing wealth and productivity of the nation. It cannot be supposed that the 56,000 members of highly skilled and organised trades who, at the present moment (September, 1908), are returned as unemployed and for the most part in receipt of allowances from their unions, are all unemployable. It cannot be supposed that the employers who write to Distress Committees, as they do write in hundreds and thousands, giving the characters of men now out of work but formerly employed by them, are all in a conspiracy of deceit. Unemployment is not to be explained away as the idleness of the unemployable. As little can it be treated as a collection of accidents to individual workpeople or individual firms. It is too widespread and too enduring for that. While the final absorption of the growing population in growing industry is accepted as being for this country still happily the rule, it is no less necessary to admit the existence of facts modifying the completeness of this absorption at certain times and places—indeed, at all times and places. There is no general want of adjustment between the natural increase of the people and the expansion of industry, between the rate of supply of fresh labour and the normal growth of the demand for it. There are specific imperfections of adjustment which are the economic causes of unemployment.

One of these has long been recognised. While industry, as a whole, grows, specific trades may decay, or change in methods and organisation. The men who have learnt to live by those trades may find their peculiar and hard-won skill a drug on the market and themselves permanently displaced from their chosen occupations, while lacking both the youth and the knowledge to make their way into new occupations. "There cannot," said John

Stuart Mill, " be a more legitimate object of the legislator's care than the interests of those who are thus sacrificed to the gains of their fellow-citizens and of posterity." It will be seen later that changes of this character are best considered, not by themselves but, from a slightly different point of view, as only one among several ways in which part of the labour supply may come to lose or lack the industrial qualities required of it.

A second type of maladjustment between the demand for and the supply of labour is found in actual fluctuations of industrial activity. Many trades, perhaps most trades, pass regularly each year through an alternation of busy and slack seasons, determined by climate or social habits, or a combination of both. Building is slack in winter and busy in spring and summer. Printers find least to do in the August holidays and most in the season just before Christmas. At the London Docks timber comes in at one time of the year; fruit at another; tea at a third. Behind and apart from these seasonal vicissitudes of special trades, and affecting, though in varying degrees, nearly all trades at about the same time, is a cyclical fluctuation in which periods of general depression—1868, 1879, 1885-86, 1893-95, 1904—alternate at irregular intervals with periods of feverish activity—1872-74, 1881, 1889-90, 1899-1900. At such times of depression the industrial system does appear to suffer a temporary loss of elasticity ; it fails for a while to keep pace with the steady growth of the population ; it gives—in a phase of falling wages and lowered standards—an object lesson of what might be expected if the supply of labour should ever come permanently to outstrip the demand.

These two elements in the problem of unemployment have long been familiar. A third, apparently far more important than either the occasional transformations of industrial structure or the periodic fluctuations of industrial activity, is only just beginning to receive attention. This is the requirement in each trade of reserves of labour to meet the fluctuations of work incidental even to years of prosperity. The men forming these reserves are constantly passing into and out of employment. They tend, moreover, to be always more numerous than can find employment together at any one time. This tendency springs directly from one of the fundamental facts of industry—the dissipation of the demand for labour in each trade between many separate employers and centres of employment. Its result may be described as the normal glutting of the labour market. The counterpart of such glutting is the idleness at every moment of some or others of those engaged.

The three factors just mentioned—changes of industrial

structure, fluctuations of industrial activity, and the reserve of labour—have been named in the order of familiaiity. They will be discussed below in a slightly different order. They represent, not indeed all, but at least the principal economic factors in unemployment. Their discussion will be preceded by a brief account of the principal sources of information; it will be followed and supplemented by consideration of the personal factor in unemployment. This will complete the statement of the problem and will lead on to a brief description of the principal remedies hitherto attempted. In the concluding chapters an attempt will be made to outline a policy for the future.

The present chapter embodies two main conclusions; one comforting and one disturbing; one negative and one positive; one defining the limits of the problem and the other indicating the problem itself.

The negative conclusion is that there is no general failure of adjustment between the growth of the demand for labour and the growth of the supply of labour. The forces which constantly tend to bring about this adjustment have not, either by excessive increase of the population or by the adoption of labour-saving devices, been brought to the limit of their power. The first objection advanced against the argument which described these forces, namely, that adjustment can only take place within limits set by the available land and capital, though perhaps sound in theory, has no practical validity to-day.

The positive conclusion is that there are specific imperfections of adjustment between the demand for labour and the supply of labour, and that these give rise to a real and considerable problem of unemployment. The forces which constantly tend to adjust demand and supply work only in the long run. There are forces as constantly tending to disturb or prevent adjustment and having often a run long enough to determine the fate of individuals. The second objection advanced against the argument for ultimate equilibrium is not to be denied.

Both these conclusions are important, and both appear to be justified by the evidence. Both therefore have been advanced here. They are, however, by no means equal either in certitude or in importance for the present inquiry. The statement that the country is not over-populated, and that its industrial system is still capable of absorbing the growing supply of labour, must always be something of the nature of a prophecy. It is impossible to bring statistics more than up to date. Because up to date industry has expanded, the inference is made that it is still expanding and capable of further expansion. Because this expansion in the past has taken place through alternations of good years and bad years, the inference is made of any particular period of depression that it is only a temporary phase and will give way to renewed prosperity. All this, however, is far from inevitable. It is likely enough that industry will at some time lose all or much of its power of growth. It is possible that any particular depression may be not a temporary phase but the beginning of a lasting decline. The negative or optimistic conclusion—that unemployment is not now being caused by general over-population—must therefore, by its very nature, be always open to a doubt. The positive conclusion, that there are other factors which have caused unemployment in the past and are liable to cause it in the present, is not open to any doubt at all. From the beginning to the end of fifty years of unprecedented industrial expansion unemployment has been recorded continuously, and has passed at intervals of seven to ten years from a normal to an acute phase. This, in itself, is enough to show that unemployment depends not so much on the volume of industry as upon the methods of industry, and, while the methods remain unchanged, will continue or recur however the volume grows. A falling demand for labour may come as a symptom of national decay. A rising demand for labour will be no cure for unemployment.

CHAPTER II.

THE SOURCES OF INFORMATION.

1. The unemployed percentage: Returns from trade unions paying unemployed benefit. Percentages 1894-1908. Returns fairly complete as to unions reporting. Not a fair sample of the whole of industry. Stable trades unrepresented. Fluctuating trades over-represented. No account taken of short time. The unemployed percentage no indication of the volume of general unemployment but only of its growth or diminution.
2. Records of Distress Committees. Include only distressed unemployed. Detailed information as to applicants.
3. Subsidiary sources of information. Statistics of commerce and manufacture. Days worked in coal-mines. Trade union reports. Pauperism.
No possibility of numbering the unemployed. Analysis must be of unemployment.

THE two main sources of information as to unemployment have been indicated in the preceding chapter. They are, first, the returns made by trade unions to the Labour Department of the Board of Trade; second, the reports of Distress Committees administering the Unemployed Workmen Act, 1905. Each of these will be so constantly referred to in the following chapters, that a short description of them, as well as of the character and limits of the information supplied by them, is indispensable. Each, as will appear, deals with a distinct social stratum. Neither by itself gives any fair representation of the problem. The two together need to be supplemented from many subsidiary sources.

(1) THE UNEMPLOYED PERCENTAGE.

A large number of trade unions include among the benefits provided to their members an allowance during unemployment. These allowances are of two kinds. The first, variously known as "donation," "stationary," "local," or "unemployed" benefit, is paid on the spot, and is intended simply to support men till they can obtain employment again in the place where they are. The second type of allowance is generally known as travelling benefit, and is intended to facilitate the movement of workmen in search of employment elsewhere. The member desiring to travel receives a ticket entitling him to draw for board and bed money upon the branches of the union in other places. In 1904, 81 out of the 100 principal unions, having a membership of about

16

950,000, gave one or other or both of these benefits at a cost for the year of nearly £650,000. The importance of unemployed and travelling allowances as a means of preventing distress will be considered later. For the present their significance is this—that the unions concerned have necessarily to keep a register of the men to whom these payments are made. It is, indeed, almost invariably made a condition of receiving benefit that the recipient should sign regularly, sometimes every day and sometimes every other day, the vacant book or register at the office of his union or branch. This serves both as evidence of the fact of unemployment—the time of signing being commonly fixed during working hours—and as an opportunity of getting the member off the fund by notifying to him, when he comes to sign, any suitable situation of which the union officials have cognisance. Unions giving unemployed benefits are therefore in a position to supply regular records of their unemployed members from time to time, and a large number of them now make voluntary monthly returns on this point to the Board of Trade. The return states, for the union or branch concerned, (a) the total membership, (b) the members unemployed at the end of the month. In each case persons on strike or locked-out, sick or superannuated are excluded. The comparison of the two figures gives an "unemployed percentage" for that union or branch. The combination of the returns for the unions in some particular trade or group of trades, e.g., shipbuilding, yields an unemployed percentage for that trade or group of trades. The combination of all the returns gives a result commonly cited as the "general unemployed percentage," and taken as an index of the state of employment as a whole. These results—both for particular trades and for all the unions covered by the returns—are published each month in the *Labour Gazette* issued by the Labour Department of the Board of Trade. The form of statement of the "general unemployed percentage" is typified by the following: "In the 272 Trade Unions with a net membership of 649,789 making returns, 40,580 (or 6·2 per cent.) were reported as unemployed at the end of January, 1908, as compared with 6·1 per cent. at the end of December, and 4·2 per cent. at the end of January, 1907".[1] The following table gives the general unemployed percentages for the past fifteen years:—

---

[1] This description of the *Labour Gazette* returns, as well as much of the subsequent criticism, is taken from the evidence of Mr. (now Sir) H. Llewellyn Smith before the Select Committee of the House of Commons in 1895. The evidence as a whole should be consulted by those who make any use of the returns (*Distress from Want of Employment*, Third Report, 1895, pp. 46-67).

TABLE III.—UNEMPLOYED PERCENTAGE, 1894-1908.

(ALL TRADE UNIONS MAKING RETURNS.) R.

	Jan.	Feb.	March	April	May	June	July	Aug.	Sept.	Oct.	Nov.	Dec.	Mean for Year.
1894	7·0	5·6	6·5	6·1	6·3	6·3	7·5	7·7	7·6	7·4	6·9	7·7	6·9
1895	8·1	7·9	6·5	6·5	6·0	5·5	5·2	5·2	4·9	4·8	4·2	4·8	5·8
1896	4·4	3·7	3·3	3·0	3·1	3·0	3·0	3·3	3·4	3·2	2·8	3·1	3·3
1897	3·1	2·7	2·2	2·2	2·0	2·5	2·5	3·4	4·2	4·5	4·6	5·1	3·3
1898	4·7	4·2	2·9	2·7	2·4	2·4	2·4	2·5	2·3	2·2	2·0	2·6	2·8
1899	2·7	2·1	2·0	1·7	2·0	1·8	1·8	2·1	2·0	1·9	1·8	2·3	2·0
1900	2·3	2·4	2·0	2·0	1·9	2·1	2·2	2·5	3·0	2·8	2·7	3·5	2·5
1901	3·5	3·4	3·1	3·4	3·0	3·0	2·9	3·4	3·2	3·2	3·3	4·2	3·3
1902	4·0	3·9	3·2	3·4	3·5	3·7	3·5	4·0	4·5	4·5	4·4	5·0	4·0
1903	4·9	4·3	3·9	3·6	3·5	3·9	4·4	5·0	5·2	5·6	5·5	6·3	4·7
1904	6·1	5·6	5·5	5·5	5·8	5·5	5·6	5·9	6·3	6·3	6·5	7·1	6·0
1905	6·3	5·7	5·2	5·2	4·7	4·8	4·7	4·9	4·8	4·6	4·3	4·5	5·0
1906	4·3	4·1	3·4	3·2	3·1	3·2	3·1	3·3	3·3	3·9	4·0	4·4	3·6
1907	3·9	3·5	3·2	2·8	3·0	3·1	3·2	3·6	4·1	4·2	4·5	5·6	3·7
1908	5·8	6·0	6·4	7·1	7·4	7·9	7·9	8·5	9·3	9·5	8·7	9·1	7·8

What is the bearing and value of these statistics? What do they show or fail to show?

They are obviously not a complete register of unemployment. They do not cover directly more than a small fraction of the industrial field. The 650,000 trade unionists included in the returns are less than a third of all the trade unionists in the country. All the trade unionists in the country are less than a quarter of the industrial manual workers. The questions that have to be answered are therefore two. Are the trade union returns a complete record of unemployment within the limited field that they cover directly? To what extent and for what purposes can inferences be drawn from them as to the number of the unemployed or the state of employment in the much larger field outside their direct scope?

The completeness of the returns within their direct scope depends, of course, upon the completeness with which the unions secure the registration of all their unemployed members. Unless these members are under some strong constraint to sign the register there is no certainty that they will sign, and thus a certain proportion of the unemployed will be left out of the statistics. Herein lies the significance of the payment of unemployed benefit. Where regular signature of the vacant book is the means of obtaining a weekly allowance it is not likely to be neglected. The Board of Trade, therefore, in calculating the unemployed percentage, uses no returns except from unions providing this benefit. On the other hand, the returns are not absolutely confined to men in receipt of allowances. The intention is to include all who are out of work in these unions, whether they are at the time receiving allowances or not, and there is no doubt that this intention is substantially effected. In all but a few unions, indeed, there is a limit to the number of consecutive weeks for which unemployed benefit may be paid, and there is thus the possibility that a member may exhaust his claims before recovering employment. He will then remain unemployed while lacking his former motive for registering at the union office. There is here, then, and must remain, the possibility of incompleteness in the statistics. All that can be said is that the resulting error is almost certainly inconsiderable. The unions making returns are asked to include all their unemployed members whether in receipt of benefit or not. The great bulk of them continue their payments for periods so considerable that those who at any time have run out of benefit are a very small fraction of all the unemployed. Even as to these the obligation to register generally remains; the rules almost invariably provide that all members out of work must sign the vacant book regularly whether in receipt of benefit or not. Nor is the obligation to register merely formal. In a good many unions, even after the actual allowance has come to an end, members continuing to sign the books are excused from payment of their contributions. In most unions which are sufficiently organised to provide unemployed benefit, the union or branch office becomes also to some extent a labour exchange. Vacant situations are notified there through members at work or even directly by employers and foremen; the unemployed man goes there to seek employment.

There is, therefore, no reason to doubt the substantial completeness of the returns made, at least as to the members who are wholly unemployed. These numbers and percentages do not, of course, necessarily indicate the total loss of employment at any time. In some occupations—such as coal-mining—depression of trade is customarily met, not so much by discharging individuals, as by shortening the working week for the whole body of men. The comparatively small percentage of men who become wholly unemployed by no means represents the real depth of the depression.

The second question is as to how far the trade union returns can be used to supply inferences as to the general state of the labour market. That depends, of course, upon the extent to which the men covered by them can be taken as a fair sample of the industrial population. A very brief examination is sufficient

2 *

to prove that they are not a fair sample at all. The following table shows the principal trades from which they are drawn, together with the proportions contributed by each trade in 1908 and in 1894.

TABLE IV.—TRADES REPRESENTED IN UNEMPLOYED
PERCENTAGE.

Trade.	No. of Unionists included in the Returns, Jan. 1908.	Proportion contributed by each Trade, Jan. 1908.	Proportion contributed by each Trade, 1894.
Building	61,057	9·4 } 14·8	21
Woodworking and furnishing	35,200	5·4	
Coal-mining	126,725	19·5	19
Engineering . . .	164,088	25·2 } 39·1	
Shipbuilding	58,424	9·0	46
Other metal trades . .	31,751	4·9	
Printing and bookbinding .	56,376	8·7	10
Textiles	93,990	14·5	3
Miscellaneous . . .	22,178	3·4	1

It will be seen at once that the returns do not by any means cover all trades and occupations. In particular they neglect altogether the more stable ones, such as railway and municipal service, as well as domestic service and agriculture. Moreover, even those occupations which do appear are by no means fairly represented. The 223,000 men from the engineering and shipbuilding trades form a far larger proportion of all the men in these trades, than the 61,000 from building do of all those engaged in building, or the 94,000 from textiles do of all textile operatives. In other words, even amongst the trades which do appear some are over-represented and some under-represented. Nor does this over-representation come by chance. One of the essential facts about fluctuations of employment is that their severity varies enormously from one industry to another, and, as a necessary consequence of the basis of the trade union returns, the more fluctuating industries predominate in them unduly. The greater the fluctuations the more will the need for unemployed benefit be felt by the trade unions, that is to say, the more likely are they to figure in the Board of Trade returns. The experiment was tried in 1895 of applying the unemployed percentage for each trade, not to the numbers of unionists for whom returns were made, but to the numbers shown by the census to be actually employed in each trade. The result of this correction was to reduce the general unemployed percentage in the particular month taken from 7·0 to 4·2.[1] The danger of generalisation is illustrated in another way by comparing two years of exceptional depression, such as 1893 and 1904. According to the actual trade union returns the former depression appears to have been the most severe. If, however, the unemployed percentages for each trade are applied to the census figures for that trade, the opposite result is reached; 1904 appears as really worse than 1893. The explanation is that the depression of 1893 was severest in the over-represented engineering and shipbuilding trades; that of 1904 was far more general, and was severest in the relatively less-represented building trades.

The points just mentioned suggest that the trade union returns show a much higher percentage of unemployment than would be found in the country generally. There are, no doubt, considerations on the other side, that is to say points in regard to which the trade union returns are an under-statement. They exclude, for instance, the most casual occupations. They take no account of loss of employment and earnings through working short time. They give inadequate representation to some seasonal trades, such as building. It is probable that they thus understate the difference between winter and summer employment. On the other hand, there appears to be really no foundation for the statements commonly made as if they were axiomatic that the Board of Trade returns show an unduly low percentage of unemployment because they are confined to the skilled men and to trade unionists. It is by no means axiomatic that the proportion of unemployment is lower amongst skilled men as a whole than amongst unskilled, or amongst trade unionists than amongst non-unionists. The skilled man holds out for a job in his own particular line; the unskilled man will take anything he can do. The unionist will rather be unemployed than work below his rate, even when, as may happen, the rate is being maintained in times of depression at a height greater than the trade will bear; the non-unionist more readily adjusts himself to a falling market.

It is best, therefore, to give up all attempts to use the trade union returns as an index to the actual volume of unemployment in the whole of industry. There are points in respect of which the percentage based upon them is clearly too high. There are other points—though not so many or so important as is generally assumed—in respect of which the percentage tends to be too

[1] *Distress from Want of Employment*, Third Report, 1895, p. 51.

low. In any case the magnificent generalisations reached by applying the trade union unemployed percentage directly to the whole industrial population are out of court. When 5 per cent. of the 650,000 trade unionists are out of work it does not in the least follow that there are 5 per cent. of the 11,000,000 manual workers, say 550,000, in the same case. The percentage totally unemployed is under such circumstances at least as likely to be one as five; the percentage losing some, even if not all, of their working time is equally likely to be ten or more.

As a measure of the volume of unemployment the trade union returns must be disregarded or used only with careful limitation to specific trades. As an indication of the movements of the labour market they retain their value unaffected by the foregoing criticisms. They are drawn, though unequally, from a considerable variety of trades. There can be no doubt that the principal movements shown by them are reflected, though unequally, throughout the greater part of the industrial field. The economic tendencies which from time to time make employment brisker or slacker for the skilled men in trade unions, must be felt, whether in greater or less degree, by the unorganised members of the same trades and by the labourers and auxiliaries dependent upon them. The carpenters and joiners, who form the great bulk of those included under the building trade returns, cannot as a rule suffer from depression without the other branches of the trade being simultaneously affected. With them too will go large sections of the woodworking and furnishing trades. So too the engineering and shipbuilding returns represent, as respects period and direction of movements in the labour market, though not as respects extent of movement, a much larger field than they cover directly. Again, many of the most important occupations which do not appear in the trade union returns—those connected with conveyance of men and goods—are specifically of an auxiliary character, and directly governed by the activity of the productive industries. The connections between various occupations are, indeed, very numerous and complex. Even if there is no connection on the side of production, there is one on the side of consumption. Diminished prosperity in a big industry, such as shipbuilding, means a falling off in the effective demand of the men engaged for food, housing, furniture and all else. These *a priori* arguments are, as will be shown later, confirmed by actual results. There can be no doubt that the various industries are so far inter-dependent, and the trade union returns drawn from a field so wide as to make the movements of the general unemployed percentage over a period of years fairly

representative of labour conditions as a whole.[1]   That is to say, a
rise in the percentage from one year to another means almost
always a worsening of conditions generally and not only in the
trades directly represented.   A fall in the unemployed percentage
means a general improvement.   This inference is on the whole
as legitimate as inferences with regard to the total volume of
unemployment are illegitimate.   The peculiar value of the trade
union returns is then simply this: that they give a continuous
record of the course of employment irrespective of the precise
numbers concerned, of the fortunes of particular employers and
of the general growth of population.   The unemployed percentages have been published monthly in the *Labour Gazette* since
1893.   They have been carried back by the records of some of
the older trade unions to 1860.   By their means one trade can
be compared with another trade at the same time.   For the
same trade or group of trades one time can with due precautions
be compared with another time.

(2) THE RECORDS OF DISTRESS COMMITTEES.

Under the Unemployed Workmen Act of 1905, Distress
Committees have been established in all the chief industrial
centres.   The first business of these Committees is to register,
investigate and classify unemployed persons applying to them
for assistance.   Their second business is, of course, to give such
assistance as they can, by temporary work, by emigration or in
other ways, to applicants satisfying certain conditions.   Some of
these Committees have taken little or no action.   The majority
have opened their registers at least during each winter, and have
received and investigated applications.   The results of their
activity have been described in their own reports and those of
the Local Government Board.   This registration is, of course, as
far from indicating the total number of the unemployed as are
the *Labour Gazette* returns.   In some areas there has been no
registration at all.   Everywhere only those have been registered
who were or who stated themselves to be in distress, and who
thought it worth while to apply for help.   Though the assistance
given carried no disqualification or stigma of pauperism, there
was no doubt among the better-class workmen a strong disinclination to apply so long as they could avoid doing so.   In fact

---

[1] This statement, it should be noted, is carefully limited to movements over a
period of years.   The course of the " general unemployed percentage " from month
to month is not a good indication of seasonal fluctuations.   It shows, for instance, as
a rule, an improvement from October to November, which can be traced directly to
the influence of the over-represented printing trades, and which would almost certainly
not be found if all occupations were equally represented.

it was found that few applied who belonged to any trade union
and still fewer who belonged to a union giving out-of-work pay.
The industrial class dealt with by the Distress Committees is thus
quite distinct from that appearing in the unemployed percentage.
This is a point of considerable importance and one which is continually overlooked. When the question is that of relieving immediate distress, attention can be confined to the men registered
by Distress Committees, since it may fairly be assumed that the
great bulk of those in urgent need of help will have applied.   No
objection can be raised to any particular relief method proposed,
e.g., the provision of rough labouring work, on the ground that it
does not suit a class of men, *e.g.*, highly skilled artisans, who do
not apply for relief.   When, however, the question is that of
preventing unemployment itself by discovering its causes, the
Distress Committee records cannot possibly be taken as giving
a complete picture.   The argument, for instance, that unemployment is due to deficiency of technical education, because so few
skilled men apply to Distress Committees, is palpably unsound.

Though, however, the Distress Committee records are incomplete in one sense—that they include only an uncertain proportion of the unemployed—they are very valuable as involving
much more than a mere counting of individuals.   The original
"Record Paper" drawn up by the Local Government Board contained eighteen paragraphs involving at least fifty different questions to be asked of and answered by every applicant for assistance,
together with six more paragraphs for information to be entered
after subsequent inquiry.   The information asked for included
the age, occupation, last and preceding employers with rates of
wages and average earnings, number of children, rent, rooms
occupied, and many other details intended to show clearly the
industrial and social status of the applicant.   The answers to the
most important questions were directed to be verified by reference to independent sources of information.   For the whole cost
of this registration and investigation the Committees were given
practically unlimited funds by being allowed to draw upon the
rates.   The result has been to accumulate a mass of information,
no doubt of unequal value, since different Committees took very
different views of their work, but of peculiar importance.   In the
first place the applicants to Distress Committees, if they are not
all the unemployed, are the unemployed for immediate practical
purposes.   They are those in urgent need of relief.   In the
second place the applicants are of a class as to which information has hitherto been wanting—an industrial stratum intermediate between the skilled trade unionists recorded in the *Labour*

Gazette and the paupers and vagrants known to Boards of Guardians. In the third place these applicants have not been simply counted. A sufficient volume of descriptive information has been obtained about them to define fairly clearly the character and causes of their distress.

(3) SUBSIDIARY SOURCES OF INFORMATION.

The two sources of information already described are those to which most constant reference will be made. They can, however, be supplemented and checked in many different ways.

First, there are many general evidences of commercial and manufacturing activity—the volumes and values of foreign trade, production and consumption of raw material in some of the principal industries, the course of prices, wages and the like.

Second, there is a great variety of statistics, bearing rather on employment than unemployment, collected by the Board of Trade each month and summarised in the *Labour Gazette*. In coal-mining, for instance, the degree of activity at any time is indicated by the average number of days per week on which coal was hewn and wound at a large number of collieries making regular returns. The following table gives the figures for the United Kingdom in each month since the beginning of 1895.

TABLE V.—COAL-MINING—DAYS WORKED PER WEEK.
1895-1908.

	Jan.	Feb.	March	April	May	June	July	Aug.	Sept.	Oct.	Nov.	Dec.	Mean for year.
1895	4·70	5·00	4·93	4·46	4·57	4·23	4·53	4·71	4·80	5·03	5·08	4·88	4·74
1896	4·94	4·91	4·81	4·69	4·88	4·58	4·83	5·00	4·89	5·02	5·31	5·16	4·92
1897	5·15	5·34	5·14	4·84	5·20	4·82	4·95	4·92	5·24	5·37	5·32	5·31	5·13
1898	5·06	5·24	5·29	4·98	5·38	4·95	5·13	5·19	5·37	5·44	5·46	5·54	5·25
1899	5·16	5·63	5·62	5·24	5·64	5·42	5·25	5·23	5·46	5·58	5·64	5·65	5·46
1900	5·13	5·69	5·67	5·19	5·63	5·18	5·52	5·43	5·65	5·63	5·45	5·46	5·47
1901	4·80	5·19	5·30	4·91	5·23	4·71	4·83	4·91	5·36	5·36	5·33	5·46	5·12
1902	5·26	5·39	5·35	4·90	4·89	5·17	4·82	4·94	5·35	5·52	5·51	5·51	5·22
1903	5·22	5·28	5·10	4·82	5·21	4·64	4·84	4·89	5·22	5·21	5·24	5·40	5·09
1904	5·10	5·19	5·28	4·86	5·09	4·95	4·79	4·76	5·16	5·16	5·14	5·30	5·07
1905	4·95	5·33	5·10	4·95	4·94	4·59	4·63	4·76	5·13	5·32	5·28	5·39	5·03
1906	5·01	5·54	5·50	5·08	5·37	4·84	4·99	4·95	5·30	5·49	5·50	5·60	5·26
1907	5·48	5·69	5·67	5·17	5·57	5·49	5·38	5·22	5·63	5·64	5·60	5·63	5·51
1908	5·44	5·56	5·49	5·05	5·48	4·75	4·93	4·93	5·34	5·23	5·19	5·29	5·22
Mean for each month, 1897-1906	5·08	5·38	5·34	4·98	5·26	4·93	4·98	5·00	5·33	5·41	5·39	5·46	5·21

Similar statistics are available for iron-mining and for iron and steel works. In the building and textile trades and in certain branches of clothing, returns are made by considerable numbers of employers as to the number of workpeople to whom wages were paid in the last week of each month, or even as to the actual amount paid. In one case, London dock and wharf labour, the numbers employed by all the dock companies and a large proportion of the shipowners, contractors and wharfingers are given day by day.

Third, from trade union reports and similar sources a great deal of information can be gathered as to the actual distribution of unemployment between individuals over a period of time. One defect of the ordinary unemployed percentage is that it does not indicate this. An average unemployed percentage of four throughout a year might mean that four particular men out of a hundred were unemployed the whole time, or it might mean that every one of the hundred became unemployed at some time for about two weeks in the year. What it actually means can only be discovered by studying individual records.

Fourth, the record of unemployment has to be completed by the record of pauperism. The trade union returns and the reports of Distress Committees represent practically the only occasions on which any considerable numbers of unemployed individuals are brought under review and counted. As has been said, they deal with two distinct sets of men. The unemployed workmen reported by the unions are with few exceptions members of skilled and highly organised trades. The unemployed applicants to Distress Committees are predominantly general labourers, and for the rest either half-skilled or the least efficient members of skilled trades. Yet a third and still lower stratum of society appears in the returns of pauperism compiled by the Local Government Board. A Parliamentary paper gives for England and Wales and for London separately the numbers of indoor and of outdoor paupers in receipt of relief at the end of each month, exclusive of lunatics in county and borough asylums, registered hospitals and licensed houses, casual paupers, persons receiving outdoor medical relief only, and patients in the fever and small-pox hospitals of the Metropolitan Asylums Board. The same return gives also the numbers of casual paupers relieved on each Friday during the month. In the annual reports of the Local Government Board further classification is made between males and females, able-bodied and not able-bodied, and so on. In this case, however, the number is not given at the end of each month but only on two particular days in the year, 1st January and 1st July, together with their mean.[1]

[1] For the benefit of those unfamiliar with Poor Law terminology it may be explained that the workhouse is reserved for persons resident in the union concerned

The first question asked with regard to the unemployed is generally as to their number. It should by now be clear that this is about the last question to which any scientific answer can be given.

There is no single universal system for registering all the unemployed. Its place is very inadequately taken by three separate registrations—by trade unions, by Distress Committees, and by Boards of Guardians—each governed by a practical motive which in effect makes each apply to an entirely distinct class of the community while supplying no basis of inference as to other classes. The three are not capable of being added together. If they were added together, they would not by any means cover the ground.

The difficulty in numbering the unemployed is, however, a far more serious one than would be represented by mere absence of a universal system of registration. Even if such a system could be set up, even if it were possible to determine for any particular moment how many persons were standing idle though able and willing to work at something, the result, from either a scientific or a practical point of view, would be all but worthless. The difficulty is fundamental—that there is no homogeneous unit which can be numbered. The hand boot-maker who has been permanently superseded by a new machine and will never be wanted again ; the compositor out of work in the August holidays and certain to be in demand in the November publishing season ; and the casual labourer on one of his off days but likely to be in demand the day after to-morrow are not really in the same case at all, and cannot be added together as if they were. Yet these are only some out of many types of unemployment. For purposes of immediate relief the unemployed may be taken as defined by the applicants to Distress Committees—110,000 in 1905-6, 87,000 in 1906-7, 90,000 in 1907-8. For purposes of scientific investigation or preventive organisation the analysis must be not of the numbers unemployed but of the causes of unemployment, and the extent to which they are essential or accidental in the existing economic order or in human nature. To this, therefore,

though "residence," for the purposes at least of first admission, implies only that one night has been spent in the district. Admission is normally secured by an order from the relieving officer. It has, however, been thought necessary to provide also in each union for the temporary reception of destitute wayfarers from other districts. For these consequently there has been established practically everywhere a separate casual ward to which they can as a rule gain admission merely by asking at the door, and where they receive lodging and board subject to the performance of a task of work and to detention for a second night.

the following five chapters will be devoted. Later it may be possible and profitable, in discussing remedies, to reach some estimate, not indeed of the number of the unemployed, but of the importance of the various types of unemployment, relatively to the whole of industry and to one another.

CHAPTER III.

SEASONAL FLUCTUATIONS.

A familiar and common phenomenon. Spring and summer trades. Winter trades. Trades dependent on social habits. Differences of period, range, regularity and cause. Seasonal fluctuations met (a) by reduction of hours; (b) by use of subsidiary trades; (c) by private or collective saving. A surface movement. A question less of unemployment than of wages.

SEASONAL fluctuation is a well-recognised feature of certain trades. Every one realises that there is, on the whole, less work for bricklayers in winter than in summer and for court dress-makers in August than in May. Few people perhaps realise how common seasonal fluctuation is. Detailed inquiry shows that it is almost the exception rather than the rule for any trade to maintain fairly equable activity throughout the year. Most trades have their regular alternation of busy months and slack months.

The most general view of the subject is afforded by a study of the trade union unemployed percentages. By taking the average for each month over a period of years the effects of special circumstances, cyclical fluctuation and general changes of level may be assumed to be eliminated or made inappreciable. The seasonal fluctuation alone will be left. In Table VI. and the accompanying chart the result is given for four principal industries, the period of years being 1897 to 1906. In a good many cases the monthly returns published in the *Labour Gazette* make more detailed analysis possible. The unemployed percentages, however, though they cover a considerable variety of trades, by no means cover the whole industrial field. Fortunately, they can be supplemented for the present purpose by returns of a different nature, relating either to the actual or proportional numbers employed by a representative body of employers or to the number of days or shifts worked per week.

These and other statistics show a great variety of seasonal movements in different industries. No doubt the commonest is that from slackness in winter to activity in spring and in summer and *vice versâ*. Building, for instance, shows a steadily decreasing unemployed percentage from December to May, a fairly busy time from then to the close of September (the actual minimum of unemployment being reached in August), and thereafter a percentage increasing steadily again. The closely related furnishing trades follow, as might be expected, a similar course, with the busiest time falling in spring rather than in summer. There are, however, many trades which are governed by quite different influences and show very different movements.

TABLE VI.—SEASONAL FLUCTUATION—UNEMPLOYED PERCENTAGES AT END OF EACH MONTH (MEAN OF 1897-1906).

Month.	Building (Carpenters and Plumbers).	Furnishing.	Engineering.	Printing, etc.
January	5·43	7·88	4·54	4·84
February . . .	5·20	6·47	4·42	4·26
March	4·39	3·25	3·97	3·57
April	3·65	2·38	3·79	4·18
May	3·39	2·45	3·59	4·51
June	3·69	3·20	3·67	4·40
July	3·50	4·09	3·69	3·74
August	3·34	4·05	3·96	5·82
September . . .	3·76	4·19	4·24	5·44
October	4·40	4·45	4·42	4·49
November . . .	4·76	4·93	4·52	2·88
December . . .	5·93	7·07	5·33	4·24

In some cases, for instance, climatic conditions have an effect directly opposite to that which they have on building. Coal miners are distinctly less busy in the warmth of summer than in winter. During the ten years 1897-1906 the average number of days worked per week in all the coal mines making returns was 5·46 in December and only 4·93 in June. The summer is also, according to the Board of Trade returns, the slackest time for iron and steel works and tin plate and steel sheet mills. So it is again, beyond question, in some occupations for which no statistics are available, e.g., at gas works.

In other cases marked and very characteristic seasonal fluctuations may be traced to social habits. The printing trades follow practically the same course year after year. The summer holidays always put an end to much work in connection with business and government. The season before Christmas is invariably the busiest. Then comes a falling off at the end of the year, a revival (in connection perhaps with the re-assembling of Parliament) in February, followed by a falling off in May and June and then a fresh burst of activity just before the holidays in

July.   Another industry violently affected by social habits is that of dressmaking.   Extreme pressure of work in the height of the London season—May and June—alternates with almost complete stagnation at its close.   Thus returns obtained by the Board of Trade from a number of representative firms in the West End show a falling off of nearly 50 per cent. in the number of dressmakers employed between July and August.   In the special branch of court dressmaking the fluctuation is, as a rule, even more violent.

CHART I.—SEASONAL FLUCTUATION—TRADE UNION UNEMPLOYED
PERCENTAGES AT END OF EACH MONTH (MEAN OF 1897-1906).

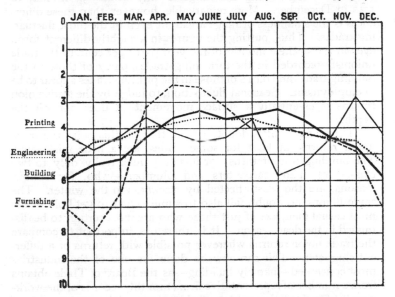

The seasonal movements of different occupations do not, therefore, by any means coincide in point of time.   They vary also very greatly in two other points of importance—regularity and range.   As to the former it has to be noted that in some trades, such as printing, building, furnishing, dressmaking—as also at gas works and in certain forms of dock labour—seasonal fluctuation is a dominant characteristic and employment runs much the same course in each successive year.   In other trades seasonal influences, though not absent, are liable to be over-ridden by influences of a different character.   Here, though over a period of years the unemployed percentage for some months may average out distinctly above or below that for other months, in any particular year the relative position is quite commonly found reversed, *e.g.*, by general expansion or contraction of trade. This is the case in iron and steel works, engineering, shipbuilding, and, speaking generally, in all trades connected with the production of metals and machinery. Such trades, it will be noticed later, are as a rule the most violently affected by cyclical fluctuation.

In regard to range of fluctuation the trade union returns show considerable differences between different trades. Thus, in furnishing, the range of the unemployed percentage is from 2·38 in April to 7·88, or nearly three and a half times as much in January, whereas in engineering the range is only from 3·59 in May to 5·33 in December. More remarkable, however, than these differences is the smallness of range apparent even in the most fluctuating trades. Thus, putting the figures in a slightly different form, even in the slackest months of the year 92·12 per cent. of the trade unionists recorded in the furnishing trades, 94·07 of those in the building trades and 94·18 of those in the printing trades appear to be in employment. Seasonal fluctuation, to judge by the trade union returns, is essentially a surface movement; it does not stir the depths.

There can be little doubt, indeed, that on this point the trade union returns, at least for some trades, are a little misleading. The building trade returns, for instance, refer really only to two classes of men—carpenters and plumbers—who, for various reasons, are the least affected by slackness in the winter. The trade unions, no doubt, fail also to some extent to get hold of the most casual men, *i.e.*, of just those who are most certain to be dismissed in the dead season. It is, therefore, important to compare the trade union returns wherever possible with returns of a different character. This can now be done for one of the industries most concerned—namely building—as the Board of Trade obtains from a number of representative firms monthly records of the workpeople of various classes employed by them. The total number of workpeople covered ranges from forty to over fifty thousand. The following table shows, for skilled and unskilled men separately, the percentage changes in the numbers employed from October, 1906, onwards :—

TABLE VII.—BUILDING TRADE—INCREASE OR DECREASE PER CENT. IN NUMBERS EMPLOYED BY FIRMS MAKING RETURNS R.

	1906.		1907.		1908.	
	Skilled Men.	Labourers.	Skilled Men.	Labourers.	Skilled Men.	Labourers.
January . .			+ 1·7	+ 1·4	− 1·2	− 3·1
February . .			+ 4·8	+ 1·2	+ 4·2	+ 2·0
March . .			+ 4·3	+ 7·6	+ 3·1	+ 5·0
April . . .			+ 2·1	+ 2·9	+ ·6	− ·6
May . . .			− 1·0	− ·8	+ 2·5	+ 3·8
June . . .			− 2·5	− ·6	− 3·0	+ ·1
July . . .			+ ·5	− 2·2	+ 1·7	+ 4·1
August . .			+ 2·9	+ 1·9	+ 5·0	+ 1·8
September . .			− 5·4	− 4·1	− 4·6	− 4·5
October . .	− 5·2	− 3·3	− 6·5	− 3·5	− 7·3	− 8·6
November . .	− 3·3	− 4·7	− 5·4	− 3·7	− 3·7	− 3·5
December . .	− 9·5	− 8·8	− 4·3	− 5·1	− 7·9	− 8·9

It will be seen that changes of more than 5 per cent. either way in a month are quite unusual, and that in this respect there is little difference between skilled men and labourers. Indeed the average of all the monthly changes is distinctly lower for the latter, about 3·6 as against 3·9 per cent. in the case of the skilled men. Taking 1907 as a whole it will be seen that in regard to labourers the first four months witness increases totalling up to 13·1 per cent., and the last four decreases totalling up to 16·4 per cent. Allowing therefore a liberal margin above the latter figure, it is reasonable to give 20 per cent. as the limit of difference between the numbers in the busiest and those in the slackest month, and therefore about 10 per cent. for the difference between the number for the busiest month and the mean for the year. The employers' returns in the building trade, while they show more fluctuation than do those from the unions, confirm the general impression of the relatively small loss of employment due to seasonal causes alone.[1]

The causes of seasonal fluctuations are sometimes classified as climatic or social. It is better perhaps to say that each type of cause is to be found in nearly every case. Climatic conditions necessarily give rise to social habits; indeed nearly all social habits involving regular annual fluctuation in the demand for labour may be traced ultimately to differences of temperature and

---

[1] In the case of building the decrease in the volume of employment during winter is slightly greater than is indicated by decrease in the numbers of employed because the working week is shorter. The difference due to this is not, however, very great; it is fully allowed for in the calculation on p. 36.

weather. On the other hand, social habits once established generally go beyond climatic necessities. It is, for instance, not so much impossible as unusual to build in winter. Sometimes fluctuation combines purely climatic with purely customary influences. At the London docks, for instance, tea comes in at one season of the year, timber at another, fruit at another according to climate. The net result is to make the general level of employment higher in the months about Christmas and again in July than it is in the early spring or in August and September. But with this goes a fluctuation dependent upon the customary dates of the wool sales for which large masses of additional labour are required. As a rule the sales take place six times a year and produce a regular up and down movement in the aggregate volume of employment. Sometimes, again—as is conspicuously the case with fluctuations of dock employment—the climate to be considered is not that of the United Kingdom but that of some other country whence goods come.

Seasonal fluctuation implies a falling off, in slack months, of the demand for labour. It is a cause of lack of employment entirely independent of the wishes and character of the individual workman, or, in general, of the individual employer. It does not, however, necessarily or indeed commonly involve acute distress.

In the first place, seasonal fluctuation may not lead to the actual discharge of workmen at all. In coal mining it is represented almost entirely by a reduction in the average number of days worked. In many other industries part, though not the whole, of the effect of seasonal fluctuation is carried off in this way—by a shortening of the working hours. For building operations, for instance, the London working week in summer consists of 50 hours, in winter of 44 hours. Here, therefore, the diminution in the numbers employed during the winter represents only part of the total diminution of employment. Part of the loss, by a reduction of working hours, is spread over all the men still employed.

In the second place, the difference in the period of fluctuation for different trades makes it possible for men thrown out of their usual occupation in a slack season to find a subsidiary occupation in some other industry which is then busy. Labourers engaged in the building trade or at brickfields in the summer can and often do find winter occupation at the docks or in gas works. Conversely labourers finding nothing to do at the riverside in August and September go regularly to pick hops or fruit or to help with the harvest. There are plenty of men in London who have been to the same farm for temporary work summer after summer. There are in the same way plenty of men who get taken on year after year by the Post Office or by some of the big shops to meet the Christmas pressure. This use of subsidiary trades in slack seasons has, no doubt, its limits. Practically it is confined to low-skilled or unskilled work. A man cannot be a cabinet-maker in April, a bricklayer in August and a compositor in November. On the other hand, by the spread of information and by deliberate organisation, the use of subsidiary trades might be made far easier than it is at present. There is more variety in the seasons for different occupations than is commonly supposed. They are as far as possible from all growing slack together in one month and all growing busy together in the next month. They offer, therefore, large possibilities of transference from one to the other, not indeed in the case of skilled men, but in respect of labourers and auxiliaries of every kind. In other words, they offer this possibility of dovetailing employments just where it is most necessary. The bricklayer cannot become a compositor in the winter months and may reasonably object in the intervals of his skill to doing the rough work of a gas stoker. But then just because of his skill he has higher wages; he can, therefore, better afford to save and stand idle entirely during slack seasons. The bricklayer's labourer with lower wages and therefore less room for saving can and does take up subsidiary work.

In the third place, seasonal fluctuation, being so common and regular a phenomenon, is to a large extent provided for in the expenditure of wages. This is one of the functions of the unemployed benefit paid by many trade unions. One or two unions, it is curious to note, only pay this benefit during the slack season.[1] Outside these unions the matter has of course to be dealt with and is very commonly dealt with by individual effort. Though bricklayers, for instance, have no unemployed benefit they are seldom to be found among the applicants to Distress Committees as a result of seasonal depression alone. Even where the individual has made no provision for slack times beforehand he can often get through them by running into debt and clearing himself during the following busy season. This is a form of retrospective saving made possible and common by the institution of the pawnshop and the readiness of small shopkeepers and landlords to grant credit to men ordinarily in good work.

In practice, therefore, it is found that acute recurrent distress at times of seasonal depression is confined to the unskilled occu-

---

[1] This is the case with two unions of painters.

3 *

pations, and even in them to men who at all times are irregularly employed. The natural tendency is for the fact of seasonal fluctuation to be recognised as a normal incident of the industry and to be allowed for in the standard both of expenditure and of wages. Estimated by the hour the rate of pay even in the unskilled branches of the building trade is relatively high—that is to say, it allows a margin for provision against slack times. This is illustrated by the following calculation.

The wage of a builder's labourer in London for a full week in summer is sevenpence an hour for fifty hours or twenty-nine shillings and twopence. Since the working hours are a little shorter in winter his average earnings throughout the year for constant employment would be slightly less than this, or roughly twenty-eight shillings and sixpence. The difference between the number of labourers employed in the busiest month and the mean number for the whole year may be put at 10 per cent., that is to say, *so far as seasonal fluctuation alone is concerned*, the wages of all builders' labourers in London might average out at over twenty-five shillings a week.[1] In fact, of course, the average is very much lower,[2] because even in the busy seasons many builders' labourers fail to get steady work. They are subject not only to seasonal fluctuation but also to under-employment.

That, of course, is the root of the trouble. The men who winter after winter are in acute distress are the men who summer after summer can only live from hand to mouth, men whose earnings even in the busy months are cut down by irregularity of employment. They have no reserves and no credit. They almost certainly do not spend to the best advantage even such money as they do earn, for their whole life is an education in the futility

---

[1] This takes no account of the possibility of the work even of those who are employed being more broken on account of weather in winter than in summer. On the other hand, it omits also the important possibility of overtime in summer. These two considerations must be left to balance one another.

[2] Estimates of the average earnings of builders' labourers as a class are impossible, because there is no homogeneous class. At one extreme are picked men in practically continuous work under one or two well-known foremen; at the other end is the lowest type of casual. In Charles Booth's *Life and Labour of the People; Industry*, vol. i., p. 127, the actual earnings of an individual labourer for the years 1891 and 1892 are recorded, and work out at twenty-five shillings a week all through. Apart, however, from the fact that 1891 at least was a year of exceptional activity in the London building trade, it is clear that a man with sufficient method and character to keep a record of his earnings would be an unusually favourable example of his class. Other estimates given in the same place vary from seventeen shillings to thirty-one shillings and average twenty-three shillings and threepence. In his evidence to the Select Committee of 1895, Mr. Aves, the writer of the chapter quoted and a high authority on building trade conditions, estimated that in London the average earnings of a man who was really a builders' labourer by calling and not merely a " general labourer " would be not less than twenty-one shillings throughout the year.

of foresight. They find themselves at the first pinch in the streets.

Ultimately, therefore, seasonal fluctuation becomes a question not of unemployment but of wages. From an economic point of view no industry is self-supporting unless it pays wages sufficient to keep men, not only while they are at work, but also while they must stand idle and in reserve. Where in any occupation seasonal fluctuation year after year brings round acute distress, that occupation must be judged as one in which wages are too low or ill-spent, because they do not average out to a sufficiency for the slack months as well as for the busy ones. It is from this point of view that the problem must be regarded. It is upon this basis that its treatment must be attempted.

CHAPTER IV.

CYCLICAL FLUCTUATION.

Alternate rise and fall of average unemployed percentage in periods of years. All principal trades affected together. Fluctuation in the labour market part of general economic ebb and flow. The pulse of the nation. Shown in bank rate, foreign trade, marriage rate, consumption of beer, crime, pauperism, company formation, railway receipts, bankers' clearances, wages, prices. Peculiar features since 1900. Material life of the nation governed by alternations of expansion and contraction.
Causes of cyclical fluctuation still in dispute. Distinction between financial crises and industrial depressions. Two types of theory untenable, *viz.*: those not applicable to all advanced industrial countries alike and those requiring fixed periods. Foreign trade fluctuation of principal countries. Three types of theory still possible. (1) Fluctuation in supply of gold and silver. (2) Misdirection of productive energy. (3) Superfluity of productive energy. The "under-consumption" theory. The competition theory. Cyclical fluctuation as the necessary form of progress under competition.
No final theory as to cyclical fluctuation can yet be given. Fluctuation itself certain to continue. Average rate of growth of demand for labour adequate for growth of population; actual rate sometimes greater, sometimes less. Recurrent pressure in labour market more or less successfully met in some trades. Not met by unorganised workmen. Mansion House Relief Funds. Better measures of palliation needed.

IN the table on p. 18 the last column gives for each year the unemployed percentage obtained by averaging the percentages for each separate month. This column shows, in fact, the changes in general level from year to year, after the effect of purely seasonal fluctuations has been eliminated. It is at once evident that the general level changes very considerably and with some regularity. The mean unemployed percentage first falls steadily from the 6·9 at which it stood in 1894 to 2·0 in 1899, rises to 6·0 in 1904, falls to 3·6 in 1906, and is now rising again (1908).

These figures are one illustration of the remarkable phenomenon which will be described in the present chapter under the name of cyclical fluctuation of industrial activity.

The unemployed percentages in certain important trade unions are now available for a good many years back and have been published in the Second Series of *Memoranda on British and Foreign Trade and Industry*, p. 98. From this the following table has been adapted showing the mean annual percentages of unemployed trade unionists in four principal industrial groups separately and in all together during the past fifty or sixty years.

TABLE VIII.—CYCLICAL FLUCTUATION—TRADE UNION UNEM-
PLOYED PERCENTAGES AND PRODUCTION. *R.*

Year.	Engineering, Shipbuilding and Metal.	Building.	Woodworking and Furnishing.	Printing and Bookbinding.	All Unions making Returns (Corrected Weights). Percentage Un-employed.	Percentage *not* Un-employed.	Raw Cotton. Lbs. consumed per Head.	Pig Iron. Cwts. produced per Head.	Shipbuilding. Tons built per 1,000.
1860	1·9	0·2	—	2·1	1·85	98·15	37·7	2·6	7·88
1861	5·5	1·8	—	3·1	3·70	96·30	34·8	2·6	7·02
1862	9·0	1·8	—	3·5	6·05	93·95	15·3	2·6	8·97
1863	6·7	1·2	—	3·2	4·70	95·30	17·5	3·0	12·86
1864	3·0	0·4	—	1·3	1·95	98·05	18·9	3·2	15·52
1865	2·4	0·3	—	2·0	1·80	98·20	24·0	3·2	14·98
1866	3·9	1·1	—	1·8	2·65	97·35	29·8	3·0	12·61
1867	9·1	3·0	4·8	2·7	6·30	93·70	31·3	3·2	10·06
1868	10·0	2·9	5·0	2·5	6·75	93·25	32·5	3·2	11·80
1869	8·9	3·6	4·5	2·8	5·95	94·05	30·4	3·4	12·56
1870	4·4	3·7	4·8	3·5	3·75	96·25	34·5	3·8	12·64
1871	1·3	2·5	3·5	2·0	1·65	98·35	38·3	4·2	12·38
1872	0·9	1·2	2·4	1·5	0·95	99·05	36·9	4·2	14·87
1873	1·4	0·9	1·8	1·3	1·15	98·85	38·7	4·2	14·13
1874	2·3	0·8	2·1	1·6	1·60	98·40	38·9	3·6	18·58
1875	3·5	0·6	2·0	1·6	2·20	97·80	37·6	4·0	14·39
1876	5·2	0·7	2·4	2·4	3·40	96·60	38·5	4·0	11·38
1877	6·3	1·2	3·5	2·6	4·40	95·60	36·7	4·0	13·42
1878	9·0	3·5	4·4	3·2	6·25	93·75	34·7	3·8	13·89
1879	15·3	8·2	8·3	4·0	10·70	89·30	34·3	3·4	11·84
1880	6·7	6·1	3·2	3·2	5·25	94·75	39·8	4·4	13·61
1881	3·8	5·2	2·7	2·8	3·55	96·45	41·4	4·6	17·45
1882	2·3	3·5	2·5	2·4	2·35	97·65	41·4	4·8	22·25
1883	2·7	3·6	2·5	2·2	2·60	97·40	42·4	4·8	25·20
1884	10·8	4·7	3·0	2·1	7·15	92·85	41·1	4·4	16·48
1885	12·9	7·1	4·1	2·5	8·55	91·45	37·0	4·2	12·25
1886	13·5	8·2	4·7	2·6	9·55	90·45	40·4	3·8	9·14
1887	10·4	6·5	3·6	2·2	7·15	92·85	40·7	4·2	10·31
1888	5·5 6·0	5·7	3·6 3·1	2·5 2·4	4·15	95·85	41·3	4·4	15·55
1889	2·0 2·3	3·0	2·6 2·4	2·1 2·5	2·05	97·95	41·2	4·4	22·98
1890	2·4 2·2	2·2	1·5 2·5	1·9 2·2	2·10	97·90	44·2	4·2	21·67
1891	4·4 4·1	1·9	1·7 2·1	2·9 4·0	3·40	96·60	44·1	4·0	21·42
1892	8·2 7·7	3·1	2·4 3·8	3·6 4·3	6·20	93·80	40·0	3·6	21·04
1893	11·4	3·1	4·1	4·1	7·70	92·30	38·5	3·6	15·18
1894	11·2	4·3	4·4	5·7	7·20	92·80	41·6	3·8	17·21
1895	8·2	4·4	3·6	4·9	6·00	94·00	41·8	4·0	16·55
1896	4·2	1·3	2·0	4·3	3·35	96·65	41·6	4·4	18·61
1897	4·8	1·2	2·2	3·9	3·45	96·55	40·6	4·4	16·12
1898	4·0	0·9	2·3	3·7	2·95	97·05	43·1	4·2	21·55
1899	2·4	1·2	2·1	3·9	2·05	97·95	43·1	4·6	23·26
1900	2·6	2·6	2·8	4·2	2·45	97·55	39·4	4·4	22·92
1901	3·8	3·9	3·7	4·5	3·35	96·65	39·6	3·8	23·63
1902	5·5	4·0	4·1	4·6	4·20	95·80	39·0	4·1	22·63
1903	6·6	4·4	4·7	4·4	5·00	95·00	36·7	4·2	17·89
1904	8·4	7·3	6·8	4·7	6·40	93·60	36·6	4·1	20·66
1905	6·6	8·0	5·8	5·1	5·25	94·75	42·8	4·4	24·27
1906	4·1	6·9	4·8	4·5	3·70	96·30	43·6	4·6	26·47
1907	4·9	7·3	4·6	4·3	3·95	96·05	44·7	4·6	23·52
1908	12·5	11·6	8·3	5·5	8·65	91·35	39·1	4·1	13·44

The table discloses at once a remarkable series of waves of good and bad employment affecting all four groups nearly simultaneously. From the bad time of 1862, employment, as indicated by the general unemployed percentage, improves till 1865, and falls off as steadily till 1868, when it begins to improve again till 1872, and falls off very gradually again till 1879. From that it recovers till 1882 to relapse again in 1886, and recovers till 1890, to relapse again in 1893-94, and, subject to a break occasioned by the engineering strike of 1897, recovers till 1899 to relapse again till 1904, and recovers slightly till 1906 to relapse again in 1907-8. This summary, based on the movements of the general unemployed percentage, can, with a very slight adjustment of dates, be fitted to any one of the four groups separately. All four share prosperity and adversity in turn and together. It is only necessary to note, first, that so far as any difference is observable in the periods for the separate groups, there is a tendency for the movements of the most important one—engineering, shipbuilding and metals—to precede those of the others (*e.g.*, in the bad years about 1868 and 1893-94, and the good years about 1872 and 1890); second, that though the periods of fluctuation are as stated, roughly the same for each group, the range of fluctuation varies extremely. In the engineering, shipbuilding and metal groups the range is very great. The average unemployment at the four minima, 1872, 1882, 1890, 1899, is 2·0; that for the four maxima, 1868, 1879, 1886, 1893, is 12·5 or more than six times as great. In building the range is less; from an average for the four corresponding minima of 1·7 to one for the four corresponding maxima of 6·1 or three and a half times as great. In furnishing and wood-working the range is from 2·1 to 5·3, or two and a half times. In printing and book-binding it is least of all; from an average minimum of 2·3 to an average maximum of 3·9 or only one and three-quarter times. It is noticeable that this order for cyclical fluctuation is almost exactly the reverse of that for seasonal oscillation. So far as the unemployed percentages may be trusted, the trades which are most regularly affected by a seasonal movement from month to month are those least affected by a cyclical movement from year to year.

The figures cited embrace a fair variety of trades. They do not by any means cover the whole industrial field. Some of the principal industries of the country—coal-mining, textiles, iron-mining and manufacture—are not at all or quite inadequately represented in the unemployed percentage. The degree of industrial activity in them may, however, be indicated in other ways.

The last three columns of the table just given show in proportion to population the consumption of raw cotton, the production of pig iron, and the tonnage of ships built in the United Kingdom during each year since 1860. In each case fluctuation corresponding in dates to that of the unemployed percentages is apparent. The years 1872-74, 1882, 1889-90, 1899 are marked by exceptional activity; the years 1879, 1885-86, 1893-94 and 1903-4 by relative slackness.

In regard to coal-mining the average number of days worked per week can be given for each year since 1895.[1] During that period there appears first a definite improvement to a maximum in 1900, followed by depression becoming most acute in 1905, and now again by an improvement which has made 1907 a record year.

This fluctuation of industrial activity has clearly nothing to do with the wishes or characteristics of the men employed. It is not within the control of individual employers. It is not limited to particular trades. It represents alternate expansion and contraction in the general demand for labour and is only one aspect of a still more general ebb and flow dominating the economic life of the nation. The fluctuation just traced in the records of the labour market and of production in one or two principal industries is more or less closely reflected in almost every series of commercial and social statistics. The evidence for this statement is to be found in the annexed table and chart.

The central position in the chart is occupied by a curve of employment in trade unions, which is simply the curve of unemployment reversed, so as to represent an unemployed percentage of 2·5 as an employed percentage of 97·5 and so on. Lines drawn through the successive lowest points of this curve—1868, 1879, 1886, 1894, 1904—cut it up into waves of unequal length, representing successive industrial cycles. The crest of each wave is at about 98; the depressions are anywhere between 89 and 94. The point of the chart is this, that the same lines cut up every one of the other curves into corresponding waves.

The uppermost curve, for instance, represents the bank rate, that is to say, the average minimum rate per cent. of discount charged by the Bank of England in each year. Rising when money is in brisk demand and falling when it is not, this rate is a general indication of the degree of financial and so of commercial activity at any time. The chart shows a quite unmistakable tendency for the curve of the bank rate to rise and fall with the curve of employment. In the successive years of minimum em-

[1] Cf. Table V., p. 25.

TABLE IX.—THE PULSE OF THE NATION. *R.*

Year.	Bank Rate (Average Minimum Discount Rate of per cent.).	Imports and Special Exports per Head.[1]	Employed Percentage (Trade Unions).	Wholesale Prices (1900=100).	Wages (1900=100).	Companies Registered during Year. Nominal Capital per Head.	Railway Receipts: Net per cent. of Paid-up Capital.	Marriages per 1,000 of the Population, England and Wales.	Consumption of Beer per Head (Gallons).	Crime. Drunkenness. Prosecutions per 100,000.	Crime. Indictable Offences Tried (in Thousands).	Pauperism. Indoor, England and Wales, per 10,000 (Mean of No. at end of each Month).	Pauperism. Vagrants, London (Friday Nights).
	1.	2.	3.	4.	5.	6.	7.	8.	9.	10.	11.	12.	13.
		£ s. d.				£	£						
1856	6	10 5 8	—	—	—	—	—	16·7	22·6	—	—	—	—
1857	6¾	10 19 10	—	—	—	—	—	16·5	22·6	—	54·7	63·0	—
1858	3¼	9 17 10	—	—	—	—	—	16·0	23·6	—	52·5	61·2	—
1859	2¾	10 16 1	—	—	—	—	—	17·0	24·8	—	50·1	56·1	—
1860	4¼	12 0 3	98·15	—	—	—	4·19	17·1	23·8	—	48·5	55·7	—
1861	5¼	11 15 10	96·30	—	—	—	4·06	16·3	24·3	—	56·0	61·0	—
1862	2½	11 19 7	93·95	—	—	—	3·86	16·1	24·1	—	61·3	64·2	—
1863	4½	13 9 5	95·30	—	—	4·8	3·99	16·8	25·4	—	61·4	62·8	—
1864	7½	14 12 11	98·05	—	—	8·0	4·23	17·2	26·7	—	58·4	60·6	—
1865	4¾	14 12 0	98·20	—	—	6·9	4·11	17·5	29·8	—	59·9	60·9	—
1866	7	16 1 3	97·35	—	—	2·5	4·02	17·5	29·4	—	57·6	61·2	—
1867	2½	15 0 0	93·70	—	—	1·0	3·91	16·5	28·1	—	59·5	65·2	—
1868	2¼	15 9 2	93·25	—	—	1·1	—	16·1	28·2	—	62·4	68·0	—
1869	3¼	15 13 5	94·05	—	—	[4·5][4]	4·22	15·9	29·1	—	61·3	67·7	—
1870	3⅛	16 1 9	96·25	—	—	1·2	4·41	16·1	30·2	—	56·1	66·8	—
1871	2⅞	17 11 3	98·35	136·0	—	2·2	4·66	16·7	29·3	—	53·1	63·2	1,123
1872	4⅛	19 3 5	99·05	145·8	—	4·1	4·74	17·4	32·2	—	51·9	59·9	—
1873	4¾	19 9 5	98·85	152·7	—	4·7	4·59	17·6	33·5	—	53·5	59·2	603
1874	3¾	18 15 2	98·40	148·1	91·7	3·4	4·37	17·0	34·0	783	53·5	58·2	603
1875	3¼	18 4 0	97·80	141·4	90·3	2·5	4·45	16·7	33·3	850	50·0	56·6	451
1876	2⅝	17 7 0	96·60	138·0	89·4	1·4	4·36	16·5	33·7	842	51·9	57·1	609
1877	2⅞	17 13 6	95·60	141·6	88·3	2·0	4·32	15·7	32·3	810	53·8	59·8	699

1878	$3\frac{3}{4}$	16	11	1	93·75	132·6	85·1	2·0	4·25	15·2	32·2	778	56·0	62·5	726
1879	$2\frac{3}{8}$	16	3	6	89·30	126·6	83·3	2·2	4·15	14·4	28·0	703	55·0	66·8	718
1880	$2\frac{3}{4}$	18	6	7	94·75	129·6	83·1	4·9	4·38	14·9	27·0	673	60·7	67·9	795
1881	$3\frac{1}{2}$	18	1	4	96·45	127·3	84·6	6·0	4·29	15·1	27·8	670	60·6	68·4	802
1882	$4\frac{1}{8}$	18	11	9	97·65	128·4	85·8	7·2	4·32	15·5	27·6	720	63·3	67·2	814
1883	$3\frac{9}{16}$	18	16	2	97·40	126·8	85·9	4·7	4·29	15·5	27·2	724	60·8	66·7	482[3]
1884	$2\frac{13}{20}$	17	8	10	92·85	114·7	85·2	3·9	4·16	15·1	27·8	736	59·6	66·3	510
1885	3	16	4	4	91·45	107·7	83·8	3·3	4·02	14·5	27·1	673	56·4	65·8	580
1886	3	15	9	10	90·45	101·6	83·1	4·0	3·99	14·2	26·9	600	56·2	65·9	578
1887	$3\frac{1}{3}$	15	19	2	92·85	99·6	83·3	4·6	4·00	14·4	27·3	585	56·2	66·2	738
1888	$3\frac{1}{5}$	16	17	5	95·85	102·7	85·0	9·6	4·06	14·4	27·2	591	58·5	65·9	1,136
1889	$3\frac{1}{2}$	18	4	0	97·95	104·0	87·6	5·5	4·21	15·0	28·9	613	57·6	64·4	960
1890	$4\frac{1}{2}$	18	5	1	97·90	104·0	90·6	5·4	4·10	15·5	30·0	660	55·0	62·0	858
1891	$3\frac{1}{3}$	18	1	3	96·60	107·4	91·7	3·5	4·00	15·6	30·2	644	54·1	60·9	842
1892	$2\frac{1}{2}$	17	1	5	93·80	101·8	90·3	2·7	3·85	15·4	29·8	591	58·3	61·7	919
1893	$3\frac{1}{25}$	16	3	8	92·30	100·0	90·5	2·5	3·60	14·7	29·6	568	57·4	64·1	957
1894	$2\frac{1}{9}$	16	1	4	92·80	94·2	89·7	3·0	3·77	15·0	29·5	593	56·3	65·4	1,086
1895	2	16	7	10	94·00	91·0	89·2	6·0	3·80	15·0	29·6	557	50·8	66·5	1,129
1896	$2\frac{1}{2}$	17	4	6	96·65	88·2	90·1	7·8	3·88	15·7	30·8	608	50·7	65·2	1,063
1897	$2\frac{5}{8}$	17	2	9	96·55	90·1	91·0	7·3	3·73	16·0	31·3	620	50·7	64·8	1,045
1898	$3\frac{1}{4}$	17	8	8	97·05	93·2	93·2	6·7	3·55	16·2	31·8	643	52·5	65·0	1,064
1899	$3\frac{3}{4}$	18	3	2	97·95	92·3	95·6	6·0	3·61	16·5	32·6	672	50·5	63·8	1,009
1900	$3\frac{15}{16}$	19	11	8	97·55	100·0	100·0	5·4	3·41	16·0	31·6	634	53·6	62·4	916
1901	$3\frac{11}{16}$	19	1	8	96·65	96·9	99·1	3·3	3·27	15·9	30·8	643	55·5	63·7	969
1902	$3\frac{1}{3}$	19	4	9	95·80	96·5	97·9	3·7	3·42	15·9	30·3	636	57·1	65·0	985
1903	$3\frac{3}{4}$	19	12	6	95·00	96·9	97·4	2·9	3·42	15·6	29·7	690[2]	58·4	66·8	1,089
1904	$3\frac{1}{8}$	19	17	9	93·60	98·3	96·9	2·1	3·39	15·2	28·8	674	60·0	71·1	1,133
1905	3	20	13	11	94·75	97·6	97·3	2·7	3·41	15·3	27·7	642	61·5	71·8	1,168
1906	$4\frac{17}{60}$	22	9	8	96·30	100·5	98·7	3·1	3·50	15·6	28·0	615	59·1	72·5	1,190
1907	$4\frac{37}{40}$	24	5	7	96·05	105·8	102·2	3·1	3·47	15·8	27·6	601	61·4	72·5	1,121

[1] Excluding Ships throughout. [2] Licensing Act, 1902. [3] Casual Poor Act, 1882.

[4] The abnormally high figure is due to a single Company with a Registered Capital of £100,000,000, of which not £200 was subscribed.

Unless the contrary is stated all the statistics apply to the United Kingdom.

CHART II.—THE PULSE OF THE NATION.

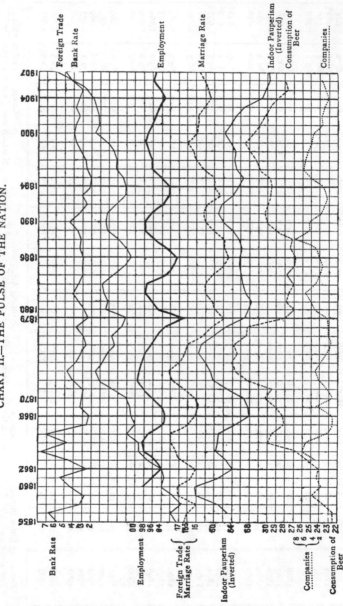

The scales at the left-hand side indicate respectively the actual Bank Rate of discount per cent., the percentage of trade union members not returned as unemployed, the number of marriages in England and Wales per 1000 of the population, the number of indoor paupers in England and Wales per 10,000 of the population, the gallons of beer consumed, and the nominal capital of new companies registered, in pounds, per head of the population. No scale is given for the Foreign Trade curve. Unless the contrary is stated, all figures apply to United Kingdom generally.

ployment—marked by the heavy vertical lines of the chart—the average rate of discount has been $2\frac{1}{2}$, $2\frac{1}{4}$, $2\frac{3}{8}$, 3, $2\frac{1}{9}$, $3\frac{1}{3}$. In the successive years of maximum employment it has been $4\frac{1}{4}$, $4\frac{3}{4}$, $4\frac{1}{8}$, $4\frac{1}{8}$, $3\frac{1}{2}$, $3\frac{3}{4}$. The correspondence of dates in the fluctuation is not, indeed, absolute. The bank rate often reaches its actual maximum or minimum in the year just before or just after employment, as shown by the trade union percentages, does so. The bank rate is also affected by a variety of exceptional and temporary causes. It rises when commercial expansion is increasing the demand for money. It rises also at times of financial panic when credit is overthrown and business practically at a standstill. The distinction between such financial crises, with a high bank rate, and industrial depressions, with a low bank rate, is a point whose importance is perhaps hardly sufficiently realised. It will come up for consideration later. In the meantime attention may be called to another peculiarity of the bank rate, apparent in the periods 1868-79, 1886-94, 1894-1904. In each of these there are, in addition to the main fluctuation leading to a maximum at about the middle of the period, two minor fluctuations resulting in subsidiary maxima one on each side of the principal one. Thus from 1868 the bank rate rises to 1869, falls slightly to 1871, rises to its greatest height in 1873, falls to 1876 and then rises again to 1878 before completing the cycle with a fall to 1879.

The curve designated "Foreign Trade" marks the values, per head of the population, of exports (British and Irish produce) and imports. Expressing values not quantities, it is liable to distortion by fluctuation of prices. It shows also a general change of level in the period up to 1872 and, apparently, now again in the last few years of the table. Neither of these facts destroys the significance of the curve as a picture of trade fluctuation or conceals the close relation between it and the curves for the bank rate and employment. It is for this purpose alone—that of showing the movement from one year to the next—that the chart is intended. A general warning may be given here against using any of the figures in the table, without further examination, for any purpose other than this, e.g., to compare the general level as between the beginning and the end of the total period covered.[1]

---

[1] Changes due to movements of price are one source of error. Another is well illustrated by the marriage curve, which appears since 1880 to show through the fluctuations a general upward tendency. This appearance is entirely due to changes in the age distribution of the people. Owing to the falling birth rate there are proportionately more persons at marriageable age and fewer children in the population now than formerly. The number of marriages in proportion to the total population not unnaturally rises. The number of marriages in proportion to persons at marriageable age shows no tendency to rise.

The three upper curves—representing the most general facts available as to the state of finance, commerce and employment respectively—are absolutely distinct in origin and character. Yet they are all strikingly correlated. By their agreement they map out the collective economic history of the nation into definite though unequal periods, each witnessing a burst of exceptional activity followed by an interval of comparative stagnation. The influence of this movement is felt in almost every department of human life.

The tendency to matrimony, for instance, is undoubtedly related to the comparative prosperity or adversity of the times. The marriage-rate shown in the chart, that is to say, the number of marriages each year to every thousand persons, rises and falls with the bank rate, the value of foreign trade and the employed percentage.

The influences which favour matrimony also favour drinking. The consumption of alcoholic liquors per head of the population increases as a rule in good years and decreases in bad ones. The chart shows this for beer alone. The same relation holds in regard to wine and spirits. For the rich man as for the poor man the years of depression—1862, 1868, 1879-80, 1886, 1894, 1904-5— are years of compulsory temperance. Prosperity leads to riotous living. Nowhere is this so marked as in the contrast between 1874, when, for every man, woman and child in the country, there were consumed 34 gallons of beer, 1·26 gallons of spirits and ·53 gallons of wine, and 1880, when the consumption of beer per head had fallen off to 27 gallons, that of spirits to 1·07, that of wine to ·45. A similar fall has taken place in the years from 1899 onwards and has been hailed as evidence of increasing sobriety. Yet it is well to remember that the years from 1899 to 1904-5 correspond with the last period of decreasing employment, and that the recovery of trade in 1906-7 witnessed a recovery in the amount of drinking. The decrease in the consumption of alcohol in the last ten years has been great enough to justify a hope of permanent improvement, but the hope may be rudely shattered at the next period of general prosperity. Between 1874 and 1880 the consumption of beer fell off as already stated from 34·0 to 27·0 gallons, or more than 20 per cent., yet in 1899 it was up again at 32·6. The figure for 1905 ought to be compared, not with that for 1899, but with those for previous epochs of depression—29·5 in 1894, 26·9 in 1886, 27·0 in 1880, 28·2 in 1868. These figures relate to beer. In regard to wine there has indubitably been a great fall irrespective of trade fluctuation. The consumption per head in 1905 was less than 50 per cent. of that in 1873 and 1876, and less than 63 per cent. of that in the lean year of 1879.

The consumption of alcohol leads to drunkenness, and drunkenness is not only at times in itself an offence against law and order but also the fruitful source of other offences. An experienced Scottish witness before the Licening Commission, speaking indeed rather of the contrast between summer and winter than of that between successive years, went so far as to suggest the generalisation that the prisons filled as the poorhouses emptied (in times of prosperity and drinking) and emptied as the latter filled (in times of depression and compulsory abstinence). In regard to prosecutions for drunkenness itself the relation is made out. The yearly number of prosecutions per 100,000 of the population tends to rise and fall in close dependence upon the bank rate, the employed percentage, and all the other indications of prosperity. From 850 in the fat year of 1875, it sank to 673 in the lean year of 1880, rose to 736 and sank again to 585 in 1887, rose to 660 and sank to 557 in 1895, rose to 672 in 1899, and began to sink again till the changes of law effected by the Licensing Act, 1902, came into operation.[1] After that change there followed a further fall to the depression of 1904-5.

In regard to offences other than drunkenness no generalisation can be made. Criminality is a very complex phenomenon and is in its different forms the indication, not merely of distinct, but of opposed influences. There is some ground for saying that assaults and minor crimes of violence, having their origin very often in drunkenness, tend to be more frequent in years of good trade and less frequent in years of bad trade. On the other hand, the pressure to steal is increased by adversity. According to the *Report on Criminal Statistics* for 1905 there is a distinct correlation between the number of larcenies and the volume of foreign trade each year; as trade expands larcenies decrease and *vice versâ*. The result is to make the general course of crime as shown by the number of indictable offences agree with that of unemployment,[2] for the great majority of such offences are thefts of various kinds.

Another instance of connection between trade depression and

[1] This Act substituted "drunk and incapable" for "drunk and disorderly" as a ground of prosecution, and made other changes extending the scope of the law.

[2] This result shows that some, not that all or any large proportion of crime, is committed under pressure of exceptional distress by people who in normal times would be respectable citizens. It would be quite consistent with the fluctuation shown that the bulk of crime should be that of habitual offenders and be unaffected by variation of industrial conditions.

It should be noted that the table gives the absolute number of offences in each year. Since this absolute number has fluctuated at about the same level since 1856, it represents a great decrease of crime relatively to the population, which has during the period grown from twenty-eight to forty-four millions.

individual failure is afforded by pauperism. In the chart the most important statistics, those of indoor pauperism in England and Wales, are shown in an inverted form; that is to say, the numbers run downward so as to make a downward movement of the curve indicate a growth of pauperism and an upward movement a decrease. In this way direct optical comparison with the other curves is made possible. The numbers themselves give for each year the number of paupers for 10,000 of the population as the mean of twelve counts, one at the end of each month.

Once again a striking correlation with the state of trade and employment becomes evident. The correlation has, however, one peculiar feature. Since 1870 the curve of pauperism has reached its successive lowest points—indicating maxima of pauperism—not in the year of greatest industrial depression, but in the next year or the year after that; it has reached its highest points in turn, not at the actual moment of greatest industrial prosperity, but just after. The worst years for employment have been 1879, 1886, 1893-4, 1904. To these correspond maxima of pauperism in 1881, 1887, 1895, 1905-6. During the same period the best years for employment have been 1872-4, 1882, 1889-90, 1899. To those correspond minima of pauperism in 1875, 1885, 1891, and 1900. These statements refer directly only to one form of pauperism, that classified as " indoor," exclusive of lunatics, vagrants and patients in the fever and small-pox hospitals of the Metropolitan Asylums Board. Outdoor pauperism is much more affected by changes of administrative policy. Between 1868 and 1878 it fell in England and Wales as a whole from 371 per 10,000 of the population to 214, and in London alone from 335 to 111. Nevertheless it too is clearly subject to the same influences as indoor pauperism, and fluctuates between maxima and minima occurring, as a rule, in the years immediately succeeding those of greatest and least unemployment. The London statistics tell the same tale as those for the whole country. This is seen, perhaps, most clearly in regard to the inmates of casual wards, who include a certain proportion of the able-bodied unemployed or unemployables. Starting from a minimum of 482 in 1883 (the year after the passing of the stringent Casual Poor Act) the average number of paupers relieved in the casual wards of London on all the Fridays of the year rises to a maximum of 1136 in 1888, falls to 842 in 1891, rises to 1129 in 1895, falls to 916 in 1900, rises to 1190 in 1906, and, after a fall in 1907, is now rising once more. Broadly speaking, the course of pauperism in all its principal forms follows the course of unemployment at an interval of about a year. This interval may be explained in various ways.

First, it may be a phenomenon exactly parallel to that which makes the greatest heat of summer occur not at but a month or so after the longest day of the year, and the greatest cold of winter occur not at but a month or so after the shortest day. The movement of temperature depends upon the balance of inflow of warmth (during the day) and outflow (during the night). It, therefore, continues to rise in July even after the days have begun to shorten, so long as they still remain relatively long; and it continues to fall in January because the days though lengthening are still short. In the same way the increase or decrease of pauperism depends upon the relative volumes of the inflow (fresh cases of distress) and of the outflow (by death and other causes). Assuming the latter to be fairly constant, pauperism would tend to increase whenever unemployment was above a certain level, that is to say, it might increase even after the greatest depression in the labour market was over, so long as sufficient depression remained to keep the inflow of paupers above normal. In the same way pauperism would tend to decrease whenever unemployment was below a certain level, that is to say, it might continue to decrease even after trade had taken a downward turn and, though remaining good, was not as good as before.

Second, the interval between the crises of unemployment and those of pauperism may represent the actual average interval between the dislodgement of persons from the industrial ranks and their arrival at the workhouse. That there is such an interval is certain. Even the poorest families have a modicum of resisting power; loss of employment by the head of the family rarely involves immediate application to the Poor Law. There may be children earning; there may be a secret hoard kept by the wife and mother; there is, in any case, a certain investment of previous savings in furniture; there are all the resources of friends and charity and credit. The stream of men thrown out from industry is, no doubt, greatest in the years of the highest unemployed percentage and least in those of the lowest. It does not in either case reach the workhouse till an interval which may be months or may be a year and more.

There is probably an element of truth in each of these explanations. Without extensive inquiry into the records of individual workhouses it is impossible to choose between them or to regard either as proved to the exclusion of other hypotheses. Whatever the precise explanation the salient facts of the connection between pauperism and unemployment remain. First, there is a definite correlation; cyclical depression of trade sends fresh recruits to the workhouses. Second, the correlation is not direct.

4

The workhouses do not begin to fill with the first contraction of the demand for labour or to empty with its first expansion. They do not serve as reservoirs of labour in immediate connection with the industrial world. This negative conclusion merely confirms the almost unanimous testimony of Poor Law officials, that respectable, able-bodied workmen practically never enter the workhouse. The men who enter the workhouse or go on the tramp, leaving their families to the Poor Law, are, as a rule, those whom adversity, combined, no doubt, with their own weaknesses, has made no longer able-bodied or respectable. Having once entered, they seldom return to industry again. The interval which elapses between loss of employment and recourse to public assistance is too often only an interval in which idleness becomes acceptable, drink the refuge from despair, and privation the origin of disease and infirmity. Losing daily in industrial value and harried from place to place by the unsatisfied rent-collector and tradesmen, the unemployed workman thrown out by industrial depression becomes perhaps at last hopelessly demoralised and hopelessly out of touch with old associates and employers just at the time when revival of trade would give him a chance again if he remained fit to take it. Missing that chance he continues the downward course which leads him, a full-fledged unemployable, into the workhouse or the casual ward.

It would be possible to extend almost indefinitely the foregoing review of social statistics and almost everywhere to meet the same familiar phenomenon. The formation of new joint stock companies is subject to the most remarkable and regular fluctuations, in which it is interesting to observe that the turning points —maxima and minima—tend, as might have been expected, to precede by a year or so the times of greatest and least actual prosperity in commerce and industry.[1] Wages rise in years of expanding trade and fall or remain stationary as an increasing unemployed percentage heralds an era of acute distress. Subject to general changes of level, prices, both wholesale and retail, follow the same course. Other things being equal the manufacturer pays more for his raw material, the trader for his stock-in-trade, and the workman for his food and clothing in good years than in bad. In the net receipts of railways per cent. of paid up capital, in the activities of the London Bankers' Clearing House, and in countless other branches of economic activity the same alternation is perceptible. It is hardly too much to say that,

---

[1] The exceptionally high figure in 1869 is due to the registration of one company with a nominal capital of £100,000,000, of which not more than £200 was ever subscribed. Apart from this the registrations amounted to only £41,000,000 or £1·3 per head of the population, about the same as the years 1868 and 1870.

apart from the death-rate, the only prominent social and economic records in which the pulsation of the nation's aggregate activities cannot be traced as a significant factor, whether cause or symptom, are the price of Consols[1] and the price of wheat. By a curious though explicable perversity the first of these records— the least reliable of all because subject to the greatest variety of unconnected influences—is the one that has hitherto had most popular favour as a symptom of the nation's economic condition. The second refers to an element at one time, no doubt, of primary importance, but long driven from that position by developing industrialism.

It is only necessary to add that the period since 1900 exhibits in some respects peculiar features. Foreign trade, after dropping slightly to 1901, at once began to move upwards again, and made fresh records successively in 1905, 1906 and 1907. Meanwhile employment declined steadily to 1904, improved only slightly to 1906 and is now once more severely depressed. The recovery of foreign trade immediately after the decline in 1901 is paralleled by the course of railway receipts and of activity in some of the leading industries, e.g., pig-iron, cotton and coal. All these, however, are industries with a large export trade. There can be little doubt that the employment curve more truly represents the condition of the whole people, since it is supported by the most general indications of all—the marriage rate, the consumption of beer and pauperism. The rise of the foreign trade curve is not indeed to be dismissed as one of appearance only. It is far greater than can be accounted for by any change of prices. It probably does represent, all over the world, an increase either in the efficiency of production or in the amount of manufactures for export relatively to manufactures for home consumption.[2] On the other hand, the comparatively high unemployed percentage in 1906—a year of great commercial prosperity—is to a large extent due to exceptional circumstances in the building and allied trades which are unrepresented in the returns of exports.

The formal fact of corresponding fluctuations in nearly every branch of the material activities of the nation has thus been established. The life of the nation is not one of smooth unbroken development or of equably sustained activity. Rather is it, like life in any other form, a matter of perpetual ebb and flow, of growth through alternating periods of expansion and contraction, of diastole and systole. The causes of this remarkable phenomenon are still a subject of keen dispute. They are, indeed, so

[1] See now ch. xv, p. 342-3. [2] Cf. Table X and Chart on p. 56.

4 *

much a subject of dispute that nothing more than the outline of a discussion of them can be attempted in the space here available. Fully treated, they would by themselves afford material for a bulky volume.

The first point to notice is that the successive periods of adversity described in the present chapter and pictured in the chart are periods of industrial depression rather than periods of financial crisis. The terms are defined by an American writer as follows :—

" The word *crisis* describes a brief period of acute disturbance in the business world, the prevailing features of which are the breakdown of credit and prices and the destruction of confidence. It has especially to do with the relations of debtor and creditor. The word *panic* describes a different phase of the same general condition—a situation which is essentially mental or psychological. . . . The adjective financial is properly used with each of these. . . .

" The term *depression* or *period of depression* describes a disturbance of a much longer duration, and which cannot be designated as financial. It pertains rather to industry and includes the whole field of production and exchange. It is properly described as *industrial and commercial*." [1]

The outward and visible signs of a crisis are a frantic demand for money and an abnormally high rate of discount. The essence of a crisis is a sudden contraction of the effective currency, due to promises to pay becoming no longer current. The fabric of modern commerce is built up on the use of credit as the principal medium of exchange, that is to say, on the habitual acceptance of promises and orders to pay in place of money down. Without the use of this medium the immense developments of national and international trade would have been impossible. With the advantage, however, comes an inevitable danger. The general acceptance of promises and orders to pay in lieu of actual money may at any moment be exchanged for an equally general refusal to accept them. This is what happens in a crisis. Every man as creditor, having lost confidence, demands not bills but money down, and as debtor consequently finds it very difficult to secure money down to liquidate his obligations. Often the difficulty culminates in some dramatic failure such as that of Overend, Gurney & Co. in 1866, drawing many lesser failures in its train.

The outward and visible signs of an industrial depression are a high unemployed percentage and falling wages and profits. The essence of it is the inability of manufacturers to find markets

---

[1] *Financial Crises and Periods of Industrial and Commercial Depression.* Theodore E. Burton (D. Appleton & Co., New York, 1902).

at what they regard as remunerative prices. There follows stoppage or diminution of production till stocks are cleared or shortage of supplies raises the price once more. Stoppage of production means less earning, less spending, less marrying, less drinking, and hard times for all. The financial aspect of industrial depression is a low rate of discount for money. Herein it presents a striking contrast to a crisis. Lord Goschen wrote of the crisis of 1866 under the title "Seven per cent.," and of the depression of 1868 under the title "Two per cent.". He noted also how through all the financial disasters of the earlier year "the mighty wave of our foreign trade rolled on little disturbed," [1] but how in the latter year almost every department of industry was at a standstill and cheap money found no hirer.

It is essential to distinguish crises from depressions. Failure to make this distinction is responsible for half the obscurity that surrounds the subject. It is, however, almost as important to recognise their frequent connection with one another. Crises occur, as a rule, at the height of periods of exceptional activity. More accurately, perhaps, they may be said to mark the close of such periods and to herald the coming of industrial stagnation. Such was the case in 1866 in this country, and in the American crises of 1873, 1893 and 1907. It is indeed quite possible for crises to occur, not just before, but in the middle of an industrial depression, as with the Glasgow Bank failure of 1878, or without any depression at all, as with the Baring failure of 1890, just as it is possible for a depression to come unheralded by any crisis, as did those of 1886 and 1904. The two things, in fact, are connected not always but only sometimes ; not necessarily but only by probability. A time of rapid industrial expansion will probably be accompanied by rash speculation, and will probably be ended by a more or less sudden and simultaneous recognition of the fact that the principal markets have been glutted. In that case there will follow that "sudden application of a critical conservatism to business transactions" [2] and breakdown of credit which constitute a crisis. If, however, the amount of pure speculation has been relatively small or the failure to find markets comes less suddenly and at different times for different industries, the period of industrial expansion may pass into a period of industrial contraction gradually and without any formal crisis. Again,

[1] *Essays and Addresses on Economic Questions* (Arnold, 1905). Lord Goschen, no doubt, judging by foreign trade alone, exaggerated the prosperity of 1866. It was beyond question a more prosperous year than 1868, but it also quite unmistakably witnessed the beginning of the decline which brought the depression in that year.
[2] *Economic Crises*, p. 3. Edward D. Jones, Ph.D. (Macmillan Co., New York, 1900).

approaching the matter from the other side, it may be said that the delicate equilibrium of finance is likely to find one of its disturbing causes in industrial fluctuation. Disturbance, however, may come and critical conservatism be induced in place of credit through many other causes.

Here these other causes may be left out of account. From the point of view of unemployment, a financial crisis is of interest only as an incident in industrial fluctuation. A crisis as such lasts only a few days or weeks. It may come and go without affecting for more than a moment the progress of industry. It is, at its best, only a storm which clears the air, and it is, beyond question, a storm of a type which in this country at least shows decreasing violence. What then, in turn, is the cause of industrial fluctuation? No full answer to that question can be attempted here. Certain theories may be ruled out as untenable. Those that remain must simply be stated, compared and left to the judgment of later study and experience.

In the first place, all explanations may be ruled out which do not apply to all advanced industrial countries alike. There may, in particular, be eliminated, as responsible causes, " different economic or fiscal regulations established by custom or governmental policy ". " Crises and depressions have occurred almost contemporaneously in different countries, under every prevalent system of banking; in monarchies and republics; in countries having free trade alike with those maintaining revenue or protective tariffs; in those having only metallic money and in those having metallic and paper money; in such as have irredeemable paper money and in those having paper money redeemable in coin; in such as have gold as the standard alike with those having silver; also in countries having gold and silver with a fixed ratio between them." [1] This statement is illustrated by the following table and chart showing the course of foreign trade per head in some of the principal industrial countries of the world.

It will be seen that all the countries show a broadly contemporaneous fluctuation. The actual range of fluctuation appears, as a rule, to be greatest in the United States. Thus between the two maxima about 1890 and 1900 the foreign trade of the United States sank 20 points (from 96 to 76), that of France 16, that of the United Kingdom 11, and that of Germany 10. According to one of the American authorities already cited, "crises are more severe and frequent in the United States than in any other country. They are felt with diminishing force in England,

---

[1] Burton, *op. cit.*, p. 66.

TABLE X.—FOREIGN TRADE OF PRINCIPAL COUNTRIES. *R.*

(Values of Special Imports and Exports Per Head of Population. 1900 = 100.)

Year.	United Kingdom.[1]	United States of America.[2]	Germany.	France.	Belgium.	Norway.
1865	75	—	—	—	—	—
1866	82	—	—	—	—	—
1867	77	—	—	—	—	—
1868	79	58	—	70	51	—
1869	80	63	—	72	53	—
1870	82	72	—	65	52	—
1871	90	82	—	78	70	—
1872	98	89	—	90	74	—
1873	99	94	—	89	81	—
1874	96	91	—	87	75	—
1875	93	80	—	89	74	—
1876	89	75	—	91	78	73
1877	90	77	—	85	77	76
1878	84	81	—	87	78	58
1879	88	80	—	92	81	55
1880	94	102	69	100	87	63
1881	92	103	71	99	87	70
1882	95	95	75	99	83	69
1883	96	96	77	96	84	68
1884	89	87	76	88	79	66
1885	83	80	67	88	72	59
1886	79	77	68	86	70	57
1887	81	81	71	84	74	57
1888	86	80	73	85	76	66
1889	93	82	79	92	82	76
1890	93	88	82	93	85	79
1891	92	92	79	96	89	82
1892	87	96	75	88	78	76
1893	83	86	75	82	77	78
1894	82	76	72	80	76	77
1895	84	76	77	81	79	79
1896	88	79	81	83	83	85
1897	87	87	84	86	88	94
1898	89	85	89	91	96	94
1899	93	87	95	99	103	98
1900	100	100	100	100	100	100
1901	97	100	94	95	96	98
1902	98	97	96	98	101	96
1903	100	101	101	102	110	96
1904	101	100	105	101	114	93
1905	105	104	115	109	122	101
1906	114	116	127	123	140	109
1907	123	127	136	133	146	118
1908	111	115	121	120	128	113
1909	114	110	128	134	141	119
1910	125	120	137	150	165	133
1911	127	129	147	158	175	148
1912	138	136	160	166	190	164
1913	144	148	168	170	186	178
1914	141	145	—	—	—	—
Base 1900 = 100.	391.67 s.	$29.18.	185.2 marks.	226.4 fr.	618 fr.	215.5 kr.

[1] The figures refer to *all* imports (*i.e.* including re-exports) and special imports as in Table IX. Ships are excluded throughout.

[2] The figures are for years ended 30th June.

See Statistical Supplement for notes on this table and on revised chart following.

Germany, France, Holland and Switzerland." [1]   Two subsidiary
points of interest in the table are the designation of the years from
1901 to 1907 as a period of record trade expansion for all countries
concerned, and the exceptional development of Germany both in
that period and before.

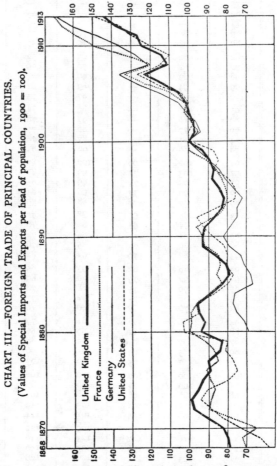

CHART III.—FOREIGN TRADE OF PRINCIPAL COUNTRIES.
(Values of Special Imports and Exports per head of population, 1900 = 100).

In the second place, explanations by reference to regular
physical or astronomical phenomena, such as the sun-spot theory
advanced by Professor W. S. Jevons, have also become untenable.

[1] Jones, *op. cit.*, p. 9.

The characteristic of industrial depressions is that, though their coming appears to be inevitable, the date of coming is within broad limits quite uncertain. During the past century the interval from one depression to the next has varied from seven to eleven years.[1] The period of sun-spot fluctuation has not varied.

After the exclusion of manifestly untenable explanations a good many different theories hold the field. They are of three main types.

In the first type of theory the prime cause of industrial fluctuation is found in fluctuation of the volume of metal currency, involving a corresponding rise and fall of prices. When, owing to increased production of gold, prices rise, manufacturers hope for profits and make as many goods as possible. When, owing to decreased production of gold, prices fall, manufacturers fear a loss and cease their activity. An explanation of this nature is not impossible. Its weak points are, first, that the precious metals form but an insignificant part of the actual means of exchange to-day; second, that evidence is yet lacking of any fluctuation in the supply of precious metals at all corresponding to the remarkable alternations of prosperity and adversity pictured in the present chapter.

In a second type of theory emphasis is laid on " misdirection of productive energy" as the cause of subsequent depression. The phrase covers a great many distinct explanations. Some writers imply by it merely over-production of particular commodities. Manufacturers in one or more important industries, it is said, over-estimate the demand and produce more than they can sell at a remunerative price. Sooner or later they have to cease producing and perhaps to clear stocks at a loss. The resulting unemployment in that particular industry diminishes the demand for other commodities and thus spreads distress and dislocation over a wide area. The weak point in this theory is that, in spite of the last suggestion, it seems hardly adequate to explain a really general depression.

Other writers imply over-production not so much of a few particular things as of a whole class of things, *viz.*, those which are not immediately consumable as compared with those which are. "The remote cause of these commercial tides . . . seems to lie in the varying proportion which the capital devoted to permanent and remote investment bears to that which is but temporarily invested soon to reproduce itself."[2] "The important

---

[1] The present depression (1908) appears to be coming within four or five years of the last one (1904). [The following sentence exaggerates the regularity of the sunspot period (1930)].

[2] W. S. Jevons, *Investigations in Currency and Finance*, pp. 27, 28.

feature in the occurrence of crises and periods of depression, is the increasing proportion of expenditures in preparation for increased production, manifesting itself in the formation and prosecution of new enterprises, and the building on a large scale of railroads, ships and factories. . . . At times these expenditures for increased production attain an unusual proportion as compared with the ordinary expenditures for annual consumption and support." [1] The suggestion appears in fact, to be, that at times there takes place over-investment for a distant return. The nation thereafter passes through a time of stress. It has over a period of years devoted so large a proportion of its energies to building railways that it has not sown enough corn or made enough boots. It has abundant means of transport but nothing to be transported.

This theory agrees with many of the facts to be explained. Mr. Burton, for instance, is able to connect each of the principal depressions of the past century in the United States with some exceptional development of the means of transit and production in the years just before. Yet even so the theory has its weak points, and seems to explain only some, not all, of the facts. Why should such exceptional developments occur and recur so inevitably every ten years or so? Is it the case in times of depression that, though there may be an excessive supply of one thing, e.g., ships, there is insufficiency of others, e.g., boots? Is it not the case that at such times all trades alike seem to be suffering from want of markets? The question leads to consideration of yet a third type of theory, in which emphasis is laid, not on misdirection, but on actual superfluity of productive energy. To this type belongs the theory of unemployment maintained by Mr. J. A. Hobson. [2]

The product of industry, it is said, is now so unequally divided that while one class—the workmen—have but the bare necessaries for existence, another class—the capitalists—have more than they can possibly spend. They therefore "save" without effort and as it were compulsorily; they can only save by investing in fresh factories and means of production. This, no doubt, gives employment while the factories are being built; in the end, however, productive power is established without reference to, and altogether out of proportion to, the demand. The new factories soon glut the market. Their operation is checked. Unemployment results. The root of the disease, in fact, is "over-saving," or, from another point of view, "under-consumption". The only radical remedy

---

[1] Burton, op. cit., p. 308.
[2] The Problem of the Unemployed. J. A. Hobson (Methuen. New Edition, 1906).

is to raise the standard of spending so as to limit saving, and to reform the distribution of consuming power, by imposing fresh taxation on large incomes, by raising wages, by shortening the working day, and by other measures of like character.

The "under-consumption" theory thus outlined is of value as emphasising the general character of the stagnation apparent at times of depression. It is, however, open to two serious objections. The first objection is that it gives, as a cause of unemployment, that which is simply the cause of the industrial growth to which unemployment is incident. To this point fresh reference will be made below. The second objection is that the theory does not in fact explain the generality of the over-production and subsequent stagnation so much and with so good reason emphasised by its advocates. If an excessive amount of capital is seeking investment, it will no doubt glut some industries. Why should it glut all alike? The natural course would be for it to pour into one or two industries which have been particularly prosperous of late, and to leave others severely alone. Mr. Hobson's theory really explains little or nothing that cannot be explained as mere misdirection of productive energy.

To account for a tendency to over-production in all industries some element common to all industries must be indicated. In the theory next to be put forward, as being perhaps up to the present time the most tenable of all, this common element is found in the simple and well-nigh universal fact of industrial competition. The argument may be put briefly as follows :—

There is at times in the community a demand for more boots or ships or houses. The demand is felt and met not by one producer but by many, and not by many each providing a definite share in agreement with the rest, but by many each acting independently and dominated by the desire to do as much business as possible, *i.e.*, to engross as large a share as possible of the market. Inevitably therefore all the producers together tend to overshoot the demand and to glut the market for a time. This is a result not of wild speculation nor of miscalculation of the total demand ; it must be a normal incident wherever competition has a place at all. Every one of ten bootmakers may accurately estimate the total demand for boots, say 10,000 pairs, at the lowest remunerative price. Each of the ten, however, desires to have the supplying of as large a share as possible of this demand—say of a fifth rather than of a tenth. The ten together will therefore set about producing twice as many boots as can be sold at a profit. This will involve great industrial activity and a vigorous demand for labour. Sooner or later, however, the glutting of the market becomes apparent. Prices fall, production is checked, and a period of stagnation and unemployment ensues till accumulated stocks can be cleared, perhaps below cost price, perhaps by waiting till the demand grows up to the supply once more. Upon this in turn follows appreciation of a demand in excess of the supply and another burst of competition to glut the market once more.

A good deal can be said in support of this argument. It is no more than a generalisation from what is actually observed in such an industry as shipbuilding. It is in accord with the evidence showing that the most violently fluctuating trades are the instrumental ones—concerned with manufacturing the means of further production and distribution—in which, since they stand most removed from the ultimate consumer, over-production is likely to proceed furthest before it is checked by information that the market has already been glutted.[1] It deduces fluctuation from a fundamental feature of all industries in all countries, and therefore explains the universality of the phenomenon. It accounts both for the certainty with which either condition—prosperity or adversity—gives way to the opposite condition within a few years, and for the uncertainty as to the precise number of years required. It makes fluctuation inevitable. It allows of external events—wars, disputes, pestilences, earthquakes, inventions, droughts—accentuating or mitigating, hastening or postponing, lengthening or shortening the depression on each occasion. Its one weak point is that while it involves fluctuation in each trade at some time, it does not in itself involve the fluctuations of all trades being simultaneous.[2] This last fact—in so far as it is a fact—must be accounted for by the close connection existing between different industries either on the side of production or on that of demand.

Though, however, the theory just propounded does not in itself completely explain simultaneous over-production followed by stagnation in practically all industries, it makes such a result probable. At the same time it in no way offends economic doctrine as to the impossibility of general over-production. It is no doubt true in the abstract, since commodities are only produced to exchange, and since ultimately they exchange for one another, that there cannot as a permanent state of affairs be

[1] Cp. Table VIII. and *Distress from Want of Employment*, Third Report, p. 48. Competition, *i.e.*, the power to over-produce in any trade, *e.g.*, in boot-making, involves an actual over-production of boot-making machines.

[2] Mr. Hobson's theory seems to be quite consistent with many if not most trades escaping fluctuation altogether.

over-production of all the good things of life while any single want remains unsatisfied. Since, however, commodities exchange for one another not directly but only ultimately and through the medium of money or credit, it seems quite possible that as a quite temporary phenomenon there should be a glut in every market, because every one is holding out for too high money prices. If all would agree together to lower prices all might do good business, recovering through the cheapness of what they bought the loss involved in the cheapness of what they sold. Ultimately, indeed, something of this sort does take place, not by agreement but under pressure of economic forces. The fall of prices through a period of stagnation enables stocks to be cleared.

How, then, does this competition theory stand with regard to the "under-consumption" theory? Briefly, it involves the same analysis of facts as Mr. Hobson's *plus* the additional fact of competition but *minus* his practical inferences.

The competition theory, it will have been seen, shares with the under-consumption theory one central assumption. It assumes that the aggregate product of the nation's activities each year is normally such that, after meeting immediate needs according to existing standards, a substantial surplus remains for increasing the means of production for the future. It assumes, in other words, the possibility of material progress. The ample justification for this assumption is to be found in the recorded growth of capital and of industry. There can be no doubt that, with the present amount and distribution of the national dividend, an abundance of wealth is each year set free from urgent uses to increase the agencies of future production, and so makes it possible to set up these agencies in excess of present requirements. There can be no doubt again that in a competitive system of industry this excess in the means of production is commonly realised. In other words, such a system normally works with a reserve of capital as well as with a reserve of labour; the machinery in a trade is never or seldom all fully employed at the same time; a fraction of it would probably suffice to satisfy the whole existing demand. This is forcibly illustrated whenever complete combination amongst employers replaces competition. The normal accompaniment to the formation of a trust is the closing down of many of the factories acquired.

"Before the establishment of the combinations hardly any industry had been able to utilise its full capacity. For instance, even before the days of the Cotton Oil Trust, numerous presses and refineries had been for a long time inactive. The Trust closed at once more than a dozen of the old-fashioned mills. The same thing happened with the Sugar Trust, which can supply the whole market with the product of one-fourth of the plant it owns. The Whisky Trust immediately closed sixty-eight of its eighty distilleries, and with the remaining twelve was enabled to furnish the same output as before and soon largely to increase it." [1]

Up to this point it is possible to be in fair agreement with Mr. Hobson. There is some reason for saying that cyclical fluctuation of trade depends directly upon the abundance of capital available for new enterprises and upon industrial competition; that it represents, in fact, the incessantly renewed attempt and partial failure to put into operation productive forces normally in excess of the existing demand. There is no justification for a practical inference from this that an attempt should be made to prevent cyclical fluctuation by destroying competition or drying up the springs of capital. " It may very well be . . . that a means of solving a difficulty may not be commendable because it creates greater difficulties than it adjusts." [2] This remark is made by an American writer in regard to one particular remedy—that of combination in trusts to regulate production. It has a much wider application. It may be applied with peculiar force to the line of treatment advocated by Mr. Hobson. This is essentially an attack upon saving, and the present large possibilities of saving,[3] based on the ground that under-consumption is the root-cause of trade fluctuation. In one sense this statement is undeniable. If the whole of the national dividend each year were devoted to immediate consumption and none to multiplying the means of production, if, in fact, there were no saving, there would be no possibility of industrial growth and therefore no possibility of the dislocations incidental to that growth.

In exactly the same sense credit may be said to be the root-cause of bankruptcies and birth of death. Mr. Hobson, no doubt, would reply that his attack is not upon saving but over-saving, and that he quite recognises the need of some provision for future production. His point is simply that this provision is now excessive because saving is too easy; his remedy is to make

---

[1] Von Halle, *Trusts*, p. 66.

[2] Jones, *op. cit.*, p. 52. The reference is to a suggestion in the report of Mr. Carroll D. Wright—the Special Commissioner on American Trade Depression in 1885-6—that " if the employers in any industry would combine under an organisation that should have positive coherence, there would be no difficulty, so far as that industry is concerned, in regulating the volume of production in accordance with the demand ".

[3] This language, of course, is not intended to do Mr. Hobson the injustice of implying that he advocates individual thriftlessness.

saving harder. In just the same spirit, Mr. Bradlaugh and Mrs. Besant, thirty years ago, would have explained that they were attacking, not all increase of the population, but only excessive increase. They started a movement, however, which shows no sign of regarding this nice distinction and yearly brings the nation into increasing alarm lest it cease to grow at all. So Mr. Hobson, in making saving harder, can hold out no guarantee that he will not make it too hard and thus stop industrial progress altogether. If incomes were so far equalised that all saving meant sacrifice of a keenly desired present good for a future one, it is extremely likely that no sufficient provision for new capital would be made at all. There is, indeed, no possibility of determining *a priori* how the national dividend can best be allocated between immediate consumption and investment in the means of future production. In other words, there is no criterion for saying beforehand what is *over*-saving and what is not. The right adjustment, however, comes about naturally through economic forces.

It may be that with the present distribution of wealth many people save simply because they cannot spend, and are therefore constantly trying to invest in the means of fresh production more than can with the existing demand be profitably invested. What, however, happens when they begin to operate the new means of production? Even the very rich will not produce indefinitely without markets, and being driven to the choice between abandoning their investments or lowering prices to increase demand, will normally, as Mr. Hobson himself realises, take the latter course. This may mean going with less or no profits. It more often in fact means increasing the efficiency of production. In either case, however, the very change desired by Mr. Hobson is brought about. The real standard of consumption is raised by a lowering of money prices. The balance between the demand for commodities and the supply is reached. No doubt the adjustment takes time and may only be accom plished with a certain amount of friction and loss. The need for adjustment can, however, only be avoided by abolishing either the possibility of producing beyond existing demand, or the competitive stimulus to such production, that is to say, by abolishing either the possibility of, or the principal factor in, material progress.[1]

[1] Criticism of Mr. Hobson's policy in regard to unemployment by no means implies opposition to all the measures mentioned by him as agreeing with that policy. Higher wages and shorter hours for workmen are excellent things in themselves. Taxation of large incomes rather than small is, no doubt, also a good thing in so far as

Trade fluctuation is, indeed, at times obviously and directly the means by which the standard of production and of comfort is driven upwards. When trade is expanding many new factories are built; they have then their chance to overcome initial difficulties and to get a footing while competition is less severe. When trade contracts again it is not the new but the old and relatively obsolete factories that have to close. The next expansion starts from a higher level of efficiency. In this way fluctuation appears intimately bound up with the possibility of material progress. The recurrent failure to operate means of production ahead of the existing demand is only partial. Each wave leaves wages higher or prices lower and productivity greater than did the wave before.[1]

No one theory as to the cause of trade fluctuation can yet be taken as proved. All those mentioned must be treated at best as no more than hypotheses to be tested by the facts. It may well prove that no one of them will fit all the facts, just as it is certain that they are by no means mutually exclusive. Whatever, however, the explanation to be finally adopted, there seems now some reason in theory for regarding fluctuation as inevitable or at least as preventible only at the cost of greater harm. There is in any case ample warrant in experience for regarding it as certain for the time of practical politics—the next few decades. Whatever the cause or causes they must be deep-seated. They will continue to produce the same results as they have produced hitherto.

These results are not everywhere the same. The pressure in the labour market is not felt equally in all departments. In certain relatively stable occupations—railway and domestic service —as in agriculture it is hardly noticeable. In shipbuilding and engineering it is very great indeed. Between these extremes is found every variety of range in fluctuation.

Again, the pressure is met with very varying success in different trades. It may involve hardly any complete unemployment of individuals; in coal-mining, for instance, as the volume of employment shrinks, the required adjustment is reached by

money is needed for public purposes; it is perfectly arguable, indeed, that a certain amount of wealth which now goes to increase future productivity might be more advantageously used in meeting immediate necessities (*e.g.*, for education, for sanitation, etc., etc.). All this, however, is very different from Mr. Hobson's advocacy of taxation for its own sake.

[1] As a matter of history it may be noted that the index number for wages has after each boom since 1870 sunk only to a point well above'that reached in the previous depression, except in 1886, when the nominal rate was about the same as in 1879. Owing, however, to a remarkable fall in prices the real wages were much higher.

reducing, for the whole body of men, the number of days worked per week. It may produce complete unemployment of individuals, but little acute distress; in many of the skilled and organised trades the men thrown out of work are, through payment of unemployed benefits, more or less supported by the general body of their fellows. In these two distinct ways—elasticity of working hours and union benefits—cyclical fluctuation is met on the same principle though not so completely as is seasonal fluctuation. The liability to loss of earnings is distributed over the whole trade so as not to crush individuals. Wages are averaged over good and bad times. In a very large part of the industrial field subject to the same liability neither method is available. Each involves a high degree of associated action. Each is in practice confined to a certain number of skilled and organised trades. Masses of semi-skilled and unskilled workmen are affected by the same fluctuations in the demand for labour as those which appear in the trade union returns. Yet they have in general neither the machinery nor the clear motive for insurance against its consequences. Their wages are low; they are not organised in trade unions. In forming the instinctive standard of life and expenditure which ultimately determines the wage for which they may be hired, they fail to take account of the fluctuations which are an inevitable incident of their industry. The measure of their failure is to be found in those periods of clamant distress which evoke Mansion House Relief Funds.

There remains, indeed, in the history of these funds one more index to add to those already given as to the course of trade fluctuation. During the past fifty years the coming of each industrial depression, as now shown retrospectively by the trade union returns, has been heralded or accompanied by the raising of relief funds for exceptional distress, by the appointment of committees of inquiry, by agitations and marches of the unemployed. Of this the table given on next page is significant.

Cyclical fluctuation means discontinuity in the growth of the demand for labour. The total supply of labour, that is to say, the population, grows, on the whole, steadily or at least with little variation from year to year. The demand for labour grows unsteadily. Thus it has happened that though, throughout the past fifty years, the average rate of its growth has been fully sufficient to absorb the growing population, the actual rate has been alternately greater and less than this. At times, therefore, labour has been scarce; wages have risen rapidly and employment become brisk. At other times labour has been in excess;

TABLE XI.—CYCLICAL FLUCTUATION AND RELIEF FUNDS.

Year.	Unemployed Percentage.	Special Relief Funds.			Other Measures.
		London.	Glasgow.	Elsewhere.	
1858	[11'9]		1857, £ — , 10,051 families assisted.		
1862	6'05		1862, £36,000, 18,797 persons assisted.		
1868	6'75	1867, Mansion House Fund, £15,000.			
1879	10'70		1878-79, £33,000.	1878-79, Manchester, £26,000; Liverpool, £4,100; Leeds, £5,700, and many other places.	
1886	9'55	1885-86, Mansion House Fund, £79,000.	1884-87, £28,000.		1886, Local Government Board Circular advocating Relief Works. Trafalgar Square riots. Royal Commission on Trade Depression.
1893-94	7'70	1891-94, Mansion House Fund, £2,500 (about).	1892-93, £3,100. 1894-95, £9,000.		1895, House of Commons Select Committee.
1904	6'40	1903-04, Mansion House Fund, £4,000. 1904-05, Mansion House Fund, £52,000 (Mr. Long's scheme).			1905, Unemployed Workmen Act.

1905-06, Queen's Unemployed Fund, £154,000.

wages have fallen or remained stationary, and unemployment has been rife. At these latter times the sphere of industry may be said to have lost its elasticity, yet always to recover it again in a few years. Till that recovery there results a pressure felt in every quarter of the industrial world.

The causes of this fluctuation are obscure, but, beyond question, deeply seated. They are at work in all industrial countries. They must spring from one or more of the fundamental facts of modern life. They probably cannot be eliminated without an entire reconstruction of the industrial order. They certainly will not be eliminated within the next few decades. Within the range of practical politics no cure for industrial fluctuation can be hoped for ; the aim must be palliation. Measures of palliation, however, may be bad or good, hasty or well thought-out, retrospective or prospective. The actual measures to be taken depend upon consideration of the effect of trade depression upon individual men and in combination with other factors. The need for some measures is undoubted. Cyclical fluctuation of trade may have economic justification. Its course is strewn with individual disasters.

CHAPTER V.

THE RESERVE OF LABOUR.

1. The irreducible minimum of unemployment. Unemployed percentages of skilled men never down to zero. Chronic distress of unskilled men. The paradox of the labour market: general and normal excess of supply over demand. Constitution of irreducible minimum shown by distribution of unemployment in trade unions. Loss of time by many, not chronic idleness of a few. Men out of work on any one day only that day's sample of labour reserve. Confirmation by experience of Distress Committees. The typical applicant is not a chronically unemployed man but a casual labourer, is industrial not parasitic upon industry.
2. Economics of casual employment: Labour reserves swollen (a) by lack of mobility, (b) by chance engagement. Abstract analysis illustrated by London riverside labour. Work at the docks and wharves. Reform by London and India Docks Company. Organised fluidity. The bulk of employment still unorganised. The observed excess of labour. Average earnings of casual dockers.
3. The glutting of the labour market: Other ports than London. Other forms of casual employment. The building trades. Casual employment only acute form of general phenomenon. Dissipation of fluctuating demands causes over-recruiting of all trades. The sense in which methods of employment may be said to call excessive reserves of labour into being.
4. Under-employment: Irreducible minimum only a sample of irregular reserves of labour. Reserve of labour not necessarily so great or so irregular as to involve distress or under-employment. Tendency to glutting of labour market varies in strength and meets with varying obstacles in different occupations. Distinction between skilled and unskilled. "Under-employment" as a form of sweating. The beating down of average earnings to subsistence level. Charity and public relief as subsidies to casual employment. The problem one of business organisation—How to provide properly maintained reserves of labour for fluctuations of demand.

THE trade union returns have yet one lesson to teach. The unemployed percentage, however it may rise or fall, never falls to zero. The lowest figure recorded in the table of general unemployed percentages for the last fifteen years (1894 to 1908) is 1·7 at the end of April, 1899.

In itself this result may appear susceptible of a simple explanation. The general unemployed percentage represents a considerable variety of separate trades, between which no transference of labour does or can take place. May it not be that these trades reach their busiest stages at different times, and that so, though every one of them may at some moment have no men out of work at all, yet there never comes a moment when all together are in that case, or a moment when one at least is not relatively depressed and able to yield an appreciable percentage

68

of the unemployed? The suggestion is reasonable, and explains some part of the irreducible minimum of unemployment. It does not explain the whole.

The irreducible minimum of unemployment does not appear only in the general percentage for all trades taken together, it is shown also by each trade or group of trades taken separately. During the past twelve years the lowest figures recorded for each of the principal industrial groups have been as follows :—

Building	.	.	0·8	.	.	.	.	May, 1897
Engineering	.	1·8	.	.	.	.	May, 1897
Shipbuilding	.	1·4	.	.	.	.	July, 1899
Printing	.	.	2·3	.	.	.	November, 1899
Furnishing	.	0·5	.	.	.	.	April, 1897

This result, moreover, holds true not only of each trade or group of trades but also of separate unions. It holds true not of decaying industries but of those on which the development of the nation's prosperity has been based. From 1881 to 1901 the persons returned as occupied in the census group corresponding to " engineering, shipbuilding and metal trades " increased in number from 978,000 to 1,475,000, or more than 50 per cent., while money wages in engineering rose as from 89·36 to 100·29. The numbers in the building trades rose from 926,000 to 1,336,000, or 44 per cent., and the money wages from 85·55 to 100·0. The numbers in woodworking and furnishing rose from 219,000 to 308,000, or 41 per cent., and those in the paper and printing trades from 196,000 to 334,000, or over 70 per cent. During all this growth in the numbers employed—a growth in each group at twice or more than twice the rate for the general population— there has never in any of the groups been a year without an appreciable number of skilled and organised workmen out of employment. For each group, indeed, taken as a whole, there appears to be much the same irreducible minimum below which the year's unemployed percentage never falls. Depression of trade is marked by very varying maxima. In the best years all the groups alike tend to have about 2 per cent. unemployed. An excess of the supply of labour over the demand appears to be a normal condition in the skilled and organised trades.

It is hardly necessary to argue at length that the same condition is found in the unskilled and unorganised occupations. The glut of labour in them is notorious. Has there ever, in the big towns at least, been a time when employers could not get practically at a moment's notice all the labourers they required? Is not this indeed the root of bewilderment and despair in regard to the unemployed problem that there appears to be always and

everywhere an inexhaustible excess in the supply of labour óver
the demand? It is difficult to get statistical evidence of excess
on the industrial side. Yet if the Unemployed Workmen Act of
1905 has done little else, it has at least cleared up all doubt upon
this point. It has shown that distress through want of employment is not a temporary but a chronic evil.

The generality of the problem makes it all the more puzzling.
A chronic excess of labour in one occupation or one grade of
industry might be explained in many ways. If, for instance, it
were confined to unskilled work, it might be attributed to
deficiencies of industrial training. But the trade union returns as
to unemployment in all the most skilled trades put this explanation and remedies founded on it out of court. If, on the other
hand, the excess were confined to the organised trades, it might
be attributed in one way or another to trade union action. It
might be said that the unions, having forced up wages in particular
occupations above the natural level, were now suffering from the
increased flow of labour attracted to those occupations. But the
experience of Distress Committees shows that the excess of the
labour supply is probably greatest and certainly a more serious
evil in the occupations which are unskilled and unorganised.

A general and normal excess of the supply of labour over the
demand appears to be explicable only by an excessively rapid
increase of population. But such an explanation leads only to
still greater perplexities. It is repudiated by the leading modern
economists. It appears to be quite inconsistent with the broadest
facts of industry set forth in the first chapter—the increasing
productivity of the nation and the rising remuneration of labour.
It does not square with the special facts showing the irreducible
minimum of unemployment precisely in those industries which
have grown with exceptional rapidity in recent years. The condition of the labour market appears to present a standing con-
tradiction of economic laws. Whatever the demand for labour,
the supply tends always and everywhere, not to coincide with it,
but to exceed it.

This is the central paradox of the unemployed problem.
Why should it be the normal condition of the labour market to
have more sellers than buyers, two men to every job and not at
least as often two jobs to every man? The explanation of the
paradox is really a very simple one—that there is no one labour
market but only an infinite number of separate labour markets.
To see this it is necessary first to examine a little more closely
the nature of the irreducible minimum of unemployment. How
is it constituted? Does it represent mainly the chronic idleness

of a few individuals, or does it represent mainly incessant loss of time now by some now by others of a much greater number of men, each of whom on the whole gets a fair amount of employment?

The returns ordinarily made to the Labour Department throw no light on these questions. They do not show the distribution of unemployment among individuals. An unemployed percentage of two for a year in a union of 10,000 might mean that 200 particular men were out of work and the other 9,800 in work the whole time, or it might mean that every man in the 10,000 lost about one week in the year. To determine what, between these extremes, it does mean, recourse must be had to further sources of information. It is necessary to know not only how many men are out of work together on specified dates, but also how many fall out of work at some time or other during a specified period, say a year. The following table, covering the ten years 1894-1903, gives information of this nature for certain important unions:—

TABLE XII.—PERCENTAGE MEMBERSHIP OF CERTAIN UNIONS UNEMPLOYED AT SOME TIME IN A YEAR.

Union.	Mean of Ten Years.		Best Year.			Worst Year.		
	Unemployed Percentage.	Percentage of Individual Members claiming Benefit in a Year.	Year.	Unemployed Percentage.	Percentage of Individual Members claiming Benefit in the Year.	Year.	Unemployed Percentage.	Percentage of Individual Members claiming Benefit in the Year.
London Society of Compositors	4·3	20·9	1898	3·0	18·0	1894	5·7	26·3
London Bookbinders . .	5·2	38·6 [1]	1902	3·3	28·3	1894	6·4	38·1
Amalgamated Millsawyers and Woodcutting Machinists .	2·5	26·0	1897	1·5	21·8	1902	3·9	28·2
Associated Shipwrights . .	—	19·2 [2]	1899	—	6·6 [2]	1894	—	44·2 [2]
Associated Blacksmiths of Scotland	4·6	27·4 [3]	1900	1·6	22·5	1894	12·5	45·6

The table shows that while even in a bad time the majority of members retain practically continuous employment from year's end to year's end, yet even in a good time unemployment is

[1] Omitting 1899, for which the figures are uncertain.
[2] The percentages are based only on members entitled to benefit, not on the total membership.
[3] Omitting 1898 and 1901, for which the figures are uncertain.

widely distributed. Omitting the Associated Shipwrights and taking a rough average for the other four unions, it may be said that the percentage of those claiming benefit at some time or other is in a good year ten times, in a bad year five times, and in an average of years seven times the mean unemployed percentage throughout the year.

In two cases—the Amalgamated Society of Engineers and the London Society of Compositors—more detailed analysis is possible. The table[1] on the next page shows the distribution of loss of time through want of employment in certain branches of the first-named union for each of the years 1887 to 1895.

The period covered by the table includes, it will be seen, two very good years, 1889 and 1890, in each of which the unemployed percentage for the branches taken was 2·1, and two very bad years, 1893 and 1894, in which the unemployed percentages were 10·2 and 8·9 respectively. The table shows that in bad years as in good years there is, even in a fluctuating industry such as engineering, a very large proportion of men—from 60 to 80 per cent.—who escape unemployment altogether. Irregularity in each year is concentrated on a minority. But, in good years as in bad years, this minority is always a fairly large one. Comparison of 1890 with 1893 yields indeed the rather striking result that almost as large a proportion of members (21·4 per cent.) became unemployed during one of the best years as during the worst (26·4 per cent.). To this point reference will be made later. For the present it is sufficient to show that the minority of irregular workmen is far too great to be dismissed as a residuum of inefficients. The principal factor in maintaining the irreducible minimum of unemployment is not the chronic idleness of a few but the incessant loss of time now by some, now by others of a comparatively large body of men, most of whom are more often in employment than out of it.

These statistics, drawn from a trade characterised rather by cyclical than by seasonal fluctuations, may conveniently be supplemented by others relating to a trade which is markedly seasonal. The following tables deal with unemployment in the London Society of Compositors. The first table shows the average percentages unemployed at the same time, and the percentages unemployed[2] at some time during each of the years

---

[1] *British and Foreign Trade*, Second Series, 1904, p. 101.
[2] The figures refer formally to those claiming unemployed benefit. This, however, includes all those who became unemployed, since each calendar year is treated as a separate unit, and a man may claim in it irrespective of the amount claimed by him in the year before.

TABLE XIII.—DISTRIBUTION OF UNEMPLOYMENT—AMALGAMATED SOCIETY OF ENGINEERS (MANCHESTER AND LEEDS DISTRICTS).

	1887.	1888.	1889.	1890.	1891.	1892.	1893.	1894.	1895.	Mean for nine years.
Mean number of members in districts (excluding superannuated members) .	5,701	5,637	5,988	6,344	6,690	6,956	6,934	7,045	7,265	6,507
Average number unemployed at same time during the year . .	460	362	128	134	307	520	706	627	383	403
Average percentage unemployed at same time during the year . .	8·1	6·4	2·1	2·1	4·6	7·5	10·2	8·9	5·3	6·1
Number unemployed for some time during the year[1] .	2,251	1,832	1,079	1·356	2,593	2,770	1,832	1,939	1,708	1,929
Percentage unemployed for some time during the year . . .	39·5	32·5	18·0	21·4	38·8	39·8	26·4	27·5	23·5	29·7
Percentage unemployed for :—										
Less than 3 days . . .	60·5	67·5	82·0	78·6	61·2	60·2	73·6	72·5	76·5	70·3
3 days and less than 4 weeks .	16·1	14·4	11·4	14·1	23·5	17·4	5·8	8·3	7·2	13·0
4 weeks and less than 8 weeks .	7·2	5·5	3·0	3·5	6·2	6·8	2·4	2·6	5·0	4·6
8 weeks and less than 12 weeks .	4·6	3·1	1·1	1·6	2·9	4·5	2·1	1·8	3·0	2·8
12 weeks and over . . .	11·6	9·5	2·5	2·2	6·2	11·1	16·1	14·8	8·3	9·3
Aggregate number of working days lost through unemployment .	140,749	110,488	39,029	40,825	93,481	159,791	215,874	191,484	116,777	123,166
Number of days lost per member .	24·7	19·6	6·5	6·4	14·0	23·0	31·1	27·2	16·1	18·7
Number of days lost per member unemployed for some time during year .	62·5	60·3	36·2	30·1	36·1	57·7	117·8	98·8	68·4	63·1

[1] Excluding those who lost less than three days in the year.

1898-1903 and during 1894, a year of maximum unemployment. The second table gives a detailed analysis for 1904. It should be explained that as the weekly allowance is 14s., amounts up to £3

TABLE XIV.—DISTRIBUTION OF UNEMPLOYMENT—LONDON SOCIETY OF COMPOSITORS.

	1894.	1898.	1899.	1900.	1901.	1902.	1903.	Mean of 1894-1903.
Membership	10,011	11,079	11,415	11,287	11,355	11,244	11,270	11,094
Average percentage unemployed at the *same* time during year	5·7	3·0	4·0	4·8	4·9	5·1	4·5	4·3
Number unemployed for *some* time during year . . .	2,636	1,991	2,166	2,546	2,552	2,511	2,294	2,281
Percentage unemployed for *some* time during year . . .	26·3	18·0	19·0	22·6	22·5	22·3	20·4	20·6
Estimated days lost per member	17·8	9·4	12·5	15·0	15·3	15·9	14·0	14·3
Estimated days lost per member unemployed for *some* time .	67·6	52·2	65·7	66·3	68·0	71·3	68·6	64·1

TABLE XV.—DISTRIBUTION OF UNEMPLOYMENT—LONDON SOCIETY OF COMPOSITORS.

Provident Benefit Drawn During Year.	Claimants in 1904.	Estimated[1] Amount Drawn by each Group.		Of Claimants in 1904.		
				Number not claiming 1905.	Number claiming 1905.	Number claiming 1905 or 1906.
		£	%			
Less than £1	385	200 ⎫		181	204	243
£1 and less than £3 . .	491	1,000 ⎬ 7·3		197	294	335
£3 and less than £6 . .	424	1,900 ⎫		100	324	350
£6 and less than £9 . .	292	2,200 ⎬ 24·9		47	245	261
£9 and less than £12 .	182	1,900 ⎫		24	158	167
£12 and less than £15 . .	137	1,800 ⎬ 33·9		19	118	123
£15 and less than £18 . .	117	1,900 ⎭		5	112	113
£18 and less than £21 . .	81	1,600 ⎫		4	77	79
£21 and less than £24 . .	45	1,000 ⎬ 33·9		3	42	43
£24 and up to maximum of £26 12s.	114	3,000 ⎭		17	97	98
	2,268	£16,500	100	597[2]	1,671	1,812

correspond roughly with less than four weeks' unemployment, those from £3 to £6 with four to eight and a half weeks, those

[1] The estimates are based on the assumption that each group may be represented by its average, e.g., £3 and less than £6 by £4 10s., with a certain adjustment in the last group. The estimates are confirmed by the good correspondence of their total, £16,500, with the true total, £16,126.

[2] Including 19 men who ceased to be members between 1904 and 1905.

from £6 to £9 with eight and a half to thirteen weeks, and those over £13 with over eighteen weeks. The maximum number of weeks' benefit that can be drawn has varied from year to year, being thirty-eight in 1904 and 1905, thirty-six in 1906, thirty in 1907. These differences affect, of course, the comparison between successive years in respect of the total sums expended, though not in respect of the total number of claimants.

The tables show that unemployment in each year is confined to a minority which forms generally much the same proportion of the total membership, varying only between 18 and 26 per cent. Within this minority there is an inner ring of men who are unemployed for practically the whole of the year. It will be shown in a later chapter that these men are much the same individuals in each year, and deserve the description of the "chronically unemployed". They are probably inefficient and certainly superfluous. They are, however, too few to account for more than a traction of the normal or even of the minimum numbers unemployed at any one time. In 1904, a bad, though not exceptionally bad, year, men unemployed for not more than four weeks out of the fifty-two represented more than a third of all the claimants to the society, and men unemployed from four to twelve weeks represented another third. On a rough estimate of the amounts drawn by various groups a third of the total loss of employment in 1904 was that of men idle for less than thirteen weeks in the year, a third that of men idle between thirteen and twenty-six weeks, and a third that of men idle more than twenty-six weeks. No doubt more accurate estimates would give a higher proportion to the last of these groups, since there should be added thereto the time lost by men who remain unemployed after they have exhausted their claim to benefits. A large proportion of the total loss of time would still remain attributable to men who are more often in work than out. This may be illustrated by an analysis of the men out of work in the last week of November, 1904, close on the busiest season of the year. In that week 370 men actually drew provident benefit, and another thirteen would clearly have drawn it had they not exhausted their claims. Of these 383 men (3·3 of the total membership) representing the irreducible margin of unemployment, 65 drew during the whole year over £26 (37 weeks), 91 between £18 and £26 (26 to 37 weeks), 131 between £9 and £18 (13 to 26 weeks), 30 between £6 and £9 (8½ to 13 weeks), 35 between £3 and £6 (4 to 8½ weeks), and 31 less than £3 (4 weeks). Even at the height of the season appreciable numbers of men normally in good employment may find themselves exceptionally unemployed.

The permanent maintenance of a small group of the chronically unemployed is a curious feature of the London Society of Compositors. It only modifies slightly the co-incidence of the general results of the analysis here with those already reached in regard to the Amalgamated Society of Engineers. In each case the great majority of men even during the worst years retain constant employment. In each case a substantial minority —say one in five—even during the best years have to submit to loss of time and earning between successive jobs. In each case one part or other of this minority—say one in ten, or one in fifty of the whole body—is at every moment standing idle. The general formula for the supply of labour in an industry appears then to be this : for work requiring, if concentrated at one spot, at most ninety-eight men, there will actually be eighty in regular employment and twenty in irregular employment ; there will be a hundred in all, so that at all times two at least are out of work. The twenty, however, are as much part of the industrial system as are the eighty ; the reserve is as indispensable as the regulars. The idleness, now of some, now of others, of the reserve is mainly responsible for the irreducible minimum of unemployment. The figures here given have only an illustrative value ; the proportions of regular and reserve and irreducible minimum vary from trade to trade. The principle is of the greatest generality. The rule for each trade is to have more men than are called for together even at the busiest moment, but for the excess to show itself in the loss of some time by a large minority rather than in the chronic idleness of a few. There is leakage, occasional in regard to the individual, incessant as regards the whole body of men. The one or two per cent. to be found out of work on any one day are but that day's sample of the twenty or thirty or more per cent. subject to irregularity of employment.

The picture to be derived from the records of Distress Committees is really the same though with heightened colouring. There are, no doubt, among the applicants for relief under the Unemployed Workmen Act a few who strictly deserve the title of the chronically unemployed—a few who, without getting any work at all, and perhaps without being able or willing to do work if they should get it, contrive to subsist indefinitely upon charity or larceny or their wives and children's earnings. They may be compared to the chronically unemployed in the London Society of Compositors. They are not industrial but parasitic upon industry. They are persons of private means, whether their own or other people's. The bulk of the applicants to Distress Committees are not of this class. They do get work sometimes; without it they would be driven to the workhouse. The essence of their position is not that they are unemployed but that they are irregularly employed. The applicants on any one day are but that day's sample of a much larger number of men constantly dropping into and out of employment. They get enough work just to keep them where they are, though it may not be enough to provide a reasonable subsistence. The typical applicant to Distress Committees is not unemployable, since it pays a business firm on occasion to employ him; and he is not individually superfluous, since he is occasionally called on. He is not parasitic upon industry but industrial. He is not a man chronically unemployed but a casual labourer. The understanding of his case involves examination, not of unemployment only, but of the conditions of employment as well. The next stage in the argument must be an analysis of the economics of casual employment illustrated practically by the leading case of London dock and wharf labour.

ECONOMICS OF CASUAL EMPLOYMENT.

What will be the economic and social effects of a system of employment in which rapid and irregular fluctuations of work at a number of different centres are met by the engagement for short periods of irregular hands, who in part at least are taken on by chance as they present themselves? Casual employment implies these two elements—of short engagements and of want of selection. Each of these is best considered separately, and with the help of an abstract illustration.

Suppose that ten centres of casual employment—say ten similar wharves—each employ from 50 to 100 men on any one day, so that each considered separately requires a regular staff of 50 and a "reserve" of 50 more. In so far as the variations of work depend upon general causes, affecting all the wharves simultaneously and similarly, the busy and slack times respectively will tend to coincide and the variations in the total work to reproduce proportionately those of each separate wharf. In so far, however, as the variations at different wharves are unconnected, they will, in the total of men required at all the ten from day to day, tend to neutralise one another, because a busy time at some wharves will coincide with a slack time at others. Suppose that in fact the numbers employed at the whole ten from day to day range from a minimum of 700 to a maximum of 800. These daily numbers, whatever they are, will give the numbers of "regular" and "reserve" labourers who may theoretically find work at the whole ten wharves taken together. They must be taken as unalterable, determined solely by the necessary irregularities of trade and tide. They would presumably be the actual numbers employed supposing all the ten wharves were combined into a single wharf having the same mass and flow of custom. But so long as the wharves remain distinct, the number of individuals who will practically be required to do the same work is affected also by quite a different set of considerations. It is clear that if each separate wharf forms an absolutely distinct labour market so that no man works at more than one, then, however the variations of business neutralise one another, the number of individuals required to do the work will be 100 for each wharf or 1,000 in all. It is clear, on the other hand, that if the whole ten form a single labour market within which labour is absolutely fluid, then the full number of individuals required will coincide with the maximum of 800 employed on any one day. The total number of men practically required to do the work without delay (and by consequence the number of reserve labourers) is, in fact, increased by every barrier to free movement from one wharf to another, and can be correspondingly decreased by everything tending to the organisation of the whole ten into a single labour market. The greatest barrier to free movement in any area is ignorance among the men as to the demand for labour in different directions; every means taken to remove this ignorance enables the work of any area to be done with a smaller reserve of labour. But the general distribution of the most accurate information as to the amount of work at each centre is only a first step. Even if every man knows exactly how many men will be wanted next day at each wharf, this will not of itself (i.e., unless each knows also exactly how his fellows will act) prevent too many individuals from applying at one wharf and (perhaps) too few at another. If it is desired to do the work with the smallest possible reserve of labour, some means must be adopted for directing the right number of specified individuals to each wharf from some one centre or exchange.

This leads to a second point, the influence of chance in the competition for employment. It, too, is best introduced by another imaginary (and indeed absurd) case. Suppose that a wharfinger who required 100 men regularly every day were to take on that number afresh each morning, selecting them by chance (i.e., by some process analogous to drawing names out of a hat) from among a crowd of applicants.[1] Suppose further that, the daily

---

[1] The "crowd of applicants," that is to say, the existence of vigorous competition, is assumed here. The correctness of the assumption and the responsibility for the excessive competition are discussed later.

wage being five shillings, the subsistence level with reference to the class of men applying for the work was represented by an average of fifteen shillings or three days' work a week. Now, since each of those who applied regularly for work would have an equal chance, each would tend to obtain over a long period the same amount of work. So long as this amount was above subsistence level—*i.e.*, gave an average of more than three days a week—any fresh-comer would tend to stay and become a regular competitor. If the average fell below three days a week, some of the regular competitors would tend to leave and try their luck elsewhere, thus restoring the required average for those who remained. The number of regular competitors among whom the work would be evenly distributed, would thus tend always to be just sufficient to give each an average of three days a week. That is to say, with the present hypothesis, the work of the wharf, requiring 100 men daily, would come to be done by 200 men applying every day, and obtaining work, on an average, every other day.

This foregoing imaginary case shows that the effect of allowing chance to influence the selection of men for employment is to increase quite unnecessarily the number of individuals among whom any definite total of work is distributed. No actual employer of course would act like our imaginary wharfinger, and pure chance nowhere enters into the formation of industrial relationships. But the relevance of this illustration to real life becomes clear the moment it is remembered that the decision of a competition by chance does not mean that the choice goes one way or the other without reason, for nothing happens without a reason, but simply that the choice is determined by causes external to the competitors, and not by their abiding personal characteristics. If the success of A. over B. to-day is the result of personal differences between them, we expect the same differences to tell in exactly the same way in a similar competition to-morrow—to make A. once more successful and B. once more disappointed. If, however, A.'s success to-day is the result of external causes, not inherent in the personalities of either, it is as likely as not that these causes will favour B. instead of A. to-morrow. A competition between two men based solely on personal characteristics will, however often repeated, result always in the success of the same man. A competition determined solely by facts external to the competitors, will distribute success in the long run equally over both. In the special case of a daily competition for employment, it will result in two men doing the work and drawing the wages of one. The illustration, assuming as it does a perfectly steady amount of work, shows that chance selection of men for employment is an independent factor additional to all other factors in producing chronic under-employment.

The foregoing arguments may now be summarised. For the work of a group of casual employers a certain theoretically determinable number of men may be regarded as necessary; the number will be fixed by conditions of trade which must be taken for the present as unalterable. And, in so far as these trade conditions involve rapid and irregular variations of work within fairly definable limits, a part of this total number will have the character of an inevitable reserve of partially employed labour. But the actual number of men by whom the work is done, and its relation to the theoretically necessary number, will be affected also by another set of considerations, quite unconnected with the total volume of work or the unalterable conditions of trade. In the first place, every hindrance to the perfect fluidity of labour from centre to centre will swell the actual number of individuals doing the work by an amount representing the degree of friction. To return to the numerical instance, the work of ten wharves, which, if they had become for purposes of employment one wharf, might have been done by 800 men, would, with a certain degree of friction, require the services of 900. In that case there would, even when the wharves, as a whole, were busiest, be at least 100 men out of work. In the second place, every element of chance in the competition for employment, whether at one centre or over a district, tends to swell the actual number of individuals between whom any definite amount of work is distributed and to decrease the share of each, down to a limit fixed by the standard of subsistence. If each of the ten wharves in the numerical instance takes on its daily number of men largely by chance, each may find 100 or more applicants at its gates every morning, and the ten together may spread their total of work over 1,000 or more men, though not more than 800 are required to meet all possible local irregularities of work, and though the probable amount of work at each from day to day is well known. In that case, even when the wharves as a whole are busiest, there will be at least 200 men out of work.

One difference must be noted between the positions of those men who will in practice be added to the theoretical maximum for any area by friction between its separate centres and by chance in the competition for work respectively. The former, though the product of disorganisation, are a true reserve of labour without which, given that degree of disorganisation and friction, the industry could not be carried on. The latter are in no sense a *necessary* reserve of labour. The employer who has been supposed to select 100 men daily by lot will in practice employ perhaps 200 different men, but the existence of so many individuals is irrelevant to him. So long as he has at least 100 applicants his work can proceed. The extra 100 are not a necessary reserve of labour. Still he does in effect employ them; however unintentionally, he by haphazard selection puts forward a demand for their services which, in relation to the sources of supply, is an effective demand. His system of employment brings this additional body of labour to his gates.

In the total reserve of labour for any occupation it is thus possible to distinguish three elements. There is first the body of men representing the fluctuations in the volume of work to be done at all centres of employment taken together. In the numerical instance given this consists of the 100 men making the difference between the 700 engaged on the day when the ten wharves collectively are slackest and the 800 engaged on the day when the ten wharves collectively are busiest. These men are required by the conditions of the trade as a whole. There is, second, the body of men required by the fact that, owing to distance, ignorance or custom, the supply of labour cannot move with perfect freedom and instantaneously from any one centre of employment to any other, and that therefore separate centres, to meet their fluctuations of work, must to some extent keep separate reserves. These men represent the friction of the labour market. In the numerical instance given they are the 100 men between the 800 required on the busiest day for the wharves collectively and the 900 required because the men just dismissed from one wharf which is slack are not necessarily or immediately available for work at any other which happens to be busy. There is, third, the body of men required neither by the fluctuations in the total volume of work nor by the fluctuations of separate business but liable to be attracted and retained by the perpetual chance of work. They are the 100 men between the 900 who would meet all the demands of the ten wharves, disorganised and separate as these demands are, and the 1,000 men each of whom in fact manages to get a share of the work by constant competition.

The economic bearings of casual employment have been analysed with the aid of imaginary cases. The conditions of London riverside labour may now be described by way of practical illustration.

Work at the London docks and wharves consists of the loading and unloading of ships and the handling of cargoes in lighters,

6

upon quays, and in warehouses. This work is spread over a large area and distributed between many different employers. The distance from London Bridge to the Albert Dock along the north bank is ten miles. That from London Bridge to the new entrance of the Surrey Commercial Docks along the south bank is three and a half miles. On each side there is a nearly continuous succession of wharves and docks between these points. Outside the ordinary London area altogether, yet forming an integral part of the port, is Tilbury Dock, twenty-six miles by water from London Bridge. The employers are of four main types—dock companies[1], shipowners, contractors and wharfingers. The dock companies are three in number, viz., the London and India Docks Company on the north side, dealing with cargoes of all kinds; the Millwall Dock Company on the north side, dealing almost entirely with grain and timber; the Surrey Commercial Docks Company on the south side, dealing predominantly though not solely with grain and timber. These companies employ respectively about 20, 4 and 10 per cent. of the labour covered by the daily returns to the Labour Department. The number of shipowners employing men directly either for export or import is uncertain, but, omitting Tilbury, is not less than thirty and may be fifty. About 13 per cent. of the men covered by the statistics of the Labour Department are employed by shipowners. The number of contractors is also uncertain, as indeed the term itself is uncertain, and includes many grades of employers. The London Post Office Directory gives the names of twenty firms of Master Porters or Stevedores, who form the important element in this group. About 12 per cent. of the men covered by the statistics of the Labour Department are employed through those and other contractors. The wharfingers are the most numerous of all employers. The report of the Royal Commission on the Port of London gives a list of 165 wharves on the north side and 155 on the south side, making a total of 320. About 115 of these, employing 41 per cent. of the labourers included in the statistics, make returns to the Labour Department.

The cardinal features about dock and wharf industry from the point of view of each separate employer are, first, considerable irregularity in the arrival and departure of cargoes by ship or by barge; second, the small extent to which machinery has been able to displace more or less unskilled manual labour in the work of loading, unloading and otherwise dealing with goods in transit. The first fact causes great hourly, daily or weekly variations in the amount of work to be done at any one centre of riverside employment; the second causes all the effects of this varying demand to

---

[1] Replaced since 1908 by the Port of London Authority.

be thrown upon the labourers, whom, beyond certain limits, it is uneconomical to employ regularly, and who are taken on and put off at short notice as they are wanted or not wanted. Every separate centre of riverside employment requires for its smooth working to have immediately available a larger number of men than it can employ regularly or even adequately.

The work of course is not all unskilled. On the ground of the special skill required Mr. Charles Booth in 1891 excluded from his statistics for the Labour Commission all the men engaged in actual stowage of export cargoes, as well as lightermen and coal porters, and he has been followed in this by the Labour Department. According to this distinction, dock and wharf labour in the strict sense is the employment offered by the import trade in discharging goods into lighters or on to land, trucking along the quay, warehousing and handling in warehouses, and by the export trade in handling goods on the quay in preparation for loading. The distinction has some though decreasing validity; the men engaged in the actual stowage of goods—generally known as stevedores—not only as a rule receive a higher rate of pay but over a considerable portion of the port are marked off by a separate trade organisation. More fruitful, however, than any absolute distinction between skilled workman and labourer is the perception of dock and wharf work as including every possible gradation, from that which any man of average or even less than average physique can turn to at once, to that which requires years of special experience. The work of corn and timber porters, though counted in with the "dock and wharf labour" from which that of stevedores and coal porters is excluded, is in fact hardly less specialised. The men engaged in it may earn ten shillings or fifteen shillings in a day; men unfamiliar with it would be useless. To a lesser degree the advantage of previous experience is felt with all the main classes of cargo, and affects the method of employment. Most of the large employers have a nucleus of permanent men whose knowledge of the details of the business makes their services important, while at nearly all centres of employment there is a body of irregular men known individually and receiving a formal or informal preference. Such men naturally acquire in time a familiarity with particular classes of work or premises and become of special value to the employer. He would rather have them than any chance-comer, and perhaps recognises their position by placing them on a definite preference list or by the issue of preference tickets. More often no formal steps are taken, and the position even of the known man, depending upon the recollection or the favour of a particular foreman,

6 *

becomes correspondingly less secure. Outside the permanent men, the preference men and the men known in varying degrees to a particular foreman, there is a broad fringe of absolutely casual and undistinguished labourers, taken on as they come to meet exceptional demands. They are men who in their own phrase work here, there and everywhere; who can seldom, if ever, name any of their employers; and whose employers still more seldom know anything about them. The element of chance in the daily competition for employment increases with every step from the permanent to the utter casual. In practically no case are characters either given or required. In the lowest grade every man, whatever his past, however small his experience, has his chance of a day's employment like any other.

These are the general facts of London dock and wharf labour. They correspond in all essentials—multiplicity of independent demands for labour, friction and chance engagement—with the abstract analysis by which they were preceded.

(1) The demand for labour in the port is not single, but distributed between a multitude of different employers. The needs of each of these employers fluctuate greatly. To some extent these fluctuations are seasonal in character. In the port as a whole, for instance, the general level of the numbers employed is from 1,500 to 2,000 higher in winter than in summer. In some of the main sections into which it may be divided the proportional seasonal change is naturally much greater. To some extent again the fluctuations if not exactly seasonal are general. The aggregate number of men employed at the docks and wharves may without apparent rule rise or fall 1,500 (about 10 per cent. of the whole) between one day and the next, or vary by several thousands between two successive weeks. To a very large extent, however, the fluctuations of different businesses are independent. They do not all grow busy or all grow slack together; a large demand in one place is neutralised by a small demand in another. The sum of the separate maxima over any period exceeds very greatly the maximum of all taken together on any one day. In 1891, for instance, Mr. Charles Booth, grouping the employers at all the docks and wharves in ten principal groups,[1] showed that their maxima during the year added up to

---

[1] Labour Commission, *Group B, Evidence,* vol. iii., Qu. 24727 *seq.* and Appendix clv.; *cf.* also *Life and Labour: Industry,* iii., p. 409 *seq.* The ten main divisions are: London and St. Katherine's Docks, East and West India Docks, Victoria and Albert Docks, Town Warehouses (all these four under the then existing Joint Committee of the separate London and India Docks Companies), shipowners in the Victoria and Albert Docks, shipowners in London Docks, North Side Wharves, Millwall Dock, Surrey Commercial Docks and South Side Wharves.

21,353—that is to say, on the supposition that each group was a separate and single labour market, the number of individuals required for the work would have been at least 21,353. But so far were the busy times for the different groups from coinciding that the maximum number employed on any one day in them all taken together was under 17,994 ; that is to say, if the port of London had been a completely unified market for waterside labour, with perfect fluidity between its different parts, 17,994 individuals would have sufficed for exactly the same work. Even these figures, however, have only an illustrative value. None of Mr. Booth's groups was in fact rigidly cut off from all the others. On the other hand, each of them included many distinct centres of employment. The sum of the separate maxima for each of these centres in a group would probably have been found to exceed the aggregate maximum for the whole group on any one day at least as much, proportionately, as the sum for the separate groups exceeded the maximum for the whole port. Unquestionably the case of the ten wharves is realised in practice. Fluctuations at different centres of employment are sufficiently disconnected to make the question of the mobility of labour between them a matter of prime importance. The actual number of men between whom the work is distributed will approximate to the arithmetical aggregate of those required on the busiest day, or will exceed it, in proportion as the movement of labour is or is not rapid and organised.

(2) There is, with one notable exception, no attempt to make the movement of labour rapid or organised. There is practically no co-operation by different employers in regard to the engaging of men. Each employer engages them as and where he can get them. Each requires and requiring tends to collect a separate small reserve of labour in his immediate neighbourhood. For the most part this is done quite unconsciously. Men naturally return to the place where they have once been successful in getting a job ; they wait about where they hope they may be known in preference to trying chances far afield. To some extent, however, there can be no doubt that more or less deliberate measures have to be adopted to keep the reserve together. Work which might be done always by the same men is given out in rotation so as to have men always in close attendance for emergencies. Thus at certain London wharves it was found that the permanent staff averaged only 70 per cent. of the minimum numbers employed on the very slackest days. The remaining 30 per cent. of constant work, together with the casual work, was distributed over a large reserve

of irregular hands.[1] It is, moreover, not at all unknown for employers and foremen to resent those whom they employ by preference though not regularly seeking work with a rival in off times.[2] Here another motive enters to reinforce the main motive and to break up the supply of labour into a multitude of small separate reserves. As a consequence, all these reserves together add up into a total far in excess of the maximum number required at the riverside on the busiest days. Some proportion of these reserves is always standing idle.

(3) Though no individual employer engages men by lot, though even without formal preference lists the foreman at each wharf gets to know and to choose again and again the same regular applicants for work, the element of chance in the labour market as a whole is a very real one. The individual has, first, to forecast the probable demand for men at different centres with, in many cases, so little means of knowledge that success becomes a matter of luck rather than of skill. Second, the number and quality of his competitors at any centre he may choose is determined partly by similar vague forecasts on the part of his regular fellows, partly by the infinitely various accidents which may send a discharged prisoner, a sturdy tramp, a time-expired soldier or an unemployed member of any other trade to try the luck of the docks. With these he must then compete for the favour of a foreman's roving eye in an undistinguished crowd, where the decision will go largely by chance, since the multitude of different centres prevents more than a small percentage of men getting known and practically preferred at one place. Given indeed a number of distinct centres of irregular work, unless the engagement of men is deliberately *and co-operatively* organised, the following dilemma is reached— either men will tend to stick to one centre or they will move freely from one to the other. With the former alternative, chance will be diminished (because each man will become well known at his centre), but friction will be at a maximum. Each centre forming a separate labour market, local fluctuations in work will be unable to neutralise one another, and the separate reserves for labour at each centre will add up to a total enormously exceeding the aggregate maximum for the whole industry. With the second alternative, friction will be diminished, but chance at a maximum. The mobility of the labour supply will diminish the numbers

---

[1] *Unskilled Labour.* Report of a Special Committee of the Charity Organisation Society, 1908, p. 34. At the Millwall Docks in 1905 the permanent staff was less than 50 per cent. of the minimum number employed on the slackest day of the year. *Cf. Dock Labour and Poor Law Relief*, 1908. Cd. 4391.

[2] *West Ham*, E. G. Howarth and Mona Wilson (1907, J. M. Dent), p. 402. This Report and that cited just above on Unskilled Labour are among the most valuable recent contributions to the subject of unemployment and deserve full study.

of individuals required to meet the fluctuating demands of the many different employers, but it will also exclude the formation of local and personal connections and preferences, and will allow chance to scatter jobs over a needless multitude of casuals. This dilemma is no imaginary one. It is illustrated by the experienced inadequacy of the plan of "preference lists" which formed the first part of the staff reorganisation at the London and India Docks. Mere mobility of labour is not enough. It must be organised movement and backed up by organised selection. Separate preference lists at each centre of employment are not enough; the lists must be amalgamated. The account of the notable labour reform carried out during the last seventeen years by the largest of the London dock companies provides the best comment upon these conclusions.[1]

Up to the time of the great strike of 1889 the bulk of the work at the docks on the north of the river was performed by purely casual labourers taken on by the dock companies' foremen from a struggling crowd at the entry to each department.[2] It was estimated that for work sufficient, if evenly distributed throughout the year, to give 3s. a day to 3,000 men, at least 10,000 competed *regularly*.[3] The quality of these men was no less notorious than their quantity. The knowledge that any man, whatever his experience, however bad his antecedents, might get a job at the docks, attracted to their neighbourhood a perpetual stream of blackguards, weaklings and failures from every other occupation. The experience, soon made, that regular attendance was not necessary to secure selection on days when work hap-

---

[1] The earlier stages of this reform are described in the evidence of Mr. W. E. Hubbard, Chairman of the London and India Docks Joint Committee, before the Labour Commission (*Group B, Evidence*, vol. i., Qu. 4581 *seq.*). For the later stages, see the *C.O.S. Report on Unskilled Labour*, p. 64, and Evidence of Messrs. H. H. Watts and S. Ward, and Howarth and Wilson, *op. cit.*, pp. 190 *seq.*

[2] The following description by a foreman in the dock companies' service is worth quoting : " The position of a ' taking-on foreman ' (before the preference system) was an extremely dangerous occupation, and while he was thus employed it was advisable to look after his money and valuables, also look to himself; in fact it was necessary to know a little of the art of self-defence. There was a place in London Docks which was called the cage, where men were taken on after the first call. When I went there for the first time I was astounded. Firstly, the constable un-barred the door, then a gigantic roar went up from hundreds of throats calling my name. A long platform about a foot from the ground was erected, upon which I stood to give out the tickets. A great mass of faces and hands through iron bars appeared before me, fighting and struggling, so much so, that it was difficult to detect which face the hand belonged to. Some would be struggling to secure as many tickets as possible, so that they might be able to sell them to other men who had not been fortunate enough to get one " (*Unskilled Labour*, p. 183). Fighting for work is by no means unknown at the riverside even to-day; *cf.* Howarth and Wilson, *op. cit.*, pp. 200, 201.

[3] Miss Potter (Mrs. Sidney Webb) in Charles Booth's *Life and Labour of the People : Industry*, vol. iv., p. 25.

pened to be plentiful, and the daily alternations of hard exercise and idleness, rapidly developed in those who came, if they had it not before, the greatest irregularity of habits, and physical or moral incapacity for continuous exertion. The low physique and half-starved condition of many of the labourers made their work dear at 4d. an hour. The London dock casual was popularly regarded as "the scum of the earth"; the system of dock employment was aptly described as, in effect, "a gigantic system of out-door relief".[1] All could get occasional shillings, few a decent living.

The attention drawn to these evils by the strike of 1889, and the investigations of authorities such as Mr. Charles Booth, led to the initiation in 1891 of a reasoned policy of reform by "de-casualisation". This reform had two sides. The first was the formation of "preference" lists. Men were ranked as "permanent," "A," "B," "C" and "casual". The "permanent" and "A" men, on weekly wages, formed the practically regular (much increased) staff; men in the other classes were engaged and paid daily and had no certainty of employment on any day, but the "B" men had a preferential right to be employed next after the regular staff and before any "C" men were taken on, while the "C" men had a similar preference over the casuals. Within the "B" and "C" classes there was a similar grading of men according to their place on the lists. This system was directed to the exclusion of that element of chance in the selection of men which, as was recognised, must distribute the work over an unnecessarily large number. It was intended to put a premium upon regular attendance for work and good behaviour, since men were to be moved up and down the lists according to their merits; to enable the decent man, protected by his "preference," to obtain a living; and to discourage the casual application of loafers and the incursion of fresh competitors. This reform undoubtedly did something, but not quite as much as was expected. Each department had a complete set of separate preference lists, but could not offer at all times a sufficient chance of work to secure the regular application of even all its "B" men. Owing to the great local variations of work a man might hope sometimes to do better as a casual at one place than as a "B" man at his proper department. He would accordingly compete as a casual elsewhere; the list system was in danger of being nullified. It was seen that the dock departments were too small to stand apart and to maintain each its own reserve of labour. A second line of reform

---

[1] Miss Potter, *loc. cit.*

was adopted, aimed at making the whole of these northern docks into a single labour market, within which the required supplies of men should be directed from a central office to the different work places. This organisation, developed gradually during the past ten years, has now proceeded so far that 80 per cent. of the work done by the London and India Docks Company is performed by weekly labourers, and 20 per cent. by preference men and casuals. The preference lists are now of quite minor significance; the "C" list has disappeared altogether, and even "B" tickets are not much regarded. The permanent and "A" classes engross nearly the whole field of employment, forming a mobile body of labour constantly employed, though sometimes in one place, sometimes in another.

The table just below [1] shows the course of the reorganisation since 1894. It began, however, considerably before then. According to figures given by Miss Potter (Mrs. Webb), the proportion of work at the London and St. Katherine's and East and West India Docks performed by permanent labourers was in 1887 only 16 per cent. In 1891-92 the work performed by the weekly staff under the London and India Joint Committee was 45 per cent. of the whole. For the years 1894-1901 it averaged, as shown in the table, 64 per cent. For the years 1902-4 it averaged 78 per cent.

TABLE XVI.—LONDON AND INDIA DOCKS—PERCENTAGE OF WORK
PERFORMED BY EACH CLASS OF LABOUR.

Year.	Permanent.	A.	Total Weekly.	B.	Casual.	Total Extra.	Average Number Employed each Day.
1894	30·7	34·9	65·6	28·8	5·6	34·4	5,079
1895	28·4	31·8	60·2	30·9	8·9	39·8	5,330
1896	30·2	33·0	63·2	29·4	7·4	36·8	5,017
1897	29·4	32·4	61·8	28·0	10·2	38·2	4,947
1898	32·7	35·4	68·1	25·7	6·2	31·9	4,232
1899	32·1	35·3	67·4	26·0	6·6	32·6	4,127
1900	28·8	33·9	62·7	25·8	11·5	37·3	4,483
1901	28·0	35·4	63·4	28·4	8·2	36·6	4,579
1902	34·4	40·6	75·0	22·2	2·8	25·0	3,839
1903	39·8	42·4	82·2	16·3	1·5	17·8	3,290
1904	41·2	37·2	78·4	19·7	1·9	21·6	3,054

[1] *Unskilled Labour.* Statement of Mr. H. H. Watts, p. 114 *seq.* and p. 64.

LABOUR STAFF, 1ST JANUARY, 1905 (EXCLUSIVE OF LABOURING BOYS AND GIRLS).

1305 Permanent Labourers. *Guaranteed Wages:* 24s. per week of six days of eight working hours between 6 A.M. and 6 P.M. Overtime pay at current rates. *Leave:* Three days annually in addition to general holidays. *Pension:* After at least fifteen years' service. Actual average weekly earnings, 31s. 3d.

1176 List A—Registered Labourers. *Guaranteed Wages:* 24s. per week of forty-eight working hours in summer and 21s. per week of forty-two working hours in winter. Overtime at current rates. *Leave:* Three days annually after twelve months' service on the list. Actual average weekly earnings, 29s. 10d.

2077 List B—Preference Labourers. *Guaranteed Wages:* 6d. per working hour between 6 A.M. and 6 P.M., and 8d. per hour between 6 P.M. and 6 A.M. No man discharged with less than 2s. pay, except in regard to special short engagements in the afternoon.

Casual men, as required, are employed when there is pressure of work, and at the same wages as those on List B.

The reorganisation has, beyond question, had the effect of improving the type of men employed. " The dock labourer who is employed by the company is, as a rule, industrious, steady and honest. The system which obtains has the effect of shaking down to the tail-end of the lowest list the men who cannot be so characterised; they only get work in emergencies, and the tendency is for them to drop off altogether. Men do not attend at the India and London and St. Katherine Docks on the off-chance of work as numerously as heretofore, and those who do attend appear, on the whole, to be of a better character and class than formerly." The improved efficiency of the men is given as at least one cause of the decrease in the actual numbers employed.[1]

It was, of course, fully recognised by the authors of this reform that the effect would be to concentrate employment upon one section of the men hitherto employed, at the expense of others who would be thrown out of work altogether. Part of the former reserve of labour became regularly employed, or nearly so; another part became no longer a reserve but an absolute surplus. This latter fact did not, of course, affect the social advantage of the change; one man fully employed and fed is preferable in the state to two men on perpetual half rations. It did, however, suggest the desirability of taking steps to drain off the surplus caused by transition from casual to regularised employment, and the Mansion House Fund of 1892 was directed or diverted to this object. Temporary work was offered at Abbey Mills to unemployed dock labourers with a view to testing their capacity and leading to permanent improvement in their position by emigration, migration, transference to new industries or otherwise. The

---

[1] *Unskilled Labour.* Statement and Evidence of Mr. H. H. Watts. Qu. 442.

proved success of this attempt, which is described in full in the Board of Trade Report of 1893,[1] appears to have been small. It is interesting, however, as one of that extremely rare type of relief schemes which have consciously attacked a clearly conceived problem.

The reorganisation of their labour by the London and India Docks Company is a reform of historic importance in the treatment of the unemployed problem. Yet to this day there is altogether insufficient appreciation either of the nature of the reform or of its limits. On the one hand, more people have heard of the preference lists than of the unification of the docks as a labour market; the relative importance of the two changes is misappreciated even where the latter is not altogether ignored. On the other hand, it is seldom realised how small a proportion of the total field of dock and wharf labour is really covered by the reform. There is a common impression that waterside employment in London has been " organised," or at least made as constant as is humanly possible in a business state; and that any further reform must take the line of paying regular wages to men who will be idle half their time. As a matter of fact, the London and India Docks Company unload less than a tenth of the total tonnage entering the port; including all the men occupied at the up-town warehouses and in preparation for loading, they employ about a fifth of the total daily average of dock and wharf labourers. Their share in the work, indeed, has fallen considerably since the dock strike, by the transference to shipowners and contractors of some of its most fluctuating portions.[2] To this extent the apparent effects of their reform must be discounted. Outside the work of the dock company preference lists have been tried here and there. The separation of the interests of wharfingers, shipowners and contractors has prevented any movement upon the other and more effective line of reform—the organisation and unification of the labour market.

---

[1] *Agencies and Methods for Dealing with the Unemployed*, 1893. Cd. 7182, pp. 238-63.

[2] In 1891 the London and India Docks Joint Committee employed at all their docks (including Tilbury) a maximum on any one day of 8,720 men, a minimum of 4,120, and an average of about 6,000. The regular (permanent and A) men at that date numbered 2,750, *i.e.*, about two-thirds of the minimum number employed on the slackest day, and less than half of the average number. For 1904 the corresponding figures were: maximum, 4,322; minimum, 2,348; average, 3,054; regular (permanent and A) men, 2,481. In other words, the regular men were fully up to the minimum number required on the slackest day (there is always some leakage through illness and the like), and were four-fifths of the average number required daily throughout the year. These figures show both the progress that has been made and the way in which it has been made, *viz.*: by keeping the regular staff nearly up to the original strength while the volume of work declined.

The problem of London waterside labour remains in essence what it was twenty years ago. This does not mean that there has been no improvement at all. There has been improvement in several ways. First, the higher hourly rate of pay for even the least skilled work, secured by the great strike of 1889, has drawn a slightly higher class of men, and the memory of a historic movement perhaps still lends some measure of self-respect to the once despised calling of dock labourer. Second, for special types of work there has been a selection of abler types of workmen ; it has been found in an increasing number of cases that the best paid labour is the cheapest labour.[1] Third, the reorganisation of the labour staff of the London and India Docks Company has improved conditions just where they were formerly at their worst. Yet all these improvements have been either indirect or very limited in scope. The dock company employ only a fifth of the labour of the port ; even in that fifth are included a great many irregular hands. In waterside labour as a whole the methods of the past continue ; the same economic forces are at work and produce the same consequences. "The central evil," says the *Report of the Charity Organisation Society on Unskilled Labour*, published this year, "is the maintenance of a floating reserve of labour far larger than is required to meet the maximum demands of employers. This is brought about by the independent action of the separate employing agencies each seeking to retain a following of labour as nearly as possible equal to its own maximum demand."

It is not indeed possible to give trustworthy statistical estimates as to the extent of this floating reserve. There is no full record of the number of those who compete regularly for waterside work in London ; there is no record at all of those who compete only from time to time ; there is no means at present of estimating the proportions of casual to regular workmen. Mr. Booth in 1892 gave it as a rough estimate that the number of men actually needed in the port under the system of casual employment was 20,000, and that the number competing regularly for work was 22,000. At the same time the full number employed on the busiest day of the year was 18,000, the average throughout the year was 15,000, and the number on the slackest day was 10,000. In other words, the system of casual employment necessitated the presence of 2,000 and left room for 4,000 regular competitors over and above the number who could find work on the busiest day. On the slackest day 12,000, and on an average throughout the year 7,000, men would be standing idle.

---

[1] *Unskilled Labour*, p. 34, and Evidence of Mr. Scrutton.

In addition to these, of course, there would be all those who took to the docks as an occasional or last resource.

The census, unfortunately, gives very little help in this matter. The number of those returning themselves as dock and wharf labourers in London and West Ham together was 25,291 in 1901. For the same year the maximum number employed on any one day in the port, exclusive of Tilbury, according to the Board of Trade returns, was 18,643, and the average number 16,454. For 1904 the maximum number was 15,616, and the average 12,988. Close comparison between these figures is, however, impossible. On the one hand, the Board of Trade figures cover only a part of the labour of the port. Some employers do not make returns ; some types of workmen, *e.g.*, stevedores, are excluded. On the other hand, only those who followed up riverside work pretty regularly would be likely to describe themselves as dock or wharf labourers. Many men appearing in the census under other headings—particularly those of general labourer and builder's labourer—would be occasional competitors at the docks. How many, it is, unfortunately, impossible to say. The experience of Distress Committees, however, makes it clear that very large numbers of those who call themselves labourers or builders' labourers find part of their living at the waterside.

The intensity of the distress involved is, unfortunately, as little capable of general statistical record as is its extent. There are no data to show the average earnings of a casual dock labourer. Such an average, indeed, would be at best but an arithmetical abstraction. In riverside employment above all things there is every gradation from getting fair continuity of work to getting hardly any work at all ; no average would fairly represent the class. In the absence of comprehensive figures all that can be done is to cite from Mr. Howarth and Miss Wilson's report on West Ham[1] one or two individual cases as to which the facts seem pretty certain. The first is the case of a glass-bottle maker, who, failing to get regular employment at his own trade, worked sometimes as a docker proper, sometimes at ship repairing or in the yard of a dock engineering works. He kept a weekly record of all his takings from every source—including odd jobs at his original trade and canvassing—for nearly three years, till he recovered regular employment. In the report this record is set out in full ; here it seems sufficient to give to the nearest half-crown the average weekly earnings for successive months.

[1] *Cf.* p. 198.

TABLE XVII.—AVERAGE WEEKLY EARNINGS OF CASUAL DOCKER.

	1904.	1905.	1906.
	S. D.	S. D.	S. D.
January . . .	—	22 6	12 6
February . . .	—	12 6	10 0
March. . . .	—	22 6	17 6
April	10 0	22 6	17 6
May	15 0	42 6	5 0
June	7 6	12 6	22 6
July	17 6	12 6	22 6
August . . .	12 6	22 6	17 6
September . . .	10 0	17 6	12 6
October . . .	12 6	20 0	15 0
November . . .	12 6	7 6	17 6
December . . .	17 6	12 6	—

During seventeen of the thirty-two months covered by the
return, the average weekly earnings were fifteen shillings or less;
during twenty-five months they were twenty shillings or less. As
much as sixty-seven and ninepence was earned in one particular
week (May 20-27, 1905), and in twenty-two other weeks out of
138 the earnings were over thirty shillings, but seventeen weeks
were absolutely blank, and twenty-eight more produced less than
ten shillings each.

Two other cases are those of "Royals," that is to say, of men
on the preference lists of some particular employer, whether shipowner or contractor. Such men have the best chance of work at
the docks, and are "considered to be in quite a superior position
to the ordinary casual docker". One of these two men, a contractor's "Royal," in seventeen out of the thirty months for which
the returns are given, averaged seventeen shillings and sixpence
or less per week. The other, a shipowner's "Royal," in forty-
five out of the forty-eight months covered by his returns averaged
twenty shillings a week or less; in thirty-three, averaged fifteen
shillings or less; in eighteen, averaged ten shillings or less.

The figures in these cases are of peculiar value for several
reasons. They are founded not on vague estimates but on regular
weekly records, and can therefore be relied on with some assurance.
They represent the experiences of men all of whom, from the
mere fact of their keeping such records, may fairly be presumed
to be rather picked men in respect of character among the docker
class, and two of whom had their superiority recognised by inclusion in preference lists. Finally, as the most important point
of all, the inclusion of these two men in preference lists marks
them formally as men having definite places in industry, places

which on their departure would remain to be filled by others as surely as if they had been in the civil or municipal service. This is a point to which reference will be made later.

The difficulty of securing statistical estimates in no way obscures the main features of the position. The system of casual engagement to meet fluctuations of dock and wharf business requires the maintenance of reserves of labour at all the points at which men are engaged. A considerable part of these reserves is so irregularly employed as to be in chronic poverty. On every day some part of them is standing idle.

THE GLUTTING OF THE LABOUR MARKET.

The work of the London docks and wharves affords perhaps the leading instance, but still only one instance, of casual employment. Casual employment itself is only the most acute form of a general economic phenomenon. These are the two points that form the subjects of the present section.

London is only one port amongst many. Its labour conditions have always attracted peculiar attention. Yet they are clearly to be paralleled, in kind if not in degree, by the conditions of waterside labour at every other port in the country.[1] Each port, no doubt, has its peculiar customs, its characteristic forms of cargo or types of employers, and its own methods of remuneration. In none is the number of separate centres of employment so great or the area covered by them so wide as in London. In few has trade union organisation had so transient a success. Yet in all these ports the problem is at bottom unmistakably the same. In all of them the incalculable irregularities of trade, weather and tide are provided for by the maintenance of reserves of casual labour. Everywhere the dockers' district is an area of chronic distress able to yield on every day in the year a mass of the unemployed. The *Report on Unskilled Labour* gives a brief account of conditions in Glasgow and Southampton. In Hull the Distress Committee report that a great number of the unemployed are dock labourers. In Bristol the Distress Committee, realising at once that casual employment is one of the main problems to be dealt with, have under consideration the possibility of diminishing and organising such employment at the docks and elsewhere. In Liverpool the matter formed the main subject of a Commission of Inquiry which reported in 1894. It has been specially dealt with

---

[1] The undesirable pre-eminence of ports in respect of unemployment extends beyond Great Britain. In the German census of unemployment (1895), the six towns showing most unemployed per cent. of population were the capital, Berlin, and Altona, Hamburg, Danzig, Königsberg, Stettin (five ports).

also in a pamphlet by Miss Rathbone,[1] which shows that "the present irregularity of employment is much greater than is arithmetically necessary to balance the irregularity of work in the port, taking it as a single labour market". The position indeed is analysed exactly on the lines of the foregoing analysis of London conditions. The number of different "stands" for the engagement of men is indicated as the principal factor in maintaining a body of casual labour altogether in excess of the total requirements of the port. Co-operation between employers in taking men from a few main centres instead of from these "stands" is advocated as the most hopeful line of reform.

The problem even in this extreme form is by no means one of waterside labour alone. Everywhere Distress Committee records reveal men whose conditions of employment approximate to those at the docks, who pick up a day here or a day there, or wait outside factories or works to be taken on at a moment's notice and dismissed in the evening. Among these the casual carman holds a peculiar position. He is often of no higher type than the least skilled labourer, but he tends generally to become attached to some particular firm. Each firm has its little collection of men waiting to be called; since the firms are never all busy together there is never a time when some men are not out of work.

The problem, again, is not confined to the extreme form of which waterside labour is the type, and in which the common unit of engagement is a day, or at most two or three days. The different classes of builders' operatives and labourers head another variety equally important and even more widely spread, in which the common unit of engagement is the "job" of weeks or months. Here the same incalculable irregularity of work, especially in regard to any one employer, issues, through the same limited use of machinery, in extreme irregularity of employment and the need for a large labour reserve. The method of engagement is in form fully as casual as at the docks; it is an almost universal rule for men to be engaged subject to an hour's notice on either side, and without characters being either given or required. Wages, however, are paid weekly, and men once engaged are, unless distinctly incompetent, in practice retained till the conclusion of the job or of their part of it. They do not have to compete, as so many waterside labourers do, for fresh engagement every morning. This fact, and to a less extent the higher rates of pay, distinguish the occupation of the builder's labourer favourably from that of

[1] *Report of an Inquiry into the Conditions of Dock Labour at the Liverpool Docks.* Eleanor F. Rathbone.

the dock labourer.   The men are, on the whole, of a higher type,
and distress among them is rather recurrent, with bad weather
or the end of a job, than chronic.   Such a generalisation has, of
course, to be made subject to a good deal of qualification.   There
is probably hardly any occupation in which formal similarity of
conditions is combined with such great practical differences.   A
job at sevenpence an hour may last a week or it may last two
years.   There are some men who seldom get anything better
than the first of these.   There are others who, by their connection
with a large firm or two or three foremen, obtain practical continuity of employment throughout their working life.   While, however, the bulk of builders' employees, skilled and unskilled, are
of a higher type than the bulk of the waterside labourers, there
is a floating mass of labour more or less common to both occupations.

The building trade has, indeed, to set against the advantages
mentioned, the great disadvantage of lacking fixed centres of employment.   By the nature of things no two pieces of work follow
closely on one another in the same spot.   The foremen, to whom
the whole business of engaging men is entrusted, move continually
from one job to another, from one end of a town to the other, or
even from town to town.   Each foreman tends to take on with
him the pick of his men and others follow, but, as a general
rule, of all the men under him at any time the proportion whom
a foreman has consciously employed before is not very great.
He starts on a job with a few leading hands.   The rest are taken
on as they come—guided by recommendations from their mates
or stray hints in public-houses, following up a load of builder's
materials or a contractor's travelling office on a van, tramping
without guidance about likely districts.   Obviously such a system
or want of system could not work unless there was an army of
men always on the tramp, a reserve of labour drifting perpetually
about the streets.   How it does work is shown eloquently by the
practice of "weeding out" at the beginning of a job.   All likely
men are taken on as they come without inquiry; a certain proportion commonly prove unsatisfactory on trial, and after a few
days, or it may be a few weeks, are dismissed as better men
gradually come along; efficient gangs are got together by a
process of selection; the men dismissed are free to go on and
repeat the same process elsewhere.[1]   The obvious result is to
maintain in a state of permanent demoralisation a mass of low
grade casuals.   Their occasional doles of work are insufficient for

[1] *Unskilled Labour*, p. 47, and " Evidence," Qu. 430-32, 305-7.

a decent living; while they are getting their doles, the more efficient men who are to displace them are probably already unemployed and seeking for work, but seeking for it in the wrong direction. To call employment in the building trade a lottery is to use the language not of metaphor but of literal description. The analysis already made as to the effects of chance in the competition for work applies forcibly; casual jobs are scattered over a quite unnecessarily large number of individuals. The lottery, indeed, is one mitigated by many formal and informal connections between particular foremen and particular workmen. Each foreman is the centre of a more or less definite group; he may keep their addresses; so far as possible they follow him about and retain touch with him. Yet clearly even this mitigation has its bad side. The more men stick to particular foremen the less is the influence of chance but the greater is the leakage of time through the breaking up of the total labour market into separate groups. The foreman system, again, increases enormously the uncertainty of employment, since with the death or dismissal of a particular foreman all those customarily dependent on him lose their ground in the labour market. Finally, the door is opened to abuse of patronage; convivial drinking and even direct bribery are not unknown as a means of securing employment.[1]

The course of the argument is already making it clear that casual employment cannot be treated as a thing apart. There is no saying, and there is no profit in trying to say, with precision, what is and what is not to be regarded as casual employment. The phrase implies, no doubt, primarily shortness of engagement, and secondarily engagement of first-comers. But no rigid distinction can be drawn anywhere between "short" hirings and "long" hirings, between employing "known" men and "unknown" men, between selecting by chance and selecting by personal characteristics. The most casual employment in the world—say that of the cab-runner—stands at one end of a continuous series of all possible relations between employer and employed of which the other end is represented by the lifelong contracts of hiring still possible in law, or by the actual permanencies of civil and municipal service. Wherever employment in practice falls short of this degree of permanence, there is the possibility of a certain number of men having to stand off for a time from their usual work, or even leave one centre of employment to try their chance at another. In every industry the aggregate demand for labour is distributed among many separate employers at many

---

[1] *Problems of Unemployment in the London Building Trades.* N. B. Dearle (1908, J. M. Dent). *Cf.* specially pp. 87-8.

different places. In nearly every industry the fortunes of these separate employers ebb and flow; the separate demands for labour fluctuate; while there is a call for some men to spend their lives practically in one service, there is a call for others to stand idle now and again or shift occasionally or frequently from place to place, according to local needs. Every industry, in fact, shows in some degree the features which have been discussed at length in regard to casual employment at the docks. To every industry the analysis there made is relevant. The dissipation of the demand for labour between a number of separate employers actually increases its effectiveness in calling for a supply of labour. Employer A. may be dismissing men while employer B. is calling for more of exactly the same type, so that the aggregate demand for that class of labour remains the same; if the business of A. and B. were amalgamated there would be no change at all. As it is, however, since the two factories are perhaps at different ends of the town or different ends of the country, B.'s demand may not be felt by the men turned off by A.; it may be felt instead by people not already in that trade—by the generation coming to working age or by men of other occupations. It will to that extent tend to increase the aggregate supply of labour in the trade even while the aggregate demand remains the same. The case of the two employers is also the case of any two industrial districts.

What, for instance, happens when in any town—say London —some particular industry becomes very prosperous so that the demand for labour begins to outrun the supply? The demand will be met either by the migration of men already in the trade from some other town—say Manchester—where employment of that class is slack, or it will tend in London itself to attract fresh people into the trade—to hasten the promotion of learners and apprentices to adult work and wages, to make mechanics at need out of semi-skilled assistants and labourers, to cause a transference from cognate but less desirable occupations. If the demand in London is at once felt in Manchester, and if the movement of men from Manchester to London is easy and rapid, the former alternative may meet the case. On the other hand, just to the extent that London's demand is not felt instantaneously at a distance, just to the extent that labour falls short of perfect mobility between the two places, the trade will actually be recruiting fresh men in London while fully qualified men are unemployed in Manchester. The labour market of that trade will in respect of its total needs tend to become overstocked.

There is, in truth, no such thing as the demand of an industry

7 *

for labour, except as an arithmetical abstraction. The actual demand is that of each of many separate employers in many different places. Because of this separation the actual aggregate force of these demands is normally in excess of the arithmetical aggregate; opposite variations are not set off against one another in practice as they are in the statistics. The actual supply tends of course to conform to the actual demand; that is to say, it tends normally to be in excess of the arithmetical aggregate of the separate demands. In other words, the normal state of every industry is to be overcrowded with labour, in the sense of having drawn into it more men than can ever find employment in it at the same time. This is the direct consequence of the work of each industry being distributed between many separate employers each subject to fluctuations of fortune. It depends upon the nature of the demand for labour, not upon the volume of the whole supply. It is the simple explanation of the irreducible minimum of unemployment shown by the trade union returns. These returns cover many widely separated districts. In some, the trade may be at its fullest activity, using up all its local reserves, calling for fresh men, and even held back because it cannot get them. In other districts the trade will be relatively slack and there will be men unemployed. This phenomenon, indeed, may be observed in only a slightly different form even where, as in coal mining, there are practically no unemployed men at all. There fluctuations are met, not by variation in the numbers employed, but by variation in the number of days worked per week. The average numbers for the United Kingdom in each month from January, 1895, onwards have been set out in a table on p. 25. The maximum is 5·69 days per week in February, 1900, and again in February, 1907. Neither of these, however, is a period of maximum activity for each of the different districts—Northumberland, Durham, Yorkshire, Lancashire, Cheshire, Derbyshire, Staffordshire, South Wales, West Scotland—taken separately. In other words, there is not one moment at which all the men in the trade in all parts are occupied to the full. In this sense there is always an unused reserve of labour, an irreducible minimum of unemployment, even in this most completely organised of industries.

The last illustration brings out perhaps more clearly than anything else the character of the reserve of labour as a normal industrial phenomenon. The maintenance of this reserve need not involve distress, and does not in fact do so where, as in coal mining, the reserve consists in the power of men already engaged to work more regularly rather than in the possibility of engaging fresh men. But whatever the form taken by the reserve, its economic character is the same. It is a thing required and produced by the character of the demand for labour—a demand dissipated between many different centres and different employers each subject to fluctuation.

At this point a general criticism may suggest itself. Modern industry, it may be said, no doubt requires a reserve of labour. Can it, however, be said to produce that reserve? How can methods of engagement bring a body of labourers, casual or otherwise, into being? That surely is the work of their parents. If no man were willing to accept irregular work, there would be no reserve of irregularly employed labourers. If there were not too many men in the country altogether, there would be no material from which to form the reserve. These two points have to be considered separately.

The first point is, no doubt, formally valid. If no man would tolerate the life of a casual labourer, there would be no casual labourers. It is, however, equally true that if all men were as honest as we should like them to be, there would be no thieving and there would consequently be no danger in leaving valuables lying about or in placing men of small means in positions of exceptional trust and temptation. As matters stand, however, common-sense puts upon those who multiply opportunities for thieving responsibility for much of the evil that results. If there were fewer opportunities of living by theft, there would be fewer thefts. If there were fewer opportunities of casual employment, there would be fewer casual labourers. No doubt many casual labourers now could hardly, if at all, accommodate themselves to regular work. The whole body of them may at any time be divided into three groups. Some are casuals by necessity; they could and would work regularly if they got the chance. Some, having begun as casuals by necessity, have become casuals by inclination; they have at one time been in good employment but now through long years of insufficient employment and irregular habits have become unfit for anything else. Some, perhaps, were born with an invincible distaste or incapacity for regular exertion. There is, indeed, not much evidence for the existence of this third type in any large numbers; it will be considered later in dealing with the unemployable. For the second as for the first type the system of casual employment is clearly to a large extent responsible. If that system were abolished, these men, whatever else they were, would not be casual labourers.

The second point raises again the issue discussed in an earlier chapter. The facts there adduced show that the general demand for labour is fully keeping pace with the general supply. In other words, as the population grows, so industry grows to absorb the population. It is perfectly consistent with this that part of the population should be only irregularly employed, and that the demand for labour in each trade should be such as to draw into it not only a regular body of workmen but also a reserve for emergencies. The potential supply of labour is, in respect of each occupation, inexhaustible. The adaptable new generations are perpetually pressing in upon all known avenues for employment. Once, however, they have been drawn into any particular line they become no longer available for development in other directions; though only partially employed they may be fully absorbed in their industry, *i.e.*, they may be prevented from effectually seeking work elsewhere. There would be nothing paradoxical in a steady growth of the demand for labour though each man by law could work only four hours a day, *i.e.*, stood idle half his time. The men who now stand idle half and more than half their time as casual labourers are really in the same case. They are chained down to their half-places in industry by ignorance and habit more binding than any law. They are under-employed rather than unemployed. No doubt somewhere or other fresh industries are arising or old ones developing and calling for more labour. These men do not and cannot answer the call. They are already part of current industry. They are not available as a force for fresh growth.

UNDER-EMPLOYMENT.

The irreducible minimum of unemployment shown by the trade union returns points to a problem in some ways wider, and in other ways narrower than itself. Discussion of it widens necessarily to embrace the whole reserve of labour and narrows again in practice to the topic of under-employment.

The reserve of labour means simply the men who within any given period are liable to be called on sometimes but are not required continuously. The men of the reserve are all those who over a given period are subject to irregularity of employment. The phrase has always to be taken in this way, that is, with reference to a specified period. Men who over a short period work regularly and men who in that same period are not called on at all, may over a longer period alike appear as members of a reserve—in action part of the time, waiting to go into action during the other part. In the statistics as to distribution of employment given at the beginning of the present chapter, the period under consideration was always a year. The labour supply in various industries was divided into regular and reserve according as it did or did not work continuously from year's end to year's end. This division, however, is different for different years, and is altogether changed again if the period be lengthened so as to include several years as a single unit and to bring into play not only local and seasonal but cyclical fluctuations. To speak of the reserve of labour in a trade may become, in fact, only another way of speaking of the whole volume of unemployment in it. The change, however, is not one of words alone. It implies a revolution of mental attitude. It involves perception of unemployment, not as a thing standing by itself—an inexplicable excrescence on the industrial system—but as a thing directly related to that system and as necessary to it as are capital and labour themselves.

The widening of the discussion from the irreducible minimum of unemployment to the reserve of labour is necessary because the individuals who at any moment constitute the minimum are an indistinguishable part of a much larger body of men subject to irregularity of employment, subject, that is, to constant leakage of earning power. The special significance of the irreducible minimum of unemployment is merely this: that in nearly every industry the fringe of irregular workmen is greater in fact than is arithmetically necessary. It is never all needed at once; some part is always standing idle. The actual leakage of labour power through irregularity of employment is more than that involved in the fluctuation of the industry as a whole. The number of men drawn into a trade by the scattered demand of a multiplicity of employers is normally in excess of what would be the maximum requirements of the trade, if its activity—remaining unchanged in amount and fluctuation—were concentrated at one place in the hands of a single firm. In other words, the irreducible minimum of unemployment in any trade indicates the degree of friction in the movement of labour. It represents that proportion of the total reserve which might be dispensed with if the labour market in the trade, instead of being broken up into many markets, were unified and organised.

The reserve of labour is a feature of nearly all industries. Incessant leakage of labour power is found to some extent in nearly all occupations and among nearly all grades of workmen. The actual form, however, and the amount of the leakage, and still more its social consequences, may differ enormously from one occupation or one grade to another. It is perfectly possible for an industry to carry its reserve of labour without producing

distress. The wages may be so high as to allow of adequate individual provision for idle times. There may, as in the case of
trade unions giving unemployed benefits, be an organised collective
provision. There may, as in coal mining, be a plan of distributing
the loss of employment over the whole body of men, so that it is
not felt as an evil at all. It is, however, also perfectly possible for
the leakage of employment to be such as to reduce the average
earnings of considerable numbers of men, who yet form an integral part of the industrial forces, below the level of a tolerable
subsistence. In other words, the leakage of employment may be
so great relatively to the hourly wages as to involve "under-employment" and to give rise to a problem of chronic distress. The
special circumstances under which this problem arises may briefly
be considered.

The tendency to accumulate reserves of labour itself varies
greatly in strength according to the nature of the demand for
labour in each trade. The tendency springs from the multiplicity
of separate employers and from the irregularity of their separate
businesses. Broadly speaking, therefore, the more numerous
and more widely scattered the separate businesses and the greater
and more rapid the fluctuations, the larger will be the reserves
of labour required and the stronger the tendency to their accumulation. Each fresh engagement of a workman in an occupation is a way into that occupation ; it is a chance and therefore an
incentive to a fresh man to enter and seek to live there. Where,
as at the London docks and wharves, thousands of fresh engagements are made daily with a minimum of previous knowledge of
applicants, the tradition is set up that any one may get a job
there. At least it appears worth every one's while to try and to
continue trying. The man who does not succeed to-day may
succeed to-morrow ; meanwhile he lives on hope and charity and
his wife and children's earnings. Where, on the other hand, fresh
men are taken on only at rare intervals and at comparatively few
places there is little to attract or to retain men in attendance.[1]

Again, the tendency is only one out of many factors governing the relation of demand and supply. It may, in any particular
case, be overborne, or held in check, or strengthened by one or
more of the other factors. A trade may, for instance, be growing
with exceptional rapidity, so that the demand for labour altogether

---

[1] The competition for posts in the civil service is probably severer than the
competition for any other employment, yet the civil service does not maintain a large
fringe of casuals in constant attendance because the competition, when it is decided,
is decided once for all. The man who has failed to get into the War Office one day
does not come down and have another try next day. He knows that he must try
somewhere else. The casual docker *never* knows this.

outruns the supply.   This is a common feature of new industries or of established industries at epochs of fresh development.   It is quite possible that for a while there should be no unemployed in such trades anywhere.   The argument of the present chapter would in no way be vitiated by the discovery that some trade at some time had no unemployed percentage at all.   The argument is not that the demand for labour can never outrun the supply, but that ultimately the supply always adjusts itself to the demand at a point allowing of reserves of men for local fluctuations.   Again, a change of social feeling may over a prolonged period depress the supply below the demand, as in the case of domestic service.   Finally, the requirement of technical skill in an occupation introduces a variety of distinctions which must be mentioned in detail.

1. The pressure of competition to enter a skilled trade is less, or less immediate.   The pressure comes practically from the rising generations alone, because they alone can learn new arts. The unskilled occupations are subject to the pressure of those dislodged from all other ranks of life.   This difference has often an important bearing on the action of employers.   An employer cannot rely upon an almost infinite instant supply of carpenters as he can on one of sandwichmen.   He has therefore a motive to steady his demand for the former class which does not exist in respect of the latter.   The possibility of getting casual labourers makes employment more casual, and casual employment in turn attracts the labourers and gradually unfits them to get other work. In the skilled trades, on the other hand, it is common enough for employers to experience delay in getting men in some particular locality, though, as the trade union returns show, even in these cases there are almost always men unemployed somewhere else.

2. Organisation among the men themselves helps to unify the labour market and de-casualise the demand.   Every trade union naturally and instinctively becomes an instrument for promoting the mobility of the labour supply and so for limiting the entry to already overcrowded trades.   Some trade unions have developed this side of their work into regular systems of labour exchanges.

3. The character of the work is more likely to be such that it cannot be done so well

(a) by men unfamiliar with the business and methods of the particular employer ; or

(b) by men subject to the physical and moral demoralisation of casual employment.

There are some classes of work—most clerical work, for instance —in which regular employment is the rule because, even though there may not always be sufficient work to occupy the staff, nothing but a regular staff could do it when it came.

4. The instinctive standard of life is normally higher and the men are therefore unwilling to submit to the same degree of under-employment. In other words, they must get work more regularly if they are to be prevented from seeking work elsewhere.

5. The higher wages give a larger margin for provision against loss of employment. In the trade unions making returns to the Labour Department, this provision takes the form of subscription for unemployed benefits. The reserve of labour is partially paid for out of the wages of the whole body of men.

For practical purposes, then, it is sufficient to consider, not the whole reserve body of labour, but only that part of it which is "under-employed," that is to say, which is called on often enough to be prevented from drifting away elsewhere, but not often enough to obtain a decent living. This is clearly the position of the casual labourer—at the docks, in the building trade, on the fringe of almost all occupations. His nominal wages are lower ; he cannot on 6d. or 7d. an hour stand the same degree of ir- regularity as a skilled man on 10½d. an hour. He is exposed to the competition of all who at any time in any trade are at a loss for a day's work. He is protected by no trade union organisa- tion and his employer finds no sufficient motive to improve the conditions or the regularity of his employment. Yet for all that he is part of the industry which he serves, not outside it. He and his like form the reserve of labour without some of which casual employment would not work, for the whole of which casual employment constitutes an effective demand. They are men not unemployed but badly employed. Their distress is an incident of dock industry or of the building industry just as lead-poison- ing is of pottery. They are the victims of an indirect but there- fore all the more dangerous form of sweating.

To see this it is only necessary to refer to the summary given on page 94 of the actual earnings of certain dock labourers. These earnings are over prolonged periods altogether insufficient for a living. Yet they are the earnings of more or less picked men, and, above all, of men having recognised places in their industry, men listed for preference as "royals". If these men went away, their places would remain to be filled by fresh comers. The casual labourer, as typified by these men, is neither unemployable nor superfluous. He is what he is in response to an effective demand. He waits about at the dock or factory gates only because every now and again he is taken on there. He tramps the streets only because that is the way in which every now and again he finds a job. His wages are wages, not only for working occasionally, but also for being there and available to work always. He has perhaps a high hourly rate of pay, but his earnings are cut down by the normal irregularity of his work to a point involving chronic distress. The social consequences of this under-employment and of under-payment or sweating in the ordinary sense are ultimately indistinguishable. Each means the maintenance, as an integral part of industry, of a low and miserable form of life. Where the two differ the disadvantage is with under-employment as the subtler and therefore the more dangerous disease.

Men can be got to follow up work which gives them five shillings a day about four times in a fortnight when they would repudiate with scorn a regular situation at fifteen or eighteen shillings a week. Public opinion and custom often maintain the nominal rate of wages even in the face of unlimited competition for employment; the conception of a certain rate per hour of work done readily becomes part of the instinctive standard of life. There is not the same check upon the cutting down of real earnings by irregularity of employment. Here if anywhere is to be seen the beating down of the remuneration of labour under competition to bare subsistence level.

A casual occupation is one in which, whatever the number of competitors for work, each has some chance; the more casual the employment the more equal the chances. It is also one in which the door is always open to fresh comers. If it is unskilled as well as casual, it is further an occupation subject to a constant and practically unlimited pressure of competition downwards from every other grade of industry. Under these circumstances the number of regular competitors for the work will tend to be determined simply by the subsistence standard of those from whom the occupation is recruited. If, to recur to the former illustration, a chance of five shillings a day three times a week is sufficient to keep men capable of dock labour struggling on outside the workhouse, then the number of dock labourers will tend to rise and the average share of each to fall till that level of earnings is reached. Only when that level is passed will the occupation be saturated and fresh comers, finding the chance of work inadequate, will either be repelled themselves or will find room only by expelling others. Now in practice not only are the potential sources of supply of labour to a casual unskilled occupation such as that of the docks unlimited, but the supply is largely composed of men whose instinctive standard of life is low to start with or has been beaten down by misfortune. In any complex and living industrial community men are perpetually passing into and out of employment. There must at all times be men who for the moment at least are in difficulties, whether through their misfortune or their faults, and to whom the chance of ten or fifteen shillings a week at the riverside, without questions asked or previous experience being required, will appear a godsend.

By casual employment therefore real earnings may be and are driven down to a normal level far below the lowest rate possible in regular industry however plentiful the competition and unorganised the workmen. This, however, by no means exhausts the peculiar evils of this indirect form of sweating.

First, such wages as are earned are seldom used to the best advantage. Irregular earnings averaging twenty-five shillings a week are for ordinary human nature by no means the equivalent of a regular wage of that amount. They are certain to a large extent to be wasted in alternations of extravagance and privation. How is household expenditure to be regulated on an income which in successive weeks varies as follows: 22s. 8d., 40s. 4d., 28s., 22s. 2d., 9s. 8d., 17s., 13s. 8d., 29s. 11d., or as follows: 38s. 4d., 5s. 10d., 11s. 3d., 7s. 3d., nil, nil, 42s. 9d., 4s.?[1]

Second, casual employment by demoralising men largely increases its own evils. Men who find their chance of employment not reasonably increased by good behaviour and not destroyed by bad behaviour naturally become slack. They work badly; they take the chance of lying in bed now and again, since work is always uncertain but will not be made more uncertain to-morrow by the fact that it has not been sought to-day. It is, however, needless to dwell upon this point. There is general agreement that casual employment, as was said of the casual wards, " acts as a trap to catch the unemployed and turn them into unemployables ".

Third, casual employment is one of the most potent causes of sweating in the ordinary sense. When the head of the family cannot get enough work, his wife and children are driven out to take what they can get at once. The tendency of low-grade women's industries—jam making, sack and tarpaulin work, matchbox making and the like—to get established in districts where casual labour for men is rife has often been noticed.[2] The effect,

---

[1] These are actual cases taken from Miss Rathbone's *Report on Dock Labour in Liverpool*, p. 43, and Howarth and Wilson, *op. cit.*, p. 249. Reference should be made also to the *Report on Unskilled Labour*, p. 56. The saving of the irregular and seasonal worker is to a large extent done backward. His earnings in good times go in working off arrears of rent and redeeming furniture from pawn; his cost of living is increased for he has to pay heavily for credit to the grocer and for rent (to cover the risk of bad debts) to his landlord.

[2] Howarth and Wilson, *op. cit.*, p. 400.

of course, is to increase the immobility of the labourer ; even if his earnings dwindle away to almost nothing he is kept from effectively seeking work elsewhere by the occupation of his family. " Much is now being said of the evils of home work and the low wages paid to women. But these evils in the great majority of cases are effect not cause. They generally originate in the fact that women, unskilled and unable, even not desiring to work regularly, compete in low-grade occupations at the time when their casually employed husbands and fathers are out of work. Reduce the extent of casual labour among men and the supply of out-workers will decrease except at wages and under conditions that are worthy acceptance. It is useless to give by means of a minimum wage to women the means for transforming the woman into the main supporter of the family and so leaving the man free to accept even worse pay or more casual condi-tions." [1]

Fourth, and following directly upon the foregoing, the danger of subsidising casual employment by public or private relief with-out improving the conditions of the casual labourer is a very real one. It is not easy to get evidence of the nominal rates of wages in a district being affected injuriously by lax administration of out-door relief or of charity ; probably custom and public senti-ment are at all times sufficient to hold in check the theoretical tendency of " grants 'in aid of wages " to depress wages directly. But in regard to casual employment, while it is equally difficult to get direct evidence of harm done by charitable subsidies, it is clear that there are no such practical obstacles to the working of economic laws. People who would be aghast at charity or public assistance given to a man in receipt of low wages, are quite ready to help an " unemployed " casual labourer, though if the analysis on p. 79 is sound, the ultimate effect must be to lower the average share of work required for subsistence and thus increase the number of casual labourers till a fresh equilibrium is reached at that lower level. It is obvious that the perennial stream of charity descending upon the riverside labourer and his wife and becoming a deluge at Christmas or on the birth of a new baby is a great convenience to the industry which needs his occasional services and frequent attendance. It amounts to nothing more or less than a subsidy to a system of careless and demoralising employment. The bulk of the relief work doled out winter after winter by municipalities has the same economic character. Casual employment, in fact, makes possible a widespread form of the " grant in aid of wages " far more dangerous because far more

[1] *Unskilled Labour*, p. 57.

insidious than the direct forms which were the object lessons of the old Poor Law. The new subsidy works, not by lowering the rates of pay, but by making labour immobile and so increasing irregularity of earning.

The economic parallel here drawn between under-employment and under-payment implies of course no moral censure. Least of all does it imply criticism of any one set of employers as more thoughtless than others. Casual employment runs throughout the industrial system. Nearly every one at times takes on casual labour. Hardly any are in a position to appreciate the true bearings of their action.

Upon under-employment then attention must first be concentrated. The evil is most pronounced in certain occupations such as waterside labour and building. It is by no means confined to them. The experience of Distress Committees shows a fringe of under-employed labour almost everywhere and in dependence upon an enormous variety of trades. On the other hand, actual under-employment is less general than the economic forces to which it may be ultimately attributed. These forces produce or tend to produce everywhere reserve bodies of labour. They involve almost everywhere a certain irregularity of employment and leakage of labour and earning power. The leakage, however, need not be so great as to cause actual distress. To belong to a reserve of labour is not necessarily to be under-employed.

While, however, the problem of under-employment is in this sense limited and narrower than that of the reserve of labour, it cannot profitably be considered without reference to the wider aspects. It has to be seen as a problem, not of rescuing individuals, but of reforming an industrial method; as a problem, not of grappling with an emergency, but of raising a general level of life. It is in essentials a problem of business organisation—that of providing a reserve of labour power to meet fluctuations in such a way as not to involve distress. This is done in some industries. In the possibility of doing it for all lies the only hope of a cure for one of the most inveterate of social evils.

CHAPTER VI.

LOSS AND LACK OF INDUSTRIAL QUALITY.

1. Changes of industrial structure: Illustrated by census. Decay of particular trades. New processes or machines. New forms of labour. Shifting of locality. Common feature the destruction of established livelihoods. Not, however, of great apparent importance. Such changes best considered under a more general heading as one type of factors producing qualitative maladjustment in the labour market. Other factors are age and deficiencies of industrial training.
2. Influence of advancing years: Applicants to Distress Committees drawn in comparable proportions from all ages though more from the later ones. Unemployment not specifically a disease of old age. Popular idea that men get displaced at earlier ages than before contradicted by statistics of superannuation in two important unions. Old men and the standard rate. Advancing years destroying adaptability increase the difficulty of obtaining new employment.
3. Deficiencies of industrial training: The bulk of applicants to Distress Committees have taken to "blind-alley" and uneducative employments on leaving school. Inference from this that improvements of industrial training are the principal remedy for unemployment not justified. Distress Committees register only some, not all, the unemployed. Casual labour market recruited from many sources and at all ages; age distribution in residuary and skilled occupations compared. Casual labour dependent upon casual demand. Possible influence of industrial training upon unemployment limited. Need for revival of principle only of apprenticeship—that every boy should be learning something as well as earning.

CHANGES of industrial structure are constantly occurring and constantly throwing men out of employment. The very life and growth of industry consist in the replacement of old machines by new; of established processes by better ones; of labour in one form and combination by labour in fresh forms or fresh combinations. The demand for labour is thus in a state of perpetual flux and reconstruction both as to quality and as to quantity. Men who for years have satisfied the demand in one form may find the form suddenly changed; their niche in industry broken up; their hard-won skill superfluous in a new world; themselves also superfluous unless they will and can learn fresh arts and find the way into unfamiliar occupations. They are displaced by economic forces entirely beyond their control and taking little or no account of personal merits. They are, in the words already cited from John Stuart Mill, "sacrificed to the gains of their fellow-citizens and of posterity".

The changes which may have this effect are very various. Each indeed is so far individual and specific as to make ex-

haustive description impossible. All that can be done is to note
the main types, and to illustrate them, as they can most conveniently be illustrated, by reference to the census reports on the
occupations of the people.[1]

First, while the industry of the country as a whole grows,
particular industries or forms of production may decay. The
most striking instance in this country is, of course, that of
agriculture. In 1851 this gave employment to 1,544,087, or
nearly a quarter of all the males aged ten years and upwards in
England; in 1901 to only 1,153,940, or less than the tenth. On
a smaller scale the changes in several forms of mining have been
even more revolutionary. Tin and lead mines employ in 1901
respectively about a half and a quarter of the numbers employed
in 1851. Copper mining has practically disappeared, occupying
789 males in 1901 as against 18,449 fifty years before. Coal
mining alone of the chief extractive industries shows a steady
and rapid growth alike in output and in numbers occupied.
Another clear case of decay is presented by silk manufacture,
where the numbers employed have fallen from over 120,000 in
1851 to under 35,000 in 1901. The causes of this, so far at least
as the "throwing" branches of the trade are concerned, were
summarised by one of H.M. Inspectors of Factories as follows:
"(1) smaller production of silk goods, owing to the competition of
foreign countries. (2) The change in the demand for a finer and
more level silk fibre. (3) The gradually improving conditions
through the Chinese reeling their silk on an improved principle
which obviates the necessity of 'throwing' under the old conditions."[2] Often of course the decay of an occupation is brought
about not so much by changes of the character here outlined, as
by the substitution of one industry for another. Thus all occupations connected with horse traction and transport—from grooming
to saddle making—are at the moment threatened by the development of motor traction.

Second, an industry may be transformed by the introduction of
new processes or new machines. From this point of view the lace
trade is particularly interesting. The total number of persons
employed declined steadily from 61,726 in 1851 to 34,746 in
1891. No doubt this was in part due to the increased importa-
tion of foreign laces. In part, however, and probably in larger
part, it represented a supersession of pillow made or bone lace by
bobbin net, first made on hand machines but more recently by

---

[1] Cf. in particular the *General Report of the Census of* 1901, from which most of
the following particulars are taken.
[2] Quoted in the *General Report of the Census of* 1901.

water power or steam power. At first the diminution of the hand workers was far greater than the increase of the machine workers, but in the decade 1891 to 1901 the tide turned. The increased demand for machine products drew into that branch of the trade numbers more than sufficient to counterbalance the continuing diminution in the other branch. The total numbers employed rose from 34,746 in 1891 to 36,439 in 1901. This change, it may be noted, has involved also a change in the localisation of the industry. The counties of Nottingham and Derby, where lace is principally made by machinery, show an increase at every census since 1871; in Bedford, Buckingham, and Northampton—the seats of hand-made lace—the numbers have fallen continuously from 23,450 in 1861 to 2,350 in 1901.

Third, perhaps as an accompaniment of new processes or machines, one type of labour may be substituted for another. Thus, in boot making, where the number of persons employed remains, in spite of the increased total population, practically the same in 1901 as in 1891, there has been, according to the census, not only a substitution of machine work for hand work, but also of females for males, and of younger for older males. Other cases in which the census shows a replacing of males by females are brushmaking, hosiery, and carpet making. Sometimes, however, a contrary move ment appears, as in straw hat manufacture, where owing, it is said, to the introduction of straw hat sewing machines, male labour has grown considerably at the expense of female.

Fourth, the chief seat of an industry may shift from one part of the country to another. This, as in the instance of the lace trade mentioned above, may happen as the accompaniment of other changes. Sometimes—as in the removal of the main ship-building centres of the country from south to north—it may be independent of them.

The common feature in all these types of change is the destruction of established livelihoods, or from a slightly different point of view, the destruction of industrial quality. The character of the demand for labour is changed; old ways of making a living are blocked up; the old qualifications will no longer serve. Undoubtedly changes of this sort are incessantly occurring. Undoubtedly also individuals are from time to time precipitated by them from comfort and security to poverty or even to absolute destitution. At the same time one of the points that stands out most clearly in the experience of recent years is the relative unimportance of such changes as factors in the problem of unemployment.[1] The man just displaced from a good situation by the destruction of an industry or the application of a new process is,

---

[1] See now ch. xvi.

8

indeed, to be found amongst the unemployed but is hardly ever to be found in appreciable numbers. He is a familiar figure in abstract discussions. He is far from prominent in the reports of Distress Committees or any other authorities dealing practically with the problem. For this lack of prominence the reasons are not far to seek.

On the one hand, changes of industrial structure are as a rule far more gradual than is allowed for by popular imagination. The typical alterations noted above have been spread over intervals of ten to fifty years. The industrial population is constantly changing, by death or retirement at one end of life and the entry of fresh generations at another; the numbers in any industry may decline continuously without any one being displaced from it, but simply through no new men entering to take the places of those who get past work. Industries seldom die in a night. So too new machines and new processes are seldom introduced everywhere at one blow. They come gradually and experimentally. Even where the substitution of the new process for the old is direct, the existing workmen or some of them have naturally the first chance of learning the new one. Often the substitution is quite indirect; machine production grows slowly in one district or set of factories as hand production slowly declines elsewhere. It is not of course suggested that these changes are normally accomplished without loss or friction of any sort. Every transition has its difficulties. The point to be made is that in industrial transitions the difficulties are as a rule far less acute than is commonly supposed.

Second, there is a logical objection at any time to describing a change of industrial structure as in itself a cause of unemployment. The cause of a man's being unemployed is not that which led him to lose his last job but that which prevents him from getting another job now. A change of industrial structure may displace men from their chosen occupations. It does not in itself prevent their immediate re-absorption elsewhere. If, therefore, the men fail to be re-absorbed it is reasonable to look for some further reason of their failure and to assign that as the cause of their unemployment. It may be that the displacement has occurred during a time of general trade depression, when the whole labour market is temporarily overstocked. It may be that the men displaced have got caught up into casual employment and have thus been kept from seeking effectively for regular work. In each case the cause of their being and remaining unemployed is to be found in the continuing factor—trade depression, or casual engagement rather than in the change of industrial structure.

The distinction here made between the cause of displacement and the cause of continuing unemployment is no mere logical subtlety. It is, indeed, essentially a practical distinction. The most important practical question with regard to an unemployed man is, not how he came to lose his last job, but how it comes that he cannot get a fresh job now. More than this, in considering remedies for unemployment, no one can seriously propose to put an end to changes of industrial structure. These changes are the very life of industry. The points to which attention must be directed are the easing of transitions and the hastening of the re-absorption of the displaced men into regular work elsewhere. Two factors which may for a time or permanently prevent that re-absorption have already been noted, viz., general trade depression involving a temporary contraction of the demand for labour in all directions and casual employment acting as a trap to catch men at a loss and turn them into the chronically under-employed. A third and yet more general factor has now to be considered. It may be that, though trade is good and though little casual work is to be had, yet the men displaced fail to get new regular work simply because they do not know where to look for it or cannot adapt themselves to it if they do.

There is thus brought into view a new form of possible maladjustment in the labour market, maladjustment either of place or of quality. There is no such thing as a demand for labour generally. Every demand is specific both in place and character—for a man to carry bricks in London or set up type in Manchester or do some one other thing in a specified place. Equally there is no supply of labour generally. There are merely millions of individuals with varying abilities and limitations, scattered in a thousand towns and villages. An unsatisfied demand for labour may thus and habitually does co-exist with an unemployed supply. The demand may be in one place; the supply in another place. The men required are often of one sort ; the men offering of another sort. There are, of course, economic forces which in the long run tend to bring supply and demand into adjustment locally and qualitatively as well as quantitatively. Men move from place to place in search of work. They move to a less extent from trade to trade. The rising generations, above all, are adaptable and can be moulded to the demand. The character of the demand again is ultimately governed by the possibilities of supply. All these adjusting forces, however, clearly leave room for much friction and delay. They are perfectly consistent with the existence of long-continued unemployment owing to the fact that the men seeking

8 *

work are not suited for any work with which they can get into touch.

There is no need to labour this point. The possibility of local or qualitative maladjustment between demand and supply of labour is obvious. Maladjustment which is merely local calls for no further analysis here. It is covered by the discussion of the preceding chapter. It remains only to consider the most important forms in which the possibility of qualitative maladjustment is realised or thought to be realised in the actual industry of to-day. Three only call for special attention—loss of industrial quality through a change in the character of the demand for labour, loss of industrial quality through advancing age, lack of industrial quality through deficiencies of training.

The first of these has already been considered. It simply presents changes of industrial structure from a fresh point of view. Men displaced by such changes have to start industrial life afresh. They are put back into the position of the boy just leaving school. They lack his mobility and adaptability. They have often not the slightest idea of where and how to look for work, for they know only the ways of the trade by which they have lived hitherto. They are probably hampered in their movement by having a house and family to maintain. They have become stiffened by age and habit, and lost their power of learning. The capacity of the industrial system to absorb fresh labour is no doubt far from exhausted, but this capacity depends entirely upon the labour being of a sort to be absorbed, that is to say, being suited or able to become suited to the particular developments of the time. The rising generations get absorbed because they are adaptable. The men put back at middle age into the position of schoolboys often fail to get absorbed because they are no longer adaptable. Fresh demands for labour may be opening all round them; they do not and cannot respond to the demand. It is small comfort to the displaced saddlemaker in London that men should be wanted in the motor industry at Coventry. He will, so far as that chance is concerned, remain unemployed. At the same time he will remain unemployed not simply because his original industry has decayed but because after its decay he cannot find the way into a new industry. The cause of his unemployment will be lack of mobility and adaptability under circumstances making these qualities essential.

From this point of view changes of industrial structure as factors in employment fall into line with changes of a more limited and individual character. The man who has for years worked with a particular firm may on the failure of that firm experience just the same difficulty in finding a new opening as if his whole industry had decayed. Such cases are, indeed, often the most pitiable of all in the ranks of the unemployed, and lead to the most complete destitution. Prolonged continuity of employment with one firm is apt to make a man peculiarly helpless when that one firm dismisses him or fails. He has no previous experience in looking for work ; he has no personal connections with other employers or foremen ; at a time of general depression he often goes under completely and rapidly when men of a more casual habit survive. The point is well illustrated in the Report of the Stepney Distress Committee for 1906-7. The cases of 104 applicants who appeared to have lost permanent work through the bankruptcy or retirement of their employers were specially examined. Over 70 per cent. of these men had failed to recover regular employment, though over 60 per cent. were still in the prime of life when they applied to the committee and another 20 per cent. were between forty-five and fifty-five. The men peculiarly liable to this complete reversal of fortune are those who, without being in the ordinary sense skilled, acquire by proved trustworthiness, by familiarity with the course of business, or by old associations a special value for one particular employer, but who when that employment fails cannot prove their worth to another.

The second topic—that of the influence of advancing age— is best introduced by consideration of the actual age distribution of the unemployed. The following table is based on the report of the Local Government Board as to the administration of the Unemployed Workmen Act in 1907-8. The figures for each of the earlier years of the operation of the Act are substantially the same.

TABLE XVIII.—AGES OF APPLICANTS TO DISTRESS COMMITTEES— ENGLAND AND WALES, 1907-8.

Ages.	No. found Qualified for Assistance under the Act.	Being per cent. of all Qualified Applicants.	Being per 1,000 of all Males at each Age.
Under 20	1,256	2·3	[0·8][1]
20 and under 30 . . .	14,020	25·7	5·0
30 and under 40 . . .	16,249	29·7	7·4
40 and under 50 . . .	12,823	23·5	7·7
50 and under 60 . . .	7,687	14·1	6·8
Over 60 years . . .	2,578	4·7	[3·8][1]
	54,613	100·0	—

[1] Calculated on males between 15 and 20 and 60 and 70 respectively.

The second column of this table shows that nearly 60 per cent. of all the qualified applicants were under forty years of age, and over 80 per cent. were under fifty. The corresponding figures for London alone are not substantially different from those for the rest of the country.

These figures are, however, in various ways unsatisfactory. First, they relate not to all applicants but only to those whom the Distress Committees, acting on various principles, regarded as qualified for assistance. Second, they are not in the form required to show the direct influence of age upon unemployment. For that purpose it is necessary to compare the number of the unemployed at each age, not with the total number of the unemployed of all ages, but with the total number of those who might be unemployed at that age, i.e., with all persons of that age.[1] The third column of the table given above makes this comparison by showing the number of the unemployed at each age for every thousand of the male population at that age. It will be seen that each decade from twenty to sixty contributes substantially, but that the proportion in the first decade—from twenty to thirty—is distinctly lower than that in the later ones. A better comparison, however, is not with all the males, but only with the occupied males at each age. This cannot be made for the country as a whole, because the returns furnished by the Distress Committees to the Local Government Board classify unemployed applicants upon one basis (20-30, 30-40, 40-50, etc.) while the census classifies the occupied population on another (15-19, 20-24, 25-34, 35-44, etc.). For London, however, and for West Ham the comparison can be made and is made in the tables next following.

---

[1] On this point a certain amount of misapprehension is not uncommon. Thus Professor M. E. Sadler, writing to the *Morning Post* of 27th August, 1908, calls attention to the fact that in London "considerably more than one-half of the total number of applicants who after investigation were found qualified for assistance under the Act were under forty years of age" and that "more than one out of every four (28 per cent.) of the total number of qualified applicants was under thirty". He thereupon expresses considerable apprehension at the "large proportion of young men among the unemployed," and advocates the development of industrial training and improvement in the conditions of boy labour as one of the remedies for unemployment. Now, from one point of view—that of relief measures—the proportion of relatively young men among the applicants to Distress Committees is very important. That is the proportion in regard to which it may be worth while to try methods—emigration, training for new industries, etc.—which would be obviously hopeless in the case of older men. As a basis for preventive measures, however, this proportion has little or no value, because it throws little or no light upon the causes of unemployment. To get that, the comparison made in the text—between the age distributions of the unemployed and that of all males or all occupied males—is essential. Only in that way can it be seen whether unemployment is more prevalent amongst the young or amongst the old. As a matter of fact it is found that the large proportion of young men amongst the unemployed corresponds with an even larger proportion of young men in the whole population.

These, it may be noted, deal with all the applicants, not only with those whose cases were entertained.

TABLE XIX.—AGES OF UNEMPLOYED APPLICANTS (LONDON).

Age.	Occupied Males, 1901.	Unemployed Applicants (Male), 1906-7.	Being per 1,000 of Occupied Males at that Age.
15-19 . .	188,367	664	3·5
20-24 . .	209,537	3,110	14·8
25-34 . .	363,988	8,146	22·4
35-44 . .	274,435	7,410	27·0
45-54 . .	187,493	4,641	24·8
55-64 . .	104,421	1,818	17·4
65 . . .	40,669	366	9·0

TABLE XX.—PROPORTIONS AT EACH YEAR IN SUCCESSIVE AGE GROUPS. (Numbers at each Year 20-24 = 100.)

Age.	Occupied Males, England and Wales (1901).	Occupied Males, London (1901).	London Unemployed, 1906-7.	London Riverside Labour (1901).	London General Labour (1901).	West Ham Unemployed, 1906-7.
15-19 .	103	90	21	49	77	25
20-24 .	100	100	100	100	100	100
25-34 .	84	87	131	122	94	143
35-44 .	66	65	119	126	83	155
45-54 .	47	45	75	94	59	129
55-64 .	28	25	29	45	31	98
65-74 .	11	8	[6]	12	9	26

The figures here given must of course be taken with caution. Men past the prime of life tend to understate their age when applying for work, so that beyond question some of those who are recorded in the middle groups should come later. After allowance has been made for this, however, it appears safe to say that the proportion of unemployed to occupied population increases in every age group up to 35-44, but that comparable proportions are found at all ages after twenty.

The second table shows the same facts in a different way and calls perhaps for a little explanation. In a normal self-contained population, that is to say one recruited mainly by fresh births, not by immigration, the numbers at each year of age decrease steadily from youth onwards, because those at each year represent the survivors of those who twelve months before were at the preceding year of age. Thus, comparing for convenience groups of years rather than particular years, the persons between forty-five and fifty-five at any moment are the survivors of and less numerous than those who were between thirty-five and forty-five ten years before. Unless therefore the population is changing very rapidly in number or age distribution, they will be less numerous also than those who are between thirty-five and forty-five now. Accordingly the first column of the table shows that in England and Wales, at the time of the last census, for every 100 occupied males per year of age from twenty to twenty-four inclusive, there were on an average only eighty-four per year of age from twenty-five to thirty-four, sixty-six per year of age from thirty-five to forty-four, and so on in decreasing order. For the occupied males in London the corresponding figures are substantially the same; the slightly greater number between twenty-five and thirty-five shows the influence of the rural invasion, and the slightly smaller numbers in the later groups the lower expectation of life in industry than in agriculture. To both these sets of figures those for the unemployed applicants present the strongest possible contrast. For every 100 unemployed per year of age from twenty to twenty-four there are not eighty-four but 131 per year of age from twenty-five to thirty-four, there are not sixty-six but 119 per year of age from thirty-five to forty-four. This means of course that the unemployed are largely recruited from those who fall out of employment after their first youth. The comparison with riverside and to a less extent with general labour points the same moral. Here too there are proportionately far more men in the later age groups than among occupied males as a whole. They are both residuary occupations to which men have recourse when driven out of their chosen trades.

The statistics given above certainly do not indicate advancing years as a factor of great importance in unemployment. The unemployed applicants to Distress Committees are drawn, not indeed in equal, but at least in comparable proportions from all age groups. The great bulk of them are men in the prime or in the vigorous maturity of life. The steady workman dismissed directly on account of his grey hairs plays but a small part in the statistics. On the other hand, advancing years undoubtedly make their influence felt. The number of the unemployed is proportionately greater at the higher ages.

The influence of advancing years is not, indeed, always unfavourable. There are some sorts of work at which men continue to become more skilful almost to the end of life itself. There are some industrial qualifications—proved trustworthiness, regularity, experience—to say nothing of old associations which get stronger not weaker with increasing age. There is, however, one industrial quality which almost inevitably deteriorates—adaptability—and this, in the flux of industry, is one of the most important qualities of all. The adverse influence of advancing years is thus seen less when it is a question of retaining old employment than when it is a question of finding new employers. The man of middle age who through trade depression or changes of method or the misfortunes of particular firms loses his ordinary place in industry is hard put to it to prove his worth among strangers. He may have admirable qualities, but he does not carry the proof of them with him as he does that of the years through which he has lived.

So much may be said with regard to age as a factor in the returns of unemployment to-day. There remains the question as to whether it is a factor gaining or losing in importance. The idea appears to be almost universal that the world is becoming increasingly harder for the man who is past his prime and that the age of compulsory retirement from industry is falling—that men in fact from being too old at sixty are coming, as a rule, to be too old at fifty-five or even before.

This proposition is commonly advanced as if it were axiomatic. It is thought to follow from the continual "speeding up" of industry that the older men who cannot be speeded up must be falling more and more behind. Whether this is really happening it is extremely hard to say. It is no doubt the case that the proportion of all persons over sixty-five who returned themselves as occupied fell in 1901 to 60·6 per cent. as compared with 64·8 per cent. in 1891. The census returns of occupation have, however, a very indirect and doubtful bearing upon questions of employment. The more relevant figures to be derived from the returns of superannuation benefit in two of the leading trade unions appear to show a tendency directly opposed to the current view. These are given in the tables on the next page.

In each of the unions concerned the superannuation benefit is payable not at a fixed age but only upon proof of incapacity either to follow the trade or to earn the ordinary rate of wages.[1] The age of superannuation is therefore the age of compulsory retirement from the trade through increasing infirmities. It will be noted that in each case there has been a distinct rise in the age within the past twenty or thirty years by the tables, and that, taking five yearly periods, the rise has been fairly though not absolutely steady. In the Amalgamated Society of Engineers the average age of compulsory retirement is now (1906-7) $63\frac{3}{4}$ or over

[1] There are also a low minimum limit of age—55 (formerly 50) for the Engineers —and a requirement of a certain number of years' membership.

TABLE XXI.—AGE AT SUPERANNUATION—AMALGAMATED SOCIETY OF ENGINEERS. *R.*

Year.	No. of Members Superannuated during Year.	Average Age at Date of Superannuation.	Average Age at Death of Superannuated Members.
1885. . .	174	61·9 61·9	65·8
1886. . .	223	63·1	
1887. . .	194	62·0	
1888. . .	250	61·9 } 62·2	67·3
1889. . .	303	62·5	
1890. . .	300	61·5	
1891. . .	289	62·3	
1892. . .	416	62·0	
1893. . .	295	63·5 } 62·7	68·8
1894. . .	407	62·7	
1895. . .	429	62·9	
1896. . .	526	61·9	
1897. . .	365	63·1	
1898. . .	629	62·5 } 62·8	69·2
1899. . .	494	63·3	
1900. . .	552	63·2	
1901. . .	628	63·4	
1902. . .	614	63·6	
1903. . .	718	63·8 } 63·6	70·1
1904. . .	715	63·6	
1905. . .	653	63·5	
1906. . .	631	63·7 } 63·8	71·0
1907. . .	691	63·9	

TABLE XXII.—AGE AT SUPERANNUATION—FRIENDLY SOCIETY OF IRONFOUNDERS. *R.*

Mean of Years.	Average Age at Death of Superannuated Members Dying during Year.	Average Time on Fund.	Average Age at Date of Superannuation.
1882-1885 . .	69·1	6·9	62·2
1886-1890 . .	69·8	7·0	62·8
1891-1895 . .	70·4	7·4	63·0
1896-1900 . .	70·5	7·8	62·7
1901-1905 . .	70·8	8·2	62·6
1906-1910 . .	71·6	8·6	63·0

1½ years greater than it was from 1886 to 1890.   In the Friendly Society of Ironfounders, where the figures for each period relate not to those superannuated but to those dying in each period, the difference shown is between 62·2 in 1882-5 and 63 in 1906-10. The following table shows the contrast in another form :—

TABLE XXIII.—AGE AT SUPERANNUATION—AMALGAMATED SOCIETY
OF ENGINEERS.

MEMBERS SUPERANNUATED.

Age.	During 1885.		During 1907.	
	No.	Per cent. of All.	No.	Per cent. of All.
Under 60 .	67	38·5	157	22·7
60-65 . .	61	35·1	251	36·3
65-70 . .	34	19·5	201	29·1
70-75 . .	10	5·7	73	10·6
75-80 . .	2	1·2	9	1·3
	174	100·0	691	100·0

It will be seen that in 1907 only 59 per cent. of those claiming superannuation were under sixty-five as against 73·6 per
cent. in 1885, while those over seventy were nearly 12 per cent.
as against 6·7 per cent.[1]

The experience of these important unions, therefore, runs
directly counter to the popular view. In them at least men
seem able to work on to a later age now than they could a
generation ago. This experience cannot of course be taken as
conclusive on the general question. The figures given are too
limited for that.[2] They are, however, sufficient to make the popular
view a thing to be proved rather than assumed. They serve also
to suggest inquiry into another statement that has obtained very
general currency. This is the statement that trade unions by insisting upon the full standard rate even for men who are too old
to do the full amount of work prevent them from getting any
employment at all.

Unfortunately, the available facts are here also insufficient to
justify any final judgment. Obviously the application of a hard
and fast standard rate irrespective of age must tend to drive men

[1] The statistics given illustrate another point which, while not bearing directly
upon unemployment, is of the greatest social importance. While the age of superannuation has risen the age at death in each of these unions has risen yet more
rapidly, i.e., the actual burden of old age upon the unions has increased. The whole
period of life has lengthened more than the period of industrial life.

[2] In one other important union—the London Society of Compositors—for which
similar averages can be given, the comparison between earlier and later years is affected
by an important change of the rules in 1901 whereby any member of sixty years of age
and of a certain standing in the society was allowed to claim a pension of ten shillings
a week without proof of industrial incapacity or submission to medical examination.
Since 1902 the average age of superannuation in each year has varied only between
62¾ in 1905 and 63¾ in 1904 and 1907, with a mean of 63¼. In the decades 1881-90
1891-1900, the means were 63¾, and 65¼ respectively.

out of employment the moment they begin to fail and long before they are completely past work. It is not the case, however, that all trade unions insist on a rate of this character. Express exceptions in the rules in favour of members over sixty, allowing them to work at any rate they can get or at a reduced rate to be approved by their branch, are by no means uncommon.[1] It is of course possible that in some of these unions an exception formally permitted by the rules is made practically inoperative by the custom of the trade or the branch. On the other hand, it is quite certain that many unions in fact make exceptions for their aged members without possessing any formal rules on the subject. This is the case with the Amalgamated Society of Carpenters and Joiners,[2] and, to a less extent, with the Amalgamated Society of Engineers. The question is indeed very largely one of the strength and feeling of the particular branch concerned. If the standard rate is firmly established it may appear safe to make exceptions for the older men. If the standard rate is at all in danger, the making of any exceptions may be dreaded as likely to be treated as a precedent. There is undoubtedly a possibility that insistence upon a rigid standard may bear hardly on older men. There does not appear to be as yet much evidence that trade union action has this effect now to any very serious extent.

The two topics just discussed—changes of industrial structure and the influence of advancing age—are clearly very closely related. Indeed, regarded as factors in unemployment, each derives importance largely through connection with the other. The characteristic effect of changes of industrial structure is to make adaptability essential. The characteristic effect of advancing years is to destroy adaptability. If all men remained throughout life as adaptable as in their school years, the labour supply might follow closely every variation in the character of the demand. If the demand remained always for the same types of work, increasing years and experience might more often strengthen than weaken men's hold on employment. Changes of industrial structure or of individual firms place men out of harmony with their environment. Ignorance and lack of adaptability prevent them from recovering harmony. Unemployment results because, though men may be required, they are no longer of the sort required.

---

[1] They occur, for instance, in the rules of several furnishing trade unions, and of others in the printing, leather and building trades. In one union indeed members over fifty-six years of age may not only be allowed but be compelled by their branches to accept less than the standard rate (so as to clear the unemployed fund).

[2] *Home Work. Report of Select Committee of the House of Commons*, 1907 (290) : Evidence of Mr. G. R. Askwith, Qu. 3965, 4196-7.

The last topic to be considered is the effect of deficiencies of industrial training in producing a labour supply out of harmony with the demand. The great bulk of the applicants to Distress Committees are unskilled or low-skilled irregular labourers. From this the inference is commonly made that the great bulk of the unemployed are of the same type. From this in turn comes the inference that unemployment itself is due to men's becoming un-skilled irregular labourers and that in preventing them from doing so lies the main hope of a remedy for the disease. The argument, in other words, is that, owing to deficiencies of industrial training, there is taking place as between demand for and supply of labour a maladjustment of quality which is a principal or the principal cause of unemployment. Skilled regular workmen are wanted ; unskilled casual workmen are being produced. This is the argu-ment to be examined in the following pages. It will be well first to set out a little more fully the facts upon which it is based.

On the one hand, it is clear that a great many boys and girls on leaving school enter occupations in which they cannot hope to remain for more than a few years and in which they are not being fitted for any permanent career. With the decay of ap-prenticeship or rather with the development of trades and processes to which apprenticeship has never been applied, there has come a break up in the continuity of industrial life. The principle of apprenticeship was that people should enter in early youth the craft in which they would remain to the end. Each craft, there-fore, would show the same age distribution as the general popula-tion ; each would be self-contained and self-supplying from start to finish. At the present time the separate industries and oc-cupations show every variety of age distribution. Some want comparatively few boys from school and only recruit at later ages. Some use far more boys than they can possibly find room for as men. It is these latter that make the problem under discussion. They are the "blind-alley" occupations which have to be aban-doned when man's estate is reached. They are of two main types. First, the boy or girl may be employed in a factory upon some special light work—minding a simple machine, paper folding, packing and the like. Second, the employment may be of a more general and outdoor character ; the thousands of newspaper boys, shop boys, messenger boys and van boys in private or public em-ploy are prominent instances. In each type, however, the position of the boys or girls is the same. They enter, not as learners, but as wage earners, doing some work too simple or too light to require the services of grown people. When, therefore, they themselves grow up and begin to expect the wages of grown people, they must go elsewhere to obtain these wages. They leave or are dismissed and their places are taken by a fresh generation from the schools. They find themselves at eighteen or twenty without any obvious career before them, without a trade in their hands, and with no resource save unskilled labour. They go therefore—very likely after an interval of military service—to overcrowd that already crowded market. Moreover in many cases they have not merely wasted in uneducative labour the years in which they might have been learning a trade; they have often actually been unlearning what they had learnt at school—the habits of obedience and regularity. This is particularly the case with some employments of the second type noticed above, where the conditions of work are such as to foster casual habits or expose to many temptations. The van boy, for instance, learns to put in half his time in waiting about, and the newspaper boy spends all his in the streets. Neither is learning the lesson of assiduity; each is thus on the way to become a " casual by inclination ".

On the other hand, it is clear that the great bulk of applicants to Distress Committees, as they are now unskilled and casual labourers, are men who as boys have entered " blind-alley " occupations. This appears at once from any inquiry into their previous history. In Stepney, for instance, it was found that out of 333 men only thirteen had been apprenticed and only twenty-three had as boys gone to work where they could pick up some sort of useful skill. All the rest on leaving school had taken to unskilled and uneducative labour, and between then and the age of twenty-one had held on an average three different situations, mainly as van-boys, errand-boys, packers and the like. " Nothing," says the Distress Committee, " is more characteristic of boy labour than its extreme mobility, and the ease with which each job can be exchanged for another has, no doubt, an important influence on industrial character later in life." There is no question that this sort of evidence could be multiplied indefinitely, in regard to all districts and all times.

These two sets of facts are unquestionable. There can be no doubt as to the tendency of certain very prevalent forms of youthful employment to turn out men who take necessarily to unskilled and naturally to casual labour. There can be as little doubt that the great bulk of those in distress through unemployment at any time are persons whose early years have been spent in employments of this character. Do these facts, however, justify the inference that entry into such employments in youth is in itself an important or the most important cause of unemployment in later life? Do they really support the view that unemployment

could be cured or greatly diminished simply by directing boys
from unskilled to skilled occupations? In several respects such
an inference appears to be over-hasty.

In the first place, the applicants to Distress Committees are
by no means all the unemployed. They are simply the men who
have thought it worth while to register. Speaking generally, they
are those of the unemployed who happen to be in distress.
There are at all times quite indubitably many other unemployed
men who are not in distress or at least not in such distress as to
apply for public assistance. Of one section of these record is
made in the trade union returns; the men covered by these
returns consist almost entirely of skilled workmen, not of irregular
labourers, yet they never fail to have from 2 to 10 per cent. of
their number unemployed. It is indeed as far as possible from
being proved that, if all the skilled men out of employment were
ranged on one side and all the unskilled men out of employment
were ranged on the other, the latter body would be the largest.
The unskilled, in proportion to their numbers, make the bigger
show, not only because they fall more readily into distress, but
because they are of the nature of a stage army. They are less
specialised. Each of them can, and does, apply for a greater
variety of situations. Suppose, for instance, that of a hundred
men in each of ten trades ten are out of work, making altogether
a hundred unemployed in a thousand artisans; then the offer of
a job in any one of these skilled trades will at most produce ten
applications. Only the men in that particular trade will apply.
Suppose, on the other hand, that out of a thousand labourers a
hundred are out of work. Then the offer of one labourer's job may
produce a hundred applications. Any one comparing the two experiences would be apt to conclude, as from similar experiences
people argue in actual life to-day, that unemployment was far
greater in volume and degree amongst unskilled than amongst
skilled workmen. Yet he would obviously be wrong in his facts
and he would not get very far if he started to abolish unemployment by converting as many as possible of the unskilled workmen
into skilled workmen. It may indeed be that unemployment, not
merely distress from unemployment, is greater amongst labourers
than amongst artisans. It may be that the unskilled labour
market is overcrowded relatively to the skilled one. The simple
fact of industrial gravitation would tend to produce this result.
Men can pass downwards from a skilled trade to compete for
unskilled work at times of depression or industrial reconstruction;
there is no possibility of an opposite movement. All the probabilities, therefore, point to a relative overcrowding of the unskilled

occupations. In the present state of our knowledge, however, they are still only probabilities. The overcrowding is still a matter of inference rather than of evidence, and is certainly less than would be suggested by a study of the Distress Committee records alone.[1]

In the next place, whatever overcrowding there may be in the market for general labour has to be attributed in part at least to causes other than the entry of boys into uneducative "blind-alley" employment. No doubt a certain number of youths go direct from such employments to the ranks of casual labour and chronic distress. A great many others, however, reach the same point by other routes and much later in life. The casual labour market is liable to be recruited from all who at any time are in difficulties; from all who through any cause whatever—illness, accident, personal default, depression, changes of method—have lost their last job and do not know where to turn for the next; from those who have failed as well as from those who have never fairly started in life. The statistical record of this is to be seen in the table given on p. 119. If dock labourers or the unemployed were mainly or predominantly recruited direct from those who have to leave a "blind-alley" occupation at eighteen or twenty, they should, as in the case of a normal self-contained population, show decreasing numbers at every year of age from that time onwards; the men between thirty-five and forty-five, for instance, would be predominantly the survivors of those who ten years before had been ranked under the same heading between twenty-five and thirty-five. Their actual age distribution, as has already been pointed out, does not fall under this rule at all. For every 100 riverside labourers in London at each year of age from twenty to twenty-four there are 122 at each year from twenty-five to thirty-four, or 45 per cent. more than the eighty-four to be expected if their age distribution followed that of the whole occupied male population. To this extent, therefore, the group of riverside labourers is recruited by the transference of men from other groups between the ages of twenty-five and thirty-five. The figures show proportionately an even greater recruiting in the next period—between thirty-five and forty-five. The age dis-

---

[1] "It is cruel mockery," observes the General Secretary of the Amalgamated Society of Engineers in writing of unemployment in the society, " to tell us to revert to old-fashioned apprenticeship or to improved methods of technical education as having any bearing on the question. Our unemployed members are men who have served apprenticeship and many of them are otherwise technically trained. Carpenters, shipwrights and mechanics of all sorts are standing in the market-place even in larger numbers, and are also duly trained and educated" (Amalgamated Society of Engineers, 57th Annual Report, 1907, p. xi.).

tribution of applicants to the metropolitan Distress Committees shows the same features, *viz.*, 131 men against eighty-four in the period twenty-five to thirty-four, and 119 as against sixty-six in the period thirty-five to forty-four.

CHART IV.—AGE DISTRIBUTION IN CERTAIN OCCUPATIONS.

England and Wales, 1901.   Males at each year, 20-24 = 100.

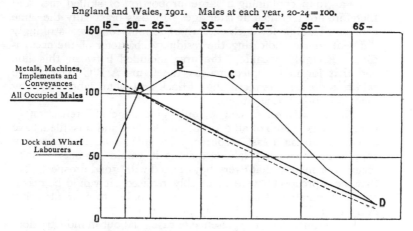

The same point is brought out perhaps still more clearly in the above chart of Age Distribution in Certain Occupations in England and Wales.   The figures corresponding to the chart are given in the following table :—

TABLE XXIV.—AGE DISTRIBUTION IN CERTAIN OCCUPATIONS.

Age and Group.	All Occupied Males.	Metals, Machines, Implements and Conveyances.	Dock and Wharf Labourers.
15-19	103	111	55
20-24	100	100	100
25-34	84	83	118
35-44	66	61	113
45-54	47	43	82
55-64	28	25	41
65-74	11	8	11

The table is to be read thus: For every 100 occupied males at each year of age from twenty to twenty-four inclusive, there are on an average at each year of age from twenty-five to thirty-four inclusive 84 occupied males, at each year of age from thirty-five to forty-four inclusive 66 occupied males, and so on.

It will be seen that the line for all occupied males is an almost straight downward slope.   That for metals, machines, etc.—a group containing a large proportion of skilled men and therefore not recruited at later ages—follows practically the same course.   The line for dock and wharf labour follows a strikingly different course, indicating the residuary character of the occupation.   Roughly speaking, the area included between this line and that for all occupied males—the figure A B C D—may be said to represent the recruiting of dock and wharf labour ages by men from other occupations.

These statistics, of course, only give a general reflection to familiar facts.   Men of all occupations, skilled and unskilled, have casual labour as a last resource.   To cut off all the sources of supply to the casual labour market it would be necessary to secure, not merely that every boy started with good prospects, but that these prospects were invariably realised; it would be necessary, not merely to teach every boy a trade, but to guarantee that every trade should be uniformly prosperous.

In the third place, the presence of casual labour in industry does not depend directly or mainly upon the unfitness of a certain number of men for other work.   It depends upon the nature of the demand for men.   When a dock labourer engaged on Monday is dismissed on Tuesday this does not happen as a rule because he refuses to work longer but because the job for which he was engaged is finished.   It may very well be that more men are trying to live by dock labour than are necessary, even under the existing system of casual employment, and that, being there, they cause such work as comes to be yet more discontinuous than it would be without them.   It might, in other words, be possible to diminish the supply of casual labourers without either stopping the industry or forcing a change in the method of employment.   The fact, however, remains that every man there, so long as he ever gets any work at all, is there in response to a definite economic demand, whose intermittence makes it none the less a force to attract and retain a body of casual labour.   It may be, again, indeed it is certainly the case, that many casual labourers have an incapacity or at least a disinclination for steady work; they may have started with this incapacity but far more often they have acquired it through long habituation to odd jobs. Casuals by necessity are always on the way to become casuals by inclination. The fact remains that industrial conditions are now such as to call for large numbers of casuals by necessity. An employer who wants men for only one day will only employ them for one day whatever their assiduity.

The results of the preceding discussion may now be summed up.

The improvement of industrial training like every other increase of efficiency must raise the general level of prosperity. Its direct value as a remedy for unemployment is somewhat limited—it cannot touch the causes of industrial fluctuation or in practice prevent casual employment. Yet the emphasis laid on it springs from appreciation of a very real defect in modern industry. The decay of apprenticeship and the development of factory life have involved at once a break up of the continuity of industrial careers and an actual step backwards in regard to education. A fresh point of stress—the point of passage from unskilled boys' work to men's work at eighteen or twenty—has been set up; from this, as from other points of stress, there is a constant discharge into the pool of casual labour. A time of life formerly directed to learning has become one of ordinary wage-earning; boys and girls attain independence and freedom from discipline before they are fit for it; employers lack their former responsibilities. There is needed beyond question to-day a revival, not indeed of apprenticeship, but of the principle underlying apprenticeship—that no youthful worker should be regarded merely as cheap labour, that every youthful worker while being employed should also be undergoing preparation for a future career. The disregard of this principle, though it does not create casual employment, undoubtedly facilitates it by helping to swell the supply of unskilled labour. The practical application of this principle is one of the tasks of the future.

The topics discussed in the present chapter are somewhat various. They are, however, clearly related. They show how in different ways part of the apparent labour supply may come to be unsuited to the demand. They all represent points or causes of stress or transition from which men are recruited for unskilled and casual employment. Their common feature is loss or lack of industrial qualifications. Men may come to lose their former qualifications through an objective change in the methods of production. Men may gradually lose their former qualifications through the subjective change brought by advancing years. Men may from the beginning lack industrial qualifications through deficiencies of industrial training. There is thus opened a wide

9 *

field for maladjustment of quality between supply and demand. The narrowing of that field must depend mainly upon the possibility of spreading more accurate information as to the character of the demand from time to time, and of securing the mobility and adaptability of the supply.

CHAPTER VII.

THE PERSONAL FACTOR.

Defects of character and the volume of unemployment : The vagrant and " unemployable ". The half-employable. All instability of character increases unemployment.
Defects of character and the incidence of unemployment : Unequal efficiency of workmen. The less efficient are dismissed and thereby further demoralised. Concentration of unemployment upon the inferior men illustrated by (a) costliness of relief works, (b) proportions of unpunctuality in good and bad times, (c) statistics of unemployed claims in trade unions. The casual fringe among compositors and bookbinders. Influence of personal character upon the incidence of unemployment a dominant fact of the situation.
The unemployed present as a rule many economic and personal factors in combination : The limbo of casual labour. The main visible effect of exceptional depression is to accentuate normal poverty—making more casual those who were casual before. Trade union statistics. Numbers unemployed and average period of unemployment in good and bad years respectively. Complication of many factors impedes direct treatment of the unemployed.

THE present inquiry began by an analysis of factors in unemployment lying outside the character and beyond the control of individuals. The casual labourer engaged on Monday is dismissed on Tuesday, not because he refuses to work longer, but because the work for which he was engaged is at an end. The percentage of unemployed carpenters rises from two in August to six in December, not because 4 per cent. of the men have become unfit or unwilling to work, but because winter is a bad time for building. When two handicraftsmen are replaced by one man at a machine the change is not in themselves but in economic conditions. In discussing these factors the problem of unemployment could be approached mainly, if by no means exclusively, from the side of demand for labour. The nature of the supply could be touched on lightly or taken for granted. The last chapter, however, already witnessed a departure from this first position. The discussion of changes of industrial structure was widened into a discussion of all the principal ways in which men might come to lose or lack industrial quality. There was involved in this some examination of the supply of labour and of the relevance of certain characteristics in it to the problem of unemployment. The discussion, however, was general; the characteristics examined were of a broad, impersonal character—such as the progressive loss of adaptability through advancing years, or the possible shortage of skilled men through deficiencies of industrial training. It is, however, clearly necessary to take also a more individual view—to analyse, in a word, the influence of the personal factor. To what extent do personal excellences—industry, ability, initiative—prevent unemployment? To what extent and under what circumstances can personal deficiencies—weaknesses of body or will or intellect—be regarded as its causes?

There are here two distinct questions. It may happen, indeed it constantly does happen, that economic conditions determine that a certain number of men shall be dismissed, while personal considerations determine which individuals shall be selected for dismissal. Under identical circumstances, therefore, the question whether unemployment is due to personal defects may be answered in opposite senses according to the point of view of the questioner. The fact that a man is inclined to be lazy or insubordinate or irregular may be the cause why he rather than another is unemployed, though it is in no sense the cause of there being unemployment. So the fact that a workman has been well trained may cause an employer to prefer him to others and prevent his being unemployed, without in the least affecting the total numbers for whom there is no demand. In considering the influence of the personal factor, the two questions, as to the volume and the incidence of unemployment, must always be carefully distinguished.

Defects of Character and the Volume of Unemployment.

There are, no doubt, a certain number of men who, though apparently able-bodied, form no part of the industrial world and do not wish to do so. They swell the volume of idleness in a country but hardly in a strict sense that of unemployment; they cannot appropriately be described as men out of work because they are never in work. They are the social parasites most prominently represented by the habitual criminal and the habitual vagrant. Each of these is in truth as definitely diseased as are the inmates of hospitals, asylums and infirmaries, and should be classed with them. Just as some suffer from distorted bodies and others from distorted intellects, so these suffer from a distortion of judgment, an abnormal estimate of values, which makes them, unlike the vast majority of their fellows, prefer the pains of being a criminal or a vagrant to the pains of being a workman.

It is beside the point for the moment to inquire whether this moral disease is inborn or acquired, and whether it is curable or incurable. Very possibly if it were made easier for men once branded as criminals to get back to a reputable life or for those once habituated to idleness to acquire the opposite habits of energy and regularity, a certain number of cures might be effected; that is to say, the distorted judgment might be corrected and men produced who would not willingly prefer crime or idleness to industry. It is sufficient to say that at present this is not done; cures are not effected. There is a definite though small class of men always in and out of prison. There is a definite though not very large class of men always in and out of the workhouses, shelters, and casual wards. These are "unemployable" in the full sense of the word.

The men who are completely parasitic and never work at all might logically be excluded from consideration here altogether. Practically they cannot be excluded, for they shade off gradually into those who work occasionally but either cannot or will not retain regular employment. Men are, of course, often dismissed from situations or leave situations, not because the demand for labour has changed or fallen, but because they are unfit or unwilling to remain. This may happen at times to almost any man. There is, beyond doubt, a fluctuating class of men to whom it happens constantly or repeatedly, a class of men getting work from time to time but normally leaving it after a shorter or longer period as a direct consequence of inefficiency, idleness or the like. These are men on the downward grade through drink or dishonesty. These are the men who are always being "weeded out" on building jobs. They get turned off, not because the demand has changed, but because they do not satisfy the demand; they go and their place is taken by another. Their case is quite different from that to be discussed later, where in a slack season the relative inefficiency of certain men decides that they and not others shall go, but where in any case some one has to go and, having gone, leaves no place to be taken by new-comers. There the influence of personality is selective; here it is primary. The men are not fit to meet a demand for regular labour. They are in this limited sense "unemployable".

The popular term "unemployable," used to describe alike these hangers-on to the fringe of industry and the vagrants who are permanently outside industry, has, indeed, no precise meaning. Whether a man is employable or not depends strictly upon the work which has to be done. The best carpenter in the world is unemployable as a compositor. Even if differences of technical

skill be disregarded and attention paid only to general character
and ability to do unskilled work, it is difficult to attach any scientific
interpretation to the word "unemployable". The fixed distinctions suggested by it between "can works" and "can't works" or
between "will works" and "won't works" are in reality fluid and
indefinite. A man whom it does not pay to employ in one industrial grouping may be fully worth his wages in another. The
aged or lazy or stupid John Smith may be useless by himself or with
nine others like himself. He may be invaluable as the tenth man of
a gang which would otherwise stand idle and in which he is kept
up to the mark by the example or public opinion of those around
him. Again, a man able and willing to work hard for a few hours
or days or even weeks may be physically or morally incapable of
working with sufficient regularity to earn a reasonable living. He
will thus be employable from one point of view, but unemployable
from another, according to the period of time taken into consideration. Finally, a man who will not work under some conditions
may be perfectly ready to do so under others, or, from the other
side, an employer may welcome at one time the sort of man
whom he would not consider for a moment at another time. The
decision of the workman to work or not depends to some extent
upon what happens to those who do not work; the less tolerable
the lot of the idler, the greater the incentive to industry. The
decision of the employer that a particular man is or is not worth employing depends upon the chance of getting a better man in his
place; his standard will rise and fall with the fluctuations of the
labour market. It is, therefore, quite impossible to make hard
and fast distinctions, or to segregate a definite class of the unemployable. Not only is the line between this class and the rest
of the community very hard to define even in theory; in practice
men shift from one side of the line to the other and the line
itself shifts according to the point of view of the observer.

From the present standpoint, however, the difficulty of definition is not a matter of any consequence. The obvious defects
of industrial character—laziness, dishonesty, intemperance, irregularity, stupidity—produce their effects on the body politic
whether or not they are sufficiently marked in any one individual
to entitle him to the name of unemployable. So, too, do the
less obvious—or, as they might almost be called, the technical
defects—lack of enterprise and lack of adaptability—which limit
men to one mode of life and unfit them to follow the constant
changes of the demand. Everything that involves unnecessary
change of situations may involve unnecessary leakage of time
between one situation and the next. Everything that makes the

labour supply unstable strengthens the influence of chance in the competition for employment and thus spreads work over a larger fringe of casual men.   Everything that narrows men's scope— to one branch of a trade or to one district—makes industrial transitions less tolerable.

The volume of unemployment, or at least that of idleness, is thus appreciably increased by defects of character in part of the population.   There are, first, at the bottom of society certain purely parasitic types—criminals and vagrants who have learnt to live without work and whose lot is practically unaffected by industrial changes.   The Departmental Committee on Vagrancy which reported in 1906 put the permanent vagrant class—the men who live always in casual wards, shelters or the open, the tramps who may be professedly in search of work but have certainly no desire to find it—at from twenty to thirty thousand for the whole country.[1]   Second, there are men willing to work every now and again but unfit or unwilling to work continuously. They are men who, if they get a permanent situation, fail to keep it and who drift naturally into the position of not looking for permanent situations at all.   They are, for the most part, on the way to join the purely parasitic class just beneath them ; they are constantly being recruited from all the grades of industry above them.   " Under present conditions," says the Vagrancy Committee, " the casual workman who takes to the road is almost certain sooner or later to join the ranks of habitual vagrancy." [2] While he remains, however, attached to industry, even in the least degree, he is affected by industrial fluctuations.   Trade depression, just as it increases the volume of crime, increases also the volume of vagrancy.   Along both lines of failure it sends amateurs to reinforce the professionals and probably in time to become professionals themselves.[3]   Third, there are, in all classes of men, common faults and occasional self-indulgences which, whether pronounced or slight in the individual, do each and all in their degree increase economic waste and unemployment.   This merely amounts to saying that from an industrial point of view human nature is not yet perfect.

If, therefore, certain degenerate human types could be abolished, and if the common level of human nature—in respect of assiduity, sobriety, adaptability and all the other virtues—could be raised the volume of idleness, whether voluntary or involuntary, would

---

[1] Report, p. 22.   [2] Report, p. 24.
[3] The Vagrancy Committee estimated that the number of persons with no settled home and no visible means of subsistence was in times of industrial activity less than 40,000, and in times of industrial depression would run to 70,000 or 80,000.

no doubt be diminished. To this extent it is right to urge improvement of human character as a remedy for unemployment. The limitations on this admission have, however, to be carefully noted. First, the number of the entirely unemployable class, though uncertain, is certainly not very great. Second, the most practical way of improving human character lies often in abolishing industrial or social conditions which induce or pander to the vices of idleness, slovenliness and irresponsibility. Third, no conceivable improvement in the character of the workmen will eliminate the main economic factors in unemployment.

DEFECTS OF CHARACTER AND THE INCIDENCE OF UNEMPLOYMENT.

The bearing of personal character on the incidence of unemployment raises a question far wider and more important than that just considered.

Between individual workmen, even of the same general type, there exist differences of every kind and degree. In the men of each trade is to be found every gradation of industrial value. Some differences affect the most obvious technical qualities; one man is stronger or speedier or more intellectual or more skilled than another. Others affect the less obvious qualities which make for continuance in employment—assiduity, regularity, punctuality, power of obedience and co-operation. Others affect rather the power to pass from one type of work to another, *i.e.*, adaptability. There can be no doubt either as to existence of these differences or as to their effect in determining the incidence of unemployment. "Whilst many men in almost every trade work with practically no loss of earnings, and some do so even in the most irregular and uncertain employments, others are habitual half-timers. No point has been more emphatically emphasised by the present inquiry than the unequal efficiency of the members of any industry, and the relatively disadvantageous position of the less efficient. To them, competition deals out stern justice, whatever the cause of their inefficiency may be." Thus Mr. Charles Booth summed up his experience in 1897.[1]

The selective influence of personal character is perhaps most obvious at times of exceptional depression. As manufacturing activity diminishes employers have to reduce staff and naturally do so by dismissing those men who appear the least valuable. The form taken by the process varies, of course, greatly according to the violence of the depression and the character of the industry.

[1] *Life and Labour of the People : Industry*, vol. v., p. 280.

Sometimes it is a case rather of retaining the few who have shown themselves particularly able than of selecting for dismissal a few who are subject to grave or slight faults; men go unless they have distinguished themselves favourably as above the average. If the depression is less severe or knowledge of individual men more detailed, perhaps only those will go who have distinguished themselves unfavourably as below the average. They are the men who always come on last as trade expands and go first as it contracts. They are the men in regard to whom their former employers, after stating perhaps that they were dismissed through "slackness of trade," then add some such comment as: "a good man when he gets to work," "fond of his glass," "too slow," or "not an early riser". Employers, indeed, sometimes welcome a slack time as an "opportunity for weeding out the black sheep; any men inclined to unsteadiness or idleness, drunkenness or sedition, are then generally got rid of".[1] What is said here of exceptional trade depression holds true of normal irregularity of employment. The better workmen tend to attract the attention of employers and foremen; the worse workmen form the casual fringe, and become still further worsened by irregularity.

The last point, indeed, is one of great importance. The "stern justice" which competition deals out to the inefficient has also the effect of accentuating their inefficiency. "We have always found," said a large employer of labour, "as to the artisan, that, if he happens to be out of work for three months, he is never the same man again. He becomes demoralised."[2] That, no doubt, is an over-statement. It embodies a very important truth. The man who is continually tramping the streets in search of employment is losing quite certainly in nearly all the qualities that go to make for industrial value.

For two reasons, therefore, the unemployed at any time are likely, on the whole, to be on a lower level than their fellows. Inferiority has caused them to be selected for dismissal. Dismissal and the resulting idleness accentuate their inferiority. From the point of view of the employer "the second-rate men are the casuals taken on when wanted".[3] From the point of view of the trade union "the same men are always signing the book" for out of work pay. The considerations urged above are so clear as hardly to need confirmation by detailed evidence. They may, however, be confirmed or at least illustrated in several ways.

[1] Charles Booth, *op. cit.*, vol. v., p. 238.
[2] *Exceptional Distress*, Report of a Special Committee of the Charity Organisation Society, 1886, Evidence, Dove, 1634.
[3] This and the following quotation are given by Charles Booth, *loc. cit.*

One is the experienced costliness of relief works. Details will be given in the following chapter. Here the general statement may be made that Distress Committees almost invariably find expenditure on work provided for the unemployed greater, and sometimes far greater, than the value obtained. No doubt this is due partly to men being engaged upon work with which they are not familiar, partly to slack conditions of employment, and partly to the privations experienced by the men before being assisted. There can, however, be no doubt of the relatively low efficiency of a good part of those engaged even on familiar or nearly unskilled work.

Another is the fact recorded in the Board of Trade Memorandum on Fluctuations in Employment,[1] that loss of working time among engineers through unpunctuality in the morning is " considerably greater on the average in times of active trade than in years of depression ". " This fact," it is said, " is partly attributable to the greater readiness of the workmen to lose time in years of good wages and full employment, partly to the greater prevalence of overtime in such years, but largely to the fact that the worst timekeepers are usually the first to lose their situations in times of depression."

A third illustration is to be found in the records of certain trade unions showing how many of the same individuals apply for unemployed benefit year after year.[2] Such records could, no doubt, be obtained for a good many trades. Here two only will be dealt with—compositors and bookbinders :—

In the London Society of Compositors 2,268 men or 19·8 per cent. of the total membership drew unemployed benefit during 1904. Of these, 1,671 or 74 per cent. claimed again in the following year and 1,402 or 62 per cent. in the year after. 1,261 or 10·8 per cent. of the total membership claimed in each of the three years 1904-6 ; and 1,006 or 8·6 per cent. in each of the four years 1904-7. Moreover, the greatest tendency to claim repeatedly was shown by those who drew the largest sums. Of the 876 men drawing less than £3 (4 weeks' unemployed pay) in 1904, 498 or 57 per cent. claimed again in 1905 ; in the 968 who drew £6 (8½ weeks) or more the proportion claiming again was nearly 88 per cent. The same point is put in another way by saying that about seven-eighths of the total payments in 1904 (£14,000 out of £16,000) went to men who had to claim again in 1905.

---

[1] *British and Foreign Trade*, Second Series, p. 100.
[2] The facts here given differ from those in Chapter V. (" The Reserve of Labour ") in that they involve tracing individuals from one year to the next. In the earlier chapter each year was treated by itself as a separate unit.

Peculiar interest attaches to the 1,006 men who claimed relief in every one of the four years from 1904 to 1907. These men, being in need of out of work pay year after year, may fairly be regarded as the casual fringe. They form in each year something less than half (40 to 44 per cent.) of the total number of unemployed claimants, but account for something more than half (54 to 59 per cent.) of the total sum claimed. During the four years taken together they cost the society over £40,000. In other words, more than 56 per cent. of the total of £71,000 expended on unemployment in these four years was taken by men forming less than 9 per cent. of the average membership.

These figures, no doubt, owe something of their striking character to the presence of a small but appreciable body of men who are to all intents and purposes chronically unemployed and draw full or nearly full benefits each year. Of the eighty-one men who drew within 2s. 6d. of the maximum benefit allowed in 1905 (£26 12s. for 38 weeks out of 52), fifty-eight drew the maximum also in one or more of the years 1903, 1904, 1906, 1907 ; and another seventeen drew £18 at least (26 weeks' unemployment out of 52). Every one of the remaining six drew substantial though smaller sums. Of the fifty-eight men, twenty-one drew the maximum in two years out of the five with, in every case but one, sums over £18 in one at least of the other years ; twenty-five drew the maximum in each of three years ; seven in each of four years ; and five in all the five years under consideration. Every one of the five received in addition nonprovident benefits—special grants from funds raised by voluntary subscription—ranging from £4 to over £14. The aggregate cost of these five men to the society during five years has been £667, or at the rate of over 10s. 6d. a week each for the whole period. The aggregate cost of the eighty-one men in the five years, excluding non-provident benefits, has been over £7,500. Facts such as these indicate a small group of men in regard to whom the function of unemployed benefit is rather to keep them out of the market altogether, lest they cut the rate of wages, than to tide over slack seasons.

In this respect the exceptionally liberal benefits afforded by the London Society of Compositors perhaps make its position peculiar. In respect of the more important fact—the much broader fringe of casual workmen who really do get work at times but who do not get it regularly—its experience agrees substantially with that of the other union for which the analysis has been made, namely, the London Consolidated Society of Journeymen Bookbinders Here, 572 members out of a total of

1,342 signed for out of work pay in 1903. Of these 572, 377 or 66 per cent. signed also in 1904; 279 or 49 per cent. in 1905; 298 or 52 per cent. in 1906. One hundred and sixty men signed in every one of the four years, for an aggregate of 4,419 weeks out of 12,448 for the whole society. The casual fringe appearing here is about 12 per cent. of the average membership for the four years and accounts for nearly 36 per cent. of the recorded unemployment.

In these two cases, therefore, statistical analysis strikingly confirms the generalisations already made and shows the fringe of casual workmen in actual being. There can be little doubt that other unions in other trades would, through considerable varieties of detail, present the same general phenomenon. It is not urged, indeed, that the selective influence of personal character is always appreciable. The analysis made above, while it shows the casual fringe of men applying for benefit year after year, shows also a large proportion of applications which are not repeated. The best and most regular of workmen may in a changing world find himself exceptionally unemployed. New methods and new machines often render whole classes of labour useless. Depression of trade may involve a particular firm, not in reduction of staff, but in absolute bankruptcy. In either case good, bad and indifferent alike are thrown upon the market. Indeed, the disaster is often the more complete in such cases in proportion as the previous employment has been regular. The longer and more continuously a man has been in one employment the less able is he to find his way into a new occupation. He has no experience in looking for work. He lacks the art of living casually.[1]

After all allowance has been made for special cases, the selective influence of personal character stands out as one of the dominant facts of the situation. Every employer, where he has the choice, dismisses the less satisfactory workmen and keeps the more satisfactory. In every organised trade the more regular and more efficient men have to pay for the less efficient and less regular. Almost inevitably, again, irregularity of employment reacts upon the man and accentuates the weaknesses with which he started. The net result is that the unemployed at any time, though they may include men of every grade, are as a whole below the general level in the qualities that make for

---

[1] Even here, however, personal character may from one point of view be regarded as retaining its selective force. It determines, not perhaps the first incidence of unemployment, but its continuance. After a disaster the man of resource and adaptability may find a new opening where the man of more limited range goes under altogether.

industrial efficiency. The bulk of them are in no sense unemployable. They are equally removed from being the picked men
of their trades. They are not useless or vicious. They are
simply, taken in the mass, less competent, less industrious, less
temperate or less regular than their fellows who have retained
employment.

THE UNEMPLOYED.

The discussion has now been carried to a point at which it is
desirable to review all that has gone before. In the first chapter
the problem of unemployment was broken up into many component factors. In the following chapters these factors have been
treated successively and, so far as possible, in isolation from the
rest. Without such analysis no understanding of the problem can
be reached and no final remedies can be suggested. In the world
of practice, however, the problem is not presented in this form.
The different factors are found there, not in isolation, but together ;
unemployment in each concrete individual case is, as a rule, the
product of many and infinitely various forces, some economic,
some personal ; some transient, some persistent ; some superficial,
some deeply rooted in the social fabric or in human nature. The
description of the problem, therefore, is not complete till something has been done to show the various factors, not in isolation,
but in action and reaction, and to picture for a moment, not the
causes of unemployment, but the unemployed men themselves.

All along the base of industry there lies now a region of
casual labour—a limbo between sufficiency and destitution. Into
this men are falling every moment through every form of human
weakness and misfortune, from every point of stress and transition in the working world above. From it some few may escape
or be drawn upwards again. More fall swiftly further into
vagrancy and crime. Most struggle on in it indefinitely, living
by odd jobs, decaying surely in physique and character. They
form the class B of Mr. Charles Booth's analysis—the class of
the very poor living from hand to mouth on casual earnings—a
class estimated by him at 7·5 per cent. of all the London population. " The labourers " of this class " do not, on an average, get
as much as three days' work a week, but it is doubtful if any of
them could or would work full time for long together if they had
the opportunity." The families of this class are "at all times
more or less in want"; their "whole income is absorbed by
necessary expenditure". " It is only by evading the payment of
rent, or going short of food, that clothes or household things can

be bought."[1]   Of this class or a part of it Mr. Booth wrote again in his final volume : " Humanly speaking, therefore, the existence of this class, consisting so largely of the inefficient and the worthless, may be inevitable, but economically their services are not wanted at all.   The work of the world could be performed better and more cheaply without them ; what they do could be easily done by the classes above them in their now partly occupied time ; and the money earned be better spent."[2]

This may be true.   Yet since, as matters stand, these men do at times get work, they must be regarded as meeting some demand.   Their removal would leave a place to be filled ; their poverty is to be explained, not by their character alone, but by that and their environment together.   In these lowest types, no doubt, personal inefficiency appears to be the dominant cause of distress ; the men would be unfit for anything else ; the demand for casual labour simply gives their weakness an opportunity. Yet often this weakness has itself been induced or fostered by casual employment, and, in any case, the lower types shade off imperceptibly into the higher ones—class B into class C—the poor through intermittence of earnings—and this into the fairly comfortable class above.   Here it is the demand for casual labour that appears as the dominant factor ; casual work is not so much chosen as tolerated unwillingly.   Yet here again it is insufficient to look at one factor alone.   Unless men were willing to take casual employment, the demand would remain ineffective.   Whichever, therefore, of the two factors appears dominant each is present to some extent in every grade.   The casual workman of every grade is the resultant of demand and supply—of the need of employers for casual labour and of the readiness of men to meet that need.   Employers want men only irregularly ; men have not learnt to fight against irregularity of earning as they have learnt to fight against low rates of pay ; as a consequence they submit to a sweating by under-employment far worse than the more familiar sweating by under-payment.   These are the two sides of the problem of normal poverty which is being forced on public attention in the shape of a problem of unemployment.

At times poverty becomes worse than normal.   The balance of casual demand and under-employed supply is disturbed by exceptional trade depression.   Yet even there it is the standing conditions of the labour market that shape the results.   The existence of casual employment means that trade depression can

---

[1] *Life and Labour of the People : Poverty*, vol. i., ch. ii. and v. and vol. ii., ch. ii.
[2] *Life and Labour of the People : Notes on Social Influences and Conclusions*, p. 207.

and does show itself to some extent, not in the dismissal of regular men, but in the lengthening of the average loss of time by the irregular man. On this point the experience of some of the principal trade unions is instructive.

The table given on p. 73 shows for certain branches of the Amalgamated Society of Engineers the distribution of unemployment between individuals in each year from 1887 to 1895. It is, possible therefore, to compare good times with bad, years of depression with years of prosperity. 1890 is a good year with an average unemployed percentage of 2·1 and a loss of working days per member of 6·4 ; 1893 is a bad year with an unemployed percentage and a loss of working days per member of nearly five times as much. Yet only a very small part of this difference is accounted for by an increase in the numbers becoming unemployed at some time or other ; the percentages for the two years are 21·4 and 26·4 respectively. The great difference is in the average amount of time lost by each of those who did become unemployed. In 1890 this was 30·1 days ; in 1893 it was nearly four times as great, viz., 117·8 days. Here is a very striking instance of a trade depression marked not so much by an increase in the proportions of irregular to regular workmen, as by increased loss of time within the irregular margin.[1]

In other unions this characteristic is less marked yet never absent. In the London Society of Compositors, for instance, the average unemployed percentage rose from 3·0 in 1898 to 5·1 in 1902, an increase of 70 per cent. But the percentage of individuals drawing unemployed benefit at some time during the year rose from 18·0 to 22·3, an increase of only 24 per cent. While the average time lost by each of those drawing benefit in 1898 was 52 days, the average time lost by each of those drawing benefit in 1902 was, on the same basis, 71 days. In the Associated Blacksmiths Society of Scotland, during the good year of 1899, 14·5 per cent. only of the members drew on an average 4·4 weeks of unemployed benefit. During the bad year of 1903 the proportion of members drawing benefit was much greater, 26·7 per cent., but so also was the average number of weeks' benefit drawn by each, viz., 6·7. In the Amalgamated Union of Millsawyers and Wood Cutting Machinists the average unemployed percentage in 1900 was 2·1, the percentage of members drawing benefit was 21·2, and the resulting average amount of unemployment per member drawing was 5·1 weeks. For 1904 the average unemployed percentage was 5·6, the percentage

---

[1] These are the years of maximum and minimum unemployment in the table. Comparison of other years gives somewhat different results.

of members drawing benefit was 32·7, and the resulting average amount of unemployment per member drawing was 8·6 weeks.

In the table on the next page these facts are set out in a slightly different form. The attempt is made to estimate in a few typical cases what proportions of the increase of unemployment in a time of depression may be attributed respectively to an increase in the number of men becoming unemployed, to an increase in the average period of unemployment, and to both these factors in combination.

The table, it will be seen, shows great variation in the different cases. In every case, however, increase of the average claim to benefit has a considerable share, and in some cases a principal share, ranging up to 82 per cent., in the increase of aggregate unemployment.

Exceptional depression as experienced by trade unions means partly that a certain number of men lose their regular employment, partly that irregular men become still more irregular. The experience of Distress Committees is the same, but with enormously heightened emphasis on the second effect. The man at the bottom of the industrial scale appears there as the principal sufferer, not only because he is in fact often the hardest hit— employers dispense with their casual staff before they part with their regular men—but also because he has a smaller reserve for emergencies. At the first pinch he passes from want to destitution.

The central fact of the situation is the maintenance, as an integral part of industry, of a body of men constantly passing into and out of employment, of a reserve as well as a regular army of labour. It is this that sets up the permanent conditions upon which and within which all the other factors have to work, that obscures their results and makes their direct treatment difficult or impossible. The man displaced from his former position by changes of industrial structure or by advancing years finds in casual employment a resource from immediate want— of a kind that paves the way to chronic poverty. The youth ill-trained, the man displaced through personal fault or inefficiency and the sturdy loafer find in casual employment a livelihood— of a kind that perpetuates and accentuates their various weaknesses. The problem presented by these factors is therefore made indefinite instead of definite ; a poor resource stands in the way of effective treatment. Still more marked is the significance of casual employment in making indefinite the effects of cyclical depression, in giving them the shape of a slight worsening of chronic distress rather than that of a displacement of men hitherto in good positions.

TABLE XXV.—EXCEPTIONAL DEPRESSION IN TRADE UNIONS.[1]

Trade Union and Years compared.	Basis of Comparison.	Percentage of Increase of Unemployment represented by		
		Increase of Unemployed Claimants alone.	Increase of Average Claim alone.	More Claimants at Increased Average.
Associated Blacksmiths— 1889, Good } 1893, Bad }	Weeks of Benefit drawn.	28	17	55
1899, Good } 1904, Bad }	Do.	45	27	28
Associated Shipwrights— 1890, Good } 1893, Bad }	Amount drawn.	17	17	66
1899, Good } 1904, Bad }	Do.	27	13	60
Amalgamated Millsawyers— 1900, Good } 1904, Bad }	Do.	28	47	25
Amalgamated Cabinetmakers— 1902, Good } 1904, Bad }	Do.	12	82	6
London Compositors— 1890, Good } 1894, Bad }	Weeks of Unemployment, calculated from Unemployed Percentage.	35	43	22
1898, Good } 1904, Bad }	Do.	26	61	13
Amalgamated Society of Engineers (Selected Districts)— 1890, Good } 1893, Bad }	Days of Unemployment.	6	76	18

In every case allowance has been made for changes in the total membership between the years of comparison.

[1] The construction of this table may be illustrated by the following instance. In 1899 507 out of 7,644 members of the Associated Shipwrights drew £417 of benefits, or £·8 per man. In 1904 4,163 out of 11,125 drew £10,591. On the basis of the 1899 membership this would have meant 2,860 men out of 7,644 drawing £7,277, or £2·55 per man. The difference between 2,860 and 507 = 2,353 multiplied by £·8 is taken as the increase of payments due to increase of claimants alone. This = £1,882, or 27 per cent. of £6,860, the difference between £7,277 and £417. The difference between £2·55 and £·8 = £1·75 multiplied by 507 is taken as the increase of payments due to increased claims alone. This is £887, or 13 per cent. of £6,860. The remaining 60 per cent. goes in the last column as due to both factors in combination.

"The unemployed," then, as they present themselves for public sympathy and instant aid, as they figure in the records of Distress Committees, are predominantly men whose earnings from being intermittent have been made casual, or from being casual have dropped to nothing at all. Other types, of course, are not wanting. There are the men of higher position who have been peculiarly unfortunate or peculiarly improvident. There are the men of lower position who make harvest in a season of aroused philanthropy. The great bulk of the distressed unemployed came from neither one end of the scale nor the other; neither from A—the class of loafers and criminals—nor from D and E—the regular labourers and comfortable artisans—but from B and C, who lie between. In class B—the very poor of casual earnings—"the whole income is absorbed by necessary expenditure" and yields no reserve whatever for emergencies. Class C—the poor of intermittent earnings—"are, more than any others the victims of competition, and on them falls with peculiar severity the weight of recurrent depressions of trade".[1] "The unemployed," therefore, present almost always a combination of two distinct economic factors in poverty—under-employment and fluctuation of industrial activity. They present also, with almost as great certainty, the personal factor—the selection of men for dismissal or casual employment according to deficiencies of ability or character or training, and the further weakening of men by irregularity and want. In this complication and interaction of many factors, industrial and personal, chronic and temporary, lies the difficulty of all direct dealing with "the unemployed". To expect from them the normal standard of efficiency and industry is only too often to be disappointed. To equalise their position to that of the employed is to run the risk of demoralising the people by taking from inefficiency its punishment and from assiduity its reward. To give them relief work on conditions as attractive as their ordinary life is to leave them with no incentive to return to independence, yet their ordinary life is such that the relief can hardly in practice be made less attractive without being made inadequate or degrading. To give them temporary work in times of exceptional depression is to throw them back upon chronic poverty at its close; it is like saving men from drowning in order to leave them on a quicksand. This, indeed, sums up the problem. A great body of workmen to-day are men living on a quicksand, which at any moment may engulf individuals, which at uncertain intervals sinks for months or years below the sea surface altogether. Many of them, no doubt, become used to

[1] Booth, *loc. cit.*

their place of habitation; they have learnt its ways and continually escape destruction; they might be unfit for any other life; they have come there, perhaps, not by disaster, but by their own weakness. Yet while this quicksand and its movements are part of industry, society cannot escape some responsibility for those who live there; cannot treat as criminals those whose industrial services are there required; cannot end the evil by rescuing individuals.

CHAPTER VIII.

REMEDIES OF THE PAST.

1. The able-bodied under the Poor Law : Relief in the workhouse. Relief of family outside and head of family inside the workhouse. Outdoor relief with a labour test. Outdoor relief without a labour test. The casual ward.
2. Municipal relief works : The circulars of 1886 and 1892. "Work" with no standard of competence.
3. Special charitable funds : Development in London 1860, 1867, 1885, 1892-5. The "colony system" of 1903-4. Mr. Long's scheme of joint committees, 1904-5.
4. The Unemployed Workmen Act : Summary of provisions. A conglomerate of ideas from Poor Law, municipal relief work and special charitable funds. Working of Act 1905-8. Numbers and occupations of applicants. Difficulties of investigation and selection. The predominant casual labourer. Cost of relief work. Absence of permanent benefit. Farm colonies. Emigration. Labour Exchanges.
5. Conclusions as to Unemployed Workmen Act : Departures from original policy in respect of finance, persons to be assisted, conditions of assistance, effect of assistance. Failure to deal with exceptional distress. Assumed advantages of relief by work rather than by money gifts unreal. Need for improved industrial conditions. A country cannot treat its dependents less badly than its citizens. Need for measures of organisation not of relief.

UNEMPLOYMENT in the past has been treated by many different agencies—public and private. To write the history of them all would probably be impossible and in this place certainly unprofitable. Some account of the principal agencies, however, will have far more than a merely historic value, for it will illustrate all the main difficulties that arise and all the principles that need discussion. With this in view it will be worth while to deal shortly with the action of the Poor Law, the municipal authorities and Special Relief Funds, and then more at length with the principles and administration of the Unemployed Workmen Act.

THE ABLE-BODIED UNDER THE POOR LAW.

From the point of view of the Poor Law the unemployed are the able-bodied, and the central principle of their treatment is that their situation "on the whole shall not be made really or apparently as eligible as the situation of the independent labourer of the lowest class". From this principle flows the general prohibition of outdoor relief, at least to the male able-bodied, except subject to the performance of a task of work. From this, amongst other reasons, follows the disfranchisement of those accepting public assistance. In effect the treatment of the unemployed by Poor Law guardians may take one or other of the five following forms :—[1]

1. Relief in the workhouse. This, the most "deterrent form of assistance," is not commonly accepted, as it is not intended to be accepted, by even moderately respectable families unless they are literally destitute. It is criticised, therefore, as involving extreme suffering and perhaps permanent demoralisation in the effort to hold out, and also because in breaking up the home it destroys a social asset of great value. The offer of the workhouse has almost always been considered too hard a measure to mete out to the respectable unemployed in periods of exceptional distress.

2. Relief of the family outside the workhouse on condition of entry of the head of the family into the workhouse. This plan—that of the modified workhouse test—was originally applied in the Whitechapel Union by co-operation with the Charity Organisation Society, the latter undertaking in suitable cases to maintain out of voluntary subscriptions the homes and families of men admitted to the workhouse. Later a special order sanctioning the plan, and enabling the guardians themselves to give relief to the family, was obtained from the Local Government Board by the Whitechapel Board of Guardians and one or two others, but was only very sparingly used. Recently the order has been applied a little more freely. Its great advantage is that while maintaining a stringent test of destitution it avoids the breaking up of homes; it leaves the man when he emerges from the workhouse somewhere to go to other than a common lodging house or a casual ward. The disadvantage is that the unemployed man himself is still as much exposed as under the ordinary plan to degradation by evil associations and to loss of self-respect; he is also, while in the workhouse, quite cut off from the chance of seeking employment. The principle underlying this plan—that of an institu-

[1] Boards of Guardians have also power to buy or rent land to the extent of fifty acres "within or near" their union in order to set the poor to work upon it. This power originated in the Act of 1601 (43 Eliz. c. 2, § 1) which directed the overseers to provide work for children whose parents were unable to support them and "persons who use no ordinary or daily trade of life to get their living by". In 1819 (59 Geo. III. c. 12) the overseers were empowered to acquire for the purposes of the Act of 1601, not more than twenty acres of land in or near their parish, and in 1830 (1 and 2 Will. IV. c. 42) the maximum area was raised to fifty acres. These Acts were not taken advantage of under the reformed Poor Law, but in 1895 the law officers of the Crown gave the opinion that the powers had passed to the Boards of Guardians and might be exercised under the control of the Local Government Board.

tional test for the head of the family as a condition of relief to the family itself—is, however, of the greatest importance in the recent treatment of the unemployed.

3. Outdoor relief subject to the performance of a labour test. By Article 6 of the Outdoor Relief Regulation Order[1] of 1852, "Every able-bodied male person, if relieved out of the workhouse, shall be set to work by the guardians, and be kept employed under their direction and superintendence so long as he continues to receive relief". "One-half at least of the relief so allowed shall be given in articles of food or fuel, or in other articles of absolute necessity" (Art. 1). The actual amount of the relief appears to be within the discretion of the guardians. The fact of giving such relief, together with the place or places at which the men are set to work, the sort, times and mode of work, and the provision made for superintendence, must however be reported within thirty days to the Local Government Board, and the guardians "shall forthwith discontinue or alter the same if the Board shall so require" (Art. 8). These regulations have generally materialised at times of assumed exceptional distress in the opening of labour yards for the employment of men in stone-breaking, oakum-picking or wood-chopping. This plan is not open to the objection that it breaks up the home, and it is not so deterrent as to drive men to starve rather than to apply. Its defects lie rather in the other direction, that men of a low grade will readily apply for it rather than seek ordinary employment, and, having obtained it, will be still further demoralised by engagement upon work in which industry is at a discount. The winter of 1894-5 was distinguished by a good many disastrous experiments with stone yards,[2] and furnished the Select Committee of the House of Commons with many criticisms. "Further

---

[1] This is the order in force in London and most large towns. Agricultural districts and the smaller towns are for the most part subject to the Outdoor Relief Prohibitory Order of 1844 which forbids all outdoor relief of the able-bodied, whether male or female, except widows having dependent children or in the first six months of their widowhood. This order, however, may be, and at the request of the guardians on cause shown, normally is, supplemented by the issue of an Outdoor Labour Test Order, practically assimilating the position in respect of able-bodied males to that in London and the large towns.

[2] The most striking of these was at St. Olave's (Southwark). The stoneyard was opened from 7th January to 28th March, 1895, the relief given being "at the rate of trades union wages," i.e., 6d. per hour for seven hours, part in money, part in kind. As many as 1,759 men were set to work in one day and the average throughout the period was nearly 900, the numbers showing an unmistakable tendency to drop every Monday and Tuesday, but comparatively little tendency to drop with the disappearance of the frost and the revival of trade. The cost per ton of stone broken was £7, the market price of this amount being 12s. The effect of the test was later described by the chairman of the board as very demoralising and calculated rather to increase pauperism than to diminish it.

objection to the stone-breaking test is to the effect that it is more
eligible than an offer of admittance to the workhouse, and that
it is attractive to the least deserving.   Moreover, where the employment of applicants is only partial the test may partake of
the character of relief in aid of wages, unless careful inquiry as to
the proceedings of such persons in their off days is from time to
time instituted. . . . Perhaps, however, the principal objection
to the stone-breaking test is the premium on idleness that it involves.   No specified task can be enforced.   The capability of
the persons employed varies and it can only be required that each
person shall perform the amount of work that he appears to be
able to accomplish. . . . The standard of accomplishment is
practically fixed by the unwilling worker."   " Your Committee
are of opinion that the casual and deserving poor suffer by being
brought into contact with the loafing class in the stoneyard." [1]
Though these objections are made to refer expressly to stoneyards it is clear that they apply with much the same force to all
the other forms of outdoor labour test available, unless the test is
reinforced by careful investigation and selection among the
applicants or is stiffened by a quite extraordinary amount of
supervision.

4. Outdoor relief without a labour test in cases of " sudden
and urgent necessity ".   This is one of the exceptions permitted
by the Outdoor Relief Regulation Order [2] (Art. 7).   Another
is made by Article 10 allowing the guardians " upon consideration of the special circumstances of any particular case " to depart
from the regulations contained in the rest of the order, reporting
such departure and the grounds of it within twenty-one days to
the Local Government Board, which has thereupon power either
to approve or disapprove of the continuance of this departure
from the established rule.   Each of these exceptions has in its
time been used to nullify altogether the prohibition of outdoor
relief without a labour test to the able-bodied.   In 1895, for instance, the St. Olave's Board of Guardians passed a resolution
that " every application should be deemed to be one of sudden
and urgent necessity," and in the winter of 1904-5 the Poplar
Board of Guardians gave immediate outdoor relief without a
labour test in practically all cases of distress, relying at first

[1] *Distress from Want of Employment* (1896).
[2] In the General Consolidated Order of 1847 the words used with regard to the
duties of relieving officer to give immediate assistance are " sudden *or* urgent" not
" sudden *and* urgent ".   The difference is of course very considerable and has been in
fact the subject of much controversy between the central and local poor law authorities,
since the wording of the 1847 order appears to justify the continuous assistance, by
outdoor relief on the ground of " urgency," of men in a state of chronic distress.

upon Article 10 but subsequently upon the General Consolidated Order of 1847.

5. Relief in the casual ward. This is the provision made by the Poor Law for the destitute wayfarer irrespective of his place of residence. Bare board and lodging may be obtained subject to performance of a task of work and to detention for an additional night. Repeated application to the same casual ward within one month is penalised by detention for four nights. The principal function of the casual ward system to-day is to provide an infinite variety of free hotels for an army of habitual vagrants whom it neither repels nor reforms nor keeps from want. Its secondary function is to act as a trap to catch the decent unemployed and turn them by evil association into the unemployable. Fortunately its operation in this last direction is limited; genuine workmen in search of employment form a very small proportion of those who visit the casual wards—according to the Association of Workhouse Masters not more than 3 per cent. Detailed criticisms of the casual ward system and suggestions for its reform are to be found in the Report of the Departmental Committee on Vagrancy, presented in February, 1906.[1]

MUNICIPAL RELIEF WORKS.

At all times of considerable distress through want of employment men have been apt to turn to the nearest local authority and expect it to provide work. During the depression of 1886, this expectation received a fresh impulse through the action of the Local Government Board. In a circular calling attention to the evidence of " much and increased privation . . . in the ranks of those who do not ordinarily seek parish relief," the Board recommended that " in districts in which exceptional distress prevailed . . . the guardians should confer with the local authorities, and endeavour to arrange with the latter for the execution of works on which unskilled labour may be immediately employed ".

The object of this recommendation was to avoid any relaxation of the ordinary Poor Law. The requirements of the respectable unemployed were summarised as follows :—

" 1. Work which shall not involve the stigma of pauperism.

" 2. Work which all can perform whatever may have been their previous avocations.

[1] Cd. 2852; cf. also The Homeless Poor of London, Report of a Special Committee of the Charity Organisation Society, 1891, and Toynbee Record, February, March and July, 1905.

" 3. Work which does not compete with that of other labourers at present in employment.

" Lastly, work which is not likely to interfere with the resumption of regular employment in their own trades by those who seek it."

The types of work suggested as meeting these requirements included spade husbandry on sewage farms; laying out of open spaces, recreation grounds, new cemeteries, or disused burial grounds; cleansing of streets not usually undertaken by local authorities; laying out and paving of new streets, etc.; paving of unpaved streets and making of footpaths in country roads; and providing or extending sewerage works and works of water supply. The two principal conditions for the execution of the work were laid down as follows :—

" In all cases in which special works are undertaken to meet exceptional distress, it would appear necessary, first, that the men employed should be engaged on the recommendation of the guardians as persons whom, owing to previous condition and circumstances, it is undesirable to send to the workhouse or to treat as subjects for pauper relief; and second, that the wages paid should be something less than the wages ordinarily paid for similar work, in order to prevent imposture, and to leave the strongest temptation to those who avail themselves of this opportunity to return as soon as possible to their previous occupations."

This circular, first issued to local authorities and Boards of Guardians in England and Wales under the presidency of Mr. Chamberlain in the spring of 1886, was substantially repeated under the presidency of Sir Henry Fowler in November, 1892. In accordance with it local authorities, during the past twenty years, have taken a considerable part in relieving distress through unemployment. In a few places municipal relief works have become almost an annual institution.[1] More generally they have been limited to times when there appeared to be exceptional distress. During the winter of 1892-93, for instance, 96 authorities in Great Britain provided relief work for the unemployed men in their districts; 77 of these gave employment altogether to 26,875 persons.[2] In the six months, ended 31st March, 1905, the Metropolitan Borough Councils spent £103,926 from

---

[1] Thus at West Ham the corporation provided work for the unemployed in 1895-96, 1898-99, and then in every winter from 1902 onwards. (*West Ham*, Howarth and Wilson, book iii., ch. iv.).

[2] *Agencies and Methods* (1893), p. 212. *Distress from Want of Employment* (1895), Third Report, p. 65.

the local rates in wages alone upon special works for the unemployed.[1]   This, it may be noted, was additional to the £50,000
that was raised at the same time by voluntary subscriptions
under Mr. Long's scheme and disbursed by the Executive Committee of the London Unemployed Fund.   There is, however,
no need to write in detail the history of the experiments and
expenditures of municipalities in this direction.   It will be sufficient to note one or two general features.

First, the principle has become established that the assistance
given by the local authorities though called "work," should be
work in which no standard of competence is required and upon
which men are under no obligation to earn their wages.   Really
unskilled work, of the type contemplated by the circular—"which
all can perform, whatever may have been their previous avocations"—hardly exists in the world of practice.   The unemployed at
a time of depression are a collection of persons from many occupations, and, as a rule, the weakest members of these occupations.
To insist upon a standard of competence might mean discharging
many of the most "deserving" men who could not do just the sort
of work provided.   All that has seemed possible has been to insist
upon each man doing as much as he appeared capable of doing.
The adoption of this course by the local authorities has perhaps
been natural.   It has, however, exposed municipal relief works to
the danger of setting a standard of output by the ability of the
weakest or idlest worker, and has made them almost always more
expensive—often much more expensive—than if they had been
performed by labourers under ordinary conditions of hiring and
discharge.[2]   Clearly, moreover, it affects in a very vital manner
the character of the operations undertaken.   To pay men wages
irrespective of their earnings is to provide them not with work
but with relief.

Second, both the "necessary" conditions laid down in the
circular have come to be widely disregarded.   At any rate till the
passage of the Unemployed Workmen Act, it has been the exception rather than the rule for local authorities, when providing
work for the unemployed, to consult with the guardians or any
one else in the selection of men for assistance, or to make any
serious attempt at discrimination between applicants.   It is by now
also quite the exception rather than the rule for anything less than

---

[1] *Unemployed Relief (Work)*, *(London)*.   House of Commons Return, 1905 (193).
[2] *Cf.* the return on *Unemployed Relief (Work)*, *(London)* already cited, and
Past Experience in Relief Works by Helen Bosanquet.   The former also contains
instances of work specially put in hand at a time of distress but conducted under
ordinary conditions and estimated to have cost no more than usual.

the ordinary or trade union wages to be paid on public relief works.[1]

Third, great difficulty has often been experienced by local authorities at times in finding, at a few days' notice, work which both could be done by the unemployed and would not in the ordinary way be done by their regular staff or at least by ordinary contractor's labour. Few authorities, indeed, have been reduced to the plan adopted by one London borough council in 1904—of discontinuing for a few months the use of their machine brooms in order to get the streets swept instead by the hands of the unemployed.[2] Many have done work which had in fact little greater utility or necessity than this.

Fourth, the plan of distributing such work as could be given between the greatest possible number of individual men—giving each perhaps only two days a week or two days in a month or a season—has been very largely adopted.

SPECIAL CHARITABLE FUNDS.

The third type of agency to be considered here is that of the special funds which have from time to time been raised by appeal to the charitable public in order to meet an assumed emergency of exceptional and urgent distress. It will be sufficient for this purpose to confine attention to London. The following table gives the principal funds raised and expended there on various occasions during the past fifty years with a view to alleviating unusual distress :—

EMERGENCY RELIEF FUNDS IN LONDON.

1860.	£40,000.	Estimate of sums raised by various agencies to meet unusual distress. Direct Temporary Relief.
1867.	£15,000.	Mansion House Fund. Direct Temporary Relief.
1885.	£78,629.	Mansion House Fund. Direct Temporary Relief.
1892-5.	£2,500.	Mansion House Fund. Temporary test work at Abbey Mills as a means to permanent removal. About £400 of this fund was carried over to 1903-4.
1903-4.	£4,000.	Mansion House Fund. Colony Relief Works.
1904-5.	£51,904.	London Unemployed Fund. Mr. Long's Scheme.
1905-6.	£63,455.	London's share of the Queen's Unemployed Fund used for Unemployed Workmen Act.

[1] The principle of paying the standard rate under such circumstances appears to have grown gradually—under pressure of the objection to under-selling the ordinary industrial worker. In 1892 even the Trades Council at Greenock was prepared to admit the payment of less than trade union rate of wages on special works for the unemployed (*Agencies and Methods* (1893), p. 221). At West Ham, however, in 1894-5 the Town Council, under pressure from the local trade unions, withdrew from co-operation in a scheme to pay for unskilled labour by the piece with a minimum time rate below the current one.

[2] *Unemployed Relief (Work)*, (*London*). Stepney. During the present month (Nov., 1908) identically the same proposal has been submitted by the Borough Council of Bermondsey to the Central (Unemployed) Body for London.

In the administration of these funds a distinct progression may be noticed. The first in the list—that of 1860-1—represented to a great extent largesse pure and simple. The police courts were the most important centres of distribution. At the Thames police court "generally a number of persons, sometimes to the amount of 2,000, collected about the court. There was a large amount of silver and it was given to the applicants as they passed along, as fast as possible."[1] At Westminster money was paid out in response to begging letters, the writing of which became in consequence a regular trade performed by a special class of men. In the city "the circumstance that two magistrates were sitting, distributing relief indiscriminately to all who chose to apply to them, was as if two additional relieving officers were put on, one at the Mansion House and the other at Guildhall—distributing money instead of provisions; and instead of its coming out of the poor rates it came from public subscription ".

By 1867 public opinion had so far developed that some attempt was made to secure distribution of the fund through committees having knowledge of the various localities and experience in dealing with distress. The local committees were, however, for the most part self-constituted. In many cases they partook rather of the character of deputations, and almost without exception they acted on the principle of giving infinitesimal doles to as many people as possible. In Poplar and Limehouse 43,000 persons were "relieved" to the extent, on an average, of sevenpence each. In Bethnal Green the average amount of relief per head was twopence farthing.

The Mansion House Fund of 1885 was the most famous of all. There are men still living amongst the unemployed of to-day who can recall with regret those golden days. There are men experienced in observing and dealing with distress who say that East and South London have scarcely yet recovered from the demoralisation of that orgie of relief. Yet the operations of 1885-6, while exceeding in scale anything that had gone before, also represented a distinct advance in administration. The sums granted to individuals were on the whole larger. Certain new and excellent objects of expenditure, e.g., the payment of club arrears, were recognised. The central committee of the fund not only took positive steps to secure the formation of representative local committees for the work of distribution, but even formulated rules for their guidance. The first of the rules was " that no part

---

[1] *Exceptional Distress*, Report of a Special Committee of the Charity Organisation Society, 1886, p. iii. Most of the subsequent quotations come from this same source.

of the funds be used for the relief of cases of chronic distress".
Others proscribed the payment of back rent and the giving of
money, except through payment of club arrears, to applicants in
receipt of outdoor relief. In some districts, no doubt, attempts
were made to adhere strictly to these rules. In others they were
frankly abandoned almost from the start. In others they—and
especially the first one—had to be relaxed simply owing to the
character of most of those applying. "We should have had
difficulty in finding anybody to participate if we had excluded
chronic cases altogether," said one almoner.[1] "The tendency of
the fund was to drift to the relief of the permanent poor. Do
what we would to avoid it, we could not help it drifting," said
another.

The operations of 1892-1895 had a quite special character,
since they were directed, not so much to carrying men over a
time of acute depression, as to removing them altogether from an
area in which the re-organisation of labour at the docks was
making them superfluous.[2]

With the Mansion House Fund of 1903-4 begins the last
stage in this history. A letter appearing in the London papers
on 23rd November, 1903, over the signatures of the Bishop of
Stepney, Canon Barnett and others, gave the outlines of a scheme
which aimed "at putting before every head of a family a means
of living, sufficient to keep up the full strength of his family and
of a character which would enable him to retain his self-respect
while at the same time affording a real test of need and of manful
purpose". Under this scheme work was to be offered at some
distance from London to heads of families settled in London.
The men were to go down to the works and get lodging, board
and pocket money, returning only at stated intervals to see their
families and look for ordinary employment; their wives were to
receive at home adequate allowances varying with the number of
dependent children. The separation of the man from home and
London was put forward as a "test" making the relief work less
attractive than ordinary work without making it either dishonour-
able (as under the Poor Law) or irregular and insufficient to
provide a maintenance (as in the case of most municipal schemes).
The letter itself was not an appeal for funds, but led to the re-
assembling of the old Mansion House Committee which undertook
the "colony" scheme there outlined. Altogether about £4,300
were spent during a period of three and a half months in providing

---

[1] *Exceptional Distress.* Evidence of Fletcher 61 and Roberts 1610; *cf.* also Qu.
821, 858, 972.
[2] See p. 90 above.

work at Osea Island and Hadleigh Farm Colony to 467 heads of families (representing 2,500 persons) resident in the four East End boroughs of Stepney, Poplar, Bethnal Green and Shoreditch. The work was mainly spade work in the open air. Men once set to work were allowed to remain there, subject to good behaviour, till the close, returning at first once a fortnight, but later only once a month to London. The average relief to each family was estimated at 23s. 3d. a week. At first it was hoped that the condition of removal from London would suffice to keep the numbers within bounds and render investigation and selection amongst applicants unnecessary. This expectation was at once disappointed, and after the first four weeks all cases were investigated as fully as possible, by reference to employers and otherwise, with a view to selecting for assistance those who, having had regular work in the past, might be presumed to have the best chance of recovering it in the future if enabled to survive a period of exceptional depression.

The "colony" scheme of 1903-4, therefore, for practically the first time in the history of charitable relief funds, witnessed the application of several important principles. Work was given, not money. Regular work, continued to each individual so long as the fund lasted and he behaved well, was given in place of doles of irregular work. The principle of making relief less attractive than industry was recognised and applied by the device of rustication. The conception of a specific industrial evil —cyclical trade depression—needing to be treated scientifically led to a selection of men, not simply according to their distress, but according to their industrial record. Finally, the committee followed up their work by an attempt to ascertain its effect upon those assisted. An investigation at the end of July, 1904, four months after the close of the scheme and in the height of the summer, showed 26 per cent. to have recovered "more or less regular employment according to the nature of their occupation," 36 per cent. to have obtained casual or irregular employment (one month or so in four or five), and 38 per cent. to have been out of work ever since leaving the relief works or to have had a few days' or one or two weeks' work but to be once again unemployed. The main effect of the scheme was to demonstrate the magnitude of the problem to be solved.

All through the summer of 1904 trade remained depressed and employment slack, and it became clear that much distress was to be anticipated during the coming winter. Accordingly, at a special conference of Metropolitan Guardians convened on 14th October, Mr. Walter Long, then President of the Local

Government Board, propounded a scheme for the organisation of special relief throughout London.[1]

To these proposals, as developed in subsequent official circulars, practical effect was given during the month following. Joint Committees representative of the borough councils and boards of guardians were set up in twenty-seven out of the twenty-eight Metropolitan boroughs and in the City of London In many, but not in all cases, the Committees included also, as suggested by Mr. Long, representatives of charitable associations. A Central Committee—numbering at full strength seventy—was formed of delegates from each of the Joint Committees and of persons nominated by the Local Government Board.

The functions of the Joint Committees were " to receive applications for work or relief, to examine into the cases and to divide them into two classes : (i.) those who were respectable men temporarily distressed owing to inability to obtain employment; (ii.) those who should be regarded as ordinary applicants for poor-law relief". The latter being excluded, the Joint Committees were left to deal with the first class " by recommending them to the borough councils for employment, by affording facilities for the interchange of information between applicants for work and employers, and by recommending them for employment upon special works undertaken by the Central Committee ". Their administrative expenses were in part thrown on the Metropolitan Common Poor Fund. The functions of the Central Committee apart from co-ordination of the work of the Joint Committees were " to collect and administer funds, and to deal with cases referred to them by the Joint Committees, by the provision of special works beyond the limits of any particular borough, by the establishment of labour colonies, or by making grants towards special works undertaken by local authorities ". The funds of the Central Committee were, in the event, drawn entirely from voluntary subscriptions received partly through the agency of Mr. Long, partly in response to a Mansion House appeal. Mr. Long had himself strongly repudiated the project of an Exchequer grant, while his own rather daring offer to sanction contributions made by local authorities out of the rates met with little response.

The Joint Committees, being formed, proceeded to register large numbers of the unemployed and to recommend the great bulk of them to the Central Committee for employment. Up to

---

[1] The scheme is referred to elsewhere and generally under the title of the London Unemployed Fund. The principles of the scheme were applicable and were applied also outside London. In view, however, of the subsequent Unemployed Workmen Act, no special account of them seems necessary.

31st March, 1905, 45,996 men had been registered and about 26,000 recommended as falling in Class I. while not more than 11,000 were ruled out as belonging to Class II.   Some of these men—an unascertainable number—were assisted indirectly by the Central Committee through grants in aid of work put in hand by public authorities.   Altogether £5,614 went in such grants. The bulk of the committee's funds was in employing men directly and served to provide work for 3,496 individuals during periods varying from one day to thirty weeks and averaging eight weeks. These works were of three main types.   About a third of the men were employed in London itself by co-operation with the County Council, the City Corporation, the Home Office, mainly on ground work in the parks.   The men were paid the standard rates of wages, making their weekly earnings for the hours worked 22s. or 25s. 8d., or in the Royal Parks 24s.   About another third of the men were employed by co-operation with the County Council in preparing ground for a garden at Long Grove Asylum near Epsom and travelled daily to and fro by special train.   The wages were the standard ones of 6d. an hour, but the obligation of paying half their railway fares (2s. a week) reduced the weekly earnings to 23s. 8d., and the amount was still further reduced later to 21s. 8d. by cessation of Saturday work and pay.   The remaining third of the men were employed by co-operation with the Salvation Army at Hadleigh, by co-operation with the Garden City Company at Letchworth and on the farm colony at Holles-ley Bay leased to the committee by Mr. Joseph Fels.   These men were employed on the "colony" system introduced by the Mansion House Fund of 1903-4.   They received merely board, lodging and pocket-money; their wives in London had allow-ances ranging from ten to twenty shillings.

THE UNEMPLOYED WORKMEN ACT.

The Unemployed Workmen Act, 1905,[1] has followed up and generalised the semi-official scheme of 1904-5.   It establishes for every municipal borough and urban district with a population of not less than fifty thousand a Distress Committee composed in specified proportions of councillors, guardians and "persons experienced in the relief of distress".   These Distress Com-mittees must make themselves acquainted with the conditions of labour in their area; may receive, inquire into and discriminate between any applications made to them by persons unemployed;

---

[1] 5 Edward VII. ch. 18.   The principal orders made under the Act by the Local Government Board are Statutory Orders, 1905, No. 1035, dealing with the powers and duties of Distress Committees, and No. 1071, known as the Regulations (Or-ganisation for Unemployed), and referred to shortly as the Regulations.

may "if satisfied that any such applicant is a person honestly desirous of obtaining work but is temporarily unable to do so from exceptional causes over which he has no control and that his case is capable of more suitable treatment under this Act than under the Poor Law," endeavour to obtain work for him or themselves undertake to assist him.   This assistance may take several forms :—

(*a*) Aiding emigration.

(*b*) Aiding migration or removal to another area.

(*c*) Providing or contributing towards the provision of temporary work "in such manner as they think best calculated to put him in a position to obtain regular work or other means of supporting himself".

It is expressly laid down that "the provision of temporary work or other assistance for any person under this Act shall not disentitle him to be registered or to vote as a parliamentary, county or parochial elector or as a burgess".   Power is also given to establish, take over, or assist labour exchanges or employment registers.   The rates are made available—to the extent of a half-penny or, with the consent of the Local Government Board, a penny in the pound—for certain expenses incurred under the Act, *viz.* :—

(*a*) Establishment charges, including expenses incurred in respect of labour exchanges and employment registers and in the collection of information.

(*b*) The cost of emigration and migration.

(*c*) Expenditure in relation to the acquisition, with the consent of the Local Government Board, of land for the purposes of the Act.

For all other purposes—including actual provision of work—reliance must be placed on other sources of revenue, upon voluntary contributions or, since 1906, upon an Exchequer grant.   In the Bill as originally introduced the cost of providing temporary work on a farm colony was made chargeable on the rates but this was dropped in Committee.   Certain other very important conditions governing the provision of relief work—that the total weekly remuneration shall be "less than that which would under ordinary circumstances be earned by an unskilled labourer for a full week's work," and that such work should not "except with the consent of the Local Government Board be given to the same person in more than two successive years"—were also omitted from the Bill and subsequently inserted in the orders issued after it had passed.   At the same time the operation of the Act was limited to three years.

In London the organisation is more complicated, the functions of the provincial Distress Committees being divided between twenty-nine Distress Committees—one in each of the Metropolitan boroughs and including borough councillors, guardians, and persons experienced in the relief of distress—and a Central Body composed of sixty-two representatives from those Distress Committees, four from the London County Council, eight co-opted members and not more than eight persons nominated by the Local Government Board. The Distress Committees have the business of making themselves acquainted with the conditions of labour in their area and of receiving, inquiring into and discriminating between applications, but may not themselves provide work. They can only refer men to the Central Body and can in practice incur no expenditure without the consent of the latter. The Central Body has the business of co-ordinating the work of Distress Committees; assisting applicants by emigration, migration or temporary work; establishing, taking over or assisting labour exchanges or employment registers; levying the halfpenny rate, and collecting voluntary subscriptions.

Provision is made for the extension of the whole or part of this machinery to municipal boroughs or urban districts with populations under fifty thousand and to the country generally.[1]

The Act, it will be seen, represents in two distinct senses a convergence of existing agencies and methods for the relief of distress through want of employment. On the one hand, the authorities set up by it were formally composed of representatives of the Poor Law, of the municipalities, and of charity. The general aim of the Act was clearly to co-ordinate the action of these three types of agency, to prevent overlapping, and to secure appropriate treatment of every class of distress. On the other hand, the ideas underlying the Act, at least in regard to its main object of temporary assistance by relief work, were no less clearly drawn in varying proportions from these same three sources. From the Poor Law came the general principle that the condition of the assisted person should remain less eligible than that of the independent labourer; the total remuneration payable was limited accordingly. From the Poor Law also, through the Mansion House Fund of 1903-4, came the idea of the "colony" system, a plan practically indistinguishable from the modified workhouse test first adopted in Whitechapel.

[1] These provisions are not altogether happily conceived. In one town at least—that of Dalbeattie—it proved necessary, in order to secure the application of the Act, to appoint both a Distress Committee for the town and a Central Body composed of practically the same persons for the county in which the town was situated.

From the practice of municipal authorities came the idea of " relief work " itself, that is, of work upon which men should be employed at weekly wages without being under the obligation to earn them. The terms of the order 1071 of 1905 expressly exclude the idea of full competence. " Each person employed on the work shall perform every task allotted to him with diligence and shall throughout his employment attain a standard of efficiency such as, *with due regard to his ordinary calling or occupation and his age and physical ability,* may be properly required of him." [1] From the Mansion House Funds of the preceding fifty years came the conception of exceptional depression of trade as an emergency for spasmodic charitable action. The principal object, in a word, was not to do any new thing but to do slightly better what had been done before. The Poor Law principle of deterrence was to be retained in a milder form, without the stigma of disfranchisement, the breaking up of homes or the evil associations of the stoneyard. Municipal " relief work " was to be retained with a few improvements of detail—greater regularity and continuity of employment—but without any attempt to clear up the dangerous confusion of ideas implied in its very name. Permanent channels were to be constructed to guide the streams of charity to a better end than before, subject to discrimination of the deserving from the undeserving and without the danger of shirking administration in order to see that every shilling went in direct relief.

The Act was passed on 11th August, 1905, and began to come into effective operation during the following autumn.[2] There have been established under it in England and Wales altogether eighty-nine Provincial Distress Committees and twenty-nine Metropolitan Distress Committees together with the Central (Unemployed) Body for London. The total population of the districts covered in 1906 was 16,341,553. Three of the Committees—at Coventry, West Hartlepool, and Rhondda—have taken no action of any kind.[3] Others have been operative only in one or two out of the

---

[1] Regulations, Art. V. (1) (c).

[2] The following account of its operation is taken principally from the three returns published by the English Local Government Board on *Proceedings of Distress Committees* in the years ending 31st March, 1906, 1907, 1908, respectively, and from the annual reports published by the Central (Unemployed) Body and most of the Distress Committees. The *Preliminary Report of the Central (Unemployed) Body* up to 12th May, 1906, and its *Second Report* from 12th May, 1906, to 30th June, 1907, have been placed on sale with Messrs. P. S. King & Son, 2 Great Smith St., London, S.W. The working of the Distress Committees in Scotland is described in two Reports of the Local Government Board for Scotland, Cd. 3431 and Cd. 3830.

[3] Up to September, 1908. The two first of these, at least, have commenced operations since that date.

three winters following the passage of the Act. The majority, having opened offices for the registration of the unemployed, have each year, in varying degrees, investigated their cases and have endeavoured to assist a larger or smaller proportion of them, mainly by the provision of temporary relief work, but also by training for rural occupations, emigration, removal to other areas in England and Wales, and in other ways. There has, in these various activities, been expended under the Act, up to 31st March, 1908, a total sum of £541,146, exclusive of sums raised by way of loan for the purchase of farm colonies. About two-thirds of this is entered under the head of provision of work; the remainder was for administrative expenses, labour exchanges, emigration (between £80,000 and £90,000) and other purposes. London accounted for nearly 60 per cent. of the total expenditure. Of the total receipts during the same period about two-fifths came from the rates, two-fifths from the Exchequer, and one-fifth—almost entirely during the first two years—from voluntary contributions.[1]

The administration of the Act is best considered under three main headings: (1) number and type of applications registered; (2) methods of registration, investigation and selection; (3) methods of assistance.

TABLE XXVI.—DISTRESS COMMITTEES IN ENGLAND AND WALES.

1905-6.

	No. of Committees Taking Proceedings.	Estimated Population (1905).	Applications Received up to 31st March, 1906.	Applications Entertained.		Total of Columns 4 and 5 per 1,000 of Population.
				Applicants.	Dependants.	
	1.	2.	3.	4.	5.	6.
London .	29	4,684,794	39,728	23,838	69,038	20
Provinces	85	—	71,107	49,979	130,927	16
Total .	114	—	110,835	73,817	199,965	17

[1] All these figures refer to England and Wales alone. In Scotland there were established up to May, 1907, fourteen Distress Committees, covering a population of 1,856,520. In each of the first two years almost exactly the same number of applicants was registered, viz., 8,860. Operations in Scotland have not differed essentially from those in England and Wales. Cf. Distress Committees in Scotland, 1905-6 and 1906-7.

TABLE XXVI. (*continued*)—

1906-7.

	No. of Committees Taking Proceedings.	Estimated Population (1906).	Applications Received up to 31st March, 1907.	Applications Entertained.		Total of Columns 4 and 5 per 1,000 of Population.
				Applicants.	Dependants.	
	1.	2.	3.	4.	5.	6.
London .	29	4,721,217	28,181	13,070	37,656	11
Provinces	76	10,528,850	58,820	47,346	115,145	15
Total .	105	15,250,067	87,001	60,416	152,801	14

1907-8.

	No. of Committees Taking Proceedings.	Estimated Population (1907).	Applications Received up to 31st March, 1908.	Applications Entertained.		Total of Columns 4 and 5 per 1,000 of Population.
				Applicants.	Dependants.	
	1.	2.	3.	4.	5.	6.
London .	29	4,758,218	32,624	14,291	42,765	12
Provinces	69	10,153,161	57,433	40,322	108,206	15
Total .	98	14,911,379	90,057	54,613	150,971	14

The total number of applications, as shown, fell off considerably between the first two years and rose again slightly in the third. In respect, however, both of these movements and of the proportion of applicants to population, different districts varied greatly. The decrease between the first two years was very marked in London itself and in the manufacturing towns of Lancashire and the Midlands; the London suburbs showed an actual increase. The increase in the third year was also considerable in London, but was still more marked in some of the shipbuilding and engineering centres, such as Sunderland and South Shields. On the other hand, several important towns, such as Birkenhead, Bolton, Leeds, Leicester, Liverpool, Portsmouth, Southampton, showed decreases. The number of applicants per thousand of the population in 1907-8 varied in London from 2·2 in Hampstead and 3·2 in St. Marylebone to 12·8 in Bermondsey and 17·5 in Poplar; outside London it varied from 0·4 in Bury and Manchester to 27·0 in Edmonton and 34·7 in Sunderland.

The numbers registered, though considerable, fall very far

short of the estimates of distress sometimes made by applying to the whole industrial population the unemployed percentage obtained by the Labour Department of the Board of Trade from the returns of certain trade unions. The proportion of the total number of men applying to the total number of occupied males in the districts where applications were received is given as 2·4 per cent. in 1905-6, 1·9 per cent. in 1906-7, and 2·1 per cent. in 1907-8. The unemployed percentages for the corresponding periods, *i.e.*, the six months from October to March in each year, averaged 4·6, 4·3 and 5·9. The Distress Committee records, moreover, count all the men who applied at any time during the period of registration—generally six months or more—even though they may have been out of work only a small portion of it. The unemployed percentage gives the average number unemployed at the same time throughout the period; the number of separate individuals who became unemployed at some time or other in the period would probably be at least twice as great.

The ages of the applicants have been dealt with in a previous chapter.[1]

The occupations of the applicants whose cases were entertained are shown in the following table :—

TABLE XXVII.—OCCUPATIONS OF UNEMPLOYED APPLICANTS, 1907-8.

Occupations.	London.	Percentage of Total of all Occupations.	Total (London and Provinces).	Percentage of Total of all Occupations.
General or Casual Labour . .	6,129	42·9	29,104	53·3
Building Trades	3,792	26·5	10,569	19·4
Engineering, Shipbuilding and Metal Trades	1,002	7·0	4,719	8·6
Boot and Shoemaking . . .	207	1·5	1,236	2·3
Furnishing and Woodworking .	463	3·2	1,109	2·0
Food, Drink and Tobacco Trades	342	2·4	684	1·3
Domestic Service	329	2·3	1,109	2·0
Textile Trades	8	·1	192	0·4
Tailoring and Clothing . .	286	2·0	326	0·0
Printing, Bookbinding and other Paper Trades	130	·9	268	0·5
Other Occupations . . .	1,603	11·2	5,227	9·6

Here, again, the results each year are very much the same. In each year " general or casual labour " accounts for more than half of all the applicants whose cases were considered and building for another fifth. As between London and the provinces the table appears to show in the latter a larger percentage of

---

[1] Chapter VI., p. 117 *seq.*

"general or casual labour," and a smaller percentage of men from the building trades. In part this may represent a real difference of conditions. It is probably, however, to a much larger extent a difference less of substance than of form, men being entered as builders' labourers in London who would appear as labourers or general labourers elsewhere.[1]

The table, as it stands, throws some light upon the class of men applying to Distress Committees. It is, however, inadequate from several points of view. There is nothing to show what proportions of the men ascribed to various occupations are skilled and unskilled respectively. There can be little doubt again that some cases of applicants entered under the heading of other occupations belong more properly to the class of general or casual labour.[2] The true predominance of this type can only be shown by the much fuller analysis which will be made best in considering the methods of investigation and selection adopted by Distress Committees.

The registration of applicants for assistance has taken place on a form prescribed by the Local Government Board.[3] This form or "Record Paper" as originally drawn up consisted of eighteen paragraphs, involving fifty distinct questions and requiring, if the work was carefully done, some twenty to thirty minutes for each case. The present "Record Paper" is only slightly shorter, including questions not only as to the age, occupation, earnings, last and other employers of the applicant during the past twelve months, but also as to his residence, rent, number of rooms, family, present income from all sources and other matters. The Local Government Board has prescribed also certain rules of investigation and selection, of which the following are the most important :—

"(I) . . . :—

"(iii.) An officer, a member, or any other person authorised by the Distress Committee to receive and investigate applications, shall visit and make inquiries at the home of the applicant for the verification of the statements of the applicant, and shall also, where the circumstances so require, with the same object, communicate with a Board of Guardians or with any other body,

---

[1] The difference noticed is peculiar to the year 1907-8. In 1906-7 London by itself had practically the same percentages of general and casual labour (51·1) and building (19·7) as had the whole country (52·5 and 17·2). Seeing how closely connected the two groups are in practice, it may fairly be assumed that the difference between the London figures for 1906-7 and 1907-8 represents mainly a change of classification.

[2] *Proceedings of Distress Committees,* 1907-8, p. 5.

[3] Regulations : Schedule. Amended by No. 6 of 1906.

authority, or person able to supply useful information with respect to the applicant.

"(iv.) In the case of each applicant the Distress Committee shall call for and consider the Record Paper which, in pursuance of these Regulations, has been provided and is in use in relation to the case, and shall satisfy themselves—

"(a) That the applicant is of good character;

"(b) That he has not from any source sufficient means to maintain himself and his dependants;

"(c) That he is not, and has not been during the period of twelve months immediately preceding the date of the application, in receipt of relief (other than medical relief) at the cost of the poor rate;[1]

"(d) That he has not in two successive periods of twelve months immediately preceding the date of the application, been employed on work provided by a Central Body, or on work towards the provision of which a Central Body have contributed; and

"(e) That his case is in other respects one which the Distress Committee, with due observance of the requirements of the Act, may properly entertain.

"(2) The case of an applicant as to whom the Distress Committee have satisfied themselves—

"(a) That in the past he has been regularly employed, has resided in their area for a continuous period of twelve months at the least, and has been well-conducted and thrifty;

"(b) That at the time of his application he has a wife, child, or other dependant;

"(c) That, in respect of age and physical ability, he is qualified for such work as the Distress Committee may be able to obtain; and also

"(d) That, in other respects, the case of the applicant is one which may be entertained in accordance with the conditions prescribed by this Regulation,

shall be treated by the Distress Committee in preference to cases of a different character."[2]

The carrying out of these regulations has necessarily involved a good deal of administrative machinery. The amount of this can best be judged from the fact that during the period from 10th November, 1906, to 30th June, 1907, the establish-

---

[1] This and the next clause have now been withdrawn (Nov., 1908).
[2] The Regulations (Organisation for Unemployed), Art. II. (1, 2), (Statutory Rules and Orders, 1905, 1071).

ment charges of the Metropolitan Distress Committees and Central Body amounted to £11,090, averaging 7s. 4d. per case registered, 9s. 6d. per case investigated, £3 2s. 6d. per case assisted by the provision of work.[1]

Spite of the Local Government Board regulations the extent and quality of the investigations have varied very greatly from one committee to another and the principles of selection have varied yet more. In London, for instance, during the winter 1905-6 the percentage of applicants adjudged after inquiry to be ineligible or unsuitable for treatment under the Act ranged from one in Battersea and five in Hackney to thirty-three in Poplar and seventy-five in Stepney. Outside London contrasts no less pointed can be found—between Manchester which in 1906-7 rejected none of its applications and Salford which rejected 38 per cent., between York which in the same year entertained all its applications but five and Bradford which entertained 150 out of 1,292.[2] It is hardly necessary to argue at length that very little significance attaches to the published statistics as to the proportions of applicants found qualified or not qualified for assistance under the Act. There can be very little doubt that in judging of eligibility and still more in giving preferential treatment Distress Committees, after excluding manifest idlers, have very commonly looked less to the industrial status of the applicant than to the urgency of the apparent distress and the number of dependent children.

The plain fact is that the Committees have had to deal principally with a type of distress to which the industrial criteria

---

[1] This includes a certain amount of central establishment charges properly attributable to heads other than the provision of work, e.g., to emigration. It does not, however, include the office expenditure at the colonies and other works, and, in that it deals only with just over half the year, it amounts to a considerable understatement. From 30th June, 1907, to the reopening of the registers at the end of the following October very few additional men were registered or assisted, but a considerable establishment had of course to be maintained. Direct expenditure on emigration or employment exchanges is excluded from the expenditure here considered.

[2] This want of co-operation is well illustrated by the fact that the Central Body, in apportioning the benefits of its fund between different parts of London, has never felt able to base its decision on the numbers and recorded quality of the applicants registered by Distress Committees, but has gone upon inferences from the census figures and other general indications of poverty.

These contrasts are not confined to England and Wales. " The Board in their last report drew attention to the apparent difference in the methods adopted by the various Distress Committees in determining whether an applicant was qualified for assistance. That the standard of eligibility varies considerably is suggested by the following figures. Taking those Distress Committees having more than 500 applicants it will be observed that in Edinburgh all the applicants were considered qualified for assistance; in Greenock 96·31 per cent.; in Dundee 96·06 per cent.; in Aberdeen 81·09 per cent.; whereas in Glasgow only 39·19 per cent. were passed as qualified " (*Distress Committees in Scotland*, 1906-7).

suggested by the Act and regulations were inapplicable. Investigation of the past employments of casual labourers has proved a hopeless and unprofitable task.[1] Discrimination between men all substantially on the same level of irregularity has appeared obviously futile. This is put plainly by some of the Metropolitan Committees. "The committee, in selecting applicants, has not drawn a sharp distinction between those usually in regular work but temporarily unable to find employment, and those in a normal condition of chronic casual employment. The latter class constitute the great majority of those registered" (Fulham). "With the exception of known bad characters and those disqualified by certain regulations the majority of applicants have been much of the same class, with almost the identical claims for preferential treatment. . . . Owing to the large number of casual workers who made application for relief work or emigration it was impossible to carry out to the letter general instruction C. B. 19th October, 1906" (Poplar). "The vast majority of the applicants to the committee are men who have been unable to maintain their families decently for some years past" (Finsbury). "The first class of applicants contemplated by the Act, that is men usually in regular employment but temporarily out of work through some dislocation of trade, are practically non-existent so far as this borough is concerned" (Bermondsey).[2]

The Stepney Committee out of 1,421 applicants, as the result of most elaborate inquiries, found only eighty-four with a recent record of regular employment and seventy-nine with a recent record of fairly regular employment lost without fault on their side. Having given or offered work to all these and to a certain number of special cases the committee were able to offer work to seventy-four others classified as having "a fair or at any rate some record of casual employment" or as having been "dismissed from their employment for slight faults". It should be added that single men without dependants and men not in urgent need were excluded from consideration along with those showing serious defects of character, physique, etc.

As a result there is no apparent difference of industrial status

---

[1] In 1905-6 the Stepney Committee, spite of repeated efforts, failed in 9½ per cent. of its cases to get any verifiable reference of employment at all. The Hammersmith Committee record, as the special difficulty experienced in their work, "the inability of many deserving applicants to remember the addresses of employers and the date of their employment".

[2] These particular quotations appear in the *Second Report of the Central (Unemployed) Body*, p. 18. They might be multiplied indefinitely by reference to the reports of Distress Committees. *Cf.* those for Chelsea, City of London, Lambeth, Hackney, Paddington, Stepney.

between the whole body of men applying and the men selected for assistance. Of the London applicants in each of the years 1905-6 and 1906-7, 80 per cent. are accounted for by the groups "Building" and "Locomotion, Transport and Labour". These include a certain number of skilled men and a much smaller number from grades of industry in which regular employment is not uncommon. The overwhelming majority are men whose employment is both casual and low-skilled or unskilled—who are builders' labourers, or dock labourers, or general labourers pure and simple. Of the 20 per cent. falling outside these groups many are described as labourers of various kinds, and many more are unclassified or ranked as potmen, window-cleaners, night-watchmen and the like.

The records of those actually assisted or recommended for assistance by these Distress Committees show a picture indistinguishable from this. In 1905-6 and 1906-7, as also in 1904-5 under Mr. Long's scheme, 80 per cent. or more of the men selected from crowds of applicants with a searching preference for those formerly in regular employment are in fact drawn from the same two typically casual groups of occupations—from "Building" and from "Locomotion, Transport and Labour". The same point is put in another way by saying that 71·3 per cent. of them are men reckoning their wages by the hour, while only 28·7 per cent. are sufficiently established to reckon by the week. Among the latter are 11·7 per cent. with wages under 25s., 10·9 per cent. with wages between 25s. and 30s., and 7 per cent. with 30s. or more. Apart from the exceptional cases introduced by the discharges from Woolwich Arsenal the men at weekly wages among those recommended for assistance are less than four for every 100 applicants.

It is possible that the predominance of the casual labourer is more marked in London than elsewhere. It is certain that such difference as exists is one of degree rather than of kind, or even one of form rather than of substance. In some districts this predominance may be modified by special circumstances, e.g., the introduction of machinery in the boot and shoe trade, as within London itself it has, during the past few years, been modified at Woolwich by the discharges from the Arsenal. Yet "investigation of the cases registered showed that, while there even in the centre of the boot and shoe trade at Leicester were a considerable number of men unemployed through no fault of their own, many of them were general (and unskilled) labourers, and about a third of the whole number may be classed as persons who had earned a precarious living by doing odd jobs, casual labourers, aged and inefficients ".[1] Almost everywhere the broad facts are the same, and are such as to make natural the remark of the Local Government Board with regard to Nottingham : " It is doubtful if the class of men who form the major portion of the applicants to the Distress Committee are much affected by the better or worse conditions of labour ".

The work of the authorities established by the Unemployed Workmen Act has fallen into several distinct branches—the provision of temporary relief work, assisted emigration or migration, and the establishment of labour exchanges. The predominant branch and the only one to be considered here in any detail is the first of these. The conditions governing it are set out in Article V. of the regulations already quoted :—

"(a) That the work shall have for its object a purpose of actual and substantial utility;

"(b) That each person employed on the work shall throughout his employment be subject to effectual supervision;

"(c) That each person employed on the work shall perform every task allotted to him with diligence, and shall throughout his employment attain a standard of efficiency such as, with due regard to his ordinary calling or occupation, and his age and physical ability, may properly be required of him;

"(d) That each person employed on the work shall, as far as possible, be afforded continuous occupation thereon day by day, with such absence only as may be needed to facilitate his search for regular work or other means of supporting himself; . . .

"(f) That when the person employed has no wife, child or other dependant, or has a wife, child, or other dependant, but is not employed on temporary work necessitating, during a period or a succession of periods comprising in each case four consecutive days at the least, his continuous absence from home, the total remuneration of that person for any given period of continuous work shall be less than that which would under ordinary circumstances be earned by an unskilled labourer for continuous work during the same period in the place in which the work was provided;

"(g) That when the person employed has a wife, child, or other dependant, and the remuneration of that person is subject to deduction for the purpose of defraying the cost of the lodging and maintenance of the wife, child or other dependant, the total remuneration of the said person for any given period of continu-

---

[1] *Proceedings of Distress Committees*, 1905-6. *Cf.* also Sunderland, Bootle, Kingston-upon-Hull, Grimsby, all of which call attention to the chronic poverty of the casual labourer.

ous work shall be less than that which would under ordinary circumstances be earned by an unskilled labourer for continuous work during the same period in the place at which the wife, child, or other dependant is lodged and maintained." [1]

The substance of these conditions is that men should be engaged upon undertakings of actual and substantial utility, should be made to work continuously and with such efficiency as can properly be required of them, and should earn less than would be earned by an unskilled labourer. Another clause lays it down that the work provided to any one individual shall not, except with the consent of the Local Government Board, last more than sixteen weeks. [2]

The great bulk of the work provided has been of a rough labouring description, *e.g.*, road making and repairing, sewerage construction, street cleansing and preparing of pleasure grounds and open spaces, though in some cases a certain amount of more skilled work, *e.g.*, painting and building, was available. A few committees, however—at Southampton, Leicester, Oldham, Manchester, Hull and West Ham—leased or bought land for experiments in cultivation. The Central Body for London, besides setting up the Hollesley Bay Farm Colony, to be described later, carried out schemes of sea-walling at Fambridge and Osea Island and constructed a railway siding at Garden City.

There has been a great and on the whole an increasing difficulty in finding work which should be of actual and substantial utility without being work which would in any case have been done at the cost of the rates. In some cases at least work has been done by hand which in the ordinary course would have been done by machines. [3] In others the work has been " anticipated," that is to say, done by unemployed labour a few months before it would ordinarily have been done by competent labour. [4] In others there appears to have been a direct diversion of employment from the channels of industry into those of relief.

The conditions of pay and employment have varied greatly. In London the bulk of the men have received wages at the full standard rate per hour but have worked less than the ordinary

---

[1] Regulations, Art. V. (i.).   [2] *Ibid.*, (iv.).

[3] *E.g.*, at Liverpool (*Distress Committee Report*, 1906-7, p. 5) and at Norwich (*Distress Committee Report*, 1906-7, p. 7). *Cf.* also *Report of London Unemployed Fund*, 1904-5, p. 52, for another instance.

[4] The Central Body for London during the first three years of its existence formally refused to contribute to the cost of merely " anticipated " public work, on the ground that this meant interfering with the ordinary labour market. In October, 1908, however, it felt constrained, by the need of finding openings for employment, to abandon this principle.

number of hours each week, so as to bring their earnings below what they would have got on full time. A good many men, however—especially during the first two years—have been employed at distances from London on the "colony" system introduced by the Mansion House Committee of 1903-4; that is to say, the Central Body has provided board, lodging and pocket money for the men at the works and weekly allowances proportionate to the size of the family at home. Alike on the ordinary works and at the working colonies the principle of continuity has been applied very thoroughly; that is to say, any man once engaged was allowed to remain, subject to good behaviour, for the full sixteen weeks permitted by the regulations. Outside London, payment at the ordinary rates per hour appears to have been the general though not universal rule, but the work has seldom been so continuous. A good many Distress Committees have, in spite of the regulations, retained the old plan of distributing the work in scanty doles over the largest possible number of men.

In one respect almost all the works have been alike—that there has been on them no attempt to apply the ordinary standards of competence and to dismiss men, as they would be dismissed in real life, simply because their output was insufficient. As a result, the cost of the work done has uniformly exceeded its value. In London, for instance, the Central Body and the semi-official committee which preceded it, spent over £58,000 on works subsequently valued at less than £13,500.[1] There can be little doubt that in some instances the valuation, being made by the officers of the authority which was to pay the ascertained value, was distinctly on the low side, nor can all the difference be attributed to the unemployed men themselves. The difference itself is such as to leave ample proof of inefficiency after all allowances have been made. In three cases where the total value of the work is not in dispute, the average value of each week's work done by the men works out at from 8s. 9d. to 10s. 3d. In regard to quite a distinct set of works the following estimates are given by the bailiff of the royal parks in which the men were employed :—

(1) Willingness to work, 70 per cent.

(2) Fitness for the work on which employed, 50 per cent.

(3) Improvement during the progress of the work, 45 per cent.

(4) Value of the work done as compared with average labour, 50 per cent.[2]

[1] *Morning Post*, 31st January, 1908, "Work for the Unemployed". The works referred to were for the most part straightforward ground labouring. The experiment of sea-walling at Fambridge, which in fact proved the most expensive, is excluded.

[2] Minutes of Central Body, 15th May, 1908.

Estimates made by the Central Body's own superintendent of works put the value of the unemployed labour somewhat higher—at 60 per cent. in the London County Council parks generally and up to 90 per cent. in one or two other cases.[1]

Results such as these are by no means peculiar to London. In Portsmouth the cost of unemployed labour is put at three times that of ordinary labour.[2] In Birmingham work carried out by the Distress Committee for one of the other committees of the Corporation cost £1,882 as against an allotment of £640.[3] In Glasgow £8,950 was spent in wages alone and £9,977 altogether on work valued at £3,045.[4] In Govan the value of the work done in 1906-7 varied from 33·3 to 66·6 per cent. of the wages paid.[5]

These are no doubt picked instances. The point that they illustrate is a perfectly general one. Distress Committees, even where the standard wage is paid, do not get and do not expect to get the standard output from the men for whom they provide work. In other words, they act as relief authorities not as employers.

What, then, has been the cost of the relief system thus established, and what have been its apparent effects upon distress through want of employment?

It is, unfortunately, impossible to give any estimate of the average cost of each week's relief work for the country as a whole because no record is to hand of the total number of weeks of employment provided. The following figures refer to London alone. During the first two complete years of its existence (ending 2nd Nov., 1907) the Central Body provided about 50,000[6] weeks of relief work for men in and about London and 36,000 on the colony system. The gross expenditure on these works was £124,000, against which may be set recoupments of about £10,000,[7] while establishment charges accounted for another £27,000. During the third year of its existence—from 2nd November, 1907, to 3rd October, 1908—the Central Body provided 32,003 weeks of relief work in and about London and 10,798 at Hollesley Bay at a gross cost for the works directly of £67,709 and for establishment charges of £13,676. The

[1] *Proceedings of Distress Committees*, 1907-8, p. 18.   [2] *Ibid.*, p. 29.
[3] *Report of Birmingham Distress Committee*, 1906-7, p. 9.
[4] *Distress Committees in Scotland*, 1906-7, p. 21.
[5] *Ibid.*, p. 22.
[6] This is the mean of two not altogether reconcilable estimates.
[7] This is exclusive of Hollesley Bay for which the accounts are somewhat complicated. As, however, the farm and garden account of the estate showed from December, 1905, to September, 1907, a trading loss of £2,644, a sum exceeding the estimated value of the unemployed labour put into it (£1,154) and nearly equalling this value plus the increased value of the estate itself (£1,933), the recoupment appears negligible.

recoupments amounted to £10,944. On this basis the net cost
of relief per week, *i.e.*, the cost over and above the recoverable
value of the work done, works out at practically the same in
each period, namely, just under £1 13s. per family.[1] The experience of the Central Body does not support the suggestion
that the provision of relief work is to be preferred to direct money
gifts on the ground of cheapness.[2]

In considering the effect of the assistance given it is well to
recall the objects of this assistance as defined by the Unemployed
Workmen Act itself. Temporary work, according to section 1
sub-section (5), is to be provided in such manner as is best calculated to put the recipient " in a position to obtain regular work
or other means of supporting himself ". It is clear that the degree
to which the work provided has visibly had this desired effect is
very small indeed. On this point an interesting light is thrown
by the record of repeated applications in London.

TABLE XXVIII.—REPEATED APPLICATIONS—LONDON.

Total Applicants, 1905-6		31,534
Re-applied to same Distress Committee, 1906-7 . .		7,160
	Being . .	22·7 per cent.
Applicants Assisted, 1905-6		6,392
Re-applied to same Distress Committee, 1906-7 . .		2,720
	Being . .	42·6 per cent.
Applicants not Assisted, 1905-6		25,142
Re-applied to same Distress Committee, 1906-7 . .		4,540
	Being . .	18·1 per cent.

The foregoing table, taken from the *Second Report of the Central
Body*,[3] shows not only that the percentage of re-applications

[1] A small portion of the establishment charges should in strictness be excluded
as having reference to other branches of activity, *e.g.*, emigration. As regards the first
period, however, this deduction would be more than counterbalanced by the addition
which should properly be made for the interest on capital expenditure (about £47,000)
in connection with Hollesley Bay. As regards the last period it is—owing to the
diminished emigration—of small importance. The figures given omit the expenditure
on women's workrooms. This totalled nearly £13,000 in the three years.

[2] During the first year of its existence the Central Body in order to give £35,000
to the men and their families, spent £13,000 on auxiliary purposes (tools, supervision,
etc.) and £12,000 on establishment charges. If the total recoupment received on
these works—£6,000—be set against the auxiliary expenses, there remains, as the net
cost of assisting by work rather than by money gifts, £7,000 auxiliary and an uncertain
proportion of the £12,000 administrative expenditure. This calculation deals with
relief work pure and simple, *i.e.*, is exclusive of Hollesley Bay, where there has naturally
been special expenditure.

[3] Pages 18 and 90. For several reasons these percentages must be regarded as a
minimum rather than a full record. First, being compiled for each Distress Committee separately, they take no account of those who, having been assisted in one
borough the first year, move into another and apply there the next year. Second, they

among men assisted is very considerable (42·6) but that it is very much higher than the percentage among those not assisted. That of course is only what might have been expected. Those who got something one year naturally tried again the next.[1] Those who got nothing would give up applying and make shift without assistance.[2] The fact that the result is only what might be expected does not affect it as a ground for judging the value of temporary relief work. The work as given, instead of showing any signs of enabling men to obtain regular work or other means of supporting themselves, has as its main visible consequence the effect of making it more than twice as likely that they will ask for similar assistance next year.

With one exception none of the provincial Distress Committees appear to have made any similar investigation. The exception is West Ham, where of those not assisted in 1905-6 42·1 per cent. and of those assisted 67·6 per cent. re-applied in 1906-7. The following table, however, is suggestive.[3]

TABLE XXIX.—MEN ASSISTED AND MEN APPLYING.

	No. of Applicants 1905-6.	Percentage of these Applicants provided with Work.	No. of Applicants 1906-7.	Applicants per 1,000 of Population 1906-7.	Change per Cent. of No. in 1905-6.
29 Metropolitan Distress Committees . . .	39,728	23·8	28,181	6·0	− 29·2
10 Distress Committees in Outer London [4] .	13,931	55·2	15,322	12·1	+ 10·0
All other Distress Committees . . .	57,176	34·0	43,498	4·7	− 23·9
	110,835	37·3	87,001	5·7	− 21·5

make, except in a few cases, no allowance for men who could not be expected to re-apply because they had emigrated. Third, all the by no means negligible possibilities of error are on the side of under-statement. One or two districts show quite remarkable contrasts, e.g., Bermondsey with 76·4 per cent. of the assisted men re-applying as against 16·4 of the unassisted; Chelsea with 71·6 per cent. as against 18·8 per cent.; Camberwell with 63·0 per cent. as against 20·0 per cent.

[1] "It was found that a large number of applicants considered that having once worked for the unemployed, they were entitled to do so whenever such work was available" (Greenwich Report, 1906-7).

[2] It is quite certain from the statistics of pauperism that these unassisted unemployed did not in the years under review to any large extent have recourse to the Poor Law.

[3] Sociological Review, Jan., 1908.

[4] Croydon (5·4), West Ham (16·2), East Ham (12·0), Hornsey (2·9), Edmonton (22·0), Erith (8·1), Leyton (7·4), Tottenham (20·2), Walthamstow (10·6), Willesden (11·2). The bracketed figures give the number of applicants per 1,000 of the population.

The proportion of assisted applicants was, owing no doubt to the practice of giving larger spells of work to each individual, lowest in London; next came the provincial committees; last the suburban committees. This is also the order of the three groups in comparing the 1906-7 applications with those for 1905-6. The group which assisted fewest men in 1905-6 experienced the greatest falling off of applications in 1906-7; the group which spread the benefits of employment relief most widely in 1905-6 shows an actual increase of applications in 1906-7.

More striking, however, than any statistics is the consensus of opinion, on the part of all those actually engaged in the work, as to the failure of sixteen weeks of temporary assistance to confer any permanent benefit. "The committee is of opinion that those assisted are undoubtedly benefited in being able to tide over a time when in the ordinary course of things there would be a period of unemployment. It is a more open question, however, as to any permanent benefit, and the proportion of those given work in 1905-6 who have again applied is rather discouraging. Whilst, however, the casual labourer exists—and the bulk of those registering under the Act belong to this class and to that of the men whose trade is seasonal—it is not easy to see how this can be obviated" (Lambeth Report, 1906-7). "The committee gladly recognises that many families have been helped over a severe time of distress by the work found for the men by the Central Body. We are obliged, however, to repeat the statement of last year, viz., that as the distress in this district arises from a permanent excess of unskilled labour over the demand, the men on completing their terms of employment found their local labour a drug in the market, just as it was before" (Bermondsey Report, 1906-7). In one district—Stepney—the general impression has been put regularly to the test of subsequent investigation into the position of those assisted. In July, 1906, 46 per cent. of those who had been assisted during the previous winter were still without work and in most cases without any definite prospects of obtaining it, 23 per cent. were in casual work, 31 per cent. were in "fairly permanent work" (a description including jobs of a few weeks or for the summer only). "Relief work has not been effective in preventing a general downward tendency. In 1906 42 men could be classed as regular as against 58 who were casual; in 1907 for the same men the figures are 29 regular and 71 casual. Relief work has not been 'educational'. It has not stimulated determination and good industrial habit. Neither apparently has it made it easier for men to find work. Nothing is more remarkable in the after-history of cases assisted by the committee, than the length of time men have remained out of employment after their discharge from relief work. Their prolonged absence from home has apparently resulted in a loss of touch with employers" (Stepney Report, 1906-7).

It remains only to conclude this description of the proceedings of Distress Committees by noticing two or three activities of a type distinct from the provision of temporary relief work.[1]

The first is the attempt to remove men altogether from the urban labour market by training for new occupations on the land. The most noteworthy example of this is the farm colony established by the London Unemployed Fund in February, 1905, at Hollesley Bay in Suffolk. This colony, which has now been purchased by the Central Body for London, comprises a total area of 1,300 acres, 600 being arable, 250 heath, and the residue pasture, woodland, etc., and has living and sleeping accommodation for nearly 350 persons. At its commencement three main objects were laid down :—

" 1. The provision of special work for periods of exceptional distress.

" 2. The provision of more continuous work for men who are not only in exceptional need of work, but who either have already lived upon the land, or show a marked aptitude for country life.

" 3. The establishment of suitable men and families in agricultural or other rural industry, in various forms, e.g. :—

(a) Ordinary farm situations, preferably in districts where wages and conditions are good and where a movement

---

[1] The work already described has dealt only with men. The Central Body for London, however, has also given employment in tailoring and the manufacture of underclothing to a fair number of women. Up to 30th June, 1907, 308 women out of 802 applying received periods of work varying from sixteen weeks to twenty-four. From 1st July, 1907, to 3rd October, 1908, 434 women received periods of work averaging 16·62 ; the number of applicants up to April of this year was 1,666. The rate of pay has been from 10s. to 17s. a week according to the number of dependent children, plus a daily dinner of the value of 6d. and fares to and from the workroom in excess of 2d. a day. A woman with two children would thus receive, apart from the fares, the value of 17s. a week, a sum of course considerably in excess of what any but the most skilled workers would earn in any woman's industry in London. As a matter of fact many of the women assisted have earned only a few shillings a week for years past and some have not earned at all, having been reduced to distress not by their own loss of employment but by the unemployment, sickness or death of their husbands. Great difficulties have been experienced in getting rid of the goods made. An attempt has been made to give the women training as well as relief, but not, apparently, with any greater success than among the men in enabling those helped to obtain other employment after leaving the workrooms. The proportion of the applicants who were assisted appears to have been considerably higher amongst the women than amongst the men.

towards small holdings, allotments, market gardening, co-operative farming, etc., is developing.

(*b*) Market gardening or ordinary gardener's situations.

(*c*) The establishing of small holdings in the neighbourhood of the colony or elsewhere (either with or without some intervening period of service elsewhere under '*a*' or '*b*'). This will be the hope held out to the picked men on the colony.

(*d*) Emigration."

In the administration of the colony emphasis has been more and more laid on the third object and particularly on the establishment of men on co-operative small holdings. The Central Body has not, however, been able itself to establish small holdings, the Local Government Board having ruled that this was a purpose outside the scope of the Unemployed Workmen Act, and great difficulties have been experienced in placing the men elsewhere. "The settlement of men in ordinary farm situations, paragraph 3 (*a*), or in market gardening or ordinary gardener's situations, paragraph 3 (*b*), has proved in most cases impossible. Consequently, the only considerable outlet for the men trained at Hollesley Bay has been that mentioned in paragraph 3 (*d*), *i.e.*, emigration."[1]

As to emigration, it appears from the returns of the Local Government Board that 3,386 men, representing altogether with their dependants over 10,000[2] persons, were emigrated, principally to Canada, during the three years under review. The total expenditure met in this case, from the rates, has been £80,000. It does not appear that emigration as conducted by the Distress Committees deserves as a whole either the criticism that it amounts to a dumping of undesirables upon the Colonies, or the opposite criticism that it amounts to exporting the best manhood of the nation. Neither the one extreme nor the other has been strongly represented among the men selected, and in many cases the claim seems fairly made out that people who were finding difficulty in keeping above the surface in this country became readily self-supporting in the more buoyant labour market of Canada. Since the spring of the present year, however, the industrial depression on the North American continent

[1] *Second Report of Central Body*, p. 38. A table in this report shows that between 11th December, 1905, when the colony was taken over by the Central Body and 30th September, 1907, 1,597 men passed through it receiving an average of 12·34 weeks' work and training per man. The net cost during the same period is put at £31,068, or £1 11s. 6d. per man and family per week.
[2] The total number of persons entering Canada during the same period is estimated at 600,000. (Mr. Walter Hazell in *The Times*, 29th October, 1908.)

has very largely closed the main outlet for emigration from this country.

The establishment of Labour Exchanges, though included in the powers of the Provincial Distress Committees and of the Central Body, has lain somewhat outside their main scope. A good many Distress Committees have endeavoured to exercise their powers in this direction, but this has not always meant more than inviting private employers to engage men off the ordinary register of unemployed applicants for assistance.[1] In London special interest has been taken in the matter, leading to the establishment, during the latter part of 1906, of a system of Employment Exchanges working on a uniform plan throughout nearly the whole of the metropolitan area, and connected by a Central Exchange or clearing house. These Exchanges are under the direct control of the Central Body as a branch of its work in officers, staff and management altogether distinct from and additional to the organisation of Metropolitan Distress Committees for the selection of unemployed applicants for relief work. They register men only for the business requirements of ordinary employers and concern themselves, therefore, only with the industrial qualifications of men and not also with the size of their families, distress, thrift or other sources of income. In accordance with a decision of the Local Government Board they are precluded from enforcing upon those who use them any specified rate of wages or conditions of employment. In regard to strikes and lock-outs the instructions issued to superintendents declare the express intention of the Central Body to prevent the unfair use of the Exchanges to prejudice the conduct of trade disputes and forbid the superintendents to take action as to either vacancies created or men unemployed owing to a dispute, without the distinct orders of the Central Body. In practice the Central Body has always taken the line of refusing to notify such vacancies to applicants. The legality of this rule and practice are still under consideration by the Local Government Board. The expenditure of the Central Body on the Metropolitan Exchanges was £8,379 for the year ending 2nd November, 1907, during the first two months of which only a part of the system was open,

---

[1] The Distress Committees at Birmingham, Manchester, Newcastle-on-Tyne, Plymouth, Reading, Salford, Warrington, and West Ham are mentioned as having provided separate registers and in some cases separate staff and offices for labour bureau purposes (*Proceedings of Distress Committees*, 1907-8, p. 8). " In several cases," it is stated, " the operations of the Committees in this direction met with some measure of success." The Board of Trade now receives and summarises each month in the *Labour Gazette* returns from nineteen Provincial Labour Bureaux in addition to those for London. Most of these are under Distress Committees.

and £9,035 for the period from 2nd November, 1907, to 3rd October, 1908.

The activity of the Exchanges since their establishment, and with greater detail, during the year ending June, 1908, is shown in the following tables.

TABLE XXX.—METROPOLITAN EMPLOYMENT EXCHANGES, 1906-9.

	Situations Offered.	Situations Filled.	Percentage Filled of Situations Offered.	Placed through Central Exchange.	No. of Applications.	Mean No. on Register throughout Period.
1906, Aug.-Dec. . .	5,974	3,626	60·7	480	34,071	—
1907, Jan.-June .	13,975	8,903	63·7	1,298	47,115	4,674
July-Dec. .	11,955	8,332	69·7	1,145	} 129,760	6,109
1908, Jan.-June .	16,001	11,696	73·1	2,747		7,134
July-Dec. .	17,119	13,321	77·8	2,839	—	8,276
1909, Jan.-June .	17,593	13,278	75·5	3,248	—	8,901

TABLE XXXI.—METROPOLITAN EMPLOYMENT EXCHANGES.
(Year ended 30th June, 1908.)

Occupation.	Applications Registered.[1]	Persons Registered.	Situations Offered.[2]	Situations Filled.
Building	18,402	11,539	2,437	2,241
Woodworking . .	4,786	3,127	945	611
Metals	11,555	7,688	1,380	1,097
Printing	2,224	1,611	369	227
Dress	1,631	1,116	401	208
Food and Tobacco . .	2,908	2,120	500	364
Glass and Leather . .	1,148	706	217	135
Transport and General .	36,217	27,602	4,629	4,027
Other Occupations . .	9,489	7,002	2,365	1,750
Total Men . .	88,360	62,511	13,243	10,660
Boys . .	15,656	11,712	4,440	3,504
Women . .	19,201	14,999	7,155	3,982
Girls . .	6,543	5,128	3,118	1,882
Grand Total . .	129,760	94,350	27,956	20,028

Persons placed in districts other than their own through Central Exchange: Males, 2,785 ; Females, 1,107—Total, 3,892.

Transport and general labour provide 41·0 per cent. of all the registrations of men, building 20·8 per cent. and the metal trades 13·1 per cent. The corresponding proportions amongst the situations filled are 37·8, 21·0 and 10·3. 36·5 per cent. of the situations filled are described as " skilled," 21·7 per cent. as for " skilled labour," and 41·7 per cent. as "unskilled". The percentage of situations filled among those offered is for men 80·5, boys 78·9, women, 55·7, and girls 60·3.

[1] Including re-registrations but not renewals.
[2] Situations for indoor domestic servants are not registered.

There has thus, spite of the unfavourable conditions of the labour market, been a fairly steady if gradual growth in the volume of work done—particularly noticeable being the developed use of the Central Exchange for enabling men to find situations outside their immediate neighbourhood. The third column—showing the steadily increasing proportion of situations filled amongst those offered—is another direct indication of improved efficiency. There has been development also in ways not appearing in statistical record. The type of men registering has, beyond question, improved as the character of the Exchanges came to be known. The co-operation of existing associations of workmen has been secured in a good many places, there being an increasing tendency for trade union branches to keep their vacant books at the Exchanges. Though, therefore, the Metropolitan Employment Exchanges are still extremely modest institutions and hampered by many difficulties, some inevitable, some unnecessary, they have succeeded in obtaining at least a footing in the industrial world and appear to be strengthening it from day to day.

THE UNEMPLOYED WORKMEN ACT—CONCLUSIONS.

The Unemployed Workmen Act is a composite measure. It has suggested or made possible a good many distinct experiments such as rate-aided emigration, farm colonies, and labour exchanges. Its main object was undoubtedly the direct assistance of the unemployed by the old method of temporary relief work. By its policy and its effect in this field it must stand or fall.

The policy of the Act in regard to temporary relief work is unmistakable. Its authors had clearly before them the fact of cyclical fluctuation as shown by the trade union returns—the unemployed percentage rising from its minimum of two or three to seven or more and returning to its minimum again. They aimed at providing a temporary refuge for the 5 per cent. or so of men thus exceptionally displaced ; at catching competent and industrious men as they fell out on one side of the depression and landing them—still competent and industrious because preserved from want and the Poor Law—upon firm ground on the other side. They viewed trade depression, in fact, as a chasm through which men might slip through to the abyss of chronic pauperism below and they wished to construct across it a bridge of temporary relief. All that it seemed necessary to secure was that the bridge should be constructed only where a real chasm could be seen to exist ; that it should be used only by men hitherto competent and industrious ; that, being costly, it should not be used too long or unnecessarily; that it should yet be such as to carry men well over to the other side. In fact it has not proved possible to carry out any part of this policy. The construction of the bridge has not been limited to times of exceptional depression nor its use to persons exceptionally unemployed; it has not been made less attractive than ordinary labour, and it has not been made long enough to land men upon the firm ground of regular work once more. These four main points, as they are illustrated in the Act and regulations and as they have worked out in practice, will be taken in order.

First, temporary assistance by relief work was to be provided only in times of exceptional trade depression. The administration of the Act on this side was deliberately made dependent upon the raising of voluntary contributions from the charitable public. If there was not sufficient distress to call forth voluntary contributions, nothing could be done. If there was distress, the charitable public might subscribe more freely, knowing both that adequate machinery was in existence to turn their money to the best advantage and that, since the cost of this machinery fell on the rates, all that was subscribed would go in direct relief. During the first year the Act was in fact financed in this way. A public appeal on behalf of the unemployed, made by the Queen on 13th November, 1905, resulted in the subscription of over £150,000, of which the bulk—close on £125,000—was distributed to the authorities established under the Unemployed Workmen Act. It was clear that such an appeal and such a result would not be repeated. In 1906 Parliament put a sum of £200,000 at the disposal of the Local Government Board to supplement voluntary contributions, and this precedent has been followed in 1907 and 1908. Practically voluntary contributions have disappeared altogether and their place has been taken by grants from the Exchequer.

Second, this temporary assistance was to be given only to men honestly desirous of obtaining work but temporarily unable to do so from exceptional causes over which they had no control (Unemployed Workmen Act, sec. 1, sub-sec. 3), and preferentially to men who in the past had been regularly employed and had been well conducted and thrifty [Regulations, Art. II. (iv.)(2)]. It is certain, from the description already given, that a very small proportion of the applicants have been men able to produce any record of regular employment within recent years, or any definite evidence of thrift. It may fairly be questioned whether any large proportion, either of those who have applied or of those who have been assisted, fall strictly within either the

words or the spirit of section 1, sub-section 3.   The great bulk
have been labourers or low-skilled irregular workmen with whom
distress through want of employment was neither temporary nor
exceptional.   They have stood so much upon the same level of
chronic poverty that investigation and discrimination have often
appeared obviously futile.   They have been so little removed
from the most destitute classes of all that Distress Committees
have been constantly in revolt against the further regulation
which was meant to distinguish the Unemployed Workmen Act
from the Poor Law by making receipt of relief under the latter
a disqualification for work under the former.[1]   This distinction
is during the present winter to be removed.

Third, any recourse to temporary assistance under the Act
was to be made unattractive by the rule that the " total remuneration . . . for any given period of continuous work should
be less than that which would under ordinary circumstances be
earned by an unskilled labourer for continuous work " [Regula-
tions, Art. V. (i) (f) (g)], and prolonged or repeated recourse was
to be made impossible by the rules that the work should not,
except with the consent of the Local Government Board, be
continued for more than sixteen weeks [Art. V. (iv.)] or be
given in more than two successive periods of twelve months
[Art. III. (iv.) (d)].

The first of these rules has been construed as permitting the
payment of full trade union rates per hour so long as the average number of hours per day or of days per week was reduced,
and this plan has been followed very generally in regard to men
employed for wages.   The regulation itself has thus been observed ; the Poor Law principle clearly intended to be imported
by the regulation—that assistance should be less attractive than
independence—has been disregarded altogether.   The majority
of those assisted, being men accustomed to casual earning, have
obtained from Distress Committees either a regularity of employment and weekly income far above their average, or a succession
of casual jobs exactly corresponding to their tastes.   In neither
case have they had to reach the ordinary standard of competence.
On the " colony " works to which the regulation also formally
applies, an attempt has been made to secure the object of the
regulation in another way.   Removal from London to unfamiliar
surroundings and the absence of money wages would, it was
hoped, act as a deterrent.   Work on this system is undoubtedly
unattractive at first sight, *i.e.*, it is refused without trial by men
who would go readily to relief work in the London parks.   Upon

[1] Regulations, Art. II. iv. (c).

those who do try it the effect wears off rapidly and often disappears.[1] The surroundings become familiar instead of unfamiliar. The food and accommodation are necessarily on a high scale: a public body which pays in kind cannot afford to risk grumbling and is really bound to give the men better than what they would provide for themselves. The men are not, in practice, deprived of the use of money and through it of alcohol. A certain proportion of the family allowance constantly finds its way to the husband at the colony.

The difficulty here is not superficial but essential. No doubt relief works might be rendered less attractive than they are if the policy of paying a fair day's wage without demanding anything like a fair day's work were abandoned. No doubt the administration of most "colonies" might be made more bracing and less philanthropic. The root of the difficulty would remain : that no scale of relief can be made less attractive than the ordinary life of the casual labourer without being made ludicrously inadequate. The root of the difficulty lies in the inconceivably bad conditions of employment and earning in the lowest ranks of independent industry.

The rules limiting the period and the frequency of temporary assistance have, like the Poor Law disqualification, failed to commend themselves to Distress Committees having practical experience of the problem. There has been visible a distinct tendency, at least in London, to multiply reasons for obtaining special exemptions from the sixteen weeks' limit—at Hollesley Bay in order to allow for training ; at Fambridge in order to keep on men who had become familiar with the work ; in the women's workrooms because quite obviously the women had nothing to turn to when temporary assistance should come to an end. The other rule—that against assistance in more than two successive years—has been the subject of continual protest. It too is this winter to be repealed.

Fourth, the temporary assistance was to be such as the Distress Committees thought best calculated to put the recipients " in a position to obtain regular work or other means of supporting themselves". The contrast between this pious hope and the reality is too glaring to need emphasis. The bulk of the applicants to Distress Committees have not for years been in regular employment; they could not, therefore, hope to re-

---

[1] " Whilst men who are new to the committee invariably show a preference for non-colony work, old hands who 'know the ropes' usually ask to be sent to a colony. 'They could do' with the 'regular grub' and the work is 'all right'" (Stepney Report, 1906-7).

cover it after tiding over a period of exceptional slackness upon relief work.   From all sides come complaints of the inadequacy even of the full sixteen weeks of assistance to secure permanent benefit.

At every point, therefore, the provision of relief work under the Unemployed Workmen Act has broken down, or at least has broken away from its original intentions.   The Act started as a carefully guarded experiment in dealing with a specific emergency—exceptional trade depression—by assistance outside the Poor Law.   One by one all the guards and restrictions have been swept away, or have become forgotten.   The assistance, for the most part, has been given neither out of the resources contemplated by the Act (voluntary subscriptions), nor to the persons contemplated by the Act (workmen temporarily and exceptionally distressed), nor in substantial accordance with the principles of the Act as interpreted by the Local Government Board (that assistance should be less eligible than independence), nor so as to achieve the purpose defined by the Act (restoration to regular employment).   All this has happened, not through defects in the machinery of the Act—though there are obvious defects—nor through perversity or carelessness in its administrators, but simply and inevitably because the Act itself was founded upon an incomplete diagnosis of the problem.   Its authors correctly appreciated the fact of cyclical fluctuation in the demand for labour.   They took no account of the irregularity of employment which in good times and bad times alike is a normal feature throughout so large a part of industry.   Yet this is the one fact which by itself makes the whole policy of the Act unworkable.   The characteristic and conspicuous result of trade depression is, not to reduce to destitution men formerly in regular employment (though no doubt this also happens to some extent), but to precipitate into distress men who are always on its verge.   For poverty of this type the sixteen weeks of relief work is obviously no remedy.   To men of this type a reduction of earnings brought about by shortening the hours is no deterrent.   The problem as conceived by the authors of the Unemployed Workmen Act was that of a definite breach in employment hitherto continuous—a disaster analogous to those caused by famine or war—a chasm over which a bridge might be thrown from firm ground to firm ground.   The actual problem has none of this convenient definiteness of outline.   The passage of the unemployed percentage from two to seven and back again to two does not mean the extrusion of 5,000 specific individuals out of every 100,000 in one year and their re-absorption the year after.   It means, for practical purposes, the gradual and barely perceptible worsening, through three or four years, of conditions of life which are always bad, and their equally gradual and imperceptible return, in the next three or four years, to being not worse than usual. The analogy with wars and famines does not hold. The metaphor of the chasm is premature. In the lowest grades of industry— those which most feel the weight of exceptional depressions— there is no firm ground at all. There are quicksands to be drained before there can be any talk of building bridges.

The Unemployed Workmen Act has, however, not merely failed from the point of view of its authors. The difficulties experienced in its working have a far wider application.

First, they reflect on the whole policy of relief work. It has been observed by a German authority[1] that in England the natural tendency is to regard relief works with favour, because they once had some measure of success—in the cotton famine— while in France the memory of the *ateliers nationaux* of 1848 makes them the last thing to be tried. It is perhaps not out of place to suggest that England has now some reason to regard relief works from the French standpoint. The experiences of the past few winters, though by no means comparable to those of the *ateliers nationaux*, are certainly not encouraging. Two advantages generally claimed for relief by way of work are, first, that it is cheaper, and, second, that it is less demoralising than any other method of relief. The operations of Distress Committees have certainly not erred on the side of cheapness; the auxiliary expenses—on materials, etc.—have not infrequently exceeded the value of the work when done; the net cost of relief in London has been three times the allowance which the best organised trade unions think necessary for their unemployed members. There may, again, be demoralisation in receiving a grant of 10s. to 15s. a week in idleness. Is there not risk of even worse demoralisation in being paid 20s. a week as wages for exertion worth 15s. or 10s. or 5s.? The objection noted by the Select Committee of 1896 to the labour yard applies to every form of work in which no standard of competence is applied: the standard of accomplishment gets fixed by the unwilling worker. "Relief work" has proved not a happy but a disastrous combination. It generally implies something that degrades the name of work and disregards the principles of relief.

Second, the difficulties experienced throw doubts upon the practicability under present conditions of any form of public assistance outside the Poor Law. The agencies described in the

[1] Dr. Schwander, the head of the Poor Law Administration in Strassburg.

present chapter have all been so many attempts to give effect to the principle of the "ineligibility" of assistance while avoiding the harshnesses of the Poor Law. All these attempts with their various devices—a shorter working week, irregularity of relief, rustication under the colony system—have substantially failed to make assistance less eligible than independence—simply because of the bad conditions of independence. A nation cannot treat its dependants less badly than it treats its citizens. Only when it has humanised industrial conditions can it safely humanise the Poor Law.

Third, the difficulties reflect fatally upon the sufficiency of any policy of relief whatever.

The operations of Distress Committees may be criticised from many points of view—on the ground of the expense; as involving interference with independent labour; as weakening the incentive to self-help and individual or collective thrift; as demoralising men by accustoming them to earn only half their wages. There is weight in all these criticisms. The main criticism and the one emphasised by all the history of the past is that these operations are altogether inadequate and misdirected. The Unemployed Workmen Act has done a good deal in the way of collecting information. It has done a little to co-ordinate existing agencies and improve in minor points the administration of special relief. It has not made any appreciable impression upon the problem. Its main service has been to demonstrate beyond question its own essential inadequacy and the inadequacy of all measures which, like itself, leave industrial disorganisation untouched and deal only with the resultant human suffering.

CHAPTER IX.

PRINCIPLES OF FUTURE POLICY.

I. The Organised Fluidity of Labour.

Summary of preceding discussion : Unemployment a matter of fluctuations and changes in the demand for labour. Its treatment a matter of business organisation—to provide reserve power for fluctuations and to ease transitions. Criticism of proposals for State employment as a reservoir of labour for ordinary employment.

The labour market : Different treatment of labour and other commodities to-day. The hawking of labour. Wastefulness of this plan shown in two ways, (a) delay of production or (b) maintenance of excessive reserves of labour. Abolition of this plan by organisation of labour market the first step in the treatment of unemployment. De-casualisation. All men not regularly employed under one firm to be engaged only from an Exchange in touch with many firms. Concentration of work on some, displacing of others. Theoretical and practical answers to objection on ground of this displacement. Organisation of labour market as an increase of industrial efficiency. Subsidiary use of emigration, afforestation, etc. Analogies between casual employment and casual relief, and between under-employment and under-payment. Principle clear ; practical application varied. De-casualisation only special form of general labour market organisation. Organised and therefore limited fluidity of labour a protection to those in each trade or district.

Labour Exchanges and other factors in unemployment : Seasonal fluctuations. Changes of industrial structure. The problem of age. The problem of youth ; relation between Labour Exchanges and industrial training. The unemployable. The Labour Exchange test of unemployment. An alternative to deterrence.

Conclusions : The demand of economists for mobility of labour. Ignorance a principal barrier to movement. The two functions of the modern workman. Organisation of the search for work increases working efficiency. Need for this on any view of relations between population and industry. The cardinal principle of social policy—to make youth adventurous and keep old age secure.

THE main factors in the problem of unemployment have now been named and analysed. The principal remedies of the past have been described, the extent and character of their failure noted. It remains to define, if possible, a policy which may afford more hope of success in the future. This is the attempt to be made in the present chapter. It must be premised by two cautions. First, the policy is one for the permanent and preventive treatment of the problem ; it is not concerned with what may here and now be the best available palliatives for present distress. Second it can only be given in outline; the practical details of administration and machinery must be left to be filled in by practice.

The definition of a general policy must be premised further by some attempt to get a general view of the problem, and to sum up under a few main aspects the whole results of the first seven chapters. Briefly the gist of these chapters may be put as follows.[1]

Unemployment is a question not of the scale of industry but of its organisation, not of the volume of the demand for labour but of its changes and fluctuations. The changes are of several types; trades decay or are revolutionised by new machines. Through these changes particular parts of the labour supply get displaced. Unemployment arises through their difficulty in getting re-absorbed. The fluctuations, also, are of several types : some co-extensive with the economic life of the nation ; some peculiar to certain trades ; some purely local or individual. To meet these fluctuations—cyclical, seasonal and casual—there are required reserves of labour power. Unemployment arises as the idleness of these reserves between the epochs when they are called into action. The solution of the problem of unemployment must consist, therefore, partly in smoothing industrial transitions, partly in diminishing the extent of the reserves required for fluctuation or their intervals of idleness, partly, when this plan can go no further, in seeing that the men of the reserve are properly maintained both in action and out of it. The problem is essentially one of business organisation, of meeting without distress the changes and fluctuations without which industry is not and probably could not be carried on. It is not a problem of increasing the mere scale of industry. It is not a problem of securing a general balance between the growth of the demand for labour and the growth of the supply—for this general balance is already secured by economic forces—but one of perfecting the adjustment in detail. This conclusion rules out a number of current proposals as possessing no direct bearing upon unemployment, whatever may be their value in other ways.

One of these is the creation of new industries. New industries have been created and old ones expanded at an unparalleled rate during the past fifty years, without appreciably affecting the problem of unemployment. Under these circumstances there is no need to discuss either the possibility or the means of giving a fresh stimulus to industrial growth. Any such proposals have to be attacked and defended on ground alien to the present inquiry. They may or may not bring increased prosperity, and with it a rising demand for labour. All history shows that a rising demand for labour is no cure for unemployment.

[1] See now Preface to 1930 Edition, p. xi.

Still less is the cure to be found in a falling supply or diminished efficiency of labour. The restriction of births, the removal of population to other countries, and the permanent reduction of working hours are all alike irrelevant to the main problem. They have all indeed been tried on a considerable scale without putting an end to unemployment. Since 1876 the birth-rate has fallen from 36·3 to 26·3 per thousand. The number of native emigrants from the United Kingdom during the same period has been close on four millions. The constant tendency of working hours is downward. Here again are movements and proposals as to which much may be said from points of view other than the present one. In regard to unemployment their only influence is an indirect one and their use can be at best but subsidiary.

The paradox has to be faced—that the creation or provision of work is the one thing that is no remedy for unemployment. It may palliate immediate distress. It may increase general prosperity. It may cause unemployment for a while to be forgotten. It does not banish disorganisation from the State.

It may, however, be said that if the problem is that of maintaining reserves of labour to meet fluctuations, then the simplest and surest solution is to be found just through one of the proposals now ruled out as irrelevant. Let new industries—afforestation, land reclamation and many more—be created, not indeed for their own sakes but as reservoirs of labour, as the sources of an elastic demand able to expand and contract instantaneously as the demand in the rest of the labour market contracts and expands. Let there stand ready, for every workman to turn to in moments of idleness, some useful work to be done for the community, some employment by which he may live till he can return to his usual avocation once more. This or something like it appears to be the aim of the Unemployed Workmen Bill of 1908—the "Right to Work" Bill of the Labour Party.[1] Might not this or something like it be reached by increasing the powers and making inexhaustible the resources of the authorities already established by the Unemployed Workmen Act of 1905?

The questions of principle involved in the assertion of a "Right to Work" would in themselves furnish matter for a very interesting discussion.[2] Here it must suffice to consider in its

[1] The Bill is intended to establish "local unemployment authorities" with an obligation to provide work for every man within their area who cannot get work at the standard rate of wages.

[2] The main objection to such proposals on the side of principle is that they ignore the personal factor in unemployment. Though differences of personal character have

practical aspects alone the proposal to provide through State employment a reservoir of labour for industrial fluctuations. Three main criticisms at once suggest themselves.

First, such employment would inevitably become to a very large extent relief employment, upon which the men were paid wages in excess of their earnings. Strictly speaking, it is impossible by any exercise of State authority to guarantee useful work to all and sundry of the unemployed, if " useful " be taken to imply work whose product shall be worth more than it cost to produce. The value of the product in relation to its cost depends upon matters some of which are beyond the control of the State, *e.g.*, the competence and industry of the workman or the demand of consumers. To provide work which should be even approximately within the capacity of all the unemployed—a heterogeneous collection with an undue proportion of inferior men—would be an impossibility; there is in fact hardly anywhere any such thing as purely unskilled work, *i.e.*, work in which competence does not tell. If the State employment were conducted on business lines, it would fail to act as a reservoir of labour for any but the particular trades requiring the same abilities. If it were not conducted on business lines, it would involve a loss, not a profit, to the State, and, a much more important point, would almost certainly demoralise the men given work by lowering their standards of industry, and paying them money that they had not earned. There can be no doubt that in practice the State employment would prove very costly. No business can be conducted with a constantly shifting body of men—the leavings of other businesses dropping in and out as occasion calls.

Second, it would in practice prove impossible to make any system of State employment act as a reservoir for the ordinary labour market. The men might flow in; they would not naturally flow out again unless the State employment was made in some way less attractive than ordinary employment. Yet this is just what it could not be made without being made either degrading or inadequate for a living. The State employment might in a time of depression draw off a large part of the dock labourers

probably little effect in increasing the volume of unemployment, they do very commonly determine its incidence. To give the individual a State guarantee against unemployment is therefore undoubtedly to condone inferiority and to weaken the incentive to industry. It is quite another matter to endeavour to regularise employment—by State action or otherwise. Devotion to the principle of struggle for existence need not go the length of desiring that the struggle should be intensified every few years by cyclical depression simply for the sake of weeding out the unfit; though there is something to be said even for this (see p. 64 as to cyclical fluctuation). In any case the State's undoubted responsibility in regard to unemployment must be treated as part of its general responsibility for public welfare and not as a duty to the individual.

13 *

in London; what chance is there that these labourers would ever want to return to the docks? Yet, if they did not return, their half-places in industry would simply remain to attract and to be filled by fresh-comers. The State would have a new industry; under-employment would continue. There is indeed the possibility that, if State employment continued to drain off the casual labourers, the employers, in order to get men at all, would have to improve their conditions of employment.[1] This is no doubt an idea contributing to the form of the " Right to Work " Bill. If the State cannot persuade or directly compel employers to regularise their work, may it not indirectly put pressure on them to do so by competing for the labour supply? It can only be said that in practice the competition would cost more money and do more incidental harm—the State continually draining off into the enervating environment of relief works the men demoralised by the employers—than can be contemplated with any equanimity. For every reason direct reform would be preferable. This leads naturally to the last and most important criticism.

Third, to set up a reservoir of labour at the public cost is simply to perpetuate industrial disorganisation. It is possible, as has just been suggested, that State employment would within certain limits put pressure upon private firms to amend their own methods of employment. This would happen, however, only in so far as the State employment ceased absolutely to be a reservoir of labour for the ordinary market and became instead a competing market with higher standards; in this way industrial reforms might be brought about indirectly and expensively. In so far, however, as State employment in any way served the object for which it is here supposed to be started—that of affording a universal refuge for men in involuntary idleness—it would be a support to the methods making that idleness inevitable. This is the main objection. This is the final criticism not only upon the present plan but on all others which either deal merely with individuals or merely add a fresh industry to those already existing—that they are not thorough enough. They accept the industrial system as it stands, and tack something on outside. They leave untouched the economic causes of unemployment.

The creation of new State industries may be a good thing. The provision of a public refuge from destitution is a necessary thing, and has been recognised as such in this country for three centuries and more. The two things—public business and public relief—

---

[1] When the South African War suddenly drew off thousands of reservists, one of the London Dock Companies found itself compelled to increase its regular staff in order to be sure of having men.

cannot be combined. Neither singly nor in attempted combination can they dispose of the need for attacking the causes of unemployment. The first step in this attack must be the organisation of the labour market.

THE LABOUR MARKET.

Every one has seen in a window at times the notice, "Boy Wanted". No one, it is safe to say, has ever seen in a window the notice, "Boots Wanted". Yet people in fact want to buy boots as much or at least as often as they want to buy the labour of boys. The contrast just noticed indicates a deep-reaching difference of industrial methods.

In regard to all ordinary commodities the rule holds that there are more or less definite places to which the would-be purchaser goes or sends, and at which the seller is to be found. Moreover, it is a commonplace of economic observation that the business of bringing commodities to market, *i.e.*, of putting would-be buyer and seller into communication, has become, and is continually becoming, the subject of more and more specialised attention and organisation. For every commodity important and well-known market places!get established and concentrate in large proportions all the business done. The characteristic term for such a market-place is "Exchange". According to its industrial character every important town has various types of Exchange—for corn, or wool, or stocks, or hops, or iron, or meat. The development of these institutions springs directly from the needs and the convenience of business.

In regard to labour the position remains fundamentally different. The prevailing method of obtaining employment is still that of personal application at the works. In other words, the prevailing method of selling labour is to hawk it from door to door. The purchaser's activity is at most to put up a notice that he does or does not want hands, *i.e.*, that hawkers of labour need or need not apply. So much may be said of general knowledge. On closer examination two points become clear. First, there do exist within defined and limited spheres organised methods for bringing would-be employers and employed together. Second, even apart from formal organisation, there grow up almost inevitably in each trade customs and informal relations guiding the movements of workmen and directing the inquiries of employers. The hawking of labour is seldom without method. The newcomer to a trade or district is at a definite though by no means decisive disadvantage as compared with a man who " knows the ropes ".

These formal and informal methods of seeking employment in Great Britain are described elsewhere.[1] It will be seen that such organisation as exists is very limited in scope and as a rule quite elementary. The methods described do less to meet the need than to show it. They do not so much modify as illustrate the general statement that a matter which cries out for organisation, and which in regard to every other commodity meets with an increasing measure of organisation, is in regard to labour still left to ill-informed individual action. There alone the cumbersome, antiquated and wasteful custom of hawking still holds the field. The abolition of this custom—in other words, the deliberate organisation of the labour market—is the first step in the permanent solution of the problem of unemployment.

The organisation of the labour market means simply that there shall be known centres or offices or Exchanges, to which employers shall send or go when they want workpeople, to which workpeople shall go when they want employment. When for any trade this has been carried so far that all employers in it send to the same Exchange or one of a series of connected Exchanges for every man they require, and take no man through other avenues at all, then the labour market for that one trade may be said to be completely organised. When for any industrial district this has been carried so far that all the trades in it use the same Exchange or all the separate trade Exchanges are connected, then the labour market for that district may be said to be completely organised. When all over the United Kingdom and for every trade in it there is a connected system of Labour Exchanges so that no man thinks of applying anywhere else either for workpeople or employment and would not get either if he did, then the labour market for the United Kingdom may be said to be completely organised. Then, or indeed with advantage some time before then, attention can be turned to organising the labour market for the British Empire or the world.

These, of course, are Utopian dreams. There are some good reasons to show that perfect organisation of the labour market is impracticable. There are many bad reasons which will no doubt stand effectively in its way. The perfect organisation just described is, however, the ideal and must be the aim. Every step towards it, everything done to concentrate the demand for labour at known connected centres, will be an advance towards the State's mastery of unemployment. Every point of deficiency

[1] Appendix to Part I, pp. 239-250.

from the ideal involves a less complete realisation of one or other of the several objects for which this organisation is required.

What then are the objects of organising the labour market? What good purpose can be served by any or the most complete system of Labour Exchanges?

In reply to that question it may be observed in the first place, and as following directly from what has gone before, that all the general probabilities are in favour of the usefulness and need of such a system. The spread of information is a matter that cries out for organised rather than for individual action. The need for markets and the wastefulness of not having them are recognised in every other branch of economic life. The point for comment is not that Labour Exchanges should be advocated now but that they should never have been seriously tried in this business country before.

The explanation of this point is indeed a perfectly simple one. The wastefulness of hawking as an industrial method has not been perceived in regard to labour as much as in regard to other things, because the waste appears in two distinct forms— one obvious, one indirect.

The waste is direct and obvious when an employer has to wait for men though just the men he wants are out of work and looking for it somewhere else. Production is checked or delayed. The employer loses for the time the use of his capital, simply because hawking has not brought labour to his door at the right moment. The men lose earning time which they cannot replace, simply because they have sought their market in the wrong direction. Such cases undoubtedly occur. Indeed during times of prosperity it is quite usual for employers to be short at least of skilled men, though, as the union returns show, even in such times there are always men in all the principal trades standing idle somewhere or other. It may safely be prophesied that practical experience would show economic waste of this direct type to be far commoner than is popularly supposed. Even the limited operations of the Metropolitan Employment Exchanges include a considerable amount of transference of unemployed men from one part of London to meet unsatisfied demands for labour in another. In every such case it must be supposed that without the machinery of the Exchanges there would be an appreciable delay and checking of production.

It will, however, be urged that waste in this form, though it does occur, is relatively rare. Very few occupations—or at least very few of those coming under the notice of authorities dealing

with the unemployed question—ever attain the happy condition
in which employers have to wait for men.   In the unskilled or
low-skilled occupations, an employer can normally get at his own
gates or just outside them as many men as he wants whenever
he wants them.   What is there for the organisation of the labour
market to do under such conditions?   The answer is that the
economic waste involved in such conditions is just as real as and
far more harmful than in the cases considered before.   The employer does not have to wait—simply because an additional
amount of waiting is done by the men.   If without any attempt
at organisation each employer can find just by his gates all the
men he wants to meet all the fluctuations of his business however
irregular, this can only mean that men are always waiting at all
points to be taken on; it can only mean that each employer or
each small district is contriving to maintain a separate reserve of
labour.   In the illustration given in an earlier chapter, each of the
ten wharves might in practice find the whole hundred individuals
sometimes required by it always in attendance at its own gates,
or might even deliberately secure this attendance by a judicious
rotation of employment.   The work of the ten wharves would
then be spread between a thousand individuals; the work of each
wharf would be carried on without a moment's delay for labour.
Yet clearly such a system would be extraordinarily wasteful.
Never less than two hundred men of the thousand would be
standing idle at one time.[1]   If the wharves were amalgamated or,
if without that, they could use a common list of men, exactly
the same mass and flow of work could be done by eight hundred
instead of a thousand.

It has already been shown that this abstract illustration
corresponds to facts.   The business of independent employers of
the same class of labour does fluctuate independently; one firm
does grow busy while another grows slack; one requires twenty
men this week and not next week, while another requires twenty
men next week and not this week.   The two employers acting
independently may employ entirely distinct sets of men, distributing the two weeks of work over forty men each idle half their time;
each indeed, by taking men on at his own gates, will tend to have
a separate string of men in attendance.   The two employers acting together—using a common list of casuals—may concentrate
their work on the same set of men, twenty getting full employment instead of forty being half-employed.   It is this principle

---

[1] On the supposition made in the former chapter that the wharves were not all
busy together so that the number employed by all on one and the same day never
exceeded eight hundred.

of the common list that has now to be considered. The first object of the organisation of the labour market is to make possible a policy of " de-casualisation ".

The policy of de-casualisation is simply this—that all the irregular men for each group of similar employers should be taken on from a common centre or Exchange, and that this Exchange should so far as possible concentrate employment upon the smallest number that will suffice for the work of the group as a whole; that successive jobs under different employers should, so far as possible, be made to go in succession to the same individual, instead of being spread over several men each idle half or more than half his time. In such a policy is to be found the remedy, and the only remedy, for the most urgent part of the unemployed problem—the chronic poverty of the casual labourer. To see this it is only necessary to consider shortly the working of other remedies. The provision of temporary relief, whether in the form of work under the Unemployed Workmen Act or otherwise, is useless, because there is no further shore of good employment upon which the casual will land when the relief is over and worse than useless, because it increases his immobility. The removal of the under-employed, whether to Canada or to afforestation schemes or to permanent national workshops, may benefit the men removed, but leaves their half-places in industry to attract and to be filled by fresh-comers. If the making or finding of new openings for labour would solve the unemployed problem, why is it unsolved to-day? Private enterprise is perpetually making new openings for labour; that is the one thing which it does really well. The eight hours' day may be a good thing for other reasons. As a device for absorbing the unemployed it is out of place. To halve the working hours of an employer who needs two hundred men this week and only one hundred next week, is to leave him with a demand for four hundred men this week and two hundred next. Thrift, sobriety, adaptability, initiative are good things for many reasons. They are all apt to be too good for the casual labourer. An individual here and there may rise superior to overwhelming odds. The mass is inevitably demoralised by a system of employment which panders to every bad instinct and makes every effort at good hard and useless; which by turning livelihood into a gamble goes far to take from idleness, slovenliness and irresponsibility their punishment and from assiduity its reward. The casual labourer is the rock upon which all hopes of thrift or self-help or trade union organisation, no less than all schemes of public assistance, are shattered. When it is asked what is to be done for the casual class, the answer must be that the only thing to be done either for or with the casual class is to abolish it, and that the only way of abolishing it is to abolish the demand which it serves.

The chronic under-employment of the casual labourer is no inexplicable or exceptional phenomenon. It is the resultant of normal demand and supply—of the need of employers for irregular men and the readiness of men to do irregular work. It cannot be cured by any assistance of individuals. It can be cured, theoretically, either by cutting off the supply or by cutting off the demand, that is to say, either by making all men unwilling to do irregular work or by making it impossible for them to get it to do. Practically, however, the first plan is purely Utopian. The sources of supply to the casual labour market include every form of human weakness and misfortune and every point of industrial stress. Something may indeed be done to affect particular sources—to divert boys from uneducative to educative employments, to mitigate the hardships of industrial transitions, to lessen the pressure of competition in the towns by making the country less repellent to the countryman. All this will leave abundant sources untouched. The closing of all ways by which men fall into misfortune must be the last step, not one of the first steps, in the destruction of poverty. Moreover, if it were possible to cut off or seriously to diminish the supply of men to the casual labour market, the stoppage of the industries now dependent on their services could, in that case, be avoided only by a reformation in the conditions of employment, making it no longer casual or degraded. Diminution of the supply of casual labour would be at best but an indirect way of forcing a modification of the employers' demand for casual labour. It is, therefore, to the modification of their demand, in other words, to its " de-casualisation," that attention must ultimately be directed. About this there is nothing Utopian except the solid improvement it would effect in social conditions.

It is an empirical fact, demonstrable and repeatedly demonstrated by simple observation, that the demands of separate employers of similar labour fluctuate independently ; men pass from one to another. It is a commonplace of business organisation that a firm with many departments may use a man, now in one department, now in another, and, if it absorbs other undertakings or adds new departments, may continually go further in regularising the employment while proportionately reducing the number of those employed. The reorganisation of employment at the London Docks, described in an earlier chapter,[1] was nothing

[1] Pp. 88-90.

more nor less than the application of a Labour Exchange or common list of men to the work of all the separate departments. Its effect, as stated, was to raise the proportion of regular labour from 20 to 80 per cent. A Labour Exchange or common taking-on place for many separate undertakings may do for them what in a single firm is done for different departments. It may become the headquarters of a compact mobile reserve of labour, replacing and by its mobility covering the same ground as the large reserve which drifts slowly and blindly about the streets to-day.[1] The larger and more varied the area of employment covered by an Exchange, the more completely will it be able to regularise the work of this reserve, because the more nearly will the independent fluctuations of many businesses neutralise one another to yield a steady average. There are, of course, limits to the movement of labour—limits of space and limits of skill. Men cannot be transferred in a morning from London to Glasgow or from carpentering to bricklaying. Obstacles of space would in part yield to every improvement of organisation; would in part have to be accepted as ultimate.[2] As to the requirement of special skill the important point has to be noted that, while it limits the range of movement, it also makes a large range of movement unnecessary. It is harder to regularise skilled employment than unskilled, but the skilled workman, because of his higher wages, can bear greater irregularity without falling into distress. The casual employment of the barrister or the doctor, the artist or the journalist, does not as a rule involve chronic distress. Moreover, it is not necessary to argue that all irregularity can be abolished by simply organising the movement of labour, or that nothing will remain to be done later. It is sufficient to say that each step in this direction is a step in advance. Wherever any two wharfingers, by using a common list of casuals, reduce the number of individuals between whom their work is shared from fifty to forty-nine, they have to that extent reduced under-employment.

[1] This involves no interference with the employer's control of his staff. Men who are of sufficient value to him to be required regularly will be employed regularly; the others will be chosen from among men at the Exchange instead of from a crowd of applicants at each factory gates. In one sense no doubt there will be a limitation of choice; the whole object of de-casualisation is to diminish the excessive number of individuals trying to live by each trade. In another and far more important sense there will be a better choice; the best men at any moment available will all be found concentrated at the Exchange. In practice, of course, no employer concerns himself about the individualities of his really casual men.

[2] The Labour Exchange affects only one obstacle to movement of labour—namely, ignorance of where to go. It neither removes nor ignores other obstacles: least of all does it, as some of its critics have urged, ignore the fact that "workmen have homes". Its aim is to give the workman a choice, wherever possible, between starving at home and getting work away from home. At present lack of information leaves him in nine cases out of ten without this choice.

They have, however, left one man without any work at all. The time is ripe to consider the obvious criticism upon de-casualisation that, in making work more regular for some, it throws others out altogether. The fact is undeniable. The avowed object of de-casualisation is to replace every thousand half-employed men by five hundred fully-employed men. What of the *dis*-placed five hundred? To this question there are two answers; one theoretical and important, the other practical and subordinate.

The theoretical answer takes the form of a dilemma—either the men displaced will find work elsewhere or they will not. If they do find work elsewhere the difficulty is at an end; a thousand half-employed men, say dock labourers, have been turned into five hundred fully-employed dock labourers and five hundred men employed elsewhere. If the men do not, and cannot, in spite of all Labour Exchanges, find work elsewhere, this must be either because there is no work for them to do—*i.e.*, because the country is already more full of men than it can hold—or because they are inefficient.[1] On either of these last suppositions, de-casualisation becomes even more necessary than before. If the country has already more men than it can hold, *i.e.*, is over-populated, then it is a matter of crying urgency to replace every thousand half-employed men (all potential fathers of unnecessary families) by five hundred fully-employed men, and to leave for the others no choice but emigration. If the men are inefficient, *i.e.*, capable of working only occasionally and not often enough for a living, then they cannot safely be left at large to bring up in semi-starvation fresh generations of inefficients.

The foregoing argument no doubt sounds formal. Yet it is only the formal way of justifying the general principle which few would care to controvert—that on any view of society, one man well-fed and capable is preferable to two on half rations. Where, therefore, a system of employment is such as to keep two men perpetually half-employed though one regular man would serve, that system must in the public interests be changed. The change, beyond question, involves risk of hardship to individuals—just as does any other increase of industrial efficiency, any new machine and any improvement of business organisation. Its possible influence in displacing labour must be judged by the same canons. By raising the efficiency of each workman—each unit in production—it enables the same amount to be produced by fewer units. The change may threaten hardship to individuals,

---

[1] There is, of course, also the possibility that the country may be passing through a general depression of trade. This, however, being a temporary phenomenon, does not affect the argument. Of course a time of exceptional depression is just the wrong time at which to attempt de-casualisation.

and the case of these individuals must be borne in mind in making the change. The change itself cannot for their sakes be abandoned, nor is the difficulty caused by them anything more than that of a temporary surplus. To compare the case for de-casualisation to the case for new machines is indeed to omit one important qualification. The benefit of a new machine, going as a rule first to the employer, filters down gradually to the workmen and the general community; even the workmen retained may not get higher wages at all but may profit only later as consumers through the lowering of prices. The benefit of de-casualisation goes first to the workmen retained—in the substitution of regular for casual earning—and to the community thus relieved of a source of demoralisation; it filters through only in the second place to the employer through the improved quality of labour.[1]

The practical answer to the supposed objection is to be found in the manner of applying de-casualisation in practice. In the first place, the change could and should be made in a time of good trade rather than in one of bad trade, so as to give those displaced the chance of at once finding other situations; the Labour Exchanges which as centres of de-casualisation brought about the displacement would be the best means of hastening re-absorption elsewhere. In the second place, the change could and should be made gradually. There need be no visions of a vast unmanageable surplus thrown by de-casualisation upon the hands of the community at a moment's notice. De-casualisation, it may conveniently be noted at this point, implies something more than the mere provision of Labour Exchanges. It implies also a definite policy at those Exchanges of concentrating work on the smallest possible number instead of spreading it out over many men. The rate at which this concentration shall be carried out is very largely within the control of the Exchange. De-casualisation, in

---

[1] There can be no doubt that ultimately the organisation of the labour market must be beneficial to the employer in so far as it gives him better and more responsible service. Employing men casually he gets men who have perhaps had nothing to do and little to eat for some days, and who, knowing that their employment is casual, have little to gain by working hard or to lose by misbehaviour. Engaging men from an Exchange he may and, as the system develops, will get for his casual work men who have only just left a job elsewhere and who, depending for their regular livelihood upon the Exchange, will have a motive to do well. Casual employment, indeed, combined with payment by the hour, is a method almost ideally suited to discourage industry. The man taken on for one particular job and knowing that he is to be dismissed and no more remembered at its close can have no conceivable interest except that of lengthening the job as much as possible. " Ca' canny " becomes a common-sense policy for the individual needing no trade union to enforce it. *Cf. Unskilled Labour*, Report of a Special Committee of the Charity Organisation Society, Evidence, p. 105, for the opinion of a builder's foreman that his preference men worked better than the casual men, because they knew that even when the job in hand was finished they would almost certainly be taken on to another job.

other words, could, once the Exchanges were at work, be made to proceed as slowly or, within limits, as quickly as was desired. A great part of it would be accomplished by squeezing out the very lowest class of men who now live really on sources other than their own labour—upon their family or upon charity; the day's work that they now get once a week or once a fortnight, and that does them no real good, might go to some other man now getting three or four days a week and make for him all the difference between sufficiency and slow starvation. A great part again could be accomplished by squeezing out the highest class—the young and vigorous—who, if forced to it, might find other openings. Another part would consist simply of preventing any entry of fresh men to replace those who died. In the third place, since a great many of those thrown out, especially at first, would be men of a very low class, unfitted by privation and bad habits for immediate undertaking of regular work, it would be necessary to have available some form of training or convalescent institution where they could be dieted and disciplined into other ways. It would be necessary to have available also the means of emigration—much the surest, simplest and cheapest method at the moment for disposing of a genuine surplus of labour.[1] It would certainly be very convenient also and would disarm much opposition if at the time of de-casualisation some obvious fresh openings for labour—afforestation schemes and the like—were being started by public action.

The exact bearing of these last suggestions must be carefully noticed. Approval of training colonies, emigration, afforestation schemes and the like at this point in no way runs counter to the criticism of such proposals as remedies for unemployment at an earlier stage. The removal of individuals is no remedy for unemployment while the system causing unemployment remains— while, to take only the point immediately at issue, the casual demand of employers continues to collect casual reserves of labour. When, however, the system is being changed, when de-casualisation is turning part of the reserve into regular men and part into a sheer surplus (a fundamentally different thing from a reserve), then the removal of this surplus to newly created industries, whether in this country or in Canada, is just what is required. It meets the inevitable difficulty of transition. Its use and need, however, are simply subsidiary to the principal reform and are quite temporary. The surplus disengaged by de-casualisation has only to be absorbed once and for all; there will be nothing to collect a fresh body

---

[1] The possibilities of emigration have for the moment been enormously curtailed by depression in North America.

of the under-employed; there will simply be five hundred regular jobs filling up regularly as fresh men are required.

The policy of de-casualisation is supported by convincing analogies. If it is true, and undoubtedly within limits it is true, that a community can have as many paupers as it chooses to pay for, then it must be equally true that a community can have as many casual labourers as it chooses to pay for or to let employers pay for. If indiscriminate gifts of money breed a class of beggars, no less surely must indiscriminate doles of work breed a class living by such doles. There is no breach of continuity throughout the series from the beggar, through the pavement artist, the cab-runner, and the casual bag carrier, up to the dock labourer and beyond. Every argument that can be brought against casual relief applies with undiminished force to casual employment. The remedies to be applied in each case are the same in principle. The aim of the Charity Organisation Society to-day is neither more nor less than the de-casualisation of relief, the making of each temporary gift have reference to permanent needs, and be, not merely a support for the day, but part of a coherent scheme of adequate subsistence. The policy here proposed is the exactly corresponding organisation of employment. The attack on casual giving has failed, indeed, to a very large extent just because it has been an attack only on casual giving and not on casual employing as well. It may be true that a community can have as many paupers as it chooses to pay for. The obverse—that it can have as few paupers as it chooses to pay for —is not true, so long as industrial methods are tolerated which breed a half-employed class inevitably lapsing into pauperism in every depression and with advancing age.

Again, if the principle of the living wage means anything at all, it means not simply a certain rate of pay but also a minimum continuity of employment. The best rate per hour is a mockery unless the average number of hours per week and of weeks in a year keeps up to a certain level. The "docker's tanner" [1] to-day represents a tragedy of misdirected enthusiasm. Under-employment infringes upon the standard of life just as much as does under-payment; it is, indeed, only an indirect form of under-payment, a sweating by irregular earnings more disastrous than any sweating by low wages. The perception of this affords also the clue to a remedy. The rule has to be established that no man shall be engaged in a manner making under-employment possible, *i.e.*, that every man who cannot be guaranteed a reasonable sufficiency of earnings from one employer shall be engaged

---

[1] The 6d. an hour which was the object of the London Dock strike.

only from an Exchange in touch with many employers and able
to organise for him a sufficiency under several in turn. The whole
principle of factory legislation—the proscription of industrial
methods disastrous to the souls and bodies of the workpeople—is
at the back of this proposal. Every argument which can be used
to justify the legal prohibition of under-payment [1] applies with
undiminished force to the prevention of under-employment.

The de-casualisation of employment is thus at one and the same
time an extension into the industrial field of the Charity Organisation principle which proscribes casual relief and a development
of the trade union principle of the living wage. It may appeal
to the Socialist as a part of that industrial organisation in regard
to which academic socialism—national ownership of the means
of production—is but a means to an end. It may appeal to the
individualist, because by diminishing the chances of the labour
market it gives more decisive influence to individual merit.

The principle is clear—that every man who cannot be regularly
employed by one firm should be engaged only from an Exchange,
should be one of a list common to many firms. The definition
of the principle is all that lies within the limits of the present
discussion. Whether the use of Exchanges should be voluntary
or compulsory, whether they themselves should be set up by
public authority or by industrial associations, are questions which
may for the moment be left on one side. The practical application of the principle involves, no doubt, some system of
public Labour Exchanges to cover the large amount of ground
which will certainly not be covered in any other way. It admits,
however, also of all kinds of private and sectional experiment—
of common lists set up by voluntary co-operation of employers,
of trade union registration, and much besides. The principle is
universal ; the practical application of it may be infinitely varied.
It must indeed be varied to meet the case. Casual employment
is no local disease ; it is found in all towns and to some extent
in nearly all trades. Nor is it one type of employment rigidly
cut off from other types.

Casual employment in all its varieties and its ubiquity is but
the acute form of a general phenomenon. So de-casualisation is
only a special form of labour market organisation. The under-
employment of the dock labourer is paralleled by the constant

---

[1] On 21st Feb., 1908, a Sweated Industries Bill to establish wages boards with
compulsory powers obtained its second reading without a division and in an almost
unanimous House of Commons. Both the economic objections to compulsion in this
case and its administrative difficulties are incomparably greater than they would be
in the case of under-employment. What the casual labourer loses by irregularity
no man really gains ; he is not cheap labour but dear labour.

leakage of employment and earnings affecting substantial minorities in nearly all occupations, skilled and unskilled alike. The excess of individual dock labourers above the number ever required at any one moment is paralleled by the irreducible minimum of unemployment in the trade unions. The problem in the trade unions and even among the skilled men outside them is not as a rule urgent, simply because the wages are as a rule high enough, particularly when spread out through unemployed benefits, to allow for an ample margin of idleness. The problem, however, differs only in degree not in kind. The crowding of the labour market is common to the highest and the lowest ranks of industry, and in all ranks arises from the same central fact— the division of the total demand for labour in fluctuating proportions between different employers and different districts. In all trades there is, just in proportion as the market is unorganised and labour immobile, a possibility and a tendency for fresh men to enter under the influence of local developments at one place though men of the trade are standing idle elsewhere. The dissipation of the demand actually increases its effectiveness in producing a supply. The concentration of the demand at common centres is required in order to bring about the recruiting of trades in accordance with their real growth, not by local accidents, and to give to employment in each occupation as a whole something of the continuity and the orderly progression which characterise employment in a single large undertaking. This is simply the dynamic aspect of the change which has already been considered statically and with reference to one extreme form of overcrowding, under the title of de-casualisation.

Some measure of protection for those within a trade or district against the competition of those outside is an essential, if somewhat paradoxical, consequence of a system of Labour Exchanges. The aim of such a system is, not simply the fluidity, but the organised and intelligent fluidity of labour—the enabling of men to go at once where they are wanted, but at the same time the discouraging of movement to places where men are not wanted. The organisation of the labour market for a trade or district gives the men of that trade or district the first call upon all the work in it which they are competent to perform. It enables them to satisfy at once demands which if there is any delay may be satisfied not by them but by the recruiting of an outsider.[1]

---

[1] Suppose, for instance, that the labour market for London carmen were completely organised, *i.e.*, that all carmen out of work registered at once at an office to which all vacant situations were at once reported. Then any vacancy would naturally be filled from that register, *i.e.*, so long as any competent London car-

SPECIAL USES OF LABOUR EXCHANGE ORGANISATION.

The organisation of the labour market has now been considered with special reference to casual employment and generally with reference to the normal crowding of occupations. These were the factors in unemployment forming the principal theme of Chapter V. There are, however, other factors in unemployment. The bearing of Labour Exchanges on some of these must be noticed.

First may be mentioned seasonal fluctuations. Here, in so far as seasonal fluctuations tend to affect the whole of each trade simultaneously, there is no room for transference of men from one employer to another in the same trade. In so far, however, as the seasonal fluctuations of different trades differ in point of time there is room for a transference at least of the low-skilled and unskilled men. A good deal of movement does in fact now take place; resort to the gasworks or the docks in winter by brick-makers or builders' labourers is not uncommon. A great deal more movement might no doubt be made to take place. The organisation of the labour market might, indeed, bring about an extensive dovetailing of winter and summer occupations not distinguishable in principle from the dovetailing of irregular jobs which is the essence of de-casualisation, and involving of course the same incidental difficulty—the displacement of some men altogether. Two men, one working at the docks in the early winter and tramping idly in the summer, and one working as a builder's labourer in the summer and starving or doing "useful" relief work in the winter, would be replaced by one man doing necessary work all the year round. How far the process of seasonal dovetailing could be carried is uncertain and must remain uncertain till it is attempted in practice. Building, with all the country occupations—harvesting, fruit-picking, hopping—on the one hand, and the gas-works, the docks, and all the exceptional Christmas demand in the Post Office, in shops and elsewhere, offer ample material for a start.

Second may be considered the changes of industrial structure which displace men from their chosen occupations. Here the function and need of labour market organisation are obvious. If the community is under an obligation to take thought for men thus "sacrificed to the gains of their fellow-citizens and of posterity," it certainly does not fulfil that obligation by provid-

---

man remained unemployed there would be no opportunity for any outsider to get employment. As it is, of course, the London employer, not being able to lay hands on the London carman, may bring one up from the country and thus glut the market.

ing them with sixteen weeks of relief work. Men who by a new machine or method have been driven from their established livelihoods are not at all in the position of those who are suffering from temporary depression ; they need, not support during a crisis, but guidance to new occupations. It is, indeed, often merely for want of guidance that men under such circumstances go under completely. The longer they have been in one occupation the less do they know of how to find work outside it. They may be men of sterling qualities such as many an employer would welcome, yet outside their own trade, which has come to an end, they have no idea of how and where to look for employment and make their qualities known.

It would, however, be idle to suggest that ignorance of where to look for fresh employment is the one thing that hinders the re-absorption of those who have been displaced by industrial changes. There is commonly added also the disability of age. Men are apt to be thrown out when they are already stiff with years and habits, unable readily to learn new ways and still less able to commend themselves for trial by strange employers.

Here is yet a third factor in unemployment, and perhaps in some ways an ultimate one. Yet even here, though the Labour Exchange alone may not serve, the Labour Exchange governed by a definite policy may reveal unexpected capacities. In any large single undertaking, *e.g.*, a railway company, there is always a certain number of old men's places—light situations— kept for those who have grown grey or become injured in the company's service. In industry as a whole there are no doubt also a good many such places, yet nothing to keep them for those whom they best fit. Work which older men could do, now, perhaps, by the chances of the labour market, falls to younger men and wastes their youthful vigour and adaptability. A Labour Exchange backed by sympathetic public opinion might do much to get all the old men's places for the older men and leave to the younger generations the task of finding and forcing fresh openings for themselves.[1] It should be noted that, though "old" men's places are spoken of, the actual men would often be at most middle-aged, and with a long character to back them might be just those whom an employer would in any case choose if he got to know them.

Fourth, and following upon the problem of age, comes the

---

[1] It may be noted here that some of the most important German Labour Exchanges, without in any way forfeiting their character as business organisations, make a special point of finding places for old and enfeebled workmen who are yet capable of doing something.

problem of youth—the factor in unemployment represented by deficiencies of industrial training. A great deal of attention has been devoted to this matter in recent years, and a great variety of proposals for its treatment have been put forward. There is even a tendency in some quarters to look to improvements of industrial training as the principal remedy for unemployment. This view represents an inadequate examination of the problem. It seems to be based, in part at least, on a mistaken interpretation of Distress Committee experiences. It ignores the striking facts of industrial fluctuation, and the reality of the demand for casual labour, just as many of the proposals based on it ignore the gulf which separates modern from mediæval industry. At the same time it points to a real defect in existing arrangements. There can be no question but that unemployment to-day is swollen as a consequence of some of the conditions of youthful labour. In any thoroughgoing attack upon unemployment there must be included, on the one hand, the better guidance of boys and girls in the choice of careers, and, on the other hand, the extension of industrial training. It will be seen that each of these proposals in its various aspects either presupposes or would be enormously assisted by the organisation of the labour market.

The better guidance of boys and girls in the choice of careers may be said to have three main objects. The first is the adjustment of individuals to the sort of work which suits them—the fitting of round boys into round holes, and of square boys into square holes. The haphazard methods of to-day leave ample room for individual maladjustment, involving sometimes waste of abilities and sometimes failure and unemployment. The second object is the adjustment of the general flow of labour as among different trades. Now some trades may be starved for labour while others are glutted; the notorious temporary prosperity of some particular class of workmen may continue to attract recruits long after the prospective demand is fully satisfied. The third object, which is really only a special development of the second, is the discouragement of one particular sort of employments, the "blind-alley" employments which necessarily set up a fresh point of stress in industry—the transition to a new occupation at manhood—and are sometimes positively demoralising as well. These being the objects, how are they to be obtained?

The guidance of boys and girls in the choice of careers means simply the extension of labour market organisation in connection with the schools. It means substituting for the haphazard entry into industrial life—the taking of the first job that offers—entry informed by wider knowledge of possibilities and prospects.

Moreover, in order to be effective this guidance must be fairly general.   It implies a juvenile Labour Exchange dealing with a substantial portion both of the supply of and the demand for boys and not one starting out with the idea of rigidly proscribing all but the best employments.   No general effect can be produced by sending a few selected boys to the best employers and ignoring all the other employers.   The latter simply get their boys in other ways; the evil is ignored not cured.   So long as "blind-alley" openings for boys are not absolutely illegal—which they never can be—the choice of them can only be discouraged generally by bringing them into direct competition with better openings at a general Exchange.   A boy choosing a career now often becomes a vanboy without ever having any idea that better careers are possible. If he came to an Exchange he might still become a vanboy, but he would at least learn that other occupations existed, and he might be advised—he could not be compelled—to choose them.

The improvement of industrial training may affect unemployment in two ways.   First, the forcing up of as much youthful labour as possible into skilled occupations is required to allow for the inevitable gravitation downwards of labour at all later ages. Men displaced from skilled work by misfortune, depression or changes of industrial structure may take to unskilled work ; the opposite process is substantially impossible.   This fact implies a constant tendency for the unskilled labour market to be relatively overcrowded.   The compensation for it must be found in an effective system of technical education—a force-pump to raise the level from which men start.   Second, the diversion of as much youthful, i.e., adaptable, labour as possible to new and growing trades is required, both to facilitate industrial development and to secure the older men in their established livelihoods.

Each of these requirements involves, of course, much more than labour market organisation.   Yet each stands in the closest relation thereto.   Technical education, for instance, needs to be guided by accurate knowledge of industrial conditions.   Not all forms of skilled workmen are in demand at any time.   Skilled occupations may decay and change like any others.   Nothing can serve so well to give continuous, automatic and general information about the nature and tendencies of the demand for labour as can a connected system of efficient Labour Exchanges. Again, it is utterly impracticable to teach all men skilled trades or even to proscribe absolutely all "blind-alley" employments. To cut up industry into water-tight compartments, insisting that every occupation should be self-contained and self-supplying from start to finish, each with exactly identical proportions of boys to men, would be to impose restrictions altogether out of accord with economic tendencies and not really necessary to meet the case. There are unskilled occupations, *e.g.*, builders' labouring, with very little room for boys at all, and quite ready to take in at eighteen or twenty those who have up to then pursued a "blind-alley" occupation. Practically therefore it must be sufficient to insist, not that every youthful worker should be learning a trade, but that he should be learning something—to keep his intelligence alive and growing.[1] With this must go on the one hand a discouragement of "blind-alley" occupations (by spread of information as to other possibilities) and the facilitation— through Labour Exchanges—of the transition at manhood from one employment to another, wherever transition of some sort cannot be avoided.[2]

Improvement of the conditions of youthful labour would, however, not only be in various ways assisted and made more effective by organisation of the labour market. It is at bottom identical in principle with this organisation and a necessary complement to it. Apart from the general fluctuations of industry—seasonal and cyclical—unemployment is simply a matter of local and qualitative maladjustment. Throughout a period of rising demand for labour men may be unemployed because they are not in the right place or not of the sort required. They lack mobility or adaptability or both. Mobility may be given by Labour Exchanges. Adaptability is partly a matter of education,

---

[1] The suggestion of compulsory continuation schools is supported by the example of Germany, where in twenty-one out of twenty-six constituent parts of the Empire, containing all but one forty-sixth of the total population, attendance at continuation schools is made compulsory for varying periods after the termination of the ordinary school course.

[2] Yet one point of some importance has to be mentioned. Even when it is clear that an occupation is with reference to the future a "good" one, there are often great social difficulties in getting boys to choose it rather than one that is bad. For very obvious reasons the commencing wages tend to be higher where a boy is merely a wage-earner than when he is learning. He is engaged upon simple light work where he acquires his full value at once; there are as a rule no expensive tools or materials which he is likely to damage in learning their use; he is not occupying the time of a teacher. The "blind-alley" occupation, therefore, very commonly offers to the boy, or rather to the boy's family, considerable immediate advantage in wages over an apprenticeship; perhaps six or eight shillings a week as against two or four. Where, as in all really poor families, the earnings of the elder children are an integral and long-expected part of the general income it is only natural that such a difference should be decisive. Thus poverty perpetuates itself. In a docker's family the children have to take the first job that offers on the day that they are fourteen. If on the day after they hear of another job, paid a shilling a week more, they must take that without further inquiry as to the ultimate prospects. The mother, who has the deciding of these things, in nine cases out of ten has no knowledge of better openings; if she had, she might still choose the worst rather than let the younger children go hungry. The children of the casual labourers of to-day become thus the casual labourers of to-morrow. The de-casualisation of adult labour is necessary to prevent children growing up under conditions which make any choice of occupations impossible.

but in much larger part simply the natural possession of the young, and should be used in them for meeting new and unfamiliar demands. It is waste of qualities to let a boy from school do anything that an older man could learn to do—waste resulting both in the unemployment of the older man and the holding back of some new industry.

Fifth, it may be asked, what the organisation of the labour market would do for the unemployable. The answer is, that by regularising employment it would sift them out of the industrial world altogether. De-casualisation would gradually make it impossible to live by working two days a week and lying in bed for the rest, or by being " weeded out" for incompetence on one building job after another. The work lost by these men—the unemployables on the fringe of industry—would go to make up a reasonable subsistence for others. These men would be left for disciplinary or hospital treatment under the Poor Law.

Sixth and last, an aspect of labour market organisation has to be mentioned, lying perhaps a little apart from the present subject but of fundamental importance. This is the function of an efficient Labour Exchange in affording a direct test of unemployment. The central problem of the Poor Law is to relieve without relieving unnecessarily. The only principle on which it has hitherto attempted to secure this is the principle of deterrence— the making of relief so repellent that men might be presumed to have exhausted every other resource before they would accept it.

Deterrence is, in fact, in regard to the able-bodied, an indirect test of unemployment ; unless they are really unable to obtain work they will not accept relief under harsh conditions. To deterrence the Labour Exchange offers an alternative and a supplement. If all the jobs offering in a trade or a district are registered at a single office, then it is clear that any man who cannot get work through that office is unemployed against his will. He may be relieved without deterrence, yet without any fear that he is being relieved when he could get work, or is being drawn needlessly from industry to pauperism. So long as the community leaves the search for employment to individuals, it must put pressure on them to continue the search—by giving public relief only under harsh, degrading or otherwise repellent conditions. Even then the community is entirely at the mercy of the individual's ignorance ; it may be relieving him though there is work if he only knew where to find it. Still more is it at the mercy of the individual's increasing callousness. The defect of deterrence in every form is that its effect weakens with familiarity—the much-whipped schoolboy gets hardened to whipping, the criminal to prison fare, the vagrant to the bath and plank bed of the casual ward. So soon, on the other hand, as the State itself undertakes the search for, *i.e.*, the registration of, employment, it is on the way to get all and more than all the security it had before against unnecessary pauperism. It can with perfect safety help the unemployed more freely because it knows that so soon as work is to be had it will have notice thereof and be able to hand on the notice to those who are being relieved. The Labour Exchange thus opens a way of "dispauperisation" more humane, less costly and more effective than that of the "workhouse test"—the way of making the finding of work easy instead of merely making relief hard.[1]

The object of labour market organisation is the close, continuous and automatic adjustment of existing demand and supply over the largest possible area. The weakness alike of theory and practice in regard to unemployment in the past has been the assumption that this adjustment was already substantially secured ; in other words, that the force of friction might be neglected. The demand for labour has been taken for purposes of argument as if it were single and concentrated; the supply of labour as if it were infinitely mobile and adaptable. The demand is, in fact, broken up by distinctions of place and quality, and subject to perpetual change and fluctuation. The supply is rendered immobile by ignorance and less adaptable by every year of age. Adam Smith and his followers were right in emphasising the mobility of labour as a cardinal requirement of industry. The practical application of their teaching has been inadequate because it has been confined to abolishing visible and legal obstacles to motion, such as the laws of settlement and of apprenticeship. It has left untouched the impalpable but no less real barriers of ignorance, poverty and custom. If friction and the waste involved in friction are to be eliminated from the labour market, there must be, not mere absence of legal obstacles, but organised and informed fluidity of labour.

Friction again is equally real and wasteful whether it takes the form of a visible delay in production or the form of a requirement of excessive reserves of labour. A Labour Exchange

---

[1] It is not suggested here that the whole principle of " deterrence " can ever be dispensed with in regard to the able-bodied. That principle serves not only to drive men to work but also to drive them to make personal provision for their unemployment, sickness, etc. It is, however, suggested that the Labour Exchange test may ultimately be made the basis of a relief system, whether or not it is supported also by a modified deterrence. It is to be noted that the policy here suggested is already in full operation in Strassburg.

is as much needed in those occupations where employers never
have to wait for men as in those where they sometimes have to
wait; it aims, not at supplying more workpeople, but at supplying them by a less wasteful method; its object is, not to enable
employers to produce more rapidly, by avoiding delays for men,
but to enable them to produce either more rapidly or as rapidly
with smaller, because more mobile, reserves of labour.

A more mobile reserve is, of course, a more efficient reserve.
The organisation of the labour market may be treated as first and
foremost a means of increasing industrial efficiency.   In the
stereotyped and local industry of the middle ages the workman
had one function—to do the work that came to him to do.   In
the flux of national industry the modern workman has two
functions—to work and to be perpetually finding and following
the market for his labour.   It follows that the less time and
energy he spends upon this second function, the greater will be
the time and energy he has free to devote to the first function.
He will be more effective as a workman the less he is a mere
seeker for employment.   Herein lies a fresh clue to a difficulty
already considered.

The increasing of individual efficiency is desirable whatever
view be taken as to the general relations of population and
industry.   If the country is not yet becoming over-populated,
then to get the present volume of work done by a smaller body
of labour is to release the residue for fresh developments.   If the
country is in danger of over-population, then the forcing up and
holding up of the standard of individual efficiency and production must be the corner-stone of social policy.   The danger of
over-population is simply that of a diminishing return to each
fresh unit of labour—a multiplication of the people forcing a progressive lowering of standards.   The only safeguard against this
danger must lie in insisting that standards shall not be lowered—
that fresh supplies of labour shall not be taken up by industry
unless there is room for them without diminishing the average
room for all.

Yet, in truth, to meet such a supposition at any length is a
work of supererogation.   All the evidences justify the view that
in this country at least labour is still an asset not a liability; that
the return to it and the demand for it will rise in the future as
they have risen in the past; that the sphere of industry, so far
from having lost, except for the moment of depression, its
elasticity, would expand yet more rapidly to more vigorous
pressure from within.   This has now to be inferred as a rule
from general statistics; it cannot be seen in detail because we

lack points of observation. Yet somewhere at all times fresh men are being absorbed in industry; somewhere, almost certainly, there are, at normal times and perhaps even in times of depression, places where more hands are wanted than can be had, unsatisfied demands for labour, industrial developments consciously or half-consciously held back for want of men. These unsatisfied demands are, of course, often of little use to the existing unemployed. Industry will not absorb all and sundry but only those who fit or can be made to fit the new forms of its growth. These are predominantly the rising generations. The broad principle of social policy thus emerges—to keep those in an established trade in constant touch with all the work of that trade, and thus to place upon the young rather than on the old the burden of finding and forcing the fresh openings which expanding industry is always offering for labour.

CHAPTER X.

PRINCIPLES OF FUTURE POLICY.

II. THE AVERAGING OF WORK AND EARNINGS.

The averaging of work and earnings : Elasticity of working hours. The example of coal and cotton. Unemployed insurance. The example of the trade unions. Expenditure on unemployed benefits. Cost per member per week. Flexibility of the provision made. The burden of unemployment borne by the trade as a whole. Foreign examples. The German report. Value of the method of insurance. Possibility of extension depends upon test of unemployment.
Minor and collateral measures : Systematic distribution of public work on business lines. Elasticity of wages. Absorption of temporary surplus. General progress. Poor Law Reform. The principles and functions of public relief.

WHEN all has been done that can be done to organise the labour market, many further measures will still be needed. The problem of cyclical fluctuation will not have been touched directly at all. The problem of seasonal fluctuations will have been affected only to a small extent by the extended and organised use of subsidiary trades. The incalculable changes and irregularities of economic conditions will still make nearly all men insecure. No amount of Labour Exchanges can guarantee that every man falling out of one job shall at once find another job suited to his powers.

The need for further measures must be fully recognised. The consideration of those measures in this chapter may, however, be premised by two general considerations. First, though the organisation of the labour market can have no direct influence upon cyclical fluctuation and certain other factors in unemployment, it may have, and indeed is certain to have, a very important indirect influence on the degree and volume of distress involved in these factors. De-casualisation will reconstruct the whole conditions of life in the lowest ranks of industry, sifting out for remedial treatment a certain number who are unemployable, and forcing up the level of all the rest. It will replace the casual class—always on the verge of distress, always without reserves for an emergency —by a class for whom the words foresight, organisation and thrift may represent not a mockery but a reality. Exceptional depression of trade, therefore, will far less certainly mean acute or immediate distress. Second, unemployment itself must be accepted as in some degree inevitable. The influence of seasons will survive any change of human institutions. Cyclical fluctuation, if the hypothesis put forward in an earlier chapter be correct, will survive any change which does not threaten the very principles of industrial growth, and is in any case quite certain to recur for many decades to come. Changes of structure also are inevitable unless industry is to become stereotyped and unprogressive. Finally and quite generally, so long as the direct demand for labour remains distributed among and dependent upon the fortunes of a host of individual employers, the demand may in certain times and places fall out of perfect adjustment to the supply; the vicissitudes of the numberless separate groups of producers means insecurity for the individuals composing those groups. They are constantly passing from one group to another; it will always be possible for an individual to fall out of one group without immediately finding another to receive him. To a very large extent therefore it must suffice to aim at preventing, not unemployment itself, but the distress which it now involves. This, indeed, is the aim of the two principal measures now to be suggested—elasticity of working hours and insurance against unemployment.

Elasticity of working hours means that the reserve power to meet growth in the demand for labour should, up to a certain point, be found rather in the ability of the men engaged to work longer, than in the presence of unemployed men standing ready to be employed. Conversely it means that the loss of employment due to a diminution of the demand should by a reduction of hours for all be spread over the whole body of men instead of being concentrated, by complete dismissal, upon a few.

This method of meeting fluctuations is, of course, by no means unfamiliar. It is found very completely developed in coal-mining, where, according to the state of trade, the pits remain open for varying numbers of days each week. The actual fluctuations to be met are very considerable. Thus for 1895, 1900, 1905 and 1907 respectively the average number of days worked at all the coal-mines making returns were 4·74, 5·47, 5·03 and 5·51 respectively. In other words, they were in turn 79, 91, 84 and 92 per cent. of the theoretical maximum of six days a week. The fluctuations, however, being met in the manner indicated, involve hardly any dismissal of individual workmen and therefore substantially no acute distress.

In this respect coal-mining occupies the premier position. Many other industries, however, apply the same method less completely. In ironstone mining, for instance, there is also a

considerable fluctuation in the length of the working week.   At
iron and steel works it is the number of shifts rather than the
number of days that varies.   In quite another industrial field—
that of cotton spinning—the working of short time during depression has become a regular practice organised and advised by
the employers' associations.[1]   The same plan is less completely
carried out, usually by individual rather than by organised action,
in the other principal textile industries, and outside them in a
great variety of trades and branches of trades.[2]   Even in building
a similar device exists in the differentiation of winter and summer
hours ; to the extent of this difference the loss of wages through
winter slackness is spread over the whole trade in exoneration
of individuals.

The more general application of this method is obviously to
be desired.   It is above all suited to those definite and general
contractions in the demand for labour which have been considered under the title of cyclical fluctuation.   The difference
between a ten hours' and a nine hours' day, for instance, would,
other things being equal, carry off a depression of 10 per cent.
The difference between ten and eight hours would carry off a depression of 20 per cent.   Except in one or two industries depressions hardly ever reach this magnitude.   As measured by the
general unemployed percentage the deepest depression ever
recorded   that of 1879—represented a fall of only 10 per cent.
from the most prosperous of the years before.[3]   As measured by
statistics of production or consumption of raw materials per head
of population the most marked contractions since 1880 have
been :—

[1] The method was applied with notable success in the very severe depression of
1903-4. In May of the earlier year the Federation of Master Cotton Spinners passed
a resolution to close their mills during the whole of Whit-week and on every Saturday
and Monday from 27th June onward. The effect was to reduce the normal week from
55 to 40 hours.   This first period of short time ended in the autumn of 1903, but
after a short interval of slightly improved activity short time was re-imposed in the
spring of 1904 and lasted till September or October, when the depression gave way to
extreme prosperity. During part of the latter year the reduction of hours was less
than that just stated, i.e., to 47½ not 40 hours per week.

[2] There is of course hardly any important trade—except perhaps shipbuilding—in
which short time is not occasionally applied to avoid the dismissal of workmen. Thus
in the Labour Gazette for October, 1908, short time was reported in many branches of
the engineering, miscellaneous metal and cutlery, linen, jute, hosiery, silk, carpet,
dyeing, leather, printing, glass, pottery, brick and tile, boot and shoe, and hat trades.
There is, however, a great difference between the practice of occasional short time by
individual employers and the organised methods of the cotton and coal trades.

[3] This figure, it must be admitted, has only an illustrative rather than a scientific
value.   On the one hand, it takes no account of short time—reckoning all as employed
though they might only be half-employed. On the other hand, it is based to an
excessive degree upon returns from some of the most fluctuating industries.

Coal Production, 100 to 87 [1891 to 1893].
Pig-iron Production, 100 to 79 [1883 to 1886].
Raw Cotton Consumption, 100 to 82 [1904 to 1907]

Only in shipbuilding are the changes altogether greater. The years 1883 to 1886 witnessed a falling off in the tonnage built from 769,000 tons to 293,000, or, allowing for growth of population, as from 100 to 37. From 1892 to 1893 there was a fall from 100 to 70.

It is not, indeed, suggested that a general eight hours' or six hours' day in slack times should be imposed by direct legislation. The matter is certainly not now one for legislation, even if it ever can be. It is one for the associations of employers acting in agreement or in sympathy with the associations of workmen, and it is a matter for each trade more or less by itself. It will be found probably that in some trades organised short time is impracticable; in others that it would increase merely the length of the job, not the numbers whom it was possible to employ; in others that it would add excessively to the cost of production.[1] All these considerations must make procedure tentative. Yet there can be little doubt that a large field for reform in this direction lies open, if once the principle of elasticity in working hours be accepted by the great industrial associations.[2]

The principle of elasticity in working hours, it will be noticed, implies a sharp distinction in policy between times of good and times of bad trade. In the former it is desirable to concentrate the work as much as possible so as to avoid drawing men into the trade who are certain to be unemployed during a depression. In the latter it is desirable to spread the work so as to keep together and out of distress the men who will be required with any return to prosperity. Half-employment as a normal condition is nothing but bad; as a method of meeting an emergency it has everything in its favour.

[1] The question of cost depends upon a great variety of considerations—standing charges, the keeping of a skilled staff together, etc., etc. As a rule, short time develops most naturally in piecework trades. Where payment is by the hour an employer might lose through adopting short time instead of dismissing some altogether, for he would be keeping good, bad and indifferent, whereas now he selects the least efficient for dismissal. On the other hand, he might gain by cutting off the hours during which least was done or during which he had extra charges for lighting and heating.

[2] It is to be noted that elasticity may be attained, not only by short time in depressions, but by overtime in years of exceptional activity. Trade unions have of course rather a tendency to oppose or limit overtime under all circumstances. Yet it is clearly better for them, as for the whole industry, that some of those in it should work longer to meet an exceptional demand than that fresh operatives should be recruited who must inevitably glut the market so soon as trade becomes slack or merely normal.

The definite and obvious depressions induced by seasonal changes in some trades and by cyclical fluctuation in most trades may in time be dealt with more and more by making working hours elastic.   There is needed, however, also some other method applicable both to general depression in trades where organised short time proves impossible and to all the incalculable varieties of individual misfortune.   This, it is here suggested, is to be sought in some form of insurance against unemployment.

The term "insurance" in this connection cannot be used as a term of art.   It must be taken to apply loosely to any process whereby each of a number of workmen sets aside something of his wages while earning, in order to obtain an allowance in case of unemployment.   It need not be taken as excluding the possibility of grants to the insurance fund from other sources.[1]   Its essence is for the individual workman an averaging of earnings between good and bad times, and for the body of workmen a sharing of the risk to which they are all alike exposed.

In this looser sense insurance is already one of the most important methods of dealing with unemployment.   It is found, that is to say, in the form of benefits paid by many trade unions to their unemployed members.   These benefits, as has been stated,[2] are of two principal types—the stationary or unemployed benefit strictly so called, and the allowance given to assist travelling in search of work.   Some unions give travelling benefits only; this is particularly common in many branches of the building trade.[3] Others give a stationary benefit only.   This is typical of strongly localised societies such as some of those in textile trades.   More commonly both benefits are given, or one and the same grant may, with slight differences of form, be used for either purpose.

In the present connection it will be sufficient to consider solely or principally unemployed benefits strictly so called—that is to say, the weekly allowances paid by unions to their members at the place of unemployment.   These vary greatly from one union to another both in amount and in duration.   At the one end of the scale comes the Amalgamated Society of Gasworkers, Brickmakers and General Labourers, with an allowance of 6s. a week for four weeks in any fifty-two.   This appears to be the only important labourers' union making provision of the kind. At the other end are the wealthy organisations in the highly skilled trades.   The London Society of Compositors grants 14s.

---

[1] These make the process strictly one of " assisted insurance " as in the various foreign schemes mentioned below.
[2] P. 16.
[3] A short description of the system of travelling benefits is given in Appendix to Part I, Methods of Seeking Employment in Great Britain.

a week for twenty weeks in each calendar year as a minimum, and generally extends the period by special vote to thirty or more. In 1904 and 1905 the period was in each case thirty-eight weeks, so that as much as £26 12s. could be drawn by a single member. The Amalgamated Society of Engineers has a sliding scale. Members over ten years' standing can draw 10s. a week for fourteen weeks, 7s. for thirty weeks, and thereafter 6s. so long as unemployed. Members in the lowest section, *i.e.*, of less than five years' standing, may draw 10s. for fourteen, 7s. for fourteen and 6s. for another twenty-four weeks. The National Flint Glass Makers Society gives allowances ranging from 10s. downwards for a period of two years in all cases, and thereafter 2s. a week (the amount of the contribution) indefinitely to members of fifteen years' standing. Between the two ends of the scale is to be found every variety of amount, period and conditions. Every trade has its own characteristic forms. The textile unions, for instance, confine themselves commonly to payment for breakdowns and fires. One or two painters' unions give an allowance only during December, January and February. Apart from these, the carpenters and plumbers stand almost alone among the building operatives in making any stationary allowance at all. The treatment of those who have drawn the whole benefit is also very various. In some cases, *e.g.*, the London Compositors, men may start afresh and draw the full amount each calendar year. More often a substantial interval has to elapse between drawing the full amount and claiming again; in a fair number of cases it is laid down, as an obvious precaution against letting the union become saddled with "unemployables," that during this interval the claimant must have worked for a stated period at his trade. With all this variety two general observations may be made. First, the allowance is never by itself adequate for the maintenance of a family. The highest rate per week for ordinary unemployment appears to be the 15s. paid by the Amalgamated Society of French Polishers, though one or two textile unions pay more for breakdowns. The most common rates are 10s. or 12s. to start with and less in subsequent periods. Second, the duration of the allowance is often very considerable. Of the forty-four "principal" unions outside the cotton trade paying unemployed benefit in 1899, twenty-seven made allowances for twenty consecutive weeks or more.

The expenditure involved is very considerable. During the ten years 1898-1907 the 100 "principal" unions, having a membership in 1907 of 1,457,856, or 61 per cent. of that of all unions, spent over four million pounds in assisting their members when out of work.[1] This sum was 23 per cent. of their total expenditure for all purposes during the same period.

The amount spent in each year varies of course with the state of trade. For the 100 "principal" unions in question it ranged from 3s. 2¾d. per member in 1899 to 11s. 1d. in 1904. For individual unions the changes are often very remarkable. The Associated Blacksmiths' Society, for instance, in 1889 spent £234, or 2s. 3d. per head, on unemployed benefits. In 1894 it spent £3,728, or £1 11s. per head. The Associated Shipwrights' Society in the three good years 1899-1901 spent £2,685 ; in the three bad years 1903-1905 spent £25,081. The average expenditure per head of membership entitled to this benefit was in 1899 1s. 1d., in 1904 19s. 1d. The Amalgamated Society of Carpenters and Joiners in 1899 spent £15,341, or 4s. 11½d. per head, on unemployed and travelling benefits. In 1904 the corresponding expenditure for this one union amounted to £90,814, or 25s. 8d. per head.

The system of trade union benefits thus briefly described probably does more than any other existing agency to provide against distress through want of employment. It does this without injury to self-respect and at a cost which in comparison to the effect produced is extremely small. It has the outstanding merit of flexibility. By substituting collective for individual saving it shifts on to each trade as a whole, part of the burden of the necessary margin of idleness. These points may be taken briefly in order.

The effectiveness of the system is to be judged by the fact that members of unions paying any substantial unemployed benefit are hardly ever to be found among the applicants to Distress Committees. The allowance given is not, indeed, in itself adequate. It has to be supplemented and does get supplemented by the earnings of wife and children, by private saving, by assistance from fellow-workmen and neighbours, by running into debt, by pawning and in other ways. It serves, however, as a nucleus. It keeps the rent paid. In practice it prolongs almost indefinitely the resisting power of the unemployed. Since it does this at a cost of only 10s. to 12s. a week it is, in proportion to the results achieved, extraordinarily cheap.

This may be shown from another point of view by estimating the average expenditure on unemployed benefits per member insured. The figures for a few of the most important unions are

---

[1] Practically the whole of this expenditure is attributable to about 80 unions, the remainder giving no unemployed benefits at all or only in one or two years out of the ten.

as follows. In the Amalgamated Association of Cotton Spinners during the ten years 1895-1904 the average cost of unemployed benefits was 7d. per member per week, but this as a sustained rate is somewhat exceptional. In the Friendly Society of Iron-founders during the same period the average was 5¾d., and in the London Society of Compositors 5½d. In the Amalgamated Society of Engineers it was 3½d. and in the Amalgamated Society of Carpenters and Joiners as low as 2½d. These figures for two reasons fail to represent the full cost of the insurance system—first, because they include nothing for administration; second, because they are based upon total membership and not strictly on the membership entitled to benefit. In none of the societies named, however, is this latter error an important one. On the other hand, all of them are societies with a liberal scale of benefit and subject to great fluctuations of employment.

The method of insurance is flexible as no provision of relief by employment can be flexible. No temporary or accidental stoppage is too small for it. The machinery of assistance is always ready; so soon as a man becomes unemployed, from whatever cause,[1] he has only to begin signing the vacant book in order to become entitled at once or in a few days to an allow-ance. On the other hand, the severest depression of trade is hardly too great to be dealt with in this way. The relief once begun can be and practically is continued for the great bulk of men so long as proves necessary. This flexibility is strikingly reflected in the figures already given of the contrasted expendi-tures in good and bad years.

The method of insurance throws upon each trade as a whole the burden or part of the burden of its margin of idleness. Unionism substitutes the collective for the individual conscious-ness, and thus enables the risk of unemployment in all its forms to be appreciated as a normal incident of industry. The in-dividual finds the risk very hard to appreciate and still harder to provide against. He may expect and allow for occasional loss of earnings through bad weather or ill-luck or in passing from one job to the next. He may expect and allow for seasonal fluctuation. Cyclical fluctuation stands practically on a different footing. It comes at far greater and less regular intervals; it lasts, not for weeks, but for months or years. Moreover, it tends to strike always the older or weaker members of a trade. In the strength of his youth a man may pass unscathed through two or three depressions, to be thrown out by the next when

---

[1] He has, of course, as a rule to satisfy his branch that his unemployment is in-voluntary and not the result of gross misbehaviour.

he is forty years old and more. In the life of the individual exceptional depression appears often as a unique disaster. In the life of a great organisation, such as the Amalgamated Society of Engineers, exceptional depression is but the downward phase of cyclical fluctuation—a phenomenon impressive and familiar, writ large in the records of recurrent increase of the unemployed percentage, recurrent pressure on the funds, recurrent decline or stagnation of membership. For such an organisation the provision of unemployed benefits becomes provision against an absolutely certain danger. Appreciation of this certainty reacts on wages. To keep its members together the union helps them when unemployed; it must therefore hold out for wages sufficient to cover the heavier subscriptions involved.[1] In the shape of these higher wages it transfers on to the trade as a whole the burden or part of the burden of unemployment.

Unfortunately the application of the system is at present very limited. The 650,000 men covered by the *Labour Gazette* returns of unemployment probably include the great bulk of those who are at all effectively insured against unemployment. The other two-thirds of the trade unionists have no system of benefits. Outside the trade unions insurance is unknown.

Clearly, indeed, in this particular field of activity trade unions possess certain natural advantages. Unionism involves an exceptional motive for insurance—the desire to provide, not merely for one's own unemployment, but for that of all one's fellows, so that they may not be led by distress to cut wages. Unions, again, come nearer than any other bodies to possessing a direct test of unemployment by which to protect their funds against abuse. They have, first, the knowledge of one another and of the trade possessed by individual members, and second, at least the beginnings of a Labour Exchange system. They are better able, therefore, than any one else at the present time to assist the unemployed on honourable terms without imminent risk of encouraging unemployment.

To these two advantages of the union in regard to insurance many would add a third—that the members of skilled and organised trades alone are able to afford the necessary premiums. Is this view, however, justified by the facts? The figures given show a weekly cost of unemployed benefit—on a fairly liberal scale and

[1] From 1900 to 1906 the membership of the three principal unions in those branches of the building trade where no stationary unemployed benefit is given, *i.e.*, bricklayers, masons and plasterers, declined 25 per cent. During the same period the membership of the three principal unions in those branches where this benefit is given, *i.e.*, carpenters, plumbers and painters, in spite of the severe depression, actually increased 2½ per cent

in some of the most fluctuating industries—of 2½d. to 7d. per member per week. It cannot really be suggested that premiums of this character are out of the reach of any considerable part of the population. There are, no doubt, workmen whose average earnings now do not suffice to pay for the bare necessaries of healthy life. Yet there are probably few, even of these, who do not on an average spend at least the amount of those premiums on luxuries with which they could well dispense. The question is simply one of the standard of duties recognised and of opportunities, not of income. The great majority of workmen fail to insure against unemployment, not because they could not afford it, but partly because the idea of doing so has never come into their heads, and partly because no opportunity of insurance is open to them.

The principle of insurance affords the most satisfactory, because the most flexible, method of making general provision for unemployment. The means of giving extended practical application to the principle need to be most carefully considered. There are, no doubt, great difficulties in the matter. There are also great possibilities. The value of the principle of insurance, indeed, is widely recognised, and abundant foreign examples of its application can be cited. There are schemes of direct voluntary insurance with municipal assistance in Berne, Basle, Cologne and Leipzig. There has been one attempt at compulsory insurance in St. Gall. There is—now meeting with increasing favour in many countries—the "Ghent system" of supplementing grants made to their unemployed members by trade unions and other associations. This plan having spread from Ghent to other Belgian towns, has now been adopted experimentally by the national Governments of France, Norway and Denmark, and within the last two years by the city of Strassburg. In the German Empire as a whole the matter is in the stage of active discussion not of practice. The possibility of a general compulsory scheme to set beside the existing provision for infirmity, sickness and accident, has been much considered. The whole subject was fully investigated by the Imperial Statistical Department, and an invaluable Report published in 1906.[1] The conclusion was reached that the facts of unemployment presented no insuperable difficulties of a technical character to the formation of an insurance system. The limits of the problem were ascer-

---

[1] *Versicherung gegen die Folgen der Arbeitslosigkeit.* Bearbeitet im Kaiserlichen Statistischen Amt. 3 vols., 1906 (Carl Heymann, Berlin). A useful summary of the conclusions of the Report and of the principal foreign insurance schemes described is given in the Report of a Special Committee of the Charity Organisation Society on *Unskilled Labour,* pp. 67-77.

tainable and not very wide. The real difficulties were held to lie in a different direction—in defining the conception of the " unemployment" which should entitle to benefit, and the obligation of the insured workman to take such work as should be offered to him. The real difficulty in fact is that of the test of unemployment. " On one point," the first volume of the Report concludes, " all proposals agree, one point emerges clear in the adjudication upon every practical scheme, that in every form of unemployed benefit or insurance an adequate system of Labour Exchanges is of the first importance." A second volume of the Report is thereupon entirely devoted to describing the existing Labour Exchange organisation in Germany.

The point here made is of fundamental importance. No scheme of insurance—or of any other honourable provision for unemployment—can be safe from abuse unless backed by an efficient organisation of the labour market, i.e., by a fairly complete registration of all the employment offering. On the other hand, with that complete registration the insurance or relief fund has an absolute protection ; the men if they too are compelled to register at the same office, cannot remain on the fund one moment after there is work anywhere available for them to do. Once the community or the insurance fund undertakes the notification of work the necessity of making relief allowances inadequate or degrading in order to drive men on the search for work disappears. The trade unions cannot safely now make their benefits really adequate simply because, though they have something of a registration system, they have very little ; they still rely mainly upon their members finding work by personal application.

Insurance against unemployment, therefore, stands in the closest relation to the organisation of the labour market, and forms the second line of attack on the problem of unemployment. It is, indeed, the necessary supplement thereto. The Labour Exchange is required to reduce to a minimum the intervals between successive jobs. Insurance is required to tide over the intervals that will still remain. The Labour Exchange mobilises the reserves of labour for fluctuations and hastens re-absorption after changes of industrial structure. Insurance is needed to provide for the maintenance of the reserves while standing idle and of the displaced men while waiting for re-absorption. No plan other than insurance—whether purely self-supporting or with assistance from other sources—is really adequate. The provision required is one adaptable to an immense variety of individual cases—that is to say, it must be far more flexible than anything to be attained along the lines either of relief works or of elasticity in working hours. The provision required is one made in part by the individual himself; by simple grants of money—whether under the Poor Law or otherwise—his self-respect is endangered. The provision required, however, cannot be made by the individual acting alone; unemployment may never come to him at all, but when it does come, may exceed all possibilities of private saving. The principle of insurance—which is simply that of spreading the wages in a trade so as to provide for the necessary margin of idleness in the trade—is therefore essential. It is at the same time adequate. The spreading of the burden of unemployment over all the men of the trade would make the burden tolerable in all but the most casual occupations. The premiums required for insurance in the principal unions are small relatively to the total wages—smaller indeed in most cases than the amounts added to those wages within recent years. There is no reason why the trade unions themselves should not extend the system of unemployed benefits. There is ample warrant in foreign example for giving State encouragement to such extension. There would, according to the opinion of those best qualified to judge—the authors of the German report already quoted—be no impossibility in the State's applying the principle of insurance to the risk of unemployment quite generally and comprehensively, once a test of unemployment had been made available.

In the third line of attack may be placed a variety of minor measures—the systematic distribution of public work, the steadying of the ordinary labour market by elasticity of wages, the greater exemption of old men in respect of standard rates, the smoothing of industrial transitions and the checking of rural depopulation.[1] Only the first two call for special notice.

1. The systematic distribution of public work. Though it may not prove possible to eliminate the causes of industrial fluctuation, it may be possible up to a certain point to counteract the fluctuation itself by getting as much public work as possible done when private work is slack, but done under the usual business conditions. This plan is something radically different from the provision of work either under the Unemployed Workmen Act, or as it has been generally practised by municipal authorities. It means simply that so far as it can be done

---

[1] In so far as this means simply the revival of rural industry it belongs to the type of proposals noticed below which may relieve pressure for a while by making fresh openings for labour, but do not touch the springs of unemployment. In so far, however, as the country can be said now to be positively repellent to the countryman, the making it attractive instead would have a permanent and direct bearing on the problem.

without extra cost,[1] public authorities should get their painting and building done in winter rather than in spring or summer, and should hasten forward the giving out of contracts when the unemployed percentage is at six or seven, holding back when it is at two or three.   It implies that in every case the work should be carried out under business conditions and the men hired, paid and dismissed in the ordinary way.[2]   Its aim, in fact, is not the relief of distress but the steadying of the labour market by making the demand in one direction—that of public bodies—expand or contract as the demand in other directions contracts or expands.   It does not help all and sundry, but only men competent at the particular work that can be given.   It does not necessarily help all of them, but only so many of them as can profitably be employed.   Its applicability therefore is strictly limited by the extent to which public authorities have the control of work, and spite of any extension of public activities, e.g., in the way of afforestation, must always remain inadequate to the immense variety of needs and capacities.   It is, finally, a matter not for legislation but for administration—for the acceptance of a principle to be worked out by the national and local authorities with due regard to business necessities.

2. Greater elasticity of wages.   The possibility of steadying employment is not confined to the systematic distribution of public work.   Fluctuation of the rate of wages between good and bad times already goes some way to put a premium on getting work done in the latter rather than in the former.   Might not the principle be applied more widely?   The possible effect, for instance, of a differentiation between winter and summer rates of pay in building is worth considering.   Building in winter is avoided now not so much because it is impossible as because it is or may be more costly ; there is greater risk of bad weather and there is increased expenditure on lighting and heating.   If the builder could get back some of this extra cost in a lower rate of wages, if, for instance, instead of paying a painter 8½d. an hour all the year round, he paid 9d. in the summer and 8d. in the winter months, he would have less reason to avoid the latter ; that is to say, he would be able to tender at much the same rates all the year round.   The difficulty in starting such a differentiation lies

---

[1] It is quite possible that work done at an unusual time, if it can be done then at all, should actually be cheaper—because wages and prices are apt to be lower and a better quality of labour available.

[2] The only desirable variant upon ordinary conditions might be, where the work was that of a local authority, that the contractor should be required to choose his men in the first instance from those resident in the district, e.g., from the men registered at the local Labour Exchange.

of course in settling the general level from which differentiation should take place. The suggestion of a lower rate than they now pay for the winter is quite frequently made by employers.[1] The workman, no doubt, would be equally ready to accept a higher rate than he now gets for the summer. The principle of differentiation is, however, independent of the general level—a benefit to both parties, not an advantage to one at the cost of the other. Here again it must suffice to indicate the principle; the possibilities and methods of its practical application must be left to those practically engaged in each trade.

The foregoing enumeration leaves out three classes of measures: first, those which may provide for the absorption of a temporary surplus of men; second, those which simply increase the general efficiency and prosperity of the working classes; third, those which are measures not of industrial organisation but of relief. The measures of the first class—emigration, reduction of working hours, creation of new industries—have already been mentioned in their place as subsidiary to de-casualisation and other types of industrial re-construction. Those of the second class baffle description. They may be taken for granted. Obviously larger wages, better conditions of work and a higher standard of life, whether or not they decrease unemployment, increase the power of resisting distress. The measures of the third class fall outside the scope of the present inquiry. Yet some indication of them, or at least of the main requirements to be satisfied by a once more reformed Poor Law, is clearly indispensable.

The first requirement of a reformed Poor Law is that it should be unmistakably Poor Law and should not admit of relief measures masquerading as industry. The attempt typified by the Unemployed Workmen Act to combine the alleviation of distress with the performance of useful work has failed in practice. The confusion of thought implied in the phrase "relief work" runs counter to the fundamental principles of social policy. It blurs the line which above all things should be kept distinct— the line between industry and relief, between the man who by his labour is adding to the wealth of the community and the man who is being supported in whole or in part by the labour of others. The new Poor Law, whatever else it may be, must not be such that men can come to it when they might be at work or such that they will be encouraged to remain as burdens on it by the idea that they are there earning their livings.

---

[1] Cf. *Unskilled Labour*, p. 49, for replies from employers.

Though, however, in the new Poor Law the line between industry and relief, blurred by the Unemployed Workmen Act, must again be drawn sharply, this need not imply the retention of all the harshnesses of the present Poor Law. Assuming an effective organisation of the labour market, the task now performed by the workhouse test—that of keeping men at a distance—will in two ways be simplified. First, de-casualisation by improving industrial conditions would make it possible to improve relief conditions without sacrificing the principle of deterrence. Second, the registration of all employment at Labour Exchanges would, as has been pointed out already, provide a direct test of unemployment apart from any deterrence at all. In other words, it would be possible, especially at times of emergency, to give relief under far easier conditions than at present without any danger of unnecessarily multiplying applications.

The second requirement of a reformed Poor Law is that it should be able to apply different measures to different cases. In respect of the able-bodied—to whom of course the discussion is here limited—three distinct forms of treatment are needed : provision of sustenance to keep men alive till they can recover employment ; provision of restorative or educational treatment for those who are apparently not now fit to take employment even if it came their way ; provision of disciplinary treatment subject to detention for those clearly beyond restoration by weaker measures, and perhaps beyond restoration by any measures at all. The present Poor Law, it will be seen, aims at meeting only the first of these three possible requirements of the able-bodied ; it has in effect only one type of institution—whether called a workhouse, a casual ward or a stoneyard—where sustenance subject to deterrence is meted out to all and sundry. The reformed Poor Law must be prepared to meet all three requirements. It must have, first, the means of temporary assistance—something to correspond to the workhouses, casual wards, stoneyards and relief works of to-day. This is for the " unemployed ". It must have, second, the means of restoring to physical vigour and perhaps of training for new occupations those who are proved incapable of supporting themselves as they are—something corresponding or akin to the free farm colonies at Hollesley Bay and elsewhere. This is for the " unemployable " or " half-employable " who can be restored. It must have, third, the means of separating from society those who are clearly unfit to belong thereto—something corresponding to the penal colonies in Belgium and Switzerland. This is for the " unemployable " who perhaps cannot be made good again. Each of these three grades of treatment must be provided.

An important distinction, however, is to be noted. The aim of social policy will be to make the first grade of treatment—that of simple tiding over—less and less necessary; to get mere depression of trade met by individual action or by measures of industrial organisation,[1] of which insurance is the chief; and to leave to measures of relief only the more difficult cases of failure where training for new occupations or segregation from the body politic is required. In other words, all tiding over should become ultimately a function of industry; all relief should be educational.

[1] Insurance against unemployment deserves this title because it is essentially an averaging of earnings over good and bad times, and it may be held to retain that character in spite of a certain amount of public assistance. As practised by the trade unions it is as completely a measure of industrial organisation as is short time in the cotton trade or in coal-mining.

CHAPTER XI.

CONCLUSION.

IN conclusion, the problem discussed in the preceding pages and the lines of its solution may be presented under a few general aspects.[1]

Unemployment is not to be identified as a problem of general over-population. There is no reason for thinking that the industrial system has lost permanently anything of its former power to absorb the growing supply of labour. There is no reason for thinking that any new stimulus to the expansion of industry is required. There is conclusive reason for holding that no such stimulus can make any lasting impression upon the causes of unemployment.

Unemployment arises because, while the supply of labour grows steadily, the demand for labour, in growing, varies incessantly in volume, distribution and character. This variation, in several of its forms at least, flows directly from the control of production by many competing employers. It is obvious that, so long as the industrial world is split up into separate groups of producers—each group with a life of its own, and growing or decaying in ceaseless attrition upon its neighbours—there must be insecurity of employment. It is probable that at least one of the most striking specific factors in the problem—namely, cyclical fluctuation of trade—may be traced ultimately to this same source. Unemployment, in other words, is to some extent at least part of the price of industrial competition —part of the waste without which there could be no competition at all. Socialistic criticism of the existing order has therefore on this side much justification. The theoretic reply to that criticism must take the form, not of a denial, but of a gloss—that there may be worse things in a community than unemployment. The practical reply is to be found in reducing the pain of unemployment to relative insignificance. In this there seems to be no impossibility. If the solution of the problem of unemployment means that every man should have the certainty of continuous work throughout life in the occupation for which he has been trained, then no solution is to be expected, or, indeed, desired. If, however, by a

[1] See now chapters xvi. and xvii.

235

solution is meant that no man able and willing to work should come to degradation or destitution for want of work, then a solution is not indeed within sight but by no means beyond hope. Its direction is certain and its distance not infinite. The demand for labour cannot be stereotyped save in a stagnant industry. The supply of labour may be made immeasurably more capable of following and waiting for the demand.

This on its two sides—of following the demand and waiting for the demand—is the policy outlined in the last two chapters. The policy may be variously described.

It is a policy of industrial organisation; of meeting deliberately industrial needs that at present are met wastefully because without deliberation. Fluctuations of demand are now provided for by the maintenance of huge stagnant reserves of labour in varying extremities of distress. There is no reason in the nature of things why they should not be provided for by organised reserves of labour raised beyond the reach of distress. To be able to follow the demand men must possess greater powers of intelligent movement from place to place; they must possess also power to move from trade to trade, or—a more essential point— they must have better guidance in the first choice of occupations. To be able to wait for the demand men must have a reserve for emergencies; they must not be living from hand to mouth; they must through insurance or its equivalent be able to average wages over good and bad times and to subsist without demoralisation till they can be re-absorbed again after industrial transformations. These two measures are complementary and, in some sense indeed, alternative to one another. The better the supply of labour is able to follow the demand, the less will it have to wait for the demand. The greater the power of waiting for the demand, that is to say, the higher the rate or the better the distribution of wages, the less need is there for movement.

It is a policy of establishing the standard of life upon a longer and broader basis. An individual is not self-supporting unless his earnings amount to a sufficiency for life and not merely to a sufficiency for the time of working. An industry is not self-supporting unless it yields wages not only for the time of employment but also for the time of inevitable unemployment as well— unless it maintains all the men required by it both while they are in active service and while they are standing in reserve. So far, therefore, as the problem arises from fluctuations of industrial activity, it becomes essentially one of wages—of their amount, division and expenditure, and, on this side at least, it falls within ascertainable limits. Fluctuations of trade vary in range but do not vary indefinitely.   So far as the problem arises from changes of industrial structure or loss of industrial quality, it is not so measurable.   In practice, however, causes of this nature are relatively unimportant, and in any case the resources—whether provided by individual saving or by way of insurance—which would enable men to tide over periods of temporary depression, would also serve to keep them while searching for new occupations.

It is a policy of making reality correspond with the assumptions of economic theory.   Assuming the demand for labour to be single and the supply perfectly fluid, it is not hard to show that unemployment must always be in process of disappearance—that demand and supply are constantly tending to an equilibrium.   The ideal for practical reform, therefore, must be to concentrate the demand and to give the right fluidity to the supply.

Finally, it is a policy of introducing organisation and unity where, and only where, they involve no harmful limitation of individual risks and responsibilities.   Industrial competition involves that for every piece of work to be done, two separate producing units should offer—that there should be two tenders for every contract.   With an unorganised labour market, this means that each of the two contractors tendering has to keep in his neighbourhood, or within touch of him, a separate reserve of labour to be called on in case he should be successful.   Whichever contractor is successful, one of these reserves will be unemployed.   In the Socialist state there will be no separate producing units; the two contractors will have been made one for all purposes.   In the competitive state with an organised labour market there will still be the two contractors, but they will draw their men from a common centre and so use the same reserve of labour.   Whichever contractor is successful the same men will obtain employment.   The only loss of employment will be that of the unsuccessful contractor and his permanent staff.   The heaviest stress of competition will fall where it can be borne with the least suffering and where it is most needed to prevent stagnation.

APPENDIX TO PART I.

EXISTING METHODS OF SEEKING EMPLOYMENT IN GREAT BRITAIN.[1]

FOUR organised methods of bringing would-be employers and employed into communication are of sufficient importance to call for individual notice; namely, newspaper advertisement, private or profit-making registries, trade union registration, and public labour exchanges. In addition to these the industrial world is permeated by informal connections and channels of information guiding the movements of workmen in search of employment and directing the inquiries of employers. These various topics may be taken in order.

1. NEWSPAPER ADVERTISEMENTS.

Advertisement in a newspaper is available as a last resource for finding work or workpeople in all occupations. It is a normal or important method only in a few. An analysis of the advertisements in fifteen papers made by the Board of Trade in 1893 showed that of 1,606 advertisements dealing with women more than three-quarters related to domestic service and half the remainder to shop assistants; while of 1,482 dealing with men, 521 related to shop assistants, 173 to clerks and warehousemen, and 216 to domestic service, leaving only 572 for all the other trades together.[2] For more recent times the position may be indicated by the following notes as to advertisements in some of the London newspapers on one day during the present year—the busiest day of the first week of May, 1908,[3] being taken in each case.

Daily Telegraph.—Men and boys: 301 places offered and 95 places wanted. Clerks, agents and shop assistants form the great majority in each case. Anything in the nature of industrial employment is very little represented. Women and girls: 248 places offered and 43 places wanted. About a third of these relate to domestic servants; nearly all the remainder to clerks and shop assistants.

Daily Chronicle.—Men and boys: 43 places offered and 335 places wanted. Here industrial occupations are somewhat better represented—the metal, woodworking and building trades all yielding appreciable numbers of places wanted. Substantially the only men's

---

[1] This Appendix was written before the passage of the Labour Exchanges Act, 1909.
[2] *Agencies and Methods*, 1893, pp. 131-34.
[3] This month is taken as being probably on the whole that of briskest demand for labour.

places offered, however, relate to watchmaking and jewellery.[1] Women
and girls : 113 places offered—all for domestic service.

Daily News.—This practically deals only with the printing trades—
yielding 7 places offered and 78 places wanted. Among the latter
are a good many advertisements by compositors specifying in some
cases whether they are unionists or non-unionists. It is interesting to
notice that comparable numbers come from both categories. Taking
four successive Tuesdays in May, 1908, there appear 55 advertisements
by non-unionist compositors as against 30 by unionists and 66 unspecified. This indicates a tendency for the employers to look elsewhere than to the trade union registry even when they want union men.

Morning Post.—Here advertising is confined to domestic service
and is considerable.

Morning Advertiser.—This is the recognised medium for the public
house trade.

The tendency for particular papers to specialise in certain lines is
noticeable. It is also somewhat noticeable that the only occupations in
which newspaper advertisement appears to play an important part—the
commercial ones and domestic service—are distinctly outside the strictly
industrial sphere and are at the same time those in which alone private
registries have any hold.

2. PRIVATE REGISTRIES.

Private or profit-making registries are of importance only in two sets
of occupations—the commercial and clerical, and those connected with
or akin to domestic service. Those dealing with the latter types of employment are to be found everywhere and need no special description.
Those dealing with commercial situations are naturally to be found only
in great centres of business such as the city of London. They charge
fees as a rule both to employers and applicants, the latter commonly
having to pay both a fixed sum on registration (up to £1 1s. or even
more) and a percentage of the first twelve months' salary in any situation
found, whether the situation lasts twelve months or not. A charge of
this nature, though quite consistent with straightforward dealing, also of
course opens the door to fraud by collusion between the registry and an
employer. The latter may constantly be engaging clerks and discharging
them after a few weeks, while the former takes its twelve months' percentage from each. There is nothing indeed to prevent registry and
employer from being the same persons under different names.

Often, it may be added, a registry dealing with commercial occupations stands not by itself but as an adjunct to some training establishment, *e.g.*, a school of typewriting.

---

[1] The day taken is not in this case typical. The first Tuesday in November, 1908,
for instance, yields 122 advertisements for men and boys (in a fair variety of trades)
as against 290 by them.

3. Trade Union Travelling Benefit and Registries.

A trade union necessarily becomes to some extent a means of assisting its members to obtain employment. Even if nothing more is done its members, in work and out of work, come together at branch meetings, and information spreads as to the places where trade is active or expected to become so. Very commonly, however, a good deal more is done. First, many trade unions provide "travelling benefits," that is to say, allowances for board and lodging whereby their members may be enabled to go from one district to another in search of work. Second, the union organisation itself becomes a means of collecting and distributing precise information as to the state of the labour market in each district, developing sometimes into a recognised registry or exchange to which employers and foremen send direct so soon as they need men. Much valuable information on both these points is collected in the Board of Trade Report of 1893 on Agencies and Methods for dealing with the Unemployed. The following summary may be quoted :—

"*Travelling Benefit.*—Many unions which provide unemployed benefit give additional payments to unemployed members travelling in search of work. In addition to these there are several societies, notably among the building trades, which have no unemployed benefit proper, but which make allowances, amounting usually to 1s. 6d. a day, to travelling members. Precautions are taken against imposition, and members in receipt of this benefit must be continually on the move, strict limits being placed upon the number of days' benefit which they may draw within a given district. It is found, however, by some unions that the benefit is largely taken advantage of, especially in the summer, by members of a roving disposition, and the payment is thought by many to encourage tramping. Some unions (*e.g.*, the Scottish Typographical Association) have, therefore, discontinued it altogether. The same difficulty on a more serious scale was found by the Ironfounders Society when it introduced a special emigration benefit in 1885 ; members used that allowance to obtain a holiday trip, and then returned, and it had to be dropped after eighteen years' trial."

"*Assistance to Members in Obtaining Work.*—In the case of some societies (*e.g.*, the London Society of Compositors) it is the custom of employers to apply frequently to the society for men, and the office, therefore, acts as a kind of labour bureau. A few unions (*e.g.*, the Dublin Bakers) go so far as to prohibit members from applying for work except through the society. In most societies, however, the main bulk of the work of obtaining employment is done by individual application, but many of the societies assist their members in the search for work by announcements, made at branch meetings, of jobs vacant or of members wanting jobs, and in many other ways. In some societies (*e.g.*, the Steam Engine Makers) considerable pains are taken to find places for unemployed members. Others (*e.g.*, the Amalgamated Society of Carpenters and Joiners) pay a small 'bonus' of 6d. to any member who takes another 'off the books' by finding him a situation."

16

" The chief important societies publish periodical reports showing the state of employment in the districts in which they have branches, and distribute these reports gratuitously to their members. Some (*e.g.*, the Engineers, Ironfounders, Compositors and others) publish lists of the workshops in each district at which their members may apply for work."

No comprehensive inquiry of a similar character appears to have been made of recent years. Yet there can be no doubt that the foregoing summary applies more or less accurately to-day, both as regards travelling benefit and as regards guidance in the search for employment.

Travelling benefit in its crude form implies the issue of a tramp card or certificate entitling the holder to draw for board and lodging upon any of the union branches while leaving him free to roam at will and at hazard from town to town. In this crude form it is still largely given, but is, beyond question, of diminishing importance. It is discountenanced by many union officials on the ground already indicated, that it encourages idle tramping and demoralises the workman. It involves often a rather cool welcome from the branch to which the tramp comes. In so far as he has come more or less on chance he is likely to find men unemployed on the spot; the local unionists will be more concerned to hasten the passage of the tramp to the next town than to encourage his settling down where he is. It is, finally, an obviously inferior method of conducting the search for work. A union having branches in many towns can do better by using its organisation to discover where work is to be had and sending men there direct and rapidly, than by assisting them to tramp without definite guidance. In the Board of Trade Report the opinion of the general secretary of the National Society of Amalgamated Brassworkers is quoted to the following effect: " Travelling from town to town in search of work has greatly decreased. The trade tramp is dying out and the sooner the system is dead the better. One of the oldest trade unions only recently expunged the travelling rule, on the ground that travelling in search of work tended to degrade members. Travelling after work where there is some evidence that it exists, and where the workman receives help either from his society or his friends, is in my judgment on the increase. Leaving home or the town is not so much dreaded as formerly, railway excursions being so cheap, frequent and speedy." In the same report a decrease of travelling in search for work is noted in such important unions as the Friendly Society of Ironfounders, the Boilermakers and Iron Shipbuilders, the Amalgamated Society of Carpenters and Joiners, the Operative Bricklayers, and the Operative Stonemasons as well as in many others. The statistics as to the first named of those unions are sufficiently full and interesting to be worth giving in detail.

TABLE XXXII.—TRAVELLING BENEFIT—FRIENDLY SOCIETY OF
IRONFOUNDERS, 1873-1907.

	Total No. of Tramp Cards Issued.	No. of Tramp Cards Issued per 1,000 Members of the Society.	Average No. of Members Constantly on Travel.	No. of Members at any Time Travelling per 1,000 Members of the Society.
1873	940	81	60	6·3
1874	1,648	138	86	7·2
1875	1,762	142	70	5·7
1876	1,925	152	108	8·6
1877	1,912	151	155	12·3
1878	1,897	150	177	14·0
1879	1,963	159	213	17·4
1880	1,430	123	139	12·0
1881	1,286	114	89	7·9
1882	1,194	104	57	5·0
1883	1,213	101	63	5·3
1884	1,511	121	99	8·0
1885	1,418	114	113	9·1
1886	1,345	111	108	9·0
1887	1,243	106	101	8·6
1888	1,056	87	57	4·7
1889	883	64	22	1·6
1890	1,253	85	45	3·0
1891	1,542	101	77	5·0
1892	1,502	99	119	7·8
1893	1,286	84	106	7·0
1894	1,329	87	123	8·1
1895	1,175	77	100	6·6
1896	1,134	72	50	3·1
1897	1,066	64	51	3·1
1898	1,062	63	44	2·6
1899	881	50	26	1·5
1900	1,129	62	49	2·7
1901	1,469	80	101	5·5
1902	1,298	71	98	5·4
1903	1,233	67	98	5·3
1904	1,431	78	155	8·4
1905	1,083	59	116	6·3
1906	913	48	55	3·0
1907	1,089	56	78	4·0

The table shows, first, a considerable fluctuation with the state of
trade; second, a general decrease. Both points are clearly brought out
by calculating the average for successive periods of expansion and
depression, taking three years in each case.

16 *

XXXIII.—AVERAGE NUMBER OF MEMBERS CONSTANTLY ON TRAVEL PER 1,000 MEMBERS IN THE SOCIETY—FRIENDLY SOCIETY OF IRONFOUNDERS.

Good Trade.		Bad Trade.	
Years Taken.	Average.	Years Taken.	Average.
1871-1873	—	1877-1879	14·6
1881-1883	6·1	1885-1887	8·9
1888-1890	3·1	1892-1894	7·6
1898-1900	2·3	1903-1905	6·7

As regards guidance in the search for employment the position appears to be still much as it was in 1892. A few of the most strongly organised societies habitually receive applications for workpeople direct from employers or foremen. Such is the case with the Boilermakers and Iron Shipbuilders, the Patternmakers, the London Compositors, the London Printing Machine Managers, the Typographical Association, and others. A good many more receive applications occasionally —according to the state of trade. But even in the most highly organised trades the use of the union office as a labour bureau is hardly ever exclusive of other methods of seeking employment or obtaining workpeople. It is not a method to which employers lend themselves very readily. They do not wish to become altogether dependent upon a possibly hostile organisation. They have a natural objection to the not infrequent rule that men on the vacant list shall be sent to jobs in the order not of capacity but of signature. Generally speaking, the union has to rely upon reports by its own members for notice of situations offering. One or two have tried to secure such reports by a small payment to any working member taking another off the books by finding work for him.[1] Other unions have endeavoured to organise a regular system for the notification of vacancies. The Associated Society of Carpenters and Joiners, for instance, at one time issued addressed postcards for the purpose to all its members, but found it impossible to get them used. The Wheelwrights and Coachmakers Operatives' Union (London) maintained a system of this nature till quite recently, issuing stamped and addressed postcards to employers, foremen and its own members for return to its labour bureau notifying vacancies. During the year 1907 677 postcards were received and 40 men placed, at a cost (exclusive of any salary to the superintendent) of £4 10s. 7d., or 2s. 3d. per situation. Complaint is made in the report for 1907 of the apathy and indifference of some members in notifying vacancies, and it is clear that the bureau is far from being the main avenue to employment. The report refers to "the members who are out of employment who become disheartened by merely walking over the same ground and calling upon the same employers week after week

---

[1] E.g., the Amalgamated Society of Carpenters and Joiners, as mentioned above.

with the result that the employers form an opinion that these are worth-less workers being always out of employment". This union has now transferred all its vacant books to the Metropolitan Employment Exchanges.

These, however, are rather exceptional cases. For the most part the union contents itself with imposing a formal obligation upon its members to insert a notice of any vacancies within their knowledge in the vacant book. Very commonly a fine may be inflicted for neglect of this duty, and commonly also it is accompanied by a prohibition of any assistance to non-unionists in obtaining employment.

Broadly speaking, the unions serve rather to enlarge the scope of the personal search for work, by travelling benefits, and to guide it, by general indications as to the state of the labour market, than to replace it altogether. In giving this help and guidance they render a very important service to industry. At the same time their activity here falls immeasurably short of any organisation of the labour market. In scope it is limited entirely to trade unionists—a fifth or a sixth of the working population. In character it is, except with a few of the strongest societies, more akin to the help which every man gets from his mates—unionist and non-unionist alike—than to the formal organisation of a labour exchange.[1]

4. PUBLIC LABOUR EXCHANGES (1909).

In almost any country but the United Kingdom the present section would be lengthy and important. Public labour exchanges fill a prominent and growing place in the industrial organisation of Germany. They have been established or are being established on a considerable scale in many other European States—France, Austria, Belgium, Switzerland and Norway. In the United Kingdom they have till within the last year or two been almost without exception unimportant and unsuccessful. Those in existence at the end of 1905 are described in an official return issued by the Local Government Board. The principal experiment since then—and the largest yet attempted in this country—that of the Central (Unemployed) Body for London, has been noticed in dealing with the Unemployed Workmen Act.[2]

The first labour bureau in this country appears to have been that established by voluntary action at Egham in February, 1885. This accomplished some real though limited work—filling a maximum of 289 situations in 1891—but declined and was closed on the passing of the Local Government Act in 1894. Another voluntary bureau, at Ipswich, established a few months after the Egham bureau, continued till it was

---

[1] Calling on friends at work to let them know one's need is perhaps the most general method of beginning the search for employment to-day.

[2] *Labour Bureaux*, report by Mr. H. D. Lowry, one of H.M. inspectors for the Local Government Board, 1906, p. 86. The Board of Trade Report on *Agencies and Methods for Dealing with the Unemployed* (1893) describes an earlier epoch (pp. 97-119).

taken over by the Distress Committee in 1906. Increasing depression of trade at the end of 1892 once more drew the attention of municipal authorities to the question, and several bureaux were established. Most of these, however, served only to register men for relief works and came to an end with the winter. A few maintained a fluctuating existence up to the passing of the Unemployed Workmen Act in 1905. The most successful appears to have been that at Plymouth which for some years placed 1,000 to 1,500 men annually, but was taken over with fatal results by the Distress Committee. The Glasgow Corporation Bureau, started apparently about 1897, filled a larger number of situations, but mainly for women and girls in domestic service. The Chelsea Bureau, described at some length in the 1893 Report as being " one of the most important labour bureaux under the control of a London Vestry," ceased making returns to the Labour Department after 1894. Such of the London bureaux as survived to 1901 were suspended in that year owing to a doubt whether they could legally be maintained out of the rates by the Metropolitan Borough Councils which under the London Government Act of 1899 had succeeded to the vestries. After this doubt had been set at rest by the Labour Bureaux (London) Act, 1902, some were revived. Outside London, municipal expenditure on labour bureaux was made possible by the fact that the authorities concerned were not subject to a Local Government Board Audit.

At the end of 1905 the official inquiry already mentioned discovered 21 municipal and 3 non-municipal bureaux in existence—the total number of situations filled by twenty of them during the twelve months ending 31st August, 1905, being 16,290. Only seven of these bureaux had been in existence more than three years. Eleven of the municipal ones were in London and ten outside. The former, with the exception of those at Battersea and Westminster, were all taken over by the Central (Unemployed) Body during 1906. Only one proved to have at the time any substantial goodwill amongst ordinary employers. The rest were either moribund, merged in Distress Committee registration or practically confined to the supply of casual men to the municipality.

The provincial bureaux have also for the most part been taken over by Distress Committees.

5. INFORMAL ORGANISATION IN THE LABOUR MARKET.

The four agencies just mentioned—newspaper advertisement, private registries, trade union registries and public labour exchanges—are the only prominent forms of organisation for bringing would-be employers and workmen into communication. Yet clearly all four together cover but an insignificant fraction of the whole field. They in no sense answer the question as to how men, in fact, obtain employment. They are probably still far less important than the informal connections and customs which spring up to guide and shorten the personal search for employment in each trade. These connections are of two types—local and personal.

On the one hand, there come to be well-known spots at which situations are notified or even actual engagements made, and at which therefore men habitually congregate. At the Liverpool Docks, for instance, there is a series of "stands" each used by a group of employers. In London it is an unwritten law that stevedores for the East and West India Docks should be taken on outside the " Blue Posts " in the West India Dock Road; there are all along the waterside many other well-known spots—generally also public-houses [1]—at which men congregate and to which employers send for men. Again, to take quite another London industry, that of furniture-making, wholesale shops which supply manufacturers with tools or materials often make a practice of exhibiting for their customers notices of men required. In the Curtain Road district there arc at least three such shops which have regular notice boards for the purpose and are indeed nothing less than labour exchanges. All the unemployed of every grade in cabinet-making go the round of these three shops systematically ; having done that they feel that they have exhausted the possibilities of the trade.[2] A similar custom exists with regard to female machinists for blouse, skirt and mantle making in the city. Shops where machines are repaired serve also as labour exchanges for the group of employers with whom they are in touch. It would probably be possible to multiply such instances indefinitely. One set of economic relations leads naturally to another. The dealer in manufacturers' materials becomes very readily also their labour exchange or at least the channel of information as to their demands for labour.[3]

Local connections, it will be noticed, merge imperceptibly into those which are less local than personal. Men "follow up" some particular foreman, or when out of work call in turn upon all their mates who are in work to ask for intimation of the next vacancy. Such methods are of course of perfectly general application. They are, perhaps, most universal in the building trade. Apart from them, indeed, the building trade is the least organised of any and illustrates most perfectly the plan of hawking labour from door to door. A foreman, with a few picked and practically permanent men, goes down to a job and waits till others come along. Some of those will be men habitually following up that foreman when out of a job ; they will have got his address or he may even have their addresses and have sent them a card. Some may be known to the picked men ; each of these, indeed, will have become the centre of a spreading circle of information. Some will have seen the contractor's portable office

[1] *Cf. West Ham*, E. Howarth and M. Wilson, p. 208. The public house, as a place of common resort, develops naturally into a Labour Exchange. The disadvantages of this form of labour market organisation, especially in conjunction with the foreman system, are obvious.

[2] For the allied industry of coach-making there are three well-known shops in Long Acre where vacant situations in all parts of London are notified in books kept for the purpose and open to the inspection of workmen.

[3] In the dyeing and cleaning industry, for instance, there is at least one wholesale house (supplying dyes, soaps, etc.) whose travellers, passing continually from one employer to another, regularly convey information as to where men are wanted or are to be had.

going down the street on a lorry and will have tracked it to its destination. Others will come guided by stray hints picked up from passers by, at street corners, in public-houses, or even tramping by chance alone.[1] In one way or another the job fills up.   As to the manner of filling up two things have to be noticed.   First, a certain proportion of men who apply and get put on at the beginning of a job are frequently found to be incompetent or unsteady workmen.   After a few hours or days' trial these go or are dismissed as better men come along.   By a process of "weeding out" to which frequent reference is made by builders and foremen, efficient gangs are obtained.   The inefficient men go on to repeat the process elsewhere; they are constantly getting and losing jobs after a short trial.   Second, the foreman has often more power than he can be trusted not to abuse.   Evidence of men bribing the foreman in order to secure or to keep employment is not easy to obtain.   Yet there cannot be the slightest doubt that either in a direct form or in the indirect form of convivial drinking it is quite common both in building and in other trades where the foreman system is much developed. It is regarded, indeed, often as a matter too notorious for comment.[2] Personal connections in the labour market as elsewhere, whether through foremen or through fellow workmen, involve all the familiar dangers of patronage.

Such then are the methods by which the indispensable commodity of labour is brought to market to-day.   Here and there within a narrow scope are formal labour exchanges.   Everywhere are informal connections and channels of information.   The personal search for employment from door to door remains the dominant method.   It is seldom perhaps wholly blind.   It is almost always a groping in the half-light or the dark.   The outline already given cannot better be filled in than by the following record of actual experiences—the early experiences of one of the best-known representatives of labour, a member of a skilled trade, and a life-long unionist :—[3]

"No better fortune awaited them in London.   The young husband sought work with no success.   News reached him that his trade was thriving again in Liverpool, so he set out to tramp there a second time.[4]

.   .   .   .

[1] A carpenter—belonging to one of the smaller unions—after agreeing with my suggestion that his union was of great value to him in telling him where work was to be had, when he came to explaining how in fact he would look for work if he were then in need of it, said that his first move would be to go, nòt to the union office, but to Liverpool St. Station and leave his tools in the cloakroom (any number of men do this), and his next to tramp the streets at hazard.

[2] When asking how men found work at some of the docks I have had the unexpected answer: "Go down to X—— and hold up your hand with a penny in it".

[3] *From Workhouse to Westminster: The Life Story of Will Crooks, M.P.*, by George Haw (Cassell & Company, Limited, 1907).   The description of Mr. Crooks' tramping for work is so apposite and so telling that I have taken the liberty of quoting it at some length.

[4] He had already tramped once to Liverpool from London through Burton-on-Trent, and had with some trouble obtained work but had gone back to London on the death of his child.

"In Liverpool, again, the prospect was not what he had been led to believe. An odd job here and an odd job there still left him in want. At last, in response to the earnest entreaties of his wife, whom nothing could persuade to revisit Liverpool, he returned to take his chance again in London.

"This time Crooks determined to try to find work outside his own trade. He went down to the docks, where by the aid of a friendly foreman he got occasional jobs as a casual labourer.

. . . .

"One typical day of tramping for work in London he described to me thus :—

"'I first went down to the riverside at Shadwell. No work to be had there. Then I called at another place in Limehouse. No hands wanted. So I looked in at home and got two slices of bread in paper and walked eight miles to a cooper's yard in Tottenham. All in vain. I dragged myself back to Clerkenwell. Still no luck. Then I turned homewards in despair. By the time I reached Stepney I was dead beat.

"'That year I know I walked London till my limbs ached again. I remember returning home once by way of Tidal Basin, and turning into Victoria Docks so utterly exhausted that I sank down on a coil of rope and slept for hours.'

. . . .

"Work came at last in an unexpected way. He was returning home after another empty day when he hailed a carman and asked for a lift.

"'All right, mate, jump up,' was the response.

"As they sat chatting side by side, the carman learnt that his companion was seeking work.

"'What's yer trade?' he enquired.

"'A cooper.'

"'Why, the governor wants a cooper.'

"So instead of dropping off at Poplar, Crooks accompanied the carman to the works. . . . That work was a stepping-stone to another and better job at Wandsworth. . . . Crooks was never out of work again in his life.

. . . .

"Nothing wearies one more than walking about hunting for employment which is not to be had. It is far harder than real work. The uncertainty, the despair, when you reach a place only to discover that your journey is fruitless are frightful. I've known a man say : 'Which way shall I go to-day?' Having no earthly idea which way to take, he tosses up a button. If the button comes down on one side he tracks east ; if on the other, he tracks west."

Nothing can better illustrate the waste of time, energy and shoe leather involved in the personal search for employment. This is the lottery which industrial disorganisation makes of the workman's life. This is the process as to which comfortable ignorance has so often assured us : " The men know where to look for work all right ; they know ; Lord bless you ! *they* know ".

PART II (1930)

CHAPTER XII.

THE POLICIES OF 1909.

The Poor Law Commission of 1905-9. Majority and Minority Reports agreed on unemployment : in diagnosis of causes ; in criticism of Poor Law and relief works as remedies ; in positive proposals. Labour Exchanges and de-casualisation. Industrial training. Unemployment Insurance. Regularisation of demand for labour. Maintenance on conditions. Acceptance of unemployment proposals by Government. Mr. Winston Churchill at Board of Trade.

ONE of the last acts of the Conservative Government of 1905 was the appointment, on 4th December of that year, of a Royal Commission on the Poor Laws and Relief of Distress. The terms of reference to this Commission fell into two sections. They were to inquire

"(1) Into the working of the laws relating to the relief of poor persons in the United Kingdom ;

"(2) Into the various means which have been adopted outside of the Poor Laws for meeting distress arising from want of employment, particularly during periods of severe industrial depression" ;

and were to report, among other things, whether any, and if so, what fresh legislation for dealing with distress was advisable. After three years of inquiry and deliberation, the Commission presented two main Reports, one signed by the Chairman (Lord George Hamilton) and, with a few reservations and notes, by thirteen other members, and the other signed by four members, including Mrs. Sidney Webb. The Majority and Minority Reports were of comparable length ; each independently covered the ground ; with their attendant minutes of evidence and appendices they filled thirty-nine volumes and 19,000 foolscap pages of print.[1] They represent the last comprehensive study of unemployment in this country.

[1] Both Reports, after appearing together in the ordinary form of a foolscap " blue book" of 1,640 pages, made separate less conventional appearances. The Minority Report was published as a book in two volumes by S. and B. Webb (Longmans, 1909) ; the second volume, under the title of *The Public Organisation of the Labour Market*, contains the section of the Report concerned with unemployment. The Majority Report was officially reprinted in handy octavo form (Reprint from Cmd. 4499 of Session 1909). Page references here are made to the Reports in these later more accessible issues.

Most of the ground covered by the Reports falls outside the scope of the present volume ; the Commissioners were concerned with the distress of many others than the unemployed, with the aged, infirm and sick, with children and lunatics, with settlement and removal, with indoor and outdoor relief. The second section of their reference, however, involved a full study of unemployment and led up to the presentation, in each of the Reports, of a comprehensive programme of measures both for diminishing unemployment and for dealing with distress due to it. Moreover, though the Commissioners found it necessary to present two separate Reports, there was in respect of unemployment a large measure of agreement between them, extending both to diagnosis and to remedies. The differences were often no more than differences of emphasis or of putting the same proposition from distinct points of view.

The Reports agreed, first, in recognising the reality of unemployment. They agreed that it was not possible for all men at all times to obtain employment on reasonable terms, and that it was not possible any longer for the State to "adopt the simple principle of the Act of 1834 that, in order to drive men into independent labour, we need only apply a test that shall be sufficiently deterrent. . . . Not only is there cyclical dislocation which recurrently reduces the demand for labour, and issues either in general short time, as in collieries and the cotton trade, or in workers of all classes and grades being thrown out of employment altogether, but, going on all the time—never disappearing, and only intensified by bad times—there is this normal underemployment of casual and seasonal workers, and there is the entirely fitful employment of the 'unemployables'." [1]   The Majority, having thus found certain economic causes of unemployment, discussed two others that had been suggested to them—namely, contraction in the total demand for labour, and displacement of labour by new methods or machinery ; they ruled out the former on theoretic grounds and they dismissed the latter as real but relatively unimportant.[2]   The Minority gave the same general diagnosis in other words, by their fourfold classification of the unemployed as :

(i) The Men from Permanent Situations, discharged by changes of process or the misfortunes of their particular employer or in industrial depressions.

---

[1] *Majority Report*, Part VI., §§ 201 and 202, p. 437.

[2] " It is certainly striking to hear from great employers in how many cases such changes do not diminish the labour they employ even temporarily, and how general is the experience that they increase it permanently " (*Majority Report*, Part VI, § 220, p. 441).

(ii) The Men of Discontinuous Employment typified by those in building and other seasonal trades.

(iii) The Under-employed, typified by the casual labourer at the docks and elsewhere.

(iv) The Unemployable.[1]

With this agreement of general diagnosis went an even more noticeable agreement in emphasising as the most serious factor in the problem the practice of casual engagement of labour and the resulting under-employment. The Majority introduced the subject in a distinct section under the heading : "The New Problem : Chronic Under-employment " ; they made a special analysis of dock labour as the leading case of casual employment ; and they described casual labour in this and other forms as the greatest single cause of the production of pauperism and distress.

"Our Investigators, Mr. Steel-Maitland and Miss Squire, assign to casual labour the chief place among industrial conditions that contribute to pauperism, and this view is confirmed by a number of witnesses. The summary of previous inquiries into distress due to unemployment in Messrs. Jackson and Pringle's Report discloses a most striking unanimity in the view that the great bulk of applications for relief from unemployment come from casual labour. Another of our Investigators, Mr. Jones, also says : ' Among the most effective pauperising agencies must be placed casual labour ' ".

"This striking unanimity among our Special Investigators is absolutely confirmed by our own inquiry." [2]

"The growth of casual labour to its present dimensions is . . . a modern evil." [3]

"This typical form of casual labour, or rather of ' underemployment '—for dockers may, at any given time, with almost equal appropriateness be counted employed or unemployed—seemed to us to present so many painful features as to warrant some amount of special investigation . .

The common sense of the nation has seen for some time that the best ordinary life for the ordinary kind of man is that he should not have too much leisure or have it whenever he likes ; that his work should be so regular as to become a habit ; that he should be able to count on taking home a regular sum weekly to his wife as wage ; and that he should have some reserve to fall back upon in bad times. All these

---

[1] *Minority Report*, Part II, Ch. IV, pp. 165-233.
[2] Part VI, §§ 314-5, p. 462.   [3] Part VI, § 317, p. 463.

things are conspicuously absent in the docker's life, and it is this that makes dock labour almost a problem by itself." [1]

" If we be correct in our analysis of casual dock labour, and if such a system does economically and morally infuse and spread evils of a most serious character into the social life of the community where it prevails, then the system cannot be considered solely from the standpoint of the employer and of the employés. It is detrimental to the moral and material well-being of the community, and should, in consequence, be reduced, and if necessary by legislative regulation, to the smallest limits possible " [2]

The Minority said the same thing in almost the same words, when summing up the results of the special investigations put in hand for the Commission : " The outcome of these investigations was all the more impressive in that it was not what we anticipated. We do not exaggerate when we say that all these inquirers— numbering, with their assistants, more than a dozen, starting on different lines of investigation, and pursuing their researches independently all over the kingdom—came, without concert, to the same conclusion, namely, that of all the causes or conditions predisposing to pauperism, the most potent, the most certain, and the most extensive in its operation was this method of employment in odd jobs." [3] They concluded :

" That of all the forms of Unemployment, that which we have termed Under-employment, extending, as it does, to many hundreds of thousands of workers, and to their whole lives, is by far the worst in its evil effects ; and that it is this system of chronic Under-employment which is above all other causes responsible for the perpetual manufacture of paupers that is going on, and which makes the task of the Distress Committees in dealing with the Unemployed of other types— such as the Men from Permanent Situations, or the Men of Discontinuous Employment—hopelessly impracticable." [4]

From this agreement in diagnosis of unemployment, the Reports proceeded to agreement in condemning two of the former remedies for distress from unemployment, namely the Poor Law based wholly on deterrence, and relief works, both under the Unemployed Workmen Act of 1905 and apart from it.

For the Poor Law of 1834 the Minority naturally had no affection. The Majority were no less prepared to recognise cyclical

[1] Part VI, §§ 258-60, pp. 450-51.   [2] Part VI, § 303, p. 459.
[3] *Minority Report*, Part II, Ch. IV (C), p. 195.
[4] *Minority Report*, Part II, Ch. IV (H), 5 and 6, p. 243.

fluctuations, changes in methods of production, blind-alley employments for boys and casual labour as "modifications and developments in our industrial system which cannot be ignored," and
whose "products and wreckage, when either out of employment or
in distress, require a treatment more elastic and varied than the
simple method which, eighty years ago, was sufficient to cope with
able-bodied pauperism in agricultural districts." [1]

As to relief works both Reports quoted with approval the
same passage from two of their investigators :—

"The Municipal Relief Works, encouraged by Mr.
Chamberlain's circular in 1886, have been in operation for
twenty years, and must, we think, be pronounced a complete
failure—a failure accentuated by the attempt to organise them
by the Unemployed Workmen Act of 1905. The evidence
we have collected seems conclusive that relief works are economically useless. Either ordinary work is undertaken, in which
case it is merely forestalled, and, later, throws out of employment the men who are in the more or less regular employ of
the councils, or else it is sham work which we believe to be
even more deteriorating than direct relief." [2]

The Majority recommended accordingly that the Unemployed
Workmen Act should be dropped at once; the Minority that it
should be continued only till it was replaced by something better. [3]

Finally came the positive recommendations, again much the
same in each Report. They were summarised by the Majority in
the following order :—

I. *Labour Exchanges.*—The establishment of a national system
of Labour Exchanges was the first positive item in both Reports, and
the cornerstone of both their schemes of reform. [4] The Majority
based their recommendation primarily on two general requirements, that of increased mobility of labour and that of obtaining
accurate information as to unemployment; the need for the Exchanges appeared, however, again and again in their specific

---

[1] *Majority Report*, Part VI, § 304, p. 459.
[2] Report by Messrs. Jackson and Pringle, cited by Majority in Part VI, § 408,
p. 490, and by Minority in Part II, Ch. III (C), p. 137.
[3] The Unemployed Workmen Act remained formally in force till 1st April, 1930,
when it was repealed as part of the measure abolishing Boards of Guardians and transferring their powers to the ordinary local authorities. For most purposes it became
inoperative with the disappearance of unemployment in the war and was never revived.
The Central (Unemployed) Body for London, having failed by repeated letters and
deputations to obtain from successive post-war Governments anything else to do,
were reduced to maintaining the Hollesley Bay Labour Colony (pp. 181-2 above)
mainly for the reception of a few selected men sent by Metropolitan Boards of
Guardians. The Body published a final Report in March, 1930.
[4] *Majority Report*, Part VI, § 528, p. 516, and Recommendation (1) on p. 560.
Minority Report, Part II, Ch. V (A), p. 248.

proposals, *e.g.*, for the improvement of industrial training and the choice of careers,[1] for the dovetailing of seasonal occupations ;[2] for the control of home assistance to the unemployed ;[3] for the putting in hand of special works at times of exceptional depression.[4] The Minority, while agreeing on most of these points, found the "highest utility" of the Labour Exchange in dealing with the under-employed,[5] that is to say, as a means of de-casualisation. To secure this, the Minority proposed to make recruiting through an Exchange compulsory for scheduled trades with casual employment or for all engagements of less than a month's duration.

> " . . . it should be made legally compulsory on employers (being persons carrying on industrial or commercial operations for profit), in all those cases in which it is not convenient to them to guarantee a minimum period of employment, which might be put at a month (subject, of course, to the power of dismissal of any particular individual for misconduct, and even of arbitrary replacement of one man by another if desired), to hire such labour as they want, whether for a job, a day, or a week, exactly as is done without complaint in the mercantile marine, *exclusively through the National Labour Exchange.*" [6]

Some of the Special Investigators of the Commission had gone even further than this, by recommending the prohibition of casual hirings altogether. The Majority, while they did not at once go so far as the Minority, did not stop far short. They recommended that the Board of Trade should send officers to visit and hold inquiries in localities where intermittent employment prevailed, and should endeavour through conference with employers and employed to arrange schemes for the progressive de-casualisation of such employment. They described with obvious sympathy a plan for indirect compulsion by imposition of an 'employment termination due,' that is to say, a tax on dismissals, and in rejecting direct compulsion observed : "On the whole, we do not think that the time has yet come for any compulsory measures." [7] They were clearly prepared for compulsion later if it proved to be required.[8]

---

[1] Part VI, Recommendation (10), p. 560.   [2] Part VI, § 525, p. 516.
[3] Part VI, Recommendation (25), p. 562.
[4] Part VI, §§ 696 and 703, pp. 558 and 559.
[5] Part II, Ch. V (A) (iv) (*d*), p. 260. The Minority emphasised also the indispensability of Labour Exchanges to any system of compulsory insurance against unemployment (Part II, Ch. V (D) (i), p. 292).
[6] *Minority Report*, Part II, Ch. V (A) (iv) (*d*), pp. 261-2.
[7] Part VI, §§ 563-5, Recommendation (12), pp. 523, 524, 561.
[8] See the explicit reference to " legislative regulation " in the passage from Part VI, § 303, p. 459.

II. *The Education and Training of the Young for Industrial Life.*—Both Reports emphasised the misuse of boy labour in uneducative employments as a fertile source of unemployed and unemployable adults. The Majority recommended that "in order to discourage boys from entering occupations which offer no prospect of permanent employment, there should be established, in connection with the Labour Exchange, a special organisation for giving boys, parents, teachers, and school managers, information and advice as to suitable occupations for children leaving school"; they cited with approval proposals of one of their Special Investigators that boys should be kept at school until the age of fifteen, that exemption below this age should be granted only to boys training to learn a skilled trade, and that there should be school supervision till sixteen and replacing of the boys in school if they were not properly employed. The Minority "in order to secure proper industrial training for the youth of the nation" proposed to prohibit any employment below the age of fifteen and have compulsory half-time work and education up to eighteen.[1]

III. *The Regularisation of Employment.*—This meant in substance the use of public employment to steady the demand for labour. The Majority advised that "Government Departments and Local and Public Authorities should be enjoined : (*a*) To regularise their work as far as possible. (*b*) To endeavour, as far as possible, to undertake their irregular work when the general demand for labour is slack."[2] The Minority had a more ambitious scheme of a ten years' programme of public work to be used deliberately to counteract cyclical fluctuation.[3]

IV. *Unemployment Insurance.*—The Majority described "the establishment and promotion of unemployment insurance, especially amongst unskilled and unorganised labour" as "of paramount importance in averting distress arising from unemployment." They regarded the attainment of this object as "of such national importance as to justify . . . contributions from public funds towards its furtherance," and were much attracted by the "Ghent System" of public subsidies to insurance through trade unions and similar associations of workmen. Not being prepared, however, to approve any actual scheme brought before them, they recommended the setting up of a small Commission or Inter-Departmental Committee of experts and representatives of existing trade benefit organisations to frame a scheme.[4] The Minority, while

[1] *Majority Report*, Part VI, Recommendation (10), p. 560. *Minority Report*, Recommendation (40), p. 342.
[2] Part VI, Recommendation (11), p. 560.
[3] Part II, Recommendation (44), p. 342.
[4] Part VI, Recommendations (13) to (18), p. 561.

prepared to consider a partial scheme of compulsory insurance, preferred and definitely proposed a State subsidy to voluntary insurance through the trade unions.[1]

Even when they passed from the preventive and industrial measures just named to defining the form of public assistance to be given to such unemployed persons as should still be in distress, there was no real difference of principle between the two sides. The Majority proposed that all assistance to the able-bodied unemployed should be conditional on daily work or residence in an industrial or agricultural institution or colony, one of whose primary objects should be the restoration of the inmates to industrial efficiency and independence. They proposed also, as the last receptacle for those who defeated all efforts at restoration, a detention colony. " We believe that no system of labour or industrial colonies can be properly worked, unless there is in reserve a semi-penal institution to which those who refuse to comply with the rules and regulations of the colony can be sent upon proof of repeated or continuous misconduct." [2] The Minority, for the ultimate residuum of men in distress from want of employment, proposed maintenance " on condition that they submit themselves to the physical and mental training that they may prove to require." [3] This training was to be given in day-training depots or residential farm colonies, and was to be backed by possibility of committal to a detention colony for, among other things, neglect to apply for maintenance and training, or breach of discipline in a training establishment. The two schemes of assistance were in all essentials the same.

There were, of course, differences of phraseology and of emphasis between the two Reports and each had some recommendations, not already named, which did not appear in the other. The Minority, for instance, proposed the setting up of a separate Ministry of Labour, while the Majority left the industrial dealing with unemployment (including Exchanges and insurance), to the Board of Trade. The Minority laid stress on the need of positive measures for absorbing the surplus labour that would be thrown out by de-casualisation; the Majority contemplated more gradual de-casualisation and trusted to the absorbing power of industry. The Majority formally reiterated the principle that home assistance to the able-bodied should be in some way less agreeable than insurance benefit or other form of aid; the Minority were content to trust, without saying so, to the deterrent effect on the work-shy of having " their whole working time . . . absorbed in such varied beneficial training of body and mind as they proved capable of ".[4]

[1] Part II, Ch. V, (D) (i), pp. 290 seq.　　[2] Part VI, § 629, p. 544.
[3] Part II, Ch. V, G 13, p. 328.　　[4] Part II, Ch. V (G), 13, p. 328.

The Minority held that such maintenance and training should be given without disfranchisement; the Majority proposed to disfranchise in future those who had public assistance for three months or more in the qualifying year.

Of these differences between the Reports the first, as to the nature of the administering authority, cut deepest. The Minority contemplated that the Minister of Labour should be concerned, not only with measures for prevention of distress through unemployment, but with the problem of the distressed able-bodied at all stages, including maintenance when insurance was exhausted, training and reconditioning, and in the last resort remedial detention in a colony. This was one side of their general policy of " breaking up the Poor Law ". The Majority entrusted the prevention of distress by Labour Exchanges, insurance, and the like, to an existing department—the Board of Trade—which by name and nature could hardly go beyond organising prevention of distress, that is to say, could not undertake direct relief of individuals. This was one side of *their* general policy of keeping the Poor Law together ; all maintenance of the able-bodied from public funds, even for training and reformation, should fall ultimately under the same authority as that which administered other forms of public relief, such as that of the impotent poor.

The difference of administrative authority proposed reflects a difference of general principle between the two parties on the Commission, running through all their work and dominating all that they said as to the Poor Law. For this very reason, it throws into striking relief the substantial identity of their two Reports on unemployment. From many different standpoints all the Commissioners had been led by patient study of the facts irresistibly and almost unconsciously to agreement ; through their own inquiries, by the evidence put before them, through the reports of their special investigators they had come to practically the same diagnosis and the same programme of principal reforms. Had they wished to present a unanimous report on unemployment, it is hard to see what could have stopped them. It need hardly be added that the diagnosis and the remedies of the Poor Law Commission are practically the same as those set out in the first part of this volume.

The advice given to the Government was all substantially the same : no more relief works, organisation of the labour market by Labour Exchanges with special attention to de-casualisation and the direction of juvenile labour, unemployment insurance, and regularisation of the demand for labour by systematic distribution of public work. These were the policies of the experts in 1909.

They were fortunate to catch the interest of Mr. Winston Churchill, then President of the Board of Trade, and became for a time the policies of the Government as well.

The Reports of the Poor Law Commission were signed on 4th February, 1909, and published almost immediately. Within four months, in the course of a debate on these Reports, Mr. Winston Churchill laid before Parliament the proposals of the Government for establishing a national system of Labour Exchanges under the Board of Trade and later, a scheme of compulsory insurance against unemployment. A Bill to give effect to the first part of these proposals was introduced on the following day, and meeting with general acceptance, received the Royal Assent and became the Labour Exchanges Act, 1909, on 20th September. Sixty-one Labour Exchanges, the first instalment of the national system, actually began operations on 1st February, 1910, less than twelve months after the signature of the Commission's report. The insurance scheme followed, as Part II of the National Insurance Act of 1911, coming into operation for contributions on 15th July, 1912, and for benefits on 15th January, 1913.

This remarkable celerity in acting on the recommendations of a Royal Commission had its explanation, and was not the fruit simply of three months' thought. Six months before the Report was issued, though not in ignorance of its prospective contents, Mr. Churchill had obtained the assent of his colleagues to establishing a national system of Labour Exchanges. He had at the same time asked certain officials of the Board of Trade to devise if they could a scheme of unemployment insurance. Though in order of time this scheme came and had to come after the Labour Exchanges, it is more conveniently described before them. The history of the Exchanges has been dominated by the insurance scheme and cannot be understood till that has been explained.

CHAPTER XIII.

ESTABLISHMENT AND TRANSFORMATION OF UNEMPLOYMENT INSURANCE.

1. The coming of insurance and the scheme of 1911. A daring adventure. Arguments for compulsion and against the Ghent scheme. British Association Address by Sir H. Ll. Smith. The scheme described. Compulsion limited to certain trades. Benefits limited in time. Incentives to economy. Launching and smooth working of scheme. The first report.
2. War and the ten-year chaos. Unsuccessful efforts to extend insurance in 1916 and 1918. Donation scheme. Belated generalisation of insurance in 1920 sunk under emergency relief. Extended benefit. Incessant variable legislation. Blanesburgh Committee and Report. Income and expenditure of Unemployment Fund.
3. The New Model of 1928. Description of scheme as amended by Act of 1930; scope, contributions, benefits and dependent allowances, conditions and disqualifications, adjudication on claims. Special schemes and proportioning rule abolished. Unlimited benefit and flat contributions. Thirty contribution rule and transitional provisions. Insurance without adjustment of premium to risk. Estimated contributions and receipts by industries. Growing reliance on Exchequer.
4. From Insurance by Contract to Relief by Status. Fundamental change in character of scheme. Unemployment relief financed by tax on employment. Old arguments inapplicable. Dangers imaginary and real.

THE COMING OF INSURANCE AND THE SCHEME OF 1911.

ON 19th May, 1909,[1] Mr. Winston Churchill, as President of the Board of Trade, announced the intention of the Government to introduce compulsory insurance against unemployment. The project seemed then and was a daring adventure. Except for one ill-judged and disastrous experiment in the Canton of St. Gall,[2] compulsory insurance against unemployment had never been attempted in any country of the world. All voluntary schemes had been immediate failures or insignificant successes. The only working model on a large scale was afforded by trade unions, which undertook no legal liabilities, were armed with almost indefinite powers of raising levies, and consisted predominantly of

---

[1] In a Parliamentary debate on the recently published Reports of the Royal Commission on the Poor Laws and Relief of Distress through Unemployment.

[2] Described, with all the other schemes of unemployment insurance attempted up to that time, in a memorandum on "Insurance against unemployment in Foreign Countries," prepared by the Board of Trade for the Poor Law Commission (Vol. IX, Appendix XXI (k)).

the picked members of skilled trades. Germany, which had led the way in accident and sickness insurance twenty-five years before, was still hesitant as to the possibility of defining insurable unemployment and testing whether it had occurred.[1] In their Reports just published, the Minority of the Poor Law Commission had definitely recommended and the Majority appeared to favour, as an alternative to direct compulsory insurance, a scheme of subsidies to trade union insurance, on the analogy of what had already been done at Ghent.

The objection to the scheme of subsidies, as it had presented itself to the officials at the Board of Trade in the autumn of 1908, was the doubt whether such a scheme would do anything serious to prevent distress. In so far as the resulting insurance was confined to existing trade union membership, it clearly would not do so; very few trade unionists, and practically none from unions giving unemployment benefits, were found among the applicants to Distress Committees. Nor was there anything in foreign experience to suggest that granting of subsidies would largely increase the scope of trade union benefits or the numbers subscribing for them. If the promotion of unemployment insurance "especially amongst unskilled and unorganised labour" had the "paramount importance" attributed to it by the Majority Report, the only logical course was to try compulsion if a scheme could be framed. Mr. Churchill was fortunately prepared to will the means to effective unemployment insurance as well as the end. The officials of the Board of Trade were prepared to back their skill in making schemes, so long as they were not asked to bring all trades in at once. The resulting proposals of the Government went ahead of the Reports of the Royal Commission, alike in definiteness and in scope.

The birth of compulsory unemployment insurance is a signal instance of how much the personality of a single Minister in a few critical months may change the course of social legislation. It may be cited also to illustrate the initiative of Civil Servants. The chief official concerned—Sir Hubert Llewellyn Smith, then Permanent Secretary of the Board of Trade—happened in 1910 to be President of the Economic Section of the British Association, and took the occasion in his Presidential Address to analyse the problem of unemployment insurance and, incidentally, expound the principles underlying the scheme which he with others was framing. The following extract[2] from his address has historical

---

[1] See Vol. I, pp. 665-7, of the Report published in 1906 by the German Statistical Office on *Versicherung gegen die Folgen der Arbeitslosigkeit.*

[2] *Report of British Association for the Advancement of Science,* 1910, pp. 678-9.

importance, as a record of the hopes, anxieties and purposes with which unemployment insurance came into the world :—

"The crucial question from a practical point of view is, therefore, whether it is possible to devise a scheme of insurance which, while nominally covering unemployment due to all causes other than those which can be definitely excluded, shall automatically discriminate as between the classes of unemployment for which insurance is or is not an appropriate remedy.

"We can advance a step towards answering this crucial question by enumerating some of the essential characteristics of any unemployment insurance scheme which seem to follow directly or by necessary implication from the conditions of the problem as here laid down.

"1. The scheme must be compulsory; otherwise the bad personal risks against which we must always be on our guard would be certain to predominate.

"2. The scheme must be contributory, for only by exacting rigorously as a necessary qualification for benefit that a sufficient number of weeks' contributions shall have been paid by each recipient can we possibly hope to put limits on the exceptionally bad risks.

"3. With the same object in view there must be a maximum limit to the amount of benefit which can be drawn, both absolutely and in relation to the amount of contribution paid ; or, in other words, we must in some way or other secure that the number of weeks for which a workman contributes should bear some relation to his claim upon the fund. Armed with this double weapon of a maximum limit to benefit and of a minimum contribution, the operation of the scheme itself will automatically exclude the loafer.

"4. The scheme must avoid encouraging unemployment, and for this purpose it is essential that the rate of unemployment benefit payable shall be relatively low. It would be fatal to any scheme to offer compensation for unemployment at a rate approximating to that of ordinary wages.

"5. For the same reason it is essential to enlist the interest of all those engaged in the insured trades, whether as employers or as workmen, in reducing unemployment, by associating them with the scheme both as regards contribution and management.

"6. As it appears on examination that some trades are more suitable to be dealt with by insurance than others, either because the unemployment in these trades contains a large insurable element, or because it takes the form of total discharge rather than short time, or for other reasons, it follows that, for the scheme to have the best chance of success, it should be based upon the trade group, and should at the outset be partial in operation.

" 7. The group of trades to which the scheme is to be applied must, however, be a large one, and must extend throughout the United Kingdom, as it is essential that industrial mobility as between occupations and districts should not be unduly checked.

" 8. A State subvention and guarantee will be necessary, in addition to contributions from the trades affected, in order to give the necessary stability and security, and also in order to justify the amount of State control that will be necessary.

" 9. The scheme must aim at encouraging the regular employer and workman, and discriminating against casual engagements. Otherwise it will be subject to the criticism of placing an undue burden on the regular for the benefit of the irregular members of the trade.

" 10. The scheme must not act as a discouragement to voluntary provision for unemployment, and for that purpose some well-devised plan of co-operation is essential between the State organisation and the voluntary associations which at present provide unemployment benefit for their members.

" Our analysis, therefore, leads us step by step to the contemplation of a national contributory scheme of insurance universal in its operation within the limits of a large group of trades—a group so far as possible self-contained and carefully selected as favourable for the experiment, the funds being derived from compulsory contributions from all those engaged in these trades, with a subsidy and guarantee from the State, and the rules relating to benefit being so devised as to discriminate effectively against unemployment which is mainly due to personal defects, while giving a substantial allowance to those whose unemployment results from industrial causes beyond the control of the individual."

The analysis leads also, as might be expected, step by step, to a scheme indistinguishable from that which had been announced a year before by Mr. Churchill and was embodied a year later in Part II of the National Insurance Act. This scheme combined compulsory contributory insurance for limited benefits in selected trades with subsidies to voluntary insurance through associations in all trades. Its main features may be summarised as follows :—

The compulsorily insured trades were building, construction

of works, shipbuilding, mechanical engineering, ironfounding, construction of vehicles and sawmilling carried on in connection with any other insured trade or of a kind commonly so carried on. Every workman in those trades had to have an " unemployment book " which he handed to his employer on being engaged, and which the employer gave back to the workman when for any cause the employment ended. To this book the employer had for each week of employment to affix a 5d. insurance stamp, and was entitled to deduct half the value, that is 2½d., from the workman's wages. For an engagement of one day only the joint contribution was 2d., and for one of two days 4d. ; for anything from three to six days the full week's contribution of 5d. was due. The State contribution was one-third of the sum received from employers and workmen, that is to say, roughly 1⅔d. a week, or one-fourth of the whole; in addition, the State bore any cost of administration in excess of 10 per cent of the income of the unemployment fund, into which all contributions were paid, and from which all benefits came.

The benefit was 7s. a week up to a maximum of fifteen weeks in a year, subject to the provisos that no one should get more than one week of benefit for every five contributions paid or deemed to have been paid for him, and that no benefit should be paid for the first week of any period of unemployment. In order to prevent the one in five rule from bearing too hardly at the outset of the scheme, all those who could show substantial previous employment in an insured trade were credited with twenty-five contributions. To get benefit the workman had to fulfil certain statutory conditions and to be free of certain disqualifications. The statutory conditions were that the applicant should prove that he had been employed as a workman in an insured trade for twenty-six weeks at some time during the past five years ; that he had made application in the prescribed manner (which meant in practice that he had lodged his unemployment book at a Labour Exchange or other local office of the unemployment fund and filled in a form) and had been continuously unemployed since his application ; that he was capable of work but unable to obtain suitable employment, and that he had not exhausted his right to benefit. Notwithstanding fulfilment of the statutory conditions a workman was disqualified for benefit :

(a) If he had lost employment by reason of a stoppage of work which was due to a trade dispute at the factory, workshop, or other premises at which he was employed—for so long as the stoppage continued or till he got work again elsewhere in an insured trade ;

(*b*) If he had lost employment through misconduct or had left it voluntarily without just cause—for six weeks from the date of so losing and leaving employment.

There were other minor grounds of disqualification.

The decision whether a workman was entitled to benefit or not was given in the first instance by a statutory "insurance officer," who was an official of the Board of Trade ; if the insurance officer decided in favour of the workman his decision was final ; if he decided against the workman, the latter might appeal to a Court of Referees, consisting of an employer, a workman, and an impartial chairman, usually of legal training ; under certain conditions there might be further reference to an Umpire appointed by the Crown. The ultimate responsibility for refusing benefit in individual cases—and of explaining in Parliament why it had been refused—was thus removed from the President of the Board of Trade. He could and did give general instructions to the insurance officers, but no instructions at all to the Courts of Referees or to the Umpire ; the latter was a judge of a specialised kind, whose rulings bound the Courts of Referees and from whom there was no appeal ; his judicial position was marked by charging his salary, like that of the ordinary judges, on the Consolidated Fund and not on any departmental vote.[1]

While ingeniously side-tracking responsibility for deciding on individual claims to benefit, the Board of Trade retained direct control of the rest of the scheme, administering it through the Labour Exchanges. The workman obtained his unemployment book from an Exchange ; he claimed and received benefit there ; he proved his unemployment and capacity to work by signing an unemployed register there in working hours daily, or (if living at a distance) at other required intervals ; his inability to obtain suitable employment was meant to be tested, and was tested substantially, by whether the Exchange could offer him a job or not. With this in view, an important proviso secured that a workman should not be refused benefit merely on the ground that he had declined employment in a vacancy due to a trade dispute or at less than the usual or recognised wages. The actual wording of the proviso was elaborate ; the existing rule is the same in principle and is set out fully later.

The contributions were paid into and the benefits from an unemployment fund which was meant to be self-supporting. If the fund became exhausted, it could obtain a loan from the Treasury,

[1] The Umpire originally had also the function of deciding whether a workman was within the insured trades or not. Later (1920) this duty of demarcation was treated as an administrative function and transferred to the Minister of Labour.

but if the Treasury thought the fund insolvent, they could then require such revision of contributions or benefits or both (within wide limits) as appeared necessary to restore solvency. Though the contributions for all trades were fixed originally at the same level, provision was made for keeping the accounts so as to show how each industry was paying in and drawing out; after seven years there was to be a valuation of the fund and it was contemplated that there should then, in the light of experience, be a revision and differentiation of contributions by trades.

Such was the main structure of the scheme.[1] A number of subsidiary provisions were added to meet possible objections to compulsory insurance, at a flat rate of contributions and benefits. The most ingenious of these fancy clauses was that which entitled any workman who reached the age of sixty without drawing as much in benefit as he himself had paid in contributions, to get back any excess of his contributions above benefits, with interest at $2\frac{1}{2}$ per cent and without forfeiting a claim to future benefits. This was meant to afford, and did afford, an almost complete reply to the steady workman who might object to insuring against a risk of unemployment that for him seemed negligible. How the scheme could afford these refunds was a mystery, till it was explained that many steady men would die under sixty and that those who lived to claim their own contributions would leave in the fund the contributions of their employers and of the State; they would be highly profitable members. Other clauses gave a refund of part of the employer's contribution for men continuously employed by him during each insurance year, allowed remission of contributions where short time was being worked systematically to avoid unemployment, provided for a reduction of the high daily rates of contribution in respect of men engaged through a Labour Exchange, and authorised arrangements by Exchanges to stamp health insurance cards in all casual occupations.

Finally, the position of voluntary associations already undertaking insurance—in practice these were all trade unions—was recognised in two ways. First, any such association of workmen in the compulsorily insured trades could make an arrangement with the Board of Trade, allowing its members to draw their State benefit as well as their association benefit through their association and not directly from a Labour Exchange. Second, the State undertook to repay to approved associations of workmen, both in the insured trades and outside them, one-sixth of any unemployed benefit paid by them to their members from their own resources. This meant in effect adding the Ghent system of subventions to the compulsory insurance scheme.

[1] Section 102 of *National Insurance Act of 1911*.

Though without precedent in its own field, the scheme had regard to all available analogies. The idea of collecting contributions by stamping of cards carried by the workmen, till then unknown in Britain, was copied from Germany. The testing of unemployment by daily signatures in working hours and many other details of administration were copied from the British trade unions. The elaborate definition of insurable unemployment by statutory conditions and disqualifications and provisos, the limitation of benefit by reference to the contributions paid, and the machinery for decisions were the original fruit of hard thinking.

After its announcement by Mr. Churchill in 1909, the scheme was not formally introduced till 1911, when it appeared as Part II of the National Insurance Bill, whose Part I was the more general but later-born scheme of health insurance. Mr. Churchill had already left the Board of Trade and the piloting of the scheme through Parliament fell to Mr. Sidney (later Lord) Buxton. It had a surprisingly easy passage. No one sought to oppose it in principle, and no one outside the Board of Trade knew enough to criticise it in detail. The interval since 1909 had been fully occupied in working out the details and setting up the administrative machinery of the Labour Exchanges. Contributions became payable from 15th July, 1912, and benefits six months later.

The scheme was thus fully launched on 15th January, 1913. It took the water smoothly and found smooth water to receive it; the eighteen months from the beginning of 1913 to the outbreak of the Great War were a time of exceptional prosperity and of unemployment as low as had been known for a generation. The working of the scheme to the end of the first insurance year on 12th July, 1913, covering six months of full operation, was described in a Report published almost immediately after; a draft report on the next insurance year was prepared by me in 1915 though never published.[1]

The main features in this year and a half of opening experience may be summarised as follows :—

1. The actual number of insured workpeople proved to be below expectation, about $2\frac{1}{4}$ millions in place of over $2\frac{1}{2}$ millions. The deficiency arose mainly because the building trade was found not to have grown since 1901 at the rate expected;[2] since the building trade was also expected to have the heaviest unemployment

---

[1] The published Report is Cmd. 6965. The later Report, referred to below as *Draft Report on Labour Exchanges and Unemployment Insurance* (1915), owing to war-time pre-occupations was never approved or published but has been made available for consultation in the library of the School of Economics.

[2] The numbers occupied in building actually fell by 7 per cent from 1901 to 1911. See Chapter XV below.

of the insured trades, this was a difference favourable to the finance of the scheme.

2. The contributions materially exceeded the expenditure, and by August, 1914, a surplus of £3,185,000 had been realised. The probable loss in a severe depression, such as that of 1908 and 1909, was estimated at no more than £5,000,000; the fund was already well on the way to security.

3. The number of claims made amounted to nearly 1,100,000, or an average of 20,000 a week, in the insurance year 1913-14; the 1,100,000 claims represented about 550,000 individuals. This meant that, in a year of exceptional prosperity, one out of every four men in the insured trades became unemployed at some time or other, and that there was one claim for every two insured persons.[1] Most of the claimants, however, remained out of work for very short periods. Of the total unemployment experienced only 55 per cent ranked for benefit; over 24 per cent fell in the first week or "waiting time," in another 17 per cent the workman was disqualified for various reasons, and less than 4 per cent. occurred after benefit had been exhausted. Forty claimants out of every 100 got work again in a week and another 35 in three weeks.[2]

4. Voluntary provision for unemployment in the insured trades was increased by the scheme; about 20 trade unions with a membership of 100,000 which had not previously given unemployed benefit began to do so in order to make arrangements with the Board of Trade. Partly through this, partly through the relative decline of the building trade, and partly through the growth of trade unionism, the proportion of workmen claiming benefit through their associations was higher than had been expected; about 650,000 workmen, or nearly one-third of the whole number insured, were found to be in associations.[3]

5. Outside the insured trades, the subsidy of one-sixth offered

[1] The percentages falling out of work in the course of the year of best employment, given for certain trade unions, in Tables XII, XIII and XIV above, range from 6·6 per cent to 28·3 per cent, but are in most cases close to 20 per cent. In 1928-9 under the general scheme about 4,000,000 out of 11,500,000 insured individuals, or 34 per cent, made claims; this was a year of bad employment.

[2] In respect of recovery of work there was a significant difference by age. The average length of a spell of unemployment in 1913, taking all ages together, was 14·8 working days; for the age-group 30-34 it was 13·1 days and increased steadily for each subsequent age-group. The length of spells was above the average also in the unsettled period from 19 to 24.

[3] The proportion of association claims to benefit to total claims was practically the same—31·8 per cent in the insurance year 1913-14. "There is no substantial difference between the proportion of cases of unemployment among members of associations and among workmen who are not members of such associations." *Draft Report on Labour Exchanges and Unemployment Insurance*, 1915, § 380.

by the State, though taken advantage of by trade unions already giving unemployed benefits, had little effect in extending the scope of such benefits.   Up to July, 1914, 245 associations outside the insured trades, with a benefit membership of 520,000, had been admitted to claim the subsidy; only four of these with a benefit membership under 11,000 had introduced unemployed benefits since the passing of the National Insurance Act.   Up to this point the views of those who had doubted whether the Ghent system would materially help in dealing with distress through unemployment were justified.

In concluding, in July, 1913, his First Report on the scheme, the Director of Labour Exchanges felt able to draw the following inferences :—[1]

" First, compulsory state insurance against unemployment in scheduled trades appears to be administratively practicable. No insoluble difficulties have presented themselves as regards the definition and test of unemployment.   Some sort of de-marcation of the insured trades has been effected.

" Second, compulsory state insurance can be introduced without destroying voluntary insurance.   The amount of voluntary insurance has, indeed, been enlarged rather than reduced by the compulsory scheme.

" On the larger question of how far the benefits of this scheme will go towards preventing distress from unemploy-ment, in bad times as in good, judgment must for the present be suspended.   The next depression of trade will show.

" It is at least possible to look forward to the next depres-sion from a new standpoint.   The invested balance of the Unemployment Fund is £1,610,000, and will increase.   The machinery for distributing the Fund is established.   The depression that must come in due course will not find the country wholly unprepared."

WAR AND THE TEN-YEAR CHAOS.

In place of trade depression there came the Great War.   The anxieties and expectations of the authors of unemployment insur-ance were swept away with all their plans, first by the disappear-ance of unemployment during the war itself, then by the catastrophic return of unemployment after the war and the stream of emergency measures for which it seemed to call.   There is no need here to survey in detail the history of the fourteen years from August, 1914, to the introduction of the new model of insurance in April,

[1] Cmd. 6965, p. 46.

1928, after the report of the Blanesburgh Committee of 1927.[1] It must suffice to name the outstanding events.

First come the efforts during the war itself, in 1916 and 1918, to extend insurance betimes as provision beforehand for post-war unemployment. The moving spirits here were the same officials as those responsible for the scheme of 1911. The fruit of their activities in 1916 was a meagre addition of $1\frac{1}{4}$ million workpeople, mainly women, to the insured classes, by the Munition Workers' Insurance Act; solid opposition by employers and workpeople engrossed in prosperity and refusing to contemplate the end of the war kept out all the important trades. The fruit in 1918 was a report made in February of that year by one of the Committees set up by the Ministry of Reconstruction, pointing to the prospect of widespread industrial dislocation and urging generalisation of insurance. " Unless a scheme of general insurance is devised and launched at the earliest possible date it may be impossible to avoid the disastrous chaos of unorganised and improvised methods of relieving distress." [2]   Into this chaos, as nine months later the Armistice guns boomed out, the nation duly descended.

Second, came the " donation " schemes, ex-service and civilian. The ex-service scheme, under which each non-commissioned member of the fighting forces on demobilisation received a free policy of unemployment insurance, having been carefully planned ahead and applying to an easily-defined class, worked smoothly from 1918 to 1921. The civilian scheme, extemporised to meet the gap caused by failure to extend insurance, could not be expected to work smoothly; during its short life from November, 1918, to November, 1919, it let loose a flood of criticism, and damaged the whole principle of insurance. Thrust on the Exchanges at a few weeks' notice, it allowed no time for framing watertight regulations or collecting and training staff. The root of the difficulty, however, lay deeper. No satisfactory definition of those entitled to

[1] The history of insurance in this period is described in a chapter on " Unemployment Insurance in the War and After," contributed by myself to one of the volumes of the Carnegie Endowment Economic and Social History of the World War. This volume, entitled *War and Insurance*, was published in 1927, and should be referred to for fuller information on the history summarised in the pages immediately following. I have borrowed or adapted a phrase or two.

[2] *Report of Unemployment Insurance Sub-Committee of Civil War Workers Committee*, § 21 (Cmd. 9192). The Sub-Committee, of which I was Chairman, included Mr. C. F. Rey, the first General Manager of Labour Exchanges; Miss A. S. Lawrence, Mr. C. A. Lister, Mr. J. J. Mallon and Mr. R. Young. Its report, signed on 12th February, 1918, and giving in an Appendix the outlines of a scheme for general insurance, was unanimously approved a month later by the main Committee. After a spell of inter-departmental battledore and shuttlecock, a Committee of officials was at last, halfway through 1919, appointed by the Ministry of Labour to frame a scheme. Their proposals, not without important changes, formed the basis of the Act of 1920.

donation was possible ; as a free gift every one tried to get all he could ; casual workers and men on the border-land of being unemployable harvested the benefit, not as the result of failure of administration, but because under the scheme they were fully entitled to claim. The widespread criticism of the scheme was grossly exaggerated, and was shown to be so by a Committee of Inquiry under the chairmanship of Lord Aberconway appointed in May, 1919.[1] The Committee reported that there were " no grounds for supposing that there had been extensive fraudulent abuse of the donation scheme ". But the damage done by it to the principle and the credit of unemployment insurance cannot be doubted. From the donation scheme dates the term "dole" indiscriminately applied later to insurance benefit also ; from it dates the conception of largesse in which all were entitled to share.[2]

The third and principal event is the Act of 1920, extending insurance to nearly all employees outside agriculture and domestic service. This Act followed that of 1911 in all important details. The statutory conditions and disqualifications for benefit were repeated almost literally. The rates of benefit and contributions were raised in view of the changed value of money. The rules limiting the period of benefit to so many weeks in each year and by reference to the number of contributions paid were retained ; the number of contributions required for one week of benefit was raised from five to six. A few minor provisions, such as the re-fund to employers for continuous employment or for short-time working, which had caused more trouble than they seemed worth, were dropped ; so also was tacitly abandoned the hope of differentiating contributions for industries by the simple method of varying the insurance stamps. On the other hand, a clause was added to allow contracting out of individual industries from the general scheme and the setting up of special schemes for them.

In intention the scheme of 1920 was a generalisation of the scheme of 1911 ; its fate was shatteringly different. Introduced under the shadow of declining trade, with benefits and contributions starting on the same day, with no time for the building up of

---

[1] Committee of Inquiry into the Scheme of Out-of-Work Donation : *Interim Report* (Cmd. 196) ; *Final Report* (Cmd. 305). The Committee having received from boards of guardians, town councils, chambers of commerce and other public bodies numerous resolutions protesting in general terms against alleged abuses of the scheme, made a selection of these bodies and invited details and evidence. " The replies were generally to the effect that the resolutions were based on general grounds rather than specific cases." Some bodies blandly replied that they had passed resolutions on hearsay or at the request of other bodies ; only one of those asked was prepared to give evidence.

[2] See the evidence of Mr. Battersby to Lord Aberconway's Committee, Qns. 2971, 2977-87.

reserves either general or individual, it never had a chance ; as the country passed into the worst depression recorded in British history, this belated effort at insurance sank at once beneath the flood of emergency relief. The sinking of insurance is the fourth outstanding event of this period ; it is marked by the invention in March, 1921, of "extended benefit," that is to say, of benefit given to those who had exhausted their insurance rights to standard benefit, from the same fund and at the same rates, but subject to special conditions and to a general discretionary power of the Minister of Labour ; at first extended benefit was given only for a limited time, i.e., up to a maximum of sixteen weeks in the special period of eight months from 3rd March to 2nd November, 1921, and fresh legislation was introduced for successive special periods.

By the invention of extended benefit relief was grafted on to insurance. Other measures varied the insurance scheme itself from day to day, under veering gusts of political opinion or changing estimates of the economic situation. The custom of passing two or three Unemployment Insurance Acts each year was established ; everything that could be called system disappeared. The rate of benefit for adult men, which had been raised to 11s. at the end of 1919 and 15s. in the Act of 1920, was raised to 20s. in March, 1921, lowered again to 15s. four months later, and raised to 18s. in August, 1924. Meanwhile, in November, 1921, benefit proper had been supplemented by an allowance of 5s. for an adult dependent and 1s. for each child ; the latter was raised to 2s. in 1924. The total weekly contribution for an adult male workman, put at 10d. in August, 1920, became $13\frac{3}{4}$d. in the Act of March, 1921, but this rate, before it became operative, was replaced by the higher rate of $18\frac{3}{4}$d. under the Act of July, 1921, which in turn gave way to $25\frac{3}{4}$d. in the following November. In 1925 reduction had its turn and the total contribution was put at 23d., but this rate also never operated, being superseded in the interests of Exchequer economy by a rate of 21d. The foregoing are the benefits and the total contributions for one class of contributor— adult males ; there were other changes, sometimes consequential and sometimes not, in the rates for other classes, as well as new classifications, and there was incessant change in the shares taken by the three contributing parties. The Exchequer share, in particular, changed according to budget exigencies or the Chancellor's policy, and since 1911 has been successively about 25, 20, 26, 35, 29 and 33 per cent of the total. The most bewildering changes have been those of the "waiting-time" at the beginning of each period of unemployment for which no benefit is paid ;

reduced from six days to three by the Act of 1920, it was put up to six again in July, 1921, down to three in August, 1924, and back to six again in 1925.   The refund of contributions at the age of sixty to contributors drawing less than their own contributions was abolished in 1924.   Finally, the trade dispute disqualification, which had held its own against incessant criticism since 1911, was amended in 1924 by the Labour Government, and in 1925 partially re-amended in the opposite sense by the Conservative Government that succeeded.   Altogether unemployment insurance was the subject of fifteen Acts of Parliament in six years from July, 1920, to July, 1926.[1]

In this welter of legislation, the second Act of 1924 may be selected as a final landmark, both for what it did and what it led to.   By this Act, the short-lived Labour Government of that year made extended benefit unlimited in time and abolished the Minister's discretion ; extended benefit became a right like standard benefit, though subject to additional general conditions, and could be drawn indefinitely.[2]   This Act had to be carried through a Parliament in which the Government were outnumbered, and was secured only by acceptance of a clause bringing benefit as a whole to an end by June, 1926, a date subsequently extended to the end of 1927.   The object of this clause was to force a full review of the principle and practice of unemployment insurance; the review was undertaken in due course by a Committee[3] under the chairmanship of Lord Blanesburgh, which was appointed on 10th

[1] With the earlier Acts of 1911, 1914 and 1919 and the first and second Acts of 1929 (extending transitional provisions and raising the Exchequer contribution) the measure introduced by Miss Bondfield in November, 1929, and now forming the (first) Act of 1930 is really the twenty-first and not, as she stated, twentieth in the line.   The difference is no doubt due to her not reckoning the Economy (Miscellaneous Provisions) Act of 1926, which in fact fixed the rates of employers' and workmen's contributions now in force.

[2] The succeeding Conservative Government of 1925, while allowing the indefinite continuance of extended benefit to stand, restored the Minister's discretion.   In 1927, at the time of the Blanesburgh Committee's Report described below, this discretionary power was being used to exclude (unless hardship would be involved) :

" 1. Single persons who are residing with parents or other relatives to whom, having regard to all the circumstances, they can reasonably look for support during unemployment;

" 2. Married women—living with their husbands, who are in employment, and whose incomings provide an income for the household sufficient to justify the withholding of extended benefit from the wife;

" 3. Married men—living with their wives, who are in employment, and whose incomings provide an income for the household sufficient to justify the withholding of extended benefit from the husband;

" 4. Persons who are working short time, and whose incomings are sufficient to justify the withholding of extended benefit;

" 5. Certain classes of aliens."

[3] The Committee of thirteen persons included Miss Bondfield, later Minister of Labour in the Government of 1929.

November, 1925, and presented a unanimous Report on 31st January, 1927.   This Report, except in respect of rates of contribution, was accepted by the Government: its recommendations, embodied in an Act of 1927 and coming into force on 19th April, 1928, defined unemployment insurance as it was intended to stand for the future.   With this the ten-year chaos since 1918 may be said to have ended.

During this period—from the beginning of the general scheme of insurance on 8th November, 1920, to 31st March, 1928—the total receipts of the Unemployment Fund were £322,000,000, and the total expenditure £369,000,000 ; a reserve of £22,000,000 taken over in November, 1920, from the limited scheme of 1911 and 1916 was changed into a debt of £25,000,000.   Of the receipts, £236,000,000, or 73 per cent, came as contributions from employers and employed in respect of employment, and £85,000,000, or nearly 27 per cent, from the Exchequer, with interest and sundries accounting for a small balance of less than ½ per cent. Of the expenditure, £331,000,000, or nearly 90 per cent, went as benefit or refunds to insured persons, and £32,000,000, or 8½ per cent, was spent on administration, with interest and sundries accounting for the balance of 1½ per cent.   The expenditure on benefits includes standard and extended benefit.   Adding the £62,000,000 spent on civilian and ex-service donation and its administration, the total for the ten years' chaos is about £431,000,000.

THE NEW MODEL OF 1928.

The Act of 1927, following on the Blanesburgh Report, was in form an amendment of the Act of 1920—legislation by reference. In substance it introduced in 1928 a new model of unemployment insurance.

This model has been amended by an Act of 1930 which has itself been made terminable, expiring on 30th June, 1933.   The day of hand-to-mouth legislation is not over.   Leaving the future for later consideration, it will be convenient here first to set out the scheme as it stands to-day, and then to describe and discuss the transformation effected since 1911.   The description is made as summary and simple as possible ; it cannot be altogether simple.[1]

[1] The statutes themselves, consisting largely of wordy Parliamentary compromises and legislation by reference, with the virtually defunct Act of 1920 as the " principal Act," are almost inconceivably hard to follow.   A consolidation Act is urgently needed, but at the present moment, with the Act of 1930 made temporary, would be impracticable.

Broadly, all persons between sixteen and sixty-five employed under a contract of service in Great Britain and Northern Ireland are insured against unemployment. To this statement there are two main exceptions—of persons employed in agriculture and in domestic service respectively—and several minor exceptions, such as those of established civil servants, railway servants, the police and persons earning more than £250 a year on non-manual work; clerks and similar employees up to that salary are included. The Act of 1930 authorises the Minister of Labour to reduce the lower limit for entry to insurance to the age when compulsory elementary education ceases, if and so soon as that age shall have been raised to fifteen or more.

Every person included in the insured classes has an unemployment book which he gives to his employer on being engaged. To this the employer affixes week by week a stamp representing the joint contribution of himself and the employee; he then deducts the employee's share from the wages. The weekly contribution in respect of adult men, aged from twenty-one to sixty-five, is now 8d. by the employer and 7d. by the employee : that is to say, the employer each week fixes a stamp costing 15d. to the unemployment book and deducts 7d. from the wages. There are lower rates of contribution for adult women (7d. and 6d.), young men from eighteen to twenty (also 7d. and 6d.), young women from eighteen to twenty (6d. and 5d.), boys (4d. and 3½d.) and girls (3½d. and 3d.). To the aggregate received as employers' and employees' contributions the National Exchequer adds half, that is to say, provides one-third of the total income; the Exchequer contribution was raised to this proportion by the second Act of 1929, having up to then been about $\frac{2}{7}$ of the whole for men and $\frac{1}{4}$ for women. The total contribution for each week's employment of an adult man is thus 1s. 10½d., of which 8d. comes from the employer, 7d. from the man and 7½d. from the Exchequer.

On leaving employment the employee takes his unemployment book and lodges it at a Labour Exchange to make a claim for benefit. This benefit for an adult man is 17s. a week with 9s.[1] for his wife (or other adult dependent) and 2s. for each dependent child. For other classes there are lower rates of benefit running down to 6s. for a boy and 5s. for a girl under seventeen. To obtain benefit the insured person, having made his claim, must show that since the date of claim he has been continuously unemployed and that he is capable of work and available for work. There was, under the Act of 1927, the further condition that the

---

[1] This is the figure substituted by the Act of 1930 for 7s. provided in the Act of 1927.

claimant should be "genuinely seeking work but unable to obtain suitable employment". The last words of this condition—that the claimant should be unable to obtain suitable employment—came from the Act of 1911 and were an essential part of the original definition of insurable employment. The earlier words, requiring the claimant to be "genuinely seeking work," introduced in 1921 as an additional check on the grant of extended benefit, were made part of the conditions for all benefit by the Act of 1927, in accord with a recommendation of the Blanesburgh Committee. Both sets of words have been deleted by the Act of 1930, and replaced by a provision disqualifying for benefit a claimant who is proved to have refused without good cause suitable employment offered him by an Exchange or not to have carried out written directions given him by an officer of the Exchange as to seeking employment. For the purpose of this disqualification employment is not suitable, that is, may be refused by a claimant without penalty, if it is either:

"(a) employment in a situation vacant in consequence of a stoppage of work due to a trade dispute; or

"(b) employment in his usual occupation in the district where he was last ordinarily employed at a rate of wage lower or on conditions less favourable than those which he might reasonably have expected to obtain, having regard to those which he habitually obtained in his usual occupation in that district or would have obtained had he continued to be so employed; or

"(c) employment in his usual occupation in any other district at a rate of wage lower, or on conditions less favourable, than those generally observed in that district by agreement between associations of employers and of employees, or, failing any such agreement, than those generally recognised in that district by good employers."

The net result of all this is to restore, with two minor changes, the original practice of the Act of 1911, of making the Exchange the substantial test of whether suitable employment is available.[1]

---

[1] The abolition of the "genuinely seeking work" condition was the main subject of controversy in the passage of the Act of 1930; as the Labour Government had finally to make the Act temporary in order to secure its passage, the abolished condition, in the improbable event of there being no fresh legislation meanwhile, would revive automatically on 1st July, 1933, and may thus call for a brief comment here. In so far as this condition has been held to require that to keep in benefit a workman must not simply register at an Exchange for work, but put up some kind of show at least of looking for work in person by going the round of factory gates, it marks a complete break with the policies of 1909. In them and in the scheme of 1911, Labour Exchanges and unemployment insurance went together as two halves of a single programme. The Exchanges were to abolish the hawking of labour, so

One of the minor changes is that the Exchange official has now the additional power, if he thinks fit, of directing the workman to look for work also in some other way than through the Exchange. The other is that the period of disqualification for refusal of a job is defined as not more than six weeks.[1]

There are other grounds of disqualification : for misconduct or leaving work voluntarily without just cause ; while an inmate of a prison or workhouse or residing outside the United Kingdom or receiving sickness or disablement benefit or blind pension ; and where the claimant has lost his employment through a stoppage of work due to a trade dispute at the factory or other premises where he was employed. This last disqualification does not apply if neither the claimant himself nor any of his fellow-workmen of the same grade or class are directly interested in or financing the dispute.

Formally, over and above the conditions named, there stands in the statute a condition requiring each claimant to prove that not less than thirty contributions have been paid in respect of him during the past two years. This condition, however, has never

as to reduce unemployment to its minimum ; insurance was to maintain men in the intervals of unemployment that remained. It was hoped and assumed that before long so much of the marketing of labour would be done through the Exchanges as to make it unnecessary to test the reality of unemployment and the need for benefit otherwise than by requiring the workman to apply constantly to an Exchange. If every vacancy for workpeople were notified to an Exchange as soon as it arose, it would be impossible for any workman to draw benefit for even a day after suitable employment was available for him ; the unemployment fund would be completely protected. Till the Exchanges reached that development it was better to take the risk of occasional loss to the fund by a few idle workmen than to drive all workmen on fruitless journeys and perpetuate the disorganisation of the labour market. The "genuinely seeking work" condition implied an admission, not only that the Exchanges did not control the labour market sufficiently for the purpose of testing unemployment, but that they never would do so, and that hawking of labour, so emphatically condemned by the Poor Law Commission, ought to continue indefinitely. This is made explicit in the Umpire's elaborate decision, of about 1,500 words, interpreting the condition, which is printed as an appendix to the Report of the Blanesburgh Committee. The condition will not, it may be hoped, ever rise from its dishonoured grave. Its value from the point of view of the administrators of the unemployment fund, has lain, not in keeping out the work-shy and unemployable, or causing people to get work who would not otherwise have got it, but in the weapon of offensive defence it afforded against claims by women who on marriage had practically retired from industry and were not wanted by employers, but tried not unnaturally to get something for nothing out of the fund and add to the family income. This is a real problem, but not one fairly solved by a "genuinely seeking work" condition of universal application.

[1] There is also a change of practice whereby at many Exchanges claimants to benefit living within three miles, instead of being required to attend at the Exchange and sign the register every day as proof of unemployment, come only every other day. This change introduced some years ago as an administrative economy, to deal with the increased numbers, is significant of the former tendency of the Exchanges to become paying rather than placing agencies. Daily signature was the almost invariable trade union rule for all workmen living within a reasonable distance.

yet operated.   The Act of 1927, which introduced it, at the same time suspended it till April, 1929, and replaced it by a "transitional provision" requiring eight contributions in two years or thirty at any time, with certain other conditions.   On the approach of April, 1929, the "transitional provisions" were continued for another year and the Act of 1930 continues them to April, 1932, while abolishing one of the subsidiary conditions.   This Act makes a new departure in throwing the cost of benefit paid under the transitional provisions directly on to the Exchequer.

Subject to these conditions and disqualifications, an insured person can draw benefit without limit of time.   No benefit is payable for the first six days of any period of unemployment, but thereafter benefit continues so long as unemployment continues. For this purpose any three days of unemployment within six continuous days are regarded as continuous, and any two periods of three continuous days are regarded as continuous with one another if not separated by more than ten weeks.

Claims to benefit are considered in the first instance by a statutory insurance officer whose decision in favour of a claim is final. If the insurance officer does not allow the claim, he must[1] submit it to a Court of Referees, consisting of an impartial Chairman and equal numbers (in practice one each) of representatives of employers and employees.   If the Court of Referees decide for the claim, the insurance officer can always appeal to the Umpire; if the Court decide against the claim there can be an appeal to the Umpire only by an association to which the insured person belongs or with the leave of the Court or where its decision is not unanimous or by the insurance officer.   The Umpire's decision is final and conclusive, i.e., excludes the ordinary courts of justice.

Associations of insured persons may make arrangements whereby their members can draw benefit through the associations in place of from an Exchange; as a condition of making such an arrangement each association must pay additional benefit from its own funds to its members, at the rate for men of at least 3s. a week up to 75s. in a year, with lower rates for women, boys and girls.[2]

[1] Unless he rejects it on the trade dispute qualification. This exception is no doubt meant to save the Courts from having to consider perhaps hundreds of identical trade dispute cases.

[2] Arrangements with associations are relatively much less important in the general scheme than in the limited scheme of 1911, under which they covered nearly a third of the workpeople insured and of the benefit paid.   At the end of 1929, arrangements were in force with 124 associations having a membership of about 847,000, i.e., about one in fourteen of all insured workpeople ; the benefit paid through associations in the financial year 1927-28 was only one-twentieth of the whole.   The subsidy of one-sixth in aid of voluntary insurance provided under the Act of 1911 was dropped on the generalisation of compulsory insurance in 1920.   On the other hand, a grant for the expenses of administering arrangements was made to associations—originally at the rate of 1s. for each week's benefit paid, reduced since 1922 to 6d.

There are a number of minor provisions authorising administration of benefit by local education authorities which have undertaken juvenile employment work, allowing travelling expenses to work found through an Exchange to be paid in part out of the unemployment fund, allowing grants to be made from the fund for approved instruction for boys and girls who are insured persons and, as a consequence, requiring attendance at such courses as a further condition of getting benefit.

In form the scheme to-day is very like what was introduced in 1911; the methods of raising contributions, paying benefits, and adjudicating on claims are practically unchanged; the conditions and disqualifications for benefit follow the same lines. In substance the two schemes are different. The making of benefit unlimited in duration for an unrelievedly flat contribution amounts to a fundamental reconstruction.

The Blanesburgh Committee regarded the principle of unemployment insurance as established :—

> "We have found in all quarters a general agreement that the risk of unemployment should be insured. . . . It has been recognised by all who have appeared before us, and we ourselves share the view, that an unemployment insurance scheme must now be regarded as a permanent feature of our code of social legislation." [1]

The term "unemployment insurance," however, meant very different things in different mouths.

The Committee found themselves faced by two opposed views. On the one side were those who favoured, as they put it, "an insurance scheme, strictly so called; a scheme under which contributors receive benefits bearing some proportion to their own payments ; a scheme capable of being administered in accordance with the original intention of the 1920 Act ". On the other side were those who desired a scheme to provide "benefit for all genuinely unemployed people, no matter how long they are unemployed"; this school of thought would in principle prefer a non-contributory scheme, that is to say, one financed wholly by ordinary taxation. Between these views the Committee sought a middle course. They rejected the view, implicit in the 1911 and 1920 schemes, and urged upon them by the Association of Poor Law Unions, "that the Insurance Scheme should carry a certain part only of the risk of genuine unemployment, leaving the remainder to the Guardians ". As a practical consequence, they proposed the abolition of the two rules limiting the period of benefit to twenty-

[1] *Report of Unemployment Insurance Committee* (1927), § 49.

six weeks in any twelve months and to one week for every six contributions paid.   Benefit to any person in the insurable field was to continue as long as his unemployment ; the former distinction between covenanted and uncovenanted or extended benefit should disappear.   On the other hand, they thought that some automatic test was necessary "to ensure that the benefits are limited to contributors, or, in other words, to persons in the insured field".   They proposed, as this test, the requirement that every claimant to benefit must show that he had paid thirty contributions within the past two years.

> "It will be conceded that in the generality of cases persons with so poor a record of employment (as having done less than 15 weeks' work in 52 weeks) could scarcely claim still to be in the insured field ; that there is grave doubt as to the genuineness of their search for work ; and that the exclusion of such individuals is only fair to the general body of insured contributors." [1]

Nevertheless the Committee felt it impracticable to apply forthwith even this modest test of insurability ; some "transitional" concession must be made, to avoid cutting out large numbers of beneficiaries at the outset of the new scheme.   In practice, as has been stated above, "transitional provisions" have been in force ever since the Committee's scheme was adopted ; the introduction of even the modest test of insurability proposed by them recedes continually.   Investigation of a sample of the 1,092,000 claims authorised for benefit at the end of January, 1929, showed that about one-ninth or 120,000 would have been disqualified by the requirement of thirty contributions in the past two years.   A similar inquiry for 14th October, 1929, gave a higher proportion —130,000 out of 940,000, or nearly one-seventh. [2]

Even apart from the transitional provisions, the Committee's compromise was not half-way between the extreme opposed views, but much nearer to those who wanted unlimited non-contributory benefit.   In regard to contributions they said :—

> "That flat rates are an unavoidable feature of any workable compulsory scheme of contributory unemployment insurance we have been forced reluctantly to recognise.   But if a scheme so comprehensive as the present is to continue to enjoy the general assent of workers who are so differently circumstanced with reference to it, it must be of its essence that the flat rate of contribution is as low as is possible." [3]

[1] *Op. cit.*, § 75.   [2] *Labour Gazette*, March, 1929, p. 81 ; January, 1930, p. 9.
[3] *Op. cit.*, § 22.

In other words, the Committee, recognising the inequity of a flat rate of contribution for unlimited benefit irrespective of all variations of risk, said that the inequity ought to be kept small by keeping the contributions small. They actually proposed a somewhat startling reduction of contributions, but on this point the Government, having regard to the facts of unemployment, could not follow them.[1] Meanwhile, the answer to complaints of inequity between individuals afforded by the refund at sixty had already been abolished;[2] the Blanesburgh Committee themselves took the final step in the direction of inequity between industries by recommending abolition of the provision for contracting out under special schemes.

It is impossible, indeed, to determine directly how much each industry is paying in, and how much it is drawing out of the unemployment fund. No accounts of income and expenditure by separate industries are kept. For practical purposes, however, it is sufficiently near the mark to assume that the contribution of each industry is in proportion to its employment, and the amount of benefit drawn is in proportion to its unemployment; in so far as this assumption errs, it must err, as a rule, by understating the inequality of experience between different industries.[3] On this assumption the table given opposite has been constructed.

---

[1] The Committee proposed contributions for adult men at the rate of 5d. a week from each of the three parties or a total of 1s. 3d., with 1d. extra from each for a limited period for extinction of debt. This, in relation to the benefits proposed, assumed an average unemployment percentage of about 6. The Government kept contributions at the figure fixed in 1926, viz., for adult men, 8d., 7d. and 6d. from each party, making a total of 1s. 9d. With these contributions and with benefits substantially as recommended by the Committee, the debt of the Unemployment Fund increased from £22,640,000 at the end of 1926 (just before the Committee's Report was signed) to £36,850,000 on 9th November, 1929. The State's contribution was raised to 7½d. by the Second Act of 1929.

[2] The abolition of the refund at sixty was recommended in 1923 by an Inter-Departmental Committee on Health and Unemployment Insurance and carried out by the Labour Government of 1924. The Inter-Departmental Committee, under the chairmanship of the Government Actuary, were commissioned if possible to bring health and unemployment insurance closer together; they were impressed by arguments of a strangely academic type: "The refund provision is an arrangement dependent on the unemployment experience of the individual and has no connection with the question of the relative risks of different classes. It is, in fact, an attempt at mixing insurance and banking, and as such, is open to the serious criticism that it attempts to embody two essentially different forms of thrift" (Cmd. 1821, § 6). The Committee, at the same time, recommended that the one in six rule should be replaced by one making the amount of benefit payable in a given year depend on the average number of contributions paid in a certain period prior to that year, but this recommendation was not at that time adopted. It was put forward on grounds of administrative economy.

[3] In treating benefit drawn as proportional to the unemployment, it is assumed that in different industries the same proportion of unemployment is covered by benefit. Actually, owing to the " waiting week " at the beginning of each period of unemploy-

(Note continued on p. 286.)

TABLE XXXIV.—ESTIMATED DISTRIBUTION BY INDUSTRIES OF TOTAL EM-
PLOYMENT AND UNEMPLOYMENT AND OF £1,000 EACH OF CONTRIBU-
TIONS AND BENEFITS (GREAT BRITAIN AND NORTHERN IRELAND).

Industry.	Numbers Insured, July, 1929 (000).	Unemployed Percentage.		Share of Total.		Share of Every £1,000.			
		1929.	Mean 1924-29, Omitting 1926.	Employment. (000)	Unemployment. (000)	Raised in Contributions.	Spent in Benefit.	Raised in Contributions.	Spent in Benefit.
				1929.		1929.		Mean 1924-9, Omitting 1926.	
(1)	(2)	(3)	(4)	(5)	(6)	(7) £	(8) £	(9) £	(10) £
Commerce, Banking, Insurance and Finance	228·59	2·7	3·4	222·42	6·17	21	5	20	6
Professional Services . . .	121·73	3·2	3·2	117·84	3·89	11	3	11	3
Tramway and Omnibus Service .	154·74	3·2	3·3	149·79	4·95	14	4	14	4
Printing, Publishing and Book-binding	261·13	4·4	4·8	249·63	11·50	23	9	23	10
Laundries, Dyeing and Dry Cleaning	135·03	4·4	4·9	129·09	5·94	12	5	12	5
Dressmaking and Millinery . .	103·40	4·9	5·8	98·33	5·07	9	4	9	5
Railway Service	138·39	5·8	5·9	130·36	8·03	12	6	12	6
Gas, Water and Electricity Supply Industries	162·03	6·0	5·8	152·31	9·72	14	8	14	7
Furniture Making, Upholstering, etc.	120·34	6·2	6·1	112·88	7·46	11	6	11	6
Hosiery	105·78	6·2	6·8	99·22	6·56	9	5	9	6
Distributive Trades	1679·09	6·3	6·1	1573·29	105·80	145	83	146	79
Chemicals	105·89	6·5	7·4	99·01	6·88	9	5	9	6
Drink Industries	108·53	6·8	6·5	101·15	7·38	9	6	9	5
National Government . . .	118·84	6·8	7·1	110·76	8·08	10	6	10	7
Construction and Repair of Motor Vehicles, Cycles and Aircraft .	245·41	7·1	7·6	227·98	17·43	21	14	21	15
Bread, Biscuits, Cakes, etc. . .	144·77	7·3	7·9	134·20	10·57	12	8	12	9
Tailoring	199·35	8·2	8·6	182·99	16·36	17	13	17	13
Metal Industries not separately specified	191·37	8·3	9·5	175·48	15·89	16	12	16	14
Hotel, Boarding House and Club Services	333·70	9·2	9·8	303·00	30·70	28	24	28	26
General Engineering, Engineers' Iron and Steel Founding . .	586·75	9·7	11·6	529·85	56·90	49	45	48	53
Local Government	274·05	9·8	8·5	247·19	26·86	23	21	23	18
Road Transport not separately specified	182·57	12·2	13·0	160·29	22·28	15	18	15	18
Boots, Shoes, Slippers and Clogs .	135·25	13·2	10·8	117·40	17·85	11	14	11	11
Cotton	554·79	13·2	11·2	481·54	73·25	45	58	46	49
Building	825·98	13·3	11·3	716·08	109·90	66	87	68	73
Woollen and Worsted . . .	239·03	13·8	11·2	206·03	33·00	19	26	20	21
Coal-mining	1074·71	16·0	15·5	902·71	172·00	83	135	84	130
Textile Bleaching, Printing and Dyeing, etc.	116·23	17·4	14·0	96·01	20·22	9	16	9	13
Shipping Service	141·42	17·8	18·1	116·25	25·17	11	20	11	20
Steel Melting and Iron Puddling Furnaces, Iron and Steel Rolling Mills and Forges	178·72	19·8	21·0	143·34	35·38	13	28	13	29
Public Works Contracting, etc. .	164·43	22·7	19·3	127·10	37·33	12	29	12	25
Shipbuilding and Ship Repairing .	204·50	24·3	27·8	154·80	49·70	14	39	14	44
Dock, Harbour, River and Canal Service	171·22	30·8	28·2	118·49	52·73	11	42	11	38
Other Industries	2586·24	9·6	11·2	2337·19	249·05	216	196	212	226
TOTAL	12094·00	10·5	10·6	10824·00	1270·00	1,000	1,000	1,000	1,000

The table shows separately each of the 33 industries of the Ministry of Labour classification having more than 100,000 workpeople in July, 1929, arranged in the order of their unemployment percentages for that year; these percentages are given in column three, and the mean percentages over the five years 1924-9 without 1926 in column four. The fifth and sixth columns show how much on the basis of its numbers and percentages, in 1929, each industry contributed to the total employment and unemployment respectively of that year. The seventh and eighth columns show, on the assumptions named above, what would be the share in 1929 of each industry in £1,000 of employers' and workmen's contributions and £1,000 of benefits respectively. The last two columns give corresponding shares on the basis of the unemployment of five years 1924-9 (omitting 1926), as applied to the numbers insured in 1929. The benefits of course are paid for in part by the Exchequer contribution; the simplest way of bringing this into account is to regard the Exchequer as providing two-sevenths of the weekly rate of benefit (by its weekly payment of 6d. for the employers and workman's 1s. 3d.), and the table therefore as being concerned with the way in which the other five-sevenths are provided.[1]

Remarkable differences between the experiences of the different industries are at once apparent. Looking first at the figures for 1929, we see at the top of the table industries paying in three or four times as much as they draw out, and at the bottom of the table other industries drawing out three or four times as much as

ment, individuals with much unemployment have a larger proportion of it on benefit than do those with little unemployment. In the sample inquiry of September, 1929 (reported in the *Labour Gazette* of January, 1930), the proportion of unemployment covered by benefit rises steadily from 48 per cent for men unemployed for from 1 to 25 days altogether in the year, to nearly 99 per cent for those unemployed for 312 days, *i.e.*, throughout the year. This increase in the proportion of unemployment covered by benefit, as the unemployment itself increases among individuals, must apply also as a general rule between industries, since their unemployment is built up of individual cases. Casual industries might be an exception, if much of the recurrent unemployment in them was so separated by days of employment as not to be continuous for the purpose of benefit; it is arguable also that in such industries the contributions might be more than in proportion to the employment, in so far as a full contribution is payable for even one day's employment in a week. It is difficult to bring these hypothetical exceptions to the test of facts, but such evidence as there is tells against them; the sample investigation of 80,000 insurance accounts in April, 1926, showed that the average of contributions per account in dock, river and canal service was lower and not higher than the average in industry generally. The official estimate for dock, harbour, river and canal service in the three years 1924-26 (cited below, p. 321) agrees with the conclusion in the table, showing benefits amounting to four times the contributions.

[1] By the second Act of 1929 the Exchequer contribution has been raised to one-third of the whole. No account is taken in the table of the possible effect of the first Act of 1930 in throwing directly on to the Exchequer the cost of paying benefit under the " transitional provisions," *i.e.*, to men who have not paid 30 contributions in the past two years.

they pay in. The top eight industries with 1,305,000 workpeople draw out between them practically the same amount as "dock, harbour, river and canal service" with 171,000 workpeople, while they pay in ten times as much ; for every £11 paid in by the last industry towards the cost of its unemployment in 1929, £31 was found by other industries directly, to say nothing of £17 found by the taxpayer. Between the extremes is every possible gradation of experience.

The scheme should not be judged by the experience of a single year, which might be abnormal. The last two columns, however, giving averages for five years, show substantially the same picture, with the two extremes toned down very slightly. The most important differences between the five year averages and those for 1929 alone, are that in the latter year general engineering, and to a less extent shipbuilding and repairing, unspecified metal industries, and chemicals are better, while building, public works, boots and shoes, dock and harbour service, and most of the textile trades are worse. The improving trades show recovery from excessive war expansion. The declining trades were nearly all trades restricted during the war ; presumably they drew in during the temporary boom of 1920 more labour than they needed permanently. These changes, though interesting in other connections, do not affect the main lesson of the table. Over the five years 1924-9, as in the single year 1929, the risk of unemployment in different industries is startlingly unequal—in some industries eight or nine times as much as in others. The employers' and workmen's contributions for insurance amount to little more than a device for taking money from one industry and giving it to another—that is to say, they are a mode of taxation.

There is thus no relation between the contributions and receipts of particular industries. It need hardly be added that there is nothing like an actuarial basis for the scheme as a whole. Benefits have been fixed at whatever seemed indispensable to prevent acute distress or meet political pledges ; contributions have been put as high as employers and workpeople would stand them ; the resulting deficits have been met, partly by increasing directly the State contribution, partly by going more and more deeply into debt to the Exchequer, and raising the borrowing limit as soon as the limit is reached.

Thus, when towards the end of 1928 the growing debt of the fund to the Exchequer was approaching the limit of £30,000,000 then in force, an Act was passed raising the limit to £40,000,000. Until this Act could be got through, the Ministry of Labour kept doubtfully within the law by suspending the weekly payment which they were required to make from the Fund towards the cost of administration.[1]

As during 1929 the numbers unemployed continued to exceed by 150,000 to 200,000 the numbers whom the existing income of the fund could cover, the State contribution was raised from about 40 per cent to 50 per cent of the receipts from employers and workmen. This was defended by the Government spokesman as more honest than going further into insolvency and raising the borrowing limit, and was calculated to keep the fund going till the early part of 1930 while the financial position was examined.

The fruit of this examination was a decision, embodied in a Bill in 1929 becoming law as the first Act of 1930, to put on the Exchequer directly, in relief of the Unemployment Fund, the cost of benefit paid or to be paid under the "transitional provisions" to those who had not paid 30 contributions in two years. With this the income and. expenditure of the Fund were expected to balance if the average number of the unemployed was about 1,160,000. Between a seventh and an eighth of those will presumably come under the "transitional provisions" and will cost the Exchequer at least £8,500,000 a year over and above its 50 per cent contribution.

As a further relief to the Unemployment Fund, the Exchequer payment for men under the "transitional provisions" was made retrospective. The back payment for the time past since 1st April, 1929, came, during February, 1930, just in time to save the debt, which on 25th January had reached £38,940,000, from outrunning its new limit of £40,000,000. It has not made the retention even of that limit possible. A rapid growth of unemployment in the first quarter of 1930 has been met by the second Act of 1930, raising the borrowing limit to £50,000,000 for the present.

From Insurance by Contract to Relief by Status.

Unemployment insurance as introduced, was in two senses contractual. First, it gave the insured person legally enforceable rights without Ministerial discretion and without regard to his other resources or private character. Second, it gave these rights in consideration of contributions by or in respect of the insured person ; though the contract was compulsory, elaborate measures were taken to make it something like a fair bargain for each industry and each individual. It was an extension of the kind of bargain which trade unions made with their own members, in

[1] See the critical comments by the Comptroller and Auditor-General in his report appended to the Unemployment Fund Account for 1927-8 (House of Commons Paper 28 of 1929).

giving as part consideration for the union subscription a strictly limited cover against distress through unemployment. Trade union insurance itself carried an element of compulsion ; a workman joining a union which provided unemployed benefit had to pay, as a rule, a single subscription for all purposes, fighting and friendly ; pressure to join the union became pressure to insure.

During the ten-year chaos from 1918 to 1928 unemployment insurance ceased to be contractual in either sense : donation and extended benefit were discretionary grants [1] and irrespective of contributions by the recipient. Since the Act of 1927 unemployment insurance has become contractual again in the first sense but not in the second ; an unlimited benefit claimable as of right has replaced the old combination of standard and extended benefit, but is claimable, not for contributions paid, but by virtue of belonging to the insured classes. Moving from contract to status, the insurance scheme of 1911 has become a general system of outdoor relief of the able-bodied, administered by a national in place of a local authority, and financed mainly by a tax on employment.

The authors of unemployment insurance in 1909 had to justify both a novel method of relieving distress through unemployment and a novel means of raising the funds that they required.

They had to justify, on the one hand, the giving of money unconditionally to men in idleness, without any attempt either to set them to work or to make them more fit for employment. They did so essentially on the ground that they were providing for temporary unemployment of men in a depression who had proved their industrial quality by working in the past, and, when the depression passed, would be needed again in their old trades and places. To give such men artificial relief work would be more costly than money payments and as demoralising. To train them for other occupations would be beside the point. To recondition them was not necessary.

On the other side, the new method of raising funds by compulsory contributions in respect of employment had to be defended against critics who said that workpeople would never stand deductions from their wages, or that industries which gave regular work and workpeople assured of regular employment ought not, under the name of insurance, to be made to pay for the irregularity of others. Here the scheme was defended partly as an extension of the system of trade union benefits for which workmen did in fact contribute, partly as a spreading of wages over good and bad times, a compelling of each industry with

---

[1] Except for a few months in 1924-5.

strictly limited help from the State to pay for its unemployment and to make the upkeep of its normal reserve of labour one of its costs of production. The argument of inequity between different trades and individuals was met partly by a whole string of rebates, refunds and other devices for adjusting premiums to risks or cover to premiums, partly by a promise of differentiation of contributions later. The aim of these devices was not abstract justice alone; they had the design of interesting employers and workpeople in the solvency of the fund and so giving motives for reducing unemployment; they were as practical as the rebates given by motor insurers to careful drivers. The unemployment fund was to be self-supporting; if the claims on it could be kept down, contributions would be lowered; if the claims exceeded expectations, contributions would be raised or benefits reduced. By 1920, when insurance came to be extended to industry generally, some of these fancy clauses appeared not worth the complications that they caused. But the rule proportioning benefits to total contributions, the refund at sixty, and the limitation of benefit to so many weeks [1] in a year were retained and still gave each workman ample reason for avoiding unnecessary claims; the new provision, under Section 18 of the Act of 1920, for contracting out under special schemes opened the prospect of a general adjustment of contributions to risks by industries.

The rule proportioning benefits to total contributions, combined with the refund at sixty, had several distinct objects. First, it provided automatically for those who worked partly in and partly out of an insured trade, by adjusting the benefit to the insurable employment. This was essential in the limited scheme of 1911. Though less important in a generalised scheme, it was not wholly without value even there. The requirement of thirty contributions in two years, if ever it comes to be applied, must act as a discouragement both to taking uninsured work at home, and to taking employment abroad. Second, it gave an incentive to each individual to avoid claims: he could save up for when he really was in want; under the present system he will at all times take all he can get. Third, the proportioning rule adjusted benefits to contributions, to some extent at least, by industries. Finally, by treating working life as a whole, it provided automatically for the increasing incidence of unemployment with advancing years; in his youth the workman could accumulate a claim for his old age. The test of thirty contributions in the

---

[1] Raised from the fifteen weeks of the 1911 scheme to twenty-six weeks in 1921.

past two years ignores well-known facts. How much the incidence of unemployment increases with age has been shown strikingly by a recent sample investigation of claimants to benefit at 16th September, 1929.[1] The average unemployment experienced in twelve months by each claimant to benefit was found to be 117 days in the age-group eighteen to twenty-four and to rise steadily to 183 at the ages fifty-five to fifty-nine and 182 at sixty to sixty-four; of every 100 claimants in the age-group eighteen to twenty-four, 31, while of every 100 in the age-group fifty-five to fifty-nine, 53, had been unemployed for more than 150 working days out of the past 312.

The provision for special schemes was double-edged. It was meant to allow industries which had little unemployment or for other reasons felt the general scheme unsuitable, to contract out voluntarily and set up their own schemes of contributions and benefits; the Departmental Committee of 1919, which framed the system of general insurance ultimately embodied in the Act of 1920, assumed that in all probability industries like coal and cotton, in which through the practice of short time working total unemployment had been small, would prefer special schemes. It could be used by the Minister of Labour, after consultation with the interests concerned, to frame a special scheme compulsorily for any industry for which through its peculiar conditions such a course seemed desirable; thus the dock and wharf industry might have been segregated and made to provide for its own under-employment. In the Memorandum introducing the Bill of 1920 it was estimated that from $1\frac{1}{2}$ to 4 millions of the total of $11\frac{3}{4}$ million persons to be covered by the Bill would be dealt with by special schemes.

At the height of the post-war reaction against the State, from 1920 to 1922, the possibilities of Section 18 of the Act of 1920 providing for special schemes were fully canvassed. There was much talk of "unemployment insurance by industries," and in February, 1922, the Minister of Labour by circular invited associations of employers and workpeople in all industries to consider the desirability of special schemes. The results were negative. In November, 1920, the general scheme had already come into operation ; in the catastrophic depression of trade which followed at once, Section 18 was suspended, lest all industries with low unemployment should seek to escape from paying for the others. When the embargo was lifted, employers and workpeople had got used to the general scheme, and insurance by industries, in spite of loud backing by professional critics of State action,

---

[1] *Labour Gazette*, 1930, pp. 6 *seq.*

proved to be a horse that would not run. Only two special schemes—for banking and for insurance—covering now together about 120,000 insured persons, were established. Otherwise Section 18 remained a dead letter, until it was repealed in the Act of 1927.[1]

With the repeal of the provision for special schemes and the making of benefit unlimited in time, following on the disappearance in 1924 of the refund at sixty, unemployment insurance has become an insurance in which every attempt to adjust premiums to risks or, conversely, to relate the cover afforded to the premiums paid, has been abandoned. The difference between the Blanesburgh Committee and the advocates of unlimited non-contributory insurance is simply a difference as to modes of taxation: the compulsory contributions have a fiscal significance alone.

The new model of 1927 cannot be defended by the old arguments of 1911. Can it be defended at all? Is it a necessary and serviceable portion of social structure, to be maintained indefinitely, or is it fraught with dangers which only drastic reconstruction can remove? That there are some dangers in unemployment insurance to-day no unimpassioned observer would deny. But those dangers are not to be found where the most impassioned critics of the scheme now place them.

The main danger of the present situation does not lie in the temptation to individual malingering, that is to say, in the possibilty of inducing workpeople to draw benefit when they could get work. This kind of abuse could be stopped completely and at once by employers notifying vacancies promptly and universally to the Exchanges; if that were done, no man could draw benefit for a single day on which suitable work was available for him. Even with their present limited control of the labour market, the Exchanges as a rule are able to check individual malingering with fair effectiveness.

Through all the transformations of insurance one element endures; one weapon has been added since 1911 to the permanent armoury for dealing with distress. Administration of benefit in all its forms—standard, extended, donation—has shown the possibility through a Labour Exchange system of controlling assistance of the unemployed sufficiently to prevent any serious abuse. Charges that the "dole" was helping numbers of men to live

---

[1] A *Report on the Administration of Section* 18 *of the Unemployment Insurance Act*, 1920, was presented to Parliament in 1923 (Cmd. 1613). Some of the difficulties of insurance by industries were described by myself in an article published in the *Manchester Guardian Commercial Supplement*, 1st February, 1923, with a suggestion for giving effect to the idea in a way that would have brought home very directly to each industry the responsibility of its own unemployment.

in idleness when they could get work have been made incessantly in the Press, by local authorities, by public men.   Whenever they have been investigated, they have been shown to be idle and irresponsible talk.   The conclusions of the Committee under the chairmanship of Lord Aberconway which investigated the working of the donation scheme in 1919, have been mentioned already. The Blanesburgh Committee gave the critics another chance.

> " Throughout the enquiry we have constantly had brought to our notice the conviction held by many that the system of unemployment insurance is subject to widespread abuses.   It has accordingly been one of our principal preoccupations to ascertain how far this belief is justified. . . .   It is convenient to state at once the conclusion we have reached in this matter. It is true that a certain number out of the $11\frac{3}{4}$ millions of insured persons have received relief to which they had no claim.   But it is equally true that these cases are relatively few and that result is, we think, due to the vigilance with which the Ministry, while dealing fairly with the genuine claimant, guards against abuse."

The Secretary of the Charity Organisation Society says that he began by thinking the abuses serious, but, on enquiry, had been unable to find them.

> " When this material (*i.e.*, that included in their memorandum) was read to our people on Monday afternoon last, they were much disappointed at the general character of almost all of it.   They had hoped that many more examples would be forthcoming illustrating the criticisms passed upon the present working of unemployment insurance by almost everybody who discusses the subject.   This shows the value of bringing these criticisms to the test of demanding examples, and more than one of our secretaries said that they quite expected to find from our case-papers numerous examples of abuses, but when they came to look they found very few. This does not, of course, prove that their previous impression was not a sound one ; on the other hand, it may quite well prove that unfavourable instances impress themselves upon the memory, while the proper and smooth working of a scheme passes almost unnoticed." [1]

Nor does such a conclusion mean that all the expenditure under the new insurance scheme is necessary or socially desirable. Manifestly some of the benefits go to meet needs of no great urgency, and sometimes the scheme is subject to scarcely veiled

[1] *Report of Unemployment Insurance Committee*, 1927, §§ 35, 36 and 39.

manipulation by employers and workmen in concert.[1] But if all other critics could be got to emulate both the care and the candour of the Charity Organisation Society, the way would be cleared for seeing where the real dangers of to-day's unemployment insurance scheme lie and do not lie.

Those dangers, in a sentence, lie not so much in the risk of demoralising recipients of relief, so that they do not look for work, as in the risk of demoralising Governments, employers, and trade unions so that they take less thought for the prevention of unemployment.

Relief of unemployment is after all a very bad second best to its prevention; however the giving of money during involuntary idleness be hedged round with safeguards, the idleness itself is demoralising, and becomes swiftly more demoralising the longer it lasts. The arguments advanced in 1909, for insurance rather than artificial work as a means of relieving the unemployed, assumed transient depressions, not the chronic under-employment of the casual labourer or the five-year idleness of the derelict coalminer. But once it is admitted in principle, that, either under the guise of insurance or in some other form, genuine unemployment can be relieved indefinitely by the simple device of giving money from a bottomless purse, prevention is only too likely to go by the board. The thoughts and time of Governments and Parliaments may be absorbed—as they have largely been absorbed during the past ten years—in successive extensions and variations of the relief scheme. The fear of causing unemployment may vanish from the minds of trade union negotiators and open the way to excessive rigidity of wages and so to the creation of unemployment. Industries practising casual engagement or perpetual short time may settle down to batten on the taxation of other industries or of the general public in place of reforming their ways. The immobilising influence of generous unemployment relief upon the recipient can be controlled by Labour Exchange machinery, simply and as completely as we choose. For its immobilising influence on the minds of Governments and leaders of industry the remedies needed are stronger and may be painful.

---

[1] The drains made on the fund by short-time workers are one case of expenditure whose social justification is doubtful; something more is said on this topic in ch. xviii. Another case is that of the woman who having worked till marriage, ceases after marriage to be regularly attached to industry or dependent on her earnings, but not unnaturally tries to get all that she can out of the unemployment fund, by registering as unemployed. Neither of these cases, however, is normally one in which the claimant could get work as an alternative to benefit if he or she tried for it. Each ought to be dealt with by some specific change of the insurance scheme—e.g., to the married woman a marriage gratuity extinguishing her claims to future benefit combined with adequate dependent allowance on her husband's unemployment and pension on his death.

CHAPTER XIV.

ESTABLISHMENT AND WORKING OF LABOUR EXCHANGES.

Contrasted history of Exchanges and insurance. Labour Exchanges Act of 1909 unchanged. General Regulations of 1910 unchanged. Wages and Trade Disputes. National system of Labour Exchanges described. Promising start broken by war and aftermath. War services. Diversion of energy to doles and insurance. Reaction against State and Committee of Enquiry of 1920. Statistics of registration and placing. Marked and accelerating recovery in recent years. Training Centres. Industrial Transference. Special functions in relation to juveniles and casual employment. Choice of Employment Schemes and Juvenile Advisory Committees. Early attempts at de-casualisation. Liverpool scheme. The lost opportunity of the war's end. Shaw Report. Registration schemes. No de-casualisation. Limited achievement of Labour Exchanges.

THE history of Labour Exchanges presents a singular contrast to that of unemployment insurance. In place of the endless string of Unemployment Insurance Acts—one for every year since 1911—there is a single Labour Exchanges Act, unamended since 1909; the only statutory change in twenty years is that transferring the administration of this Act from the Board of Trade to the newly-constituted Ministry of Labour at the beginning of 1917. Instead of growing out of all recognition in size and type, the Exchanges, as an organisation for placing men in employment, are much what they grew to be within three years of their beginning. Oddly enough, while unemployment insurance preserving its name has changed its substance, the Exchanges have kept their substance and changed their name; since September, 1916, they are officially Employment, not Labour, Exchanges. Instead of getting almost too much of the attention of Parliament and the public, the Exchanges have suffered at times from neglect. In the shadow of the companion scheme of insurance their own growth has been stunted and the thoughts and energy needed for their development as placing agencies have been devoted to the lesser service of paying benefit; atrophy rather than hypertrophy has been their danger.

The Labour Exchanges Act itself is a short and simple measure. Its main operative provision authorises the Board of Trade (now the Ministry of Labour) to "establish and maintain, in such places as they think fit, Labour Exchanges". This term is

295

defined to mean "any office or place used for the purpose of collecting and furnishing information, either by the keeping of registers or otherwise, respecting employers who desire to engage workpeople and workpeople who seek engagement or employment". Other provisions empower the department to assist Labour Exchanges maintained by any other authorities or persons, to take over such Exchanges, to make general regulations for the management of Exchanges maintained or assisted by them, and to establish advisory committees. By regulation power can be taken to advance the fares of workpeople proceeding to a distance to take up work found for them through an Exchange. It is an offence for employers or workmen to make false statements to an Exchange with a view to obtaining workpeople or employment.

This is practically the whole of the Act; it is a measure leaving everything to the policy of the Minister in charge. The Board of Trade under Mr. Winston Churchill in 1909 might have thought fit to set up Exchanges experimentally and sporadically, where previous discussion with employers and workpeople suggested that there was special need for them and a definite prospect that if established they would be fully used. The Board might have thought fit, in place of establishing their own Exchanges, to try to interest local authorities and by offers of financial assistance to bring into being a system of municipal Exchanges like that of Germany. The actual policy of the Board was more audacious and more direct. They set out to establish as rapidly as possible a full-blown system under their own control. They took over and absorbed into this national system all the existing Exchanges with any life in them, notably those of the Central (Unemployed) Body for London ;[1] they secured the closing of all others.

This policy would probably have been adopted even if the insurance scheme had not been in contemplation. The Poor Law Commission had advocated "a national system of Labour Exchanges" as the first requisite for dealing with unemployment ; the Exchanges were established before there was any certainty that unemployment insurance would follow. Though not certain, however, the introduction of insurance was from the first highly probable, and no policy could be contemplated other than that of making at once a complete network of Exchanges. Machinery had to be established by which it would be possible by a given early date in every part of the country to issue unemployment books for payment of contributions, to receive claims, to register the unemployed, and to pay unemployment benefit.

[1] Pp. 183-5 above.

With this task before them the Board of Trade could not afford to lose time in preliminary discussions. Steps to get premises and staff for the new organisation began long before the Labour Exchanges Act was on the statute book. Sixty-one Labour Exchanges opened their doors on 1st February, 1910, and eighty-seven more followed by the end of that year. Two years later, at the end of 1912, the insurance scheme came into full operation and the Exchange organisation reached its full extension, with 414 Labour Exchanges and about 1,000 local agencies of the unemployment fund. The latter were analogous to postal sub-offices, the agents undertaking to perform specified duties in offices provided by themselves for a commission based on the numbers of insured workpeople in their areas. The Exchanges proper were housed in premises hired and hastily adapted by the Government and staffed by managers and other full-time officials, appointed on a temporary basis by somewhat exceptional procedure. For administrative purposes the Exchanges and local agencies were grouped in territorial divisions, originally eleven in number but reduced to eight on the introduction of insurance. The whole formed a self-contained branch of the Board of Trade, under a Director and General Manager, dealing with Labour Exchanges and unemployment insurance together. The sanctioned staff in the financial year 1913-14 for both purposes was 3,243.

The organisation to-day is in essentials the same. The number of Employment Exchanges is all but unchanged at 417. The local agencies of the unemployment fund have become " branch offices," reduced in number to 745 but undertaking Exchange as well as insurance work. The divisions have been readjusted and reduced to seven in number by the passing out of Ireland ; the officers in charge have become " Divisional Controllers ".[1] The whole organisation has passed from the Board of Trade to form the bulk of the new Ministry of Labour. The staff has increased greatly, numbering at the end of 1928 about 17,000, of whom about 8,000 are pensionable civil servants. Most of this increase, however, and most other changes in the organisation are on the side of unemployment insurance.

Not only the Labour Exchanges Act but the General Regula-

---

[1] The divisions with the location of the divisional offices are : London and South Eastern (London), South Western (Bristol), Midlands (Birmingham), North Eastern (Leeds), North Western (Manchester), Scotland (Edinburgh), and Wales (Cardiff). The first of these contains more than a quarter of the total population, and for the purpose of insurance statistics is divided into an inner and an outer portion, known as London and the South East. The Exchanges and branch employment offices in Ireland were taken over in 1922 by the Government of Northern Ireland and the Irish Free State respectively; unemployment insurance in Northern Ireland is still administered, through the Exchanges so transferred, by the Minister of Labour in Whitehall.

tions made thereunder [1] have remained without change from the beginning. The most important points dealt with by these regulations are the attitude of the Exchanges towards questions of wages and conditions of employment, their action in times of trade dispute, and the advance of fares to workpeople travelling to employment at a distance.

On the first of these points the main regulation is as follows :—

> " The officer in charge of a labour exchange in notifying applications for employment and vacancies to employers and applicants respectively shall undertake no responsibility with regard to wages or other conditions, beyond supplying the employer or applicant, as the case may be, with any information in his possession as to the rate of wages desired or offered."

This is supplemented by a regulation allowing associations of employers or of workpeople to file at the Exchange agreements as to wages and conditions of employment ; the agreements are there open to inspection, and the manager of the Exchange is in a position to tell employers or workpeople what are the standard or customary terms of service in any district or occupation. It is then left to the individual to make his decision—as to what wages he will offer or accept—upon the facts before him. The Exchanges naturally do not accept from employers notification of vacancies where the wages or conditions offered conflict with a legal requirement, as under the Trade Boards Acts, but, subject to this exception, pass on to the workman whatever offer is made. A further regulation provides that no person shall suffer any disqualification or be otherwise prejudiced on account of refusing to accept employment found for him through an Exchange, where the ground of refusal is the existence of a trade dispute or that the wages are below the current rate.

The regulations as to wages and conditions have worked simply and without friction. The treatment of trade disputes raises thornier problems. Labour Exchanges, depending upon the voluntary co-operation of employers and workpeople, are clearly bound to be impartial when the two parties are in conflict, but a formal principle of impartiality goes no distance towards saying how an Exchange should act in regard to men thrown out by a dispute or vacancies created by it. As was pointed out in the Draft Report of 1915, " at least three distinct courses can be and have been represented as equally impartial."

---

[1] Dated 28th January, 1910.

"(*a*) To ignore strikes and lock-outs altogether, *i.e.*, to fill vacancies created, and register workmen unemployed through them, in exactly the same way as other vacancies and workmen, and without calling special attention to the fact of the strike or lock-out."

"(*b*) To recognise strikes and lock-outs as ground for suspending the operation of the Exchange altogether within the trade and district affected."

"(*c*) While not refusing to fill vacancies created or to register workmen thrown out by a strike or lock-out, to do so (at least as regards the vacancies) only subject to a special warning to the applicants that the vacancies have this character."

"Each of these courses permits of minor variations. For example, the third course may mean announcing the strike or lock-out generally in the Exchange, or may mean giving notice of it only to the particular workman to whom the vacancies are notified ; and the second course may mean suspending the operation of the Exchange for the whole trade and district affected, or may mean endeavouring to limit the suspension only to the particular employers and workmen affected."[1]

The third course, subject to minor variations, was that followed before the war in all the important Labour Exchanges in Germany. The same course, after repeated discussions with representatives of employers and workpeople, was adopted for the British Exchanges and embodied in the regulations in the following terms :—

"III. (1) Any association of employers or workmen may file at a labour exchange a statement with regard to the existence of a strike or lock-out affecting their trade in the district. Any such statement shall be in the form set out in the Second Schedule hereto, and shall be signed by a person authorised by the association for the purpose. Such statement shall be confidential except as hereunder provided and shall only be in force for seven days from the date of filing but may be renewed within that period for a like period and so on from time to time."

"(2) If any employer who appears to be affected by a statement so filed notifies to a labour exchange a vacancy or vacancies for workmen of the class affected, the officer in charge shall inform him of the statement that has been filed, and give him an opportunity of making a written statement

[1] *Draft Report on Labour Exchanges and Unemployment Insurance* (1915), §§ 126-7.

thereon. The officer in charge in notifying any such vacancies to any applicant for employment shall also inform him of the statements that have been received."

This regulation, while causing misunderstanding and resentment at times among the trade unions, has stood the test of time and repeated reconsideration. It has the advantage of saving the Exchanges from deciding formally on the existence or the merits of a dispute.[1] On the other hand, employers wanting men to take the place of strikers have many far more likely means of recruiting than the public Labour Exchange where the strikers themselves may be gathered. The issue, except on rare occasions, was from the beginning academic rather than practical, and has lost steadily in practical importance, through the growth of trade unionism and collective bargaining.

Not only the Labour Exchanges Act and the General Regulations but the detailed procedure of the Exchanges could be described to-day in terms applicable to them twenty years ago. The Exchanges are offices at which workpeople are invited to register when seeking employment and to which employers are invited to notify vacancies for employment. They are ready to deal with all occupations, skilled and unskilled, manual and clerical, extending formally, though not to any large extent practically, into occupations, such as agriculture and domestic service, which are still outside the scope of unemployment insurance.[2] They deal with men, women, boys and girls, usually in separate departments, sometimes in separate buildings. They make no charge for their services and they have no compulsory powers.

Registration of insured workpeople out of employment, indeed, is in practice compulsory and universal, as without it benefit cannot be obtained; this involves as a rule regular personal attendance at the Exchange. Notification of vacancies by employers is voluntary, and can be done in any way convenient, by letter, telephone or personal call. Certain information is asked for as a matter of course from workpeople and employers, but the general principle is that ultimately it rests with each party using the Exchange to

---

[1] Under the insurance scheme the Umpire has at times to decide both as to the existence of a dispute and as to the degree to which various classes of workmen participate in it, but these decisions can be given at (comparative) leisure after full investigation and hearing of both sides; an Exchange having to decide off-hand whether or not to fill a vacancy, notified perhaps by telephone, would be in a quite different position.

[2] At first the Exchanges did not deal with vacancies for indoor domestic servants in private houses, on the assumption that the ground was already covered by the ordinary registries. This restriction was removed in the war and not re-imposed, but the volume of work done by Exchanges in relation to indoor domestic servants remains small.

give as much or as little information as he thinks will serve his purpose. The fuller and more accurate the information given by either employer or workman as to qualifications required or possessed, as to wages, prospects and the like, the more likely is the Exchange to find itself in a position to help. But the Exchange does not insist on any particular information and, as a general rule, it takes no responsibility for verifying the correctness of what is told to it and what it passes on. It is simply a means of communication.

In regard to the filling of vacancies two principles of some importance are adopted : first, that the Exchange should endeavour to find for each vacancy the workman who is industrially best qualified and should pay no attention to priority of registration or need ; second, that each Exchange should deal directly only with vacancies in its own district. If an employer notifies a vacancy to an Exchange outside his own district, the vacancy is transferred to his proper Exchange, so that any suitable workpeople may be sent to him from his own locality rather than from a distance. Each workman is expected in the same way to register at his local Exchange. The object of the system is to promote advantageous mobility of labour, not wasteful wandering. If the local Exchange has no men suitable for a vacancy notified by an employer, it will try in turn, first, the neighbouring Exchanges, then, by notice to the divisional clearing house, the other Exchanges in the division, to which daily lists of unfilled vacancies are circulated by the clearing house. If local and divisional sources fail, the vacancy is reported to headquarters and included in a *National Clearing House Gazette*, issued weekly with daily supplements to all the Exchanges in Great Britain.

A substantial proportion of the work of the Exchanges consists in enabling men to find work in this way at a distance. Here their national extension gives them advantages over other agencies, and their service in reducing unemployment is most obvious. On this side of their work, they are helped materially by the power of advancing fares. Under the Labour Exchanges Act and the regulations thereunder, the advance can be made only where the employment is found through the Exchange and at a distance more than five miles from the workman's home ; the advance cannot exceed more than the workman's own railway fare ; and in practice takes the form of a voucher for his ticket. Sometimes the employer undertakes to repay the fare ; otherwise the advance is made to the workman and the employer is asked to deduct the amount from his wages by weekly instalments. The losses incurred on fares so advanced have been remarkably small. From the beginning of the Exchange system to the 31st March, 1924, about £300,000 was advanced to workpeople on terms of repayment by them or their employers; with the exception of 1½ per cent written off as bad debts and £775 outstanding at the final date, the whole of this had been recovered. A considerable part of the total fell in the period of the war, when employers would more often themselves pay the fares, but the experience of trifling loss is not confined to the war period.[1] When it is remembered that, in normal times, repayment of the loan would in most cases depend upon the workman staying long enough in the post to allow of the necessary deductions from his wages, the recovery of so large a proportion is notable evidence of the power of the Exchanges to find suitable men for work without the employer having a chance of seeing them beforehand.

Such is and was the organisation of the Labour Exchanges. What, in brief, has been their history and achievement?

The system begun in 1910 differed from earlier experiments of similar aim only in scale, in the energy put into it, and in the completeness of its dissociation from the relief of distress. It had no magic wand to enforce the support or break down the apathy and suspicions of employers or workpeople. Trade, however, in the years just before the war was good and the work of the Exchanges developed steadily. The vacancies filled by them rose from about 1,400 a day in 1910 to 2,900 in 1913 and 3,100 in the first half of 1914. Of these placings, one in eight involved transference to another Exchange district. Within a few years of their beginning the Exchanges were already filling one out of every three vacancies occurring in the insured trades; they had the vacant books of more than half the union branches in these trades voluntarily deposited with them for signature by members falling out of employment.

The war broke this steady development, by heaping on the Exchanges one new task after another. They began by supplying, under a War Book plan, much of the labour needed to mobilise the Expeditionary Force in the first days of August, 1914.

---

[1] At 31st March, 1914, advances totalling £11,686 had been made in 37,494 cases; £10,819 had already been recovered, £684 was in process of recovery, and only £183 or less than 2 per cent had been written off as irrecoverable. Later years gave a similar experience; the total advanced from 1922 to 1928 being over £70,000 in over 89,000 cases with a prospective loss of less than 4 per cent. In addition to the power of advancing fares under the Labour Exchanges Act, it is now possible for part of the fare in the case of insured persons to be paid from the Unemployment Fund, under section 30 of the Unemployment Insurance Act of 1920 and section 12 of the Act of 1930. For transfers from congested mining areas, under a scheme approved by the Government after the report of the Industrial Transference Board at the beginning of 1929, not only the fare of the workman himself but the reasonable costs of removing his household can be paid from the Exchequer.

They became, thereafter, in the words of the Committee of Enquiry appointed in 1920 to examine their work and advise on their future, "an essential part of the machinery required for the mobilisation of the national resources for the purposes of war; had they not existed, it would have been necessary to improvise some less adequate machinery for the purpose. It was fortunate that they were in existence and that the Managers and Staffs had acquired some knowledge of the psychology of employers and workmen and some experience in the transfer of labour."

"Very many workers and employers were under obligation to go to the Exchanges during this period, and the average daily number of vacancies filled rose to 4,713 during the first six months of 1916, and to 5,071 during the first six months of 1918. The staff of the Exchanges was also engaged upon much work of a special kind. Thus they were largely employed upon the selection of skilled men for release from the Forces and upon the difficult task of obtaining substitutes for men made conditionally available for military service. The Exchanges enrolled and transferred workpeople under the several special labour enrolment schemes (except the original National Service Volunteer Scheme). Thus the Exchanges enrolled 212,000 War Munition Volunteers and transferred 81,180: they enrolled 75,800 Army Reserve Munition Workers and placed 58,200 in employment; and they enrolled and placed 32,700 War Work Volunteers. The great majority of women enrolled in the Women's Service Corps were recruited through the Exchanges, including about 43,700 in the Q.M.A.A.C., 700 in the W.R.N.S., and 16,300 in the W.R.A.F. Further, the Exchanges supplied over 1,086,000 women for war work and in many cases arranged for their accommodation near their work."[1]

To this list from the Committee's Report may be added periodical collection of information as to employment and prices and inspection of factories applying for war contracts.

It leaps to the eye that not all these activities—and there were others more invidious still—were of a kind to make Exchange officials popular in the industrial world. Peace brought duties even more overwhelming; under a succession of emergency schemes for military demobilisation, civilian demobilisation, donation and unemployment insurance, Exchange work proper shrank

[1] *Report of the Committee of Enquiry into the Work of the Employment Exchanges* (1920, Cmd. 1054), §§ 10 and 15.

to less than half its war-time maximum. Peace brought also a reaction against the State, and a campaign to restrict its functions. The Committee of Enquiry whose report has just been cited found a good many witnesses in 1920 prepared to advocate the abolition of the Exchanges. There was plenty of evidence on the other side, and what the Committee would have reported as to the Exchanges alone remains uncertain. While they were sitting, however, the position was changed by the passage, in August, 1920, of the Act making unemployment insurance general. This settled the main issue for the Committee.

> "We see no alternative . . . but to continue the Exchanges as the administrative machinery of unemployment insurance. The Exchanges are analogous to the doctor in Health Insurance, since they are needed to certify that the applicant for benefit is suffering from genuine unemployment. Such machinery is necessarily costly and the best economy is to ensure that the utmost possible use is made of it." [1]

Within two years, the attack on the Exchanges was renewed with fresh force. A Committee appointed, under the chairmanship of Sir Eric Geddes, to prune the national expenditure, suggested that the possibility of placing unemployment insurance on the basis of insurance by industry should be explored.

> "If such schemes could be widely adopted the work remaining would be considerably reduced, and this seems to us to be the only effective way of reducing the vast expenditure on Employment Exchanges. They are popular neither with employer nor employee, and their continued existence practically depends on their work in connection with Unemployment Insurance. . . . We think . . . they ought to be abolished, and probably could be abolished after some such enquiry and modification as we have suggested." [2]

The negative results of the attempt made by the Government to follow up this suggestion have been described already; [3] the movement for unemployment insurance wilted under argument and disappeared as after 1922 the unemployment fund went yearly deeper into debt. Unemployment was too big a task and risk for anyone but the State; that meant the continuance of the Employment Exchanges as the State's machinery for dealing with the problem.

Though the Exchanges survived the attack made on them from 1920 to 1922, the damage done to them as placing organisations by

---

[1] *Report of Committee of Enquiry*, § 41.
[2] Committee on National Expenditure: *First Interim Report*, p. 146 (Cmd. 1581, 1922).   [3] pp. 291-2.

the war and its aftermath can hardly be questioned. For long years together they were forced to subordinate their main function of organising the labour market to other tasks more urgent but less important ; this process had begun even before the war, with the introduction of insurance.[1]

The lowest point came in 1922, when the Exchanges, though registering through insurance nearly four times as many workpeople, filled fewer vacancies than in their second complete year of working ten years before. From that point there has been a notable and now swiftly accelerating recovery. The course of this and the earlier history of the Exchanges can be seen compendiously in the following table of Labour Exchange statistics for certain years from 1910 to 1929 :—

TABLE XXXV.—LABOUR EXCHANGE STATISTICS, 1910-29.

Year.	Offices Open at End of Year.		Registration of Workpeople (in thousands).	Vacancies Notified (in thousands).	Vacancies Filled (in thousands).				
	Exchanges.	Branch Offices.			Total.	Men.	Women.	Boys.	Girls.
1910	148	—	1,400	459	374	219	82	47	27
1911	261	—	2,040	789	621	363	136	78	44
1912	414	—	2,464	1,063	828	514	168	88	58
1913	390*	932*	2,966	1,223	922	566	199	90	66
1916	363	959	3,659	2,049	1,557	636	696	117	109
1920	407	950	4,571	1,312	942	455	284	107	96
1922	379	766	8,989	859	716	411	190	50	64
1923	383	777	8,952	1,060	917	555	212	75	75
1924	382	772	11,447	1,369	1,165	679	278	112	96
1925	404	756	11,715	1,510	1,306	730	338	127	111
1927	413	750	—	1,459	1,274	684	325	140	125
1928	413	747	—	1,536	1,351	729	340	149	133
1929	417	745	—	1,863	1,631	931	382	169	149

* July, 1914. Ireland at that date had 19 Exchanges and 135 local offices.

NOTE.—The figures are taken from the *Draft Report on Labour Exchanges and Unemployment Insurance* (1915) and *Abstracts of Labour Statistics ;* they have been brought up to date by the Ministry of Labour. Up to 1925 the figures exclude certain classes of casual workers, such as dock labourers and coal-porters ; those for 1927 and 1928 include them. Figures relating to "Offices Open" refer to the United Kingdom in 1910, 1911, and 1912 ; but in all other years to Great Britain only. Figures relating to Registrations and to Vacancies refer to Great Britain and Northern Ireland only from 1922 onwards ; before that to the United Kingdom.

[1] " I may point out, in conclusion, that the Exchanges have never yet had a fair chance for development. They have always been doing something else than their main job, and there has never been time for a systematic overhauling of the administration. The Exchanges were opened gradually in 1910 and 1911. In 1911 the headquarters staff, and 1912-13 the whole staff, was absorbed in the launching of Unemployment Insurance. Then came the war, and in 1919 demobilisation. The department has never even found time to publish a report on its working." (Evidence by myself to the Committee of Enquiry of 1920, Cmd. 1140, p. 181.)

It will be seen from the note to the table that there are one or two changes in the basis of the figures, but these do not affect their substantial comparability.

The number of Exchanges proper is practically the same now as when the organisation reached full stature just before the war. The number of branch offices, formerly described as local agencies, has fallen somewhat; it has been found possible to dispense with branches in many rural areas, while increasing the size and work of those that remain.

The registrations of workpeople have increased enormously; the rises in 1913 and in 1922 are the direct consequence first of the introduction and then of the extension of unemployment insurance; 1925 is given as the last year for which these figures are available.

Under the heading of vacancies filled there is first a rapid growth as the Exchanges became established before the war. During the war, 1916 marks the peak of their activities in placing with 1917 close behind; as is natural, the greatest increase from before the war is in finding women for war work and as war substitutes; more than half the vacancies filled are for women and girls; 1920 is the only year of active demand for labour since the war, and 1922 is low-water mark. The recovery thence was checked by the year of disputes (1926), but 1928 was better for the Exchanges than any previous year since the war, and 1929 shows a jump to the highest total ever recorded, to more than 5,000 vacancies filled each working day as compared with 4,000 in 1928.[1] This improvement, in a state of trade as bad as ever, is the direct result both of increased attention to placing by the Exchanges and of the dawning recognition among employers and the public of the part that the Exchanges alone can play in bringing about the needed redistribution of labour.

Statistics of placing generally may be supplemented by the following table, showing from 1921 onwards the vacancies filled by applicants from Exchanges other than that dealing with the vacancy. Such placings do not necessarily involve transference over considerable distances or moving of the workman's home; large cities and industrial areas are served by numbers of Exchanges, each with its assigned district; a workman may find work within easy distance of his home through an Exchange other than his own. But even in such cases the service rendered

---

[1] 1929 shows interesting contrasts with the earlier record of 1916. The placings of men and boys have increased nearly 50 per cent while those of women have decreased almost in the same proportion. The placings of girls have risen proportionately almost as much as those of men or boys.

by the Exchange system both to employer and to workman is substantial ; in many other cases included in the total the transference of labour is over a considerable distance and the service rendered by the Exchanges could hardly have been given in any other way.

TABLE XXXVI.—LABOUR EXCHANGE PLACINGS
IN OTHER DISTRICTS.

Year.	Total Vacancies Filled.	Vacancies Filled by Applicants from Other Districts.	
		Number.	As Percentage of all Vacancies Filled.
1921	782,391	65,503	8·4
1922	669,331	69,422	10·4
1923	865,335	103,277	11·9
1924	1,114,449	136,501	12·2
1925	1,241,032	159,252	12·8
1926	1,082,917	137,784	12·7
1927	1,211,986	180,570	14·9
1928	1,287,693	212,580	16·5
1929	1,564,503	275,617	17·6

NOTE.—The figures have been supplied by the Ministry of Labour ; they relate to Great Britain only and exclude Post Office Christmas placings, for which complete statistics are not available over the whole period.

The tendency shown by the figures in the table is striking. While in eight years the total of vacancies filled has doubled, the number filled by applicants from other districts has more than quadrupled, and the percentages in the last column show an all but unbroken rise from 8·4 to 17·6. In 1913, as has been stated, one in eight of all vacancies was filled from another district ; after the war, in 1921, the proportion begins at one in twelve but by 1929 has risen to more than one in six.[1] The real growth in the work of the Exchanges and their service to the community is thus more than in proportion to the total of vacancies filled.

The statistics given above record the work of the Exchanges

[1] While placings in other districts by the Exchanges have increased relatively to their other placings, the somewhat perplexing fact remains that apparently, of all employment found, a smaller proportion is found through the Exchanges and more by other agencies where the employment is in another district than where it is in the Exchange's own district. Detailed figures for a recent short period have just been published and are given below on p. 322, n. 2. Their exact meaning is doubtful. To some extent they may be accounted for by the relatively large proportion of cases in which men return by direct communication to a former employer at a distance, or as due to the necessarily artificial boundaries of neighbouring Exchange areas in large towns. Finding employment "in another district" may for a workman mean finding it with his nearest employer. But it may be that finding work in other districts, otherwise than through the Exchanges, represents sometimes an undesirable mobility of labour.

in general terms as employment agencies. In dealing with exceptional unemployment since the war, their general activities have been reinforced by the establishment of training centres and by the industrial transference scheme.[1]

The work of the training centres, begun in 1925, is directed partly to preparation for agricultural employment overseas, partly to preparation for industrial employment in Britain. Under the first heading the total number admitted to training, from 1925 up to the end of 1929, is 9,640, and the number completing training and proceeding overseas is 7,262; more than half the total is in 1929, during which a special effort for overseas settlement was made. Under the second heading, out of 13,429 men trained wholly or completely, 10,823 or over 80 per cent have been passed into employment. The training given has been in connection with particular trades—building, furnishing, coach-building and certain metal trades—and has lasted commonly for five or six months. Though the numbers dealt. with are inconsiderable in relation to the total volume of unemployment, there can be little doubt that the trainees' prospects of obtaining and retaining employment have been materially increased. Unfortunately this kind of help, in order to be effective at all, has had to be confined almost entirely to young unmarried men. Only in the last year has it seemed worth while to experiment with a few married men and with men above 25 years of age. The reasons for this limitation will appear in the discussion of industrial transference.

The industrial transference scheme, set on foot after the report of the Industrial Transference Board of 1928,[2] is simply an intensive effort to find places in other districts for men from depressed mining areas. Within limits it has undoubtedly succeeded in lightening the burden of unemployment in those areas; men who but for the Exchanges would all but certainly have remained in corrupting, unwilling idleness at home have moved and made good elsewhere. The numbers reckoned as transferred under the scheme are 10,000 in 1928 and 32,000 in 1929. But the process has been one of laborious individual treatment. The possibilities of transference, as is pointed out in the latest report of the Ministry of Labour, are limited in practice by many factors, of which the two most important are domestic immobility and unsuitability for work in new conditions. The surplus of mining labour includes a large proportion of married men with large families; even if

---

[1] The account here is based mainly on the relevant portions of the general *Reports of the Ministry of Labour* for 1928 and 1929 respectively. Reference should be made to these Reports for the facts cited.

[2] Cmd. 3156.

work is available for them elsewhere, to find housing, particularly in districts with expanding industry, has often proved impossible; domestic immobility has restricted transfer in the great majority of cases to juveniles or men without dependants.   As regards employability, a significant change has been experienced during the currency of the scheme.   At the outset no difficulty was found in selecting from the congested areas men who would make good elsewhere, but early in 1929 it became evident, "mainly through the increased extent to which transferred men were failing to retain their jobs, that there was a change in the quality of the men coming forward for transfer".   Partly, no doubt, this was due to the fact that the men of most enterprise and highest industrial quality would be the first to come forward or be selected; partly, it reflected the damaging effect on character of prolonged unemployment.   The Ministry of Labour found itself driven to establish "transfer instructional centres," intended, in a course shorter and simpler than that of the training centres proper, to re-condition men who in long idleness appeared to have lost the habit of regular hours and steady work.   This new scheme was "directed primarily to men in the depressed areas who had a record of employment so poor as to make direct transfer to employment in some other part of the country impossible without risk of failure, and who were either unsuitable for, or not prepared to accept, the longer course of training in a Government Training Centre." [1]   How much something of the kind is needed and how much more of the practical problem of the depressed areas even so is left untouched, is suggested by an examination made in October and November, 1929, of the 40,000 men aged 18 to 45 in those areas who had been unemployed for more than three months.   Of all this number only about 7,500 appeared both available and suitable for immediate transfer to industrial employment, nearly 10,000 stood in need of a transfer instructional course and 4,000 of more specialised training, while the remaining 20,000 were held to be unsuitable for transfer whether with or without training because of their families.   This analysis is in part subjective, representing the judgments of the Exchange officials, but it shows strikingly how the problem of transfer presents itself in practice to those who have to solve it. Behind the men examined stands the army of the unemployed over 45 years of age—a still less tractable problem.

The factors named—of domestic immobility and industrial quality reduced by unemployment—do not exhaust the difficulties of transfer.   Throughout the period since 1921 the Exchanges have been faced by the further difficulty of finding districts with a

[1] *Report of the Ministry of Labour for* 1929, p. 37.

shortage of unskilled labour to which transfers could be made. There have been no places without unemployment and few with unemployment at pre-war levels. If the Exchanges had clung rigidly to the original conception, that vacancies should be notified to other districts only when every effort to find labour locally had failed, they would hardly have done any transference at all. It seems clear that as a national organisation they have adopted a less parochial view of their functions, and have made the draining, however slowly, of the depressed areas a cause more sacred than that of keeping local work for local men. To some extent, with their extension into small towns and country districts, they have by the offer of transferees led to the making of openings for them. To some extent they have, directly or indirectly, given a first chance of openings not to local men but to men from the depressed areas. This has led naturally at times to difficulties and local objections, but the justification of such a policy up to a certain point is beyond question. In many depressed areas a man remaining there would clearly never get work again at all. Even if the immediate effect of his transfer elsewhere is that he takes a job which would otherwise have gone to one of the local unemployed, it does not follow that the latter will remain unemployed indefinitely. Even without a definite job in prospect it is advantageous to transfer men from areas where industry is dead to those where it is living and growing. From a national point of view a condition of 40 per cent of unemployment in one district and 4 per cent in another calls for redress rather than argument, and the Exchanges are fortunately national.[1]

Training centres and industrial transference illustrate new problems thrown at the Exchanges by the war. There remain for discussion two special functions which have been theirs from the beginning—the guidance of boys and girls in the choice of careers, and de-casualisation, particularly of dock labour.

With a view to the first of these duties, the Board of Trade in 1909 prepared, in dealing with boys and girls at the Exchanges, to set up in each important district a Juvenile Advisory Committee, with representatives of educational interests to secure that the necessary guidance was given. In some quarters, however, the view was taken that the transition from school to employment should be assisted and supervised, not by an industrial authority like a Board of Trade Labour Exchange,

---

[1] One of the possible weaknesses of allowing juvenile employment to be dealt with by local authorities in certain areas (as described just below) is that these authorities may take a too parochial view of their functions, concerning themselves solely with placing local juveniles in local jobs and not opening the door to juveniles from depressed areas.

with or without a committee, but by the education authorities themselves. A Choice of Employment Act, passed in 1910, accordingly gave those education authorities that wished it the power to set up their own employment bureaux for juveniles, and the Board of Trade agreed, where this was done, themselves to cease dealing with juveniles, that is to say, young persons under 18.[1] Some of the authorities exercised their powers under the Choice of Employment Act, while others did not, so that the country became divided into two classes of areas, in which juvenile employment was dealt with by the Board of Trade and by the education authorities respectively. The introduction of unemployment insurance caused a complication, as the administration of this remained at first with the Board of Trade, even when the placing of juveniles was being dealt with under the Choice of Employment Act. The difficulty was resolved in 1923, as the result of a report by Lord Chelmsford, by handing over insurance administration in respect of juveniles to the education authorities, when these had adopted schemes for employment; by that time the powers given by the Choice of Employment Act had been embodied in section 107 of the Education Act of 1921. Finally, in 1927, the two systems were brought together again by providing that the central supervision of local authorities in administering choice of employment schemes should be exercised, not by the Board of Education, but by the Minister of Labour.

At the end of 1929, 112 education authorities in England and Wales had choice of employment schemes, while there were in other areas 174 juvenile advisory committees appointed directly by the Minister of Labour. The former group included most of the larger industrial centres and had about 400,000 insured juveniles; the latter included, as notable exceptions, London, Bristol, and Sheffield, with most of the smaller areas and about 500,000 insured juveniles. Practically there seems to be no substantial difference between the two forms of administration; both alike represent a widespread concerted effort to apply the knowledge and interest of Exchange and educational officials, teachers, and persons of goodwill to the placing of the coming generation to the best advantage in industry.[2]

---

[1] In Scotland, similar powers had been given to education authorities at an earlier date, by the Education (Scotland) Act of 1908.

[2] The working of the system during 1928 in both groups indifferently is described in a Ministry of Labour *Report on Advisory Committees for Juvenile Employment* (36-75-0-28). Separate reports are issued from time to time by the Committees for London and several of the other large cities. In Scotland, the only local education authority exercising its own powers is Edinburgh; in Glasgow and elsewhere throughout Scotland there are Ministry of Labour Committees.

As is pointed out in a later chapter,[1] this side of the
Exchange work is likely to be of growing economic significance
under post-war conditions of falling birth-rates and changing
industrial structure.   The number of young people relatively to
the rest of the population, that is to say, the proportion of the
total labour supply that is ductile and readily adaptable to new
needs, is falling rapidly ; it is all the more important that as
little as possible of this diminished proportion shall be misdirected into blind-alley occupations or decaying industries.   At
the same time the practical possibilities of what can be done
here to diminish mal-distribution of labour should not be
exaggerated.

It is a definite gain that the first choice of work by a boy or
girl should be made under guidance, rather than without guidance.   But even the first choice is not free ; the possibilities for
juvenile labour are determined by the nature of local industries,
and after the first choice has been made the boy or girl passes
sooner or later out of supervision into the chances of the industrial
world.   No choice of employment schemes can affect the alternate
over- and under-recruiting of trades, as illustrated for building in
Chapter XV, or save men from the decay of their industries
when they are already too old to find other openings, or prevent
casual employment from making casuals.   While it is safe to
assume that the bringing of reason to bear on a matter previously
left largely to tradition and chance has made conditions definitely
better than they would have been otherwise, the degree of improvement and the service here rendered by the Exchanges and
juvenile employment bureaux cannot easily be measured.

On the work of the Exchanges in de-casualisation and prevention of chronic under-employment a more definite judgment can
be passed.   Here, as the Minority of the Poor Law Commission
said, was to be found their highest utility.   Here, in the leading
case of dock and wharf labour, they have achieved just nothing
at all.

This failure of the Exchanges has not been for want of trying
on their part.   The Act incorporating the Port of London
Authority in 1908 had made it one of their express duties "either
by themselves or in co-operation with other bodies or persons, by
establishing or maintaining or assisting in the establishment or
maintenance of offices, waiting-rooms and employment registers,
and by the collection and communication of information and
otherwise" to "take such steps as they think best calculated to

[1] Ch. xvii.

diminish the evils of casual employment".[1]   The Majority of the
Poor Law Commission, referring both to this specific provision
as to London and to the ports generally, had recommended in
1909 that the Board of Trade "should send officers to visit . . .
localities where intermittent employment prevails, and should
endeavour through conference with employers and employed
to arrange schemes for the progressive de-casualisation of such
employment".   As soon as the Exchange organisation was
established, or even before, the Board of Trade followed up this
recommendation in every considerable port in the kingdom and
in other fields of casual work.   With the passage of the National
Insurance Act of 1911 they tried to bring another weapon to
bear.   Though dock labourers were not insured against unemployment under Part II of the Act, they were insured against
sickness under Part I; section 99 of the Act allowed the Board
to make arrangements for keeping and stamping the contribution
cards of men engaged through the Exchanges and so saving the
employer the burden of all this work for casual employees.   The
result of the Board's efforts to promote de-casualisation from 1909
to the outbreak of war is summed up in a few paragraphs of the
Draft Report of 1915.

In London, Southampton, Bristol, Manchester Docks, Preston,
Hull, Leith, Glasgow and (for ship-repairers) on the Clyde, the
negotiations pressed by the Board had accomplished nothing;
one or two experimental Exchanges opening in hopeful antici-
pation—as at Leith and Avonmouth—had not been used and
had been closed again.   In Liverpool and Goole, for dock labour,
and in the South Wales ports, for ship-repairing, schemes had
been set up and were operating under section 99 of the National
Insurance Act, but these "had the character of insurance schemes
as much as or even more than that of Labour Exchange schemes":

" . . . while many attempts have been made by the
Board of Trade to carry into effect the recommendation of
the Poor Law Commission . . . difficulty has generally been
experienced in first obtaining the voluntary co-operation of
the parties concerned.   It has not often been found that the
employers were ready seriously to consider a scheme, and

---

[1] Section 28 of the Port of London Authority Act of 1908.   The section concludes
with a proviso that nothing in it "shall deprive any person of any legal right which he
would otherwise possess with regard to the engagement of labour," and the proviso
seems to have been treated by the Authority as making the section a dead letter from
the start.   "It would be difficult to point to any reform, accomplished or attempted,
for which the Authority could claim credit as a contribution towards the task laid upon
them by this section" (Lascelles and Bullock, *Dock Labour and Decasualisation*, p. 9).

where this first difficulty has been overcome, it has often proved impossible to frame a scheme that would be accepted both by employers and workmen. The latter have, on more than one occasion, voted against a scheme put before them by their representatives. . . . The reduction of the number of separate centres for the engaging of men and the consequent concentration of their engagement upon a limited number of Exchanges, which has constantly been urged by the Board's officers as the main means of improving the conditions of employment, has not in fact been realised at Liverpool, Goole, or in the South Wales ports. . . . On the whole it cannot be claimed that any substantial progress has yet been made with the de-casualisation of labour in the principal centres where such labour is employed. The powers of the Board (of Trade) have not proved adequate to secure that change in the methods of engagement which alone appears to offer a prospect of real improvement. At the same time much valuable experience has been obtained and co-operation between employers and workmen established." [1]

Of these early schemes, the best known and the only one surviving to-day is that for dock labour at Liverpool. As introduced in 1912, it was stated to have four main features :—

"(a) the registration of all dock labourers, the issue of metal tallies to the men registered, and the limitation of employment to men provided with such tallies.

"(b) the use of 'surplus stands' to direct dock labourers to the points at which they are needed, when they have failed to get work at their ordinary places of employment.

"(c) the payment of all the wages earned by each man in a week from any number of different employers in a single sum to him at a Clearing House.

"(d) the keeping and stamping of the health insurance contribution cards at the Clearing Houses, the deduction of the workmen's contributions from them there on payment of wages, and the pooling of the employers' contributions according to the amount of labour used by them." [2]

The third and fourth of these reforms have been carried out, and the third has removed a hardship peculiar to the Liverpool

---

[1] *Draft Report on Labour Exchanges and Unemployment Insurance* (1915), §§ 223-5.
[2] *First Report on Unemployment Insurance*, § 121.

dock labourer.[1] The first has also been carried out, but not the second, because the employers and their foremen in practice never telephoned to the surplus stands for labour and the men naturally never went there ; the stands have been abolished and the telephone boxes set up for communicating with them have been removed. This very mild first step towards a change in the places of engagement—the only part of the scheme that could make any real difference to regularity of employment—has thus been formally retracted. Failing the increase of mobility that might have resulted from this feature of the scheme, it has been found necessary at all times to keep the number of men registered for work far in excess of the number employed on the busiest days. Registration and the Liverpool scheme generally have served only to show up once more the evils of casual labour and to furnish for the first time comprehensive statistics of weekly earnings.

One of the striking results disclosed in the starting of the scheme was the combination of a large surplus of labour in the port with repeated shortages of labour at particular stands. A preliminary investigation in January, 1912, showed that the number of men employed on the busiest day of that month was under 20,000 ; that the total number seeking work there was 27,000 ; that, nevertheless, at one or other of a number of stands chosen for observation there were, on every week day in the month, shortages of labour totalling sometimes over 1,000 combined with surpluses at other stands never falling below 1,000.[2] When the scheme got to work in July, 1912, the preliminary investigations were fully confirmed. The number of men registered for work and actually doing some work in the first twelve months was over 29,000 ; the average number employed each week was 20,000 and the number in the busiest week was 23,000. Employment in a week did not by any means represent full employment even for that week. The number of men paid each week through the Board of Trade averaged 17,555 and the amount paid averaged £19,818, that is to say, 22s. 7d. per head, but individual earnings departed widely from the average ; one man in ten got 40s. or

---

[1] Formerly dock labourers at Liverpool, though hired casually as elsewhere by the day or hour, were paid, not daily as in London, but only at the end of each week, and a man who had worked for several employers in a week would have to collect his wages from several, perhaps widely scattered pay offices, on Saturday. This was naturally felt as a hardship by those who suffered it, though their numbers have not proved to be as great as might have been supposed : during 1923 on an average 77 per cent of those working in each week worked for one employer only in the docks and only 4 per cent worked for more than two. See table in Lascelles and Bullock, op. cit., p. 186.

[2] Lascelles and Bullock, op. cit., pp. 84-5.

more and one man in three 15s. or less.[1] Yet with all this underemployment, there were constant complaints of shortages of labour and demands by some of the employers to have more men registered. One inference drawn by the officials in charge of the scheme was that there was a substantial body of men who had become casual by inclination and, though registered, did not present themselves for work on more than two or three days in a week or in more than two or three weeks in each month.[2]

The statistics of Liverpool dock labour before the war showed it as an occupation of men sweated by chronic under-employment and demoralised by irregularity. The picture since the war is in essentials the same. The numbers registered for work and obtaining work have both fallen, but are in much the same relation to one another. In 1928 and 1929 alike the average number of men paid wages by the Board of Trade each week is a little over 14,500, and the maximum number in any one week is just over 16,000 but the number of tallies in circulation averages over 20,000, that is to say, is 25 per cent above the maximum of the busiest week. The amount paid per head of those paid each week averaged in 1928 £2 12s. 4d. and in 1929 £2 11s. 8d. ; these amounts represent respectively 4·4 and 4·3 times the standard wage of 12s. for a day of eight hours.[3] The £1 2s. 7d. paid in 1913-14 represented 4·5 times the standard daily wage of those days, 5s. for nine hours. The abnormal addition of 170 per cent to the docker's rate of pay per hour since the war has increased

---

[1] These are not all the possible earnings of the men. Some might have received "subs" or advances of their pay direct from the firms, or have worked for firms in the docks outside the scheme, or have worked outside the docks altogether. The average additions to be made under these heads, however, are small. See Statistical Supplement, p. 438.

[2] See *The First Year's Working of the Liverpool Docks Scheme*, by R. Williams (P. S. King & Son, 1914). The number of men actually taking out tallies in the first twelve months was 31,471, but of these 2,138 did no work at all at the docks; 5,249 worked in thirteen weeks or less, 4,836 in fourteen to twenty-six weeks, 5,228 in twenty-seven to thirty-nine weeks, and only 14,020 in as many as forty weeks in the year, though the minimum employed in the slackest week after the scheme was in running order was over 18,000. In the five weeks ending January 31st, 1913, the numbers of men employed in each week fluctuated only from a minimum of 21,482 to a maximum of 22,984, but only 16,258 individuals worked in each of the five weeks. The effect of casual engagement in spreading a steady total of work over an excessive number of men and making work needlessly irregular could not be better exemplified. Mr. Williams (*op. cit.*, p. 103) gives the earnings over a year of 600 men on the preference lists of certain firms, *i.e.*, the most favoured class of dockers; 10 per cent averaged 20s. a week and under, and another 19 per cent averaged between 20s. and 25s.

[3] The post-war averages like the pre-war averages cover widely divergent individual figures. In 1923 the percentage of men receiving less than three times the standard day wage in a week averaged 29 per cent. In 1913 the percentage was 35 during the slack month of June and 31 during the busy month of January (*First Report on Unemployment Insurance*, § 131).

his income and has made the service of the port far more expensive to the consumer without making the calling any less casual or demoralising to the labourer. The one certain change made in the lives of the dock labourers by eighteen years' working of the Liverpool dock scheme is that each Saturday three or four thousand men, in place of getting paid in two or three places, get paid in one place. Yet the evils of casual employment were no new story in Liverpool even in 1912. They had been shown up by Miss Rathbone's enquiry years before.[1]

The experience of the Liverpool scheme from 1912 to the present day is typical of dock labour generally. Whatever else is changed, the methods of casual engagement continue and with them continue demoralisation and under-employment. In the war itself the need for keeping in the ports and exempt from conscription sufficient men to carry on their work led to various systems of more or less formal registration.[2] With the end of the war there came a unique opportunity of abolishing chronic under-employment in the docks. Since the evil is under-employment of a body of men too large for the real needs of a port but kept there through the chances of casual work, the cure, in normal times, involves concentrating employment by deliberate organisation on some of the men and leaving the rest without employment at all; a small mobile force is made to cover the same ground, do the same work, and earn the same total of wages as a large immobile one. This extrusion of some of the men formerly under-employed is the practical difficulty—the only real one—in the way of de-casualisation; and this by 1918 the war had removed. The work of most of the ports had diminished greatly; by the Armistice the number of men employed in dock and wharf labour was 27 per cent below the number so employed in July, 1914; of the dockers who had joined the fighting forces a large proportion would never return. Then was the time by a rigid registration system to stop, till de-casualisation was complete, the entry into the industry of men not previously connected with it; to replace the innumerable disconnected taking-on places by a few connected centres mobilising the labour supply; to guarantee registration to every man who could prove a past real connection with the industry; finally, in lieu of ordinary unemployment insurance, to guarantee to every registered man a minimum weekly income, and to raise the funds for this in such a way as to give direct discouragement to registration of more men than were needed. A detailed scheme for this purpose was in fact prepared in 1916

[1] *Report of an Enquiry into the Conditions of Labour at the Liverpool Docks* (1904).
[2] Lascelles and Bullock, *op. cit.*, pp. 100-2.

by the officials then concerned with such matters and was discussed with the parties concerned.[1] For a moment it looked as if sufficient assent might be won to find a place for the scheme in any reconstruction legislation. But disastrous suspicions broke in on the negotiations; soon after these particular officials lost their influence on labour affairs; ministers, employers, and trade union leaders would not think of the war's end till it ended. The golden opportunity of painless reform came and went by unused.

The problem of dock labour was not, indeed, out of sight in the immediate aftermath of war. On the contrary it received peculiar prominence.[2] The various dockers' unions, amalgamated during the war into the Transport Workers' Federation, adopted at the end of 1918 a general policy of limiting dock work to registered men and securing for those men maintenance while standing in reserve. At the beginning of 1920, this policy, pressed with a demand for higher wages, on an Industrial Court under the Chairmanship of Lord Shaw, achieved a resounding victory. The Court recommended the higher wages and the introduction of a system of registration of dock labour in all the ports, docks and harbours of the United Kingdom; they approved the principle of maintenance; they devoted several sections of their Report to denouncing afresh the evils of casual employment.[3]

"The Court is of opinion that labour frequently or constantly under-employed is injurious to the interests of the

[1] The principle of the scheme was that every registered docker in any week in which his earnings fell below a certain minimum, say 30s., should have them made up to that amount, and that the funds for this should be raised from the employers by charges for each man registered, probably both an entrance fee on first registration and an annual subscription thereafter. The amount of the charges would thus depend in the first instance on the number of men whom the employers considered necessary for the work of the port; but the rate per head would be raised or lowered according to the maintenance required. By registering an excessive number of men the employers would thus increase their costs both directly and, by causing unemployment, indirectly. It was contemplated further that, as in insurance generally, the employers should be allowed to make deductions from the workman's wages and keep what they deducted, so that they would gain still more by regularising employment, but this was not an essential feature of the scheme. The essential thing was that the industry, through the employers, should pay, not as under the insurance system, in proportion to the employment given, but in proportion to the numbers of men kept attached to it by registration and the chance of employment.

[2] A full and valuable account of dock labour in this period up to the beginning of 1924 is contained in the volume on *Dock Labour and Decasualisation*, by E. C. D. Lascelles and S. S. Bullock (P. S. King & Son, 1924), to which reference has already been made.

[3] *Report of a Court of Enquiry concerning Transport Workers' Wages and Conditions of Employment of Dock Labour*, §§ 17-19 (House of Commons Paper 55 of 1920). The Report was signed by seven out of the nine members of the Court; the two others dissented mainly on the proposal as to a minimum daily wage of 16s., but approved, in principle, of registration and of allowances to unemployed dockers on condition of their being mobile. On these points, therefore, there was unanimity.

workers, the ports, and the public, and that it is discreditable
to society. It undermines all security, and is apt to under-
mine all self-respect upon the workers' part. It is only among
those who have sunk very far, and whom the system itself
may have demoralised, that it can be accepted as a working
substitute for steady and assured employment. In one sense
it is a convenience to authorities and employers, whose requirements are at the mercy of storms and tides and unfore-
seen casualties, to have a reservoir of unemployment which
can be readily tapped as the need emerges for a labour supply. If men were merely the spare parts of an industrial
machine, this callous reckoning might be appropriate; but
society will not tolerate much longer the continuance of the
employment of human beings on those lines.

"The system of casualisation must, if possible, be torn up
by the roots. It is wrong. And the one issue is as to what
practical means can be adopted of readily providing labour,
while avoiding cruel and unsocial conditions.

"So serious has the position become that it has evolved
habits of mind and body on the part of the workmen themselves which are detrimental to them and on a wide scale
deeply injurious. Many workers have got into the habit of
thinking that day labour is a sign of independence, and that
labour secured even for a week leaves them devoid of that
liberty to do nothing which they have come to prize.

.   .   .   .

"Casualisation, in short, and that on a large scale, seems
to have become part and parcel of the dock industry, and
this has been accentuated since the outbreak of war. It was,
and it remains, one of the most appalling problems which
confront all those engaged in social amelioration or philanthropic effort. Since the war it has reached the dimensions
of a serious social disease. The spectacle of men who, after
all, have the obligations of citizenship resting upon them,
being assembled at the dock gates, uncertain whether they
are to enter the ranks of Labour for even half a day or be
left a prey to those temptations which spring from idleness,
poverty and a sense of neglect, is not one which can be
treated by any independent and humane mind with
equanimity."

Unfortunately from all this very little that endures has come,
and nothing that makes a difference to the conditions of dock
labour. The victory of the Shaw Report has proved yet hollower

than the victory of the "docker's tanner" thirty years before.[1]
The daily minimum of 16s. fixed by the Shaw Report in March,
1920, disappeared in the crash of 1921, and the present minimum
is 12s.; towards tearing up casualisation by the roots hardly a
step has been taken. There are, originating mainly before the
Shaw Report, Port Labour Committees in most of the ports,
theoretically charged with the duty of registration. Four years
after the Shaw Report, as the result of another dispute and another
hearing by an Industrial Court, a fresh Committee was set up
under the Chairmanship of Sir Donald Maclean to consider the
principle of maintenance set out in the Shaw Report. The Committee issued in 1924 two interim reports of which the first emphasised the importance of having a registration scheme in every
port, while the second, dealing with the proposal for a guaranteed
week, pointed out that the basic question was that of cost and that
the cost could not be determined till registration was effective.[2]
Thereupon, having shelved the guaranteed week pending registration, the Committee was not publicly heard of again till 1928,
when it made a report advocating reduction of taking-on places;
within the past few months it has been asked to resume its
activities.[3]

Meanwhile maintenance of a kind during the intervals between
successive jobs has resulted from the inclusion of dock labour
in the general insurance scheme of 1920. For the individual
docker the scheme of benefit for days of continuous unemployment often works out unfairly; one man, having earned high
wages for two days or nights of almost continuous work, may
and does get unemployment benefit as well for the rest of the
week, while another man, working a few hours on each of three
or four days, has lower earnings and no benefit. For the industry
as a whole the insurance scheme is a subsidy from other industries

[1] See p. 207 n. above. The 6d. an hour won by the London Dock strike of 1889
was never lost, in spite of the continuing fall of prices to 1897. The attention directed
to the evils of casual employment at the time led to the reform of the dock companies'
system of employment which is described on pp. 88-91 and which remains the one
piece of large-scale de-casualisation on record.

[2] The Reports are printed in the *Labour Gazette* for July, 1924. The first gives
a list of eighteen ports, including London, Liverpool, Manchester, Bristol, Southampton.
Swansea, Newport (Mon.), and Aberdeen as already having registration schemes, and
another list of thirty-three including Hull, Grimsby, Tyne and Wear, Leith, Dundee,
Glasgow, Greenock, Barrow-in-Furness, Falmouth, and Harwich as not having them.
A report a year later, in the *Labour Gazette* for July, 1925, makes it clear that in
London at least the previous registration scheme must have been shadowy. One of
the most effective schemes (apart from Liverpool) appears to be at Bristol (*Labour
Gazette*, June, 1926). At Bristol, because the port starts with the advantage of a
single taking-on place, there has probably been some real improvement in the con-
ditions of the labourers through registration.

[3] See *Labour Gazette*, February, 1928, and January, 1930.

in aid of casualisation. An official estimate puts the total contributions from employers, workmen and the State in canal, river, dock and harbour service during 1924-26 at £2,388,000 and total benefit at £9,625,000.[1] This is a subsidy to casualisation of over seven million pounds in the three years or about 5s. per head per week for every man in the industry.

It is now clear that, for abolition of distress through chronic under-employment in dock and wharf labour, three things are required, first, registration to prevent the inflow of unnecessary labour; second, re-organisation of methods of engagement and pooling of the labour supply so as to get the work of the port done by the smallest possible number of individuals with as little unemployment as possible; third, maintenance of the men in those intervals of unemployment or of waiting in reserve which remain. The second of these is the essential step urged in the first part of this volume but left out of all practical schemes hitherto. Registration without re-organisation of engagement, means that to avoid local shortages enough men have to be registered to do the work of the port in its disorganised state, that is to say, many more men than the number required on the busiest day. To add maintenance and still leave out re-organisation means that men are to be maintained indefinitely while working three, two, or perhaps one day a week; whether the maintenance be an adequate one for their needs or a pittance this is equally demoralising and all but equally extravagant.

Failure to secure de-casualisation of dock labour by persuasion need cause no surprise. The Majority of the Poor Law Commission in 1909, while convinced of the need for de-casualisation, had recognised abundantly the difficulties of bringing it about. In addition to the obvious difficulties of getting employers to combine for labour, the attitude of the trade unions had to be taken into account, and behind the trade unions that of the men themselves.[2] The experience of the Board of Trade in the five years before the war amply confirmed the fears of opposition expressed by the Majority. After twenty years it seems fair to say that the appeal to reason and public spirit in this industry has failed. The way is open to the compulsion which the Majority of the Commission were prepared to apply when needed and which the Minority advocated from the start.

Apart from the special case of the docks, there will be general agreement in 1930, as in 1920, that "the Exchanges have not

[1] *Hansard*, 29th November, 1927, col. 284, vol. 211.
[2] See *Majority Report of Poor Law Commission*, Part VI, Chapter I, §§ 296-300.

succeeded in displacing, so far as was expected, other methods of finding work."[1] They could probably not point to any specific achievement of de-casualisation elsewhere than in the docks. They have not abolished the hawking of labour. There has even in some occupations since the war been a development of Exchange service by trade unions for their members. Four out of every five engagements of insured workpeople are made otherwise than through the national system of Employment Exchanges.[2]

This limitation of their achievement is not to be laid at the door of the Exchanges themselves. They had no compulsory powers and could rely only on gradual voluntary conversion of employers to their use; their promising early start in this direction was broken by the war, and since then, till within the last year or two, they have always had other work to put before placing. Nor have employers at any time proved easy to convert. The tendency to get labour in the old ways normally and try the Exchanges in emergencies only has been common. Those who

[1] *Report of Committee of Enquiry into Labour Exchanges* (1920, Cmd. 1054), § 95 (7).
[2] The proportion of Exchange placings to all placings during 1913, when insurance applied only to selected trades, was 33·9 per cent. The proportion of 20 per cent named in the text for the present time was given by the Minister of Labour in a memorandum on the financial effects of the Bill which became the Act of 1930. The following table, printed in reply to a Parliamentary Question of 26th June, 1930, gives details for the period from 31st December, 1929, to 24th March, 1930. It should be noted that the table refers to adults only. The proportion of Exchange placings to all placings is presumably higher among juveniles.

ADULT CLAIMANTS FOR UNEMPLOYMENT BENEFIT REGISTERED AS WHOLLY UNEMPLOYED.

Engagements in Insured Work.

Group.	Percentages of Engagements Effected through Employment Exchanges.								
	In Area of Exchange at which Claimant was Registered.			In Area of some other Exchange.			All Areas.		
	With Former Employer.	With New Employer.	Total.	With Former Employer.	With New Employer.	Total.	With Former Employer.	With New Employer.	Total.
Men . .	12·7	30·4	23·5	4·8	12·4	9·9	10·5	24·3	19·2
Women . .	13·7	49·9	35·2	7·6	28·7	22·1	12·0	42·4	31·0
Total	12·8	32·6	24·9	5·1	14·4	11·4	10·6	26·4	20·4

In the above table the former employer means the employer with whom the applicant was last employed.

have then found the Exchanges unable to meet the emergency have seldom thought of applying to their case the commonplace observation that a supplier of labour, as of any other article, on whom one wants to rely in emergencies should also be given one's daily custom ; only in this way can he keep a stock at call. The statistics given above of the growing proportion of Exchange work that involves the co-operation of two Exchanges in finding work for men or men for employers in districts other than their own, is in itself a sign of their being used by employers too much for emergencies and too little by way of daily routine. The achievement of the Exchanges, however, must not be under-estimated. Their achievement in fact is normally in excess of the credit given to them [1] and is more than the mere statistics of placing suggest. In so far as they are used disproportionately for emergencies rather than as daily sources of supply, their 5,000 daily placings include a relatively large proportion of difficult cases—of finding men for employers from a distance and of slowly draining the stagnant pools of mining labour ; the placings in the insured occupations which they do not make include probably a disproportionately large proportion of cases where workmen laid off for a few days or weeks return automatically to their regular employer. If the Exchanges have not yet substituted an organised for an unorganised labour market, if their success has been least when it would have been most striking and is still most needed— in relation to casual labour—they have proved themselves in peace as in war an indispensable piece of national machinery. They have experienced within the past year a marked and encouraging revival.

[1] The Committee of Enquiry of 1920 received many representations from employers and some from workpeople as to the uselessness of the Exchanges to their particular industries. On these representations they observed : " In assessing the value of some of the evidence just mentioned we would refer to the statistical statement which appears in Appendix V. This shows that in certain of the industries which do not consider the past services of the Exchanges to have been of value, large numbers of employers and workpeople make successful use of them." (§ 49.)

CHAPTER XV.

FLUCTUATION—CYCLICAL AND OTHER.

Multiplicity of writers since 1909. The monetary explanation of the trade cycle. Inherent instability of credit and prices. Points for further enquiry. Points of advantage over other explanations. Monetary theory does not explain all fluctuations. Hyper-cyclical fluctuation of building trade. Difficulty of finding trade cycle before 1860. Instability of credit only one of several factors of economic instability.

THE examination of the causes of cyclical fluctuation attempted in the first part of this volume twenty years ago was admittedly inadequate. The preface then written spoke of turning back "unsatisfied from whole fields of inquiry as fascinating as they are important". It named particularly among these fields of enquiry "the problem of the underlying causes of cyclical fluctuation in trade and employment".

The gap thus left in 1909 has been amply filled by other writers. In the short interval between the first publication of this book and the early days of the war, there appeared at least four works of importance almost wholly devoted to this one topic—namely *A Study of Industrial Fluctuation*, by Mr. D. H. Robertson (1915), *Les Crises périodiques de Surproduction*, by Professor Albert Aftalion (1913), *Business Cycles*, by Professor Wesley C. Mitchell (1913), and *Good and Bad Trade*, by Mr. R. G. Hawtrey (1913). Since the war has come another full length study—*Industrial Fluctuations*, by Professor A. C. Pigou (1927)—while almost as much has been contributed by other books treating the trade cycle as part of a more general problem. These include *Currency and Credit* (1919) and *Monetary Reconstruction* (1926), by Mr. R. G. Hawtrey, *A Tract on Monetary Reform*, by Mr. J. M. Keynes (1923), *Stabilizing the Dollar*, by Professor Irving Fisher (1920), *Money* (4th Impression, 1928), and *Banking Policy and the Price Level* (1926), by Mr. D. H. Robertson. The new edition of *Business Cycles*, by Professor Wesley Mitchell (1927), substantially a new book, has up to the present reached only

324

the stage of a first volume setting out facts with little or no theorising.[1]

This flood of literature makes it in part unnecessary and in part impertinent to attempt here a fresh formal investigation of the problem. On the one hand, the labour of economists in the past twenty years has not been unfruitful. The nature and causation of the trade cycle, as experienced in Britain from the middle of the nineteenth century to the beginning of the Great War, are no longer wholly mysterious. Six years ago Mr. Keynes referred to " the almost revolutionary improvement in our understanding of the mechanism of money and credit and of the analysis of the trade cycle, recently effected by the united efforts of many thinkers ".[2] Elsewhere he said : " Mr. Hawtrey has emphasised what is perhaps the main difference between the attitude of a good many economists now and their pre-war attitude, namely, their greater confidence as to the connection between monetary causes, the credit cycle and unemployment. Mr. Hawtrey himself has been a great pioneer in the exploration of that subject. I myself believe that there is no longer any reason to doubt the connection." [3] On the other hand, recognition of the monetary nature of the nineteenth century trade cycle is only one step to understanding all that has now to be explained. In spite of the explorations of many experts, much remains obscure in the relations of currency, credit, and trade, even before the Federal Reserve Act of 1913 and the outbreak of war. Since those two events, new governing conditions, new policies and new problems have succeeded one another in bewildering succession the behaviour of money and the relations of industry and finance have become a battleground of specialised study as dangerous to the outsider, and sometimes to the expert, as any in the whole field of learning. The central feature of the monetary theory of fluctuation, best described in Mr. Hawtrey's words as "the inherent instability of credit," remains intact ; its recognition is one of the recent assured advances of economic science. But the manner and times in which in varying circumstances this instability will

---

[1] Reference should be made also to *Control of Credit*, by J. R. Bellerby (1923) ; to articles on theories of trade fluctuation by Mr. L. K. Frank and Mr. W. M. Persons, (*Quarterly Journal of Economics*, August, 1923, and November, 1926); on " The Explanation of the Business Cycle," by Professor Schumpeter (*Economica*, December, 1927) and to the review of Professor Pigou's " Industrial Fluctuations " made by Mr. Hawtrey in his book on *Trade and Credit* (1928). Professor Pigou and Mr. Hawtrey have continued their discussion of " The Monetary Theory of the Trade Cycle " in articles with that title appearing in the *Economic Journal* for June and December, 1929.

[2] *Economic Journal*, 1924, p. 68.

[3] *Ibid.*, p. 169 (Report of a " Discussion on Monetary Reform " held at the London School of Economics on 14th April, 1924).

show itself, the nature of the limits now set to its influence, and the possibilities of narrowing those limits by new methods of credit control are all uncertain ; no attempt to throw light on them can prudently be made in a work mainly devoted to other problems. It will be sufficient here for one who, like myself, agrees with the opinions already cited from Mr. Keynes, first, to give in general terms the monetary theory of the trade cycle ; second, to indicate as shortly as possible how and where this theory succeeds where the principal competing theories—industrial, psychological, agricultural—fail as explanations of ascertained facts ; third, to indicate those points on which the monetary theory seems still to call for development. On this discussion of theory will follow a presentation of some new facts both as to the trade cycle in the past and as to industrial fluctuations distinct from the trade cycle.

The kernel of the monetary theory of cyclical fluctuation, as has been stated, is " the inherent instability of credit ". In every country with a banking system money is of two main kinds, described by Mr. Hawtrey as " currency " and " credit," and by Mr. Robertson as " common money " and " bank money ". Every individual with a bank account, asked how much money he has, will answer that he has so much in cash at home and so much in the bank ; when a bill has to be paid he may pay it either in cash (metallic or paper) or by cheque, either in common money or in bank money.

Common money is made by the State, or sometimes by approved banks under strict State control. Bank money is made by banks on the request of persons who wish to use it. In quantity bank money is now in all advanced industrial countries much the larger of the two kinds. Most people with bank accounts have far more money in the bank than in their pockets or safes. Most business is done by cheques. An estimate by Professor Irving Fisher gave the proportion of all transactions that were carried through by cheques in the United States as 86 per cent in 1896 and 91 per cent in 1909.

Bank money, of course, is not made by bankers on demand for everybody and anybody without conditions. For most people with bank accounts—professional men, *rentiers*, small shopkeepers—it is habitually made either on deposit with the bank of an equivalent amount of common money or on payment in of a cheque, representing transfer of a credit already created. The distinction of the two kinds of money for such people as those named is one of minor importance. Apart from the overdrafts which they sometimes require, bank money is a convenience rather than an essential condition of their economic life. The making of bank money on those terms for any one customer does not add to the total money of both kinds, because either it involves a transfer of bank money formerly held by some one else, or, if it is an actual increase of bank money, the increase is exactly offset by an immobilisation of common money.

For business firms, bank money is habitually made also on different terms. The banker gives the business man the right to draw cheques, to be met by the bank on request with cash, in exchange, not for a previous surrender of cash by the business firm, but for a promise to pay in the future; he makes a loan. The banker does this, of course, only for firms in whom he has confidence, and on certain terms as to security and interest; he does it with the intention and expectation that the credit so created shall shortly be destroyed again by repayment of the loan. Moreover, though the banker makes bank money in this way for the individual firm without requiring previous deposit of common money by that firm, he does not, for reasons to be named later, make bank money without regard to the total of common money deposited with him by all his customers. This form of making of bank money is a net addition to the total of money; other things being equal, *i.e.*, failing a contemporary increase in the demand for money by increase of other commodities or otherwise, its tendency must be to lower the value of money, *i.e.*, to raise prices. Conversely bank money is destroyed and the total of money is diminished whenever such a debt to the bank is paid off; thereby the value of money is raised and prices are lowered. There is thus in the relations between bankers and those who undertake business, described henceforth as undertakers, a constant process of making and unmaking bank money, of creating and extinguishing credits; the "undertaker" for this purpose may be either one who himself takes charge of production—as farmer, mine operator, manufacturer, etc.—or a dealer who gives orders for production to such persons. When credits are being made faster than they are being destroyed, other things being equal, prices will rise; when credits are being made more slowly than they are being destroyed, other things being equal, prices will fall. The making and unmaking of credit are the joint acts of the banker and the undertaker. What motives affect each, or influence the rates of creating and extinguishing credits?

The general desire of the banker, subject to the limitations mentioned below, is to make as much bank money as possible Doing so is the service to the community by which he lives; he makes a charge for the service. So far as he is concerned, the only limitations are first, that he should have security for repayment, second, since an essential part of his service is ability to convert bank money into common money on request, that his bank money outstanding at any time should not be altogether out of relation to his reserves of common money available for this conversion.

The object of the undertaker in securing bank money is to finance the production by himself or another of commodities from which he hopes to make a profit; the amount of bank money he wishes to make will depend on the scale of production proposed. From this point of view, the time element involved in modern production makes the question of rising and falling prices important. The undertaker uses the bank money made for him by the banker either himself to buy materials and labour at present prices or to put the actual producer in funds for the purpose; if, when he comes to sell the product later, prices have risen, he will find profits easy and large; if they have fallen, he will find profits hard, small, or non-existent. If, therefore, the undertaker thinks the course of prices is going to be such as to yield ready profit, he will try to produce as much as possible; if he thinks they are going to fall to the point of making a loss on production for him, he will produce as little as possible. In the former case, he will seek to make credits faster than he extinguishes them—to get as much bank money on loan as possible with a view to repaying it at a lower real value, *i.e.*, when commodity prices have risen. In the latter case, he will do the reverse and seek to extinguish credits faster than he creates them.

In general, therefore, the undertaker seeks to create credit faster than he extinguishes it if he expects prices to rise.[1] The banker helps him so long as the limit of relation to cash reserves is not reached. The resulting net creation of credit adds to the total quantity of money and itself tends to bring about a rise of prices. The expectation of the undertaker is justified or more than justified; this leads to expectation of a further rise and further creation of credits. Expectation by the undertaker of a fall of prices sets an exactly opposite train in motion. The interplay of prices and credits makes them both unstable.

---

[1] This is, of course, only a statement of general tendency. The undertaker's decisions involve always an assumption as to the course of prices between the time of making the bank money and selling the finished product. He may assume that prices are going to rise, yet not produce, because even with the expected rise he cannot hope for sufficient profit; or he may assume a fall, and yet produce, because even with the expected fall he hopes for a profit or at least to avoid a heavier loss through standing idle altogether. This does not affect the argument that it will be easier for the undertaker to expect a profit if he assumes rising prices and to make a profit if prices in fact rise than in the reverse case. The general tendency is clear.

Enterprise, Credit, Prices and Profits must be conceived of as locked together—four points on an unbroken circle of influence.

An expectation of profits stimulates enterprise, which expands credit, which raises prices, which raises profits, which justifies the expectation of profits and leads to more enterprise and more expansion of credit. Expectation of loss chills enterprise, which contracts credit, which lowers prices, which justifies the expectation of loss and leads to further contraction of credit. The undertaker is constantly making his dreams or his fears come true.

This assumes an initial stimulus. But the stimulus can come in at any point in the circle, e.g., at prices—if some external cause such as a strike in a competing field raises prices; or at profits—if a bountiful harvest increases demand or invention cheapens production; or at credit—if a change of banking policy or influx of gold or even extension of instalment buying increases the quantity of money; or at enterprise—if men's minds are changed by political events.

The point may be put in another way by saying that the value of money is always in unstable equilibrium. The value of money, i.e., the general level of prices at any moment is determined by an equation with the quantity and velocity of circulation of money on one side and the total supply of commodities at that moment on the other side. Unless industry is already working at full capacity, an increase in the quantity or velocity of circulation of money, involving a fall in its value, i.e., a rise of prices, should tend to bring about its own correction by stimulating the production of commodities and so lowering prices again; i.e., should start a move back to the old equilibrium. But under modern conditions the first step to the production of more commodities to meet an increase of money is the making of yet more money, i.e., is a move away from equilibrium. This is what happens in the short run, and makes the inherent instability of credit and prices. The next step is to ask what happens in the long run and how and under what conditions stability is restored.

The answer to this question is found in the consideration named above as limiting the banker's willingness to create more credit. He must for solvency keep his maximum liabilities to pay cash in some relation to his cash reserves, that is to say, keep the bank money which he creates for undertakers within a limit set by the common money that he holds.

The creation of credit naturally tends to bring the banker up towards this limit directly, by increase of credit. At the same time it sets in motion other forces tending to produce the same result indirectly by depleting cash reserves. As prices rise, those reserves, under a system based on gold, are increasingly affected by three drains—of gold into industrial uses, of cash into internal circulation to meet higher wages and prices, and of gold abroad to balance the exchanges because rising prices make the country a good one to sell in and so stimulate imports.

The inherent instability of credit will make a rise of prices and net creation of credit once started tend to continue, but it can only continue till the bankers find themselves approaching their maximum proportion of credit to cash reserves. As they approach that proportion, they will seek to check the further creation of credit—either by refusing it in particular cases altogether or more commonly by raising the charge for their services in creating it. In a country with a central bank this is done by the central bank raising its rate of discount—that is to say, its charge for creating credit—by successive stages as the activity of production and of credit creation grows. The first increase in the rate of discount may not—usually does not—check the process of adding to credit, but sooner or later a point is reached when, unless the cash reserves themselves are increased, they must and do have this effect. There follows a contraction of credit, starting a downward movement of prices which by the inherent instability of credit and prices, brings a further contraction of credit and a further fall. At last a point is reached when bankers feel safe, wish to expand credit again, and seek to do so by cheapening it, that is to say, lowering the rate of discount.

In other words, credit and prices, though unstable in the short run, are stabilised in the long run because credit is tethered to cash reserves. So long as the cash reserves cannot change rapidly, the upward and downward movement of prices and with it the upward and downward movement of trade and employment takes place within limits.

The foregoing account of the monetary theory of the trade cycle is given in its simplest terms as applicable to the financial system of Britain before the war. It is a direct deduction from the elementary facts of money and enterprise and once appreciated stands almost on its own merits as a deduction. An acute analyst knowing the credit system might have deduced the credit and price cycle and general fluctuation of trade even though these had never been observed.

In fact, cyclical fluctuation during the sixty years before the war was a notorious and dominant feature of economic life in Britain and other industrial countries.   Nor is direct statistical confirmation of the monetary theory itself—that is to say of connection between change of bank credits and the trade cycle—altogether lacking.   Though Professor Pigou is the chief modern critic of the monetary theory, as a main or sufficient account of fluctuation, he gives in his study of *Industrial Fluctuations* a chart in which bank credits are seen moving in accord with unemployment just as on this theory they should move.   The chart records the bank credits outstanding each year from 1880 to 1914.   The resulting curve is clearly correlated with the movement of employment shown in the chart of cyclical fluctuation, having maxima at 1881, 1889, 1899, 1907 and minima at 1886, 1893, 1904 and 1908.[1]

A single result like this falls far short of full confirmation of the theory, and of what more elaborate study would almost certainly produce.   In the present state of knowledge, however, further statistical study seems required less in order to test the central thesis of the monetary theory—that credit is inherently unstable—than to complete the theory itself.   The mechanism by which the course of the trade cycle is reversed—from boom to depression and from depression to boom—is still in many respects obscure.   Granted both that prices and credit once they have started upwards will tend to go on and that they cannot go on indefinitely, it is not obvious from the foregoing analysis that having reached their limit they must at once bound back again. Why should they not, under the general desire of bankers to do as much business as possible, *i.e.*, have as much credit outstanding as possible up to the ratio of their cash reserves, stay for some time or indefinitely near the top of the curve?   Again, granted that once a contraction of credit and prices has begun it tends to continue, what in practice is the barrier that stops it at last? and when it has stopped, what turns it?   Clearly a mere offer of cheap money does not suffice ; banks at times of depression may go on offering cheap money for months or even years together before any recovery happens.   The reversals of movement at the top and at the bottom of the cycle respectively, are not only

---

[1] The chart is at p. 130 with a table of the figures represented at p. 367 of *Industrial Fluctuations*.   There are intervening peaks at 1896 and 1905 in the bank credit curve.   It may be added that the clearings of London banks given by Professor Pigou in a chart at p. 118 show a similar correlation.

due to different causes but may be quite different in character. The trade cycle arises from the interaction of one unstable element in economic life—credit—and other relatively stable ones. At the top of the cycle the stable element is found in the cash reserves to which credit though elastically is tethered. At the bottom of the cycle the stable element is something different but its nature is uncertain. Is it the fixed capital of the country prescribing a minimum of industrial activity, or the savings of *rentiers* and salaried persons seeking investment, or the fundamental requirements of the population for food and necessaries, or a combination of all of these and of other elements, which finally stops the decline of production and makes enterprise raise its head once more? It is possible that enquiry will show at last that recovery from a depression is in fact less automatic than decline from a boom, less like a rebound, and more like waiting for a new impulse. It is certainly not as automatic as some of Mr. Hawtrey's writings suggest.

Completion of the theory of the trade cycle in the directions suggested above, and in other directions, is not merely desirable on theoretic grounds. It is the essential basis of any practical attempt to diminish fluctuation by control of credit or otherwise. On that practical issue no judgment can be attempted here. Mr. Hawtrey himself was at one time very doubtful whether even an all-wise banker could do much to cure the trade cycle; to-day, judging by the quotation given below, he is more hopeful. Professor Pigou has given cogent reasons for hoping little.[1]

While, however, there is ample room for and need of further statistical enquiry, instability of credit stands as the first and longest step to full explanation of the trade cycle. Whether it does or does not prove to be "one of the most important advances in economic thought ever made,"[2] it is a substantial and assured advance. The momentary equilibrium of prices is at every moment being disturbed, as is the equilibrium of a bicyclist. But as soon as the bicyclist knows his business, the correction of each disturbance is so rapid that the departure from equilibrium is hardly noticed. What has to be explained in prices is why each disturbance is not at once corrected, why trade is like an inexpert rather than an expert rider. The inherent instability of credit is a full and sufficient explanation.

---

[1] *Industrial Fluctuations*, Part II, Chapters IV, V and VI. For Mr. Hawtrey's earlier view reference should be made to *Currency and Credit*, p. 423. The question will presumably be one of the major issues before the Committee of 1929 appointed to enquire into the relations of finance and industry.

[2] These are Mr. Keynes' words, in an article already cited in the *Economic Journal*, 1924, p. 68.

As compared with other theories, the monetary theory has the decisive merits of explaining first, the continued rise of prices during the upward movement of the cycle in spite of the increasing output of goods ; second, the generality of the movement, *i.e.*, its extension over all trade simultaneously and to some extent over all countries.   It is at the same time entirely consistent with two other main features of the cycle, namely the varying period of fluctuation and the varying violence with which different trades are affected. As to period of fluctuation, inherent instability of credit makes fluctuation certain (by preventing an immediate correction of either upward or downward movements) while leaving the period uncertain ; the period may be affected by the speed of upward or downward movement, by changes in the production of gold, by good or bad harvests, by tariffs, and by other changes, all affecting in one way or another the time at which the upper or lower limits of movement are reached.   As to the varying violence of simultaneous fluctuations in different industries, the degree of fluctuation in each industry is naturally influenced by the average life of its product, *i.e.*, the proportion which the annual production bears to the total stock.   For an article with an average life of one year, reduction or increase of stock by 2 per cent will mean a 2 per cent fluctuation of production upwards or downwards ; for an article with an average life of five years, a 2 per cent reduction or increase of stock in a year involves a 10 per cent contraction or expansion of the year's production.

On the other hand, if we turn from the monetary explanation to other theories—whether mainly industrial such as that put forward by Professor Aftalion or mainly psychological such as that which seems still to be most favoured by Professor Pigou— no explanation either of the continued rise of prices in the upward phase and the continued fall of prices in the downward phase, or of the simultaneity of the movements in different trades and countries is to be found in them.   The first of these facts forces recognition of elasticity in the quantity of money, so that it can grow alternately faster and slower than goods do.   The second postulates some link between different trades and countries, such as is found only in the financial factor.[1]

[1] The weaknesses of Professor Pigou's exposition of the " mutual generation of errors of optimism and errors of pessimism " as a principal cause of industrial fluctuation are, to my mind, threefold.   First, the nature of the " errors " is never defined. Second, the suggested links between different business men (apart from the monetary factor) causing them all in many different businesses to make the same error at the same time (*Industrial Fluctuations*, pp. 79-82) are inadequate and would at best produce a substantial *net* error one way or another (p. 82), not a common simultaneous error.   The unjustified transition from multifarious *errors* (in the plural) to the one common error which makes the trade cycle, appears in the fifth sentence of ch. vii

Professor Pigou, indeed, fully recognises the connection between credit creation by the banks and trade fluctuation,[1] and that the borrowings of business men from the banks are unlike their borrowings from the public, "because the banks are ready, in response to offers of higher interest, to allow the ratio of their reserves to their liabilities to decrease". "The extra borrowings from banks, resorted to by business men when their expectations are roseate, set forces in motion which cause the general level of prices to rise." Finally, "a cumulative tendency towards expansion is set up, which continues under its own impulse until it encounters some external obstacle".

All this is singularly like Mr. Hawtrey's own language. It may be suspected that, at the last trump, the difference between Professor Pigou and Mr. Hawtrey in their analysis of economic facts will be found to be slight. The real difference is that they are to a large extent looking at different facts.

Mr. Hawtrey is concerned not with every form of fluctuation in economic activity but with "the trade cycle". His latest summary of the monetary theory makes this plain :—

"(1) Non-monetary causes do not affect general productive activity (as distinguished from the activity of the particular industries immediately affected) except through their monetary effects ;

"(2) The monetary effects of these causes, in so far as they clash with credit policy, are systematically counteracted by the banks ;

"(3) If credit policy were based on stabilisation of the price level (suitably interpreted) instead of on gold reserves, cyclical fluctuations could be eliminated altogether ;

"(4) The non-monetary causes have no tendency to periodicity."[2]

Professor Pigou's very title *Industrial Fluctuations* (in the plural) indicates that he is concerned with all forms of instability in industry, whether general or special, periodic and sporadic. Acceptance of a monetary explanation of *the* trade cycle in no sense excludes admission that there are other fluctuations, peculiar to certain industries and due to different causes. The monetary

---

on p. 83 : " The activity which is developed in industry " (when all that the previous argument justified was " in *an* industry "). The transition is made again on p. 84 in assuming a common time for the discovery of errors of optimism in industries of widely differing gestation periods and duration periods for their products, and on p. 85, in speaking of "the period of gestation of the principal instrumental goods ".

[1] He shows, as stated above, the relation between rate of change of bank credits and the state of employment, and he defends against Professor Cannan the reality of "credit creation by the banks " (*Industrial Fluctuations*, pp. 123-5).

[2] *Economic Journal*, Dec. 1929, p. 639.

theory explains one type of economic fluctuation dominant in the life of Britain from the middle of the nineteenth century to the outbreak of the Great War. It does not explain all kinds of fluctuation at all times. The limitations of the theory will be illustrated here in two ways; first by describing one particular movement of a different type, which may be called the hyper-cyclical fluctuation of the building trade;[1] second, by extending the survey of cyclical fluctuation made in Chapter IV over a longer period.

More than twenty years ago, in writing of the London building trade,[2] Mr. N. B. Dearle pointed out how it escaped at times the crises affecting other industries. He might with equal justice have pointed out how sometimes it shared very little in their booms. The accompanying chart brings out clearly the long hyper-cyclical fluctuation to which these experiences are due. The chart gives in a thick curve the unemployment percentage in the Amalgamated Society of Carpenters and Joiners for each year from 1860 to 1913, and in a thin curve the running ten-year means of the annual figures. Both curves are inverted, i.e., the unemployment scale runs down, so that a high point as at 1865 or 1898 represents little unemployment and brisk trade, while a low point as at 1886 or 1909 represents a maximum of unemployment and depression. The thick curve shows a series of waves which, with occasional shifting of dates back or forward a year, are the familiar waves of the trade cycle. But the waves do not all occur at the same general level. The first two crests in 1865 and 1875, with unemployment percentages of 0·3 and 0·6 respectively are separated by a depression in which the maximum of unemployment is only 3·7, but from 1875 the curve drops catastrophically till in 1879 unemployment is 8·2 per cent; the crest of the next wave in 1882 (3·5) hardly rises above the trough of the wave before and is followed by another depression of 8·2 in 1886. The next wave begins a tendency to return to a higher level, with a crest in 1891 at 1·9 and, after another shallow depression in 1895 (4·4), is followed by another high crest in 1898 (0·9). Then follow deep and still deeper depressions (8·0 in 1905 and 11·7 in 1909) and a rapid recovery till the curve ends with the war.

---

[1] The description and charts here are taken from a paper on *Some Aspects of Trade Fluctuation* read by myself to the Manchester Statistical Society in 1921. All the tables in that paper are given in the Statistical Supplement (pp. 451-3 below). The paper contains one or two charts not reproduced here, with a discussion of " ca' canny " and its causes.

[2] *Unemployment in the London Building Trade* (1908).

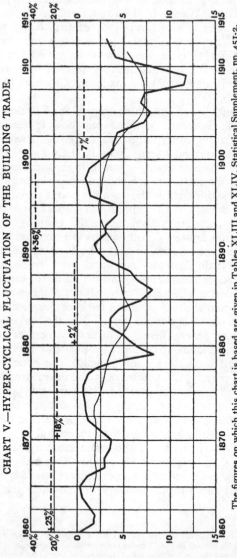

CHART V.—HYPER-CYCLICAL FLUCTUATION OF THE BUILDING TRADE.

The figures on which this chart is based are given in Tables XLIII and XLIV, Statistical Supplement, pp. 451-2.
The continuous heavy line gives the mean percentages unemployed each year in the Amalgamated Society of Carpenters and Joiners, with scale (inverted) at side.   The light line gives continuous ten-yearly averages.
The broken lines above, with figures at the side, indicate for each inter-censal period the increase or decrease in the numbers occupied in the Building Trade in England and Wales, expressed as a percentage of the numbers at the beginning of the period.   The lines are placed with reference to a base line at 0, and to the scale of percentages shown.

Unemployment in the building trade thus shows a double movement. Underlying the five to nine-year waves of the trade cycle is a ground swell—a hyper-cyclical fluctuation—with a length, in the period covered by the chart, of about eleven years. The course of this longer fluctuation is shown by the thin line of ten-year averages. From a minimum of 1·81 in 1872-3, representing the mean of the years 1868-77, the ten-year average rises (*i.e.*, the inverted curve sinks) to 5·88 at 1883-4, falls to 2·36 at 1894-5, and rises again to 7·37 at 1906-7 ; only the beginning of the subsequent recovery of employment can be shown.

To this fluctuation of unemployment correspond variations in the recruiting of labour for the industry and in the building of houses.

The first point is illustrated by the dotted horizontal lines along the upper portion of the chart, representing by their position for each inter-censal period the change per cent of the numbers occupied in building. Increases of 23 per cent and 18 per cent in 1861-71 and 1871-81 are followed by one of 2 per cent in the bad period 1881-91 ; the next decade sees a remarkable increase of 36 per cent to the boom about 1900, followed by the yet more remarkable phenomenon of an actual decrease of 7 per cent in the disastrous decade 1901 to 1911. The second point is illustrated by Table XLVI in the Statistical Supplement, comparing growth of the population and of the total number of houses from census to census. Even apart from exceptional figures such as that for 1821-31, presumably due to some change of classification, it is clear that the supply of houses grows much less steadily than does the population needing them. From beginning to end of the fifty years 1861 to 1911 the number of the population and the number of building operatives in England and Wales increased much in the same proportion—80 per cent and 87 per cent respectively ; allowing for the higher standard of housing and for buildings other than houses, this seems a reasonable relation. But accordance in movement over the fifty years is reached only through a succession of discordances and of violent oscillations in building, involving for that trade recurrent periods of prolonged unemployment and for the population as a whole recurrent shortages of housing accommodation.

The facts just set out for the building trade become more instructive through comparison with another industry. If beside the figures for the Amalgamated Society of Carpenters and Joiners are set those of the Amalgamated Society of Engineers, the latter over the fifty years from 1861 to 1910 are seen to have a higher average of unemployment—4·47 per cent as compared

22

with 3·85 per cent.   They also more often show single years or
pairs of years with an exceptionally high percentage (over seven).
But if we look, neither at the whole fifty years nor at single years,
but at ten-year means, a different picture appears; in building,
the highest ten-year mean (7·37 for 1902-11) is more than four
times the lowest (1·63 for 1860-9); in engineering, the highest
ten-year mean (5·53 for 1878-87) is much less than twice the
lowest (3·32 for 1869-78).   The recruiting of the metal trades as
a whole is, indeed, at least as uneven from census to census as
that of the building trades, but it does not lead to such prolonged
periods of heavy unemployment and it takes place at different
periods.[1]

The hyper-cyclical fluctuations of the building trade have
clearly nothing to do with the trade cycle.   They cut across the
cycle; they are not repeated in other industries; they must be
explained, not by credit or some other factor common to all industries, but by factors peculiar to building or most marked in it.
Such factors are not far to seek.

The building trade has two marked characteristics; it contains
an immense number of small employers, and its products have
a relatively high degree of permanence.   Its hyper-cyclical fluctuation seems to be directly traceable to these two characteristics.

The building trade, above all, is an industry of innumerable
small employers.   There are certainly not less than 50,000 such
employers altogether.   It is, or was till recently, comparatively
easy for their number to be increased by fresh accessions from
the ranks of the operatives; large preliminary capital was less
necessary than elsewhere.   Accordingly a rising demand for
houses, making it profitable to build houses, is met, not by one
producer or by a limited number acting in concert, but by an
immense number of separate small producers each acting without
very full knowledge either of the total demand or of what others
are doing or contemplating, and each anxious to absorb as large a
part as possible of the expected profits.   This, in itself, leads to a
tendency for the builders as a whole to over-shoot the demand, that
is to say, to produce more than can be disposed of at a price
consonant with the cost of production.   Because of the great number of employers, however, the over-production may go a consider-

---

[1] While between 1881 and 1891 the building trade was almost stationary, with a
2 per cent increase of numbers occupied, the metal trades increased 18 per cent; in
the next decade while building rose 36 per cent, metals rose only 27 per cent.   There
are naturally traces of hyper-cyclical movement in engineering, and a few points of
agreement with building, but these are sufficiently accounted for by the trade-cycle
and by the inclusion in the Carpenters and Joiners Union of a proportion of ship's
carpenters.   The contrasts of the two industries are more striking than their
agreements.

able way before it is discovered; the relative permanence of the product then makes any remedy a slow one; demand has to grow up gradually and absorb the excess.   Each upward and downward movement of building activity may be spread over many years, and may follow the demand for houses at such a distance as to appear more often than not to be a movement in the opposite direction. The fluctuation in the process by which supply of houses is adjusted to demand is reflected and magnified in the process by which the supply of labour to the trade is adjusted to the demand, and in the consequent course of employment and unemployment.

In speaking of the fluctuation now under review as peculiar to the building trade, it is not implied of course that other industries may not also have fluctuations independent of the trade cycle. Agriculture, with its dependence on harvests, is the most obvious example.   The cotton trade is affected both by the supply of raw cotton (depending on the weather in North America) and by overseas demand for piece-goods (depending largely on weather and crops in India).   Many other trades might on enquiry present corresponding peculiarities of movement.   The building trade is only one illustration of such movements independent of the trade cycle, though for several reasons specially worth choosing for illustration here.   Its hyper-cyclical fluctuation is markedly violent and regular, is exceptionally productive of unemployment, and represents a factor of instability in modern life to which perhaps sufficient attention has not been paid—the instability due to many-headed control of industry.   Other industries, like engineering and cotton, are disturbed by varying demand for their products. Building contrives to fluctuate exceptionally and violently though engaged largely in meeting demands which do not fluctuate.

Study of the building trade from 1860 to 1910 has taken us outside the trade cycle to see a fluctuation different in kind from the cycle though contemporary with its greatest development. Study of the period before 1860 will be found to take us outside the trade cycle in another way—by time.

The chart given in Chapter IV as "The Pulse of the Nation" shows the movement between 1856 and 1907 of seven economic indices—bank rate, employment, foreign trade, marriage rate, indoor pauperism, companies registered and consumption of beer. The new chart which is given below and described as "The Birth and Life of the Trade Cycle" is at once a revision and an extension of the old chart.   Several of the series given before— bank rate, marriage rate, employment, companies, consumption of beer—are reproduced with minor corrections.   One—that of

22 *

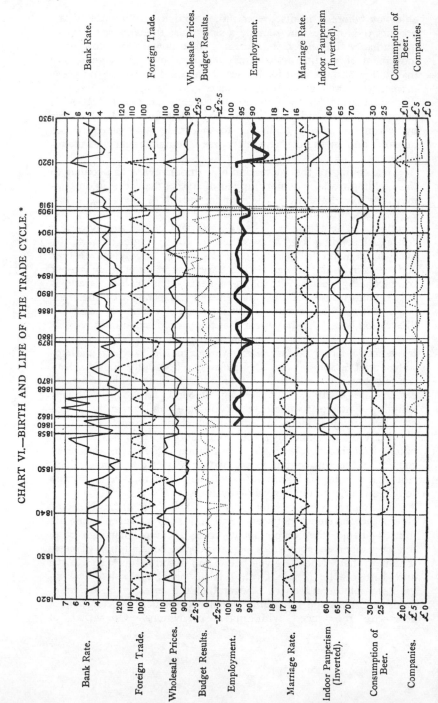

CHART VI.—BIRTH AND LIFE OF THE TRADE CYCLE.*

* The figures on which this chart is based are given in Table XI.VII. pp. 455-7.

"foreign trade"—is replaced by a series for exports alone with the trend eliminated. Two series, concerned with wholesale prices and with budget surpluses and deficiences, are added. The first is intimately connected with the monetary theory; the second is an interesting novelty, with the advantage that it can be carried a long way back.

So far as possible all the series are carried back to 1820 and forward to 1929, with the war gap left blank ; those who wish to can find such figures as exist for that period in the Statistical Supplement.

As in the old chart, heavy lines are drawn through the depression years 1862, 1868, 1879, 1886, 1894, 1904, with 1858 and 1909 added, cutting up each of the curves shown into a succession of unequal waves. This wave movement, affecting simultaneously all the separate economic records in the fifty odd years before the Great War, is the indubitable trade cycle of which the monetary theory is the explanation. How far can this movement be traced back into the period before 1860? Has it reestablished itself since the war ?

It is not easy to work back with any assurance into the earlier period. Each of the curves taken separately shows fluctuations, rather more ragged and less flowing than later but not fundamentally different in themselves. Taken together the curves in the earlier period depart from the conditions of the later period : their fluctuations are not to any marked extent simultaneous. One new depression line—at 1858—has been drawn on the chart, and thus one wave of record shortness—four years—has been added to the life of the trade cycle. But before 1858 there is no year through which another depression line could be drawn to fit even tolerably all the curves recorded. A line at 1852 would suit bank rate, wholesale prices and foreign trade (fairly) but would cut the middle of high stretches in marriages, consumption of beer, and budget results. A line at 1848 would find all or nearly all the indices below their average, but with the nadir of depression already a year past for marriages, consumption of beer and budget results and two or more years ahead for bank rate and wholesale prices. Earlier still anything like general agreement in the dates of depressions disappears completely ; with the doubtful exception of 1839, this applies also to the dates of booms. Instead, the various indices tend to go together in sets of two or three. Thus bank rate and wholesale prices have a definite though slightly changing relation from the beginning ; bank rate rising and falling at first a year later and then in step with prices. Foreign trade seems to go less with either of these than with marriage rate,

consumption of beer and budget results, notably in being depressed
at 1826, 1837 and 1842, and active at 1844 and 1853 ; such agreement as can be traced between foreign trade and wholesale prices
seems fully explicable by the fact that the values recorded in the
foreign trade curve themselves contain an element of prices.

The contrast between the times before and after 1858 is
striking.   It is not possible before then to find a cyclical fluctuation
of trade in the sense in which such fluctuation is found later, as an
influence dominant alike over finance and trade in the narrow
sense and over industry and the whole economic life of the nation.
The full inferences to be drawn from this and the explanation to
be given would themselves form the subject of a lengthy volume.
The superficial examination made here is suggestive only.   What
it does suggest is that several distinct types of fluctuation were
during the second quarter of the century gradually beaten into
time with one another under the influence of credit.   Prices and
credit were naturally linked from the beginning, but a cycle based
on credit could not become dominant till the country was mainly
industrial and heavily capitalised, and could not become regular till
the country had a central bank adopting a simple and automatic
credit control.   So long as the economic life of Britain remained
largely based on British agriculture, marriages and other indices of
prosperity and trade itself would be affected by success or failure
of harvests as much as by credit.   From this point of view, the
free trade policy of 1846 helped the coming of the trade cycle, not
simply by hastening the industrialisation of Britain, but also by
widening the area from which grain was brought and diminishing
the influence of local harvests.   Credit itself and the machinery
for its control only assumed by gradual stages the form postulated
in the monetary theory; the Bank Charter Act of 1844 and the
bank policies developed thereafter were necessary precursors of the
full trade cycle.   Once the policy of the simple ratio of credit to
cash reserves was established, the greater completeness with which
in Britain the influence of harvest fluctuations had been eliminated
made Britain the classic land of the trade cycle.

In the economic life of the later middle ages, if war be
excepted, there was only one important factor of instability—
harvest variation due to good and bad seasons.   The prices of
wheat and other crops oscillated violently; other prices remained
steady from decade to decade.[1]

[1] There were secular changes in the relation between supply of and demand for
silver, leading to the great rise of prices in the second half of the twelfth century and
to the sagging down of prices from the middle of the fourteenth century, in spite of

In modern economic life there are many factors of instability —weather and harvests as before, invention, psychological contagion, many-headed control of business, credit.   The last of these is the first subject of this chapter.   The last but one, on which emphasis was laid in Chapter IV, has been illustrated again by reference to the building trade.

With all these different factors of instability, modern economic life, as the result of complex reactions, is probably on the whole more stable than medieval life, and not less stable.   For doing much the same amount of work year after year much the same number of people year after year enjoy much the same volume and kind of necessaries and comforts.   Modern times have nothing to set beside the violent contrasts of sufficiency and starvation, resulting from harvest abundance and failure in fourteenth century England, and affecting simultaneously nearly the whole population. For this there is the simple reason that, with one exception, the various factors of instability in modern times are not simultaneous in their action; even weather variations have been neutralised for most countries,[1] by world-wide extension of the area from which they draw their food.   The one exception is the new factor whose discovery is due mainly to Mr. Hawtrey—the inherent instability of credit.   In industrialised England of the later nineteenth century this led to a fluctuation which could fairly be called the pulse of the nation.

If it be asked what this factor will lead to in the future, the answer is uncertain.   Credit has not changed its character wholly since before the war.   If we look at the right-hand end of the chart, we see from 1920 to 1921 a catastrophic downward movement of every curve; all the features of slump following boom in the nineteenth century are re-produced and exaggerated. If we note the course of events in America and in Britain and elsewhere from the end of 1929 to the time when these words are being written (April, 1930), we see fluctuation of a kind too general to be explained by other than a monetary cause.   The inherent instability of credit remains and must be reckoned with by those whose concern is unemployment.   But if the nature of credit has not changed wholly since the war, neither has it remained without change, nor is it likely to escape further changes.   The trade cycle in Britain before the war resulted, not simply from the instability

continual reduction of the silver content of the coinage.   These compare with, but are in general much slower than, the modern secular swings of prices, downwards for twenty-five years to 1896 and upwards from then to the war.   They are ignored here, both for modern and for medieval times.
[1] Excluding Russia.

of credit, but from instability controlled in a certain way; it was a by-product of a particular banking system, of credit tethered to gold by simple ratio.   It is very doubtful if the trade cycle can be traced far before 1860.   It is not certain in what form it will survive the establishment of the Federal Reserve System in America, and the shaking of institutions and policies that has followed the war.   It may be that after a time the trade cycle here and elsewhere will resume its stately swing.   It may be that the catastrophe of 1920-1 (perhaps one should now say the collapse of 1930) will prove the last kick of the dying system. Prophecy is idle.   It will be sufficient in the following chapter to study the facts already known of unemployment since the war, and if possible to draw their moral.

CHAPTER XVI.

UNEMPLOYMENT SINCE THE WAR.

Greater scale of post-war unemployment. Continuance of some old causes—disorganisation of labour market and seasonal fluctuation. New emphasis on changes of industrial structure and location. Depressed staple industries. Wages and unemployment. The argument from theory. Rise of real wages since 1913. Contrast with earlier rise. Relation to productivity. Standard of living as cause of unemployment.

UNEMPLOYMENT in Britain since the war transcends in scale anything experienced in earlier years. Before the war the annual percentage of trade union members unemployed ranged from just under one to just over ten; the mean of the corrected percentages from 1860 to 1914 is 4·5. This is also, though accidentally, the percentage taken by the Government Actuary in 1919, as the mean percentage of unemployment to be expected in the future over good and bad years, in the insured population as a whole. Experience has rudely shattered this expectation. For the nine years from 1921 to 1929 the annual percentage unemployed in the insured population has ranged from a minimum of 9·7 in 1927 to a maximum of 16·9 in 1921 and has averaged 12·0. The trade union percentages have not been continued beyond 1926. In the six years for which they overlap the insurance figures, from 1921 to 1926, they range from 9·1 to 17·2 with a mean of 13·0, while the insurance percentages range from 10·3 to 16·9 with a mean of 12·8. The two sets of figures show an unexpectedly close agreement.[1]

---

[1] As used in this chapter and in the table of cyclical fluctuation, the trade union percentages have been corrected, both before and after the war, in the manner described in the *Second Series of Memoranda on British and Foreign Trade and Industry* (Cmd. 2337, pp. 82 seq.), by giving equal weight throughout to the metal, engineering and shipbuilding trades on the one hand and to all the rest of the trades included on the other hand. The membership covered by the trade union returns was 884,444 in January, 1913, and 976,491 in January, 1926. The rate of unemployment actually cited by the Government Actuary in 1919, in reporting on the Unemployment Insurance Bill then before Parliament, was not 4·5 but 5·32 per cent (Cmd. 498, § 4). It was then thought, however, that some 3¾ millions of the insurable population, including many in industries with little unemployment, would be dealt with by special schemes; the 5·32 per cent was expected to apply to the remaining eight millions. "If, in conformity with the conditions now obtaining, the excluded classes had been limited to insurance and banking employees and to railway workers of over three years' standing, the rate would have been little more than 4½ per cent."

345

The contrast of pre-war and present experience is shown dramatically in the accompanying chart of Labour Supply and

CHART VII.—LABOUR SUPPLY AND DEMAND IN GREAT BRITAIN.

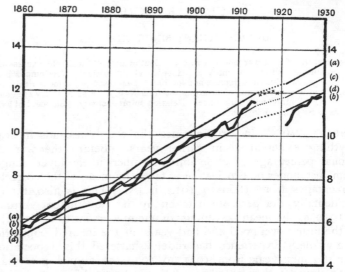

The figures at the sides of chart represent the industrial population of Britain in millions.

(a)	Labour Supply.
(b)	Labour Demand.
(c)	95 °/₀ of Labour Supply.
(d)	90 °/₀ of Labour Supply.

Demand.[1] The upper slanting line represents approximately the numbers of the employable industrial population of Britain— the labour supply—in the past seventy years and is based on

(§ 4 of Appendix 2 to the *Report of the Unemployment Insurance Committee* of 1927). The Government Actuary in 1919 reached his results by adding one-tenth, as a margin of safety, to estimates of the probable rate of unemployment in each industry supplied to him by the Ministry of Labour. These estimates are printed as an Appendix to Cmd. 498 of 1919 and yield a mean percentage for the whole industrial population of 4·1, that is to say, with the Actuary's tenth about 4·5. This identity with the mean trade union percentage from 1860 to 1914 is accidental but supports the argument in the text for taking the trade union percentages as a rough measure of the scale as well as of the movement of unemployment generally. The Actuary's tenth was, no doubt, meant to allow for the effect of insurance itself in increasing recorded unemployment.

[1] The figures represented in the chart are given in the Statistical Supplement, pp. 458-9, with critical notes. The chart, of course, is presented as substantially true rather than formally accurate.

census returns. The rate of growth is treated as uniform between each census from 1861 to 1911 ; after the war gap, the post-war line begins with the census of 1921 and is carried on by unemployment insurance statistics. The lower slanting line represents 90 per cent of the figures represented by the upper one. If the whole of the employable population were in fact employed at any time, the opportunities for employment, that is the effective labour demand, would for that date be on the upper line, and the unemployment percentage would be zero. If only 90 per cent were in employment, labour demand would be on the lower slanting line, with 10 per cent of unemployment. An intermediate fainter line represents 95 per cent of employment and 5 per cent of unemployment.

The actual course of effective labour demand is represented by the fluctuating line, based up to 1921 on the trade union percentages and thence on the insurance percentages of unemployment, as applied to the employable population. As is stated above, the trade union and insurance percentages from 1921 to 1926 agree so closely in general movement and level that the chart would look nearly the same whichever series was used ; but the insurance statistics are now more authoritative and better known. The trade union percentages are the same as those used in the chart of cyclical fluctuation ; the present chart is in effect a picture of cyclical fluctuation of employment made truer to facts by insertion of the trend, *i.e.*, the secular growth of employment.

Up to the war, labour supply and labour demand run in a well-established relation. The former grows steadily ; the latter on the whole as fast, but unsteadily, sometimes faster, sometimes more slowly or even at times declining, but never so fast as to reach 100 per cent of the former and only once for one year falling below 90 per cent. Labour supply and labour demand are kept in some kind of general adjustment to one another, never touching and never diverging completely. They are like two bicyclists, one proceeding straight and soberly along one side of a narrow road, one proceeding less soberly in a series of wobbles, but never falling off the road altogether and always coming back from the ditch side to rejoin his companion.

In the war and just after, the chart is reduced to dotted lines and crosses ; the employable population cannot be determined with accuracy. For four years of fighting, effective labour demand almost but not quite equalled labour supply and unemployment almost but not quite vanished ; for two years of peacemaking and slow demobilisation, war momentum and the meeting of needs suppressed in the war kept employment good. Then in

1921 the lines of labour supply and labour demand begin again in a different relation. Only in one year out of the nine since then does labour demand rise above 90 per cent. The drunken bicyclist may not wobble so much as he did, but has taken to riding permanently in the ditch. The irreducible gap between him and his companion has become not 1 or 2 but nearly 10 per cent; the average distance not 4·5 but 12·0 per cent.

The difference between the 12·0 per cent now experienced and the 4·5 per cent deduced by the Government Actuary in 1919, about 900,000 persons, is taken by Professor Clay " as a rough indication of the specific addition to unemployment which must be attributed to the war ".[1]

Such direct comparisons of earlier and later experience are subject to the criticism that they cannot allow for the increase in completeness of registration through recent developments of insurance. Before the war, trade union registration of unemployment was admittedly incomplete ; benefit was not commonly paid for the first few days of unemployment and was strictly limited in duration. Men who expected to be at work again soon might not think it worth while to register at all, or, if not in distress at the moment, might keep their claim intact for a period of prolonged unemployment; at the other end, those who had already drawn their maximum of benefit might cease to register. Organised short time, moreover, as practised in the coal and cotton industries, failed as a rule to be recorded as unemployment. To-day the position is changed completely. Benefit is unlimited in duration, so that men neither cease to register because they have exhausted their claims nor have any motive for holding over claims to a period of prolonged distress ; though a waiting period of six days without benefit is still enforced at the beginning of each period of continuous unemployment, the rules as to continuity make it worth the workman's while to register at once and whenever he can ; short time is organised systematically so as to count for unemployment and to quarter the employees on the fund in their idle periods. Administrative changes admittedly from time to time affect the numbers registered as unemployed. Two such changes in 1928 were responsible for adding 65,000 persons to the registers of the Exchanges as unemployed applicants for work.[2] Another addition of comparable or greater scale appears to be resulting from the Act of 1930.

[1] *The Post-War Unemployment Problem* (Macmillan, 1929), p. 29.
[2] An article in the *Labour Gazette* for November, 1929, dealing with changes in the estimated numbers of insured persons in the various industries, begins by explaining some of the general changes in numbers as the result of administrative changes. Thus a relatively rapid increase from July, 1923, to July, 1925, is attributed in part

On the other hand, the close agreement noted above between the general levels of unemployment as measured by the corrected trade union percentage and insured population percentage from 1921 to 1926 suggests that there are compensating considerations, and that the net error in taking the trade union percentages as a rough measure of the volume of unemployment generally over a period of years is less than many critics have thought it.[1] A real and serious difference between unemployment before and since the war is certain. Nor are we likely to go far wrong in estimating it with Professor Clay at something like the difference between 4·5 and 12·0 per cent.

Before considering the causes of this increased unemployment, it will be well to show briefly how it is distributed in time and among industries. This is done in the two tables that follow. The first gives the percentage of insured workpeople unemployed in Great Britain and Northern Ireland at the end of each month from the beginning of 1921 to the end of 1929. The second gives for each of thirty-three principal industries the annual percentage unemployed for each year from 1924 to 1929, with the mean for these years exclusive of 1926 ; the industries include all those shown separately in the *Labour Gazette* returns with more than 100,000 insured workpeople in 1929, and are arranged in order of unemployment from Professional Services with 3·2 per cent of unemployment at one end, to Dock, Harbour, River and Canal Service with 28·2 per cent at the other end.

to relaxations of the benefit rules made in 1924 causing larger numbers of insured persons to maintain contact with the Exchanges, and a subsequent slackening in the increase up to 1928 is correspondingly attributed to the re-imposition in 1925 of restrictions on benefit which had been removed in 1924. Then comes a more rapid increase from 1928 to 1929, due in some degree to removal of restrictions on benefit in April, 1928, and to the system under which as from July, 1928, unemployed insured persons can avoid accumulation of arrears of health insurance contributions by registering at Exchanges as applicants for work. The addition of 65,000 named in the text is the addition made by these two changes up to October, 1928.

[1] Among the compensating considerations are the probabilities that trade union provision for unemployment (a) would develop principally in trades subject to violent fluctuation, and (b) would increase unemployment by increasing rigidity of wages. On the other hand, it seems clear that the tendency to increase administratively the numbers registered as unemployed is a continuing one; the changes of administration to be taken into account are not those of insurance alone. Comparison of insurance and Poor Law statistics, after correction for seasonal influences, shows an ominous tendency for the unemployed percentages and the numbers of persons ordinarily engaged in some regular occupation who are receiving domiciliary relief to vary inversely, *i.e.*, suggests that a rise or fall of one set of figures may reflect a fall or rise of the other more than a real change of economic conditions. This inverse variation is most notable in the latter halves of 1924 and 1925, the first half of 1928 and, so far, the opening months of 1930. Both sets of figures rise and fall together, though unequally, in the mining stoppage of 1926 and since the beginning of 1927 the Poor Law figures show a large fall, unquestionably due to administrative pressure. Clearly great caution must be exercised in drawing inferences from short-period changes of either set of figures, till more detailed examination of their working has been made.

TABLE XXXVII.—PERCENTAGES OF INSURED WORKPEOPLE UNEM-
PLOYED EACH MONTH FROM JANUARY, 1921, TO DECEMBER,
1929.   (GREAT BRITAIN AND NORTHERN IRELAND.)

Year.	Jan.	Feb.	Mar.	Apr.	May.	June.	July.	Aug.	Sept.	Oct.	Nov.	Dec.	Mean for Year.
1921	[11·2]	[13·1]	[15·4]	[20·2]	[23·4]	[22·4]	[17·9]	[15·6]	[14·2]	[14·5]	[17·2]	17·9	[16·9]
1922	17·7	17·1	16·0	15·9	14·6	13·7	13·1	12·8	12·7	12·6	13·0	12·8	14·3
1923	13·3	12·4	11·7	11·5	11·2	11·3	11·6	11·8	11·7	11·7	11·5	10·6	11·7
1924	11·9	10·6	9·8	9·7	9·4	9·3	9·8	10·5	10·6	10·9	10·8	10·7	10·3
1925	11·2	11·3	11·1	10·9	10·9	11·9	11·2	12·1	12·0	11·4	11·0	10·4	11·3
1926	11·0	10·4	9·8	9·1	14·3	14·6	14·4	14·0	13·7	13·6	13·5	11·9	12·5
1927	12·0	10·9	9·8	9·4	8·7	8·8	9·2	9·3	9·3	9·5	10·0	9·8	9·7
1928	10·7	10·4	9·6	9·6	9·9	10·8	11·6	11·6	11·4	11·8	12·2	11·2	10·9
1929	12·3	12·2	10·1	9·9	9·9	9·6	9·7	9·9	10·0	10·4	11·0	11·1	10·5
Mean*	12·7	12·1	11·2	11·0	10·7	10·8	10·9	11·1	11·1	11·2	11·4	10·9	11·2

* Excluding 1921 and 1926.
The monthly figures are taken from the *Nineteenth Abstract of Labour Statistics* to the end of 1927, and from the *Labour Gazettes* in 1928 and 1929 (using revised percentages from June to August), with the annual figures as means of the monthly figures.
Figures in square brackets refer to the United Kingdom.

With these tables as basis, we are in a position to consider how far the difference of pre-war and post-war unemployment is a difference of kind as well as of degree.[1]   To what extent can unemployment to-day be attributed to the types of maladjustment diagnosed in the first part of this book—to disorganisation of the labour market, to seasonal and cyclical fluctuations of demand, to changes of industrial structure and other causes of lacking or lost industrial quality?

[1] These two tables do not give the distribution of unemployment among individuals, *i.e.*, they do not show to what extent the 1,269,870 persons who on an average are found unemployed on any given date in 1929 are the same persons at different dates and to what extent different persons.   On this question light is thrown by two sample investigations of insured persons claiming benefit at 18th March and 16th September, 1929, respectively.   About 30 per cent of the men and about 50 per cent of the women on each occasion were found to have had less than three months' unemployment in twelve, while another 30 per cent both of men and of women had been unemployed between three and six months.   That is to say, the proportion of men who were more often out of employment than in it was 40 per cent and that of women 20 per cent. The worse showing of the men is only to a small extent due to coal-mining, in which 19 per cent or nearly one in five of those claiming had been unemployed for twelve months or more while 56 per cent or nearly three out of five had been unemployed for more than six months in twelve.   Apart from mining 2·5 per cent of the men had been unemployed for twelve months or more, 37 per cent for more than six months in twelve, and 67 per cent for more than three months.   While these figures are not strictly comparable to those given on p. 271 for the limited insurance scheme in 1913 (showing 40 claimants out of every 100 getting work again in a week and another 35 getting it within three weeks), they leave no doubt as to the greater severity of the problem in the individual case.

TABLE XXXVIII.—UNEMPLOYMENT IN PRINCIPAL INDUSTRIES, 1924-1929.
(GREAT BRITAIN AND NORTHERN IRELAND.)

Industry.	Numbers Employed (000).		Unemployed Percentages.						Mean Excluding 1926.
	1923.	1929.	1924.	1925.	1926.	1927.	1928.	1929.	
1.	2.	3.	4.	5.	6.	7.	8.	9.	10.
Professional Services . . .	109	122	4·0	3·5	3·1	2·7	2·7	3·2	3·2
Tramway and Omnibus Service .	108	155	3·2	3·6	4·5	3·3	3·2	3·2	3·3
Commerce, Banking, Insurance and Finance	227	229	4·9	4·9	3·1	2·4	2·3	2·7	3·4
Printing, Publishing and Book-binding	228	261	5·4	4·9	5·3	4·7	4·4	4·4	4·8
Laundries, Dyeing and Dry Cleaning	107	135	6·2	5·7	4·7	4·0	4·0	4·4	4·9
Gas, Water and Electricity Supply Industries	173	162	6·1	6·1	5·9	5·1	5·9	6·0	5·8
Dressmaking and Millinery .	117	103	7·5	7·3	6·4	4·7	4·8	4·9	5·8
Railway Service	190	138	5·8	6·3	11·1	5·2	6·4	5·8	5·9
Furniture Making, Upholstering, etc.	94	120	7·2	6·2	7·6	5·4	5·4	6·2	6·1
Distributive Trades . . .	1,254	1,679	6·6	6·7	6·7	5·4	5·7	6·3	6·1
Drink Industries . . .	100	109	7·0	6·7	6·8	6·0	6·2	6·8	6·5
Hosiery	90	106	6·9	8·7	10·5	6·4	5·9	6·2	6·8
National Government . .	181	119	9·1	7·7	7·2	5·7	6·0	6·8	7·1
Chemicals	104	106	9·0	9·0	10·6	6·5	6·1	6·5	7·4
Construction and Repair of Motor Vehicles, Cycles and Aircraft .	192	245	8·5	7·0	8·9	7·5	7·7	7·1	7·6
Bread, Biscuits, Cakes, etc. . .	160	145	9·4	9·1	8·2	6·7	6·8	7·3	7·9
Local Government . . .	242	274	7·2	8·6	9·0	8·0	8·9	9·8	8·5
Tailoring	186	199	9·5	10·3	10·4	7·1	7·9	8·2	8·6
Metal Industries not separately specified	165	191	11·4	10·3	11·4	8·8	8·9	8·3	9·5
Hotel, Boarding House and Club Services	259	334	12·3	11·0	9·2	8·1	8·2	9·2	9·8
Boots, Shoes, Slippers and Clogs .	142	135	9·2	10·5	11·5	8·4	12·9	13·2	10·8
Cotton	568	555	13·7	8·3	18·0	9·0	11·9	13·2	11·2
Woollen and Worsted . .	269	239	7·0	14·6	15·9	8·9	11·8	13·8	11·2
Building	716	826	10·6	9·8	10·9	10·4	12·4	13·3	11·3
General Engineering, Engineers' Iron and Steel Founding . .	667	587	15·2	12·6	15·7	10·4	9·9	9·7	11·6
Road Transport not separately specified	149	183	15·4	14·1	14·2	11·6	11·9	12·2	13·0
Textile Bleaching, Printing, Dyeing, etc.	115	116	12·7	13·0	18·3	12·9	13·8	17·4	14·0
Coal-mining	1,244	1,075	5·7	15·8	9·1	18·1	21·9	16·0	15·5
Shipping Service . . .	127	141	19·5	20·8	20·5	16·4	16·1	17·8	18·1
Public Works Contracting, etc. .	128	164	17·8	17·7	20·5	17·9	20·4	22·7	19·3
Steel Melting and Iron Puddling Furnaces, Iron and Steel Rolling Mills and Forges . . .	211	179	21·1	24·5	41·2	18·5	21·2	19·8	21·0
Shipbuilding and Ship Repairing .	270	204	29·4	33·8	39·7	24·8	26·5	24·3	27·8
Dock, Harbour, River and Canal Service	191	171	25·6	29·9	30·0	24·2	30·5	30·8	28·2
All Industries . . .	11,486	12,094	10·3	11·3	12·5	9·7	10·9	10·5	10·6

Note.—The numbers employed are taken from the *Labour Gazette*, November, 1929, and the annual unemployed percentages are calculated from the monthly figures given in the *Gazettes.*

It is clear, in the first place, that disorganisation of the labour market is still a potent cause of unemployment. The Employment Exchanges have become an indispensable part of the State's machinery for dealing with unemployment, but they have been used by employers as occasional rather than as the normal markets for labour ; neither through them nor in any other way has casual employment been diminished in those twenty years seriously if at all. Dock, Harbour, River and Canal Service—the classic case of such employment—has an unemployed percentage now higher than that of any other industry, ranging in the past six years from 24 to 31. Building—the industry which stands next to the dock and wharves in disorganisation of methods for obtaining labour, in spite of every favouring circumstance, has now a percentage of over 13. Each of these industries, so far from being bloated for war purposes, was severely restricted in the war ; from July, 1914, to November, 1918, the males employed in building fell 52 per cent and those at docks and wharves 27 per cent ; the number of women in each was negligible. Neither industry, therefore, had a problem of reconstruction and scaling down like the munitions industries. Dock and wharf labour has been affected by the decline of exports, but imports have risen and the physical volume of foreign trade, taking imports and exports together, is probably greater, not less, than before the war.[1] Building has been faced by a large unsatisfied demand for houses and has been helped to meet the demand by subsidies ; as a consequence the number of insured persons has risen largely—between 1923 and 1929 from 716,000 to 826,000, or by about one-sixth. Yet in the same time unemployment in this subsidised growing industry has equalled the average of all industries and has risen rather than declined. Public Works Contracting is like Building, an industry given to casual labour, and yielding now in spite of subsidies and rapid growth of total numbers—by more than a quarter from 1923 to 1929—a percentage of unemployment exceeded only by those of iron and steel, shipbuilding and dock labour. Building and Public Works stand alone among important industries as having increased largely since 1924 both their employment and unemployment. The disorganisation of those trades which before the war contributed most to unemployment continues and produces the old results.

As to fluctuations of demand as a cause of unemployment the position is complex. The uncertainty as to the future of cyclical

---

[1] In 1927 and 1928 the combined value of exports and imports was about 105 per cent of the mean value for 1909-13, values being reckoned throughout at 1924 prices. See *Board of Trade Journal*, 24th Jan., 1929, p. 115.

fluctuation has been mentioned in the last chapter.   The possibility of sudden general depressions of trading and industrial activity has been shown sufficiently by the experience of the first half of 1930. Seasonal fluctuations naturally continue.   The unemployment insurance statistics make it possible to trace some seasonal movement in nearly every important industry.   Both the degree and the time of fluctuation vary greatly from one industry to another.   The new statistics make possible also some answer to the interesting question, raised twenty years ago in the Minority Report of the Poor Law Commission, as to the extent to which the movements of all the different industries taken together counterbalance one another, so that employment as a whole is substantially steady throughout the year.   The authors of the Minority Report argued that this would be bound to happen, and that therefore there were large opportunities of dovetailing employment in different industries.   The monthly means in the last row of Table XXXVII show that this view was only partly justified.   Even when all the insured industries are taken together, the spring months from April to July are appreciably better for employment than the winter ones of January and February.   The difference is two per cent, between 87·3 per cent employed in the worst month (January) and 89·3 per cent employed in the best month (May).   There seems to be no record of any specific achievement of the Exchanges in dovetailing employment between occupations with different seasons and so diminishing the unemployment due to this type of fluctuation. So far as can be seen it continues as before.

When we come to the third of the economic causes of unemployment recognised in the diagnosis of 1909—lack and loss of industrial quality—we meet at once a striking contrast between pre-war and post-war conditions.   Lack, as distinct from loss, of industrial quality comes about mainly through deficiencies in the training and guidance of youthful labour ; the war, sweeping all and sundry into the fighting ranks at the age of eighteen, broke for many of them their preparation for after-careers, and produced in due course the difficulty of the ex-service man of no special aptitude. This may perhaps be left on one side as not in essence an industrial problem.   More relevant are the changes of industrial structure properly so-called that resulted from the war, and the loss of industrial quality that they occasioned.   First, and most obvious of these changes, was the anomalous growth of industries ; those that directly served war purposes—engineering, shipbuilding, iron and steel—were bloated beyond any possible peace-time needs ; others —like building, printing, furnishing—were held in check.   The war, however, acted not only positively in bringing about changes

23

calling for reversal when peace returned ; it acted negatively also, by suspending " the normal and necessary adjustment to changing market and technical conditions," [1] and thus making the accumulated adjustment when it came at last sudden and painful.   Yet a third disturbing factor, following on the war, was the dislocation of international trade and consequent depression of the export industries, partly through growth of economic nationalism and of war-taught self-dependence, partly through currency difficulties. Finally, there cannot be omitted as a disturbing influence the action of Governments, whether in giving selective protection or subsidies to particular trades or in legislating as to hours of labour.

Coal is a leading illustration of all the four factors of disturbance named above.   The coal-mining industry of Britain, though not expanded in the war itself, was stimulated by overwhelming demands just after the war, as one after another of the great competing coal-fields of the world was laid largely or wholly out of action—first France and Belgium while recovering from German occupation, then the United States of America during the prolonged dispute of 1922, then the Ruhr during French occupation.   The natural adjustment to changing market and technical conditions, such as the growing use of oil, lignite, water-power and other alternatives stimulated by the war itself, or the substitution of new for old fields, such as Yorkshire for Lancashire, or the introduction of new and more efficient methods, was suspended ; every mine that worked could pay without worrying about efficiency.   The effect on unemployment of legislation, alternately shortening hours so as to draw in fresh labour and lengthening them so as to expel labour from the coal industry, is too obvious to need comment. Coal, finally, is one of the great export trades of Britain.[2]

Of the four disturbing factors named some are more transient than others in their influence.   This is illustrated in Table XXXVIII by the notable decline of unemployment in general engineering, the war munition trade *par excellence*, from 15·2 per cent in 1924 to 9·7 per cent in 1929.   It is illustrated from another angle in Table XXXIX dealing with all industries that in 1929 had more than 12 per cent of unemployment.   The mean for all those industries was 16·3 per cent ; the rest of the insured population in that

---

[1] Clay, *op. cit.*, p. 146.

[2] The difficulties of British mining are only an acute case of a general trouble. In the quarter-century before the war the coal consumption of the world rose by about 4 per cent a year.   Between 1913 and 1928 the difference (according to a report published in 1929 by the Economic Committee of the League of Nations) was approximately equal to the growth " which before the war was to be expected in a single year ". In the difficulties common to the coal industries of all countries, the greater age of the British industry, involving an earlier and less efficient lay-out of mines and greater exhaustion of easy coal, was sufficient to pick it out to be principal sufferer.

year had an unemployed percentage of 7·5.   For each of the industries thus found with heavy unemployment after ten years of war, the table brings together several sets of facts—how they expanded or contracted in the war itself, how their employment and unemployment have moved in the past five years, the relative importance to them of foreign trade, and how their exports in 1924-9 and in 1929 alone compare with exports in the last five years before the war.

The first fact leaping to the eye is that the table contains hardly any war industries : steel-melting, etc., pig iron and shipbuilding alone of the industries which grew largely in the war are now in the list for heavy unemployment ; for all three, the decline of exports is a sufficient explanation of continuing depression, though they all show some improvement from 1924 to 1929.   All the other large industries which, taking men and women together, increased their numbers in the war—general engineering, electrical engineering and marine engineering ; motor vehicles, cycles and aircraft ; chemicals, oil, glue, soap, etc. ; and theatres, music halls and cinemas [1]—have by 1929 got back to having less than the average unemployment.   Conversely, industries conspicuously contracted in the war—pottery, glass bottles, tin plates, cotton, building, public works and dock, harbour, river and canal service—are now conspicuous by heavy and as a rule increasing unemployment.   The second feature of the table is the decline of exports shown in the last two columns.[2]   The general result is to show unemployment to-day as a result less of the war itself than of its aftermath—of excessive development in 1920 and thereafter of industries which had been suppressed during the war and of the decline that has overtaken international trade.

The cramping of Britain's trade overseas appears to be one of the more enduring dislocations involved in the war.   Whether this is to be explained simply by growth of economic nationalism and tariff barriers or has some deeper cause will be considered later.   Whatever the cause, the result is a shifting of industrial structure and of the quality of labour demanded, too swift for the labour supply to follow.   From 1923 to 1929 all the staple

[1] This list is based on returns of employment collected from employers by the Board of Trade regularly during the war and for some time after.   The appearance of " theatres, music halls and cinemas " as a war industry, *i.e.*, one in which more people were employed at the Armistice than in July, 1914, is one of the most remarkable minor facts of the war—illustrating the raised standard of life and enjoyment. " Wholesale and retail corn and flour merchants, grocers, and bakers " also showed a small increase of numbers in the war.

[2] Tin-plates, jute yarn, and pottery, earthenware, etc., alone of those industries for which figures are available show increased exports as compared with 1909-13.   Their position in the table is presumably due to special causes.

TABLE XXXIX.—INDUSTRIES WITH HIGH UNEMPLOYMENT IN 1929.

Industry.	Percentage Expansion (+) or Contraction (−) of Numbers Employed between July, 1914, and Nov., 1918.		Unemployed Percentage.		Numbers Insured in July.		Numbers Unemployed 1929 (000).	Exports as Percentage of Output in 1924.	Quantities Exported as Percentage of Mean, 1909-13.	
	Men.	Men and Women.	1924.	1929.	1923 (000).	1929 (000).			1924-29, omitting 1926.	1929.
1.	2.	3.	4.	5.	6.	7.	8.	9.	10.	11.
Canal, River, Dock and Harbour Service	− 24·9	− 24·4	25·6	30·8	190·9	171·2	52·7	—	—	—
Shipbuilding and Repairing	+ 43·2	+ 48·4	29·4	24·3	270·0	204·5	49·7	11†	72	108
Tin Plates	− 39·4	− 34·3	8·5	23·6	29·9	31·3	7·4	71	111	122
Public Works, Contracting, etc.	− 40·9	− 40·2	17·8	22·7	127·9	164·4	37·3	—	—	—
Steel Melting and Iron Puddling Furnaces, Iron and Steel Rolling Mills and Forges	+ 15·6	+ 27·3	21·1	19·8	211·0	178·7	35·4	—*	86	92
Lead, Tin and Copper Mining	− 19·3	—	16·5	18·8	5·1	5·5	1·0	—	—	—
Shipping Service	—	—	19·5	17·8	127·2	141·4	25·2	—	—	—
Textile Bleaching, Printing, Dyeing, etc.	− 24·5	− 14·2	12·7	17·4	115·0	116·2	20·2	See textile figures.	—	—
Glass Bottle Making	− 35·7	− 27·4	20·3	16·6	16·3	17·3	2·9	6	84	71
Coal-mining	− 15·2‡	− 14·7‡	5·7	16·0	1,243·6	1,074·7	172·0	30	—	—
Artificial Stone and Concrete Manufacture	—	—	16·5	15·9	10·5	17·4	2·8	—§	Considerable Decline.	
Hand Tools, Cutlery, Saws and Files	− 12·9	+ 0·5	14·9	15·1	30·0	33·5	5·1	40	130	134
Pottery, Earthenware, etc.	− 46·6	− 24·4	12·7	14·7	72·1	73·9	10·9	50	—	—
Linen	− 25·5	− 10·4	10·6	14·1	81·8	79·6	11·2	—	—	—
Woollen and Worsted	− 21·7	− 8·1	7·0	13·8	269·4	239·0	33·0	{Yarn 12 / Tissues 48}	74 / 79	73 / 68
Building	− 54·4	− 51·4	10·6	13·3	716·0	826·0	109·9	—	82	77
Cotton Industry	− 47·6	− 28·5	13·7	13·2	567·6	554·8	73·2	{Yarn 12 / Piece goods 86}	66	59

	2	3	4	5	6	7	8	9	10	11
Boot, Shoe, Slipper and Clog Trades	− 30·9	− 13·2	9·2	13·2	14·9	135·2	17·8	14	85	85
Coke Ovens and By-Product Works	—	—	8·3	12·9	15·0	12·0	1·5	—	—	112
Jute	+ 32·5	− 10·4	9·9	12·4	41·0	39·5	4·9	Yarn 10 / Piece goods 40	104	44
Pig Iron (Blast Furnaces)	+ 18·4	+ 31·8	14·3	12·1	28·9	22·1	27	7	40	

* "A satisfactory comparison of ... exports with production of the main classes of iron and steel products cannot be made without bringing into account the Returns made on Schedules for other branches of manufactures."—*Census of Production*, 1924, Preliminary Report, I, p. v.

† "The form in which the statement of output in 1924 has been obtained ... renders difficult any comparison between output and exports. The ships and boats exported were completed ships and boats and the current relation of exports to production is, perhaps, seen best in the comparison of the tonnage exported with the tonnage launched."—*Census of Production*, 1924, Preliminary Report, 6, p. iii.

‡ Including Shale Oil Manufacture.

§ 38 per cent based on *factory value*.

NOTES: The industries considered are those which have more than 12 per cent unemployed in 1929.

Columns 2 and 3 are based on figures given in a confidential Report on the state of Employment in all occupations in the United Kingdom at the end of July, 1919, as compared with July, 1914, and November, 1918.

Columns 4 to 8 have been obtained from *Labour Gazettes*. Column 8 is deduced from column 7 by applying the percentages in column 5.

Column 9 is obtained by comparing the quantities exported with the total output in 1924 as given in the *Census of Production*, 1924, Preliminary Reports.

Columns 10 and 11 are based on the quantities of home produce exported, as given in the *Annual Statements of Trade of the United Kingdom*. Figures for Iron and Steel and for Woollen and Worsted Tissues have been taken from "Survey of Industries" Committee on Industry and Trade, 1928; the former are based on the mean of 1910-13.

It has been necessary to reconcile the classification of Industry or Products in the four sets of returns used: hence the results must be regarded as approximate only. Owing to the difficulty of finding a common unit for different classes of goods included in a single industry it has been necessary, in some cases, to omit certain classes in columns 9 to 11; but these classes form a small part of the whole. In columns 10 and 11 there has been the added difficulty of changes of classification during the period covered, which has again led to certain omissions.

industries on which the former prosperity of the country was founded—coal, iron and steel, cotton, wool, and other textiles, shipbuilding, even engineering have lost in numbers and suffered more than the normal unemployment. In contrast new and minor industries have expanded, with as a rule little unemployment. How far this expansion of industries connected with distribution, road transport, furnishing, electrical engineering, silk and artificial silk, motors, gramophones, scientific instruments and the like is substantial ground for optimism will be considered later. Meanwhile, it must be noted as a change of industrial structure involving a change of place. All the great staple industries except engineering are strongly localised. The new industries are scattered, but apparently strongest in the south and midlands of England. From this flows a marked differentiation by districts in the growth of insured workers and in the rate of unemployment.

TABLE XL.—DISTRIBUTION OF INSURED POPULATION AND UN-EMPLOYMENT BY DISTRICTS.

District.	Insured Persons.		Unemployed Percentage.			
	No. in July, 1929 (000).	Per Cent of 1923.	1925.	1927.	1928.	1929.
South-East	894	122·0	5·9	5·0	5·4	5·6
London	2,214	113·6	7·9	5·8	5·6	5·6
South-West	840	113·0	8·5	7·3	8·1	8·1
Midlands	1,793	109·7	9·1	8·4	9·9	9·3
North-West	2,120	105·2	11·4	10·6	12·4	13·3
North-East	1,986	104·4	15·0	13·7	15·1	13·7
Scotland	1,270	101·6	15·2	10·6	11·7	12·1
Wales	583	97·6	16·6	19·5	23·0	19·3
Great Britain	11,700	108·5	11·0	9·6	10·7	10·4

The unemployed percentages for 1925 have been supplied specially by the Ministry of Labour. The others are figures from the *Labour Gazette* and published reports of the Ministry.

In the foregoing table, the principal insurance divisions are set out in the order of their growth of numbers between 1923 and 1929. The rate of growth is well above the average for the whole country in London and the South, just above it in the Midlands, and well below the average in the North and Scotland ; Wales has an actual decrease. The order of the divisions in growth of numbers, save for a slight displacement of Scotland, is exactly the reverse order of their unemployment in 1929. From

5·6 in the South-East and in London at one end, the percentage rises to 13·3 in the North-West to 13·7 in the North-East, and 19·3 in Wales.

The latter districts, with Scotland in a less degree, are the black spots of unemployment, brought into notoriety in 1928 by the report of the Government Committee known as the Industrial Transference Board. " . . . in many of the districts concerned," reported the Board, " the idea of a cyclical or transient depression must now be recognised quite unflinchingly as no longer tenable." " Until recently, national policy has assumed that industries and areas would return, broadly speaking, to the position they held before the war ; and unemployment policy has been largely one of 'tide-over,' the aim being to maintain the labour force required for the industries in the areas in which they were normally conducted in a state as free as possible from demoralisation. . . . Our considered opinion is that from now onwards the first aim of policy should be the dispersal of the heavy concentrations of unemployment by the active encouragement of movement from the depressed areas to other areas, both in this country and overseas." [1]

In itself this is sound diagnosis and good sense. But as experience has shown the remedy proposed—of transference to other areas—is not by itself equal to the complexities of the situation ; the steps taken to carry out the policy of transference and the intractable difficulty presented by married men with large families have been described in an earlier chapter. Nor, it has now to be added, can the diagnosis of post-war unemployment implied in taking transfer as the main or sole remedy, be regarded as even approximately complete.

WAGES AND UNEMPLOYMENT.

Changes of industrial structure become sudden instead of slow and account for some of the difference between pre-war and post-war unemployment. It is hard to believe that they explain it all. In the first place, the war is now more than ten years behind us. If nothing were needed but a readjustment of the quality of the labour supply to new conditions, it would be natural to expect more progress than appears towards absorption of the unemployed. In the second place, unemployment appears too widespread to be explained by depression of particular trades. If nothing but changes of structure in a healthy industrial system were at work, there should be somewhere, as the complement to the declining industries and

[1] *Report of Industrial Transference Board* (1928, Cmd. 3156), §§ 38 and 35 to 36.

districts, other industries and districts with a swiftly expanding demand for labour. This, however, is just what in Britain to-day it seems impossible to find. There are some districts with less unemployment than others, but are there any with unemployment as low as or lower than what was normal before the war?[1] There are some new industries growing as the old ones decline, but the growth of employment in them is not such as to encourage easy optimism. For one thing it is too slow and affects too few work-people; for another thing, as Professor Clay points out, it is "not the result of a spontaneous and unaided development of the industries that have provided it. Largely it is due to Government subsidies and selective Protection. Of the first seventeen industries, arranged according to rate of increase in the detailed list of expanding industries given in the *Labour Gazette* for November, 1927, fourteen have had the advantage, directly or indirectly, of protection or subsidy."[2] British industry in general seems to have lost its former power of expansion. May there not be some general cause which blocks its progress to re-absorption of the unemployed?

The suggestion that such a general cause of unemployment might be found in excessive wages was first put forward prominently by Professor Pigou in the *Economic Journal* of September, 1927; the higher rate of unemployment since the war was there attributed to "maintenance of wages at too high a level". Professor Pigou himself referred to an article by a French economist, M. Rueff, making the same suggestion in 1925;[3] he reproduced the striking chart from M. Rueff's work to which further reference is made below. Professor Pigou's arguments were criticised by Professor Clay in an article appearing in the same journal six months later, but more recently Professor Clay, approaching the problem from a slightly different angle, in an

---

[1] As appears from Tables XL and XXXVIII none of the big divisions of the country and only three of the larger industries—containing half a million workpeople—had in 1924-29 an unemployed percentage as low even as the average of 4·5 assumed for all industries by the Departmental Committee of 1919.

[2] *Op. cit.*, p. 109. Professor Clay's comment remains substantially true for the latest figures available (up to July, 1929). The growing industries of Britain (omitting those with less than 20,000 workpeople in 1929 and less than 25 per cent increase on 1923) are, in the following order: Silk and Artificial Silk (74), Scientific and Photographic Instruments and Apparatus (26), Musical Instruments (28), Tramway and Omnibus Service (155), Brick, Tile, etc., Making (82), Electrical Engineering (84), Stone Quarrying and Mining (43), Distributive Trades (1,679), Public Works Contracting (164), Furniture Making, Upholstering, etc. (120), Electric Cables, Wire and Electric Lamps (94), Hotel, Boarding House and Club Services (334), Motor Vehicles, Cycles and Aircraft (245), Laundries, Dyeing and Dry Cleaning (135), Road Transport not separately specified (183), Entertainments and Sports (74). This (apart from the special cases of roads, electricity, and motors) is truly a remarkable list of industries serving directly the consumer rather than the production of further wealth. The bracketed numbers represent, in thousands, the insured persons at July, 1929.

[3] *Revue Politique et Parlementaire*, December, 1925, pp. 425 *seq.*

address to the British Association in September, 1929, seems to have reached much the same conclusion as Professor Pigou. " It would appear . . . that wage-fixing authorities, acting independently of one another and disregarding the general economic situation, are maintaining wage-rates at a level at which existing industries cannot provide full employment." " We have interfered with the harsh but effective correctives of wage-demands that restrict employment, namely, the loss of income by unemployment and the expansion of employment where wages are not held up. Either, therefore, we must devise alternative correctives, or we must expect unemployment on a large scale from this cause alone." [1]

The theoretical possibility that the adoption of a particular wage policy in a country may cause general unemployment is undeniable. The number of workmen who can find employment in any industry is determined by comparison of the wages paid to and the value of what is added to the total production by the "marginal workman," that is to say, the last workman whom it is worth while to employ. So long as employers find that by taking on additional men they can increase the value of their production by more than the cost of production, they will tend to demand more labour; as soon as they find that the addition of another man and his production will bring the price which they can command for their product below the cost of producing it, they will stop expanding their staffs. If in any industry in which this equilibrium has been reached, the employers ask and obtain a reduction of the wages of any section of workmen, without affecting the efficiency of production, they will be able by lowering their selling price to increase in some proportion, depending upon the elasticity of the demand, the quantity of their product that they can sell and so to employ more labour. If, on the other hand, efficiency of production remaining as before unaltered, any section of the workmen asks for and obtains a rise of wages, the employers must either secure a corresponding rise of prices, or accept a smaller return on their capital. On either alternative, forces tending to reduce the volume of production and the number of workmen employed will be set in motion; a rise of prices will restrict the demand for the product and a fall of profits will divert capital into other industries or to other countries. The number of workmen for whom the industry can find employment will fall; unless other

---

[1] Presidential Address to Section F of the British Association for the Advancement of Science, South Africa, 1929, printed as " The Public Regulation of Wages in Great Britain " in the *Economic Journal* of September, 1929. Professor Clay's earlier article, criticising Professor Pigou, appeared in the *Economic Journal* of March, 1928, and is reprinted in his book entitled *The Problem of Industrial Relations*.

industries can expand to absorb a greater proportion of the working population, unemployment will result.

Whether other industries can expand, so as to absorb the labour force extruded from one industry through a rise of wages unaccompanied by change of efficiency, depends upon two considerations : first, whether they themselves are already employing the full number they can at existing levels of prices and wages, and second, whether their wages are plastic or not.[1] If the other industries are already at full strength having regard to prices and wages, and if wages cannot be lowered in them, they will not be able to absorb additional labour. The men excluded from the other industry will remain permanently unemployed.

The theoretical argument can be carried one stage farther. If in a country conditions arise in which its industries generally find the wages they have to pay excessive in relation to the prices they can command with their existing volume of production, they will restrict production and so reduce employment till prices rise to a remunerative level ; if the competition of producers in other countries is such that prices cannot easily be raised, or if export of capital is easy and the rewards to capital attractive in other countries, production will be transferred from the first country to these others.

This potential effect of high wages policy in causing unemployment is not denied by any competent authority. Some indeed who recognise most clearly that wages can be pushed up to or maintained at a level causing unemployment regard such a policy as desirable ; they hold that it is an important stimulus to inventiveness on the part of employers and so to greater efficiency in production ; they argue that trade unions " ought consciously to try and keep wages not in exact adjustment with, but a trifle above, the current marginal productivity equivalent ; to accept the fact that this is bound to produce a variable, but permanent, margin of unemployment, which is of their own deliberate making and no inherent fault in the capitalist system ; to take all possible steps to increase the mobility and fluidity of labour, in order to facilitate the reorganisation and improvement of technique which must ensue before a fresh advance of wages is possible ; and to mitigate the incidence of unemployment on individuals in every

---

[1] There is a third consideration of great practical importance, namely, whether the men extruded can move to and have or can acquire aptitude for new work in any of the expanding industries. This consideration bears on the earlier part of this chapter and is not discussed here, as the point at issue is as to whether there are factors in unemployment other than the difficulty of transfer from declining to expanding industries.

possible way ".[1] Another recent critic of orthodox wage theory, Mr. M. H. Dobb, has argued that the equations which in that theory were held to determine division of the product of industry between capital and labour, are in reality indeterminate ; that, within wide limits, the distribution at any given time is conventional, has been determined historically by the standards of consumption of capitalists, and can be altered by altering those standards.[2]

In so far as Mr. Rowe and Mr. Dobb give academic support to popular demands for raising wages, Mr. J. M. Keynes, in recent lectures, has supplied one answer to them.[3] " . . . the High-Wage Party forget that we belong not to a closed system, but to an international system ; and to an international system, moreover, for which we have deliberately contrived a very high degree of mobility of international lending." There are thus narrow limits to the practical application of this party's notions "unless they are applied internationally, or unless we place obstacles in the way of mobility of foreign lending " ; the capitalist, in place of yielding obediently to Mr. Rowe's stimulus to greater exertion or to Mr. Dobb's stimulus-pressure to lower his standard of consumption, may simply invest in some other country where his share of the product remains greater. This is one, and in present circumstances, a sufficient answer to the High-Wage Party, but it is not the only one. Even if the opportunity for lending were cut off, it is not clear that reducing the capitalist's share of the product would have the effects contemplated by those who recommend it ; in place of submitting to the intolerable pain of thinking harder, as required by Mr. Rowe, or of giving up his conventional standard of consumption, as required by Mr. Dobb, the capitalist might save less ; collectively, capitalists might save too little to allow the existing standard of production of the population to continue. It is important to add this second argument to the argument used by Mr. Keynes. The practical application of high wage notions, if it was not to lead to unemployment, might have to lead not only to restriction of foreign lending but to collectivist saving.

Short of both these measures, the limits within which distribution

[1] J. W. F. Rowe, *Wages in Practice and Theory* (Routledge, 1928), p. 229.

[2] "A Sceptical View of the Theory of Wages," by M. H. Dobb (*Economic Journal*, December, 1929). Mr. Dobb's article is criticised on theoretic grounds by Mr. J. R. Hicks in "Edgeworth, Marshall, and the Indeterminateness of Wages," (*Economic Journal* for June, 1930).

[3] Stevenson Lecture at Bedford College, London, and Ludwig Mond Lecture in the University of Manchester, reprinted as "The Question of High Wages," (*Political Quarterly* for January, 1930). The sentences quoted here are on pp. 115 and 117.

of the product of industry can be changed directly [1] in favour of labour, without causing unemployment, are narrow. Are there grounds for supposing that these limits have been transgressed in recent years and that the theoretical possibility of high wages causing unemployment is being realised practically in Britain to-day? Professor Pigou, after citing as suggestive rather than conclusive M. Rueff's correlation of unemployment and of wages in relation to prices, relies on an argument still mainly theoretical. Professor Clay takes the *a priori* ground of showing how former methods of fixing wages with some regard to economic conditions have been replaced by new methods of a more arbitrary character. A more direct approach to the problem than either of these is that of considering the actual course of wages since the war and before it.

For this purpose valuable material is afforded by Mr. Rowe's recent study of wages in five principal industries—coal, cotton, engineering, building and railway service. Though confined to these industries, Mr. Rowe's figures, as compared with more general figures, have the advantage of dealing not simply with wage rates—some hourly, some weekly, some by the piece—but with actual earnings in a full week and per hour. The industries themselves are of cardinal importance; in each Mr. Rowe takes three grades—representing roughly skilled, semi-skilled, and unskilled labour—so that he covers fifteen different classes of workpeople; for these he gives true weekly and hourly earnings at four dates—1886, 1913, 1920 and 1926. Conclusions based on his figures are substantially confirmed by other enquiries.

The first conclusion is that there has been in Britain a notable increase of real wages, that is to say, a gain of money wages upon both cost of living and wholesale prices since the outbreak of war. For the fifteen grades Mr. Rowe's figures show from 1913 to 1926 rises in money wages per week ranging from 62 to 122 per cent with a mean of 90 per cent, and of money wages per hour ranging from 84 to 193 per cent with a mean of 123 per cent. In the same period the cost of living has risen 72 per cent and wholesale prices have risen 48 per cent. Putting these figures together real wages per week judged by cost of living have risen 10½ per cent, and judged by wholesale prices 28 per cent; real wages per hour by cost of living have risen 30 per cent, and by wholesale prices 50 per cent. It should be added that the employers

---

[1] Indirect change by taxation, as suggested by Mr. Keynes in the lecture cited, stands on a different footing.

are paying also additional insurance contributions representing from 2 to 4 per cent of the 1913 wages.[1]

These results for fifteen grades in five principal industries are in striking general accord with those given by Professor Bowley for wages generally. In a Special Memorandum prepared for the London and Cambridge Economic Service, describing *A New Index Number of Wages*, Professor Bowley puts the increase of real wages from 1914 to 1924 at about 10 per cent per week and 20 to 25 per cent per hour ; real wages here have reference to the cost of living. A further increase of 2½ to 3 per cent probably occurred from 1924 to 1926, and would bring Professor Bowley's hourly figure to but little below the 30 per cent derived from Mr. Rowe.

The full significance of the increase of real wages since 1913 can be seen only by comparing it with the course of events before the war. From 1886 to 1913, for the same fifteen grades, money wages per week rose by percentages varying from 8 to 60 and averaging 28 ; money wages per hour rose by percentages varying from 22 to 70 and averaging 35. Mr. Rowe himself treats the cost of living as for practical purposes the same at the two dates, though if anything higher at the later date. According to the estimates made by Mr. G. H. Wood in 1909 and continued on the same principles in 1913, the cost of living in 1913 was actually about 11 per cent higher in the latter year than in 1886 ; wholesale prices were 15 per cent higher. Putting these figures together as before, from 1886 to 1913 real wages per week judged by cost of living rose 15 per cent, and judged by wholesale prices rose 11 per cent; real wages per hour by the same standards rose 22 per cent and 17 per cent respectively.

On the basis of Mr. Rowe's material, and allowing for the insurance contributions, real wages per week as judged by cost of living rose in the thirteen years from 1913 to 1926 by almost as much as they had risen in the twenty-seven years from 1886 to 1913, say, 12 to 13 per cent as against 15 per cent; real wages per hour from 1913 to 1926 rose more than in the much longer period from 1886 to 1913, say, 33 per cent as against 22 per cent. In other words, the rate of increase of real weekly

---

[1] The employer's contributions for an adult workman in 1926 were 8d. in respect of unemployment and 4½d. in respect of health insurance, or a total of 12½d. as compared with 3d. for health in 1913 ; unemployment insurance in that year, with an employer's contribution of 2½d. a week, applied only to 2,250,000 workmen, say a quarter of the whole. The net addition to the employer's contributions since 1913 in respect of each adult workman was thus about 9d. The weekly wage rates of Mr. Rowe's fifteen grades in 1913 ranged from 21s. 10d. for engineering labourers to 46s. 6d. for coal-getters, with an arithmetic mean of 32s. 7d.

wages has been nearly twice as great and that of real hourly wages
thrice as great in a period of war and dislocation as it was in an
era of almost legendary prosperity and progress before the war.
If real wages were calculated, as for some purposes they should
be, by reference not to cost of living but to wholesale prices, the
contrast between recent and pre-war experience would be more
striking still.

The argument cannot indeed be pressed to the degree of precision indicated by these figures.   There are too many uncertain
elements, in the records alike of wages, of prices, and of cost of
living.   Mr. Rowe's wages for 1926 relate, for coal-mining, to the
early part of that year, and his hourly wages would thus be substantially reduced by the lengthening of the working day after the
dispute.   More important, perhaps, than this is that the period of
twenty-seven years taken for comparison before the war consists of
two nearly equal halves, with very different showing in respect of
real wages ; nearly all the progress of real wages in the twenty-
seven years was in fact achieved in the first half, and the last half
was a time of rising cost of living with stagnation in real wages.
On the other hand, Mr. Rowe's figures come down only to 1926.
The rise of real wages through maintenance of money wages while
cost of living falls has continued steadily since then; the latest
estimates prepared by Professor Bowley for the London and
Cambridge Economic Service put the rise of real wages per week
from 1913 to 1929 at just under 17 per cent.[1]   There is no
need to put more precision into the comparison than the figures
will bear.   The broad conclusion seems hardly questionable that
since just before the war, during a period of destruction of capital,
squandering of resources and dislocation, real wages have risen at
a rate faster than that which could be achieved in times of peace
and prosperity.

From what source has this rise of wages come?   Has there, in
spite of the probabilities to the contrary, been an increase in the
productivity of labour commensurate with the cost of labour?
This point also is dealt with in Professor Bowley's memorandum.
While certainty is impossible, several arguments converge to the
conclusions first, that output per head was nearly the same in 1924
as in 1914 in spite of the reduction of hours ; second, that the
money cost per unit output of labour had risen between those
years by substantially more than either cost of living or wholesale
prices.   In other words, the increased efficiency of production was
probably sufficient up to 1924 to cover the reduction of hours but

---

[1] These estimates are the basis of the index of real wages in Table XLI.

not the rise of wages as well. Since 1924 the process has continued; up to 1929, compared with 1924, output per head may have risen perhaps 4 per cent but wholesale prices have fallen 18 per cent and cost of living has fallen 6 per cent. Over the same period, 1924-9, money wages fell by less than 1 per cent. To-day the real cost of labour to the employer for each unit of output may be as much as one-sixth or more higher than before the war.[1]

If the increase of real wages since before the war is more than can be justified by increased production, may it nevertheless still be justified as a better distribution of the product of industry between capital and labour? As will be suggested in the following chapter, it is possible that in 1913 capital was in fact getting a larger proportion of the product of industry than it had done, say, twenty years before then. It does not follow that the distribution of the product could without harmful reactions be made again less favourable to capital in 1929 than in 1913. Capital on the whole in the post-war world is scarcer than ever before; the service of saving claims higher, not lower, rewards and, with a free international market for capital, gets them, in one country or another. Clearly for any one country at such a time to bring about consciously or unconsciously a redistribution of the product of its industry in favour of labour as against capital is to court the probability that industry will be transferred elsewhere and unemployment created.

The widespread enduring unemployment that we find in Great Britain is just what we should expect to find as the result of an abnormal rise of wages, unaccompanied by an equal rise of productivity or cheapening of capital. This inference of cause and effect is strengthened by consideration of how the rise of real wages since 1913 has come about. It has been the result less of bargaining between employers and workpeople, each knowing the conditions and the possibilities of their trades, than of movements beyond their control and of Government action taking no account of such conditions.

In a time of sustained material progress, such as was the last half of the nineteenth century in Britain, wages are never likely to rise to a point causing prolonged unemployment. Wages generally are a sluggish element in the economic structure, embodying customary standards. If technical advances are increasing

---

[1] Output per head at the end of 1928 was apparently no better than in 1924 (according to the *London and Cambridge Economic Service Bulletin*, for April, 1930, it was "stationary or decreasing"), that is to say, per week it was no better than in 1914. Real wages per week, however, had risen 17 per cent reckoned on cost of living (alike in 1928 and 1929), and something like 40 per cent reckoned by wholesale prices. The contrast with American experience is glaring.

rapidly the productivity of labour, it is most unlikely that wage demands will do more than follow that increase with a substantial time lag; only a deliberate policy of making life impossible for the capitalist, backed by powerful organisation or political control, is likely then to make wages outrun productivity. The same is true of a time of rising prices, such as marked the opening of the twentieth century in Britain ; whether or not there was in those years any actual check in the material progress of the country, the rise of prices, followed only slowly and incompletely by a rise of wages, ensured sufficient profit to industry. It was natural that in the first part of this volume, the possible influence of wage policy in producing unemployment should receive scant notice. The era then examined was one first, of rapid industrial development, later of rising prices, with trade unionism and collective bargaining covering thoughout but a small fraction of industry.

Yet even in that era there was one type of unemployment which might have been explained in terms of wage policy. In a time of trade depression failure of wages to share in the fall of prices was in one sense a cause of the unemployment then experienced ; complete plasticity of wages would in theory have prevented unemployment altogether. Here the natural sluggishness of wages was, among trade unionists, reinforced by a policy of maintaining, so far as possible, rates of wages once established and paying benefit to the larger numbers who at those wages could no longer get employment.[1] This was within limits a necessary and defensible policy ; experience had shown that the depression would pass, prices rise, and the unemployed be absorbed again at the old rates or more.

Apart from passing trade depressions, it is fair to say that rises of real wages before the war followed on increases of productivity, were made possible by such increases, and kept within limits set by them. The war and its aftermath present a different picture.

To begin with, in the war itself, consumption was divorced from production. The nation lived beyond its national income, lived well on savings and on borrowings. When the war ended, it had standards of life bearing no necessary relation to what it could produce, and had at the same time a sense of needing a rest from war-time exertions. To this war-time dislocation of standards succeeded the boom and depression of 1920-21, with a catastrophic fall of prices. The fall of money wages was much

---

[1] This bearing of trade unionism and unemployed benefit is recognised in Part I on p. 21 (sentence beginning twelve lines from the bottom), and on p. 141 in dealing with the chronically unemployed London Compositors.

less and was checked sooner. The return to the gold standard for 1925 gave a fresh downward kick to prices while money wages remained unchanged, that is to say, real wages rose further. For in the meantime two new factors had come in to make money wages less plastic downwards. One was the growth of trade unionism and collective bargaining ; the other was the generalisation of unemployment insurance in 1920 and its conversion into unlimited relief, by extended benefit in 1921 and by statute in 1927. Of the former Professor Clay writes that "there are few important gaps left in the provision for the settlement of wages by collective bargaining in Great Britain". Of the latter Mr. Rowe writes that "unemployment insurance has almost completely abolished the fear of blackleg labour by the unemployed, however numerous" and "has enormously strengthened the bargaining power of trade unionism". "This post-war disregard of unemployment in wage negotiations," infers Professor Clay, "is the principal and direct explanation of the loss of plasticity in wage rates."[1]

The movements of wages and prices since the war and the corresponding movements of unemployment are shown graphically in the chart below. The beginning of the chart, up to 1925, is in substance the same as that given by M. Rueff, with a revision of wage figures suggested by Professor Bowley ;[2] the end of the chart deals with years not covered by M. Rueff. The curve of wages divided by prices and the curve of unemployment move uncannily together, from minima in the first part of 1920 to one maximum in 1921 and a secondary peak in 1922, thence downwards to 1924 and since then slowly upwards once more. The unemployment curve tends every now and again to lag just behind the other, at the minima of 1920 and 1924 and the maximum of 1922, as might be expected if it is an effect and the other the cause. The most considerable discrepancy of movement, in 1926, is what might be expected from the coal dispute of that year.

To sum up, post-war Britain presents two novel features— unexampled unemployment and a rise of real wages almost equally without precedent. The former is most marked in the trades dependent on export. The latter has come about as a legacy of war-time dislocation rather than as an adjustment to improved economic conditions ; it almost certainly outruns the increase in the productivity of labour. A rise of real wages of this character,

---

[1] *Economic Journal*, September, 1929. The quotations from Mr. Rowe are on p. 180 of "Wages in Practice and Theory".
[2] *Special Memorandum 28 of London and Cambridge Economic Service.*

CHART VIII.—WAGES, PRICES AND UNEMPLOYMENT IN BRITAIN FROM 1919 TO 1929.*

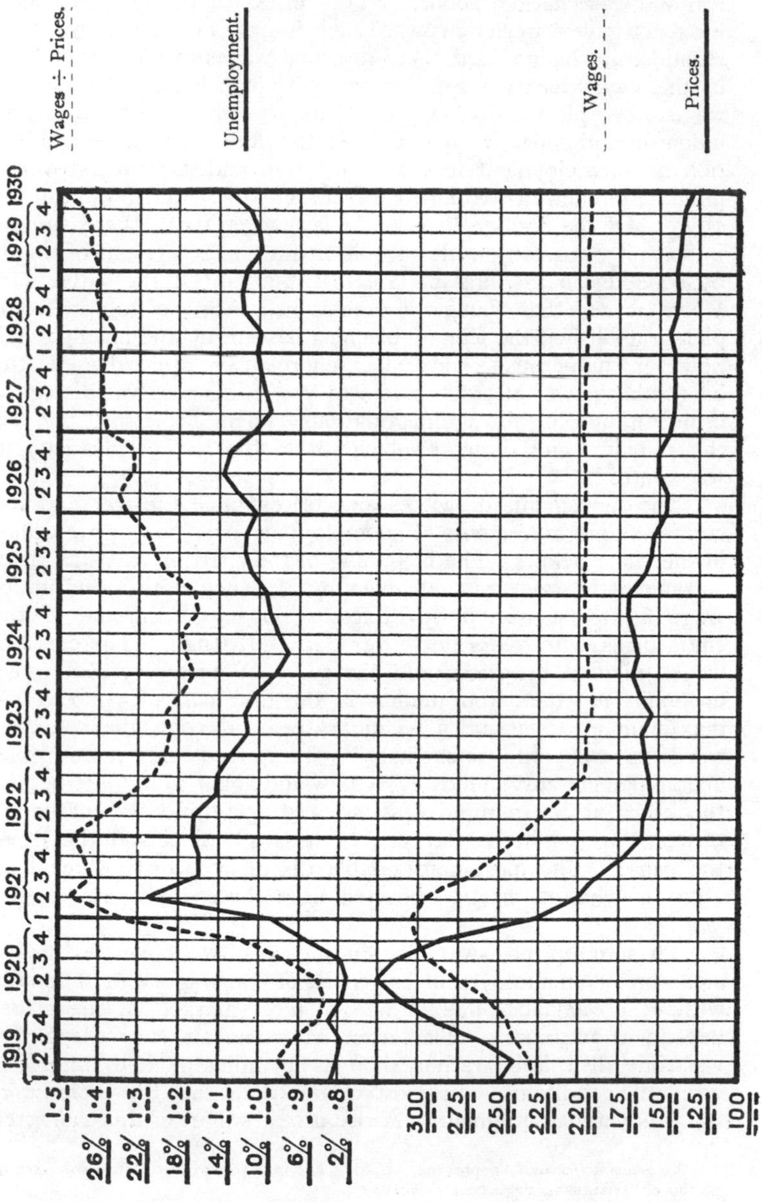

* For figures and notes see Statistical Supplement, pp. 459-60.

and so occasioned must naturally cause extensive and enduring unemployment, above all in export trades, either by raising the prices of British products in competition with those of other countries, or by reducing the margin from which capital is saved, or by causing a transference of capital to more remunerative use in other countries, or by a combination of two or more of these methods.

It is not easy, it might not be possible, to go farther than this in showing a causal connection between the rise of real wages and the rise of unemployment. It hardly seems reasonable, however, to doubt the connection.

As a matter of theory, the continuance in any country of a substantial volume of unemployment which cannot be explained by specific maladjustments of place, quality and time, is in itself proof that the price being asked for labour as wages is too high for the conditions of the market ; demand for and supply of labour are not finding their appropriate price for meeting. The deductive argument with which this discussion began leads farther than to the suggestion of mere possibilities ; any residuum of post-war unemployment which cannot be explained otherwise must be explained in this way.[1] The statistical argument that followed was needed less to show that wages were now above the market level than to show how they had come there, by a rise due more to price changes than to the initiative of wage-earners or to the adoption by their agents of the wage policy proposed by Mr. Rowe.

Nor, however unwelcome the conclusion may appear, is it in itself either novel or surprising.[2] It is only another way of putting the self-evident fact that deflation of credit and prices, however brought about and however justified, must increase costs

[1] In 1913 Professor Pigou carried the argument to the point of saying that " unemployment is *wholly* caused by maladjustment between wage-rates and demand " (*Unemployment*, 1913, Ch. V, p. 51). As a serious assertion this involves either ignoring the now well-known facts of seasonal fluctuation, casual employment, and loss or lack of industrial quality or using words in a way too artificial for daily use. As a paradox it is full of instruction.

[2] It will of course appear nonsensical to those who hold that the cure for unemployment is to be found in raising wages and so increasing consumption and the demand for consumption goods. Of course if wages could be raised without making any other change whatever, the argument would be plausible. In the real world, however, the question is whether transference of demand to consumption goods from the goods or services that the capitalist would require if wages were not raised will add more to employment of one kind than it takes away of employment of another kind. It is probable that, since demand for necessaries is on the whole less variable than demand for comforts and luxuries or instrumental goods, a community which made nothing but necessaries for itself might have more stable employment than if they made also some of the other things, but they would be miserably poor. High wages are among the many good things for which there are many better arguments than the bad argument that they cure unemployment.

24 *

of production relatively to selling prices and tend to contract employment, unless it is accompanied by an equal fall of wages, debenture interest and similar charges.   Nor, may it be added, is the argument, though applied here to wages under a capitalistic system, applicable only there.   If a community of co-operative producers working and trading with other countries were to decide that they would not sell their products except at an enhanced real price, they might find that their customers would not pay the price ; their production and employment would contract.   If a family group cultivating three equal fields with a yield of, say, 24, 20 and 16 bushels each per acre, were to decide henceforth not to work for any yield of less than 20 bushels, they would be unemployed for a third of their time, till scientific invention could raise the productivity of the poorest field ; if increase of production were impossible, one-third of them would be a surplus population that could find work at their chosen standard only by moving to a more fertile country.[1]

The counterpart of an assertion of a standard of life for working under any system, capitalist, socialist, communist, syndicalist, is a readiness to refuse work that will not yield that standard.   Assertion of a minimum standard is assertion of a determination under certain conditions to stand idle, to be, till that minimum can be won, a surplus population.   Here the argument reaches the threshold of another problem, the subject of the following chapter.   Standard of living forms the link between two questions hitherto kept distinct—that of unemployment and of population.

[1] I owe these arguments to Professor Robbins.

CHAPTER XVII.

UNEMPLOYMENT AND OVER-POPULATION.

Population and unemployment problems brought together by rigid wages. Defini-
tions of over-population. Conception of optimum density and its limited value.
A simple practical criterion needed. Tests of material progress. The Victorian
Age of rapid general growth. The Edwardian Age of wage stagnation. Doubts
as to course of national income. The post-war period. Decline of staple trades,
rise of wages, stagnation of national income.

Allegory of the Cistern : Standard of living, density of population, return to labour,
internal and external influences, inflow of fresh labour. Simultaneous upward
and downward pressures causing unemployment. Changing economic balance
of world. Tariffs. Old and new coal-fields.

Fall of birth-rate. Coming decline of population. Britain's future in grip of two
blind forces. Unemployment due to discrepancy between standard of living and
return to labour the same however reached.

THE opening chapter of this book, twenty-one years ago, was
devoted to keeping the problems of unemployment and population
distinct. In the chapter just concluded the problems have come
together across the bridge of rigid wages. Supply of labour as
a whole and demand for labour as a whole are normally kept in
general adjustment to one another, that is to say, unemployment
is reduced to the result of specific maladjustments of place, time
or quality, by plasticity of wages. If it is possible for wages to
become rigid at a point that is too high in relation to production
per head of the total population, part of the population will not
be able to find employment at those wages. This disequilibrium of wages and production may result either from a rise of
wages unaccompanied by a corresponding rise of production per
head or from a fall of production per head unaccompanied by a
corresponding fall of wages. In the former case the result will
be described as unemployment due to excessive wages ; in the
latter case it will be ascribed to over-population. In the former
case, since it is real rather than nominal wages that are in question, the movement may be occasioned either by a rise in money
wages or by their maintenance while prices fall. In the latter
case also there are alternatives ; production per head in any
country may be checked either by growing difficulties in producing, *e.g.*, through exhaustion of natural resources, or by diminished

demand for its products, *e.g.*, through competition of other countries, or through imposition of tariffs.

By all routes, the end of the journey will be the same—a part of the population standing idle, not simply as a reserve for fluctuations, but as a surplus to the needs of industry; arrival at that end will depend on the same essential condition that wages should not be plastic downward. In the preceding chapter reasons were given for thinking that a situation of this kind has been reached in Britain since the war along the route of rising real wages. In the present chapter it becomes necessary to consider whether there may not have been a converging movement along the other route of over-population. This involves a brief discussion of points of view as to population—an attempt to define what over-population means, how in the modern world it can come about, and how if at all it can be discovered and remedied.

The problem of population to-day is not so easy as it seemed to be when industry and international trade and applied science were in their infancy together. So long as economic development is envisaged mainly as the applying of successive doses of agricultural labour to a limited territory, the issue is soon reduced to the Malthusian one—of whether the capacity for increasing beyond his means of subsistence which man shares with all animals shall be offset by vice or by misery or by moral restraint; at an early stage in its history, increase of the labourers in a country begins to press downwards the return to labour.

The development of industrial technique and organisation, appearing to require for their greatest efficiency a concentration of labour far beyond agricultural standards, introduces one complication into the problem. It becomes clear that an increase of population may drive the return to labour upwards, not downwards: it is possible for a country to be under- not over-populated.

The development of international trade and national specialisation introduces another complication. It becomes clear that the return to labour in any country, or, conversely, the numbers that it can support at any given standard of comfort, may depend largely, not on conditions in that country, but on conditions outside it. The starting-point of any fruitful discussion of population problems to-day is that the population problem, for every country, is a problem of the distribution of the population of the world as a whole. Each of the varied inter-locking activities of mankind in the pursuit of material welfare—agriculture, mining, manufacturing, transport, commerce, finance—involves a special type of population and for its most efficient performance a different density. The distribution of the world's population accordingly depends on the distribution of those activities. This in turn depends partly on physical conditions of climate, geographical position, and natural resources; partly on human conditions, such as the character, abilities, and training of the people; partly on political institutions and policies, such as tariffs, subsidies, and the like. But, for any one country, the conditions—physical, human, political—to be taken into account are not those of that country alone.

The population that any one country can support at any given standard of life depends, not solely on its own natural fertility or resources and its own achievements of industrial technique or co-operation, but on how in each of these matters it compares with other countries. The return to labour in any one country may rise or fall—its optimum density of population may change—without any change of numbers, methods or activities in that country, as a result of changes elsewhere, of industrial discoveries and developments in other countries, of political re-groupings, of war and peace.

In the last sentence a phrase has been used which calls for explanation, and raises an issue of theory. Discussion of population problems in economic text-books to-day hinges as a rule, not on the unequal race between numbers and subsistence, but on the conception of an "optimum density," that is to say, of there being for each territory at any given stage of economic development a certain density of population which would make its output per head a maximum. If the population were either more or less than that optimum, the output per head would be smaller. What is the value of this conception of optimum density as a guide in the discussion of population problems?

It represents in one respect a substantial advance on earlier modes of thought. Its mere phrasing suggests that a people may fall short of maximum prosperity by being too small for its territory as well as by being too large, and that economically there may be gain and not loss to each individual through increase of numbers. But once this has been grasped, the value of the conception is largely exhausted. When it is suggested that optimum density should be taken as the criterion for judging of over- or under-population, that a country with more than the optimum density is over-populated and one with less than the optimum is under-populated, difficulties arise. As a matter of abstract reasoning there must be for every territory at each moment of time an optimum density of population which would make output per head at that moment a maximum. But for practical use as a criterion of over- or under-population optimum density suffers from the two defects of being unknowable and never the same for two moments together.

In Victorian England, as the population grew, the average real income of each individual also grew ; the country seemed to have room and to spare for all who sought to live there. It would be possible to argue, however—indeed it has been argued—that wealth per head would have grown yet more rapidly if the population had been less, *i.e.*, that the optimum density had been passed. It would be equally possible to argue that wealth per head would have grown yet more rapidly if the population had done so also, *i.e.*, that the optimum density was still ahead.

To compare such arguments to the pastime that bemused the fallen angels in Hell might, indeed, be unfair ; the subtlety of modern economic disputants is usually sufficient to save them from being in wandering mazes lost. But they can be as sure as the angels of never losing the pastime by finding an end or coming to any conclusion. There is no means of bringing these arguments to the test of facts, since repeated experiment with variations is impossible in economic science. One cannot even say as a rule in what direction the optimum lies, *e.g.*, whether a population increasing at a certain rate is moving towards the optimum or away from it.[1] The optimum itself is never still. If the optimum number of the population of Great Britain for 31st March, 1930, were divinely revealed that night to an economist in a vision, the one thing of which he could feel certain when he waked on 1st April, would be that the number was no longer the same.

[1] Professor Carr-Saunders in *The Population Problem* argues that uncivilised populations, at least, normally approximate to the optimum density, but it is impossible to follow his argument. The fact that Australian bushmen and other savage populations are above bare subsistence level (pp. 231 *seq.*), proves only that they are not *pessimum* populations and shows nothing at all as to how near they are to the optimum or whether they are above or below it. The argument (pp. 230, 236, 292) that, because uncivilised peoples by abortion, infanticide or other customs regulate their numbers, they approximate to the optimum density, either attributes to such peoples miraculous powers of economic statesmanship or deprives the term optimum density of scientific meaning. Turning from uncivilised to modern societies, probably most economists would agree that if the English-speaking people of the world were more evenly distributed over all the lands now occupied by them, the output per head would be higher ; most again, realising that even an increasing output per head is consistent with the optimum being already past, probably view with approval or equanimity the falling birth-rate of Britain. But these are impressions, not scientific judgments. How tenuously abstract the conception of optimum density is may be seen by following up a suggestion of Professor Cannan's that the optimum must be considered dynamically not statically, *i.e.*, over a period of time and not only for a single moment. The density which would make output a maximum in one year might involve a wholly unsuitable density over the next ten years. If the character of the population, *i.e.*, its age constitution and not simply its total number is brought into account, the optimum population for any one moment, *i.e.*, with maximum output per head at that moment, would be a population without either children or old people, that is to say an impossible population.

For practical discussion of population, recourse must be had almost always to another and simpler criterion than optimum density. In place of asking whether in different circumstances, which never existed and cannot be brought about, the hypothetical return to labour in a country would be more or less than the actual return to labour, we must be content to ask how the actual return is moving—whether it is rising rapidly or slowly, is stationary or is falling, whether rise or fall is tending to become faster or slower than in the past.

So long as the return to labour is rising rapidly or steadily, few men, save economists in search of argument, will concern themselves about over-population, or ask how the rise could be made greater. If it is falling, or after a rise has begun to rise much less rapidly or to hesitate, the time for serious concern is at hand. From the point of view of unemployment, indeed, the simple question of rising or falling return to labour is also the most important, because of the conservatism of popular standards. So long as the average return to labour is rising, however slowly, workmen will in general be content to ask for wages within the limits set by that return. If, however, the average return to labour begins to fall, the whole weight of conservatism will be against any corresponding fall of wages ; the effort to maintain wages may be a large factor in producing unemployment.

To answer the simple question of how the average return to labour has moved or is moving in any country is therefore a sufficient aim. Even this question is quite hard enough to answer.

In the first chapter of this volume the question was dealt with cursorily in the light of facts available in 1909. From an examination of the thesis that unemployment might be explained simply and sufficiently as the result of over-population—of a supply of labour growing more rapidly than the demand for labour—two conclusions emerged, one negative and comforting, one positive and disturbing. The negative conclusion was that in the Britain of those days there was no general failure of adjustment between the growth of the demand for labour and the growth of the supply of labour. " For the present the sphere of industry in the United Kingdom retains its elasticity. It expands, not indeed steadily, but still sufficiently for the people. It absorbs the generations as they come. It yields each fresh man on the whole more living and working room than fell to the lot of those before." The positive conclusion was that there were specific imperfections of adjustment between the demand for labour and the supply of labour, sufficient to give rise to a real and considerable problem of unemployment. "The forces which constantly tend to adjust demand and supply work only in the long run. There are forces as constantly tending to disturb or prevent adjustment and having often a run long enough to determine the fate of individuals." In other words, there was unemployment in spite of a rising return to labour.

The evidence cited in 1909 to show this rising return to labour represented a very imperfect study of the general problem of standards of living. No more seemed needed then both because the comforting lesson of the figures till then was so plain, and because the main object in view was not the comforting but the disturbing conclusion—that unemployment persisted, however prosperity grew. If to-day fresh enquiry is made as to how the return to labour is moving, a different result emerges.

The enquiry, as has been stated, is not a simple one. For Britain the application of statistical tests of the return to labour is peculiarly difficult. The yield of the soil in agriculture is clearly irrelevant ; the yield even in the great elementary industries of coal or iron is at most suggestive rather than conclusive. Britain is essentially a manufacturing, commercial, and financial country ; the return to labour in it is measured largely by its output of or gain from finished articles and services which themselves, by their infinite variety, escape all measurement. Current statistics both of production and of prices refer mainly to raw materials or food ; they miss the main features of British economic life and service.

Nevertheless, materials for an estimate of material progress since the middle of the nineteenth century are not wholly lacking. Some of the most significant of these are presented in the table on the opposite page.

The table records, at six successive epochs before the Great War, beginning with 1860 and ending with 1910, and for one epoch after it, the position of some of the principal indices of economic welfare. The chart that follows gives the same facts in graphic form. The table and chart are explained here briefly ; a full account of the sources and construction of the figures is given in the Statistical Supplement.[1]

The figure for each epoch up to 1900 is an average for ten years in which the epoch is central ; thus for "1860" the average of 1855-64 is taken ; for "1870" the average of 1865-74, and so on. For "1910" the average is for the nine years 1905-13 alone. For the last epoch, since the war, most of the

---

[1] Pp. 461-2.

TABLE XLI.—MATERIAL PROGRESS IN THE UNITED KINGDOM RELATIVE TO POPULATION.

	1.	2.	3.	4.	5.	6.	7.	8.	9.	10.	11.
Epoch.	Coal Production. Tons.	Pig Iron Production. Cwts.	Steel Production. Cwts.	Shipbuilding. '001 Tons.	Raw Cotton Consumption. Lbs.	Raw Wool Consumption. Lbs.	Exports Index. 1913=100.	Real Wage Index. 1913=100.	Real Income at 1913 Prices. £.	Consumption Index. 1913=100.	Housing [2] (Scotland).
Annual per head of unadjusted population.											
1860 (1855-64)	2·62	2·70	—	9·7[4]	28·1	—	33·5	60·7[5]	25·3[5]	69·2	43·4
1870 (1865-74)	3·59	3·60	·22[3]	13·5	33·5	10·4	49·4	67·8	28·8	74·5	46·1
1880 (1875-84)	4·21	4·20	·77	16·0	38·6	10·2	55·3	77·4	33·0	83·2	49·2
1890 (1885-94)	4·62	4·00	1·59	16·7	40·6	11·8	67·3	91·6	38·6	88·2	51·8
1900 (1895-04)	5·22	4·30	2·24	20·4	40·1	12·3	71·5	101·0	44·5	97·1	54·3
1910 (1905-13)	5·89	4·34	2·86	21·3	42·9	12·7	88·8	101·0	45·4	98·7	54·9
1925 (1922-25, 1927-29)	5·30	2·82	3·40	15·3	30·9	11·2	95·5	115·1	45·3 to 46·4[6]	107·3[7]	56·7
Index Numbers, on basis 1895-1904 = 100, adjusted for man-value of population.											
1860 (1855-64)	51·1	31·9		48·6[4]	71·4	—	47·7	60·1[5]	58·0[5]	72·5	82·2
1870 (1865-74)	70·3	47·8		68·0	85·5	86·1	70·8	67·1	66·3	78·5	87·1
1880 (1875-84)	82·6	57·7		80·5	98·7	85·0	79·3	76·6	76·1	87·8	91·7
1890 (1885-94)	89·7	83·0		83·1	102·6	97·2	95·4	90·7	87·9	92·1	95·5
1900 (1895-04)	100·0	100·0		100·0	100·0	100·0	100·0	100·0	100·0	100·0	100·0
1910 (1905-13)	111·8	113·4		104·1	106·2	102·2	123·3	100·0	101·2	100·9	100·6
1925 (1922-25, 1927-29)	98·3	105·2		72·8	74·7	87·5	129·4	114·0	98·6 to 101·0[6]	107·7	102·0

[1] The figures in this column are not per head of population or adjusted for man-value in lower half.

[2] The figures in this column are not per head of population but represent the percentage of total population living not more than two to a room at successive censuses from 1861 to 1921. They are corrected for man-value in the lower half.

[3] 1868-74.   [4] 1858-64.   [5] 1860-64.   [6] 1924 only.   [7] 1924-27 only.

See note in Statistical Supplement, pp. 461-2.

figures represent averages for 1922 to 1929, with 1926, the year of the coal dispute, omitted, and centre accordingly round 1925 ; real income and housing relate to named single years.   All years of war and its immediate aftermath are left out of account.

Five of the indices relate to particular industries—coal, iron, and steel,[1] shipbuilding, cotton,[2] wool—and measure their production either directly or by consumption of raw material.   One, described as the "exports index," shows the values of exports of United Kingdom produce divided by the Sauerbeck index of wholesale prices, so as to eliminate as far as possible the effect of changing value of money.   Another index, described as "real wages," shows the estimated average rates of money wages earned in a full week, divided by an index of cost of living, so as to eliminate the effect of changing retail prices.   The next index, described as " real income," shows the estimated national income per head divided by the same cost of living index ; the last two indices described as "consumption index," and "housing," are concerned directly with the working-class standard of life.   They show respectively the estimated consumption per head of food, drink, and other necessaries, and the proportion of the total population living not more than two to a room ; the last relates to the actual census years and to Scotland only, since similar figures are not available for the rest of the United Kingdom.

The table is divided into two halves.   In the upper half actual figures of production or consumption of exports at 1913 wholesale prices and of real income at 1913 retail prices are given per head of the total population of the United Kingdom ; for wages and housing no question of population arises.   In the lower half of the table the figures are given as index numbers, with those for 1900 (1895-1904) as basis, and with the further change that the population has been corrected for "man-value," i.e., so as to allow for changes of age and sex constitution.   A population with a smaller proportion of children will naturally, on the same standard of living, consume and produce more per head than one with a larger proportion of children ; as these proportions, particularly since 1911, have changed appreciably, allowance must be made for the change.   Presentation of the numbers per head of the uncorrected

---

[1] Pig-iron and steel, shown separately in the upper half of the table, are combined in the lower half.   To a considerable extent the two are complementary to one another, steel gradually replacing pig-iron in the economic activities of Britain.

[2] Consumption of raw cotton is an imperfect index of activity in the cotton trade owing to change in the thickness of the counts.   Progress since 1880 was greater than appeared because British industry was concentrating more and more on the fine counts, using more spindles and producing more value for the same weight of raw cotton.

population in the top half of the table makes it possible to see the changes due to this correction.

The chart gives the index-numbers from the lower half of the table in graphic form. What does the chart show? The survey will be made in three stages—up to 1900, from 1900 to 1910, from 1910 to the post-war epoch.

The chart shows, first, for every separate index a marked and almost unbroken rise, epoch by epoch, to the last but two in 1900. From different starting-points, usually of about 50 or 60, the various indices move in fifty years to 100; the general progress from 1890 to 1900 is not less than in previous decades. Unquestionably up to 1900 the average productivity and prosperity of each unit of the population rose as the number of units rose; there was an increasing return to labour as a whole.

This is the age of what Matthew Arnold called "our passionate material progress".[1] Long before 1900, indeed, Britain had lost the general economic supremacy that had been hers as first starter in the industrial race. Providence had not concentrated in these islands all the coal and iron resources of the world. As in the last half of the nineteenth century France and Germany and the United States developed their own mineral resources, as other countries followed down the industrial path, Britain was destined to find, and did find, her supremacy challenged, now in one field, now in another. In the heyday of her early start she had gone successfully into lines of business for which she had no enduring advantage. Once competitors entered the field, she came under growing pressure to discover and maintain those branches of work for which she had the greatest aptitude, and to withdraw from the rest. This process of challenge and adjustment in detail was bound to occur, irrespective of the actual growth of population, and, as it occurred, to give rise to strains and stresses. In the Victorian age, it did not threaten material progress as a whole.

The picture of the Edwardian age to the outbreak of war is more interesting because more varied; there are shadows as well as lights. From 1900 to 1910 all the special indices of production in particular trades continue their upward career; if, for shipbuilding, iron and steel, and wool, the rise is a thought less rapid than in the decade before, for coal and for cotton it is more rapid. All the general indices, on the other hand—wages, income, consumption, housing—suddenly change their course, and show barely perceptible progress or in one case no progress at all. One index,

[1] *Essays in Criticism*, First Series, 1895, p. 17.

CHART IX.—MATERIAL PROGRESS IN THE UNITED KINGDOM,
1860-1925.

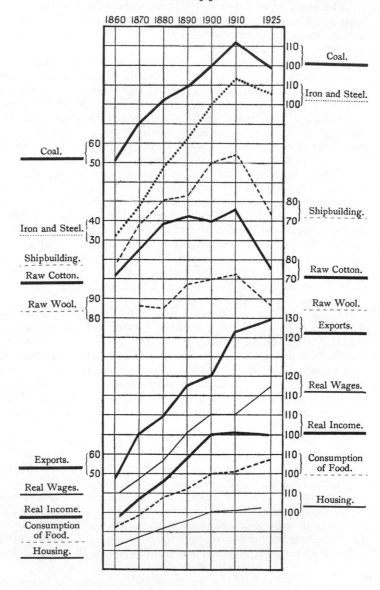

that of exports, which may be regarded either as special or as general, has an all but unprecedented rise.

How is this varied picture to be interpreted? The steady rapid growth of real wages to the end of the nineteenth century was taken before as the most definite sign that the capacity of the country for population had not been reached. Does the stagnation of real wages in the beginning of the twentieth century call for as definite a reversal of that comforting verdict?

There can be little doubt that the check to growth of real wages shown in the chart occurred in fact. Though the index of real wages is a composite structure, resting in part on estimates with a liberal margin of error, its movement from 1900 to 1910 is confirmed by the movements of the consumption and housing indices. The agreement of all three indices, resting as they do on independent material, puts the reality of a check to working class progress in the opening decade of the twentieth century beyond reasonable doubt. This does not in itself prove that the return to labour in Britain had ceased to rise, and proves still less that it would never rise again if population were not checked. One decade is too short for such judgments. A temporary check to working class progress might come, not through a check in production but through change in distribution of the product of industry. A check in production as a whole might be a transient consequence of special causes.

At the turn of the century we do in fact find special and temporary influences disturbing the economic life of Britain. One of these is the South African War; that war, like other wars, probably caused a greater loss of savings than of human life; it would leave capital scarce relatively to labour and in a stronger position to bargain. Another is the change in the movement of prices. Just before 1900 the falling tide of prices turned. From 1900 to 1913 the nation lived on a rising tide. This also is an element favouring capital as against labour,—profits rather than wages. Yet another special influence at the turn of the century is a change in the rate of labour supply, due partly to the course of birth and death-rates more than twenty years before and partly to the development of compulsory education. This point calls for explanation.

In 1876 the birth-rate in this country reached its maximum. At the same time, or just before, important steps were taken for the improvement of public health; the death-rate,, which had changed little for thirty years, began to fall, and fell steadily thereafter. There followed, a quarter of a century later, as a wave follows a distant earthquake, an abnormal growth in the supply of adult labour.   As has been pointed out by Mr. Yule, the numbers of the labouring population increased by 19 per cent from 1891 to 1901, as compared with a rise of 14 per cent from 1881 to 1891, and 10 per cent in earlier decades.[1]   If we take five-year averages, the rate of natural increase (difference of birth and death-rates) reached its highest points in the years 1881-5. Normally, this would have shown itself first by large numbers of boys entering the labour market in the early nineties.   At the same time, however, the Education Acts were withdrawing more and more boys under fourteen into the schools.   The State dammed up the rising flow of juvenile labour for a year or two. The main pressure in the labour market began to be felt later, i.e., about 1900, and presented itself as the "problem of boy labour," which was really the problem of those who had got boy's work easily enough between fourteen and twenty (replacing the younger children kept at school), but found themselves in difficulties when they reached man's estate.   This abnormal movement was bound, for the time at least, to disturb the balance between the growth of labour seeking employment and the growth of the demand for labour.   Some temporary pressure in the labour market was inevitable.   It might cause a check in economic progress as measured per head of the total population ; it would certainly, in the bargaining between labour and capital for the division of their joint product, make labour for the moment relatively weak and capital for the moment relatively strong because scarce.   Wages would lose relatively to profits.

All three special influences named above as coming to bear about 1900 favour capital against labour.   It is in accord with expectation that, of all the economic indices, that which shows worst from 1900 to 1910—the only one that shows no progress at all—is real wages, labour's share of the national dividend.[2]

It is also in accord with expectation that the index showing

---

[1] See Mr. Yule's paper on " Changes in the Marriage- and Birth-Rates in England and Wales during the Past Half-Century " (*Journal of the Royal Statistical Society*, March, 1906).

[2] Professor Bowley in his study of the distribution of national income in 1880 and 1913 reached the conclusion that the proportion falling to property and to labour respectively in these two years was much the same, but that between them came a fluctuation, by which the percentage falling to property was first cut down (till about 1900) and then increased again to its former level.   " So far as estimates can be made for the intermediate period, it appears that the proportion to property fell from 37½ per cent in 1880 to 36 or 35 per cent in the following 15 or 20 years, and increased since 1900 and since 1910 till it again reached 37½ per cent in 1913 " (*The Change in the Distribution of the National Income*, 1880-1913, p. 25).   Income from property includes income from abroad, and property's larger share in Professor Bowley's estimates is due to the growth of such income from abroad.   But the change of distribution deduced by him, for times of falling and rising prices respectively, is an interesting confirmation of the suggestions made here.

most expansion of all in this decade should be exports. This can, with high probability, be related to an abnormal export of capital just before the war, made easy by large profits. The following figures, based on a table of Mr. C. K. Hobson's, show for the periods named the mean value of capital exported each year and the value per head of population [1] :—

TABLE XLII.—EXPORTS OF CAPITAL 1870 TO 1912.

Period.	Annual Exports of Capital.	
	Actual.	Per Head of Unadjusted Population.
	£ mn.	£.
1870-74	60·8	1·91
1875-84	13·8	·40
1885-94	53·4	1·43
1895-04	24·1	·59
1905-12	139·6	3·13

Exports of capital, it will be seen, fluctuate greatly, but in their fluctuation show an interesting agreement with the movement of the exports index in the chart; the epochs of large and of small export of capital are, without exception, epochs of large and of small rises respectively in the exports index. An export of capital can in theory be effected either by increasing the export or decreasing the import of commodities; as Mr. Hobson shows, it did before the war normally involve sending abroad in large quantities rails, locomotives, mining machinery and the like. Export of capital again is increased or decreased by a variety of causes; clearly one thing making it easy is a piling up of surplus profits.[2] The high figure for 1905-12 fits in with the suggested gain of profits upon wages.

One index, that of real income, remains for consideration. This is the most general of all; if its apparent movement from 1900 to 1910—a rise of 2 per cent as against 15 per cent of earlier decades—be accepted, there can be no doubt that the twentieth century began with a check, not in working class progress alone, but in the progress of the nation as a whole. This is the

[1] *The Export of Capital* (Constable, 1914), p. 204. The figure for 1912 given by Mr. Hobson is regarded by him as open to doubt but has been used here. Even if it should be reduced slightly the inclusion of 1913 would almost certainly raise the mean for 1905-13 for comparison with the other figures in Table XLII above that given here for 1905-12.

[2] See a table given by Mr. Hobson at p. 40, showing the increased proportion of profits carried to reserve by industrial companies in years of large profits. For export of capital in the form of commodities, see his first chapter.

25

conclusion to which Professor Bowley points : "The results of the system (of production and distribution) have not produced a satisfactory livelihood to the bulk of the population, and its working in the generation before the war afforded no promise of any rapid improvement ; indeed, in the early years of this century real income increased little faster than the population." [1]

The index of real income, however, just because it is the most general, has also the largest element of uncertainty.   The estimates published by Professor Bowley and Sir Josiah Stamp and forming the basis of the index used here, relate directly to particular years— 1880, 1911, 1913, 1924. [2]   They contain two items—taxpaying income and wages—for which solid and fairly continuous data are available ; they contain two items—evasion and intermediate incomes (that is to say, incomes of clerks, shop assistants, and others not engaged by manual labour but not earning enough to pay income tax)—which can be calculated only with liberal margins of error for particular years and interpolated on general considerations for intervening years.   Moreover, though these latter items are small relatively to the other two, they are by no means fixed.   The persons with intermediate incomes certainly increased very much in the generation before the war, but how much they increased and still more what their incomes amounted to can only be guessed.   Evasion is assumed by Professor Bowley to have decreased during the same time, but it is not clear that this takes account of the facts just cited as to export of capital and of the greater opportunities for legal evasion thus offered. [3]

[1] *The Change in the Distribution of the National Income, 1880-1913*, p. 27.

[2] *The Division of the Product of Industry* (Clarendon Press, 5th Impression, 1921), and *The Change in the Distribution of the National Income, 1880-1913* (Clarendon Press, 1920), by A. L. Bowley, and *The National Income, 1924* (Clarendon Press, 1927), by A. L. Bowley and Sir Josiah Stamp.   See also the Report of a Committee of the British Association on " The Amount and Distribution of Income (other than Wages) below the Income Tax Exemption Limit in the United Kingdom " (*Statistical Journal*, December, 1910).

[3] Professor Bowley, whose figures have been used in the table and chart here, accepts the estimate of £37,000,000 given by Sir Josiah Stamp (*British Incomes and Property*, p. 324) as the total of taxable income escaping taxation in 1913 ; he puts the corresponding figure for 1880 at £60,000,000 and assumes a more or less steady decline.   The £37,000,000 includes two distinct things—income received but fraudulently concealed (put by Sir Josiah Stamp at £17,000,000) and income from foreign investments left to pile up abroad without ever being remitted to this country.   The latter was an admittedly legal form of avoidance of taxation till the Finance Act of 1914 shifted the basis of liability for taxation from the remittances to the profits arising abroad whether remitted or not.   It was estimated for budget purposes that the change would increase income tax receipts by £1,000,000 in a full year, and Sir Josiah Stamp infers from this an overseas income hitherto escaping taxation of £20,000,000.   The budget estimators, however, can hardly at that time have known what is now known of the abnormal growth of exported capital just before 1914, and would presumably also be cautious in their estimate of receipts from this source.   It is possible that the overseas income not being remitted was much above their estimate in 1913 and likely that it had increased very much in the past decade.

The index of national income accordingly, though given here on the basis of the published estimates of the leading authorities for certain years and inferred on the same principles for other years, must be taken with reserve; it cannot be stressed in conflict with other evidence. The apparent break at 1900 in the progress of national income and its stagnation in the following decade are not easy to reconcile with the continued rapid growth of production per head in every staple industry. If coal, iron and steel, shipbuilding, cotton and wool were still developing as fast as ever, from 1900 to the war, where can the falling off have been that nullified their growth and brought to a standstill the material progress of the nation? These are definite grounds for thinking that at 1910 the index of real income should be appreciably higher than it appears in the chart; there are other, less definite, grounds for thinking that at 1900 the index should be appreciably lower and that its course as a whole should thus show a steadier progression to the outbreak of war.[1]

The stagnation of real wages, on the other hand, besides being confirmed by the indices of consumption and housing, can be reconciled with the growth of other indices, if it be accepted that labour in the first decade of the twentieth century lost ground to capital in the division of their joint product. An interpretation of the Edwardian age is thus reached consistent in itself and with other than economic records. That age does not live in our memories and will not live in drama and fiction[2] as a season of hard living and hard labour. It comes back to us now rather in the guise of the ball before Waterloo, as an episode of unexampled spending and luxury; as the time when we saw our roads beset by motors, our countryside by golfers, our football grounds by hundred-thousand crowds and a new industry of bookmakers, our dancing-rooms and dining-rooms by every form of extravagance. The smooth development of Victorian days was broken, but the characteristic of the time was inequality of fortune rather than

[1] The chart shows national income from 1890 to 1900 rising more rapidly than wages, but Professor Bowley regards this as a period in which the distribution of the product changed in favour of labour as against capital. In yet another way the figures here given make the epoch 1910 appear worse than it really is in relation to 1900. The ten years 1895-1904 represented by the epoch 1900 include only one year of relatively slight depression (1904) and an undue proportion of good years, and have a mean unemployed percentage of 4·2. The nine years 1905-13 of the epoch 1910 include the end of the slight depression of 1904-5 and the very bad depression of 1908-9, and though they end with one of the best years of employment ever experienced, they have a mean unemployed percentage of 5·0. This unequal incidence of the trade cycle is reflected directly in the total of the national income and weights the comparison unfairly against 1910.

[2] *Sonia*, by Stephen McKenna; *Tono-Bungay*, by H. G. Wells; *The Regent*, by Arnold Bennett.

general misfortune; discontent rather than poverty; a gain by
capital in relation to labour, by profits in relation to wages, by
some classes of workmen at the expense of others,[1] even more than
a check to our progress as a nation.

Even if it be held that with the turn of the century, national
progress, and not working class progress only, faltered in its stride,
we are not bound to believe that the check was permanent. The
three factors described above—the earthquake wave of labour
supply, the South African War and the upward turn of prices—
are all peculiar to their time. The relative shortage of capital
would tend to produce its own corrective. Difficulty in absorbing
an abnormal flood of new labour does not prove permanent over-
population : if all the hundred million persons who now find room
and growing opportunities in the United States had landed there
at once, they would all have starved.[2] In the last three years
before the war we find in nearly all indices resumption of a rapid
upward movement. What would have happened if the war had
not come ? Would the Edwardian age have proved a passing
episode of unrest or the beginning of a serious threat to our
prosperity ? This is one of many questions whose answers are
buried in the common grave of war.

The last stage in the survey—from just before the war to the
present time—is the most critical and interesting of all. The
main results are sharply in contrast with those of the stage before.
All the special indices of the staple trades, which then had continued to rise, now show marked—almost catastrophic—declines.
Real wages, which then had stagnated, show a new rise, as fast
as anything recorded in the Victorian age ; this rise is confirmed,
as the earlier stagnation had been confirmed, by the indices of
consumption and housing.[3] Real income occupies as before an
intermediate position ; per head of total population it is, within
the limits of error, the same in 1924 as in 1905-13 ; per head of
adjusted population, as shown in the chart, it is almost certainly
a trifle less. That, in spite of the decline of the staple trades,

---

[1] Increase in capital's share of the product of industry, by changing the proportions
spent on necessaries and luxuries respectively, might stimulate the demand for and
increase the rewards to certain classes of labour at the expense of other classes, *i.e.*
while depressing wages generally, might raise them in particular occupations connected
with luxuries.

[2] This is pointed out by Mr. H. Wright, in *Population*, p. 110 (" Cambridge
Economic Handbooks," 1923).

[3] The movements of real wages and of consumption of necessaries are in reassur-
ing agreement with one another, both (a) in the stagnation from 1900 to 1910 and the
subsequent resumed rise, and (b) in the fact that the rate of increase of consumption is
uniformly a little below that of wages. Consumption relates to standard necessities ;
some part of the rise of wages would go in buying not more of these but other articles
not included in the records of consumption.

real income should show no worse than this, must be due to growth of new trades and services. That the exports index should still show a small rise is also due in part to this, in part perhaps to a relative change in export and import prices. Generally the chart in the last stage reflects from another angle the results of the last chapter—decay of the staple trades, inadequate compensation for this by growth elsewhere, gain by wages on national income and production.

For the purposes of the present chapter, the most important result is the stagnation or decline of real income. This rests upon a direct comparison of the years 1924 and 1911 made by Professor Bowley and Sir Josiah Stamp,[1] and is confirmed by, in place of conflicting with, what else is known of production. It must be taken with the reserves required by the tentative nature of some of the estimates used and by the exceptional history of recent years. It must be taken also with the comment that, if the views suggested in the preceding chapter be correct, real income would have been higher in 1924 if real wages had risen less and had allowed unemployment to be less. But the maximum addition for this is small and would not suffice to make real income in 1924 certainly better than in 1905-13.[2] It does appear as if an unprecedented upward drive of wages and of the standard of living desired had come in Britain, just at a time when the changing conditions of the world were holding back any increase in the return to British labour and were making a rise of standards most hard and most dangerous.

ALLEGORY OF THE CISTERN.

The employed population of any country may be conceived of as a fluid contained in and passing through a long rectangular cistern of peculiar construction. The top and bottom of the cistern represent respectively the demand for the services of the

[1] *The National Income, 1924* (Clarendon Press, 1927). Comparing 1911 and 1924 the authors conclude that " the real Social Income was very nearly the same at the two dates. The real income per head decreased 5 or 10 per cent, since population had grown about 7 per cent. This decrease is attributable to the falling off of income from abroad. Real home-produced income was very nearly the same per head in spite of increased unemployment and the reduced working week." These results have been adjusted here for the slight difference between 1911 and the mean of 1905-13 and also by allowing for the change in the age constitution of the population; in the table they are given with a margin, 1924 appearing as from 99 to 101 of 1900; in the chart the mean of these figures is used. The comparison being made directly between the period just before the war and 1924 is not affected by the doubts raised above as to the comparison between 1905-13 and earlier epochs.

[2] If without any reduction of wages or other change unemployment in 1922-29 had been reduced to the same level as in 1905-13, the national income would have been raised about 2 per cent.

population and the demands which they make for their services, *i.e.*, their standard of living ; both top and bottom can move up or down so as to approach or get further from one another and diminish or increase the space between them.   The two ends of the cistern are highly porous ; at one end—that of youth—the new generations of workers pass continuously with little obstruction into employment ; at the other end—that of age—men pass out yet more easily by retirement.   The sides of the cistern are also porous but much less so ; they will under pressure let some of the fluid escape, or under strong suction let it be drawn back again into employment.   They have this peculiarity that while they are almost equally porous outwards (*i.e.*, for extrusion from employment) along their whole length from youth to age, they get less and less porous inwards (*i.e.*, for return to employment) from the young end to the old ; this represents the fact that, while the chance of losing employment is not very different in different age groups, the chance of recovering employment, once it has been lost, is less for older than for younger men.

The top and bottom of the cistern are rigid ; the sides and ends are elastic and can expand or contract automatically as the space between top and bottom varies.   The whole must be pictured as moving up and down on vertical shafts at each corner. The superficial area of the top or bottom represents the area of the country (allowing for relative richness of natural resources) so that the distance between the top and the bottom represents the density of population.   The height of the top above the ground depends thus both on the standard of living (height of bottom) and the density of population (distance between top and bottom).

The stream of fresh labour entering at the end of youth exerts a continuous pressure, which, if the entry is more rapid than the outflow at the end of age, tends to drive the top and bottom further apart and increase the volume of employment ; if this cannot be done, either by moving the top upwards (finding fresh demand for services) or moving the bottom downwards (lowering the standard of living), some of those already in employment will be forced out through the sides into unemployment.

Apart from this internal pressure the top and bottom of the cistern are subject to varying pressures from outside and move with varying degrees of friction.   The bottom, representing the standard of living of the workpeople, is always under a slight pressure to move up and moves down with great difficulty.   The top, representing the demand for the products of their labour, has a freer movement but is subject to a great variety of influences. Technical improvements in industry continually tend to raise it.

Weights may be placed on it by internal taxation or external tariffs or downward pressure applied by exhaustion of natural resources or development of competing countries. While the top of the cistern is near the ground, the factors affecting its vertical movement arise mainly within the country itself; as it gets further from the ground, factors from outside become increasingly important. A dense population with a low standard of living and a population with a high standard but small density may live within a self-contained community, little affected by the developments and policies of other communities. A country which combines a high standard of living with a high density of population will bring the top of the cistern within the play of influences from outside—foreign competition and foreign tariffs. The position of the top represents both the numbers for whom the country can find employment and their standard of life.

The allegory of the cistern is susceptible of many further refinements. Casual employment may be represented by a section where the side casing is broken down so that men flow ceaselessly into and out of employment; the division between the two becomes little more than a line. Cyclical fluctuation is a rhythmic pressure and release of pressure over the whole top, driving men out of employment in all directions and then re-absorbing them by suction; other fluctuations and changes of demand are a continual quivering of the top pressing out men and drawing them back, now here, now there. The insurance system is like a trough fixed along each side of the cistern to catch men as they are pressed out and keep them in contact with employment, ready to be drawn back again as soon as the pressure that drove them out relaxes; the trough is hung directly on to the top (supported by employer's and workmen's contributions), and thus adds to the weight that has to be lifted to allow the standard of living to rise or employment to expand. So, too, the Government of the country can if they desire hang a pump (in the form of a pension scheme) at the old end of the cistern to suck men out more rapidly into retirement and lighten pressure within. Or they can hang a pump or other device at the young end (*e.g.*, a raising of the school age) to take off some of the pressure of the entering generation. But the weight of such devices will almost inevitably be added, more or less completely and more or less directly according to the form of taxation adopted, to the weight on the top of the cistern; they will to that extent tend to check expansion of industry or rise of the standard of living.

It would be inappropriate though fascinating to pursue these refinements here. The main lesson of the allegory is clear. If the reading of history given in this and the preceding chapter is right, an upward thrust of peculiar violence on the bottom of the cistern since before the war, has coincided with a downward thrust on the top of the cistern, begun perhaps before the war and greatly intensified by it. In the result the top has moved hardly at all ; the bottom has risen sharply ; the fluid has been forced out in all directions.

The origin of the upward pressure on standard of living has already been traced in falling prices combined with loss of plasticity in money wages. The downward pressure cannot be diagnosed as clearly, but has in all probability two elements. First, there has been since the war a growth of tariff weights on expansion ; war's lesson of self-sufficiency has fostered economic nationalism. Second, Britain's loss of position to other countries in respect of natural resources can no longer be ignored.[1]

The population of Britain has grown upon its coal-fields : a disproportionate share of the world's industrial work and industrial population was centred in Britain before the war, because these coal-fields had been the first to be worked and remained for long one of the cheapest sources of power in the world. But there is nothing in nature to make them so always ; there is much in nature to bring a change. Coal-mining is extractive, taking out from the soil without putting back. In this respect, industrial life based on coal stands nearer to savage life based on hunting than to the intermediate stage of farming communities. As a savage tribe, having made game scarce in one hunting ground, moves on to fresh grounds, so the industrial population of the world may tend to shift from the old coal-fields to the new ones. The savage tribe may be led to move before its old ground is cleared completely, if it finds better hunting elsewhere ; so the shifting of an industrial population need not wait for complete exhaustion of the minerals which first brought it together. The total coal resources of Britain are so great that complete exhaustion is not to be contemplated. But relative exhaustion, that is, the using up of all coal which, allowing for quality, is easier to get than the coal of other countries, is a possibility which must be faced. It is important, therefore, to ask what has been and what is the return to human labour in getting coal, in Britain and elsewhere.

The output of coal in Britain per head of all those employed in mining has been falling for fifty years. From 319 tons per head per year in the five years 1879-83 it reached 257 tons in

[1] Coal is considered here in the light of the *Report of the Royal Commission of 1925* (Cmd. 2600). For the present purpose of suggesting secular tendencies, it is not necessary to bring figures up to date, while both the stoppage of 1926 and the hours legislation of that year make fair comparisons all but impossible. The authority for all the facts given here is Chapter XI of the Report.

1909-13, and 218 tons in 1924-5, the last two years before the last big stoppage. Part of this fall, probably half or a little more, is to be accounted for by two reductions of working hours between the extreme dates chosen. The other half or a little less represents the increase in the proportion of men employed away from the face to those employed at the face, of men above ground and of men underground on the lines of communication between the shaft and the face in proportion to the hewers; for every 100 men at the face there were in 1905, 114, and in 1924, 145 employed away from the face. This increase of off-hand workers—one of the features of mining made prominent by the Royal Commission of 1925—may itself be attributed to a variety of causes—additional safety regulations, re-arrangements involved in the reduction of hours, undertaking of new services in cleaning and washing coal. But, as the Commission pointed out "the most natural and general explanation of an increase in the number of off-hand men, that is to say, of the men on the lines of communication between the face and the shaft, in proportion to the men at the face itself, is that the lines of communication as a whole may have become longer or more difficult to maintain". The Commission, while they were not able to test this hypothesis directly and precisely, did get evidence of growing physical difficulties of mining in Britain and brought out some striking contrasts between conditions here and in America. Returns from the collieries covering 1913 and 1924 showed that in the former year 55 per cent of all the coal produced in Britain came from seams 4 ft. thick and upward, but in the latter year only 51 per cent; in 1913 19 per cent, but in 1924 23 per cent of the coal came from a depth of more than 500 yards. "In the United States, the deepest bituminous coal-mining operation is less than 1,000 ft. from the surface, and the average depth of the shafts is about 260 ft. Less than a quarter of all the mines have shafts at all; the rest are approached by horizontal 'drifts' or downward 'slopes,' or are 'strip' mines worked in the open after shovelling off the earth above the coal. In Great Britain more than half the coal now being worked comes from depths greater than 300 yards." [1]

Of course physical difficulties may be overcome by science: "technical progress and wise planning often make it easier now to get coal from a hard 2-ft. seam, or from 3,000 ft. below the surface, than an earlier generation found it to work a 6-ft. seam at 300 ft.". Of course also there are no such contrasts between the British and

---

[1] Cmd. 2600, p. 116.

European coal-fields as those between the British and American.
The fact of growing physical difficulties remains, and the probability that these will be relatively more marked the older the
coal-field. Age in a coal-field means, in general, both that its easy
coal has been worked out and that it was laid out when the science
of mining was less advanced. The Royal Commission of 1925,
setting out the output per head from 1879-83 to the war, for
Britain and her principal mining rivals, drew the following contrasts :—

> "The American Bituminous output rises sharply from
> 505 tons to 698 tons per head; the French, German and
> Belgian outputs remain substantially unchanged near 200,
> 250 and 165 tons respectively; the British output falls
> from 319 to 257. In the last years before the war Great
> Britain is at the German level; in 1925 Great Britain is
> below the German level, having started 25 per cent above
> it fifty years ago. British mining, even before the war,
> was thus losing ground relatively to other European countries,
> as well as to America. The table brings out, on the one
> hand, the growing competition that British coal had to face,
> directly in the export trade and indirectly in all manufactures
> based on coal; on the other hand, the difficulty of main-
> taining for the British miner those advantages in comfort
> and in leisure over his European fellows that once had
> seemed to be his birthright." [1]

The suggestions from such facts and from others cited before
are strong and clear. From the failure of real income per
head to rise appreciably in the past twenty, perhaps the past
thirty, years, it looks as if a term was being set to the material
progress of Britain and to her capacity for population, as if the
economic balance of the world was turning against her. From
the statistics of coal mining, it looks as if one element in the
change was her increasing relative difficulty in winning her sole
source of power. From the plight of the export trades it looks
as if the known development of economic nationalism since the
war was being effective. Beyond these probabilities it is hard to
go. Their indications may be wrong; the process they indicate,
though now real, by a fresh spin of the wheel, may be reversed.
But, at the very least, they leave no room for easy optimism;
they throw a new colour over all thoughts of Britain's future.
In those thoughts, one fresh fact, of prime importance, has

[1] Cmd. 2600, p. 128. The table continued to date is printed in the Statistical
Supplement below, p. 463.

still to be brought into reckoning. The allegory of the cistern suggests one more aspect of the problem of unemployment and over-population. The new generations of labour have been pictured as flowing in to employment at one end of the cistern, that of youth. The volume of this flow may vary, and so may change the internal pressure to increase the volume of employment, pushing up the top or pushing down the bottom; the pressure behind the flow depends upon the birth-rate or rather upon the difference between birth- and death-rates.

In the period reviewed twenty years ago, this difference was such as to add rapidly and to all appearance indefinitely to the numbers seeking employment. The opportunities of employment, however, and actual employment grew as fast; the top of the cistern could move upwards freely enough both to increase the volume of employment and to let the bottom of the cistern—the standard of living—rise. In the period now under review, note has to be taken not of a single but of a double revolution. It is probable, though not certain, that in the last generation and particularly since the war, the power of British industry to absorb at former or rising standards a rising population has become less. It is not merely probable but practically certain that British industry will not for many more years be required to do so.

The rate of births per thousand of the population in Britain has been falling since 1876. The actual number of births and the natural increase of population, that is the difference between births and deaths, have both been falling since 1903. The fertility of the British people, as measured by births in relation to married women of child-bearing age, is now a little less than half of what it was fifty years ago, that is to say, in relation to the number of women who might bear children one child is born now where two were born then.[1] The actual number of births in 1927-9 averaged 749,000, i.e., 333,000 a year below the maximum of 1,082,000 reached twenty-seven years ago; for every three births then there are just over two now. The mean number of deaths in 1927-9 was 560,000; there is still, through a fall of the death-rate, a natural increase of the population but this is now little more than a third of the former maximum : 188,000 persons a year in 1927-9 as compared with 491,000 in 1903 and 459,000 over the ten years 1901-10. The last year 1929 yields 133,000 only. The flow of the new generation first into schools and then into employment is year by year swiftly and sensibly becoming less.

[1] For every 1,000 married women aged from 15 to 45 births averaged 295·5 in 1870-2, 288·7 in 1880-2, 138·3 in 1926-8, 135·4 in 1928.

The origin of this revolution—for it is no less—in human fertility is not obscure. It is the result of birth control, that is of human choice, in using applications of science to prevent births. which would otherwise have resulted from the working of natural instincts. Why, about fifty years ago, not only in Britain, but in nearly all countries peopled by European stocks, there should have begun this development of birth control is perhaps less clear.[1] The revolution itself is pictured in the accompanying chart. It is more material in this place to discuss its probable consequences than its causes.

The effect of a changing birth-rate upon the size of a population is not simple ; in estimating future population allowances have to be made for death-rates, for emigration, for age constitution as affected by these as well as by births, and for other factors. The question has fortunately been the subject of a good deal of expert study—particularly by Professor Bowley —since the war. For the present purpose it will be sufficient to cite Professor Bowley's conclusions, as given in 1924, on the figures of 1921-3, and to show how the figures have moved since then.

Professor Bowley, working on the life table of 1910-12, showed that, assuming the death-rates of that date, the rate of births per 1,000 women of age twenty to forty-five experienced in 1921-3 was just sufficient to maintain a stationary population with no surplus to spare for emigration. ". . . at the birth-rate (per potential mothers) of the years 1921-3 the population will ultimately diminish if there is any emigration, unless the death-rates fall further. As a fact emigration on a considerable scale took place in the past three years, and with the present rates of births, deaths and emigration, the population of Great Britain would increase to 45 or 46 millions about 1941 and then diminish." [2]

The rate of births per 1,000 women aged twenty to forty-five at the time of Professor Bowley's study (1921-3) was 106. The rate in 1926-8 is about 87. In actual numbers 1927-9 as compared with 1921-3 had on an average 164,000 fewer births, 29,000 more deaths, 47,000 fewer emigrants, a net shortage of 146,000 a year. Clearly Britain will never reach Professor Bowley's peak of 45 or 46 millions and will find its numbers

---

[1] An article by myself on " The Fall of Fertility among European Races " (*Economica*, March, 1925) gives the main facts of the fall and discusses its causation.

[2] " Births and Population in Great Britain," by A. L. Bowley (*Economic Journal*, 1924, pp. 191-2).

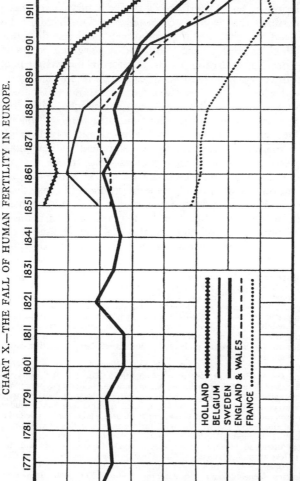

CHART X.—THE FALL OF HUMAN FERTILITY IN EUROPE.

HOLLAND
BELGIUM
SWEDEN
ENGLAND & WALES
FRANCE

The chart shows at various periods, for the chief European countries, legitimate living births per annum per 1,000 married women aged 15-49. The numbers represented are given in Table LI in the Statistical Supplement, with explanatory notes.

falling within the present decade.[1]   How far the fall will go no
one can say, for no one can say how much further or how fast in
future fertility will continue to decline.   Up to the present there
is no sign of halting.

Restriction of human fertility in the past fifty years has pro-
foundly modified the problem of population for Britain.   But it
has not solved the problem of population;[2] still less does it solve
the problem of unemployment.   Beyond a very few years there
will be no need to find room in Britain for an increasing people;
if British industry can keep its present place in the economic
structure of the world there will be room and to spare in it
at present standards.   But the condition named, that Britain
keep its present place in the economic structure of the world,
may not be fulfilled.   Changes in the economic structure of the
world—by scientific invention, by development of new markets,
by development of rival producing areas—may make it hard for
Britain to hold even 30,000,000 people at or above its present
standard, as, on the other hand, they might make life easy there for
50,000,000.   Birth- and death-rates, even if they could be managed
completely by statesmanship would be far too slow as a means of
fitting the population of the country to the capacity of the
country; in practice, death-rates can be managed only in one

---

[1] This statement is left here in the general terms sufficient for the present
purpose.   The rate of births per 1,000 women twenty to forty-five now needed to
maintain a stationary population without emigration is not exactly 106 but a little
lower, being affected both by the changed death-rates since 1910-12 and by the
increased proportion of women of this age in the population.   But the correction for
these factors would be trifling as compared with the fall from 106 to 87 births.
A more accurate forecast of future population could now be made allowing for
changes since 1921-3, but would probably be put out of date, by further fall of the
birth-rate, as soon as it was made.

[2] The practical issues calling for thought on the side of population are now those
of quality and age distribution rather than of quantity.   The fall of fertility, though
not confined to any class of the population, has been differentiated in degree; speaking
broadly, it has caused those classes to contribute by births least to the coming generation who have contributed most—in so far as such contributions can be judged by
material rewards and esteem—to the welfare of their own generation.   The fall of fertility again has diminished and will diminish further the proportion of young people in
the whole population and increase the proportion of the old.   From being 15 per cent
of males aged fifteen to seventy in 1911, boys of ages fifteen to twenty will fall to be
12 per cent or less in 1941 (*Estimates of the Working Population of Certain Countries
in 1931 and 1941*, by A. L. Bowley, prepared for League of Nations Economic and
Financial Section, Geneva, 1926).   Industry must learn to work in future with 88 men
and 12 boys in place of 85 men and 15 boys.   The change, unless deliberate correctives
are applied, is likely to have two consequences, one temporary, one enduring.   It will
cause a temporary relative shortage in the supply of juvenile labour, leading possibly to
competition for this labour among employers and a disproportionate rise of wages.   It
will lower permanently the average natural mobility of the labour supply taken as
a whole, by diminishing the proportion of it which is young, adaptable and not
weighted by family responsibilities.   In so far as it does this, it will add to the volume
of unemployment.

direction, and birth-rates as a whole probably cannot be managed by statesmen at all. Finally, whatever the general adjustment of labour supply and labour demand, of population and territory, unemployment will continue so long as the specific maladjustments described in earlier chapters are allowed to remain.

It is time to gather together the varied strands of theory and fact forming the material of this chapter.

The population problem for any one country is a problem of the distribution of the world population according to economic advantages. This general principle rests on the existence of international trade and the consequent specialisation of economic functions as among different countries. In so far as nearly every country is concerned more or less in international trade, the principle applies more or less to every country. To Britain it applies more than to most countries. Of all large nations the British nation has grown to be the least self-sufficient, the most highly specialised, the most dependent on trade and peace and world-wide co-operation.

During the nineteenth century this dependence seemed well-advised ; peace reigned ; international trade grew without visible limit. The spectre of over-population was exorcised by the incantations of prosperity. Wages and standards of life rose easily within limits set by rising productivity ; the secular fall of prices from 1870 to 1897 was itself largely a result of increasing efficiency, transmitted its gains automatically to the workpeople, and was too gradual ever to bring money wages into prolonged discordance with prices. Unemployment arose only through the specific maladjustments described in the first part of this volume.

With the turn of the century came a change. There was certainly a check in working class progress between 1900 and 1910. There may have been a corresponding check in the general progress of the country. But the change left the problem of unemployment untouched. The new movement of prices—now rising in place of falling—kept slow-moving wages within the limits of productivity, whether checked or not. There was discontent as rising cost of living filched the rewards of labour, but there was no new type of unemployment ; after the severe depression of 1908-9 came 1913, the year of lowest unemployment for a generation or more.

In the aftermath of war Britain is seen in the grip of two forces —the changing economic balance of the world and the secret revolution of the birth-rate. The two to some extent now are working in opposite directions, but neither is adjusted naturally to

the other.   Each works separately, blindly and all but uncontrollably to an unknown end.   The issues that they raise admit of no
scientific answer ; they are the playground of happy speculation
in the lecture-room or the plaything of hazardous decision at the
polls.   Shall Britain seek to hold on the course set for her eighty odd
years ago by the designers of international commerce and goodwill ;
dare she still, in face of discouragements, trust to find the world
large enough and open-armed enough and her own resources rich
enough to keep in this island one of the great and thronging
workshops of humanity ?   Shall she—can she—instead make her
unit of population and trade neither an island nor the whole world
but an empire ?   Shall she be content to be an island again,
self-sufficing or nearly for a smaller people ?   The dominance of
no nation is immortal.   With our passion of material progress
burnt out, there may still be left warmth to live by and a hearth
to cherish other less mortal household gods than empire—science
and the arts and peace and liberty.

From such spacious themes the argument turns back—to unemployment and the opening of this chapter.   Unemployment
due to disequilibrium between the demands for the service of
labour in a country and the demands of the labourers for reward
of their service, is the same in essence whether the coming of disequilibrium can be traced mainly to decline of the former demand
or to rise of the latter.   The choice of remedies is also the same
—to remove some of the labourers to another country or to bring
productivity and wages into accord once more.

CHAPTER XVIII.

A SECOND CONCLUSION.

Diagnosis and policies of 1909 reviewed. Arguments for labour market organisation strengthened. Decision of principle needed between insurance with reformed Poor Law and relief subject to Labour Exchange test. Unsuitability of money relief for long unemployment. Need to prevent insurance or relief from subsidising industrial disorganisation. Suggested scheduling of trades. Compulsory de-casualisation.
The new problem of wages and unemployment. Reduction of wages or raising of production. Expenditure on public work as a remedy for unemployment. Utility and limitations of this policy.
Unemployment still a problem of industry, not an Act of God. Organisation not spending, needed.

THE diagnosis of unemployment made twenty-one years ago in the first part of this volume was confirmed in all essentials by the Poor Law Commission of 1905-9. The recommendations of the Commission led to the policies of 1909—organisation of the labour market, insurance against unemployment, steadying of the demand for labour. To-day the problem of unemployment bulks larger than ever. Was the old diagnosis wrong or is it out of date? Were the policies wrong or was their application mishandled?

A formal answer to these questions is that the continuance of unemployment cannot invalidate the diagnosis or the policies of 1909, because these policies have not been carried through. Unemployment insurance, with all its devices for reducing claims to benefit, has been transformed into unemployment relief. Labour Exchanges, after a hopeful start, were sunk in a flood of war tasks and post-war doles; they are now reviving as employment agencies; but their special and most needed service of de-casualisation has gone by the board. Steps for deliberate steadying of the demand for labour began with the appointment in 1914 of Mr. Percy Alden's Committee on Government Contracts and ended with the vanishing of the Committee in war turmoil.

A more fruitful answer lies in recognising that unemployment to-day contains two new features. A part of it is due to changes of industrial structure, occurring with unexampled speed in the transition from war to peace, and in the aftermath. Another part is almost certainly due to disequilibrium between wages and productivity, following the abnormal rise of real wages since the

26

outbreak of war ; by raising costs of production this would have handicapped Britain's international trade, even if other conditions had remained the same. A further possibility cannot be excluded ; that the check recorded in some measures of British material progress at the turn of the century and becoming general since the war marks the beginning of a permanent shift in the economic balance of the world, transferring industry from the coal of these islands to competing sources of power elsewhere. In relation to unemployment this would operate, like the abnormal rise of real wages, to produce disequilibrium of wages and productivity ; that is to say, it would be a contributory cause of the second new feature already noted in post-war unemployment. It should be regarded, however, as a possibility rather than a certainty or a high probability. All that is certain is that before 1900 un-employment occurred in spite of a rapid expansion of employment at a rising standard of life and was presumably mitigated by this expansion, while after 1900 expansion became less general and less assured up to the outbreak of the war and since the war has been barely perceptible.

How far do these new features in the problem of unemploy-ment or our greater knowledge of old features since the diagnosis of 1909 call for a revision of the old policies? Are Labour Exchanges less needed than they seemed before or are they more needed ? What should be the future of the insurance scheme? What new policies are possible and desirable ?

The answer to the first of these questions is that effective organisation of the labour market is even more needed to-day than it seemed to be twenty years ago. New arguments have been added while the old ones remain, strengthened by new knowledge.

In the first place, in so far as unemployment to-day is due to permanent changes of industrial structure involving changes of location, rather than to transient depression, it is yet more important than before to make labour mobile, locally and between industries ; it is yet less possible than before to leave men with-out guidance in the search for work. The tables in Chapter XVI, setting out the new contrasts between growing and declining industries, between depressed and relatively prosperous districts, are sufficient illustration of this point. It has received practical recognition in the report of the Industrial Transference Board and the revival of Labour Exchange activity since that report was published.

In the second place, while some of the new conditions make fluidity of labour even more needed than before, others make it harder to secure without deliberate effort. The declining birth-rate involves a decrease of juveniles relatively to adults in the population, and thus reduces the average mobility of the whole ; it becomes each year more important to prevent diversion into wrong channels of the shrinking supply of adaptable youthful labour. The insurance scheme and the relaxation of the Poor Law are immobilising forces and need to be corrected by deliberate organisation.

In the third place, all the old elements in the problem calling for labour market organisation remain. The flux of employment —the ceaseless passing of men into and out of situations— persists ; if not greater than it was before in fact, it is greater than most people would have thought possible. Seasonal employments persist with little or no formal dovetailing between them. The hawking of labour persists. Casual employment persists ; the measure of this failure in twenty years to deal with "the most potent, the most certain, and the most extensive in its operation . . . of all the causes or conditions predisposing to pauperism" is found in the 31 per cent of unemployment in dock and wharf labour, 23 per cent in works of construction, 13 per cent in building. Each of these three industries, ending the war with numbers greatly reduced, had a golden opportunity of reform ; each was in a position then, without causing hardship, to rationalise its methods of engaging labour and to avoid building up again a needless under-employed reserve ; each has gone on in the old ways to the old result. The first of the three formally registers as required for its work enough men to make the average week for each four days or less out of six. The last two have each under the stimulus of State subsidies expanded simultaneously their employment and their unemployment. The three industries between them provided in 1929 an average of 200,000 unemployed, 17 per cent of the numbers occupied in them, one in six of all the unemployed though less than one in ten of all those insured. They are, however, only the leading examples of industries practising casual engagement ; smaller pools of casual labour are to be found scattered through many industries and between them make a formidable total.

The confirmation by new facts of the old reasons for organisation of the labour market is more important than any new reasons, interesting as some of the latter are. The experience of the Liverpool Docks scheme and other experiments in the ports since 1909 has dotted the " i "s and crossed the " t "s of every argument for de-casualisation used in the first part of this volume and in the Reports of the Poor Law Commission. It has been

26 *

shown by statistics in place of by inference and illustrations, how the demands, of individual employers in a port fluctuate independently and not simultaneously, so that the work of a group of employers is incomparably more regular than that of its units; how casual engagement by each of the separate employers collects a stagnant mass of under-employed and demoralised labour which is at once far in excess of the total needs of the port and insufficient in times of good trade to prevent local shortages; how miserably low are the average earnings over a year even of the most favoured men.[1] It has been shown by pre-war statistics and post-war experience how swiftly the building trade passes from under- to over-staffing. It has been shown by insurance records how one worker out of every four or three or less according to the state of trade becomes unemployed and employed again in the course of a year, having intervals between jobs whose reduction would mean a reduction of unemployment.

" The whole picture thus presented by the statistics of men falling out of employment and men remaining unemployed is that of a constant irregularity of employment even when employment is at its best, a ceaseless shifting from job to job, a recurrent loss of productive power and of wages in the interval between one job and the next. It seems clear that much could be done, and needs to be done, towards reducing unemployment by shortening these unproductive intervals, in other words, by hastening, through Labour Exchange organisation, the passage from employment to employment. This conclusion on general grounds is reinforced by two special considerations.

" First, there has been practically throughout the period an unsatisfied demand by employers for workmen in a good many of the insured occupations, notably in connection with shipbuilding and, to a less extent, engineering. Yet, throughout this period, never less than 7,000, and usually more than 8,000, shipbuilding operatives have been unemployed, and considerable sums have actually been paid by way of unemployment benefit to men in this trade.

" Second, unemployment has not, by any means, been evenly distributed throughout the country. Generally speaking, in the whole South of England and in Ireland there has, trade by trade, been markedly more unemployment

---

[1] See Lascelles and Bullock, *Dock Labour and Decasualisation*, ch. vi, and the record for 600 picked dockers given by Mr. Williams for Liverpool (*First Year's Working of the Liverpool Docks Scheme*, p. 103).

than in Wales, Scotland and the North of England. The mean percentages of unemployment books remaining lodged to unemployment books issued for the last six months are, in Ireland 7·6 ; in the London and South-Eastern Division 5·8 ; in the South-Western Division 4·4. No other division has a percentage above 2·6 ; two of the most important— Yorkshire and East Midlands, and Scotland and Northern— have percentages of 1·9 and 2·0. In the latter districts there has been in many directions an unsatisfied demand for labour ; in the former, while trade has on the whole been good, there have always been far larger numbers of men unemployed. The possibility of assisting men to move from the less prosperous to the more prosperous districts needs careful consideration."

This passage from the First Report on Unemployment Insurance,[1] relating to the prosperous year 1913, raises curious echoes to-day. Successive Ministers of Labour, driven one after another to extenuate the problem of unemployment which they could not solve, have pointed out how many of the unemployed are simply on the wing from one job to the next, and how, though some districts may be depressed, others are relatively prosperous. Except that the names of the prosperous and depressed districts are now exactly reversed, the Industrial Transference Board have said little that is not in the last paragraph just quoted. If it is not easy yet to point to unsatisfied demands for labour, it very soon may be ; the relative depression of wages for skilled work in engineering and other industries, as compared with less skilled work in other industries, has checked recruiting and has brought shortages of suitable labour within sight.

Finally, the problem of the man dislodged from his regular post when past middle age deserves mention. Twenty years ago, it was argued, on somewhat limited facts, that while advancing years were seldom in themselves a cause for losing employment, they were a serious difficulty in the way of regaining employment once it has been lost ; most employers taking on new men habitually preferred the younger man, even for a post well within the capacity of the older one. The suggestion was made accordingly that Labour Exchanges should work with a definite policy of helping older men preferentially to all the posts within their capacity, leaving to the younger generations the task of finding and forcing fresh openings for themselves. Post-war experience illustrates and supports this completely. [2]

[1] Cmd. 6965, §§ 248-50.   [2] See pp. 121, 211, and 440-42.

Statistically, it has been shown that older men are no more likely to lose work than younger ones; they are perfectly capable of rendering satisfactory service. Practically, apart from the casual occupations and the congested areas of mining and one or two other trades, the one intractable part of the unemployment problem for most Labour Exchanges is represented by the men of fifty-five and upwards, anxious to work, with long records of work behind them, with ten or more years of good work in them, but unable, once they have lost work with their old employer, to persuade a new employer to try them. Just because each employer, having the choice between two new men, tends to prefer the younger, the older man is never given a chance at all; youth is allowed to drive out age too soon. The one real solution of this intractable problem is that employers generally should be more ready to try the older men whom they do not know and should help the Exchanges to carry out the policy suggested above. It may be said that employers are not philanthropists and cannot be expected to engage labour in any way but that in which they think convenient to themselves. If that is so, employers must reconcile themselves to causing and paying for much needless unemployment.

The organisation of the labour market, in all its aspects—de-casualisation, recruiting of trades by total not local needs, guidance of juveniles in the choice of careers, transference from depressed to prosperous areas, retention for the older men of all the older men's places—involves changes in previous industrial methods and attitudes. How those changes are to be brought about and whether by persuasion or by regulation in each case, is a matter beyond the scope of this volume. On the special topic of de-casualisation something more will be said in discussing the future of unemployment insurance. In general the purpose of this chapter is not to be a compendium of practical reforms but to show briefly where, in the light of twenty years' experience, the diagnosis and policies of 1909 stand to-day.

The main constructive policy of 1909—organisation of the labour market—is more certainly and more urgently needed than before. What judgment is to be passed on the second policy— unemployment insurance—or rather, what is to be done with the new form of relief to the able-bodied that has grown out of the insurance scheme of 1911?

The history of unemployment insurance is very different from that of labour market organisation. In place of struggling for life against apathy and distrust, being thrust into a corner, being rejected wholly in the field of greatest service, as has been the fate of the Exchanges, insurance has grown to overshadow every other measure for dealing with unemployment. The first insurance scheme exacted a weekly contribution of $2\frac{1}{2}$d. from each of less than $2\frac{1}{4}$ million workmen and added an equal contribution from their employer and about $1\frac{2}{3}$d. from the State, in order to give the workman 7s. a week for a maximum of fifteen weeks of unemployment in twelve months. The $2\frac{1}{4}$ millions have become 12 millions, the 5d. from the employer and workman has become (for men) 15d., the 7s. a week has become 17s., with substantial dependants' allowances in addition, the benefit has become practically unlimited in duration. The income of the unemployment fund, from an average of under $2\frac{1}{2}$ million pounds a year, has become 40 millions.

With this growth of scale has come a fundamental change in the character of the scheme. It has been converted, practically since extended benefit became continuous in 1924, formally since standard benefit became unlimited on a flat rate of contributions in 1928, into a system of general unemployment relief financed mainly by a tax on employment. This has happened, under pressure of post-war conditions, because two of the main presuppositions of the insurance scheme were not fulfilled. The scheme of 1911 was meant to be accompanied both by effective organisation of the labour market reducing industrial unemployment to its minimum, and by a reform of the Poor Law, giving appropriate relief in restorative institutions to those that fell through the meshes of insurance; it was never meant to be the last as well as the first defence against destitution.

The first step towards sound decision as to the future of the unemployment insurance scheme is to realise how completely its present differs from its past, and in the light of that realisation to face frankly the alternative courses open and all that each involves —the alternatives of getting back and going forward.

One alternative is to go further along the road already travelled, to recognise the seeming logic of events, and to regard every person as entitled to maintenance up to a certain level, irrespective of any contributions paid by him, so long as by signing regularly at a Labour Exchange he proves that he is genuinely unemployed—that is to say without work, able to work, and unable to get work.

This alternative dispenses with the need for any further agency, such as the Poor Law, for relief of the unemployed. It involves, however, re-consideration of the contributory system. Once the principle of insurance is abandoned for the principle of relief, the employer's and workman's contributions under the present scheme become a tax on employment with few compensating advantages; all the arguments urged in 1911 as to the advantage of interesting employers and work-people in the solvency of the scheme and of making the work-people see it as an extension of trade union benefits have disappeared. On fiscal grounds a tax on employment is hard to defend; it does not come out of profits; it goes directly into costs of production; it discourages a desirable activity. Admission of such a specialised tax throws away the main safeguard of economy in the British financial system—Treasury responsibility for the Budget; the tax is one likely to grow, as it has grown, rapidly. If unemployment insurance is going to become unemployment relief subject to the Labour Exchange test, the present plan of financing it mainly by a direct tax on employment has little to commend it.

The other alternative is to get back to the principles of insurance embodied in the Act of 1911, of securing to every workman, in virtue of contributions made by him while working and by his employer, the right to a definite income for a limited period of unemployment. This involves, on the one hand, an attempt to adjust contributions to risks of unemployment and, on the other hand, the organisation of some kind of relief to be given to those who run out of insurance.

The first of these consequential requirements presents no serious difficulties. Even though it be decided, as possibly it must be decided, that differentiation of the stamps to be affixed to unemployment books is not practicable, except for very broad distinctions—such as that between agriculture and industry—other modes of differentiation remain. The regular workmen's case can be met by refunds, like that given at the age of sixty in the Act of 1911. Industries and employers with unemployment above the average can be made to pay for it, as is suggested later, by any one of several devices. The possibilities of raising money to pay for unemployment are not exhausted by the plan borrowed from Germany in 1911, of requiring an adhesive stamp to be stuck on a contribution card for each week of employment.

The second consequential requirement is more troublesome; it means carrying out some reform of the Poor Law in relation to the able-bodied. This was postulated alike in the first part of this volume and in both Reports of the Poor Law Commission. Here lies the main difference of principle between the alternatives named above. The giving of money without other conditions during unemployment was justified in 1911 as a means of tiding over temporary depression men who needed nothing but tiding over; the assumption that underlay limitation of the period of benefit was that those who remained unemployed beyond a certain time needed something more than tiding over in their own trades and places. Prolonged unemployment suggested that those suffering from it were superfluous, or out of place or unfit; it would tend to make them unfit if they were not so already. For such men, as Mr. Davison puts it, " maintenance is not enough ".[1] The main argument for the second alternative is that it would make easier the distinction between industrial maintenance, by spreading of wages, and relief which sooner or later must involve pressure on the individual to change his trade or place or ways. It would, no doubt, be possible in a pure relief system to graduate the terms of relief, and give it on terms of increasing discipline for prolonged unemployment. But though possible it would be much harder. What does not seem possible, without grave damage, is to continue any longer to mix up relief with insurance. The payment of insurance contributions does not now materially add to the self-respect of the workman and does not give him and his employer any sense of being interested in the solvency of the scheme. But the ghost of insurance rights haunts the scheme and makes it hard to discriminate between those for whom maintenance is enough and those who need something more.

The first step, then, out of the present troubles, is to choose between having an insurance scheme and having a relief scheme. However this choice is made, the second step is the same : to determine that assistance to the unemployed shall not stand in the way of preventing unemployment. The danger to be avoided, as has been argued earlier, lies less in the demoralising influence of a generous plan of assistance upon the individual workman, than in its effect on the minds of those in authority—governments, trade unions, leaders of industry. This danger arises under each of the alternatives named above ; it is inherent in any adequate provision for unemployment, whether by insurance or by relief.

The remedy for carelessness of Governments about the causation of unemployment lies outside the special scope of this volume. The problem to be solved is part of the general problem of persuading Governments to see economic problems steadily and see them whole, and not either in the fits and starts of inexpert Cabinet Committees or sectionally through the eyes of administrative experts, concerned each with some one object, whether it be restoration of the gold standard, or avoidance of a strike of miners, or balancing the national budget or saving the local rates. The steps taken by the present Government for the formation of an

---

[1] R. C. Davison, *The Unemployed*, ch. vii (Longmans, 1929).

Economic Advisory Council, served by a staff of trained economists, represent a notable move in the right direction; whether they go far enough time will show.[1] It is sufficient illustration of the point made here that, during ten years of unexampled unemployment, not one of the five successive Governments in charge has set on foot any scientific enquiry into the causes of unemployment; each has turned itself and Imperial Parliament into a Board of Guardians voting on rates of relief. The investigations of the Royal Commission of 1905-9 stand unrepeated.

The problem of carelessness of unemployment in wage bargains is also too general for discussion here. The second of the alternatives named before, of re-establishing something like a real insurance scheme in whose solvency employers and work-people might feel an interest, would help. For the rest, reliance must be placed on wider general understanding of the relation between wages and unemployment.[2]

The problem of how to prevent maintenance of the unemployed from subsidising and perpetuating industrial methods directly productive of unemployment bears directly on the subject of this volume and calls for discussion. This discussion will be simplified by thinking in the first instance in terms of insurance, that is, of supposing that a genuine insurance scheme is to be re-established, and is to be backed by a suitable Poor Law. The further step required is, in one way or another within the insurance scheme, to provide for differentiation between industries or employers, to penalise the unnecessary creation of unemployment and to reward and stimulate prevention. This does not involve unemployment insurance by industries, in the sense attached to that phrase nine or ten years ago, namely the breaking up of the general insurance scheme into many separate schemes, with differing benefits, conditions, procedure, and machinery, with separate funds and formal transfers of insured persons from one fund to another. There may be advantage in having a special scheme of benefits as well as of contributions for one or two well-defined occupations, such as dock labour. But there is nothing to be gained and there is much to be lost by

---

[1] Those who care to may refer to two articles by myself on "An Economic General Staff" appearing in the *Nation* in December, 1923, and January, 1924. As the copyright in the idea of such a staff has been claimed by many people and by some attributed to myself, I may be allowed to add that the suggestion of an economic general staff was the first and most emphatic recommendation of a Committee of Economists appointed in 1917 to consider the probable state of industry after the war. I was not a member of that Committee and had forgotten all about it when I wrote my two articles, but I must have read their report at some time and have plagiarised it unconsciously in 1924.

[2] See also Professor Clay's article, previously cited, in the *Economic Journal* for September, 1929.

departing generally from the plan of a uniform benefit, paid on the same principles by the same organisation, to all insured persons wherever they may be. Unity of the insurance scheme, however, and uniformity of benefit rules and procedure, can be combined with differentiation of contributions.

The specific suggestion now put forward is that the Minister of Labour should have power to schedule any industry having excessive unemployment, and that scheduling should have two consequences; first, that all engagements of work-people should be made through a Labour Exchange, so as to bring the recruiting of the industry under supervision and limitation; second, that funds required to meet the excessive unemployment would be raised by some special levy on the industry through the employers. The levy might be either in substitution for or in addition to the ordinary insurance contributions, and the form of it might vary from one industry to another. In dock labour, for instance, which would certainly be scheduled, the levy might be a fee for each man registered as entitled to seek work in the industry. In building or cotton it might take the form of an "employment termination due," that is a tax on each dismissal leading to a claim for benefit. A yet more drastic plan would be to make each employer individually liable to the unemployment fund for the whole or a proportion of the benefit paid by the fund to any workman formerly employed by him, the liability being fixed either on the last employer or on a succession of employers, in proportion to the workman's length of service with each.[1] This might have several good effects which would not be wholly lost even when employers took to insuring mutually or otherwise against their liabilities. Each employer would be under strong pressure to make his employment as regular as possible, would have a reason for taking back his old employees if available in place of opening the door to new labour, would be chary of dismissing older men, and would assist the administrators of the scheme to keep off benefit men who had left voluntarily or through misconduct.[2] The whole attitude of employers towards the solvency of the unemployment fund might be radically and beneficially changed. All these methods embody the principle of charging industries and employers, not in proportion to the employment given by them, but in proportion

---

[1] This suggestion was originally made by me in the *Manchester Guardian Commercial Supplement* of 1st February, 1923.

[2] Whenever a claim to benefit is made a form is sent to the last employer inviting him to inform the Exchange of the reason of the workman's leaving. Neglect to reply to this form is common, even when, as sometimes appears later, the cause of leaving is such as would disqualify the workman for benefit.

to unemployment or to the tendency of their methods to bring it about. It is not suggested, of course, that every excess above the average unemployment should at once lead to the scheduling of an industry. Within limits and so long as this does not subsidise the continuance or creation of unemployment, the various industries may and should help to bear one another's burdens. "Excessive unemployment" for scheduling purposes would mean something different from unemployment above the general average.

It is not to be expected that, however excessive unemployment were defined, the proposal made here would command the ready assent either of the employers or of the work-people in the industries to be scheduled. But as the eminently conservative majority of the Poor Law Commission observed of dock labour twenty-one years ago, a system of employment "detrimental to the moral and material well-being of the community . . . cannot be considered solely from the standpoint of the employer and employés". The principle of regulating engagement of labour in industries with heavy unemployment has already been admitted for coal.[1] The principle of making industries provide for the exceptional unemployment created by their methods of engaging labour or involved in their conduct of business represents the barest justice to other industries, to the taxpayer and, last but not least, to the individual workman for whom relief is the sorriest of substitutes for regular work.

The foregoing suggestions have been made in the terms of a restored insurance scheme. They, or their equivalent, are not less but more important, if, in the alternative, the tendency towards permanent public relief in place of insurance continues. A State which undertakes to relieve adequately and indefinitely from a bottomless purse all the unemployed, will soon find itself subsidising the manufacture of unemployment, unless it adopts countermeasures. The only difference, here, between a scheme of State relief and one of insurance is that with the former the countermeasures—that is to say the regulation of recruiting, casual engagements, short-time and so forth—must be stronger and more direct.

Here the subject of unemployment insurance must be left.   To

---

[1] Section 18 in Part IV of the Mining Industry Act, 1926, authorises the Minister of Labour, after consultation with associations of employers and workmen in the coal-mining industry to make regulations for securing that, in the recruitment of persons over eighteen years of age for the industry, preference should be given up to 31st December, 1929, to those who were so employed during the week ending 30th April, 1926. As an alternative to formal regulations under this section, the mine-owners agreed to carry out the principle of the section by notifying to the Labour Exchanges in the first instances vacancies for adult mining labour for which they had no miners available.

embark upon examination of details, however important, such as the definition of continuous employment or payment of benefit for short time or the means of defending the fund against married women or the rates of contribution and benefit, would be beyond the limits and the purpose of this volume. Nor is such discussion of minor problems the most urgent need to-day. It is necessary first to decide where we stand in regard to the general principles of insurance or relief and in what direction we wish to move. When that decision of principle has been taken and not before, the lines of solution for minor problems will begin to appear.

Organisation of the labour market and insurance against unemployment were the linked main policies of 1909. They were not the only policies. In the first part of this volume there are various minor suggestions, such as those for elasticity of working hours and of wages; there is an outline of principles of public relief to the unemployed, by free and detention "colonies"; there is a criticism of relief work—all finding an echo in one or both of the Reports of the Poor Law Commission. There was, besides all this, one main policy already named—the steadying of the demand for labour by systematic distribution of public work on business lines. This policy has never seriously been tried. What bearing would it have on present problems?

As set out in Chapter X and enlarged in the Minority Report, this policy was conceived essentially as a means for smoothing cyclical fluctuations of employment. The future of cyclical fluctuation in the changed and changing monetary conditions of the world is obscure. The possibilities of credit control are being canvassed more actively than ever. Whatever these possibilities, recent experience has shown that we cannot yet count on freedom from sudden and violent depressions, causing widespread increase of unemployment. It is still highly relevant to the circumstances of to-day to discuss the general question of the possible influence on unemployment of public works designed to reduce it. The policy of national development by public expenditure as a means of reducing unemployment was made a main issue by one of the political parties in the General Election of 1929. It has, however, more than the transient interest of most election issues and has been the subject of controversy between economists. The voting of the electors need not be taken as a scientific judgment on the merits of this controversy.

On one side stands "the orthodox Treasury dogma," recited by Mr. Winston Churchill in his Budget speech of 1929, "that, whatever might be the political and social advantages, very little additional employment . . . can, in fact, and as a general rule, be created by State borrowing and State expenditure ". This dogma finds expression in the last of the official " Memoranda on Certain Proposals relating to Unemployment " issued by the Conservative Government of 1929 in criticism of the Liberal programme. The economic arguments underlying the dogma have been given by Mr. R. G. Hawtrey. Mr. J. M. Keynes and Mr. H. D. Henderson have given the popular case, and Professor Pigou the academic case against the dogma.[1]

Clearly the dogma, if interpreted without its saving words "as a rule," and as an absolute barrier to any attempt to stimulate employment by public expenditure and public borrowing, is untenable. The amount of resources available for expenditure on employment is not fixed but growing ; otherwise employment could never grow. Moreover, the rate of growth is not pre-determined ; otherwise it would be folly to praise the enterprise of business men as making employment. Public expenditure can reduce unemployment, just as private expenditure can, if it does not involve as a consequence an equivalent reduction of similar expenditure elsewhere. There are at least four ways in which public expenditure can be incurred without this consequence :

1. If it reduces the consumers' unspent margin by giving an attractive opportunity for investment of their idle balances.

2. If it leads to creation of bank credit which would not otherwise have been created.

3. If it leads to imports of capital from abroad.

4. If it diminishes export of capital in the form of gold.

The last two possibilities are of theoretical importance only. The first two, though regarded by Mr. Hawtrey as practically unimportant, are admitted by him in theory. " The fundamental objection in principle," concludes Professor Clay, ". . . that public enterprise would merely divert without increasing employment, does not appear to be well founded." . . . " It is arguable that Mr. Hawtrey's two exceptions both cover the present conditions of British industry." [2] It may be argued, indeed, that the second exception would normally apply to the time of cyclical trade depression familiar before the war. One common feature of such times was stagnation continuing in face of a low bank rate, private enterprise refusing to be roused by any amount of cheap money, dealers and manufacturers still paralysed by fear of further fall of

---

[1] Cmd. 3331. Mr. Hawtrey's views are set out in Chapter VI of his volume of essays on *Trade and Credit* (Longmans, 1928), and Professor Pigou's in an article entitled " The Monetary Theory of the Trade Cycle " (*Economic Journal*, June, 1929). Mr. Keynes' and Mr. Henderson's contribution is a pamphlet entitled *Can Lloyd George Do It ?* (May, 1929).

[2] *The Post-War Unemployment Problem* (Macmillan, 1930), pp. 132-3.

prices and of making losses in place of profits.   In such circumstances public enterprise, making for use rather than for sale at a profit and thus not cowed by the same fears, might lead to creation of credit that would not otherwise have come into being.[1]

There is another case in which public expenditure may be an appropriate remedy.   Just as public expenditure on setting works in hand may diminish unemployment if it is incurred at a time of trade depression when private enterprise is slack, so it may diminish unemployment if it is planned to employ classes of labour which for some special reason are unemployed and not likely to be absorbed in the unguided expansion of private enterprise.   Where, as since the war, unemployment arises to some extent through changes of industrial structure involving decay of old-established industries or a new localisation of labour, public expenditure may be designed deliberately and beneficially to favour the employment of men who have been displaced, even at the expense of slowing down the development of some new industry and the speed with which youthful labour elsewhere is advanced into adult occupation. Selective subsidies to decaying industries or rather for the employment of men displaced from such industries may have economic advantages as definitely as may protection of infant industries. The only issue is as to whether the public expenditure is well designed for its special purpose, that is to say, whether employment can be found suitable in place and character to the class of unemployed labour in view.   The difficulties to be solved are practical—that of finding work to be done which is at once valuable for public purposes, suited to the kind of men unemployed, and either within reach of their homes or so placed that housing can be provided, without excessive cost.   Such difficulties are not insoluble, though they limit severely the application of the method.[2]

The particular problem that to-day calls most loudly for treatment by this method is the problem of those depressed mining areas which have now more population than they can ever hope to support again.   The theoretical solution put forward by

[1] Mr. Hawtrey's disregard of this as a practically important possibility is, it may be suggested, one result of his exaggerating the automatism of the credit and price cycle and the effect of cheap credit alone in producing a revival of trade. (See pp. 331-2 above.)

[2] The fact that the employment to be found on public works is terminable is an advantage rather than a disadvantage ; the object in view is not the starting of new permanent industry but the easing of an industrial transition, or evening out a cyclical fluctuation.   The practical difficulties limit the scope of the remedy more rigidly in relation to changes of industrial structure than in relation to cyclical fluctuation ; the latter is by its nature general and the resulting unemployment more widely spread, so that problems of place and housing are less serious.

the Industrial Transference Board of moving population elsewhere shatters against the practical difficulties and intolerable slowness of transfer. Juveniles and single men and men without dependents are being moved or are moving themselves; many of the older men are chained by domestic immobility. This is a fact that has to be recognised as unflinchingly as the fact emphasised by the Industrial Transference Board, that no work will arise of itself for these men in their present homes. The choice lies probably between maintaining them in idleness indefinitely and organising for them by public expenditure such work as one can within their powers and within their reach.

For one new element accordingly in post-war unemployment, though one that each year that passes makes less important—for the black spots of mining and the heavy trades—national development by public expenditure is a remedy appropriate and necessary though limited in scope. To the other new element named above, to disequilibrium between wages and productivity, it is irrelevant, as are the other remedies previously considered—organisation of the labour market, unemployment insurance or credit control—as are protection, safe-guarding, Empire trade, free trade, and the rest. If and in so far as unemployment is now resulting because, through fall of prices, real wages have risen and become rigid at a point above the productivity of the marginal labourer, the remedy must be sought in restoring the equilibrium thus disturbed. It cannot be found elsewhere.

Since, however, the equilibrium desired involves three distinct elements—productivity, wages, and numbers seeking employment at those wages—it may be approached in several ways. Theoretically at least four plans are open: to reduce numbers, to raise productivity per head, to lower wages directly, to lower wages indirectly by raising prices. Practically the order of merit of these four plans is the inverse to their order of ease of accomplishment. Reduction of numbers by emigrating the unemployed surplus, if it could be done without other change in economic conditions, would be a full and immediate solution; unfortunately the married middle-aged industrial workers who are apt to form the surplus here seldom find it easy to gain admittance to other lands. At the other end of the list of plans comes indirect lowering of wages by rise of prices; this and the absorption of the unemployed in a temporary boom could probably be achieved very rapidly by a Government prepared for inflation, but the inevitable after-effects of such a policy rule it out. Substantially the choice lies between the second and third of the plans named— raising productivity to overtake wages or lowering wages to meet productivity.   Here, too, the better plan is the harder.   To concentrate, as a remedy for unemployment, on lowering wages, is open to several objections.   One objection is that the swollen costs of production to-day include other elements than wages, e.g., interest on debentures which also have profited by fall of prices. Another and more important objection is that to admit reduction of wages as the prime means of reducing costs of production weakens the incentive to progress ; the effect of such a doctrine on efficiency has been poignantly illustrated by the coal-mining industry.[1]   This objection is only one aspect of the fundamental objection of principle to lowering standards of life in face of a risk of over-population.   On the other hand, increase of productivity cannot be achieved by wishing for it and cannot be achieved rapidly by continuing on old lines in industry.   Output per head does now rise year by year as the result of technical and other improvements, but the rise since 1924 is put by the best authorities at certainly under 2 per cent a year.   Even this has been offset of late by an equal or greater fall of prices raising real wages.   To make an early impression on unemployment without lowering wages, progress on a different scale is needed.   Whether and how it can be brought about must be left for discussion elsewhere and by others.[2]   Here three general observations must suffice.

First, since with the present levels of industrial efficiency and wages severe unemployment cannot be avoided, the obligation on those who wish to maintain wages is clear.   The higher standard of life of those who are in regular work is to some extent won at the cost of the unemployment of those who are not.   The former

---

[1] See the summary of the Mining Association policy in the *Report of the Royal Commission on the Coal Industry, 1925*, p. 225.

[2] " Rationalisation " is in some danger of becoming like the old lady's " blessed word Mesopotamia," an incantation to be repeated hopefully by all and sundry three times a day without any clear perception of its meaning.   Professor Clay defines the term clearly enough as implying " industrial combination with the object of securing not monopoly prices, but certain productive economies ".   The object in view is the general one of reducing cost by increasing efficiency of production.   The difference between rationalisation and other modes of increasing efficiency—such as technical improvements of machinery and processes or educational improvements in the training of workmen—lies in taking as the starting-point the relations of different productive units ; the assumption underlying rationalisation finds its analogy in town-planning. It is no more likely that the individualistic growth of many small separate businesses will produce an industry laid out on the lines of maximum overall efficiency, than it is likely that the disorderly uncontrolled activities of innumerable small property owners and builders will produce a well-planned town, without needless corners, duplicate streets, and traffic congestions.   At some stage or other the town planner and the industry planner should have an innings.   The assumption is reasonable in itself, and has been illustrated both positively and negatively of late years—positively by the success of the chemical industry, negatively by the failure of coal.

and their leaders are in honour bound, not merely to remove restrictions on output, not simply to avoid opposing improvements of industrial technique and organisation, but to further such improvements in every way within their power.

Second, even the most rapid rise of productivity may have little or no effect on the volume of unemployment, if its gains are at once swept away by wage demands. Output has somehow to be allowed to overtake consumption, and this means, at the very least, that for some time to come there should be no further general rises of wages.

Third, improvements of industrial efficiency, however beneficial in the end and however necessary to-day to diminish unemployment, often in the first instance make unemployment by displacing men from their previous occupations. In the long run, no doubt, such improvements increase rather than diminish the total demand for labour, but the new demands may be in other industries or places or for work-people of a different kind from those who have lost employment. How soon, therefore, the labour displaced by rationalisation or any other form of industrial progress can be re-absorbed is essentially a question of mobility. The old argument for labour market organisation returns as always.

The record of the past twenty years of dealing with unemployment is depressing. Those parts of the policies of 1909 which were aimed at the reduction of unemployment—de-casualisation and the evening out of the demand for labour—have failed most completely of adoption ; the Labour Exchanges, indispensable as they have become, have had a limited and inadequate success ; the disorganisation of the labour market continues. That part of the policies which was designed mainly, though not wholly, for relief of unemployment has grown portentously and grown always in the direction of becoming relief and nothing else.

Yet the failures of these twenty years must not be taken too hardly. After all, what a twenty years they have been ! One may dream that but for the war there would be no failure to record. And the main result of the fresh examination here made of unemployment should not be discouraging. In the concluding chapter of Part I, the policies then proposed were summed up as making the supply of labour more capable of following and waiting for the demand—of following the demand through labour market organisation, of waiting for it through insurance. To these policies another must now be added—that of adjusting production to standards of living or standards of living to production. But, with this addition, unemployment remains, in 1930 as in 1909, a problem of industry, not an Act of God.

Some things in Britain's destiny are beyond management by its governments and its leaders; the slow vast forces shaping and re-shaping the economic structure of the world and the swift changes of personal desire that determine future numbers work uncontrollably, outside their reach or beneath their feet. But unemployment is not of these. It is no mysterious visitation, but in the main the consequence of our own choices, the measure of how our industry adjusts itself to the changing world. For one great industry the changes have been too catastrophic for adjustment and have left a disaster for which there is no full remedy. The problem of the ruined mining areas stands by itself—an ill to make the best of till time ends it, by moving one by one all who can move, by expenditure in organising such work as is possible for those who cannot move. Apart from this acute but limited problem, we know what to do if we wish to get back to the level of unemployment that ruled before the war; we must either lower our standards of life or bring production up to justify them. We know also what to do if we wish to bring unemployment below that level; carry out the main preventive policy of 1909 and organise completely the labour market, abolishing the hawking of labour and casual under-employment and the anarchic recruiting of trades and the blind choice of careers. These things cannot be done in a day, but with time they can be done. They cannot be done by wishing for them but, by fixed purpose, by willing means as well as ends, by counting and deciding to pay the price, they can be done. If we prefer not to do them, if we think the cost of curing unemployment too high, we may continue instead to pay for unemployment; the post-war situation puts frankly the question, how much unemployment we are prepared to carry in order to avoid surrender of standards of life once gained.

Solution of the problem of unemployment is thus practicable to-day as it was practicable twenty years ago. The price of a solution is perhaps higher but it is payable in the same coin. " 'Practicability' is never anything but a relative term—dependent upon the urgency with which an object is desired and upon the inconveniences which men are prepared to undergo in its pursuit. It is practicable for most people to run a mile to save a life. It is not practicable for anyone to run a mile unless he is prepared to get warm. So it is not practicable for a nation to get a mastery of unemployment without being prepared to submit to some change of industrial methods and customs. The problem of unemployment—this is a point that cannot be too strongly

27 *

emphasised—is insoluble by any mere expenditure of public money. It represents not a want to be satisfied but a disease to be eradicated. It needs not money so much as thought and organisation." The repeated lesson of twenty-one years since those words were penned is how much more abundant is money than thought, how much harder it is, for the cure of social ills, to change men's habits and open their minds than to slit their purses—how much harder and how much more important.

STATISTICAL SUPPLEMENT.

THE main object of the first part of the Statistical Supplement is to give wherever available and likely to be of interest later figures corresponding to those in the original text (Part I).

These later figures are described sometimes as continuations, carrying on to 1913 or occasionally later series of annual or monthly figures which in the text end in 1908 or earlier, and sometimes as supplements, giving for later epochs figures which may be of interest as comparing or contrasting with those in the text.

Occasionally later information has led to a revision of the figures originally printed. In all these cases the table now printed in the text is marked R to indicate that it has been revised. The nature of the revision is stated in the relevant part of the Statistical Supplement.

Comment on the continuations and supplements is confined to the briefest possible indication of salient differences of tendency or result. The sources of the figures, whether appearing in the text or in the Supplement, are named in the Supplement. "Statistical Abstracts" mean the "Statistical Abstracts for the United Kingdom".

The later part of the Supplement contains figures and statistical notes dealing with points in Part II, which seemed too cumbersome for the text.

Page 7. *Continuation of:*

TABLE I.—PRINCIPAL INDUSTRIES IN UNITED KINGDOM, 1855-1907.

Period.	Coal: Production per Head. Tons.	Pig Iron: Production per 100. Tons.	Raw Cotton: Consumption per Head. Lbs.	Raw Wool: Consumption per Head. Lbs.	Shipbuilding: Tonnage per 1,000.
1905-1913	5·89	21·7	42·9	12·72	21·35
1920-1925	5·26	13·5	31·4	12·31	17·62
1908	5·92	20·5	39·1	11·80	13·44
1909	5·93	21·4	42·7	11·96	13·94
1910	5·89	22·3	36·2	13·57	15·56
1911	6·00	21·0	43·2	13·96	24·44
1912	5·73	19·3	46·1	13·19	24·10
1913	6·30	22·5	47·6	13·84	26·36
1914	5·77	19·4	45·9	11·59	22·47
1915	5·71	19·8	43·9	20·66	9·24
1916	5·86	20·7	45·4	16·14	9·70
1917	5·74	21·5	41·2	16·80	17·84
1918	5·28	21·1	34·3	12·19	19·15
1919	5·15	16·6	32·2	22·62	22·85
1920	4·94	17·3	36·9	16·27	27·50
1921	3·46	5·6	22·1	10·92	20·24
1922	5·27	10·3	29·9	15·57	13·32
1923	5·80	15·6	28·9	8·41	8·59
1924	5·57	15·2	28·1	10·03	18·31
1925	5·06	13·0	34·2	9·66	14·14
1926	2·62	5·1	32·1	11·30	8·22
1927	5·19	15·0	32·4	11·63	15·72
1928	4·91	13·6	31·8	11·07	17·98
1929	5·28*	15·6	30·7	11·71	19·16

* Provisional figure.

The figures in Table I have been obtained by dividing the total quantities produced or consumed annually by the corresponding estimated population of the United Kingdom as given in the *Statistical Abstracts*, which also supply the quantities of coal, pig iron and ships produced. The figures from 1915 to 1920 inclusive are based on civilian population only. The quantities from 1922 onwards relate to Great Britain and Northern Ireland only, but the population includes the Irish Free State. The cotton figures were obtained from the *Seventeenth Abstract of Labour Statistics* up to 1912 and subsequently from *Tattersall's Cotton Trade Review* (January, 1928) treating each bale as weighing 500 lbs. From 1905 to 1912 both sets of figures are available; though the figures for individual years differ at times (perhaps through difference of seasons) the means for the eight years are very close : 42·3 from *Abstract of Labour Statistics* and 42·5 from *Tattersall*. The quantities of raw wool consumed come from *Statistics of the Worsted, Woollen and Artificial Silk Trades*. The pig iron figures taken by themselves are deceptive because, to some extent, the place of pig iron has been taken by steel. Steel, as well as pig iron, is included in the table showing " Material Progress " in Chapter XVII.

Page 9. *Continuation of :*

TABLE II.—RATES OF MONEY WAGES AND PRICES, 1878-1907.

(BOARD OF TRADE INDEX NUMBERS, 1900 = 100.)

Mean of years.	Wages.						Prices (wholesale).
	Building.	Coal Mining.	Engineering.	Textile.	Agriculture.	Mean of five groups.	
	1	2	3	4	5	6	7
1908-1913	101·37	92·47	103·40	108·82	106·03	102·40	109·4

The figures above for 1908-1913 and those for 1888-1897 and 1898-1907 in the table now printed in the text are based on figures in the *Eighteenth Abstract of Labour Statistics ;* the latter differ slightly (through later information) but not materially from the figures in Table II as originally printed.

Retail prices are naturally better than wholesale prices for comparison with wages with a view to determining the standard of living. Mr. G. H. Wood's Index Number (*Statistical Journals,* December, 1899, and March, 1909, brought up to 1913 by figures supplied by Professor Bowley), including rent, yields the following figures on the basis 1900 = 100 :—

1878-1887 . . . 107·7
1888-1897 . . . 98·6
1898-1907 . . . 100·8
1908-1913 . . . 109·1

Page 9 :

ANNUAL VALUES OF LAND ASSESSED TO INCOME TAX UNDER SCHEDULE A.

(1900 = 100.)

Mean of: 1908-13 . . . 98·7
1914-17 . . . 98·8
1918-26 . . . 97·3

From 1915 the actual figures are not available and the results approximate only. From 1921 the classification of the source of income has been revised. From 1924 the Irish Free State has been excluded.

The figures are taken from the *Statistical Abstracts*.

Pages 16-28. *Note on Chapter II.*

The whole of this chapter has now little more than historical importance; the working of the Labour Exchanges since 1910, of partial Unemployment Insurance since 1913, and general Unemployment Insurance since 1920 has yielded entirely new sources of information. The percentage of unemployed in trade unions, having for a time been calculated and published along with the new percentages derived from the insurance scheme, has not been published since the end of 1926. A critical account of the insurance statistics is given in a paper by Mr. John Hilton printed in the *Statistical Journal* for 1923 (LXXXVI, pp. 154-193).

Page 18. *Continuation of:*

TABLE III.—UNEMPLOYED PERCENTAGE, 1894-1908.

(ALL TRADE UNIONS MAKING RETURNS.)

Year.	Jan.	Feb.	March	April	May	June	July	Aug.	Sept.	Oct.	Nov.	Dec.	Mean for Year.
1909	8·7	8·4	8·2	8·2	7·9	7·9	7·9	7·7	7·4	7·1	6·5	6·6	7·7
1910	6·8	5·7	5·2	4·4	4·2	3·7	3·8	4·0	4·3	4·4	4·6	5·0	4·7
1911	3·9	3·3	3·0	2·8	2·5	3·0	2·9	3·3	2·9	2·8	2·6	3·1	3·0
1912	2·7	2·8	11·3²	3·6	2·7	2·5	2·6	2·2	2·1	2·0	1·8	2·3	3·2
1913	2·2	2·0	1·9	1·7	1·9	1·9	1·9	2·0	2·3	2·2	2·0	2·6	2·1
1914	2·5	2·3	2·1	2·1	2·3	2·4	2·8	7·1	5·9	4·4	2·9	2·5	3·3
1915	1·9	1·6	1·3	1·2	1·2	1·0	0·9	1·0	0·9	0·8	0·6	0·6	1·1
1916	0·6	0·5	0·5	0·5	0·5	0·5	0·4	0·4	0·4	0·3	0·3	0·3	0·4
1917	0·3	0·3	0·3	0·3	0·4	0·4	0·4	0·5	1·3	1·1	1·1	1·4	0·7
1918	1·0	0·9	1·2	0·9	0·9	0·7	0·6	0·5	0·5	0·4	0·5	1·2	0·8
1919	2·4	2·8	2·8	2·7	2·1	1·7	2·0	2·2	1·6	2·6	2·9	3·2	2·4
1920	2·9	1·6	1·1	0·9	1·1	1·2	1·4	1·6	2·2	5·3²	3·7	6·0	2·4
1921¹	7·1	8·7	10·2	15·1²	19·9²	20·6²	16·9²	16·6²	15·0	15·7	16·1	16·2	14·8²
1922¹	16·5	16·2	16·2	16·8	16·2	15·5	14·5	14·1	14·4	14·0	14·2	13·8	15·2
1923¹	13·6	12·9	12·2	11·2	11·2	11·0	10·9	11·1	10·9	10·5	10·2	9·3	11·3
1924¹	8·5	8·2	7·8	7·5	7·0	7·2	7·4	7·9	8·6	8·7	8·6	9·2	8·1
1925¹	9·0	9·4	9·0	9·4	10·1	12·3	11·2	11·4	11·4	11·3	11·0	11·0	10·5
1926¹	10·6	10·4	10·1	10·0	13·2²	12·9²	13·2²	13·3²	13·6²	13·6²	13·2²	12·2	12·2²

Note.—During the War men with the forces were excluded from the base in working the percentages.

[1] The figures from 1921 onwards exclude pottery trade operatives. From July, 1924, onwards building trade operatives are also excluded from the general average.

[2] Affected by the general Coal Mining stoppage.

The table originally printed in the text was based on the *Twelfth Abstract of Labour Statistics* supplemented by the *Labour Gazettes*. In the Thirteenth and subsequent Abstracts revised figures (representing fuller and more accurate information for certain Unions) were given. The figures now printed up to 1908 in the revised text table and from 1909 onwards in the Supplement are taken from the *Nineteenth Abstract of Labour Statistics* brought up to date by *Labour Gazettes*. The effect of the revision is to make unimportant changes in 1895 and 1896 and to lower all subsequent percentages by amounts increasing gradually from ·1 to ·4 or ·5.

Page 20. *Supplement to :*

TABLE IV.—TRADES REPRESENTED IN UNEMPLOYED PERCENTAGE.

Trade.	January, 1913.		January, 1923.		January, 1926.	
	Number of Unionists included in the Returns.	Percentage contributed by each Trade.	Number of Unionists included in the Returns.	Percentage contributed by each Trade.	Number of Unionists included in the Returns.	Percentage contributed by each Trade.
Building . . .	73,708	8·3 ⎫	125,227	10·4 ⎫	—	— ⎫
Woodworking . .	⎫45,248	5·1 ⎬13·4	48,978	4·1 ⎬16·6	36,793	3·8 ⎬6·9
Furnishing . . .		⎭	25,492	2·1 ⎭	30,010	3·1 ⎭
Coal mining . .	163,614	18·5	134,396	11·2	143,869	14·7
Engineering and ship building . . .	284,918	32·2 ⎫	426,751	35·4 ⎫	342,706	35·1 ⎫
Other metal trades .	63,010	7·1 ⎬39·3	56,673	4·7 ⎬40·1	48,738	5·0 ⎬40·1
Printing, bookbinding and paper . .	62,850	7·1	95,193	7·9	105,618	10·8
Textiles . . .	124,237	14·1	130,257	10·8	125,725	12·9
Clothing (boot and shoe)	⎫54,703	6·2	74,812	6·2 ⎫9·8	81,542	8·3 ⎫13·2
„ (Other) . .	⎭		43,383	3·6 ⎭	47,878	4·9 ⎭
Miscellaneous . .	12,156	1·4	43,981	3·6	13,612	1·4
Total . . .	884,444	100·0	1,205,143	100·0	976,491	100·0

Note.—The figures are taken from the *Labour Gazettes*.

Page 25. *Continuation of:*

TABLE V.—COAL-MINING—DAYS WORKED PER WEEK.
1895-1908.

Year.	Jan.	Feb.	March	April	May	June	July	Aug.	Sept.	Oct.	Nov.	Dec.	Mean for year.
1909	5·03	5·21	5·29	4·86	5·09	4·81	4·98	5·01	5·26	5·33	5·36	5·49	5·14
1910	5·60	5·60	5·58	5·55	4·44	4·96	4·84	5·10	5·27	5·27	5·28	5·51	5·25
1911	5·56	5·56	5·53	5·00	5·33	4·49	4·82	4·65	5·44	5·56	5·50	5·54	5·25
1912	5·62	5·70	—¹	5·52	5·41	5·35	5·15	5·46	5·55	5·58	5·57	5·52	5·49
1913	5·64	5·61	5·67	5·69	5·64	5·44	5·26	5·54	5·60	5·59	5·56	5·66	5·58
1914	5·67	5·58	5·56	5·54	5·39	5·25	5·06	4·55	5·01	5·03	5·09	5·22	5·25
1915	5·49	5·62	5·68	5·69	5·63	5·65	5·01	5·60	5·65	5·63	5·64	5·70	5·58
1916	5·72	5·69	5·71	5·72	5·74	5·59	5·72	5·69	5·74	5·74	5·58	5·53	5·68
1917	5·66	5·43	5·39	5·54	5·53	5·53	5·20	5·50	5·50	5·46	5·46	5·45	5·47
1918	5·39	5·48	5·64	5·73	5·66	5·76	5·58	5·67	5·73	5·77	5·24	5·75	5·62
1919	5·56	5·73	5·65	5·59	5·74	4·92	4·80	5·70	5·66	5·68	5·69	5·71	5·53
1920	5·74	5·75	5·72	5·76	5·75	5·70	5·64	5·69	5·74	—¹	5·78	5·74	5·73
1921	5·26	4·79	4·71	—¹	—¹	5·59	4·77	4·67²	4·58	4·97	5·18		4·95
1922	5·16	5·35	5·17	5·30	4·85	4·49	4·65	5·33	5·27	5·44	5·50	5·56	5·17
1923	5·56	5·50	5·63	5·69	5·59	5·57	4·89	5·14	5·37	5·56	5·54	5·68	5·48
1924	5·17	5·66	5·68	5·71	5·31	5·07	4·61	5·17	5·18	5·13	5·26	5·36	5·28
1925	5·39	5·31	5·20	5·28	4·93	4·54	5·05	4·48	4·59	4·88	5·15	5·46	5·02
1926	5·47	5·37	5·30	5·57	—¹	—¹	—¹	—¹	—¹	—¹	—¹	5·33	5·41³
1927	5·02	5·11	4·89	5·04	4·63	4·68	4·43	4·63	4·83	4·75	4·72	4·93	4·80
1928	4·95	4·84	4·92	4·98	4·70	4·52	4·18	4·58	4·77	4·72	4·85	5·31	4·78
1929	5·24	5·46	5·59	5·00	4·95	4·86	4·56	5·05	5·09	4·93	5·07	5·19	5·08
Mean 1907-1913	5·48	5·56	5·54	5·26	5·28	5·04	5·05	5·13	5·44	5·46	5·44	5·52	5·35
Mean 1920-1929 (omitting 1921 and 1926)	5·28	5·37	5·35	5·34	5·09	4·93	4·75	5·01	5·10	5·06	5·23	5·40	5·17

¹ Disputes. No returns. ² Great Britain only henceforward. ³ Based on five months only.
Note.—The figures are taken from the *Abstracts of Labour Statistics* and the *Labour Gazettes.*

Pages 29-37. *Note on Chapter III.—Seasonal Fluctuation.*

Much fuller statistical information than that available at the time of writing this chapter was published soon after, in a Memorandum on " Statistics of Seasonal Industries and Industries carried on by Casual Labour," prepared by the Board of Trade for the Poor Law Commission of 1905-1909 and printed in Volume IX, Appendix XXI (D).   The effect of this information is to confirm nearly all that is said in Chapter III, the conclusions reached being summarised as follows, with a table " showing the slackest and busiest months in certain industries ".   There have been added to the table as printed by the Poor Law Commission certain trades for which in 1909 statistics were available only over one or two years but are now available for a substantial period. These trades are given in italics; for some of them there are two marked busy or slack seasons.

" CONCLUSIONS.[1]—(1) Seasonal fluctuation is found to a more or less marked degree in nearly every industry.

"(2) The seasonal fluctuations of different industries are by no means simultaneous.

"Both these points are illustrated by Table XIV, which forms a calendar of busy and slack times in various trades. Only those trades are taken for which it is possible to take an average over a sufficient period of years to eliminate chance variations. The bracketed figures give the unemployed percentages, the other figures are from the sources named above. It will be seen that the busiest seasons of the twenty-three industrial groups entered in the table are distributed over eleven of the twelve months in the year, the only month unrepresented being July. The slackest seasons of the said groups are distributed over ten months, the only months which escape being April and May. The greatest number of busy seasons is to be found in May, but November is also strongly represented. The greatest number of slack seasons is shown by the table in December, but this is a result to be taken with a little caution. The unemployed percentage being made up at the end of the month is liable to be affected unduly by the Christmas holidays. It does not necessarily represent the conditions throughout the month. Of the groups shown in the table as having their maximum unemployment in December, carpenters and joiners, engineers, mill-sawyers and coachbuilders have their next slackest time in January; hat makers and leather workers in November; brushmakers in August.

"(3) The importance of seasonal fluctuation varies greatly as between different trades. The seasons on the whole are least marked and least regular in industries connected with the manufacture and use of metals—engineering, shipbuilding, miscellaneous metal trades, iron and steel working, tinplate and steel sheet milling. Seasonal fluctuation is not so much absent here as liable to be overridden by other movements, in particular cyclical fluctuation. In other trades—printing, building, furnishing, clothing, and at gasworks, tramways and the London Docks—seasonal fluctuation is a prominent and regular phenomenon."

[1] *Poor Law Commission Report*, 1910, Vol. IX, Appendix No. XXI (D), page 654.

TABLE V A.[1]—SHOWING THE SLACKEST AND BUSIEST MONTHS IN
THE YEAR IN CERTAIN INDUSTRIES.

Month.	Busiest Season.	Slackest Season.
January .	London Docks, 15,236 employed daily.	Furnishing (7·88), Iron Mining, 5·46 days per week, *Bricks*, *Glass (also October)*.
February .	Paper-making (2·74).	Plumbers (7·26).
March .	Steel Smelting (2·71), Textiles.	Coopers.
April .	Brushmaking (2·42), Furnishing (2·38), *Boots and Shoes*.	
May .	Engineering (3·59), Shipbuilding (5·94), Hat-making (2·51), Leather (4·23), Coachbuilding (1·64), Clothing (1·19), *Corsets*.	
June .	Mill-sawyers (3·63), *Glass*.	London Docks, 13,560 employed daily. Coal Mining, 4·93 days per week.
July .	*Bricks*.	Steel Smelting (5·28), Iron and Steel Works, 5·35 shifts per week, Tinplates, 361 mills, *Wholesale Costumes*.
August .	Carpenters and Joiners (2·87), Coopers.	Printing and Bookbinding (5·69), Paper-making (3·64), Tobacco (9·41), *Corsets (also January)*.
September	Plumbers (5·92), Iron Mining, 5·02 days per week, *Wholesale Costumes (also March)*.	Metals, Various (2·51), Textiles, *Boots and Shoes*.
October .	Iron and Steel Works, 5·49 shifts per week.	Clothing (3·01).
November	Metals, various (2·06), Printing and Bookbinding (2·82), Tobacco (3·15), Tinplate, 390 mills.	Shipbuilding (9·86).
December	Coal Mining, 5·46 days per week.	Carpenters and Joiners (5·93), Engineering (5·33), Hat-making (4·65), Leather (5·81), Mill-sawyers (5·17), Coachbuilding (5·84), Brushmaking (12·14).

Note.—The figures in brackets after the trade represent the mean percentage
unemployed in Trade Unions.

[1] This is Table XIV of *Poor Law Commission, op. cit.*, p. 655, with the additions
noted above.

Since the War full information as to the seasonal movements
of employment in all trades is afforded by insurance statistics (see
Chapter XVI, p. 353).

Page 30.   *Supplement to :*

TABLE VI.—SEASONAL FLUCTUATION—UNEMPLOYED PERCENT-
AGES AT END OF EACH MONTH (MEAN OF 1907-1913).

Month.	Building (Carpenters and Plumbers).	Furnishing.	Engineering.	Printing.
January	10·1	10·4	5·5	5·5
February . . .	8·9	7·9	5·2	4·9
March	8·1	5·6	5·8 [1]	4·5
April	6·8	4·3	5·6	4·9
May	6·2	4·3	5·4	5·0
June	6·5	5·5	5·4	4·8
July	6·5	6·6	5·6	4·3
August	5·9	6·1	5·7	6·3
September . . .	6·7	6·1	5·6	6·0
October	7·3	6·5	5·7	5·0
November . . .	7·4	6·9	5·7	3·2
December . . .	9·0	8·9	6·3	5·1

[1] March, 1912, omitted—abnormal owing to coal dispute.
Note.—The figures are taken from the *Abstract of Labour Statistics.*

Page 33.   *Continuation of:*

TABLE VII.—BUILDING TRADE—INCREASE OR DECREASE PER CENT
IN NUMBERS EMPLOYED BY FIRMS MAKING RETURNS.

Month.	1909.		1910.		1911.		1912.		1913.	
	Skilled Men.	Labourers.	Skilled Men.	Labourers.	Skilled Men.	Labourers.	Skilled Men.	Labourers.	Skilled Men.	Labourers.
Jan.	− 2·4	+ 0·2	− 2·8	− 4·6	+ 2·0	+ 1·7	+ 0·3	+ 3·1	+ 0·3	+ 0·1
Feb.	+ 6·9	+ 2·1	+ 8·2	+ 11·0	+ 7·3	+ 2·5	+ 2·3	+ 2·7	+ 3·9	+ 4·1
March	+ 3·5	+ 1·8	+ 7·7	+ 4·7	+ 8·1	+ 5·3	+ 4·0	+ 3·7	+ 3·7	+ 0·2
April	+ 5·1	+ 9·8	+ 2·6	+ 0·6	+ 7·0	+ 7·5	+ 3·3	+ 1·4	+ 4·4	+ 6·3
May	− 0·2	− 0·3	− 1·9	+ 1·6	+ 5·1	+ 4·9	+ 0·3	+ 0·4	− 1·5	+ 2·3
June	− 2·0	− 0·8	− 2·3	+ 1·4	− 4·8	− 5·1	+ 0·2	+ 2·9	− 1·2	+ 0·9
July	+ 4·3	+ 5·1	+ 0·0	+ 2·1	+ 1·2	+ 4·3	+ 1·1	+ 0·3	+ 2·1	+ 3·0
Aug.	+ 4·8	+ 3·6	+ 6·5	+ 3·0	+ 3·9	+ 1·3	+ 5·1	+ 6·9	+ 4·6	+ 7·4
Sept.	− 4·2	− 4·6	− 5·8	− 4·5	− 3·6	− 3·0	− 2·2	− 3·5	+ 0·6	− 1·4
Oct.	− 6·4	− 5·1	− 5·4	− 5·4	− 5·8	− 4·6	− 5·9	− 3·0	− 3·3	− 2·5
Nov.	− 2·1	− 1·7	− 4·5	− 4·1	− 2·7	− 2·9	− 1·9	− 1·9	− 3·6	− 3·8
Dec.	− 7·3	− 7·2	− 6·0	− 6·3	− 6·4	− 5·5	− 3·3	− 6·6	− 5·9	− 6·4

Note.—The figures have been calculated from the numbers employed returned
in the *Labour Gazettes.*

TABLE VII A.—FLUCTUATION OF EMPLOYMENT IN THE BUILDING TRADE.

Year.	Labourers Employed per cent of Skilled Tradesmen.			Average Monthly Change per cent in Numbers Employed.					
				London.		Provinces.		Total (U.K.).	
	London.	Provinces.	Total (U.K.).	Skilled Trades-men.	Labourers.	Skilled Trades-men.	Labourers.	Skilled Trades-men.	Labourers.
1907	67·8	78·0	74·3	6·2	3·6	3·0	2·9	3·5	2·9
1908	71·3	75·8	74·2	5·9	4·9	2·9	3·7	3·7	3·8
1909	65·9	74·5	71·6	7·0	6·3	3·6	3·6	4·1	3·5
1910	66·6	75·0	72·5	7·1	5·5	3·8	4·3	4·5	4·1
1911	69·6	72·4	71·6	8·6	7·2	3·4	2·9	4·8	4·0
1912	71·8	76·6	75·4	5·6	6·7	2·5	3·3	2·5	3·0
1913	71·7	79·5	77·3	5·3	5·3	2·2	3·1	2·9	3·2
Mean for seven years	69·22	75·9	73·8	6·5	5·6	3·1	3·4	3·7	3·5

Note.—The table is based on monthly returns made by employers to the Board of Trade (*Labour Gazette*) of the numbers employed at the end of each month. The total number of employees covered by the returns is usually between 50,000 and 60,000.

The percentages in columns 2, 3 and 4 are the means of twelve monthly counts. The percentages in the rest of the table represent the mean of the changes month by month, increases and decreases alike being added together, irrespective of sign, and averaged.

TABLE VII B.—MEAN NUMBER OF WORK-PEOPLE IN BUILDING TRADE COVERED BY EMPLOYERS' RETURNS.

Year.	London.			Provinces.			Total (U.K.)		
	Skilled Trades-men.	Labourers.	Total.	Skilled Trades-men.	Labourers.	Total.	Skilled Trades-men.	Labourers.	Total
1907	9,568	6,454	16,022	16,803	13,107	29,910	26,371	19,561	45,932
1908	8,008	5,701	13,709	15,026	11,406	26,432	23,034	17,107	40,141
1909	6,958	4,595	11,553	14,196	10,564	24,760	21,154	15,159	36,313
1910	8,042	5,345	13,387	21,074	15,648	36,722	29,116	20,993	50,109
1911	9,321	6,486	15,807	22,093	15,988	38,081	31,414	22,474	53,888
1912	8,571	6,186	14,757	20,910	16,025	36,935	29,481	22,211	51,692
1913	8,271	5,929	14,200	20,889	16,606	37,495	29,160	22,535	51,695
Mean for seven years	8,391	5,814	14,205	18,713	14,192	32,905	27,104	20,006	47,110

Note.—The figures are taken from the *Labour Gazette*.

The continuation of Table VII from 1909 to 1913 shows much the same picture as in the earlier years. The mean of all the monthly changes is again slightly higher for skilled men (3·8 per cent.) than for labourers (3·6 per cent.). The sums of the decreases during the last four months for labourers are for each year as follows :—

1907	. . .	16·4
1908	. . .	25·5
1909	. . .	18·6
1910	. . .	20·3
1911	. . .	16·0
1912	. . .	15·0
1913	. . .	14·1

and over the seven years, which may be taken as a trade cycle, average 18·0, as compared with 16·4 for the one year 1907 cited in the text.

The figures in Table VII, however, deal with London and the Provinces together, and further examination shows that the conditions in the two districts are not the same. This appears from Table VII A. The mean monthly change in London is twice that in the Provinces and is greater for skilled men than for labourers (6·5 against 5·6 over the seven years 1907 to 1913); the proportion of skilled men to labourers is also higher in London than in the provinces. This last fact may mean that work treated as skilled in London is elsewhere done by labourers, or may reflect a real difference in the types of work done. The large amount of highly seasonal decorating work in London might account both for the larger proportion of skilled men (painters and paper-hangers) and for the instability of their employment.

As a check on the use of the combined London and Provinces figures, the numbers covered by the returns are given in Table VII B. The figures in Tables VII, VII A and VII B are based on returns in the *Labour Gazettes*.

Page 39.   *Continuation of:*

TABLE VIII.—CYCLICAL FLUCTUATION—TRADE UNION UNEMPLOYED PERCENTAGES AND PRODUCTION.

Year.	Engineering, Shipbuilding and Metal.	Building (Carpenters and Joiners).	Woodworking and Furnishing.	Printing and Bookbinding.	All Unions making Returns (Corrected Weights).		Raw Cotton, Lbs. consumed per Head.[3]	Pig Iron, Cwts. produced per Head.	Shipbuilding, Tons built per 1,000.
					Percentage Un-employed.	Percentage *not* Un-employed.			
1909	13·0	11·7	7·6	5·6	8·70	91·30	42·7	4·3	13·94
1910	6·8	8·3	5·4	4·9	5·10	94·90	36·2	4·5	15·56
1911	3·4	4·2	3·3	5·1	3·05	96·95	43·2	4·2	24·44
1912[1]	3·6	3·7	3·1	5·2	3·15	96·85	46·1	3·9	24·10
1913	2·2	3·3	2·4	4·0	2·10	97·90	47·6	4·5	26·36
1914	3·3	3·3	4·1	4·5	3·25	96·75	45·9	3·9	22·47
1915	0·6	2·2	2·1	3·1	1·00	99·00	43·9	4·0	9·24
1916	0·3	0·9	1·0	1·3	0·45	99·55	45·4	4·1	9·70
1917	0·2	0·5	0·6	0·6	0·60	99·40	41·2	4·3	17·84
1918	0·2	0·2	0·5	0·3	0·70	99·30	34·3	4·2	19·15
1919	3·2	1·2	1·3	1·6	2·50	97·50	32·2	3·3	22·85
1920	3·2	0·3	1·4	1·6	2·55	97·45	36·9	3·5	27·50
1921[1]	22·1	3·9	9·4	7·3	15·55	84·45	22·1	1·1	20·24
1922	27·0	7·5[2]	7·6	6·6	17·20	82·80	29·9	2·1	13·32
1923	20·6	5·0[2]	5·8	4·7	12·50	87·50	28·9	3·1	8·59
1924	13·8	1·9[2]	4·5	3·3	9·10	90·90	28·1	3·0	18·31
1925	13·5	2·2[2]	4·4	2·8	11·05	88·95	34·2	2·6	14·14
1926[1]	18·2	5·2[2]	8·2	4·3	12·70	87·30	32·1	1·0	8·22

[1] Coal stoppages.
[2] The figures from 1922 onwards are averages of the percentages unemployed at the end of each *quarter*.
[3] See note to continuation of Table I.

The unemployed percentages are taken from the *Nineteenth Abstract of Labour Statistics*, except those for all unions, which have been specially supplied by the Ministry of Labour and are corrected by the method used in *British and Foreign Trade and Industry* (the source of the earlier figures); *i.e.*, by combining, with equal weights, the mean for "Engineering, Shipbuilding and Metal Trades" with that for "All Other Trades included in the Returns". For the source of the last three columns see note to continuation of Table I.

Pages 42-43. *Continuation of:*

TABLE IX.—THE PULSE OF THE NATION.

Year.	1. Bank Rate (Average Minimum Discount Rate per cent)	2. Imports and Special Exports per Head.[1]	3. Employed Percentage (Trade Unions).	4. Wholesale Prices (1900 = 100).	5. Wages (1900 = 100).	6. Companies Registered during Year. Nominal Capital per Head.	7. Railway Receipts: Net per cent of Paid-up Capital.	8. Marriages per 1,000 of the Population, England and Wales.	9. Consumption of Beer per Head (Gallons).	10. Drunkenness. Prosecutions per 100,000.	11. Indictable Offences Tried (in Thousands).	12. Indoor, England and Wales, per 10,000 (Mean of No. at end of each Month).	13. Vagrants, London (Friday Nights).
		£ s. d.				£	£						
1908	3·00	21 14 8	91·35	103·0	101·6	2·4	3·32	15·1	26·9	576	68·1	75·7	1,114
1909	3·10	22 7 11	91·30	104·1	100·4	3·2	3·43	14·7	26·1	515	67·1	77·4	1,134
1910	3·72	24 9 9	94·90	108·8	100·8	4·7	3·59	15·0	25·3	490	66·4	77·1	1,099
1911	3·47	24 18 3	96·95	109·4	101·1	3·5	3·67	15·2	27·2	514	62·3	74·1	992
1912	3·78	26 19 2	96·85	114·9	103·7	3·8	3·55	15·6	26·8	544	67·6	73·3	699
1913	4·77	28 2 2	97·90	116·5	106·8	3·4	—	15·7	27·8	557	63·3	70·2	402
1914	4·03	24 4 10	95·75	117·2	107·8	2·5	—	15·9	26·7	549	58·6	69·2	252
1915	5·00	—	99·00	143·9	—	1·2	—	19·4	—	426	55·5	66·0	125
1916	5·47	—	99·55	186·5	—	1·1	—	14·9	—	260	58·6	62·2	91
1917	5·15	—	99·40	243·0	—	1·6	—	13·8	—	146	63·0	59·6	84
1918	5·00	—	99·30	268·1	—	3·0	—	15·3	—	91	58·4	55·3	55
1919	5·15	53 17 0	97·50	296·5	253·4	9·3	—	19·8	17·5	170	53·5	51·1	63
1920	6·71	69 15 1	97·45	358·0	303·0	12·8	—	20·2	20·8	265	60·6	51·3	140
1921	6·09	37 6 3	84·45	229·7	301·9	2·5	—	16·9	18·6	215	61·4	54·5	236
1922	3·69	35 14 1	82·80	185·0	232·8	3·0	—	15·7	15·9	211	58·2	56·2	348
1923	3·49	40 18 1	87·50	185·1	208·1	2·6	—	15·2	15·6	213	56·8	56·3	378
1924	4·00	46 3 7	90·90	193·6	210·2	2·8	—	15·3	16·4	216	57·4	55·5	385
1925	4·55	46 7 1	88·95	185·4	211·3	3·0	—	15·2	16·4	207	57·5	55·8	475
1926	5·00	41 15 11	87·30	172·5	212·3	4·8	—	14·3	15·7	184	77·6	59·7	682
1927	4·65	42 6 6	90·40	164·7	211·3	4·1	—	15·7	15·5	180	63·4	56·3	805
1928	4·50	41 14 3	89·30	163·1	209·2	5·2	—	15·4	15·2	155	61·5	56·2	713
1929	5·50	42 6 4[2]	89·60	158·4	209·2	—	—	15·8	15·0	—	—	55·4	604

[1] Excluding ships throughout.
[2] Provisional figure only.

Note.—Those figures which refer to the United Kingdom do not include the Irish Free State after 1922.

Table IX in the text has been revised in the following respects:—

(a) Imports and Special Exports from 1902 onwards.

(b) Employment from 1894 onwards, in view of the official revision of the trade union percentages mentioned in connection with Table III. The actual figures used have been furnished specially by the Ministry of Labour.

(c) Wages from 1880 onwards, in view of various official revisions of these index numbers. The figures now printed are taken from the *Nineteenth Abstract of Labour Statistics* from 1880 onwards. Before 1880 the figures are taken from the first series of *Memoranda on British and Foreign Trade and Industry* (p. 260).

(d) Crime and Drunkenness, for which figures for 1906 and 1907 have been added.

The chart on page 44 has not been revised as the changes to be made in the foreign trade and employment curves would be inappreciable.

The sources used are as follows:—

Column 1. *Statistical Abstracts* supplemented by *Board of Trade Journals.*

Column 2. *Statistical Abstracts.* The figures are the sum of the values per head of total imports and of exports of United Kingdom produce less the value of ships exported, divided by the estimated population, to bring the series into line with returns prior to 1899.

Column 3. See note to continuation of Table VIII. Up to 1926 figures refer to all Trade Unions making returns; thereafter to insured persons in Great Britain and Northern Ireland. In 1925 and 1926 the percentages for the latter are 89·00 and 87·70 as against 88·95 and 87·30 for Trade Union figures.

Column 4. *Nineteenth Abstract of Labour Statistics*, up to 1919 based on old Board of Trade index number; from 1920 onwards on the new Board of Trade index multiplied by 116·5 (the index for 1913) so as to reduce it as far as possible to basis 1900 = 100. The difference between the two indices is not great; the figure for 1920 on the old index would be 368·8 as compared with 358·0 on the new.

Column 5. *Nineteenth Abstract of Labour Statistics*, up to 1914; from 1919 onwards the mean of the revised monthly index given by the *London and Cambridge Economic Service* on the basis July, 1914 = 100 (see

Special Memorandum, Number 28), multiplied by 107·8 (the index for 1914) so as to reduce it as far as possible to the basis 1900 = 100.

Column 6. *Statistical Abstracts*—calculated by dividing estimated population into total capital.

Column 7. *Statistical Abstracts*—percentages calculated from total figures.

Column 8. *Registrar-General's Reports.*

Column 9. *Statistical Abstracts.* The figures refer to homemade beer.

Columns 10 and 11. *Annual Reports on Criminal Statistics, England and Wales*, Tables E, AB and C . The figures in column 10 for 1906 and 1914-18 had to be calculated by dividing the numbers given in Table AB by the estimated population.

Columns 12 and 13. *Reports of London Government Board* until 1919 and subsequently *Annual* and *Monthly Reports of the Ministry of Health* and *Quarterly Statements of the Numbers in Receipt of Poor Relief.* Column 12 was calculated by dividing the mean of the numbers of indoor paupers at the end of each month by the estimated population. Column 13, up to and including 1914, is the mean of all Fridays; from 1915 onwards, the mean of four Fridays only (the last in each quarter). For 1913 and 1914 these four Fridays give figures of 354 and 222 respectively, *i.e.*, in each case 12 per cent below the true figure. This suggests that the figures from 1915 onward should be increased in the proportion 100 : 88.

The continuation of Table IX shows 1909 as another year of maximum depression for employment, wages, marriages, consumption of beer, pauperism and vagrancy, just surpassing in respect of these indices the preceding year 1908, which is the worst in respect of bank rate, foreign trade, wholesale prices, companies registered, railway receipts, and indictable offences. The peak between this depression and that of 1904 is in 1906 for some indices and 1907 for others.

1913 seems designated as another peak ; as appears from the following comparison with the whole of 1913 and with the first half of 1913, all the most important indices in the first half of 1914 were suggesting a downward turn of the cycle.

Series.	Year 1913.	Jan.-June, 1913.	Jan.-June, 1914.
Employed percentage (all unions, *not* corrected)	97·9	98·1	97·7
Imports and special exports per head .	£28·1	£13·8	£13·6
Bank rate	4·77	4·79	3·17
Wholesale prices (Sauerbeck) . . .	113·0	114·4	110·3
Marriage rate	15·7	14·0	14·4
Indoor paupers	70·2	71·9	69·8
London casuals	402	447	244

The marriage rate alone is exceptional in showing the first half of 1914 slightly higher than the corresponding period of 1913. Allowing for the normal seasonal variation (as shown by Miss D. S. Thomas in *Economica*, February, 1924, page 97), the estimated rate for 1914 works out at 16·0 as compared with 15·7 in 1913. The continuing improvement of pauperism and vagrancy after the good year of 1913 presumably represents no more than the usual time lag.

In the post-war period, 1920 shows all the features of a boom, being a maximum in bank rate, foreign trade, prices, wages, companies registered, marriages, consumption of beer, and drunkenness, and being only just beaten by 1919 in employment and (inverted) pauperism.

The generally lower level of consumption of beer, drunkenness, and vagrancy after the war is striking. Indoor pauperism is also lower, but this results presumably from the greater freedom in giving outdoor relief.

Pages 55-56—*Note on Table X and Chart III.*

The figures in Table X called for general revision through the availability of later official statistics ; incidentally one or two arithmetical errors came to light. As this involved correction of the chart, it seemed convenient in this one case to combine revision with continuation. Both Table X and the chart as now printed in Part I run therefore to 1913 (or 1914). The comment in the text of Part I is confined to the period before 1908 ; this text is substantially unchanged.

The continuation of the table shows 1907 as a marked peak for all six countries, followed by an almost equally general depression in 1908. Then the figures rise rapidly again for all countries to 1913. In the United Kingdom and United States, for which alone strictly comparable figures are available, the first half of 1914 shows a slight recession from 1913, justifying the marking of that year as a maximum.

The sources used for Table X are as follows :—

United Kingdom—*Statistical Abstracts*—see notes on continuation of Table IX, column 2.

United States : *United States Year Book.*

Germany : *Statistisches Jahrbuch für das Deutsche Reich,* calculated by dividing the total of special imports and exports by the estimated population.

France : *Annuaire Statistique,* calculated as for Germany.

Belgium : *Annuaire Statistique.*

Norway : *Statistisk Aarbok,* calculated as for Germany.

Pages 84-85.—*Note on Fluctuations of Employment at London Docks and Wharves taken together and separately.*

Further statistics on the lines of those cited in the text for 1891 (from Mr. Charles Booth) are given for 1906 in a Board of Trade Memorandum on " Statistics of Seasonal Industries and Industries Carried on by Casual Labour," printed in Volume IX, Appendix XXI (D) of the Poor Law Commission Report of 1909. The main results are summarised as follows :—

" In 1906, for instance, the highest number employed on any one day in the year at all the docks and wharves making returns was 14,482, on November 20th. But this was not necessarily the busiest day for each of the five main groups into which the employers are divided. The London and India Docks were busiest on November 30th, with 4,020 men ; the Millwall Docks on November 16th, with 1,182 ; the Surrey Commercial, on November 20th, with 1,760 ; the Shipowners, on April 3rd, with 3.195 ; the wharves on September 14th, with 6,650. The sum of these separate maxima is 16,807, or 17 per cent above the maximum of the whole port on the one busiest day. If each month be taken separately a similar though less marked result is apparent, the sum of the maxima exceeding the maximum for the whole port by amounts ranging from 6 per cent in August to 13 per cent in November and April. It will be noticed that only rarely do the busiest days of any two groups for any month coincide."

" Each of the five big groups is, however, itself composed of many separate businesses or employing centres. How far do the fluctuations at each of these centres within a group coincide and how far do they neutralise one another ? Tables XI and XII show the effect of splitting up into their component parts two of the groups, *viz.,* the wharves and the shipowners in the Royal Albert and Victoria Docks. The second and third columns in each case give the maximum and minimum numbers employed on any one day of the month by the group as a whole. The fourth and fifth columns give the sums of the maxima and of the minima recorded for the separate businesses within each group during the month. The sixth column gives the average numbers employed in the group as a whole. The main interest of the tables lies in the comparison of the second and the fourth columns. The separate maxima fall generally on different days for different businesses so that their sum considerably exceeds the largest number at work on one and the same day in the group as a whole. For the 115 wharves the sum of the maxima exceeds the maximum for the whole group by numbers varying from 242 or 4 per cent in July to 1,085 or 16 per cent in November. The average difference is 632 or 9·7 per cent. In the case of the shipowners the excess is still greater, ranging from 974 or 27 per cent in May to 2,216 or 74 per cent in January and averaging 1,695 or 56 per cent."

Page 93. *Note on Average Earnings of Casual Dock Labourers.*

The working of the Liverpool Dock Labour Scheme described in paragraphs 121-132 of the *First Report on Unemployment Insurance* (1913, Cmd. 6965) made possible for the first time a calculation of the average wages earned by a large body of dock labourers. The calculation is summarised below :—

From July, 1912, to July, 1913, the average wage paid each week through the Board of Trade Clearing House was £1 2s. 7d. for each man paid anything, in the week. To estimate from this the average total earnings of dock labourers over all weeks, various adjustments are needed :—

1. Deduction for weeks with no work at all under the Scheme, say one week in six, or 3s. 9d.
2. Additions for work away from the docks (6d. a week), for " subs " or payments in advance for work within the Scheme (2s. a week), and for earnings at docks not paid through the Clearing House (6d. a week).

There results as the average total weekly earnings over all weeks of the 22,500 dock labourers in Liverpool 21s. 10d. The actual earnings of individuals vary widely. Thus, taking the mean of a busy and slack month, 33 per cent of the weekly payments through the Clearing House were less than 15s. each, 42½ per cent ranged from 15s. to 30s., 14 per cent ranged from 30s. to 40s., and 10½ per cent were above 40s.

Pages 112-113. *Note on numbers occupied in certain industries.*

The decline in agriculture continued to 1911 (1,259,254 or 9·2 per cent of all males aged 10 and over) and 1921 (1,171,298 or 8·4 per cent of males aged 12 and over). Tin mining showed a small revival (to 7,125 males in 1911), but lead and copper a further fall (to 2,968 and 279 males respectively). Silk continued to decline in 1911 (to 29,643 persons of 10 and over).

The recovery of the lace trade from 1891 to 1901 was continued, the numbers occupied rising to 41,003 in 1911 (as compared with 36,439 ten years before). The later increase, like the former, took place in Nottingham and Derby; those occupied in hand-made lace in Bedford, Buckingham, and Northampton, fell further from 2,497 in 1901 to 1,336 in 1911.

In boot and shoe making females continued to gain on males up to 1911. The replacement of males by females in the brush-making and hosiery trades continued; comparable figures are not available for carpet-making. The contrary movement towards replacement of females by males, shown in straw hat manufacture, also continued in 1911 and was more marked.

The statement in the text as to substitution of younger for older males in boot and shoe making up to 1901 is perhaps more definite than is warranted by the evidence; the 1901 figures exclude dealers, while the 1891 figures include them. The 1901 and 1911 figures are comparable in so far as both exclude dealers; they show no marked change of age distribution.

Page 117. *Supplement to :*

TABLE XVIII.—AGES OF APPLICANTS TO DISTRESS COMMITTEES, ENGLAND AND WALES, 1910-11.

Ages.	No. found Qualified for Assistance under the Act.	Being per cent of all Qualified Applicants.	Being per 1,000 of all Males at each Age.
Under 20	1,526	2·9	0·9
20 and under 30 . . .	11,547	22·3	3·9
30 and under 40 . . .	15,499	29·9	5·9
40 and under 50 . . .	12,659	24·4	6·3
50 and under 60 . . .	7,713	14·9	5·6
60 years and over. . .	2,887	5·6	2·5
All ages	51,831	100·0	—

Page 119. *Supplement to :*

TABLE XIX.—AGES OF MALE UNEMPLOYED APPLICANTS (LONDON), 1910-11.

Age.	Occupied Males, 1911.	Unemployed Applicants (Male).	Being per 1,000 of Occupied Males at that Age.
15-19 . .	175,274	1,074	6·1
20-24 . .	183,728	2,430	13·2
25-34 . .	358,218	7,306	20·4
35-44 . .	289,881	7,526	25·9
45-54 . .	208,096	4,868	23·4
55-64 . .	117,456	1,822	15·5
65 and over .	47,365	242	5·1

Page 119. *Supplement to :*

TABLE XX.—PROPORTIONS AT EACH YEAR IN SUCCESSIVE AGE GROUPS.

(NUMBERS AT EACH YEAR 20-24 = 100.)

Age.	Occupied Males, England and Wales (1911).	Occupied Males, London (1911).	London Riverside Labour (1911).	London General Labour (1911).	Occupied Males, London (1921).
15-19	104	95	35	63	103 [1]
20-24	100	100	100	100	100
25-34	95	97	178	126	97
35-44	78	79	199	131	90
45-54	56	57	159	110	77
55-64	33	32	83	62	47
65-74	13	11	20	19	26 [2]

[1] In calculating this figure the number at age 15 has been taken as half the number given by the Census at 1921 for the two years 14 and 15.
[2] For ages 65 to 69.

The occupied males in England and Wales and in London show a decline in group 20-24 as compared with all other groups and particularly the groups immediately following. London Riverside Labour and London General Labour show a remarkable growth in later age groups (25 onwards) as compared with the earlier ones and indicate a diminution of early recruiting to these occupations.

The London 1921 figures are dominated by the war gap, increasing all groups from 35-44 onwards in relation to the groups 20-24 and 25-34.

Page 121. *Note on* " The adverse influence of advancing years is thus seen less when it is a question of retaining old employment than when it is a question of finding new employers."

This statement can now be confirmed by statistical enquiry, as true both before and since the war. Before the war, enquiries made by the Board of Trade in regard to the Manchester and Leeds branches of the Amalgamated Society of Engineers in 1895, yield figures relating to nearly 8,000 men, as follows :—

Age Group.	Average Days lost in the Year per Working Member.	Percentage of Working Members losing at least Three Days in the Year.	Average Days lost in the Year per Member losing Three Days at least.
1	2	3	4
15-24 . .	8·8	15·2	57·9
25-34 . .	13·1	24·4	53·9
35-44 . .	12·3	21·0	58·6
45-54 . .	20·1	22·3	90·4
55-64 . .	33·1	30·4	108·9
65-74 . .	26·9	29·0	92·6
All ages . .	15·1	22·1	68·4

The second column of the table shows a marked increase in the amount of unemployment per head after 45, the decade 45-54 yielding an amount 63 per cent and the decade 55-64 an amount 169 per cent greater than that of the decade 35-44. The third column shows that the increase of unemployment in the decade 45-54 is not at all, and in the decade 55-64 is only partially, due to an increase in the proportion of members becoming unemployed ; for 45-54 this proportion is practically the same as that for 35-44, and for 55-64 it is only some 45 per cent greater. The fourth column shows how much the increase of unemployment is due in each of the later periods to the larger average amount of unemployment experienced by those who experienced any at all. The comparison with the earlier decade 25-34 is in some ways even more striking. So far as these figures go a man of 50 is actually less likely to fall out of work than is a man of 30, but once he has fallen out he is likely to wait more than half as long again before he gets back to work again.

For the time since the war, reference should be made to the *Report on an Investigation into the Employment and Insurance History of a Sample of Persons Insured against Unemployment in Great Britain*, published by the Ministry of Labour in 1927. On page 36 is given a table comparing the age distribution of (*a*) all insured persons, (*b*) all persons claiming benefit over a period of fourteen months from 1st February, 1925, to 31st March, 1926, and (*c*) claimants on the register at 12th April, 1926, and between

24th and 29th November, 1924. The figures are given separately for males and females, and the outstanding features of the table for both sexes are first, the close agreement between the age distribution of (*a*) and (*b*), and the difference between these and the distribution at each of the epochs in (*c*), when the proportions from later ages are higher and those from earlier ages lower. The first feature means that the risk of falling out of work during any given period—here fourteen months—is much the same at all ages. The second feature means that the risk of being unemployed at any given date increases with age, after thirty-five; since the chance of falling out of employment does not increase, this can only be explained by a decreased chance of getting back into employment, once it has been lost. These figures, relating to a sample of the whole insured population are thus strikingly in accord with pre-war results for particular trades.

Page 122. *Supplement to:*

TABLE XXI.—AGE AT SUPERANNUATION—AMALGAMATED SOCIETY OF ENGINEERS.

Year.	Members Superannuated during the Year. Number.	Age. Average.		Quartiles.		Superannuated Members dying during the Year. Number.	Age (from detailed obituary). Average.		Quartiles.		Average Age from Grouped Figures.	
1885	174	61·9		58½	65½	51	65·8		60½	70½	—	
1886	223	63·1		59½	65½	97	67·3		62½	72½	—	
1887	194	62·0		58½	64½	88	67·0		62½	70½	—	
1888	250	61·9	62·2	58½	65½	129	66·7	67·3	61½	70½	—	
1889	303	62·5		58½	65½	119	67·9		63½	72½	—	
1890	300	61·5		58½	64½	158	67·6		62½	71½	—	
1891	289	62·3		58½	65½	149	68·4		64½	72½	—	
1892	416	62·0		58½	64½	162	69·0		63½	73½	—	
1893	295	63·5	62·7	60½	66½	176	69·3	68·8	63½	73½	—	
1894	407	62·7		59½	65½	161	68·9		63½	73½	—	
1895	429	62·9		59½	65½	240	68·6		64½	73½	—	
1896	526	61·9		58½	64½	199	69·6		64½	74½	69·9	
1897	365	63·1		59½	65½	254	69·0		63½	73½	68·7	
1898	629	62·5	62·8	59½	65½	260	69·0	69·2	64½	73½	68·4	69·4
1899	494	63·3		60½	66½	305	68·7		62½	74½	69·7	
1900	552	63·2		60½	66½	299	69·6		64½	74½	70·2	
1901	628	63·4		60½	66½	317	70·0		65½	74½	70·2	
1902	614	63·6		60½	65½	307	69·9		65½	74½	69·1	
1903	718	63·8	63·6	60½	66½	309	69·8	70·1	65½	73½	70·1	69·9
1904	715	63·6		60½	66½	347	70·0		64½	74½	70·6	
1905	653	63·5		60½	66½	252	70·8		65½	75½	69·6	
1906	631	63·7		60½	66½	398	70·7		65½	75½	69·8	
1907	691	63·9		60½	67½	420	71·3		65½	75½	71·1	
1908	797	64·0	63·8	60½	66½	461	71·6	71·3	66½	76½	70·9	70·9
1909	798	63·6		60½	66½	482	71·1		65½	75½	71·1	
1910	660	63·6		60½	66½	329	72·0		67½	77½	71·8	
1911	573	64·1		60½	67½	515	72·1		67½	76½	72·4	
1912	535	64·2		60½	67½	504	72·4		67½	76½	72·3	
1913	495	65·1	65·0	61½	67½	541	72·4	72·5	67½	77½	72·7	72·9
1914	538	65·3		62½	68½	455	72·5		66½	76½	73·0	
1915	379	66·4		62½	69½	439	73·1		67½	77½	73·9	
1916	382	65·1		61½	68½	507	73·5		69½	77½	74·4	
1917	369	65·1	65·3	61½	68½	475	—		—	—	74·9	74·6
1918	377	65·0		61½	68½	487	—		—	—	74·7	
1919	768	65·9		62½	69½	406	—		—	—	74·3	
1920	—	—		—	—	—	—		—	—	—	
1921	—	—		—	—	—	—		—	—	—	
1922	2,031	66·2		63½	69½	607	—		—	—	74·5	
1923	1,506	65·1	65·3	61½	68½	663	—		—	—	74·2	73·9
1924	1,244	64·8		61½	68½	664	—		—	—	73·6	
1925	1,122	65·1		61½	68½	710	—		—	—	73·4	
1926	1,234	65·2		61½	68½	750	—		—	—	74·2	
1927	1,137	64·8		60½	68½	801	—		—	—	73·9	

Table XXI in the text has been revised, the averages being re-calculated and given to one point of decimals in place of by vulgar fractions of years.   Half a year has been added also to all the averages, on the assumption that a person stated to be aged 61 may be anywhere between 61 and 62.   *The Annual Reports of the Amalgamated Society of Engineers*, on which the table is based, simply name the age of each member at superannuation.

In the Supplement the table is given as a whole from 1885 to 1927, with fuller statistical information.   The ages at death of superannuated members dying during the year are given in the annual reports of the Society in two ways: (*a*) in individual obituaries from 1885 to 1916, and (*b*) in groups from 1896 to 1927.   The two sets of figures agree substantially where they overlap and can be treated as interchangeable for broad comparisons.

The revision of Table XXI does not affect the conclusions previously drawn from it, about six months being added to all the figures.   The later figures show the average age of retirement continuing to rise up to the war and after the war they are higher than just before.   The war itself, with its keen demand for skilled men, no doubt hastened the rise of age of retirement (though 1913 was already very high) and the last years from 1923 mark a small reaction from the war.

The right-hand side of the table shows the average age at death, rising even more rapidly than the age of superannuation, and thus increasing the drain on the superannuation fund. Bro adly in forty years about three years have been added to the working life and 6½ years to the total life of those members of the Amalgamated Society of Engineers who have qualified for superannuation.

Page 122. *Supplement to:*

TABLE XXII.—AGE AT SUPERANNUATION—FRIENDLY SOCIETY OF IRONFOUNDERS

Year.	Superannuated Members Dying during the Year.					Age at Superannuation of those Members who Died during the Year.				Time on Fund.
	Number.	Age at Death.				Average.		Quartiles.		
		Average.		Quartiles.						
1882	33	69·8		65½	74½	62·3		60½	64½	
1883	33	68·9	69·1	63½	72½	62·2	62·2	60½	64½	6·9
1884	32	68·1		63½	70½	62·4		60½	64½	
1885	32	69·6		65½	73½	62·1		60½	62½	
1886	41	69·9		64½	75½	63·7		60½	66½	
1887	43	69·4		64½	73½	62·8		60½	64½	
1888	37	70·0	69·8	66½	74½	63·0	62·8	60½	66½	7·0
1889	52	70·0		65½	74½	62·4		60½	64½	
1890	57	69·9		64½	73½	62·1		60½	63½	
1891	64	70·9		67½	74½	63·1		60½	65½	
1892	49	70·8		66½	75½	62·9		60½	64½	
1893	52	71·0	70·4	67½	74½	62·9	63·0	60½	64½	7·4
1894	58	69·9		65½	73½	62·8		60½	64½	
1895	71	69·4		64½	73½	63·2		60½	64½	
1896	64	70·3		65½	74½	62·3		60½	63½	
1897	61	72·2		66½	77½	63·2		60½	64½	
1898	59	69·7	70·5	64½	74½	62·2	62·7	60½	63½	7·8
1899	81	69·8		64½	74½	63·2		60½	65½	
1900	90	70·6		66½	75½	62·7		60½	64½	
1901	75	71·0		67½	75½	62·3		60½	63½	
1902	90	70·3		65½	74½	62·5		60½	63½	
1903	75	70·5	70·8	66½	74½	62·8	62·6	60½	64½	8·2
1904	95	70·4		65½	74½	62·7		60½	63½	
1905	102	71·7		66½	76½	62·8		60½	65½	
1906	118	71·3		64½	76½	62·5		60½	63½	
1907	92	71·5		67½	75½	63·1		60½	64½	
1908	108	71·9	71·6	67½	75½	62·9	63·0	60½	64½	8·6
1909	114	71·8		66½	76½	63·2		60½	65½	
1910	104	71·7		66½	76½	63·2		60½	64½	
1911	107	72·1		66½	77½	62·7		60½	63½	
1912	118	72·0		66½	76½	63·4		60½	65½	
1913	121	71·5	72·1	67½	75½	63·0	63·1	60½	64½	9·0
1914	155	72·1		67½	75½	63·3		60½	65½	
1915	119	72·6		67½	76½	63·2		60½	65½	
1916	153	73·5		67½	77½	63·1		60½	64½	
1917	—	—	73·4	—	—	—	63·4	—	—	10·0
1918	129	72·9		67½	77½	63·6		60½	66½	
1919	146	73·9		68½	78½	63·4		60½	65½	

Note.—The *year* of age only is given in the returns; a half year has therefore been added throughout on the grounds that this is a nearer approximation to the average. Age at superannuation is obtained by subtracting "time on fund" from "age at death," and hence the annual average applies only to those members who died during the year.

Table XXII in the text has been revised and is continued there to 1906-10 so as to get a five-year period for the final average. The complete annual table from 1882 to 1919 printed here shows a continuance of the rise both of the age of death and the age of retirement. The former, however, has risen much more than the latter: by 4·3 years, from beginning to end of the period covered, as compared with 1·2 years. The average period on pension has thus increased very markedly from 6·9 to 10·0 years.

Page 123. *Supplement to :*

TABLE XXIII.—AGE AT SUPERANNUATION—AMALGAMATED SOCIETY OF ENGINEERS.

MEMBERS SUPERANNUATED.

Age.	1912.		1919.		1926.	
	No.	Per cent of total.	No.	Per cent of total.	No.	Per cent of total.
Under 60 .	99	18·5	57	7·5	103	8·4
60-64 . .	222	41·5	285	37·0	531	43·0
65-69 . .	138	25·8	278	36·2	374	30·3
70-74 . .	64	12·0	124	16·2	193	15·6
75 and over .	12	2·2	24	3·1	33	2·7
Total . .	535	100·0	768	100·0	1,234	100·0

The percentage of those claiming superannuation who were under 65 continued to decline from 73·7 in 1885 to 59·0 in 1907, 60·0 in 1912 and 51·4 in 1926, while the percentage of 70 and over rose from 6·8 in 1885 to 11·9 in 1907, 14·2 in 1912 and 18·3 in 1926. The 1919 figures are presumably still affected by the war.

Page 129.   *Supplement to :*

TABLE XXIV.—AGE DISTRIBUTION IN CERTAIN OCCUPATIONS,
1911 AND 1921—ENGLAND AND WALES.

MALES AT EACH YEAR 20-24 = 100.

Age.	All Occupied Males.		Metals, Machines,[2] Implements and Conveyances.		Dock and Wharf Labourers.[2]	
	1911.	1921.	1911.	1921.	1911.	1921.
15-19[1]	104	108	103	115	49	48
20-24	100	100	100	100	100	100
25-34	95	91	91	84	146	130
35-44	78	87	70	72	158	174
45-54	56	73	47	54	118	178
55-64	33	45	26	30	61	102
65-74 (1911) or 65-69 (1921)	13	25	9	15	17	52

[1] The 1921 census does not give separately the numbers at age 14 and age 15 respectively. The number at age 15 has been taken as half the number at ages 14 and 15 together.
[2] The classifications of these occupations were changed in the 1921 census so that the figures are only roughly and not exactly comparable with those for earlier cenous.

The 1911 census figures show for all occupied males higher figures than in 1901 at all later age groups as compared with the group 20-24, presumably a reflection of falling birth- and death-rates (with some special explanation of the 15-19 figure). Metals, machines, implements and conveyances follow the line of all occupied males much as before, though with growing deficiency in later ages ; this is presumably a sign of an expanding occupation group. Dock and wharf labour shows a yet more exaggerated rise in groups after 20-24, with 35-44 as the most populous group of all.

Pages 166 and 167. *Continuation of:*

TABLE XXVI.—DISTRESS COMMITTEES IN ENGLAND AND WALES.

District.	No. of Committees Taking Proceedings.	Estimated Population.	Applications Received up to 31st March.	Applications Entertained. Applicants.	Dependents.	Total of Columns 4 and 5 per 1,000 of Population.
	1.	2.	3.	4.	5.	6.

1908-9.

London	29	4,795,757	49,239	22,414	71,276	20
Provinces	95	11,984,167	147,518	114,175	304,767	35
Totals	124	16,779,924	196,757	136,589	376,043	31

1909-10.

London	29	4,833,938	41,843	17,737	60,871	16
Provinces	87	11,364,974	85,223	64,012	175,223	21
Totals	116	16,198,912	127,066	81,749	236,094	20

1910-11.

London	29	4,522,961	26,531	11,053	36,839	11
Provinces	65	9,031,469	46,960	40,775	112,248	17
Totals	94	13,554,430	73,491	51,828	149,087	15

1911-12.

London	29	4,522,961	20,711	9,286	29,348	9
Provinces	45	7,483,260	33,308	28,357	76,471	14
Totals	74	12,006,221	54,019	37,643	105,819	12

1912-13.

London	29	4,519,754	16,146	7,823	27,273	8
Provinces	43	7,716,951	27,235	22,839	60,639	11
Totals	72	12,236,705	43,381	30,662	87,912	10

1913-14.

London	29	4,518,191	11,080	5,605	19,420	6
Provinces	30	4,711,606	13,220	10,744	27,898	8
Totals	59	9,229,797	24,300	16,349	47,318	7

Table XXVI in the text, with its continuation here, covers the administration of the Unemployed Workmen Act over a period of nine years. The percentages in column 6 reflect the coming and the passing of the depression of 1908-9; from 1905-6 they run as follows: 17, 14, 14, 31, 20, 15, 12, 10, 7.

Page 168. *Supplement to:*

TABLE XXVII.—OCCUPATIONS OF UNEMPLOYED APPLICANTS.

1908-9.

Occupation.	London.	Percentage of Total of all Occupations.	Total (London and Provinces).	Percentage of Total of all Occupations.
General or Casual Labour . .	7,169	32·0	64,773	47·4
Transport and Conveyance . .	3,376	15·1	7,429	5·4
Building Trades	6,767	30·2	23,047	16·9
Engineering, Shipbuilding and Metal	1,616	7·2	17,028	12·5
Furnishing and Woodwork . .	702	3·1	2,260	1·7
Food, Drink and Tobacco . .	523	2·3	1,458	1·1
Domestic Service . . .	402	1·8	2,090	1·5
Tailoring and Clothing . .	382	1·7	882	0·6
Textile Trades	25	0·1	2,649	1·9
Boot and Shoemaking . . .	339	1·5	2,437	1·8
Printing, Bookbinding and other Paper Trades . . .	186	0·8	566	0·4
Other Occupations . . .	927	4·2	11,970	8·8

1913-14.

General or Casual Labour . .	1,664	29·7	8,204	50·2
Transport and Conveyance . .	1,030	18·4	1,693	10·3
Building Trades	1,471	26·2	2,969	18·2
Engineering, Shipbuilding and Metal	279	5·0	650	4·0
Furnishing and Woodwork . .	109	1·9	196	1·2
Food, Drink and Tobacco . .	206	3·7	449	2·7
Domestic Service	233	4·2	373	2·3
Tailoring and Clothing . .	167	3·0	253	1·5
Textile Trades	8	0·1	82	0·5
Boot and Shoemaking . . .	46	0·8	438	2·7
Printing, Bookbinding and other Paper Trades . . .	49	0·9	95	0·6
Other Occupations . . .	343	6·1	947	5·8

29

It has not appeared necessary to repeat the table of occupations of unemployed applicants for every year from 1908-9 to 1913-14. The two years chosen are respectively those of greatest and of least unemployment (as recorded by the trade union percentages); the exceptional depression of the engineering and shipbuilding trades in the earlier of these two years is reflected in the larger proportion of applicants from these trades, but the total numbers are small and point to the effect of union benefits in keeping men off the distress registers.

Page 178.   *Supplement to :*

TABLE XXVIII.—REPEATED APPLICATIONS—LONDON.

Information in this form is not available for later years, but the following table, extracted from the *Sixth Report of the Central (Unemployed) Body for London,* bears on the same point :—

Year Ended 30th June.	Total Registrations.	Number Registered Previously.	Proportion Per Cent.
1907-08	31,479	} Not available.	
1908-09	49,485	}	
1909-10	42,441	20,626	48·5
1910-11	26,540	13,626	51·3
1911-12	20,907	10,022	47·8

The numbers of total registrations differ slightly from those given for London in Table XXVI and its continuation, presumably because the year of account ends in one case at 30th June and in the other at 31st March.

Page 222.   *Contraction of Production in Industrial Depressions.*

The cases cited at the top of this page remained the greatest up to the war except for cotton, where the fall of raw cotton consumption from 44·7 lbs. per head in 1907 to 36·2 lbs. in 1910 represents a fall from 100 to 81. The contraction of shipbuilding between 1907 and 1908, from 100 to 51, was exceptionally sudden but not so great as the drop between 1883 and 1886. The post-war contractions of shipbuilding from 27·50 tons per 1,000 in 1920 to 9·17 in 1923, and of raw wool consumption from 22·62 lbs. per head in 1919 to 8·97 in 1923 set up new records.

The contraction of coal and production from 1891 to 1893 cited in the text is connected with a trade dispute stoppage in the latter year, as are the low outputs per head of 1921 and 1926. Among purely industrial depressions, the contraction from 100 to 93 between 1883 and 1886 appears the worst up to the war.

Page 243. *Continuation of:*

TABLE XXXII.—TRAVELLING BENEFIT—FRIENDLY SOCIETY
OF IRON FOUNDERS, 1873-1907.

Year.	Total No. of Tramp Cards Issued.	No. of Tramp Cards Issued per 1,000 Members of the Society.	Average No. of Members Constantly on Travel.	No. of Members at any time travelling per 1,000 Members of the Society.
1908	1,178	61	132	6·8
1909	1,121	60	133	7·1
1910	902	50	73	4·0
1911	647	35	40	2·2

These figures are not returned after 1911.

Page 336. *Notes on Chart V:*

The figures for Chart V appear in Tables XLIII and XLIV.
Tables XLIII to XLVI are referred to in Chapter XV; they are taken from a paper by myself on "Some Aspects of Trade Fluctuation," read to the Manchester Statistical Society on 9th March, 1921.

TABLE XLIII.—UNEMPLOYED PERCENTAGES, 1860-1913, IN THE
AMALGAMATED SOCIETY OF CARPENTERS AND JOINERS
AND THE AMALGAMATED SOCIETY OF ENGINEERS.

Year.	Yearly Means. A.S.C.J.	A.S.E.	Decade.	Ten Year Means. A.S.C.J.	A.S.E.
1860	0·2	1·4			
1861	1·8	3·8			
1862	1·8	7·2			
1863	1·2	5·5			
1864	0·4	2·4	1860-69	1·63	4·66
1865	0·3	1·8	1861-70	1·98	4·93
1866	1·1	2·5	1862-71	2·05	4·65
1867	3·0	6·3	1863-72	1·99	3·99
1868	2·9	7·9	1864-73	1·96	3·52
1869	3·6	7·8	1865-74	1·98	3·42
1870	3·7	4·1	1866-75	2·03	3·47
1871	2·5	1·0	1867-76	1·99	3·57
1872	1·2	0·6	1868-77	1·81	3·42
1873	0·9	0·8	1869-78	1·87	3·32
1874	0·8	1·4	1870-79	2·33	3·60
1875	0·6	2·3	1871-80	2·57	3·69
1876	0·7	3·5	1872-81	2·84	3·94
1877	1·2	4·8	1873-82	3·07	4·07
1878	3·5	6·9	1874-83	3·34	4·21
1879	8·2	10·6	1875-84	3·73	4·55
1880	6·1	5·0	1876-85	4·38	4·99
1881	5·2	3·5	1877-86	5·13	5·40
1882	3·5	1·9	1878-87	5·66	5·53
1883	3·6	2·2	1879-88	5·88	5·26
1884	4·7	4·8	1880-89	5·36	4·39

TABLE XLIII—(*continued*).

	Yearly Means.			Ten Year Means.	
Year.	A.S.C.J.	A.S.E.	Decade.	A.S.C.J.	A.S.E.
1885	7·1	6·7	1881-90	4·97	4·06
1886	8·2	7·6	1882-91	4·64	4·03
1887	6·5	6·1	1883-92	4·60	4·47
1888	5·7	4·2	1884-93	4·55	5·08
1889	3·0	1·9	1885-94	4·51	5·45
1890	2·2	1·7	1886-95	4·24	5·37
1891	1·9	3·2	1887-96	3·55	4·84
1892	3·1	6·3	1888-97	3·02	4·47
1893	3·1	8·3	1889-98	2·54	4·30
1894	4·3	8·5	1890-99	2·36	4·35
1895	4·4	5·9	1891-00	2·40	4·40
1896	1·3	2·3	1892-01	2·60	4·37
1897	1·2	2·4	1893-02	2·69	4·18
1898	0·9	2·5	1894-03	2·82	3·79
1899	1·2	2·4	1895-04	3·12	3·56
1900	2·6	2·2	1896-05	3·48	3·43
1901	3·9	2·9	1897-06	4·04	3·47
1902	4·0	4·4	1898-07	4·65	3·55
1903	4·4	4·4	1899-08	5·72	4·13
1904	7·3	6·2	1900-09	6·77	4·94
1905	8·0	4·6	1901-10	7·34	5·26
1906	6·9	2·7	1902-11	7·37	5·26
1907	7·3	3·2	1903-12	7·34	5·11
1908	11·6	8·3	1904-13	7·23	4·82
1909	11·7	10·5			
1910	8·3	5·4			
1911	4·2	2·9			
1912	3·7	2·9			
1913	3·3	1·5			

The annual figures are taken from the *Seventeenth Abstract of Labour Statistics* and the second *Fiscal Blue Book*. The ten year means have been calculated.

TABLE XLIV.—BUILDING AND METAL TRADES—UNEMPLOYED PERCENTAGE AND CHANGES IN NUMBERS OCCUPIED.

Period.	Building.		Metals.		
	Mean Unemployed Percentage.	Increase (+) and Decrease (−) Per Cent in Numbers Occupied.	Mean Unemployed Percentage.		Increase (+) and Decrease (−) Per Cent in Numbers Occupied.
			A.S.E.	All Unions.	
1851-60	—	18·8	3·21	4·89	44·0
1861-70	1·98	23·5	4·93	6·29	43·8
1871-80	2·57	17·8	3·69	5·19	14·8
1881-90	4·97	2·0	4·06	6·69	18·4
1891-00	2·40	36·2	4·40	6·08	26·6
1901-10	7·34	− 7·0	5·26	7·22	15·2
Mean of five periods :					
1861-1910	3·85	14·5	4·47	6·29	23·8

Note.—The unemployed percentage for "Building" relates to the Amalgamated Society of Carpenters and Joiners only, and that for "Metals" to the Amalgamated Society of Engineers. The figures are taken from the same source as Table XLIII, and are the means of the ten years, 1851-60, etc.

The figures as to numbers occupied are taken from the first *Fiscal Blue Book* up to 1891, and from the *Seventeenth Abstract of Labour Statistics* thereafter. They relate to England and Wales alone and represent the increase per cent as between 1851 and the next census, 1861, and so on. The figures for metals from 1851 to 1891 cover the headings "Iron and Steel" and "Machine Making and Shipbuilding"; those from 1891 to 1911 cover "Metals, Machines and Implements" and "Ships and Boats". There is thus a change of classification at 1891 making direct comparison between, say, 1881 and 1901 impossible, but 1891 can be compared both with 1881 and with 1901.

TABLE XLV. — AGE DISTRIBUTION OF MALES IN BUILDING TRADE AND IN ALL OCCUPATIONS AT CENSUSES 1881 TO 1911—ENGLAND AND WALES.

The figures for each age group are the numbers at each year of age out of an average 10,000 of all ages.

Age Group.	Building Trade.				All Occupations.	
	1881.	1891.	1901.	1911.	1901.	1911.
10-14	30 [1]	33	24	12	72	56
15-19	262	212	260	138	290	264
20-24	296	233	289	196	282	256
25-34	} 228	257	225	262	241	244
35-44		224	201	216	186	200
45-54	} 103	155	156	182	132	143
55-64		85	90	116	80	85
65-74	(37)	(35)	35	45	32	34
75 and upwards	—	—	—	—	—	—

[1] This figure relates to the age group 5-14.

TABLE XLVI.—HOUSES INHABITED, UNINHABITED, AND BEING BUILT AT CENSUSES 1801 TO 1911—ENGLAND AND WALES.

Census Year.	Proportion per 1,000 Inhabited Houses of:		In each Intercensal Period Increase Per Cent of:	
	Uninhabited Houses.	Houses being Built.	Population.	Total Houses.
1801	36·5	—	—	—
1811	28·4	9·0	14·0	13·2
1821	33·4	9·2	18·1	16·7
1831	48·3	10·0	15·8	20·7
1841	58·8	9·3	14·3	19·7
1851	46·8	8·1	12·7	10·0
1861	49·4	7·3	11·9	14·2
1871	61·4	8·9	13·2	15·4
1881	80·0	9·6	14·4	15·5
1891	68·3	7·0	11·7	11·3
1901	71·7	9·9	12·2	15·5
1911	57·2	5·3	10·9	12·1

Page 340.   *Notes on Chart VI :*

The figures on which this chart is based are given in Table XLVII below.   The uppermost curve and the last five are those given in Chart II, p. 44 ; the figures are brought up to date in Statistical Supplement, p. 433, where notes on the figures used will also be found.

Foreign Trade (Exports of United Kingdom produce per head).—These figures are values, 1820-1853, from the *Statistical Journal*, 1890 (Dr. Ogle); thereafter from *Memoranda on British and Foreign Trade and Industry* supplemented by *Statistical Abstracts*.   Up to 1914 the figures used in the chart are the annual values as percentages of a fifteen-year moving average.   For the first and last seven years values of the latter have been interpolated by continuing the trend of adjacent years ; from 1919 onwards, values have been used after adjusting the scale to the level of the percentages shown previously.

Wholesale Prices.—These figures are from *An Introduction to the Study of Prices*, W. T. Layton, to 1918 (*i.e.*, 1860-1918, Sauerbeck's Index adjusted to 1900 basis, previously Jevons' Index adjusted by equating the respective figures for 1860 and correcting in this ratio); subsequently from *Statistical Journals*.   The series given in Table IX above is the Board of Trade Index, which is not available before 1871, and has therefore been replaced throughout by the figures given here.   As with Foreign Trade, the figures used in the chart are based on a fifteen-year moving average up to 1914.   From 1919 onwards, actual index numbers have been charted after adjusting the scale.

Budget Results.   (Difference of revenue received from budget estimates.)   These figures are from *Commerce and Industry Statistical Tables of the British Empire from 1815*, edited by William Page.

With the exception of "Budget Results," "Employment," "Consumption of Beer" and "Companies Registered," 1914 figures are based on the first six months only, as explained in the Statistical Supplement (notes on Table IX).

TABLE XLVII.—BIRTH AND LIFE OF THE TRADE CYCLE.

Year.	Bank Rate (Average Minimum Discount Rate per cent).	Foreign Trade.		Wholesale Prices.		Budget Results, £000.	Employed Percentage (Trade Unions).	Marriage Rate per 1,000 of Population, England and Wales.	Indoor Pauperism in England and Wales per 10,000 (Mean of no. at end of each month).	Consumption of Beer per Head (Gallons).	Companies Registered during Year Nominal Capital £ per Head.
		£ per Head.	Per cent of 15 Year moving average.	1900 = 100.	Per cent of 15 Year moving average.						
	1.	2.	3.	4.	5.	6.	7.	8.	9.	10.	11.
1820	5·00	1·55	97	172	101	—	—	16·3	—	—	—
1821	5·00	1·75	109	157	94	823	—	16·7	—	—	—
1822	5·00	1·75	109	147	90	1,411	—	16·1	—	—	—
1823	4·00	1·65	103	148	93	673	—	16·3	—	—	—
1824	3·75	1·75	109	147	93	1,978	—	16·5	—	—	—
1825	4·00	1·75	108	172	111	829	—	17·1	—	—	—
1826	5·00	1·40	87	150	101	− 2,147	—	16·1	—	—	—
1827	3·75	1·65	102	150	104	− 2,567	—	16·2	—	—	—
1828	4·00	1·60	98	135	95	1,285	—	16·5	—	—	—
1829	3·75	1·55	93	132	94	− 560	—	15·3	—	—	—
1830	3·75	1·60	97	135	96	107	—	15·6	—	—	—
1831	4·00	1·55	92	137	98	− 826	—	16·0	—	—	—
1832	3·75	1·50	88	130	93	519	—	16·5	—	—	—
1833	3·50	1·60	94	125	90	824	—	16·8	—	—	—
1834	3·50	1·65	95	130	94	647	—	16·8	—	—	—
1835	3·75	1·85	106	133	98	343	—	16·2	—	—	—
1836	4·25	2·10	119	143	106	1,962	—	16·2	—	—	—
1837	4·75	1·65	91	140	104	− 765	—	15·1	—	—	—
1838	3·75	1·95	106	140	105	62	—	15·4	—	—	—
1839	5·00	2·05	109	153	116	− 283	—	15·9	—	—	—
1840	5·00	1·90	99	145	110	− 1,023	—	15·6	—	27·2	—
1841	5·00	1·95	101	142	108	− 226	—	15·4	—	23·0	—
1842	4·00	1·75	88	125	96	− 4,484	—	14·7	—	22·6	—
1843	3 50	1·90	93	118	92	2,433	—	15·2	—	22·2	—
1844	3·00	2·15	104	115	91	2,614	—	16·0	—	23·0	—
1845	2·75	2·15	100	123	99	2,698	—	17·2	—	22·3	—
1846	3·50	2·05	91	123	100	2,140	—	17·2	—	25·6	—
1847	5·25	2·10	89	130	107	− 969	—	15·8	—	21·4	—
1848	3·75	1·90	77	113	93	1,259	—	15·9	—	22·9	—
1849	3·00	2·30	88	107	89	690	—	16·2	—	23·9	—
1850	2·50	2·60	93	107	88	1,276	—	17·2	—	25·2	—
1851	3·00	2·70	92	110	90	1,061	—	17·2	—	25·0	—
1852	2 00	2·85	92	108	88	1,618	—	17·4	—	25·4	—
1853	3 50	3·60	110	123	99	2,197	—	17·9	—	25·9	—
1854	5·00	3·50	103	138	111	0	—	17·2	—	22·6	—

TABLE XLVII. (continued).

Year.	Bank Rate (Average Minimum Discount Rate per cent).	Foreign Trade. £ per Head.	Foreign Trade. Per cent of 15 Year moving average.	Wholesale Prices. 1900 = 100.	Wholesale Prices. Per cent of 15 Year moving average.	Budget Results. £000.	Employed Percentage (Trade Unions).	Marriage Rate per 1,000 of Population, England and Wales.	Indoor Pauperism in England and Wales per 10,000 (Mean of no. at end of each month).	Consumption of Beer per Head (Gallons).	Companies Registered during Year Nominal Capital £ per Head.
	1.	2.	3.	4.	5.	6.	7.	8.	9.	10.	11.
1855	4·89	3·45	97	133	107	− 1,435	—	17·2	—	21·0	—
1856	6·00	4·15	110	137	109	594	—	16·7	—	22·6	—
1857	6·75	4·35	109	142	110	1,516	—	16·5	63·0	22·6	—
1858	3·25	4·10	98	127	97	1,557	—	16·0	61·2	23·6	—
1859	2·75	4·55	103	128	97	1,630	—	17·0	56·1	24·8	—
1860	4·25	4·75	103	132	99	− 1,964	98·15	17·1	55·7	23·8	—
1861	5·25	4·30	90	131	97	− 609	96·30	16·3	61·0	24·3	—
1862	2·50	4·30	87	135	101	554	93·95	16·1	64·2	24·1	—
1863	4·50	5·00	97	137	103	2,038	95·30	16·8	62·8	25·4	4·8
1864	7·50	5·45	102	140	105	3,185	98·05	17·2	60·6	26·7	8·0
1865	4·75	5·60	100	135	101	1,420	98·20	17·5	60·9	29·8	6·9
1866	7·00	6·30	108	136	101	2,422	97·35	17·5	61·2	29·4	2·5
1867	2·50	5·95	99	133	98	− 370	93·70	16·5	65·2	28·1	1·0
1868	2·25	5·85	95	132	98	− 558	93·25	16·1	68·0	28·2	1·1
1869	3·25	6·15	98	131	97	1,998	94·05	15·9	67·7	29·1	(4·5)[1]
1870	3·12	6·40	100	128	95	2,250	96·25	16·1	66·8	30·2	1·2
1871	2·87	7·10	110	133	100	2,416	98·35	16·7	63·2	29·3	2·2
1872	4·12	8·05	125	145	111	4,576	99·05	17·4	59·9	32·2	4·1
1873	4·75	7·95	122	148	114	3,432	98·85	17·6	59·2	33·5	4·7
1874	3·75	7·40	113	136	106	585	98·40	17·0	58·2	34·0	3·4
1875	3·25	6·55	99	128	101	1,508	97·80	16·7	56·6	33·3	2·5
1876	2·62	6·05	91	127	101	37	96·60	16·5	57·1	33·7	1·4
1877	2·87	5·95	89	125	101	643	95·60	15·7	59·8	32·3	2·0
1878	3·75	5·70	86	116	96	− 72	93·75	15·2	62·5	32·2	2·0
1879	2·37	5·60	85	110	94	− 1,817	89·30	14·4	66·8	28·0	2·2
1880	2·75	6·45	101	117	102	1,021	94·75	14·9	67·9	27·0	4·9
1881	3·50	6·70	106	113	102	681	96·45	15·1	68·4	27·8	6·0
1882	4·12	6·85	109	112	103	1,525	97·65	15·5	67·2	27·6	7·2
1883	3·56	6·75	107	109	102	841	97·40	15·5	66·7	27·2	4·7
1884	2·95	6·55	103	101	97	1,255	92·85	15·1	66·3	27·8	3·9
1885	3·00	5·90	93	96	94	− 1,209	91·45	14·5	65·8	27·1	3·3
1886	3·00	5·85	92	92	92	904	90·45	14·2	65·9	26·9	4·0
1887	3·33	6·00	95	91	92	1,667	92·85	14·4	66·2	27·3	4·6
1888	3·20	6·35	101	93	97	1,646	95·85	14·4	65·9	27·2	9·6
1889	3·50	6·70	107	96	102	3,154	97·95	15·0	64·4	28·9	6·5
1890	4·50	7·05	114	96	104	1,879	97·90	15·5	62·0	30·0	6·4
1891	3·33	6·55	107	96	106	565	96·60	15·6	60·9	30·2	3·5
1892	2·50	5·95	98	91	101	− 58	93·80	15·4	61·7	29·8	2·7
1893	3·05	5·70	93	91	101	− 507	92·30	14·7	64·1	29·6	2·5
1894	2·11	5·55	90	84	93	509	92·80	15·0	65·4	29·5	3·0

[1] This abnormally high figure is due to a single company with a Registered Capital of £100,000,000, of which not £200 was subscribed.

Year.	Bank Rate (Average Minimum Discount Rate per cent).	Foreign Trade.		Wholesale Prices.		Budget Results. £000.	Employed Percentage (Trade Unions).	Marriage Rate per 1,000 of Population, England and Wales.	Indoor Pauperism in England and Wales per 10,000 (Mean of no. at end of each month).	Consumption of Beer per Head (Gallons).	Companies Registered during Year Nominal Capital £ per Head.
		£ per Head.	Per cent of 15 Year moving average.	1900 = 100.	Per cent of 15 Year moving average.						
	1.	2.	3.	4.	5.	6.	7.	8.	9.	10.	11.
1895	2·00	5·80	93	83	92	5,812	94·00	15·0	66·5	29·6	6·0
1896	2·50	6·10	97	81	90	3,470	96·65	15·7	65·2	30·8	7·8
1897	2·62	5·85	93	83	92	3,996	96·55	16·0	64·8	31·3	7·3
1898	3·25	5·80	92	85	94	1,569	97·05	16·2	65·0	31·8	6·7
1899	3·75	6·10	95	91	101	9,255	97·95	16·5	63·8	32·6	6·0
1900	3·94	6·85	103	100	109	2,973	97·55	16·0	62·4	31·6	5·4
1901	3·69	6·52	95	93	101	449	96·65	15·9	63·7	30·8	3·5
1902	3·33	6·62	94	92	99	-575	95·80	15·9	65·0	30·3	3·7
1903	3·75	6·78	93	92	97	-2,711	95·00	15·6	66·8	29·7	2·9
1904	3·33	6·95	92	93	97	97	93·60	15·2	71·1	28·8	2·1
1905	3·00	7·55	96	96	98	1,669	94·75	15·3	71·8	27·7	2·7
1906	4·28	8·46	103	103	103	2,446	96·30	15·6	72·5	28·0	3·1
1907	4·92	9·51	113	107	105	3,703	96·05	15·8	72·5	27·6	3·1
1908	3·00	8·29	96	97	95	-1,502	91·35	15·1	75·7	26·9	2·4
1909	3·10	8·36	94	99	95	-30,894	91·30	14·7	77·4	26·1	3·2
1910	3·72	9·39	102	104	99	4,060	94·90	15·0	77·1	26·3	4·7
1911	3·47	9·90	105	107	100	3,469	96·95	15·2	74·1	27·2	3·5
1912	3·78	10·57	109	113	105	1,613	96·85	15·6	73·3	26·8	3·8
1913	4·77	11·27	113	113	103	3,418	97·90	15·7	70·2	27·8	3·4
1914[1]	4·03	10·80	105	110	99	17,488	96·75	15·9	69·2	26·7	2·5
1915	5·00	—	—	(144)	—	—	99·00	19·4	(66·0)	—	1·2
1916	5·47	—	—	(181)	—	—	99·55	14·9	(62·2)	—	1·1
1917	5·15	—	—	(233)	—	—	99·40	13·8	(59·6)	—	1·6
1918	5·00	—	—	(256)	—	—	99·30	15·3	(55·3)	—	3·0
1919	5·15	17·39	—	275	—	—	97·50	19·8	51·1	17·5	9·3
1920	6·71	28·17	—	335	—	—	97·45	20·2	51·3	20·8	12·8
1921	6·09	14·27	—	207	—	—	84·45	16·9	54·5	18·6	2·5
1922	3·69	14·52	—	175	—	—	82·80	15·7	56·2	15·9	3·0
1923	3·49	16·71	—	172	—	—	87·50	15·2	56·3	15·6	2·6
1924	4·00	17·72	—	185	—	—	90·90	15·3	55·5	16·4	2·8
1925	4·55	17·03	—	181	—	—	88·95	15·2	55·8	16·4	3·0
1926	5·00	14·34	—	168	—	—	87·30	14·3	59·7	15·7	4·8
1927	4·65	15·51	—	163	—	—	90·40	15·7	56·3	15·5	4·1
1928	4·50	15·51	—	160	—	—	89·30	15·4	56·2	15·2	5·2
1929	5·50	15·61	—	152	—	—	89·60	15·8	55·4	15·0	—

[1] Figures used in the chart for columns 1, 3, 5, 8 and 9 for 1914 apply to the first half of that year corrected as described above, pp. 435-6. The figures given here relate to the whole year with the exception of those in columns 2 to 5.

Page 346.   *Notes on Chart VII :*

The line marked "Labour Supply" represents approximately the numbers seeking employment in industry in Great Britain; and is based on the census returns of all persons occupied, subject to deductions for those working as employers or on their own account, or engaged in agriculture, professions, public administration and defence, indoor domestic service, and other forms of personal service.   The first and last of these groups, *viz.*, those working as employers or on their own account and those in forms of personal service other than indoor domestic, are not given separately before 1921 in the census reports; for earlier years they have been assumed to form the same proportion of the total occupied as in 1921.   In 1891, indoor domestic servants in the census returns included daughters and other female relatives, who at other periods were excluded; the amount here deducted for this group in 1891 is the mean of the numbers in 1881 and 1901.

For 1921 the resulting figure is 12,436,000, as compared with the 11,080,000 of persons insured against unemployment.   The difference is accounted for by young persons under the age of 16, by exclusion of permanent railway workers and certain other classes, and by minor reasons.   For 1929 the figure used bears the same proportion to 12,436,000 as the number of insured persons in 1929 bears to that of 1921.   The figures for 1914 and 1929, being estimates, are put in brackets.

The growth of labour supply has been treated as steady between each census and from 1921 to 1929.   The trend of 1901 to 1911 has been continued to 1914.   From 1915 to 1920 labour supply is affected by war conditions and the line of labour supply is not drawn.

The line marked "Labour Demand" represents the percentages of employment (in trade unions up to 1922, corrected as in Table VIII, and in the insured population thereafter) applied to the "Labour Supply" of the year.   The crosses from 1915 to 1920 are placed with reference to a line joining 1914 to 1921 labour supply.

The figures corresponding to the chart are given in the following table :—

TABLE XLVIII.—LABOUR SUPPLY AND DEMAND—GREAT BRITAIN.

Year.	Labour Supply (000).	Employed Percentage.	Year.	Labour Supply (000).	Employed Percentage.
1860		98·15	1895		94·00
1861	5,919	96·30	1896		96·65
1862		93·95	1897		96·55
1863		95·30	1898		97·05
1864		98·05	1899		97·95
1865		98·20	1900		97·55
1866		97·35	1901	10,374	96·65
1867		93·70	1902		95·80
1868		93·25	1903		95·00
1869		94·05	1904		93·60
1870		96·25	1905		94·75
1871	7,135	98·35	1906		96·30
1872		99·05	1907		96·05
1873		98·85	1908		91·35
1874		98·40	1909		91·30
1875		97·80	1910		94·90
1876		96·60	1911	11,619	96·95
1877		95·60	1912		96·85
1878		93·75	1913		97·90
1879		89·30	1914	(11,991)	96·75
1880		94·75	1915		99·00
1881	7,747	96·45	1916		99·55
1882		97·65	1917		99·40
1883		97·40	1918		99·30
1884		92·85	1919		97·50
1885		91·45	1920		97·45
1886		90·45	1921	12,436	84·45
1887		92·85	1922		85·90 [1]
1888		95·85	1923		88·50 [1]
1889		97·95	1924		89·80 [1]
1890		97·90	1925		89·00 [1]
1891	9,178	96·60	1926		87·70 [1]
1892		93·80	1927		90·40 [1]
1893		92·30	1928		89·30 [1]
1894		92·80	1929	(13,300)	89·60 [1]

[1] These figures relate to insured persons.

Page 370.   Notes on Chart VIII :

The figures used in the chart are shown in Table XLIX below.   The beginning of the Table up to 1925 is that given by M. Rueff in an article entitled " Les Variations du Chômage en Angleterre" (Revue Politique et Parlementaire, Tome cxxv, p. 430); but the wage figures have been revised as suggested by Professor Bowley (Special Memorandum 28 of London and Cambridge Economic Service).   M. Rueff's table has here been brought up to date.

TABLE XLIX.—WAGES, PRICES AND UNEMPLOYMENT IN BRITAIN—1919-29.

Quarter.	Wages. 1913 = 100.	Prices. 1913 = 100.	Wages ÷ Prices.	Unemployed Percentage.	
				Trade Unions.	Insured Work-people.
1919 : 1.	228	249	·92	2·7	
2.	230	242	·95	2·2	
3.	238	258	·92	1·9	
4.	244	288	·85	2·9	
1920 : 1.	255	309	·83	1·9	
2.	276	324	·85	1·1	
3.	294	314	·94	1·7	
4.	301	284	1·06	5·0	
1921 : 1.	304	227	1·34	8·5	
2.	295	201	1·47	20·9	
3.	269	190	1·42	16·0	
4.	251	174	1·44	16·0	
1922 : 1.	237	162	1·46	16·5	
2.	223	160	1·39	16·4	
3.	208	157	1·32	14·5	
4.	196	156	1·26	14·1	
1923 : 1.	195	158	1·23	13·0	
2.	195	160	1·22	11·2	
3.	192	156	1·23	11·3	
4.	191	161	1·19	10·4	
1924 : 1.	193	166	1·16	8·3	
2.	194	164	1·18	7·2	
3.	196	165	1·19	8·0	
4.	196	170	1·15	8·8	
1925 : 1.	195	169	1·16	9·1	11·2
2.	197	160	1·23	10·6	11·2
3.	196	156	1·26	11·3	11·8
4.	196	153	1·28	11·1	10·9
1926 : 1.	196	147	1·33	10·4	10·4
2.	196	145	1·35	12·0	12·7
3.	196	150	1·31	13·4	14·0
4.	196	150	1·31	13·0	13·0
1927 : 1.	197	143	1·38	Discontinued	10·9
2.	196	141	1·39		9·0
3.	196	141	1·39		9·3
4.	196	141	1·39		9·8
1928 : 1.	195	141	1·38		10·2
2.	194·5	143	1·36		10·0
3.	194	139	1·40		11·5
4.	194	138	1·41		11·7
1929 : 1.	194	139	1·40		11·5
2.	194	137	1·42		9·9
3.	193	136	1·42		10·0
4.	193	134	1·44		10·8
1930 : 1.	193	128	1·51		13·2

Pages 379 and 382. *Notes on Table XLI and Chart IX :*
Except when otherwise stated, the figures for successive epochs
are the means of the years 1855-64, 1865-74, 1875-84, 1885-94,
1895-1904, 1905-13 and 1922-29 (omitting 1926); and, until the
separation of the Irish Free State, relate to the United Kingdom.
After the separation, most of the production records relate to Great
Britain and Northern Ireland, but the population used for all production columns (except column 7) is that of the United Kingdom,
since the whole or nearly the whole of the former production came
from Great Britain and Northern Ireland only. Some of the
figures for 1929 are provisional. No corrections have been made
for unemployment except in column 9 or in the upper half of the
table for changes in age and sex constitution. The index numbers
in the lower half, with the exception of wages, have been corrected
for changes in the age and sex constitution of the population.
This has been done by reducing the population of each epoch to
its "man-value" for consumption purposes, in accord with a scale
adopted by Professor Bowley for the New Survey of London Life
and Labour. This scale is as follows :—

Ages.	Males.	Females.
0-5	33	33
5-14	50	50
14-16	85	80
16-70	100	100
70 +	60	60

and makes the man-value of the population at successive censuses :

Census Year.	Percentage of Total Population.	
	U.K.	Scotland.
1861	73·2	72·0
1871	72·8	72·2
1881	72·7	73·1
1891	73·5	73·9
1901	74·5	74·0
1911	75·1 [1]	74·4
1921	76·3 [1]	75·7
(1925)	(76·9) [1]	—

[1] These figures relate to Great Britain only: that for 1911 applies both to the
United Kingdom and to Great Britain. The figure for 1925 has been estimated.

The sources of the first six columns are given in the notes on
Table I, p. 422 above. The following notes deal with the other
columns :—

Column 7. Value of exports per head (excluding ships
throughout) divided by Sauerbeck Index of Wholesale
Prices. The "actual figures" are index numbers on
basis 1913 = 100.

Column 8. Pre-war figures represent Mr. G. H. Wood's
Index Number (*Statistical Journal*, March, 1909) brought

up to 1913 by Professor Bowley and reduced to basis 1913 = 100.

Post-war figures are based on Professor Bowley's revised wage rates (*London and Cambridge Economic Service*, January, 1929), base 1913 = 100, divided by the Cost of Living Index (from the same source), base 1913 = 100.

Column 9.   Pre-war figures calculated on basis adopted by Professor Bowley and divided by Mr. G. H. Wood's Index Number of the Cost of Living (*Statistical Journal*, March, 1909) brought up to date by Professor Bowley. Post-war figure based on Professor Bowley and Sir Josiah Stamp's comparison of 1911 and 1924 in *The National Income, 1924*, and adjusted, as far as possible, to be comparable with the mean of 1905-13. Allowance has been made for unemployment, sickness, extra holidays and the change from United Kingdom to Great Britain.

Column 10.   Pre-war figures based on Mr. Wood's Index Numbers of Consumption (*Statistical Journal*, December, 1899), omitting cotton, wool, wine and spirits, weighted on System V, in Mr. Wood's paper and carried forward by figures supplied by Professor Bowley. The articles included are corn, meat, sugar, rice, currants, tea, coffee, cocoa, beer and tobacco. The first figure relates to 1860, 1862 and 1864.   1913 = 100.

The post-war figure is based mainly on a comparison of consumption per head of various articles in 1905-9 and 1924-7 respectively, contained in a pamphlet on *The Agricultural Output and the Food Supplies of Great Britain*, 1929, published by the Ministry of Agriculture and Fisheries.   In making a combined index, the various articles of consumption have been weighted as in the Ministry of Labour's Cost of Living Index, articles not included in the latter being omitted; a few articles have been added from the pre-war source.   The articles included are wheat, meat, fish, eggs, milk, butter, cheese, margarine, potatoes, sugar and cocoa from the Ministry of Agriculture pamphlet, with currants, tea, coffee, beer and tobacco from the pre-war source.

Column 11.   The figures give the percentage of persons living not more than two to a room in Scotland at each census from 1861 to 1921.   Comparable figures for successive censuses are not available for England and Wales.

Pages 392-4.   *Notes on Table L:*

The following figures are referred to in Chapter XVII; they are taken from the *Report of the Royal Commission on the Coal Industry* (1925), Cmd. 2600, Vol. I, Table 13, p. 127, and have been brought up to date by the Department of Mines.

TABLE L.—OUTPUT OF COAL PER PERSON EMPLOYED IN VARIOUS COUNTRIES.

Tons.

Period.	United Kingdom.	France.	Belgium.[2]	Germany.[3]	United States.[4]		
					Bituminous.	Anthracite.	Total.
1874-78	270	154	135	209	341	323	327
1879-83	319	187	163	257	505	374	427
1884-88	319	196	173	269	449	340	398
1889-93	282	201	168	257	503	349	444
1894-98	287	208	174	262	511	336	447
1899-03	289	198	169	247	616	370	542
1904-08	283	194	162	251	617	423	568
1909-13	257	195	159	256	698	449	636
1914-18	252	152	125	286	782	498	710
1919-23	195	132	135	163	656	481	623
1924-29	242 [5]	165	155	257 [6]	797 [6]	429 [6]	716 [6]
Year							
1924	220	154	133	209	697	491	655
1925	221	158	142	234	789	345	694
1926	— [5]	168	155	278	862	456	774
1927	245	159 [7]	155	279	779	433	704
1928	253	170 [7]	168 [7]	287	856	419	754
1929	270 [7]	182 [7]	175 [7]	— [8]	Not available		

[1] Includes Alsace-Lorraine from 1919, but excludes the Saar throughout. The first figure relates to the 3 years 1876-78 only, and the next to 1882-83.

[2] Includes Limburg from 1917. The Belgian figures throughout, like those for Germany from 1914-18 onwards, are based on an assumed number of "full-workers," *i.e.*, the number of persons required to produce the recorded output if both mines and men had worked continuously without unemployment or absence.

[3] Excludes ceded territories (Alsace-Lorraine from 1918; Saar and Hultschin from 1920 and Upper Silesia from June, 1922). The German figures, as usually published from 1909 onwards and as given above from 1914-18, are calculated on a different basis from those for earlier years. The figure of 256 given above for 1909-13 is corrected and comparable with earlier but not with the later years. The uncorrected figure for 1909-13 would be 265.

[4] The American figures in 1874-78 represent only one-fifth of the industry and in 1879-83 only 54 per cent.

[5] 1926 omitted owing to protracted dispute.

[6] 1924-28 only.

[7] Provisional figure and subject to revision.

[8] It is estimated that the figure for 1929 will show an increase in the neighbourhood of 8 per cent to 9 per cent over 1928.

Page 397. *Notes on Chart X :*

The chart is based on the figures given in Table LI below; they have been obtained mainly from the Report on "Mouvement de la Population," published in 1907 by the French Ministère du Travail and subsequently from Reports of the International Statistical Institute.

The method has been to calculate the mean number of living legitimate births for decades running, as a rule, from '6 to '5 and to express this number as so much per 1,000 of the married women aged 15 to 49 in the census year falling within the decade.

TABLE LI.—EUROPEAN FERTILITY: LEGITIMATE LIVING BIRTHS PER ANNUM PER 1,000 MARRIED WOMEN, AGED 15 TO 49.

Year.	Sweden.	England and Wales.	France.	Belgium.	Holland.[1]	Prussia.	Bavaria.	Saxony.	Ireland.
1761	251	—	—	—	—	—	—	—	—
1771	240	—	—	—	—	—	—	—	—
1781	242	—	—	—	—	—	—	—	—
1791	245	—	—	—	—	—	—·	—	—
1801	232	—	—	—	—	—	—	—	—
1811	232	—	—	—	—	—	—	—	—
1821	253	—	—	—	—	—	—	—	—
1831	240	—	—	—	—	—	—	—	—
1841	235	—	—	—	—	—	—	—	—
1851	241	242	179	252	(294)	—	—	—	—
1861	248	244	172	276	(285)	—	—	—	—
1871	235	252	172	270	(292)	271	282	262	260
1881	240	250	167	264	291	273	276	267	250
1891	231	229	150	236	284	265	263	250	245
1901	219	203	134	213	270	250	259	216	267
1911[2]	196	171	116	161	233	204	214	153	247
1921[3]	166[4]	149	124	130	201	121	136	86	—

[1] For decades 5-4. Figures before 1876-85 partly estimated but substantially correct.

[2] 1908-13 for Sweden, France, Belgium; 1907-14 for Prussia, Bavaria, Saxony.

[3] Based on three years *circa* 1921 for Sweden, England and Wales, France, Belgium and Holland; Prussia, Bavaria and Saxony on five years *circa* 1925.

[4] Number of married women estimated.

INDEX.

(References to the more important topics discussed are given in heavy type.)

465   30

30 *

DAILY TELEGRAPH,
advertisements for and by work-people, 239.

DALBEATTIE,
Central (Unemployed) Body for, 164 *note*.

DAVISON, R. C., 409.

DEARLE, N. B., 335.

DE-CASUALISATION, **201-209.**
analogies in favour of, 207.
dock labour problem, 314-321.
failure of Labour Exchanges to secure, 312-314.
increases efficiency, 205.
London Docks, 88.
objections answered, 204-207.
temporary measures subsidiary to, 90, 244.
time for, 204 *note*.
work of Labour Exchanges in, 312, 313, 321-322, 404, 406.
See also Dock and Wharf Labour.

DEMAND FOR LABOUR,
aggregate of many separate demands, 4, 98-100.
always specific, 115.
bringing a body of labour into being, 101.
concentration needed, 201, 209, 237.
contraction of, considered by Poor Law Committee, 254.
course in relation to supply, 346 (chart)-348, 448, 449 (table).
disorganisation of, 352-353.
dissipation of, increases effectiveness in calling for supply, 99.
excess of supply over, explained, 70 *et seq.*
fluctuating growth, 4, 193, 235.
generally keeps pace with supply, 11, 14, 65, 102.
limited by available land and capital, 6.
London Docks, independent fluctuations, 84, 85.
need for more information, 132.
perpetual flux, 111.
reorganisation of, essential, 402-406.
rising, no cure for unemployment, 15, 193.
supply, maladjustment with, 12, 14.
ultimately governed by supply, 5.
unity assumed by economists, 216, 237.

DEMORALISATION,
by casual employment, 87, 101, 105, 108, 201.

DEPOPULATION, RURAL, 6.

DEPRESSION,
defined, 52.
effect of, in trade unions, 145-147 (table).
exceptional. *See* Charity Organisation Society.
increases crime and vagrancy, 137.
Royal Commission on, 66 (table).
worst men dismissed in, 139. *See* Industrial Depression, Cyclical Fluctuation.

DETERRENCE,
condemned as remedy for unemployment, 256.
labour exchange alternative to, 215, 216, 233. *See* "Ineligibility of Relief."

FRENCH POLISHERS, AMALGAMATED SOCIETY OF,
   unemployed benefit, 224.

FRICTION OF THE LABOUR MARKET.
   See Labour Market.

FULHAM,
   chronic distress, 172.

FURNISHING,
   applicants to Distress Committees, 168 (table), 449 (table).
   growth of numbers employed, 69.
   irreducible minimum of unemployment in, 69.
   numbers included in trade union returns, with woodworking, 20 (table),
      425 (table).
   seasonal fluctuation in, 30-31 (table and chart), 428 (table), 429 (table).
   standard rate for older men, exemptions from, 124 note.
   unemployed percentage in, since 1867, with woodworking, 39, 432 (table).

GARDEN CITY,
   relief works at, 162, 175.

GAS, WATER AND ELECTRICITY SUPPLY SERVICES,
   insurance benefits and contributions, 285 (table).
   unemployment in, 351 (table).

GAS WORKS,
   seasonal fluctuations at, 30, 210.

GASWORKERS, BRICKMAKERS AND GENERAL LABOURERS, AMAL-
      GAMATED SOCIETY OF,
   unemployed benefit, 223.

GEDDES, SIR ERIC,
   Chairman of Committee on National Expenditure, 304.

GENERAL LABOUR,
   applicants to Distress Committees, 168 (table), 169.
   applicants and situations at labour exchanges, 184 (table). *See also*
      Casual Labourer.

" GENUINELY SEEKING WORK " CONDITION, 279-280 *note*.

GERMANY,
   continuation schools, 214 *note*.
   foreign trade compared with that of other countries, 55-56 (table and
      chart).
   output in coal-mining, 394, 463 (table).
   unemployed greatest in the ports, 95.

GHENT SYSTEM OF UNEMPLOYED INSURANCE, 228, 259, 264, 272.

GIFFEN, SIR ROBERT,
   estimates of national wealth, 6.

GLASGOW,
   applicants to Distress Committees found qualified, 171 *note*.
   casual employment in, 95.
   failure of bank in 1878, 53.
   Labour Bureau, 246.
   relief funds 1857-95, 66 (table).
   relief work, cost and value, 177.

GLASS BOTTLE MAKING,
high unemployment in, 1929, 356 (table).

GLASS TRADE,
applicants and situations at London Labour Exchanges, with Leather, 184 (table).
seasonal fluctuation in, 428 (table).

GLUTTING OF LABOUR MARKET, 13, 69, 70, **95-102**, 199 *et seq.*

GOSCHEN, LORD, 53.

GOVAN,
relief work, cost and value, 177.

GRANT IN AID OF WAGES,
effect in depressing wages, 109.

GRAVITATION, INDUSTRIAL, 105, 213.
See Unskilled Occupations and Industrial Training.

GREENOCK,
applicants to Distress Committee found qualified, 171 *note.*

GRIMSBY,
chronic distress, 174.

HACKNEY,
applicants to Distress Committees disqualified, 171.

HADLEIGH FARM COLONY,
relief works at, 160.

HAMILTON, LORD GEORGE,
Chairman of Poor Law Commission, 253.

HAMMERSMITH,
difficulties of investigation, 172 *note.*

HAMPSTEAD,
applicants to Distress Committee, 167.

HAND TOOLS, CUTLERY, SAWS AND FILES,
high unemployment in, 1929, 356 (table).

HAT MAKING,
displacement of women by men in straw-hat making, 113, 439.
seasonal fluctuation in, 428 (table).

HAWKING OF LABOUR, **197** *et seq.*
example of, 248, 249.
in building trade, 247.
wastefulness, 199, 200.

HAWTREY, R. G.,
Currency and Credit, 324.
Good and Bad Trade, 324.
Monetary Reconstruction, 324.
on cyclical fluctuations, 325-326, 334, 343.
on public work, 414.

HENDERSON, H. D.,
on public work, 414.

OVER-PRODUCTION,
  as a cause of subsequent depression, 59.
  in what sense possible, 5, 60.

OVER-SAVING,
  a suggested cause of cyclical fluctuation, 58 *et seq.*

OVERTIME,
  sometimes desirable, 222.

PAINTERS,
  elasticity of wages suggested, 231.
  unemployed benefit in winter only, 35, 224.

PANIC,
  psychological phase of a crisis, 52.

PAPER-MAKING,
  seasonal fluctuation in, 428 (table).

PAUPERISM,
  caused by casual employment, 255-256.
  fluctuations with state of trade, 42-44 (table and chart), 340 (chart), 433 (table), 456-457 (table).
  interval between unemployment and pauperism, 47-50.
  statistics published by Local Government Board, 26.

PENAL COLONIES, 233.

PERMANENT LABOURERS,
  London and India Docks, 90.
  Millwall Docks, 86 *note.*

PIG-IRON,
  amount produced per head, 1860-1906, 39 (table).
  cyclical fluctuation, 41.
  production in United Kingdom, 7 (table), 39 (table), 222, 422 (table), 432 (table).

PIGOU, PROFESSOR A. C.,
  cyclical fluctuation, 332-334.
  Industrial Fluctuations, 324, 334.
  public work, 414.
  unemployment due to excessive wages, 360-361, 364.

PLUMBING,
  seasonal fluctuation in, 428 (table).

PLYMOUTH,
  Labour Bureau, 246.
  Labour Exchange established, 183 *note.*

POLICE COURTS,
  distribution of relief at, 158.

POOR LAW,
  able-bodied under, **150-154.**
  conflicting policies on the breaking up of, 261.
  difficulties of relief outside, 190, 191.
  institutions, 26 *note.*